Moscow,
St Petersburg
&
The Golden Ring

Moscow &

by

Masha Nordbye

St. Petersburg

Photography by

Patricia Lanza & Masha Nordbye

ODYSSEY BOOKS & MAPS

Odyssey Books & Maps is a division of Airphoto International Ltd.
1401 Chung Ying Building, 20–20A Connaught Road West, Sheung Wan, Hong Kong
Tel: (852) 2856 3896; Fax: (852) 3012 1825
E-mail: magnus@odysseypublications.com; www.odysseypublications.com
Follow us on Twitter—www.twitter.com/odysseyguides

Distribution in the USA by W.W. Norton & Company, Inc. 500 Fifth Avenue, New York, NY 10110, USA.
Tel: (800) 233-4830; Fax: (800) 458-6515; www.wwnorton.com

Distribution in the UK and Europe by Cordee Ltd. 11 Jacknell Road, Dodwells Bridge Industrial Estate,
Hinckley, Leicestershire LE10 3BS, UK. Tel: (1455) 611-185; info@cordee.co.uk; www.cordee.co.uk

Distribution in Australia by Woodslane Pty Ltd. Unit 7/5 Vuko Place, Warriewood, NSW 2012, Australia.
Tel: (2) 9970-5111; Fax: (2) 9970-5002; www.woodslane.com.au

Moscow, St Petersburg & the Golden Ring, Fourth Edition

ISBN: 978-962-217-855-7
Library of Congress Catalog Card Number has been requested.
Copyright © 2015, 2007, 2004, 2003, 1999, 1995, 1991, 1990, published by Airphoto International Ltd.

Grateful acknowledgment is made to the following authors and publishers:
Peter Owen Ltd for *Adventures in Czarist Russia* by Alexandre Dumas, edited and translated by Alma Elizabeth
Murch; Farrar, Straus and Giroux Inc. and Georges Borchardt Inc. for *In Plain Russian* by Vladimir Voinovich
translated by Richard Lourie, translation © 1979 by Farrar, Strauss and Giroux Inc.; North Point Press for *The Noise
of Time* translated by Clarence Brown © 1965 Princeton University Press; Princeton University Press for *The Road
to Bloody Sunday: The role of Father Gapon and the Assembly in the Petersburg Massacre of 1905* by Walter Sablinsky
© 1976 Princeton University Press; Random House Inc. and William Heinemann Ltd for *Among the Russians* ©
1983 Colin Thubron; Penguin Books for *Dead Souls* by Nikolai Gogol, translation © 1961 David Magarshack;
Chronicle Books for *White Nights* by Fyodor Dostoevsky © 1995.

Managing Editor: Masha Nordbye   Maps: On The Road Cartography 637, 645, 662–3, 666, 672
Designer: Au Yeung Chui Kwai   Index: Don Brech, Records International Management, Hong Kong

Photography by **Masha Nordbye**: cover, 2, 3, 8, 14–15, 104, 105, 106, 107, 108, 109, 110, 111, 113, 114, 115, 119,
120, 121, 184 (bottom), 186, 189, 192 (top), 222, 226, 228–229, 231, 234 (bottom left), 235 (bottom), 236
(bottom), 262, 263, 264, 265, 267 (bottom), 321, 324, 326, 327, 328–329, 330–331, 333 (bottom), 335, 336, 372,
440, 444, 447 (bottom), 451, 456–457, 458, 459, 460, 464, 546–547, 548, 549, 550–551, 552, 553, 554–555, 556,
557, 560, 596, 610 (top), 611, 612–613, 615, 616–617, 618–619, 620, 621, 623, 624, 680.

Photography by **Patricia Lanza**: 6-7, 9, 12–13, 53, 101, 124, 125, 128, 184 (top), 185, 187, 190–191, 227, 232, 234,
235 (top), 238, 266, 267 (top), 322, 323, 325, 332, 333 (top), 334, 441, 446, 447 (top), 448, 449, 461, 553 (top),
558–559, 605, 606–607, 608 (bottom), 609, 622.

Additional photography/illustrations, courtesy of **Kevin Bishop** 600, 603; **Bolshoi St Petersburg State Circus
Museum** 236 (top); **State Tretyakov Gallery, Moscow** 52, 58, 59 (bottom), 60, 61, 62 (bottom), 63; **Itar-Tass** 19;
Patrick Lucero 98, 102, 192 (bottom), 230; **Keith Macgregor** 442, 443, 455, 462, 463, 545, 608 (top), 610 (bottom),
614; **Moscow History Museum & Interbook Business** 56 (top), 57; **Museum of Advertisement** 64 (top left); **Russian
Museum of Political History** 56 (bottom); **Trillium Studios (Cary Wollinsky)** 16, 54–55, 126, 127, 182; **State
Hermitage Museum** 59 (top); 64 (bottom); **State Russian Museum, St Petersburg** 62 (top); **Carolyn Watts** 188.

Production and printing by Twin Age Ltd, Hong Kong. E-mail: twinage@netvigator.com
Printed in Hong kong

SPECIAL ACKNOWLEDGMENTS

We will preserve you Russian speech; keep you alive great Russian word.
We will pass you to our sons and heirs; free and clean,
and they in turn to theirs. And so forever.

Anna Akhmatova

In Special Memory of Leonard and Mark

And lovingly to Eleanor, who gifted me the world.

After 30 years of journeying across Russia and areas of the former Soviet Union with many extraordinary experiences, a multitude of hosts and characters have blessed my path; I am forever grateful for their generous support and assistance. I wish to especially thank my friends and family for all their help and humor during the many months of research and writing.

Keepers of the Flame

Sandushka Johnson, John Porterfield, Tom Moore, Carlichka "Bogoliubsky" Gottlieb, Corina Gamma & Rod Babcock, Dr. Angela Thompson, Andrea Anderson, Lynette Mason, Lyoni Craven, Andy Reed & Gank, Geri, Maya & Cupcake, Isabel Allende & Villie Gordon, Amy Tan, Bob "Veliki" Jones, Jane Brockman, Stuart & Ms Mabel, Linda Svendson & Kent Madin, Judy Clapp, Sophie James & Jonathan Lucas, Yanni, Kate & Charlie Feist, Michele Connor & Mt Kailash, Tom Campbell & Beth Davidow, Doria Steedman, Pam Ventura, Ritchie Gaona & the Trapeze family, Dominique Jando, Sam Keen, Cesar & Naomi Torres, KM Roadside, William Nordbye, Alexandra Baker, Sasha, Andrei, Max & Masha—the Frishkadelkamis, Archimandrite Pachomy & St Sabbas Orthodox Monastery (www.stsabbas.org), Natasha Kuznetsova, the St Petersburg Circus & Museum, Manco computer wizards, and a special hail to my Odyssey comrades, Au Yeung Chui kwai, Helen Northey, George Baily and Magnus Bartlett.

В Специальнои Памяти: Tanya Frish, Дядя АА Sonin, Uncle Murray & Crystal Gaer, Gene Sawyer, Vladimir & Vita Uspensky, Yuri Nikulin, Schneer, Robert Baker, Mek & Brud Morsey, John Roadside, Tom & Tina Roadside, Sam Orth, Brian Seeholzer, Matt Valensic, and the Slavic-blooded Бабушки и Дедушки.

And a hearty Спасибо to all those who helped through the many years in the ol' *Bolshaya Kapusta.*

Masha Nordbye

After defeating the Swedes in 1709, Peter the Great decided to build his Summer Palace, Peterhof, outside of St Petersburg, on the shores of the Gulf of Finland. The great Cascade Fountain in front of the palace has 17 waterfalls, 142 water jets and 39 gilded statues.

CONTENTS

The Kremlin's Assumption Cathedral.
Its spacious interior is covered with exquisite frescoes and icons dating from the
15th century. The screen of icons on the front wall were painted in the mid-17th century
by monks of the Trinity-Sergius Monastery in the Golden Ring town of Sergiyev Posad.

In 1870, the Abramtsevo Estate, located north of Moscow, was purchased by wealthy merchant and art patron, Savva Mamontov, who turned it into a popular artist colony. Artist Viktor Vasnetsov designed this small wooden dacha, known as the 'Hut on Chicken Legs,' named after the headquarters of the witch Baba Yaga from a popular Russian fairy tale.

INTRODUCTION

On with the journey!...
Russia! Russia!
When I see you... my eyes
are lit up with supernatural power. Oh, what a
glittering, wondrous infinity of space....What a
strange, alluring, enthralling, wonderful world!

Nikolai Gogol

Perhaps no other destination in the world has captured the traveler's imagination as much as Russia. Throughout the centuries, its visitors have reported phenomenal and fanciful scenes: from golden churches, bejeweled icons and towering kremlins to madcap czars, wild cossacks and prolific poets. Russia was, and remains, an impressive sight to behold. A travel writer in the early 20th century remarked that Russia's capital, Moscow, 'embodied fantasy on an unearthly scale... Towers, domes, spires, cones, onions, crenellations filled the whole view. It might have been the invention of Danté, arrived in a Russian heaven.'

By the 1600s, Russia was already the largest country in the world, stretching eventually from Finland to Alaska. The massive conquests deep into the Siberian wilds by Ivan the Terrible and Peter the Great had created a territory larger than the Roman Empire with the richest resources on Earth. It was so vast that in 1856, when American Perry McDonough Collins arrived in Irkutsk, Siberia to propose a railway line to link the country, it took him nearly a year to travel the 5,632 kilometers (3,500 miles) to St Petersburg. He had to change horses over 200 times.

After the 1917 Bolshevik Revolution, the countries bordering Russia fell into the Soviet Union's domain. The USSR became the world's largest nation with 15 republics stretching across 11 time zones and two continents, Europe and Asia. Its borders encompassed one-sixth of the planet's total land area with a population of 290 million speaking 200 languages and dialects.

On the historic day of December 21, 1991, after seven decades of Communist rule, the Soviet Union collapsed. The attempted coup in August 1991 was the catalyst that led to the dissolution of one of the most oppressive regimes in history. As one defender of a new and nontotalitarian government exclaimed: 'I have lived through a revolution, the Siege of Leningrad and Stalin, and I will not tolerate another takeover; let the people be in peace!' In its place was established the Commonwealth of Independent States (CIS), or the Soyuz Nyezavysimeekh Gosudarstv (SNG) with eleven member states.

(opposite) Tomb covering dating from 1630.

Moscow is the Commonwealth's largest city and capital of its largest state, the Russian Federation, which occupies 17,070,959 square kilometers (6,591,104 square miles), stretching from Kaliningrad to the eastern tip of Siberian Kamchatka. There are more than 1,100 cities and towns in Russia, and over 80 percent of the population lives in European Russia to the west of the Ural Mountains. With nearly 145 million people and over 150 nationalities and ethnic groups, Russia is truly the core of the Commonwealth. It is impossible to take in the diversity of the entire country during one, two or even three visits. However, there is no better way to learn about the Russian character and way of life than making a trip to Moscow, St Petersburg and the area of the Golden Ring.

Moscow is the center of politics, industry and culture—the heart of this giant nation—and the source of the Russian spirit, or *dushá*. The Russian poet Alexander Pushkin wrote of his first trip to Moscow: 'And now at last the goal is in sight: in the shimmer of the white walls...and golden domes, Moskva lies great and splendid before us...O Moskva have I thought of you! Moskva how violently the name plucks at any Russian heart!'

The true enchantment of Moscow begins in the city center, where you gaze upon the gilded domes of the palaces and churches of the former czars, rising up from within the old protective walls of the Kremlin. From the citadel, paths lead out to the fairy-tale creation of Ivan the Terrible, St Basil's Cathedral, which looms up from the middle of Krasnaya Ploshchad or Red Square. *Krasnaya* is an Old Russian word meaning both red and beautiful. The city, which marked its 865th anniversary in 2012, is also a place where frenzied consumerism is coupled with deep spirituality, and golden domes of long-closed churches are gleaming once again. In 1931, Stalin destroyed the immense Cathedral of Christ Our Savior, but in 1997 the next generation helped rebuild it with 360 million dollars collected in public funds. Shopping malls have popped up everywhere around Red Square; and surely Lenin would not recognize the place—even though people (mostly foreign tourists) still queue in front of Lenin's Mausoleum to view the Father of the Great October Revolution.

Like arteries from the heart of the city, long thoroughfares take one through various stages of Moscow's history. These roads offer an abundance of sights, architectural monuments and museums. Districts from the Arbat, which celebrated its 520th anniversary in 2013, to the newly-developed hip and vibrant Krasny Oktyabr or Red October complex near the Kremlin embody both Russia's long history and many transformations sweeping the country. The city offers a wealth of breathtaking and poetic creations, as the famous Russian writer Anna Akhmatova remarked: 'As you stroll through the city, you'll find...all of Moscow is truly soaked with verses, saturated with meter, time after time.'

The towns and villages surrounding the city, known collectively as the Golden Ring, reveal a quieter and quainter lifestyle. This area is considered the cradle of Russian culture. The small towns, like Sergiyev Posad (the center of Russian Orthodoxy) and Suzdal (the most ancient Russian town), were built between the 10th and 17th centuries and are magnificently preserved. Antiquated villages, onion-domed churches, frescoes and icons by the 15th-century artist Andrei Rublyov, colorful wooden dachas (country homes) and endless groves of *beryoza* (birch trees) provide a delightful contrast to the bigger cities. These serene sites are reminiscent of a 19th-century Tolstoyan novel, a portrait of Russia's past.

Photograph of the great writer, Lev Tolstoy, taken in 1910, shortly before his death at the age of 82.

Much more provincial than Moscow, St Petersburg is the legacy of Peter the Great. Images of this astoundingly beautiful city are reflected in the Neva River which winds around the many islands that comprise the area. A stroll along one of the many canal embankments takes in three centuries of ornate architecture glistening under the pastel northern lights. Sights abound: the Hermitage, one of the largest museums in the world; Peterhof Palace, rivaling Versailles in grandeur; Peter the Great's fortress; the golden-spired Admiralty; the statue of the Bronze Horseman; and scenes of numerous revolutions. Throughout the world, every time someone recites Gogol or Dostoevsky, or sees a performance of *Boris Godunov* or *Swan Lake*, St Petersburg's bounty flowers again. Liberated of the name Leningrad (and anything to do with Lenin) in 1991, the city's residents affectionately refer to their city simply as Pieter. They proudly celebrated St Petersburg's 310th anniversary in 2013.

Visitors today will be astonished by the immense transformation that has swept across the land. Russia can rightfully claim that no other place on earth has made such radical changes in so short a period of time. After a thousand years of autocratic rule and 74 years of Communism, a new democratic market economy has, slowly but surely, spun into action for the first time in the country's existence.

Since Vladimir Putin was elected President to lead Russia into the 21st century, private enterprise has firmly taken hold of the economy. A whole new generation of young Russians, who do not even remember the Politburo, have ventured into successful businesses. Government enterprise has given way to individual billionaires, state-owned land to real-estate moguls, and ideological propaganda has shifted to billboards promoting products from around the world.

Ventures between east and west have opened plush hotels, internationally stocked shopping centers and scores of entertainment and excursion opportunities.

Many travelers enter the country with an organized tour group, which includes hotels, meals and sightseeing. But, visitors can also enter on individual or business visas, and stay in Russian homes or apartments. Even though Moscow is now regarded as one of the most expensive cities in the world to visit, it now offers a wide selection of places to stay (from 5-star to budget hotels) and thousands of eateries and food store options. For the more adventurous, specialized tours are also offered, including biking, hiking, climbing and rafting.

Today, in many of the larger cities and towns, English is widely understood. If you do not read Cyrillic or speak Russian, take a Russian phrase book; a smile, some patience and the knowledge of a few Russian words is always well taken by the locals. So much so, that you may even find yourself invited to someone's home for *chai* (tea) or vodka, where you will quickly discover that Russians are truly among the warmest and most hospitable people you'll ever meet.

До свидания *Do Svidanya!*

A haze of legend will be cast
Over all, like scroll and spiral
Bedecking gilded boyar chambers
And the Cathedral of St Basil.

By midnight denizens and dreamers
Our Mother Russia most of all is cherished,
Here is their home, the fount' of all
With which this century shall flourish.

Boris Pasternak

CHRONOLOGY

700–882: The Vikings (Varangians) begin to leave Scandinavia and establish trading settlements with the Slavs in northwestern Russia. Kievan State in the south is formed and named after the Slavic Prince Kii. In 862, the Norseman Rurik defeats the important Slavic town of Novgorod and becomes one of the first Vikings to rule in Russia. In 880, Rurik's successor, Oleg, conquers the Slavic-ruled Kiev, unites the two states and makes Kiev his capital. The ruling class is known as 'Rus', (thought to be derived from the Viking word *ruotsi*, meaning rower or oarsman). This term is later applied to the people of Eastern Europe; eventually the areas are united into the Russian states.

977: Novgorod gains its independence from Kiev.

978–1015: Rule of Prince Vladimir, who introduces Byzantine Christianity into Russia in 988.

1015–1054: Rule of Yaroslav the Wise. Kiev becomes the first center of the Orthodox Church.

1113–1125: Rule of Vladimir Monomakh. The two principalities of Novgorod and Kiev are united again under his rule. The crown of Monomakh is worn by the later rulers of Russia. The decline of Kievan Rus begins after his death.

1147: Prince Yuri Dolgoruky 'Long Arms' founds Moscow. He builds a kremlin and defensive walls around the city.

1169: Prince Andrei Bogoliubsky transfers the capital from Kiev to Vladimir.

1223: First Mongol invasion of Russia.

1237: Batu Khan, grandson of Genghis Khan, invades Moscow and goes on to conquer many of Russia's other regions. The Mongol Tartars dominate Russia for the next 250 years.

1240: The Prince of Novgorod, Alexander Nevsky, defeats the Swedes in an important battle along the Neva River. Nevsky rules as grand prince in Vladimir from 1252–1263.

1299: The Church Metropolitan flees Kiev and takes up residence with the grand prince in Vladimir.

1325–1340: Reign of Ivan I, nicknamed Kalita 'Moneybags' because of his strong economic hold over the other principalities. Ivan is named grand prince in 1328, and chooses Moscow as his residence. The seat of the Orthodox Church is moved from Vladimir to Moscow. In 1337, St Sergius founds the Monastery of the Holy Trinity in Sergiyev Posad.

1353–1359: Reign of Ivan II. Plague wipes out one-third of Moscow population.

1362–1389: Reign of Dmitri Donskoi. In 1380, the grand prince defeats the Tartars in the Battle of Kulikovo on the Don, becoming the first Russian prince to win a decisive battle over the Mongol army. Two years later the Mongols burn Moscow to the ground.

1389–1425: Reign of Vasily I. Continued unification of Russian lands.

1425–1460: Reign of Vasily II. In 1445 a huge fire destroys much of Moscow.

1453: The Ottoman Turks conquer Constantinople, which releases the Russian Orthodox Church from Byzantine domination. Less than a decade later, the head of the Orthodox Church takes on the title of Metropolitan of Moscow and All Russia and receives his orders from the grand prince.

1460–1505: Reign of Ivan III (Ivan the Great). He marries Sophia, the niece of the last Byzantine emperor, in 1472 and adopts the crest of the double-headed eagle. Moscow is declared the Third Rome. During his rule, Ivan the Great rebuilds the Kremlin and annexes the city of Novgorod. He refuses to pay any further tribute to the Mongols and defeats their armies. Two centuries of Tartar oppression in Russia come to an end. Population of Moscow over 100,000.

1505–1533: Reign of Vasily III, father of Ivan the Terrible. 1510 annexed Pskov.

1533–1584: Reign of Ivan IV (Ivan the Terrible) who is crowned in 1547 in the Moscow Kremlin with the title of Czar (derived from Caesar) of All Russia. Moscow becomes the capital of the Holy Russian Empire. St Basil's Cathedral is built to commemorate the defeat of the Tartars in the far eastern provinces. He organizes the Oprichniki, a special bodyguard to prosecute the Boyars (noble-class landowners). In 1581, Ivan kills his son, Ivan Ivanovich, in a fit of rage. In 1582, Russia loses the Livonian War and access to the Baltic. Upon his death, Moscovy is left in a state of political and economic ruin.

1584–1598: Reign of Fyodor I, son of Ivan IV. When he dies childless, so does the House of Rurik. (1585–98, Boris Godunov acts as *defacto* regent)

1598–1605: Reign of Boris Godunov.

1605–1613: The Time of Troubles, an era of much instability, famine and unrest. In 1591, Dmitri, son of Ivan the Terrible, mysteriously died at the age of 10. In 1604, a false Dmitri, claiming to have survived, turns up in Poland. With the help of Polish troops he seizes the Russian throne, but is murdered shortly thereafter. When a second false Dmitri, in 1605, then tries to gain the throne, the Russian army, headed by the Cossacks, emerge victorious.

1613–1645: Following the Time of Troubles and the defeat of Polish invaders, the 16-year-old Mikhail Romanov (related to Ivan the Terrible) is elected new czar of Russia on March 14, 1613. The Romanov dynasty continues to rule Russia until 1917; there were 18 rulers in all.

1645–1676: Reign of Alexei I, father of Peter the Great. Establishes Russia's first Law Code in 1649. Patriarch Nikon sets out to reform the Orthodox Church causing a major schism between the Reformers and the Old Believers. Nikon is deposed in 1660. Ukraine and Russia unite in 1653.

1676–1682: Reign of Fyodor III. When he dies, his feeble-minded brother, Ivan V, and half-brother, Peter (Peter the Great), are proclaimed joint czars. The Streltsy (marksmen) briefly gain control over the government. Sophia, Peter's half-sister, acts as regent until 1689.

1689–1725: Reign of Peter the Great. During his enlightened rule, Peter adopts the Julian calendar, transfers the capital from Moscow to St Petersburg, introduces Western culture and customs to his country and builds the first Russian fleet along the Baltic. In 1721, he dissolves the seat of the Patriarch and creates a governing church body known as the Holy Synod. That same year, after the end of the Great Northern War, he assumes the title of Emperor of All Russia. (See Special Topic on page 479.)

1725–1727: Reign of Catherine I, the widow of Peter the Great, who becomes czarina with the help of her guard Menschikov. Academy of Sciences founded in 1725.

1727–1730: Reign of Peter II, Peter the Great's grandson.

1730–1740: Reign of Anna Ivanova, daughter of Ivan V and niece of Peter the Great. In 1731, first opera performed in Russia.

1740–1741: Reign of Ivan VI. Proclaimed Emperor at two months old, and overthrown by Elizabeth a year later.

1741–1761: Reign of Elizabeth, daughter of Peter the Great and Catherine I. In, 1754, Rastrelli begins construction of Winter Palace. In 1755, the first university is founded in Moscow. In 1757, Academy of Arts founded.

1762 (for six months) Reign of Peter III. In 1744, Peter married Sophie of Anhalt-Zerbst. After his assassination, his wife, Catherine II ascended the throne.

1762–1796: Reign of Catherine II (Catherine the Great), German-born wife of Peter III. The first foreign woman to rule as czarina. She ushers in Russia's Golden Age (for more on Catherine the Great see Special Topic, page 543).

1796–1801: Reign of Paul I, son of Catherine the Great. Builds the Mikhailovsky Palace, where he is assassinated by conspirators.

1801–1825: Reign of Alexander I, son of Paul I. In 1812, Napoleon's armies flee Moscow in defeat. Rise of the Decembrist movement, who petitioned for the end of autocracy. 1809–1815 John Quincy Adams serves as first US Ambassador to Russia.

1825–1855: Reign of Nicholas I, son of Paul I. On December 14, 1825 the Decembrists attempt to overthrow the czarist government and gain freedom for the serfs. The uprising was crushed and conspirators immediately hanged Bolshoi Theater opens in 1825. In 1842, Gustav Fabergé opens his first jewelry shop in the capital. Marx and Engels publish the communist manifesto in 1848. In 1849, Petrashevsky Circle arrested, which includes Dostoevsky. In 1851, the first railway opens between St Petersburg and Moscow (see page 760).

1855–1881: Reign of Alexander II, son of Nicholas I. In 1861, Alexander signs a decree to emancipate the serfs. 1864, trial by jury introduced. 1867, sale of Alaska to the United States, and all other land claims on the American continent. Karl Marx's *Das Kapital* is translated into Russian and the first Marxist groups formed within the country. 1869 Tolstoy completes *War and Peace*.

1881: Alexander II is assassinated in a bombing by members of the Peoples' Will group—revolutionaries. Ironically, the Czar was planning reforms and a State Duma.

1881–1894: Reign of Alexander III. The brother of Lenin, Alexander Ulyanov, along with four others, attempt to assassinate the czar. All are hung in the Kronstadt Fortress.

1894–1917: Reign of Nicholas II. Nicholas marries the granddaughter of Queen Victoria; they have five children. In 1895, workers hold public rallies to celebrate May Day, day of worker solidarity. Nicholas dismisses a call for constitutional reform that provokes the founding of the Social Democratic Workers' Party. In 1903, this Party splits into two factions: Bolsheviks and Mensheviks. Russo-Japanese War 1904–05. The first revolution takes place in 1905 (known as the Bloody Sunday massacre) in St Petersburg. Romanov dynasty celebrates 300th anniversary in 1913. World War I breaks out in 1914. In 1916, Rasputin murdered by Count Yusupov. Second revolution begins in February 1917. Czar Nicholas abdicates on March 15, 1917 and a Provisional government is formed. The prime ministers of the new government are Prince Lvov (Feb–May) and Alexander Kerensky (May–Oct). Lenin and the Bolsheviks overthrow the Provisional Government in October 1917. In 1918, Nicholas and his family are executed in the Ural town of Sverdlovsk (present-day Yekaterinburg).

1918–1924: In 1918, Lenin moves capital from Petrograd to Moscow. Civil war erupts between 1918–20. The Socialist Soviet State is formed in 1922, and the first Soviet Constitution adopted. The Bolsheviks switched the Russian calendar from the Julian to Gregorian (the last European country to do so), and announced that January 31, 1918 would be immediately followed by February 13. The Communist government nationalizes industry, introduces censorship of the press and forms the Cheka police force. Lenin introduces the New Economic Policy (NEP). When Lenin dies in 1924, St Petersburg (Petrograd) is renamed Leningrad (see Special Topic on page 598).

1924–1953: Joseph Stalin (Iosif Vissarionovich Dzhugashvili). In 1927, Trotsky is expelled from the Party. In 1928, Stalin introduces the First Five Year Plan and Collectivization. A widespread famine sweeps the nation, eventually killing ten million people.

1934–1941: Stalin's assassination of Leningrad Party Chief Sergei Kirov signals the beginning of the Great Terror. Half the delegates of the 17th Party Congress are purged, along with 90 percent of the country's generals. Of approximately 20 million people arrested, seven million are shot immediately while the rest are sent to gulag camps for rehabilitation. In 1939, the Nazi-Soviet pack is formed. In 1940, Soviet Union annexes Baltic republics.

1941–1945: World War II. Hitler invades the USSR in 1941, and the siege of Leningrad lasts for 900 days until 1944. The Soviet Union suffers 20 million casualties.

1945–1953: World War II ends in 1945. Yalta and Potsdam conferences. Occupation of Eastern Europe.

1953–1955: Georgi Malenkov is General Secretary of Communist Party.

1955–1964: Nikita Khrushchev becomes leader and founds the KGB, the committee for state security, in 1954. In 1956, at the 20th Party Congress, he denounces Stalin in a secret speech. Two-thirds of the Orthodox churches and monasteries are closed down. In 1961, the Soviets send the first man, Yuri Gagarin, into space, and the Congress votes to remove Stalin's body from its place of honor alongside Lenin in the Kremlin Mausoleum. Berlin Wall is constructed in 1961. In 1962, Cuban Missile Crisis fuels the Cold War.

1964–1982: Leonid Brezhnev forces Khrushchev's resignation, who immediately rescinds Khrushchev's Rule 25 restricting Party officials to 15 years in office. The discovery of large gas and oil reserves boosts the economy, but these benefits are undermined by poor planning and lack of incentives. Alcohol consumption quadruples in 20 years. Further repressions stimulate the dissident and Samizdat movements.

1968: Invasion of Czechoslovakia.

1979–1989: Occupation of Afghanistan.

1982–1984: Brezhnev succeeded by Yuri Andropov, former head of the KGB.

1984–1985: Andropov dies and is succeeded by Konstantin Chernenko, Brezhenev's 72-year old protégé, who dies one year later.

1985–1991: Mikhail Gorbachev (see History, page 27).

1991: December 21, the Soviet Union ceases to exist.

1992–1999: Boris Yeltsin, President of the Russian Republic, forms the 11-member Commonwealth of Independent States (see History, page 34).

2000–2008: President of Russia, Vladimir Putin. (He also served as Prime Minister of Russia from 1999–2000 and 2008–2012.)

2008–2012: President of Russia: Dmitry Medvedev.

2012 to present: President of Russia: Vladimir Vladimirovich Putin, serving a six-year term. He is eligible to run for re-election in 2018.

HISTORY

PERESTROIKA

Mikhail Sergeyevich Gorbachev was born in 1931 in a small Cossack village within the Stavropol region. While in school, he worked as a combine operator's assistant, and by the age of 18, he had been awarded the Order of the Red Banner of Labor and had joined the Communist Party.

On March 11, 1985, 54-year-old Mikhail Sergeyevich Gorbachev was elected the new General Secretary of the Communist Party. Following in the footsteps of such past rulers as Ivan the Terrible, Peter the Great, Stalin and Brezhnev, Gorbachev inherited a stagnating economy, an entrenched bureaucracy and a population living in fear and mistrust of its leaders.

Gorbachev's first actions were to shut down the production and sale of vodka and ardently pursue the anticorruption campaign instituted by former president, Yuri Andropov. In 1986, Gorbachev introduced the radical reform policies of *perestroika* (restructuring), *demokratizatsiya* (democratization) and *glasnost* (openness), now household words. He emphasized that past reforms had not worked because they did not directly involve Soviet citizens. Perestroika introduced profit motive, quality control, private ownership in agriculture, decentralization and multi-candidate elections. Industry concentrated on measures promoting quality over quantity; private businesses and cooperatives were encouraged; farmers and individuals could lease land and housing from the government, and keep the profits made from produce grown on private plots; hundreds of ministries and bureaucratic centers were disbanded. A law was passed that allowed individuals to own small businesses and hire workers so long as there was 'no exploitation of man by man'. (Twenty years later, in 2006, 75-year-old Gorbachev, published his book *To Understand Perestroika*. He also founded Green Cross International, devoted to improving the environment worldwide.)

In a powerful symbolic gesture, Andrei Sakharov and other political prisoners were released from internal exile. (After winning the 1975 Nobel Peace Prize, Sakharov, the physicist and human rights activist, was banished for nearly seven years to the city of Gorky, present-day Nizhny Novgorod. He died in Moscow on December 14, 1989, at age 68.) One hundred Soviet dissidents from 20 cities were allowed to form the Democratic Club, an open political discussion group. Glasnost swept through all facets of Soviet life.

For the 40 million followers of the Russian Orthodox religion, and people of other religious beliefs, Gorbachev stated that 'believers have the full right to express their convictions with dignity'. On December 1, 1989, Gorbachev became the first

Soviet leader to set foot in the Vatican, where he declared: 'We need spiritual values; we need a revolution of the mind... No one should interfere in matters of the individual's conscience. Christians, Moslems, Jews, Buddhists and others live in the Soviet Union. All of them have a right to satisfy their spiritual needs—this is the only way toward a new culture and new politics that can meet the challenge of our time.'

As Peter the Great understood, modernization meant Westernization, Gorbachev reopened the window to the West. With the fostering of private business, about five million people were employed by over 150,000 cooperatives. After April 1, 1989, all enterprises were allowed to carry on trade relations with foreign partners, triggering the development of joint ventures. Multimillion-dollar deals were struck with Western companies, such as Chevron, Pepsi, Eastman-Kodak, McDonald's, Time-Warner and Occidental.

At the 1986 Iceland Summit, Gorbachev proposed a sharp reduction in ballistic missiles, and in December 1987, he signed a treaty with US President Ronald Reagan to eliminate intermediate-range nuclear missiles. In January 1988, the Soviet Union announced its withdrawal from Afghanistan. Nine months later Andrei Gromyko retired and Gorbachev was also elected President of the Supreme Soviet.

During a visit to Finland in October 1989, Gorbachev declared: 'The Soviet Union has no moral or political right to interfere in the affairs of its Eastern European neighbors. They have the right to decide their own fate.' And that is what they did. By the end of 1989, every country throughout Eastern Europe saw its people protesting openly for mass reforms. The Iron Curtain crumbled, symbolized most poignantly by the demolition of the wall between East and West Berlin.

In December 1989, Gorbachev met with US President George H.W. Bush at the Malta Summit, where the two agreed that 'the arms race, mistrust, psychological and ideological struggle should all be things of the past'.

ELECTIONS AND ECONOMY

On March 26, 1989, there was a general election for the new Congress of People's Deputies—the first time that Soviet citizens had had the chance to vote in a national election. One thousand five hundred delegates were elected together with an additional 750, who were voted in by other public organizations. The 2,250-delegate body then elected 542 members to form a new Supreme Soviet.

Ousted a year earlier from his Politburo post for criticizing the reforms, the Congress candidate Boris Yeltsin won 89 percent of the Moscow district vote. As Moscow crowds chanted 'Yeltsin is a Man of the People' and 'Down with Bureaucrats', a surprising number of bureaucrats had, in fact, lost to members of such groups as the Church Metropolitan of Leningrad. Andrei Sakharov was also elected. An interesting aspect of the election rules was that even candidates who ran unopposed could lose if over half the votes polled showed a level of no confidence, a privilege not enjoyed by voters in most Western countries.

At the beginning of 1990, Soviet citizens once again headed to the polls to elect their own regional and district officials, this time with the additional opportunity of choosing candidates from other independent and pro-democracy movements. Scores of Communist Party candidates were defeated by former political prisoners, adamant reformers, environmentalists and strike leaders. Yeltsin was voted in as President of the Russian Federation, the Soviet Union's largest republic with Moscow as its capital. In June 1990, Yeltsin resigned from the Communist Party, declaring that 'in view of my...great responsibility toward the people of Russia and in connection with moves toward a multiparty State, I cannot fulfill only the instructions of the Party'.

Yeltsin's ascent underscored the fact that for all Gorbachev's unprecedented reforms and innovative policies, he had failed to bring the country's economy out of stagnation; because of this he lost his popularity at home. An extensive poll conducted throughout the Soviet Union revealed that more than 90 percent considered the economic situation critical. Some of the disheartened commented that 'glasnost has produced more copies of Solzhenitsyn than salami'. Food and fuel were in critically low supplies, and the population anticipated the worst food shortages since World War II. Ration coupons were issued for meat, sugar, tea and soap. After the launch of a probe to Mars, graffiti in Moscow appeared exclaiming: 'To Mars for Soap!'

Modernization still did not approach Western standards: there were few computers and most areas continued to use the abacus. It was estimated that 40 percent of the crops had been wasted because of poor storage, packing and distribution methods. Many Soviets felt that their living conditions had worsened: 'We live like dogs. The leash has become longer but the meat is a bit smaller, and the plate is two meters further away. But at least we can now bark as much as we want.'

Gorbachev was also faced with a budget deficit of over 100 billion rubles. The severe shortages boosted the black market, which provided goods for up to 85 percent of the population. On November 1, 1989, the government drastically cut the bank ruble exchange rate by 90 percent to curb black-market exchanges (up to 20 times the official rate) and bring the ruble closer to an open exchange on the world market. The prime minister stated that 43 million people (15 percent of the population) were living below the poverty level. There was also an estimated 23 million unemployed, the new paradox of this modern Soviet society.

Compounding failing measures and political contradictions, the nation was rocked by a series of disasters: Chernobyl, the earthquake in Armenia, ethnic unrest and extensive strikes in mines and factories across the country (a 1989 law legalized strikes). But Gorbachev remained confident and pressed on with perestroika: 'This is a turbulent time, a turbulent sea in which it is not easy to sail the ship. But we have a compass and we have a crew to guide that ship, and the ship itself is strong.'

In one of the most important changes in the country's political and economic system since the 1917 Bolshevik Revolution, Mikhail Gorbachev was elected by Congress as the Soviet Union's first executive president. This new post, replacing the former honorary chairmanship of the Supreme Soviet, had broader constitutional powers. The president now had the right to propose legislation, veto bills passed by Congress, appoint and fire the prime minister and other senior government officials, and declare states of emergency (with the approval of the republics).

Gorbachev (who celebrated his 80th birthday in 2011) summarized the results of all his policies: 'Having embarked upon the road of radical reform, we have crossed the line beyond which there is no return to the past... Things will never be the same again in the Soviet Union—or in the whole communist world.' Gorbachev's second revolution became one of the most momentous events in the second half of the 20th century.

THE COMMUNIST PARTY

If what the Communists are doing with Russia is an experiment, for this experiment I would not even spare a frog.   Professor I P Pavlov (1918)

The Bolshevik Party, formed by Lenin, began as a unified band of revolutionaries whose 8,000 members organized the mass strike of the 1905 St Petersburg revolt. By October 1917, the Bolshevik Party (soon renamed the Communist Party) had over 300,000 members, many of whom became the leaders and planners of the newly formed Soviet State.

Before the fall of Communism, there were more than 20 million Party members, a third of them women. Membership was open to any citizens who 'did not exploit the labor of others', abided by the Party's philosophy and gave three percent of their monthly pay as dues to the Party. Members were also required to attend several meetings and lectures each month, provide volunteer work a few times a year and help with election campaigns. Approximately 200,000 of these members were full-time officials, *apparatchiks*, paid by the Party. The Komsomol, or Communist Youth Organization, had 40 million additional members, while 25 million schoolchildren belonged to the Young Pioneers. Eligibility for party membership began at age 18.

On February 7, 1990, after 72 years of Communist rule, the Soviet Communist Party's Central Committee voted overwhelmingly to surrender its monopoly on power. On March 15, 1990, the Soviet Congress of People's Deputies amended Article Six, which had guaranteed the Communist Party its position as the only 'leading authority' in government. In its revised form, Article Six stated that the Communists, together with other political parties and social organizations, had the right to shape State policy. During the 28th Party Congress, the Party voted to reorganize its ruling body, the Politburo, to include Communist Party leaders from each of the 15 republics, in addition to the top 12 Moscow officials. Instead of being selected by the Central Committee, the Party in each republic chose its own leaders, guaranteeing, at the time, a voice in the Party to even the smallest republic.

Other amendments revised the Marxist view that private property was incompatible with Socialism. Individuals could own land and factories as long as they did not 'exploit' other Soviet citizens. New economic policies replaced direct central planning, instituted price reforms, created a stock exchange and allowed farmers to sell their produce on the open market. Additional new laws decreed that 'the press and other mass media are now free; censorship of the mass media is forbidden', and that all political movements had access to the airwaves with the right to establish their own television and radio stations. The monopoly enjoyed by the Communist Party on State-run radio and television ended. Even advertising, long denounced 'as a means of swindling the people' and a 'social weapon of the exploiter's class', became acceptable. These momentous changes paved the way toward a multiparty democracy and a free-market economy.

By the end of August 1991, Boris Yeltsin stood in the Russian parliament building, the White House, and declared: 'I am now signing a decree suspending the activities of the Russian Communist Party!' All Communist newspapers such as *Pravda* were temporarily shut down. Gorbachev followed by issuing decrees to end Soviet Communist rule. These decrees dissolved the Party's structure of committees and policy-making, which included the Central Committee. Archives of the Party and the KGB were seized, and the government confiscated all of the Party's assets throughout the country. It would take two years before the Communist Party regained some of its powers.

ATTEMPTED COUP OF AUGUST 1991

Gorbachev's vision of a second revolution never included an attempted coup. During his last year in office, many of his actions contradicted all that he had worked toward. After strongly supporting accelerated reforms, Gorbachev suddenly rejected the 500-Day Plan, which proposed converting the sluggish centralized economy into a market-oriented one. Then, in December 1990, he appointed the conservative Boris Pugo as his Minister of the Interior.

On January 11, 1991, Lithuania announced its independence; two days later Pugo sent in troops. Soviet troops were also sent into Latvia to quell demonstrations. During the Gulf War, the Chairman of the KGB, Vladimir Kryuchkov, charged that foreign governments were trying to destabilize Soviet society; the Russian military had become much more sensitive to the reactionary elements gathering force.

Gorbachev banned Yeltsin's rally of support in March 1991 and renewed censorship of the print and television media. The people in Moscow demonstrated anyway and troops were sent in. One of Gorbachev's aides said: 'March 28 was the turning point for Mikhail Sergeyevich. He went to the abyss, looked over the edge, was horrified at what he saw and backed away.' Gorbachev had to move closer to an alliance with Yeltsin to survive.

Those in the government became uneasy with the upcoming Union of Republics' treaty; much of Moscow's power would be usurped if signed. Leading bureaucrats realized they could lose their jobs and began planning ways to undermine Gorbachev's power. Even though he had created an unprecedented wave of changes, Gorbachev's popularity at home had now fallen to practically zero. After five years of promises, reforms had only made the living standards of average citizens worse. When prices had risen by over 50 percent, the population became increasingly reluctant to trade their goods for worthless banknotes—inflation rose to over 1,000 percent and the ruble collapsed. Despite a grossly dissatisfied population, disjointed government and repeated warnings of a plot against him, Gorbachev left for a vacation in the Crimea to work on the Union Treaty.

On the Sunday afternoon of August 18, 1991, Gorbachev was told that Yuri Plekhanov, a top KGB official, had arrived to see him. Gorbachev sensed something was wrong and tried to use the telephones; all five lines were dead. Then Valery Boldin, the Chief of Staff, entered the room, saying that Gorbachev had to sign a referendum declaring a state of emergency within the country. If he did not sign, the vice president would take over leadership duties. Since Gorbachev refused to go along with the conspiracy, thousands of troops were sent into Moscow. Ironically, the coup members failed to arrest Boris Yeltsin who, that morning, had just happened to rush off to his office in the parliament building 45 minutes earlier than usual.

The next morning, the coup leaders announced that Gorbachev, 'with serious health problems', could no longer govern. But it became obvious from the outset that the coup was ill planned. None of the opposition leaders had been arrested. Yeltsin, holed up in the White House, was receiving calls from around the world (from a cellular phone slipped in by the manager of Pizza Hut) and ate delivered pizza. The coup was doomed to fail just from the attention created by all the international media connections. At one point, Yeltsin went outside and climbed on top of a tank in front of 100,000 protesters. He appealed for mass resistance and named himself the Guardian of Democracy. By the end of the day, troops switched to Yeltsin's side, and many of the elite commando divisions were now protecting the White House.

By August 20, the coup attempt was weakening; many of the planners stayed at home. Crowds of people raised the old white, blue and red Russian flag. The famous cellist, composer and conductor Mstislav Rostropovich, a survivor of the Siege of Leningrad, even flew in from Paris and played music within the parliament building. Tank divisions descended upon the White House later in the day. Swarms of people blocked their way; after three were killed, the tanks retreated, refusing to fire on their own people.

Three days after the attempted coup, Yeltsin announced its failure. He sent officials to the Crimea to bring Gorbachev safely back to Moscow. The shaken president and his family (his wife, Raisa, later died of leukemia in 1999, at the age of 67) returned by airplane early the next morning. Seven members of the State Emergency Committee, also called the Gang of Eight, were arrested; the eighth, Boris Pugo, shot himself in the head.

The crowds cheered, not so much for Gorbachev's return, but for their savior, Boris Yeltsin. Communism had disintegrated with the attempted putsch. Thousands celebrated as the statue of 'Iron Felix' Dzerzhinsky, the founder of the secret police after the 1917 Revolution, was toppled from its pedestal in front of the KGB building. A Russian flag and crucifix were put in its place—a monument to the millions who had died in prison camps at the hands of the KGB. Unbelievably, a new era had begun.

THE END OF THE SOVIET UNION

The Soviet Union ceased to exist on December 25, 1991. The great ideological experiment began by Lenin's Bolshevik Revolution, constituted on December 30, 1922, ended nine days short of its 70th year. 'One State has died,' announced Russian television, 'but in its place a great dream is being born.' The birth was of the Commonwealth of Independent States. Four days later, Gorbachev, the eighth and final leader of the Soviet Union, submitted his resignation. He no longer had a Soviet Union to govern. Boris Yeltsin claimed his office in the Kremlin.

The patience of the Russian people was great, and it gave foreigners to believe that the Russian people were slaves at heart. Now the Russian people must show to the whole world that it is a truly free people. After this great turn of events the Russian man must rule himself.

Nikolai Berdyayev, from the journal *Narodopravstvo*, 1917–18

BORIS YELTSIN

Boris Nikolayevich Yeltsin was born into a poor family in Sverdlovsk in 1931. He went on to dismantle the entire Soviet empire. In an historic meeting in Alma Ata, the capital of Kazakhstan, Yeltsin convinced the leaders of the former Soviet republics to sign a new treaty forming the 11-member Commonwealth. In February 1992, Yeltsin officially put the Cold War to rest in a meeting with US President George H.W. Bush. He proclaimed a 'new era', in which the two nations would join as allies to seek 'an enduring peace that rests on lasting common values'.

By the time Yeltsin took control, the economy was in disarray. Without GOSPLAN (the former central planning commission) and GOSNAB (the former central supply organization), factories everywhere had no idea what to produce or where to ship their goods. With the help of economic advisor Yegor Gaidar, Yeltsin announced the lifting of price controls. Gradually, over 600 commodities exchanges were formed and the Moscow Stock Exchange building returned to its original function. Russians received government vouchers redeemable for cash, or shares in businesses that were previously State-owned. People in private enterprises began to flourish, from street vendors to entrepreneurs. Newly rich businessmen (nicknamed *Noviye Russkiye* or New Russians) operated with the latest technology and bought expensive cars. (Today Russia is the largest market in the world for luxury cars.) It was possible for some young people to make more money in one day than their parents had in months, or even years. But for many, especially the elderly, the new order meant standing in longer queues and spending hours in the cold trying to sell pitiful possessions to make ends meet.

Newspapers were also freed of censorship. Advertisements interrupted television programs. Soap operas were watched avidly—over 60 percent of the population tuned in to the Mexican series *The Rich Also Cry*. Western imports, including MTV, *Santa Barbara* and *Beverly Hills 90210*, deluged Russian television. And foreigners could now travel legally to once-restricted cities.

Yeltsin's biggest crisis since the attempted coup of 1991 arose after he dissolved the obstructionist Russian legislature at the end of September 1993, and moved to replace it with a new elective body. Yeltsin said he was acting to stem a 'senseless struggle that was threatening to lead Russia into a political abyss... the body is an outmoded Soviet-era institution sustained in office by a useless constitution'.

A growing animosity had been brewing between Yeltsin and his opposition, which had tried and failed to impeach him six months earlier in March 1993. Yeltsin had conducted a referendum in April when Russian voters had expressed their preference for him and his policies. However, the Supreme Soviet instantly claimed Yeltsin's order to dissolve the legislature as null and void. Vice President Alexander Rutskoi, now a Yeltsin rival, was immediately elected acting president and Yeltsin was impeached on a 144–6 vote. Communist and nationalist leaders appeared on the White House balcony and urged their supporters to stay on. Many were taken with the irony of the gathering, on the very site where Yeltsin, next to Rutskoi, had faced down the right-wing coup plotters in August 1991. But this time Yeltsin was the coup plotter. While both sides waged all-out political warfare, many Russians were now fed up with all the chaos. One citizen stated: 'We are tired of the political battles and want to live a normal life and earn some decent money; no one knows anymore what we're coup-ing for!'

About a week after this crisis began, parliament supporters smashed through police lines, stormed the mayor's office and attacked the headquarters of the State television company, which exploded into the worst political violence since the 1917 Bolshevik Revolution. 'There can be no forgiveness for attacking innocent people,' announced Yeltsin. 'The armed revolt is doomed.' Yeltsin then countered by creating a state of emergency and sending in armored personnel carriers, tanks and elite commando units, which fired upon the White House. A new military tactic was also employed—blasting pop group Dire Straits and Russian Rap from loudspeakers near the White House. Thirteen days later, the opposition leaders surrendered after a massive barrage by tanks and paratroopers. The battle left 187 people dead and the White House a blackened shell with nearly every window blown out. (Six months later, the arrested White House hard-liners, who had tried to topple the government in 1991 and 1993, were pardoned by the new Parliamentary Duma.)

Yeltsin continued to promise that his struggling nation would not retreat from economic reform. To aid the reform process, many countries pledged financial support to Russia. In January 1994, US President Bill Clinton journeyed to Moscow for a summit with Yeltsin. In an historic meeting, the Ukraine also participated and signed an agreement to disarm all of the 1,800 nuclear warheads that had fallen to it after the collapse of the Soviet Union. Clinton told Yeltsin: 'You are in the process of transforming your entire economy while you develop a new constitution and democracy as well. It boggles the mind and you have my respect.'

THE FIRST MULTIPARTY ELECTIONS

Two years after Yeltsin had banned Communist activity on Russian soil, the constitutional court lifted Yeltsin's order, ruling that it violated the constitution. Thus, the Communist Party participated in the country's first true multiparty election on December 12, 1993. In the election, a new Russian constitution was also voted in, which gave the president more power and Parliament less. The constitution granted Russia's 149 million citizens many economic freedoms and civil liberties that had been stifled since the Bolshevik takeover. These included the right to own land, the right not to be wiretapped and the right to travel freely at home and abroad. It also provided for a new Parliament, known as the Federal Assembly, with the Federation Council as its upper chamber and the Duma as its lower. A month after the ballot, those elected assembled in Moscow to launch the new parliamentary democracy. Yeltsin stated: 'We must preserve this for the sake of national peace and to make sure dictatorship never returns to Russia.'

Even though they were no longer the only party, the Communists again became one of the largest political forces in the land. Taking part in the election were other hard-line groups, among them the Agrarian Party, the Centrist Democratic Party and the Women of Russia Party. The pro-reform parties included Russia's Choice, the Yavlinsky Bloc and the Russian Unity and Accord Party. The Beer-Lovers Party was one of many on the fringe. Some of those elected were reactionary journalist Alexander Nevzorov, weightlifting champion Yuri Vlasov, and the psychic healer Anatoly Kashpirovsky.

Although Yeltsin's opponents won the majority of the 450 seats in the Duma, they were forced to compromise with his supporters. The upper chamber, the 178-seat Federation Council, roughly equivalent to the US Senate, met under the new State symbol, the double-headed eagle, first adopted by Ivan the Great in the 15th century. First Deputy Prime Minister Vladimir Shumeiko, a close ally of Yeltsin, was elected as the first Speaker.

The ultranationalist Liberal Democratic Party, headed by Vladimir Zhirinovsky, shocked the world by beating Yeltsin's Russia's Choice Party in these first ever parliamentary elections. Zhirinovsky's party won nearly a quarter of the Russian vote, which many saw as a protest by a population feeling the pain of reform. In the three years that this obscure Moscow lawyer rose into the national spotlight, he rashly advocated party dictatorship, Russian military expansion, the expelling of millions of non-Russians and ending payments of foreign debt. Zhirinovsky also threatened to restore Russia's imperial borders, annex Alaska and invade Turkey and Poland. With this character climbing to the forefront of Russian politics, no wonder the world was greatly concerned for Russia's fragile young democracy and its vulnerability to irresponsible leadership.

THE EFFECTS OF REFORM

A few weeks after Parliament convened, Yegor Gaidar, the architect of Russia's free-market reforms and leader of Russia's Choice Party, unexpectedly quit his post as Economic Minister. As a result the ruble plummeted. (The Russian Central Bank had already pumped more than one billion dollars into the economy—more than a quarter of its hard currency reserves—to stabilize the monetary system.) But even after the reforms, no more than ten percent of the population seemed better off, while over 50 percent complained of being worse off. The continuing credit squeeze created more unemployment, delayed pay checks and wiped out entire savings accounts of average citizens. The Russian comedian Mikhail Zhvanetsky joked about the economy: 'Much has changed but nothing has happened. Or is that much has happened and nothing has changed.' Many forecasted that nearly a century of suppressed initiative combined with a government-controlled lifestyle would take at least a generation to alter.

By 1993, inflation (2,600 percent in 1992 and 900 percent in 1993) became so rampant that savings of 20,000 rubles—that could once buy four cars—was now worth only a few pounds of sausage. One survey concluded that on his monthly salary, an average Russian could only pay rent, consume a daily ration of half a kilogram (one pound) of bread, half a liter (less than one pint) of milk, 100 grams (three-and-a-half ounces) of beef, and five cigarettes. Satire was commonplace: 'What was the nationality of Adam and Eve? Russian, of course—who else would think that being homeless, naked and splitting one apple between them was living in paradise.'

Russians began to augment their diets with vegetables grown in gardens or apartment window boxes. To supplement their incomes, many turned to vending sausages or cigarettes, pawning family goods, collecting bottles for recycling, or working as taxi drivers. An entire generation of educated people could barely afford to live. And one teacher wryly noted: 'We can't even afford to die.' (The cheapest funeral cost was over $300, while the average pension was $50 per month—the official poverty level was set at $35). One retiree summarized, 'And what good is freedom to me now? Freedom to buy a pornographic magazine, openly complain all I want, or travel to Cyprus when I can't even afford to eat? I hope and believe that things will get better. But they will never be better for us. I'll simply not live to see those days.'

During the first years of transition, the World Bank estimated that one-third of the population, or nearly 50 million Russians, had an income below the minimum sustenance level. With prices for food, gasoline and consumer goods approaching US levels, average Russian salaries were still only one-tenth of those in America. Over one-quarter found themselves unemployed and a survey reported that only ten percent of Russian males were capable of fully supporting their families. Russia's life expectancy plummeted so fast in the first half of the 1990s that a British medical journal stated that it was 'without parallel in the modern era'. Due to the severe decline in living standards a Russian man's life expectancy fell to age 58, compared to 72 in neighboring Finland. The male incidences of heart disease, suicide and alcoholism were among the highest in the developed world, and the mortality rate exceeded the birth rate. Alarmingly, if the trend continued in 1,000 years there would only be 150 people left in Russia!

For the first time in Russian history, investment and stock funds, quasi-banks, and joint-stock companies (without insurance protection) filled print advertising and the airwaves with the promise of large returns—in some cases up to 30,000 percent. In a few years alone, over 2,000 banks opened across the country. Many investors never saw their money again. One businessman stated that 'the average Russian is the most unprepared investor in the world. For 70 years all he did was put his money into State-owned banks and was raised to believe that whatever was told over TV or in the newspapers was true.' Scam operations and pyramid schemes flourished, and hundreds of thousands of victims were cheated out of their life savings in the new era of cowboy capitalism.

However, with the explosion of new commercial activities, a new class was created—that of the filthy rich or *Noviye Russkiye* (New Russians). About 60 percent of this group simply turned the socialist empires they managed into their own private companies. Others capitalized on the 'Wild East' state of mind, where practically everything was up for grabs. With both a penchant for entrepreneurship and greed, some became billionaires virtually overnight. Suddenly, the demand for office space, apartments, retail markets and shopping centers was enormous.

Consumption by the nouveaux riches is decadent even by Western standards. Protected by bodyguards, driving bullet-proof Land-rovers, building villas, sending their children to study abroad, wearing designer clothing, this elite class has built an enormous division between the haves and have-nots. One pensioner declared, 'We're back to having two classes again—the aristocrats and the peasants!' Many Russian nightclubs have no foreign customers—they simply cannot afford the prices.

It is often said that the collapse of Communism has fertilized the ground upon which gangsters and mafia thrive. But the word mafia has a different implication in Russia. It simply defines a broad range of group activity that was already flourishing under Socialism. Since much was illegal during this era—from owning a business to playing rock 'n' roll—most unsanctioned activities were commonplace; a survey in the 1980s indicated that the average Russian dealt daily with black marketeers who provided the economy with most of its goods. In turn, these types had no problem embracing capitalism and finding immediate ways to make money. Even though encountering mafia activity may be the price of doing business in Russia (the chances of experiencing any as a tourist are practically zero)—all in all, violent crime rates are still much lower than in the United States.

In 1994, after two decades of forced exile in the U.S. Russia's greatest living writer Alexander Solzhenitsyn was allowed to return to his homeland. The winner of the Nobel Prize for Literature in 1970, Solzhenitsyn was banished by the former Soviet Government in 1974 for writing *The Gulag Archipelago*, which preserved the memory of the Soviet holocaust. (In 1945, at age 27, Solzhenitsyn was arrested for writing derogatory comments about Stalin in a letter to a friend. He was accused of anti-Soviet Propaganda and sentenced to eight years in labor camps.) But before Solzhenitsyn returned to his homeland, he first wanted to complete his four-volume epic *The Red Wheel*, a history leading up to the 1917 October Revolution that he had worked on for 20 years: 'Our history has been so hidden. I had to dig so deep, I had to uncover what was buried and sealed. This took up all my years.' The work totals over 5,000 pages.

After his exile, Solzhenitsyn declared: 'All of us in prison in the 1940s were certain that Communism would fail. The only question was when... In a strange way, I was inwardly convinced that I would someday return to Russia.' It was not until late 1989 that Gorbachev finally gave permission to publish Solzhenitsyn's works in Russia: 'It was only when I lay there on rotting prison straw that I sensed within myself the first stirrings of good. The line separating good and evil passes not through states, nor between classes, nor between political parties either, but right through every human heart.' (In a recent poll, 90% of young Russians were unable to name a victim of Soviet purges and prison camps.)

In 1993, a political poll in St Petersburg showed that 48 percent of the respondents wanted Solzhenitsyn as their president. In *The First Circle*, first published in the West in 1968 because it was banned in the Soviet Union, he described that in a tyranny a real writer is like a second government. In 2006, billboards across Russia advertised the TV adaptation of Solzhenitsyn's fiercely anti-Soviet novel; and the 10-part mini-series, directed by Gleb Panfilov, became one of the nation's most watched programs. (The first complete English translation of the novel was published in 2009.) The story chronicles three days in the lives of prisoners at Mavrino, a special prison set up in an old country estate outside Moscow in the aftermath of WW II. (The title is a reference to Dante's concentric circles of hell in The Divine Comedy.) Even though Alexander Solzhenitsyn returned home to live, he knew there was a long road ahead: 'If it took Russia 75 years to fall so far, then it is obvious that it will take more than 75 years to rise back up. I know that we are still faced with incredible hardships for years to come'. (After Solzhenitsyn died in 2008, at the age of 89, Moscow changed the name of Big Communist Street to Alexander Solzhenitsyn.)

THE RESURGENCE OF THE COMMUNISTS

In February 1995, the Commonwealth of Independent States elected Yeltsin as its chairman and moved its headquarters from Minsk, Belarus to Moscow. After celebrating Victory Day, the 50th anniversary of World War II, in May, Yeltsin had to vigorously embark on his reelection campaign—for only six percent of the population approved of the job he was doing. The majority of Russians blamed

Yeltsin for the social upheavals, deplorable living conditions and unpopular war in Chechnya. In addition, many civil servants, teachers, and pensioners had not received a government pay check in up to six months. Following his elevation to near sainthood after the 1991 coup attempt, Yeltsin now had single-digit ratings, was in declining health and drinking heavily. He soon suffered two heart attacks and was confined to bed for four months.

But Yeltsin struggled on, stating: 'It is our task to prevent a Communist victory at the polls.' But, in the December 17, 1995 parliamentary elections, the Communists led the field of 43 parties. Gennady Zhuganov, who had taken charge of the reborn Communist Party in 1993, now even welcomed religious members. The Communists and Zhirinovsky's ultranationalists finished first and second, garnering 22 percent and 11 percent of the vote respectively. The astounded world questioned how a country so recently freed from socialist rule could so quickly choose a course back to renewed oppression. With a long tradition of not regarding freedom as a value, the average Russian experienced reform more as hardship than salvation. Even writer Ivan Turgenev expressed this notion after Alexander II agreed to free the serfs in 1861: 'And although you were freed from slavery, you do not know what to do with freedom.'

Foreigners find it difficult to comprehend how Russians can be skeptical of the transition to a Western-style democracy and economy. One must first understand that to them it may only be another short-lived phase in their country's history. So many promises in the past have proven hollow. Even Gorbachev warned: 'If reforms continue pushing people into a dead end, discontent could spring loose and extremism move in.'

1996 PRESIDENTIAL ELECTIONS

The architect of Russia's privatization program, First Deputy Prime Minister Anatoly Chubais, was dismissed in January 1996, but then called back in March to help with Yeltsin's presidential campaign. Yeltsin's daughter Tatyana Dachenko also played a major role. At 65, Yeltsin wanted to prove he was, indeed, capable of a comeback at the June 16 election. A few weeks before the ballot, on May 27, Yeltsin brought Chechen leader Yanderbiyev to the Kremlin to sign a peace treaty after 18 months of war that had left Chechnya ruined and over 40,000 dead. Boris Yeltsin was as determined as ever not to have the Communist Party win: 'Our responsibility to the memory of the millions who suffered in the camps and to our children and descendants is to prevent neo-Stalinists, fascists and extremists from coming to power in Russia. Russia must enter the 21st century without this filth.'

On June 16, 1996, an 11-man race took place for the presidency. Yeltsin captured 35 percent of the vote, and Zhuganov 32 percent. General Alexander Lebed, an ex-paratrooper and decorated hero of Russia's war in Afghanistan, received 15 percent. Zhirinovsky finished seventh with less than six percent of the first round vote. Since no candidate received over 50 percent a national run-off election was scheduled to take place on July 3. In a calculated move, Yeltsin appointed Lebed as his national security chief.

The Communist Party now faced a major identity crisis. People were just as uncertain of Zhuganov's politics as they were of Zhirinovsky's. Gennady Zhuganov, in his 1995 book *I Believe in Russia*, stated that 'if Stalin had lived longer, he would have restored Russia and saved it from the cosmopolitans'. Most of the population, especially the younger generation, were more interested in pay checks than politics. Many also feared that if Zhuganov won, the Communist party would not allow others to exist and would return to monopolizing the State. To the relief of the majority, the election resulted in a stunning victory for Yeltsin: he received 54 percent to Zhuganov's 40 percent.

On August 9, 1996, Yeltsin, with a stiff walk and slowed speech, swore an oath for his second term as president, with his hand held over a red-bound copy of the Russian constitution. By October Alexander Lebed was fired, accused of plotting a military coup. (Lebed was later killed in a helicopter crash in 2002.) A month later, on November 5, Yeltsin underwent a major coronary bypass operation; he had had another heart attack right before his reelection.

THE LAST YEARS OF THE 20TH CENTURY

By 1997, even though Russia was finally emerging from its post-Soviet economic slump, just six percent of Russians said they were content and seventy-two percent felt their lives had changed little over the past five years. A major role reversal had also taken place within the country. Instead of children having to live with parents (because of housing shortages), parents now found themselves living with their children out of economic necessity. The clash of extraordinary monetary achievement and oppressive backwardness continued to mar the road ahead.

In February 1998, as Russia journeyed through a seventh year of insecurity, Yeltsin felt that the 'nation needed a new strategy for upsurge', and fired three cabinet ministers along with his deputy prime ministers for failing to reverse Russia's economic and social ills. Yeltsin then pressured the Duma into voting in the 35-year-old Sergei Kiriyenko, then Minister of Oil and Energy, into the position of prime minister. Many regarded this merely as a political stunt to shift blame from Yeltsin's own sagging popularity. By May, thousands of striking coal miners, in massive protests, even blocked routes of the Trans-Siberian railway, demanding $600 million in back wages.

By 1998, Yeltsin's government had fallen behind by months, even years, with payments of State wages and pensions, which forced people in many areas to resort to barter and subsistence farming. It was estimated that nearly 70 percent of the population lived mostly off the produce grown in their small garden plots. Many villagers kept a cow, caught and dried fish from the rivers and grew cabbage, beets, potatoes and onions. The result was an almost cashless society where business was transacted and employees paid mainly by trading goods and services. Since most companies and citizens had no money, they could not pay their taxes (the government claimed that fewer than three percent of the population had filed income tax declarations the year before), meaning the state was constantly short of funds, and the deficit continued to grow.

In August 1998, the country experienced its worst economic crisis since the 1991 Soviet collapse. (A Russian saying goes: 'It is better to have 100 friends than 100 rubles.') Overnight the ruble plunged to less than a quarter of its value, shutting down the nation's largest commercial banks, which in turn caused the nation to default on most of its debt. (It owed the IMF 17.5 billion dollars for the year and the country's GNP was estimated to be lower than Belgium's.)

Yeltsin responded by dismissing the Russian cabinet, the third time in little more than a year, replacing Prime Minister Kiriyenko with Foreign Minister Yevgeny Primakov, an ex-KGB head. He also assigned Vladimir Putin to head the former KGB, now known as the Federal Security Bureau. With Russia plunging into turmoil and also suffering from one of the worst harvests since 1953 (the last year of Stalinist rule), many accused Yeltsin of trying to shift blame away from himself. A new joke circulated in Moscow: 'For too long we have been standing at the edge of the precipice; now we are taking the great leap forward.'

By October 1998, millions of dissatisfied Russians across the country took part in rallies demanding Yeltsin's resignation. (Yeltsin and other Kremlin members were also being investigated for bribery and corruption.) At the end of the month, Yeltsin was admitted to a sanatorium for rest and treatment for what was termed neuropsychological asthenia. Although no one knew what this meant, the Kremlin announced that this condition forced the president to relinquish his day-to-day duties, which would be taken over by Primakov. The question asked by Russia and the world was how the country would survive without a strong leader and a solution to its dire economic crisis.

On May 12 1999, one day before impeachment hearings were to be held (the impeachment, supported by Communists, never came to pass), Yeltsin fired 70-year-old Yevgeny Primakov (many surmised because of Primakov's increasing popularity) replacing him with yet another revolving-door Prime Minister, the more youthful Sergei Stepashin. Yeltsin continued with his unpopular erratic decisions by subsequently replacing Stepashin three months later with Vladimir Putin. Then, on September 30, a few weeks after explosions in two apartment blocks in Moscow left over 200 dead (terrorism was suspected, but never proven), Yeltsin sent ground troops back into separatist Chechnya (Russia had pulled out in 1996), in what would become an ongoing bloodbath.

Even though Boris Yeltsin had inherited a decaying and corrupt Socialist empire and created the most democratic state in Russian history (in 1990, everything belonged to the state; by 1997, almost 75 percent of property was held privately) and in the eyes of the world had accumulated a list of major international accomplishments (he slashed the nuclear arsenal by 60 percent, halved the armed forces, helped broker a Serbian retreat from Kosovo and, in October 1999, signed the order for the last Russian troops to exit the Baltic), this leader now found himself suffering the same fate as Gorbachev—ending his final days in office with only a two percent approval rating. With his health and mental acuity diminishing, many sadly compared him with the Communist leader Brezhnev who, at the end of his term, served only as a weak puppet figure. But Yeltsin asserted, 'I am not going to resign. It's very difficult to remove me. And considering my character, it is practically impossible.'

So, when on December 31 1999, the 68-year-old Yeltsin appeared on television to give a New Year's address, no one expected him to take the world again by surprise. He announced his immediate resignation, although officially in office until the following June. 'I want to beg forgiveness for your dreams that never came true. And I also want to beg forgiveness for not having justified your hopes. I beg your forgiveness for having failed to jump, in one leap, from the gray stagnant, totalitarian past to the light, rich and civilized future.' Yeltsin, once hailed as the 'Father of Russian Democracy' by former US President Clinton, handed over power to 47-year-old Vladimir Putin as acting-President of the Russian Federation (thereby forcing early elections in March 2000). Yeltsin ended his speech by stating, 'Russia must enter the new millennium with new politicians, new faces, and new intelligent, strong and energetic people. We, who have been in power for many years, must go.'

During his Presidential campaign, Putin (and his newly formed Unity Party) were well ahead in the polls of the ten other candidates, which included Primakov, Yavlinsky, Zhuganov and Zhirinovsky. Yuri Luzhkov, the popular re-elected Mayor of Moscow (who had decided not to run for the national election), helped Putin gather votes in his region. On March 26 elections were held and Putin won a four-year term by garnering 53 percent of the vote; his inauguration was held on May 7 2000. Later in the year, Putin published the book-length conversation *First Person*. He had never before held an elective office.

VLADIMIR PUTIN

Vladimir Vladimirovich Putin, born October 7, 1952, grew up in a *kommunalka* communal apartment in Leningrad, Russia's most westward-looking city. The only child of factory workers (his father was the son of one of Stalin's cooks), the driven young Vladimir became the city's judo champion (he has an 8th-degree black belt) and graduated from Leningrad State University with a Law Degree; during his studies, the KGB recruited him. (In 1975, the year Putin joined up, the agency had already sent Noble Prize winners Andrei Sakharov into internal exile, and Alexander Solzhenitsyn into forced exile abroad.) As an agent Putin received special Communist perks including free housing and travel opportunities. In 1983, he married Lyudmilia and they had two daughters, Masha and Katya. (They divorced in 2014.) Putin spent 16 years with the KGB, rising to the rank of lieutenant colonel, and was mainly stationed in Dresden, East Germany, where he witnessed the end of the Cold War.

As a young man, Putin spent the second half of the 1980s recruiting people to spy on the West. Working as a foreign intelligence operative, the goal was to steal Western technology. Fiercely patriotic, he later defended Soviet-era intelligence and said that he would 'never read a book by a defector, by someone who had betrayed the Motherland.' In 1989 (shortly after the fall of the Berlin Wall), Putin returned to Leningrad and soon rose to become the city's Deputy Mayor. For his toughness and dedication he earned the nickname 'Stasi,' after the East German secret police. With the break-up of the Soviet Union came the disintegration of the KGB, and Putin resigned from the agency in 1991.

In 1996, when St Petersburg mayor Anatoly Sobchak failed to be re-elected, Putin got a job in the Moscow Presidential Administration office. Then, two years later, the ex-intelligence officer found himself coming full circle when Yeltsin appointed him as head of the FSB (the Federal Security Bureau, what used to be the KGB). One of Putin's first moves was to try and obtain approval for the monitoring of e-mails and other Internet communications by requiring service providers to install equipment linking all their computers with the FSB. As can be imagined, critics harshly protested a return to old Soviet spying standards and the proposal never passed through the Duma. By 1999, Putin had become secretary of the Security Council, and in August of that year, he was appointed the last Prime Minister in Yeltsin's sea-sawing government.

Many Russians elected Putin because of his staunch no-nonsense, take-charge leadership which they felt necessary to tackle the country's enormous problems. One of the first things Putin did after becoming acting President was to fly to Chechnya on New Year's Day and hand out awards to Russian servicemen fighting there. He then fired Boris Yeltsin's daughter Tatyana from her Kremlin Post as 'image advisor.' (She was also under investigation for taking government kickbacks; Putin

Introducing a new supply-side economic plan for the country, Putin also allowed for a simplified flat tax of 13 percent.

Five months after the election, 73 percent of Russia approved of Putin's presidency. This tough pragmatist appealed to the masses who were downright fed up with decades of inept leadership and rampant corruption. One Russian journalist noted that perhaps what Russians really yearned for was a nationalist father-cum-czar-like figure whom they could have faith in to restore order to this apparent state of cowboy capitalism. The double entendre of Ras-Putin, was not lost within circles of discussion. (In 2000 a national poll discovered that 79 percent of Russians regretted the demise of the Soviet Union, up from 69 percent in 1992.) In his first State of the Union address in July 2000, Putin promised Russians 'a solid country, strong and pure.'

Even though rich tycoons had bankrolled Yeltsin's 1996 re-election campaign, Putin wanted them out of politics. (Many wondered how, during Yeltsin's term in office, a handful of Russian businessmen had ended up with a 30 percent share of one-seventh of the world's resources; the oils and metals tycoon, Roman Abramovich, became the world's richest man under 40.) Now Putin warned the country's wealthy oligarchs that he would not stand for anymore bandit capitalism, 'Those fishing in muddy waters will no longer be able to keep their catch.' Bank accounts were frozen, and two business and media barons, Boris Berezovsky (who had once acted as Executive Secretary of the Commonwealth) and Vladimir Gusinsky (chairman of the Media-Most empire, who had made his fortune in banking and real estate), were forced to flee the country. The latter's NTV channel, Russia's first privately-owned network, was taken over by the State gas monopoly Gazprom. Pressure was also put on the press to censor any negative stories about the new government. The world sat in wonder: was Putin really a new innovative breed or just another retainer from the old Communist-trained school?

In May 2001, Putin signed another decree that divided Russia into seven federal zones, each with its own Kremlin representative. All of Russia's 89 provinces were regrouped under the new system. Putin vowed that a 'strong central authority was essential to avoiding the breakup of the country.' The President also reinstated the Soviet-era music written by Stalin court composer Alexander Alexandrov (and first broadcast nationally on 1 January 1944) as the country's national anthem. (This had been dropped by Yeltsin in 1990, who preferred Glinka's famous 1833 choral hymn march, Slavsya (Glory)! or 'A Patriotic Song'; but, in the end, it was deemed too difficult to sing.) New words for the 'Unbreakable Union' were written by 87-year-old Sergei Mikhalkov (father of film directors, Nikita Mikhalkov and Andrei Konchalovsky), a popular children's poet who, ironically, had co-written the original words, approved by Stalin in 1943. The Soviet-era lyrics shifted from "Party of Lenin, the strength of the people/Communism's triumph, lead us on..." to something

Lenin, the strength of the people/Communism's triumph, lead us on..." to something more prosaic to better suit the modern era: "...You are unique in the world, inimitable. Native land protected by God!" Mikhalkov died in 2009, at the age of 96, and is buried in Moscow's Novodevichy Cemetery.

It did not seem to bother Russians much that Putin attempted to muzzle the media, fuel the ongoing war in Chechnya, and grossly mishandle the Kursk submarine disaster. In addition, there was the government's mishandling of the Moscow Theater Chechen Siege along with the Beslan School terrorist take-over, where over 200 people were killed. For, after nearly a decade of decline, the country was finally enjoying a mild economic boom thanks to higher oil export prices and a lower ruble exchange rate. The average monthly wage was rising, and citizens were finally getting paid on time. In addition, on September 20, 2001, eight decades after Lenin had first banned private ownership of property, Russia's parliament voted to allow its citizens (and foreigners alike) to buy, sell and own land. Putin was also the first Russian leader in a decade to enjoy a working majority in parliament, and the country had a balanced (and surplus) budget for the first time in post-Soviet history.

At this time, it was reported that a staggering 35 percent of household wealth in Russia was owned by just 110 people, the highest level of wealth inequality in the world. With such an enormous concentration of Russia's wealth in the hands of a few, it was no small wonder that the government was concerned. So, when prominent Yukos oil executive Mikhail Khodorkovsky (his personal worth was estimated at $8 billion) began to express major political ambitions, he was arrested by the Kremlin on October 25, 2003, at gunpoint, as he was about to depart on his private jet from Siberia. What brought him down is far from clear. Whether pure political rivalry and an attempt by Putin to consolidate his power or real gross misconduct, the 40-year-old Khodorkovsky was charged with fraud and tax evasion. (The company's $15 billion in assets were later frozen and put up for auction.) Khordorkovsky argued that his meteoric rise to wealth during the 1990s privatization of state assets occurred not because he did anything illegal, but because of poorly written laws. After spending ten years in prison, Khodorkovsky received a special government pardon in 2013—one that put him on a charter flight straight out of the country to Europe. He stated, 'for Russia the second decade of the 21st century will become a period of crisis for a system built on corruption and hands-on control.'

The 2003 parliamentary elections gave the pro-Kremlin and nationalist parties a landslide majority for the first time in post-Soviet history. The United Russia party, that merely ran on loyalty to the President and a 'Strong Russia' campaign, gained a majority 50 percent of the 450 Duma seats, while the nationalist Rodina or Homeland (which ran on a populist ticket of returning the riches to the people), acquired nearly ten percent.

One of the main dramas of the election was the demise of the Communist Party. Whether it is true that Putin ran a 'war of media extermination', as Communist Party leader Gennady Zhuganov claimed, or that the population split their traditionalist 'Red-White' views between the Homeland and United Russia parties, it was clearly shown that it was time for old-guard Communist ideology to move off the modern stage.

On the other side, liberals also struggled to survive, and found themselves ousted from parliament for the first time in a decade. Both Yabloko (mainly funded by Yukos-Sibneft) and the Union of Right Forces (SPS) failed to garner five percent of the vote needed to win a block of seats. One party member sadly reflected, 'The democrats no longer exist. The democratic movement has been enfeebled, decapitated and destroyed.'

After his first full term in office, Putin emerged with the dualistic reputation of being both a man of the future and a traditionalist, doing whatever was necessary to promote the stability and growth of his country, but his seemingly open embrace of democratic values, such as civil liberties and a free press, proved to be questionable. Some considered the schizophrenic standoffs of the two Putins worthy 'of the pen of a new Dostoevsky'.

On March 14, 2004, Vladimir Putin easily won a second term as President (he ran against five challengers) when he garnered well over two-thirds of the vote (of more than a 50 percent turnout), in an election widely criticized for heavy Kremlin censoring of all opposition. After this election, the government believed that Putin, now with a clear majority, had carte blanche to enforce his system of power. In 2006, the opposition journalist and human rights activist, Anna Politkovskaya, 48, was murdered in broad daylight inside her Moscow apartment building. She wrote of Chechen atrocities and government corruption, and said, 'How could I live with myself if I didn't tell the truth.' Two years earlier, she had written the book: Putin's Russia: Life in a Failing Democracy. (It wasn't until 2014 that a Russian court convicted five men of the crime.) In 2007, the poisoning of former KGB agent and dissident, Alexander Litvinenko, by radioactive polonium in London, exploded into an international espionage scandal. His wife co-authored the book, Death of a Dissident: The Political Poisoning of Alexander Litvinenko.

During his eight years as President, many expressed concern that Putin clamped down on democracy, smothered political opposition and widely suppressed the news media. Behind a façade of democracy, many questioned if a new autocracy was now governing Russia. But, in turn, Putin said that he was proud that 'Russia had a healthy democracy, a renewed sense of national pride and played a prominent role on the world stage.' Compared to the chaotic decade after the fall of the Soviet Union, and the unpredictable Yeltsin-era, it appeared that Russians were willing to trade some liberties for more stability and economic opportunities. But, with the cost of living rising each year, pensioners (the legal age of retirement is 60 for men and 55 for women) and war veterans across the country staged massive protests against major cuts in long-standing social subsidies.

In 2008 Putin's hand picked successor, Dmitri Medvedev, already serving as Prime Minister, was elected President with 70 percent of the vote. Many considered him merely Putin's puppet, and one of his first acts was to install Putin as prime minister. In 2009, by order of the Kremlin, all gambling halls and casinos were outlawed and restricted to small areas in Kaliningrad, the south and Siberia. Chechen terrorists continued a deadly series of attacks, which included a train, metro and airport bombing. Civic protests, called Strategy 31, were held on the 31st of each month at Moscow's Triumfalnaya Square (and in St Petersburg) to demonstrate the right of free assembly, guaranteed by Article 31 of the Russian Constitution. In 2010, ten people pleaded guilty to spying for Russia while living undercover in the US—in one of the biggest spy scandals since the Cold War. When deported back to Russia, Medvedev bestowed upon them the country's highest honor at the Kremlin. In August of 2010, during a deadly heat wave, hundreds of thousands of acres of parched woodlands and peat bogs burned throughout western Russia, when hundreds died, thousands were evacuated and Moscow was blanketed in thick smoke. Shortly thereafter, long-term Moscow mayor, Yuri Luzhkov, met his downfall and was fired by Medvedev who, in a power move, showed that the Kremlin was still in control of the capital.

In September 2011, following a change in law extending the presidential term from four to six years, Putin announced he would seek a third, non-consecutive term as President. (There is no limit to the number of terms a President may serve, just a limit on successive terms to two.) On March 4, 2012, Putin was reelected in the first round of voting with 64 percent of the vote; his closest rival was Communist Party leader, Gennady Zhuganov, with 17 percent. (Medvedev was appointed Prime Minister.) Despite accusations of fraud, along with large protests, Putin was sworn in on May 7. As a result of the new amendment, Putin will serve six years (instead of the previous four), and will be eligible to run again in 2018.

In June 2013, Russia passed a contentious anti-gay law that made it a crime 'to propagandize for untraditional sexual relationships to minors,' which exploded in a massive wave of world criticism. Six months later, a Moscow court sentenced former Bolshoi soloist, Pavel Dmitrichenko, to six years in a penal colony for ordering an acid attack on the theater's artistic director, Sergei Filin. Dmitrichenko was accused of hiring two men who attacked Filin outside his Moscow apartment (in January 2013) and tossed the contents of a jar of sulfuric acid into his eyes. (Filin has only partially regained his eyesight.) The attack outraged the ballet world and threw the Bolshoi into turmoil from which it is still recovering.

Also in December 2013, the Kremlin granted amnesty to hundreds of political prisoners tied to the 20th anniversary of Russia's constitution. Among those freed were 30 Green Peace activists arrested in the Barents Sea while protesting oil drilling in the Arctic, and the two still-imprisoned members of the punk group, Pussy Riot, arrested earlier in the year for staging a performance protest inside Moscow's Cathedral of Christ Our Savior. (All were arrested for 'hooliganism.')

In February 2014, the XXII Olympic Winter Games took place in Sochi. Russia spent more than $50 billion on the games, making them the most expensive Olympics in history. The Olympic torch traveled in the longest relay ever—from the Pacific Ocean and the North Pole to the bottom of Lake Baikal. An unlit torch went into space aboard a Soyuz spacecraft and was even taken out on a spacewalk.

The Olympics had barely begun as the Crimean controversy unfolded. In November 2013, the political crisis in the Ukraine ignited when President Viktor Yanukovych rejected a Free Trade Agreement with the European Union, and chose instead to seek closer economic ties with Russia. Mass protests followed and, by February 2014, the demonstrations had grown so violent, especially in Kiev, that they forced the President to leave office and flee to Russia. Soon after, Russian troops, posing as self-defense forces, entered Crimea, and armed men swept into the naval headquarters in Sevastopol, home of the Black Sea fleet. On March 16, 2014, in a referendum vote, more than 90 percent of Crimea (with two million residents) voted in favor of annexation to Russia. Five days later, Putin signed the referendum into law, which caused the biggest political crisis in East-West relations in decades. Putin advised the West to 'stop hysterics,' and in a rousing patriotic speech before Russian lawmakers, denounced the West's hypocrisy and double standards (as the German reunification), and declared that the Crimea was 'historically Russian and was returning home.' The United States and European Union responded by slapping sanctions on Russia, and the U.N. General Assembly approved a (non-binding) resolution calling the Crimean referendum to secede from Ukraine invalid.

In the meantime, a Kremlin poll released a survey that indicated that most Russians were not in favor of the intervention. And the Soviet Union's former republics wanted no part of this either, especially after Putin indicated that in the future Russia would not stay away from escalating violence against Russian-speaking populations, a very unsettling precedent for all of Russia's neighbors.

At the same time Putin was dealing with Ukraine, he was also forging a powerful alliance with China. In May, 2014, the two countries signed a 30-year, $400-billion natural gas deal—the largest in history. And Russia and China are collaborating more along political and military lines as well that include development of comprehensive military modernization and cyber warfare programs. Putin is hailed in Chinese media as a powerful leader who is not afraid to take on the West. With an imploding population of 143 million compared with China's rising one of over 1.3 billion, Putin may well look upon a Chinese alliance as a strategic merger for the future and a further way to diminish western influence.

Meanwhile, within the country, the parliament, by the end of summer, had passed 60 new laws, many of which curb civil liberties, discourage dissent and limit Internet freedom. One requires popular bloggers to register and submit their work for scrutiny, another introduces criminal penalties to anyone twice found guilty of violating rules of conduct at a public rally, and yet another now requires all Internet companies that collect personal data from Russian users (even on cloud technology, like booking airline tickets) to store that information on servers located on Russian territory. Another law bans advertising on cable and satellite television channels (virtually allowing state-run monopolies to drive the smaller independent stations out of existence). A new law even bans women from wearing synthetic lace underwear (or any made out of material containing less than 6% cotton); outraged women have been arrested wearing them on their heads while screaming, "Freedom to Panties!" There were even proposals to prohibit Russian women from wearing high heel shoes or canvas sneakers, and to ban the use of foreign words like 'hamburger' from media and the arts…Only time will tell what shall unfold throughout Russia… and Vladimir Putin has the potential to remain in office until 2024.

RUSSIA TODAY

Since Putin's reelection in 2012, even though the ruble currency, in one year alone (2014), lost nearly 40 percent of its value against the dollar, and Russia continues to warn of cold relations with the West, the President's approval rating remains at an all-time high. This support allows Putin to brush off Western critics who accuse the Kremlin of tightening its grip on society, controlling all major television stations, and retaking control of many industries and natural resources, such as the gas giant Gazprom. Most of Russia's economic activity is concentrated in Moscow and 75 percent of the nation's money has a foothold in the capital. The most successful businesses are those that never existed under Socialism, such as the restaurant and food industry, computer technology, and advertising. Even though Russia is now on the brink of recession, over the last decade, the country continued to grow, and this has fueled the consumer class and brought more prosperity to the hinterlands of the country. Even though millions continue to struggle, a middle-class lifestyle is reaching more Russians than ever before.

In few countries of the world are people under 35 playing such an important role in a nation's transformation. Unlike the elderly, they do not remember the state's promise of cradle-to-grave security and are willing to energetically take up challenges in the midst of much uncertainty. The formation of independently owned companies is increasing, and over 20 percent of business managers have studied abroad. The most important turn around for the country is that these internationally educated youth actually choose to return to Russia. For example, the computer industry in Novosibirsk, Siberia, is so successful that the area has become known as the Silicon Taiga. The younger generation is excited to participate in creating a new and enterprising Russia.

But, merely trying to graft Western models of democracy onto one of the largest nations on earth may not so easily be met with success. Although the economic front might be looking up, the legal and health care systems are still abysmal. Within the courts, many sit in jail for years awaiting trial. When they do get one, the accused are made to sit in a cage, while a judge, and twelve citizens (mainly pensioners) act as the jury to decide their fate. The country's health care has, in turn, collapsed with the country's health. Public hospitals and clinics are in dire need of funds, and doctors still earn very poor wages. And for many, homelessness, stress, and poverty (one-third of the population still live at subsistence levels) are taking a mental and physical toll. Russia's suicide rate is among the highest in the world, three times that of the US.

Alarming recent statistics indicate (in Soviet times there were no accurate records) that today only thirty percent of Russian babies are born healthy. Two thirds of adolescents are said to suffer from some type of chronic illness (and drink vodka regularly), and many cities, such as Moscow, have some of the worst air pollution on earth. In addition, Russia has one of the highest rates of tobacco use in the world. (Interestingly, historic records show that English merchants first brought tobacco to Russia in 1585. By 1655, Czar Alexei I tried to altogether ban smoking under penalty of death, but those caught smoking mainly had their noses cut off. Peter the Great allowed tobacco use again after his jaunt to Western Europe.) Today, over half of Russian adults are habitual smokers, and Russia ranks first in the world for the number of young people smoking. In 2013, Putin signed into law the first non-smoking measures and, in June 2014, stricter Western-style bans extended to restaurants, shops, hotels and trains. But, most smokers interviewed said that the ban is unlikely to be strictly implemented. Another new Russian law also bans using obscenities (*mat*, in Russian) in movies, literature and music. Books with curse words must be sold in plastic marked "18+" and labeled as containing expletives.

Today, Russia has more heroin addicts than any other country, and a cheaper homemade opiate, known as *krokodil*, is said to now account for over half of all addictions and drug-related deaths. (It gets its name from the fact that the drug mixture causes the skin to become scaly and bumpy like a crocodile's.) Because of the rise in prostitution and spread of dirty needles, the number of new H.I.V. cases from 2000 up until today has increased over six fold. Seventy-five percent of Russian women still rely on abortion to control family size. Because of the harsh transition after the Soviet Union collapsed, between 1992 and 2009, the Russian population dramatically declined by nearly 5%. Currently, two-thirds of deaths in men are alcohol related, and mortality levels from cardiovascular disease are 30% higher than in Western Europe. A quarter of Russian men die before reaching 55 (life expectancy for men is down to 64 years, compared to 78.7 in the US). The twin trends of rising deaths and declining births are canceling out the growth for Russia's future. The population peaked in 1992 and, by 2050, official projections estimate that, unless these trends reverse, the population could contract by as much as 20%, down to where it was in 1960. Many critics view Putin's increased risky behavior and patriotic rhetoric as a way to shift his citizens' attention off many of the country's woes.

After a thousand years of autocracy or dictatorship, it cannot be easy for a population to re-adjust to an entirely new and novel nation—there is ample reason for both hope and despair. But, that Russia has so quickly transformed itself is an astounding achievement. In a recent poll, three-quarters indicated that they have now adjusted to the new economic reality. After enduring an already long and tumultuous history, the odds are that Russia can, yet again, survive another turbulent transition. Russians pride themselves on their own resiliency and uniqueness, and whatever the future brings, they are firmly determined in the 21st century to create a country of their own making. And not to be forgotten is the extraordinary, indefatigable resolve of the Russian spirit.

> *Russia is baffling to the mind,*
> *Not subject to the common measure*
> *Her ways—of a peculiar kind*
> *One must have faith in Russia...*
> *For she will prevail.*   Poet Fyodor Tyutchev, 1866

(right) Bathing the Red Horse, *painted in 1912 by Avant-garde artist Kuzma Petrov-Vodkin.*

(opposite page) Even during the cold winter months, people enjoy walking in Red Square. The distinctive onion domes of St Basil's Cathedral gradually evolved from the original Byzantine cube-shaped roofs to withstand heavy snowfalls.

A large stone lion stands above the Neva by the Palace Bridge (Dvortsovy Most). The building across the river with the tower is the Kunstkammer (Cabinet of Curiosities), built in 1714 to house Peter the Great's private collections. It is now the Museum of Anthropology and Ethnography and the Lomonosov Museum. The columned building to the left is the Academy of Sciences.

(above) Moscow's Okhotny Ryad Square in the early 1900's. The Church of St. Paraskeva Pyatnitsa, built in the 1680's, was demolished in 1928.

(left) Choreographed by Marius Petipa, famous ballerina, Mathilda Kshesinskaya (1872–1971), stars in The Talisman (1898) in St Petersburg.

(opposite page) An early 1900's scene of central Moscow's Tretyakovsky Passage. In 1871, the wealthy merchant Sergei Tretyakov, who founded the Tretyakov Art Gallery, created a passage through an old part of the Kitai Gorod wall to gain quicker access to the banks along Okhotny Ryad. Today, the passage, known as Moscow's Fifth Avenue, is filled with many upscale shops.

Москва.   Третьяковскій проѣздъ.
Moscou,   Tretiakowski proiesd

(opposite page)
Lenin on a Platform, *painted in 1947 by Alexander Gerasimov, a leading artist of Soviet Realism.*

(left)
Portrait of Prince Alexander Menshikov (1673–1729), *who was governor of St Petersburg during the reign of Peter the Great; his stone palace on Vasilyevsky Island is now open as a museum.*

(below)
First Days of the October Revolution (1917), *painted by Georgy Savitsky in 1949.*

(*above*) St Basil's *(1913) by Avant-garde artist, Aristarkh Lentulov.*
(*opposite top*) Portrait of an Unknown Lady (1883) *by Ivan Kramskoi, a founder of the*
Peredvizhniki *or the Society for Traveling Art Exhibitions.*
(*opposite bottom*) *According to Abstract artist Vasily Kandinsky,* Composition VII *(1913) was*
the most complex piece he ever painted. All three can be found in Moscow's Tretyakov Gallery.
See pages 502–505 for more on Russian artists.

(above) Impressionist Valentin Serov painted Girl With Peaches (1887), a portrait of Vera Mamontova on the Abramtsevo estate; it now hangs in Moscow's Tretyakov Gallery.

(opposite top) Boris Kustodiev painted A Merchant's Wife (Kupchikha) Drinking Tea in 1918; it now hangs in St Petersburg's Russian Museum.

(opposite bottom) Kustodiev also captured the world of the Moscow Tavern (1916), where horse cabmen take a tea break; on the table is a large teapot with hot water, and the smaller one on top holds the zavarka brewed tea. It can be viewed in Moscow's Tretyakov Gallery.

(top left) The American Singer Company in Russia pictures a woman wearing a traditional kokoshnik headdress while happily operating 'The Real Singer Sewing Machine.' The Singer Building (now Dom Knigi or House of Books) still stands on Nevsky Prospekt in St Petersburg. (top right) Jean Cocteau drew posters for Diaghliev's Ballet Russes and its 1913 Grand Season in Paris. (bottom) The bedchamber ante-room, decorated with Dutch tiles, in St Petersburg's Menschikov Palace (1710), the city's first stone building. On the wall hangs a Portrait of Catherine I, Peter the Great's wife.

FACTS FOR THE TRAVELER
PLANNING YOUR TRIP

Traveling to and around Russia is not as easy as in most other European countries, and requires more careful planning. Read some literature on your destinations and areas of interest and talk to people who have been there. Locate travel agents or other specialist organizations that have experience in dealing with travel to Russia.

GROUP TOURS

There are a multitude of package and group tours from which to choose. The advantage of a group tour—especially if it is your first trip and you do not speak the language—is that everything is set up for you. Most group tours have preset departure dates and fixed lengths of stay, and usually include visits to Moscow and St Petersburg. The group rate often includes round-trip airfare, visa-processing fees, first-class accommodation, up to three meals a day, transportation within Russia, sightseeing excursions and a bilingual guide. Special interest groups also offer trips that include some sightseeing, but otherwise focus on more specific areas, such as sports, ecology and the arts, Adventure tourism has opened up a whole new array of opportunities, among them hiking, rafting, biking and climbing.

INDEPENDENT TRAVEL

Independent travel to Russia is still difficult. It is not quite as simple as going to a Russian embassy or consulate, filling out a visa form, and taking off. You must first provide proof of a hotel reservation, or business/family sponsorship. The official reason for this visa restriction is that hotel space in Russia is still fairly limited. Many hotels tend to be pre-booked in high seasons, and the government does not want visitors to arrive with nowhere to stay. The good news is that the old monopoly of mediocre Intourist hotels has dissolved along with the Soviet Union, and today choices for hotels, hostels, apartments and bed-and-breakfasts exist for any budget. Independent travelers can also arrange homestays with a Russian family. Cheap accommodation is in big demand, so try and book at least six to eight weeks in advance to guarantee space and the best rates. Today, many higher-end hotels, hostels, host family organizations and travel agencies specializing in Russia can also provide visa sponsorship invitations.

VISAS

Most travelers to the Russian Federation must have a visa. There are mainly six types: tourist, business, private visitor, work, transit and student. Normally a visa should be obtained in the country of residence (otherwise it may be more difficult to procure). Visas were issued by the Russian Foreign Ministry, but as of November 2002, this service was transferred to the Interior Ministry (RMIA), also known as OVIR. As of 2003, Russian visas are now stamped into passports. If staying more than three months, a medical certificate indicating an HIV negative status may be required. Russian consulates also reserve the right to see your return ticket or proof of onward travel out of the country. Do not panic if your visa has not arrived as your departure date nears. Russian embassies and consulates are notorious for issuing visas at the last minute. When applying, indicate with an enclosed letter that you absolutely need the visa delivered by a certain date, and follow up with a phone call, if necessary. If a passport is lost in Russia, contact your embassy or consulate. Most airlines check to see if passengers have a Russian visa before allowing them to board a flight to Russia.

TOURIST VISAS

If you are with a group or package tour, the company takes care of your visa application. There are several ways for independent travelers to apply for a tourist visa; inquire at a local travel agency that handles Russian visas, or collect a visa application at a Russian embassy or consulate. The easiest way is to Google 'Russian Visa' to find a travel website where you can download information and perhaps apply through the company. Some companies that provide Russian visas and sponsor official invitations are www.travel2russia.com, www.gotorussia.com, www.visahouse.com; www.waytorussia.net, www.visatorussia.com and www.traveldocs.com. A single entrance tourist visa is good for up to 30 days. It is not possible to extend a tourist visa while in Russia.

To apply for a Russian Visa: 1). Complete the application form and sign it; 2) Several passport-size photographs are required; 3) An original and valid passport needs to be included. (The Russian visa stamp takes up to two open pages, so make sure you have at least two blank pages remaining. 4) If staying in a hotel, a visitor must include proof of a reservation (it does not have to be pre-paid). The hotel confirmation MUST have an official Russian company registration and confirmation number on it. (If you do not have a hotel, or stay with friends or relatives, find a travel agency that specializes in Russian visas and can issue an official invitation. A Visa Support Document or Letter of Invitation from a hotel or (online) travel agency is required for all Tourist visas. (Most hostels and apartment rental agencies can provide this letter as well. 5) A Visa fee is required; this depends on your citizenship and how quickly you need the visa processed. If a travel agency provides an Invitation, an extra charge is added, along with their servicing fees. Try to give ample time—allow for up to 8 to 15 business days for processing; It is recommended to include proper postage as for FedEx or express mailing for the passport return.

By Russian law, you are required to register your visa within seven business days of arrival in Russia (see Registration under Business Visas). When staying at a hotel, the reception automatically registers the visa upon check-in (it may take a day for your passport to be returned). Some hotels (as in Moscow) can register online, but others in smaller towns will issue a stamped registration paper to you.

As an alternative to hotels, you can also book a homestay with a Russian family; agencies coordinating stays can help obtain a visa. Some of Russia's Youth Hostels are now affiliated with the International Youth Hostelling Association. RYH can help with visa processing, inexpensive hostels, travel tickets and other information. (See Practical Information sections under Accommodation and Useful Addresses.)

BUSINESS VISAS

If a traveler is going to Russia on business or is just an independent tourist who would like to visit friends, rent an apartment, or even enter the country without hotel reservations, the best way is to apply for a business visa. The easiest way is to contact a Russian specialist travel agency near you or see online list on page 66. These firms can also help find places to stay and take care of other travel needs. Many of these agencies issue an official sponsor Confirmation Letter, and with this invitation and the application forms (see requirements under Tourist Visa), a one-month or three-month single- or double-entry business visa are possible. Normally a multiple entry 6- or 12-month or 3-year visa is only available for people who have been issued a Russian visa before. A multiple entry business visa allows nationals of all countries to stay in Russia up to 90 days out of a 180-day period. You should allow yourself at least 14–21 business days to get these types of visas for the standard processing fee, otherwise fees can be considerably higher.

PRIVATE (ORDINARY) VISAS

If sponsored by a Russian host organization (or private individual), you can receive what is known as an Ordinary visa. The host must fill out an invitation form and bring it to the local OVIR office (have them contact OVIR for current requirements). When approved, a Notice of Permission, good for one year, is issued. By giving this, along with the appropriate visa application forms, to the Russian embassy or consulate, a visa is issued good for up to 60 days in the host's town. On arrival, you must register at the local visa office. (It is much simpler to obtain a business visa if planning to stay in a private residence.)

Registration: With any business visa (or tourist visa when not staying in a hotel), you must personally register in Russia at a local OVIR office within seven business days of arrival. The travel agency that sponsors and issues your visa usually has their own contact office in Moscow, at airports, and in other cities where it is easier to register—so do not forget to ask for an address. (Always keep a xerox copy of your passport and visa—for the registration office may need to hold onto your passport for a day.) Many Russian local travel agencies can also register the visa for a small fee. If seven business days are exceeded, a penalty may apply. On the other hand, if you are staying in the country (or city) less than seven business days, a registration stamp is not required. Only one registration stamp is needed per stay, but if you journey to another city for more than a week, you need to register again. If you have a double- or multiple-entry visa, another registration stamp is needed for the next period of entry. If you try to exit without a registration stamp (sometimes issued as a separate piece of paper), passport control may collect a fine, or not permit departure. (Often, though, passport control never seems to check.) You must exit the country before the visa expires. (If it has expired, report to a specialist travel agency or an OVIR office to try for an extension; you cannot get one at the airport—nor an extension for a tourist visa. If departing Russia on an overnight train, make sure the visa is valid though the day you cross a border.)

TRANSIT VISAS
For certain countries, a short-term (48 to 72-hours) transit visa can be issued (prior to entering Russia). For transit by air, it is usually good for 48 hours. For a nonstop Trans-Siberian Railway journey it is good for up to 10 days—but requirements vary depending on if traveling west or east. If arriving on a **Cruise ship**, passengers can stay in Russia for 72 hours without a visa and may participate on a city tour with an organized cruise ship group. You can only disembark independently if you have a valid Russian visa before arriving! In addition, check on guidelines before you leave. Often, a visa may not be enough, and a passenger needs to pre-book a tour or guide through a Russian Travel Agency, who meets you at the ship.

STUDENT VISAS
If you are a student with proof of enrollment at an accredited Russian school, a student visa can be issued though the Ministry of Internal Affairs which a school or university can help you to attain.

You may also need separate visas (and transit visas) to travel to or through other Commonwealth states such as the Ukraine or Belarus, but US and UK citizens do not need visas for Baltic States. Passport control may review other visas before allowing you to leave for the next destination.

WHEN TO GO
Hotel prices and itineraries of many tour programs change depending on the season. Peak season is from May to September. Alternatives are to go in the spring (April 1–May 15) or fall (September 1–October 31) when prices are lower and the cities less crowded. The summer White Nights in St Petersburg are spectacular, but at the same time the summer in Moscow can be humid and dusty. An Indian summer in the fall can be quite lovely. If you do not mind the cold and snow, the winter season

is cheapest and accommodation most readily available (but the number of daylight hours are limited). The rainiest months for both cities are July and August.

TIME ZONES

Russia has 9 time zones. (In 2010, President Medvedev eliminated two time zones. Thus, Chukotka in the far east is nine hours ahead of Kaliningrad, the westernmost territory.) Moscow and St Petersburg are in the same zone. Moscow is 11 hours ahead of the US West Coast, eight hours ahead of the East Coast, three hours ahead of London, two of Central Europe, and one hour ahead of Helsinki. Russia changes its clocks the last Sunday in March (one hour forward) and last Sunday in October (one hour back). Moscow time is five hours behind Hong Kong, seven hours behind Sydney, and nine hours behind New Zealand.

WHAT TO PACK

For your convenience, travel as light as possible. Most airlines on international flights allow up to two pieces of luggage (free of charge), weighing no more than 23 kilos (50 pounds) each, and one piece of cabin baggage. Luggage allowance tends to be very strict when traveling within Russia. Often all bags are weighed, including your cabin baggage. Each bag must weigh no more than 20 kilos (44 pounds), and often only one checked bag is allowed. You may be charged per additional kilogram (2.2 pounds) for overweight luggage.

DOCUMENTS

Keep your passport, visa, important papers, tickets, vouchers, prescription medications and money in your hand luggage at all times! Also carry a photocopy of your passport and visa, and a few extra passport pictures. Bear in mind that you may need to show identification to get into certain places or exchange money, even if it is a xerox copy of a passport. Know your credit card and pin numbers, and their emergency telephone numbers in case of loss or theft.

CLOTHES

The season of the year is the major factor in deciding what to bring. Summers are warm, humid and dusty, with frequent thunderstorms, especially in Moscow—bring a raincoat or an umbrella. The White Nights of St Petersburg are delightful in the summer, but occasionally a pullover or light jacket is needed. Winters are cold and damp, with temperatures well below freezing. It can snow between November and April, when cold Arctic winds sharpen the chill. Be prepared with your warmest clothes—waterproof boots, hat, gloves, scarf and thermal underwear (surprisingly, it is often colder in Moscow than St Petersburg). Interiors are usually well heated, so dress in layers. Bring slightly smarter attire for ballets and banquets. A must is a good pair of walking shoes that can get dirty. Wearing shorts or sleeveless shirts may prevent you from entering monasteries and churches during services.

Even though numerous clothing stores have now opened throughout both cities, Western attire and brand-name fashion is much more expensive than at home. It is best to buy necessary clothing before you leave, but otherwise you should now be able to find almost anything, especially in Moscow and St Petersburg.

MEDICINE

Many more Western medicinal products are available in Moscow and St Petersburg, but they may cost more than at home. Bring along necessary prescription drugs (know generic names) and allergy medications, antibiotics (such as Cipro) and a course of anti-diarrhea drugs (such as Lomotil), glasses and contact lenses. Also consider packing a small first-aid kit for cuts and bruises. If you take injections, bring your own needles and syringes. Even though you can now find many items in various Western-style supermarkets, they may not carry your preferred brands. To save time looking for them, bring some of these with you: aspirin, throat lozenges, cold formulas, vitamins, laxatives, lip salve, dental floss, travel sickness pills, water-purifying tablets, antibacterial handwash, handi-wipes, contact-lens cleaner, mosquito repellent/anti-itch spray and indigestion tablets. Luxury-class hotels usually have a resident nurse on hand. (See Practical Information sections for each city for listings of medical facilities, dentists and pharmacies.)

PERSONAL ARTICLES

Even though most travel supplies are now readily available, consider bringing along preferred brands of cosmetics, shampoo, lotions, razors and shaving cream, toothpaste, tampons, small packets of tissues for restrooms, a water bottle, money belt, washing powder, an all-purpose plug for bathtubs and sinks, earplugs, a sewing kit, pantyhose, adhesive tape, extra locks for suitcases, sunglasses, pens and note pads, and a sturdy tote-style shopping bag. A small flashlight and whistle are good to carry at night. If you are a student bring a student ID—many places, as museums, may offer discounts on fares or admission charges. This may also apply to senior citizens.

GADGETS

Voltage is 220V (and sometimes varies to 127V). Most major hotels have plugs for 220/110V. Pack a few adapters (Russia uses the European round two-pin plug). An IPod as well as a small tape recorder may come in handy. Bring plenty of batteries for your camera, alarm clock and watch. Also useful is a Swiss army knife or penknife that has a bottle opener and corkscrew.

FILM AND PHOTOGRAPHY

Digital flash cards and film are available in major cities, but are more expensive than at home. Using a flash is prohibited in many museums and churches. In the former Soviet Union there were many photographic restrictions, but these no longer apply. Some places still prohibit cameras (such as the Lenin Mausoleum) and others, such as museums and churches, may require a purchased permit that can be bought at the entrance. Many locals are still uncomfortable with having their picture taken. Understand that people are sometimes sensitive about foreigners photographing what they perceive as backward or in poor condition. Always remain courteous.

MISCELLANEOUS/SUNDRIES

A Russian phrase book and dictionary really come in handy. Try to master some of the Cyrillic alphabet before you leave. It is especially helpful in places like the Metro. Bring reading material and travel literature—Western books will be more expensive, and most of the Russian-published material is, no surprise, in Russian! Gift-giving is part of Russian *gostyepriimstvo* (hospitality). Bring some specialty gift items from home—picture travel books of your country or city, postcards, T-shirts, sport pins and the like are always appreciated.

GETTING THERE

INTERNATIONAL FLIGHTS

Since flying from points outside Europe can involve large time differences, consider a stay in a European city for a day or two to recover from jet lag. Stopovers are often included or provided for a minimal extra charge. Moscow has three international airports: Sheremetyevo (SVO), Domodedovo (DME) and Vnukovo (VKO). The newly rebuilt Pulkovo (LED) airport in St Petersburg opened in 2014.

CONNECTING TRAINS

One pleasant way to travel is by train from a European city to Moscow or St Petersburg. Informative websites are: www.raileurope.com, www.trainsrussia.com, and www.russiantrains.com. (Tickets can be purchased online.) For long distance train schedules: www.russianrailways.com and www.russian.rail.com. For example, after a few relaxing days in Helsinki, you can take a train to St Petersburg or Moscow. (Besides longer overnight trains, the daily high-speed train to St Petersburg takes only 3.5 hours.) Other high-speed trains—SAPSAN (Peregrine Falcon) now cover the Moscow-St Petersburg route in 4 hours, half the time of regular trains.

One can also travel by rail from other European cities, such as Berlin (35 hours) or Warsaw (26 hours). Another popular train route is from the Baltic States (Estonia, Lithuania and Latvia) to Moscow or St Petersburg. (Make sure to check if any countries you pass through require transit visas.) The famous Trans-Siberian, on its western run, starts in Beijing and routes through either Manchuria or Mongolia, then crosses Siberia (one is allowed to get off at various locations along the way) with Moscow as its destination; from here, one can also continue on to other cities in Western Europe. (See Special Topic on page 371.)

BY FERRY AND BUS

Ferries leave for Russia from numerous European countries, such as Sweden, Finland, Latvia and Germany. The journey takes about 14 hours; overnight cabins are available. Ferries arrive and depart St Petersburg from the Sea Passenger Ship Terminal on Vasilyevsky Island. Cruises are also offered that journey along inland waterways with destinations such as Kizhi Island in Lake Ladoga or Valaam Island in Lake Onega, or along the Volga River. Overland round trip bus excursions are also available to Moscow and St Petersburg from European countries, with frequent departures from Helsinki. (See Useful Addresses and Practical Information sections for more details on cruise and bus excursions.)

DRIVING

It is not recommended to drive to Russia in your own car. There are now millions of cars—with many poor drivers on bad roads in awful weather conditions! The highways and border towns are filled with police and smugglers who both make a living out of extortion and theft. Definitely make sure you have proper insurance and contact a tourist information center before you leave to set up precise routes and learn of requirements and official procedures. Once inside Russia, roads make targets for holdups, routes are poorly marked, parts are scarce or expensive, and gas stations may be hard to find. You may be asked to present an International Driving Permit with a Russian translation of your license.

CUSTOMS AND IMMIGRATION

Visitors arriving by international air must pass through a passport checkpoint in the airport terminal. Those arriving by train do this at the border. Uniformed border guards check passports and stamp visas.

On many international flights, arrival cards are no longer given. When you pass through Passport control, your visa is scanned and a departure card is printed out which you must present upon exiting the country. Some airports and train journeys require an arrival/customs form to be filled out. If you have nothing to declare, proceed through the Green Channel. Currently, visitors are allowed to take in/out US $3,000 (or its equivalent) in currency, and goods of a value of about US $2,000 (1500 Euro), weighing less than 50kg without making a declaration. If arriving with over $3,000 to $10,000 (or its equivalent), fill out a customs declaration form. A visitor cannot depart Russia with more money than brought in without paying taxes.

If you arrive with expensive items, these could be confiscated when departing if you have no proof that you brought them into the country. Any expensive cameras, videos, personal computers, jewelry, musical instruments, etc., should be declared and forms stamped in the Red Channel. If uncertain about any items, proceed through the Red Channel and double-check with a customs officer. Also note that once declared, you must then depart with these items (unless you have official permission to leave them behind) or you could be subject to a duty up to the full value of the goods in question.

Drugs, other than medicinal, are highly illegal. Do not try and leave the country with items of cultural or historical value, such as antiques (made before 1941), old icons, or very expensive works of art (even modern) unless you have an authorized certificate from the Ministry of Culture. The place of purchase can usually help obtain this. People charged with trying to export items of cultural significance without proper certification can face a prison sentence. Carry receipts so you can also prove their value if questioned. Caviar can also be confiscated (check—there is a limit). If something does get confiscated, and a friend staying behind is with you at the airport, give it to them for safekeeping; otherwise customs may keep it.

Money

The Russian Federation currency is the **ruble**, which became Russia's national currency, along with the **kopek** coin, in 1534, during the reign of Ivan the Terrible. The paper ruble notes (first circulated in 1998) come in denominations of 5, 10 (both current but no longer issued), 50, 100, 500, 1,000 and 5,000 rubles. On December 11, 2013, the official symbol for the ruble became ₽. There are 1, 2, 5 and 10 ruble coins. There are 100 kopeks to the ruble, and they come in 1, 5, 10, and 50 kopek coins. Check your change—make sure you receive the current ruble notes in your money exchange—any notes marked prior to 1997 are invalid.

Currency Exchange

Cash is the most acceptable form of currency in Russia (the country still does not have a check system). Traveler's checks are not as widely accepted. You can convert foreign currency to rubles at the airport or in your hotel. In addition, hundreds of exchange kiosks (signs in Russian say ОБМЕН ВАЛЮТЫ—*Obmyen Valyuti*) line the streets of most big cities and towns. Counterfeit dollars and euros have flooded Russia, so don't be offended if your money is carefully examined. Make sure all bills are in good condition; any old, torn, taped or marked bills may not be accepted. The exchange rates are now fixed, and thus no reason to seek out black market money trades. You can exchange unused rubles at the end of your trip in town, at the airport, or border.

Many hotels, restaurants, shops and ticketing agencies now accept credit cards. (Note: by law, businesses are required to show prices in rubles; nonetheless, you may come across prices stated in Y.E., meaning conventional units as in dollars or euros.) Carry lower denomination bills, for many places cannot provide change for larger bills; they also come in handy for cab fares, porters, etc. Tipping is discretionary, depending on the service. Usually about ten percent is acceptable.

Numerous ATMs have sprung up in cities and towns and can be used 24 hours a day. Look for signs that say Bankomat which are linked to international networks. Major banks can also give cash advances against credit cards with a commission (about three percent) based on the amount. When using an ATM, to get cash from your bank debit or credit card, you must know your international PIN number (and for use in Russia, it can only be 4 digits). Besides rubles, many machines now allow you to select to receive cash in dollars or euros as well. To receive international money transfers, Western Union has offices located in both cities.

BEWARE OF DUAL PRICING

Basically a foreigner in Russia can still expect to pay almost double at cultural and excursion sites, such as museums. (Note: the price for foreigners is often posted in English, and the lower price in Russian.) A photography/video permit is often an extra fee. The good news is that prices for hotels and transportation (bus and metro) are now the same for everyone. Showing some type of international Student ID may help get up to a 50 percent discount.

Another way to save money is to go on a Russian group excursion. Russian tours tend to be cheaper than those organized for foreigners. If you do not understand Russian, then just bring a guidebook with you. Buying excursion or theater tickets at specially marked street kiosks (kassa) can also be much cheaper than purchasing them through your hotel.

VALUABLES

Hotels usually have safe deposit boxes in the room or at the front desk. It is advisable to lock up your valuables, money, passport and airline tickets (even if in a locked suitcase in the room)—thefts have been reported in hotels. In case of loss or theft, notify the service bureau at your hotel immediately. Always put your money in a safe place, carry bags tightly around your shoulder and make sure backpacks are secured. Buy a money belt, so you can carry your money discreetly. Unfortunately, over the last few years, tourist crime has risen—pockets are picked and bags stolen. Take extra care when in large crowds and markets, or if bands of Gypsies or street urchins approach. Take the same precautions as you would in any large metropolis.

HEALTH AND EMERGENCIES

To call an ambulance in Russia, dial 03 (01 for emergency services). Since a Russian ambulance may take time to arrive, try calling one of the Western clinics immediately.

Immunizations are not required unless you are coming from an infected area. Russia does not have many health risks, but the main areas of concern are the food, water and cold weather. Some people may have trouble adjusting to Russian cuisine, which can include heavy breads, thick greasy soups, highly salted and pickled foods, smoked fish, sour cream, and vodka... In the smaller towns familiar vegetables and fruits are often in short supply. (If you do not have an iron constitution, bring indigestion or stomach disorder remedies.) If you are a vegetarian or require a certain diet, consider bringing some packaged or specialty foods and vitamins along.

DO NOT drink the tap water, especially in St Petersburg, where a virulent parasite *Giardia lamblia* can cause miserable bouts of fever, stomach cramps and diarrhea. If you feel ill, get checked by a doctor. For *Giardia*, some prescribe Metronidazole (available in Russia as Trikapol) 200mg three times per day for two weeks. Local juices or flavored sugar water, along with iced drinks, cannot always be trusted. (Most upscale hotels now have their own water-purifying systems, but it is advised to double check.) Stick to bottled mineral water. In winter be prepared for a cold, and in the spring and summer months possible allergy attacks or mosquito bites.

If illness occurs, see Practical Information sections under Medical for hospital/pharmacy/dental locations. Many of these Western clinics can also organize air evacuation in the event of an emergency. It is advisable to purchase travel/medical insurance before the trip.

CRIME, SAFETY AND HAZARDS

The reports of crime in Russia have, for the most part, been overly dramatized by both Russian and Western press. Statistically, Russian streets are as safe as in Paris, London or New York. Even though some areas of Russia are experiencing unrest, it is considered safe to walk around Moscow or St Petersburg at any time during the day or evening, though, as in any big city, use common sense and take care of your valuables. It is highly unlikely for the average tourist to ever cross paths with Russian mafia or organized crime.

As a foreigner, you are automatically assumed to have money. Do not flaunt expensive jewelry and watches or wads of cash, and try to dress inconspicuously. Never exchange a large amount of money at a currency kiosk and then continue on walking alone on the street. Pickpocket gangs, often using children to distract their targets, work areas around major hotels, popular restaurants, metro areas and tourist attractions (thieves come in all denominations—from the well-dressed or the elderly to pretty young women). As one gets your attention, another may try to pick your pocket, cut the strap off your shoulder bag, snatch your camera or open your backpack. If all valuables are secure, then nothing can be stolen—don't put all rubles and foreign cash in one place. (It has been known for muggers at night to follow intoxicated foreigners leaving a restaurant or party.) Do not walk alone down poorly lit back-alleys or in neighborhoods you are not familiar with. It is safe to ride the Metro, but from the station, at night, make sure you do not have to wait long for a bus or walk a long way to get home. The biggest nuisance is mainly over friendly drunks. If you cannot get rid of them, walk into a large hotel or restaurant, where guards are usually posted.

In addition, do not flag down a taxi or private car late at night and ride by yourself to the outskirts of town; if more than two people are in the vehicle and you are alone, do not get in. If you should experience a mugging, do not resist—the gun is probably real. It is a good idea to place a small sum of money in one pocket and hide the rest; this way, you can pull out the smaller amount, and say it is all you have. The GAI or Militsia Police wear blue or gray uniforms with red epaulettes and cap bands. Their vehicles are usually navy blue and white. If robbed, report the incident to the police; your hotel can direct you to the nearest police station (you will probably need an official report to file an insurance claim). If something major occurs, also report it to your embassy or consulate.

As an added twist, incidents have occurred where officials, looking like policemen, have pulled over tourists to question their documents and then tried to extract money. (As an example, a policeman may ask you to step inside a van and ask to see your passport. He will then remark that your documents/visas are not in order and you need to pay a cash fine (really a bribe) to get your passport back.) In Moscow, this has occurred around Red Square, and in St Petersburg along Nevsky Prospekt. If you are suddenly questioned by police and asked to pay out money, this may well be a scam. Demand to call your embassy or consulate. *Always* carry a photocopy of your passport and visa with you at all times. In this way, if questioned, just hand over the photocopy—*never* your passport.

Do be aware of the fact that police (*militsia*), stationed particularly around Metro areas, train stations and bus stops, are allowed to stop anyone and ask for their *dokumenty* (documents). In Russia, it is required that a foreigner carry identity documents with them at all times. If asked, show a *copy* of your passport and visa; never hand over your actual passport! Despite what the officer may demand, a copy is sufficient.

If someone tries to pick you up in a bar, restaurant, or hotel, remember both men and women work as prostitutes. Think twice—not only is AIDS (and hepatitis and other venereal diseases) on the rise, but there are many reports of victims being drugged and robbed (prostitutes often work with criminals to target guests). Hotel guests should also never open their doors for unexpected callers. Russia has now become one of the major routes to Europe from the Golden Triangle. Do not even think of purchasing drugs or using them—Russian jails and prisons are horrific; remember this country created the gulags.

Beware of fake art works, especially icons and lacquer boxes. A seller may try to charge a foreigner as much as possible. If the price is high and you cannot tell an antique from a modern imitation, do not buy it—scams abound. Do not buy vodka and caviar off the street or from some alley kiosk; purchase them in larger stores.

If in need of a public toilet, first try finding one in a hotel, restaurant or museum. Otherwise, look on the street for the sign WC or ТУАЛЕТ (*tyalet*)—they are hard to find and most are not in good condition. The men's toilet is marked with an M (women should go to the door marked Ж). Most train stations now have automated toilets. At the entrance, you may need to pay a small fee to an attendant. Sometimes, a few squares of toilet paper are provided; remember to carry small packets of tissues.

Do not jaywalk—cross only at appropriate crossings or lights. Drivers do not care what is in front of them, and many streets are too wide to cross quickly (use underground crossings). Also be cautious when walking on sidewalks. There are many construction sites or deteriorating areas filled with deep holes, uncovered manholes or other hazards.

Smoking has reached epidemic proportions in Russia. While tobacco companies are being hounded in the United States, they are welcomed with open arms in Russia where cigarette sales are a goldmine business. Although a 2014 anti-smoking law made it illegal to smoke in many public areas, you will encounter smoking everywhere! A recent survey reported that over 50 percent of Russian adults smoke. If you are susceptible to allergies, springtime can be a problem, especially in Moscow where pollen from trees and plants is a wheezer's anathema; at times, white fuzzy blossoms from poplar trees, called *pukh*, accumulate like snow drifts throughout the city.

GETTING AROUND

Moscow has three main airports:

Sheremetyevo (www.svo.aero/en) is located 28 km (18 miles) northwest of the city. The new $300 million Sheremetyevo International Airport currently has four operating passenger terminals: A, C are the North Terminals (A is used for business and private aviation), and D, E, F the South Terminals. Terminal D is the hub for Aeroflot and its SkyTeam partners. (This terminal is built in the image of a giant swan with outstretched wings.)

To get into the city: **Aeroexpress** trains currently run (from Terminal F with free bus shuttles here from other terminals) to/from Belorussky Train Station from 5:30am to 11pm; the journey takes 35 minutes. (On some airlines, you can check in your luggage at the Aeroexpress train station terminal no later than two hours before departure.) For more information: www.aeroexpress.ru/en.

If you have little luggage, cheaper buses and *marshrut* shuttles also run from Sheremetyevo airport to Rechnoi Vokzal or Planernaya metro stations.

Domodedovo (www.domodedovo.ru/en) is located 42 km (26 miles) south of town. From Domodedovo, the Aeroexpress runs to/from Paveletsky Train Station from 6am to 11:30pm and takes 45 minutes. From the airport, shuttles and mini buses also go to Domodedovo Metro station.

Vnukovo (www.vnukovo.ru) is located 28 km (17 miles) southwest of the center.

From Vnukovo, Aeroexpress trains run to/from Kievsky Train Station from 6am to 11pm and take 40 minutes. Buses also run to/from Yugo-Zapadnaya metro station.

St Petersburg's new Pulkovo Airport (reopened in 2014) is located 20 km (12 miles) south of the city (www.pulkovoairport.ru/en). Buses and mini-vans run from Pulkovo Airport into the city and to Moskovskaya Metro station.

Each airport has official taxis; order one from the dispatch desk for a set price depending on the area of your destination. (Try offering to share a ride with other passengers into town to split the cost.) A travel agency can also arrange someone to meet you at the airport with a car. In addition, you can pre-book rides from travel agencies, such as www.enjoymoscow.com.

Remember that traffic in Moscow is horrendous, especially during rush hour; allow ample time to get to the airport!

BY AIR

The airports used for internal flights are much more crowded and chaotic than international airports, so try to arrive several hours before departure. Passports and visas are required at check-in, and usually all luggage is X-rayed at the front of the terminal before entering. Know the baggage allowance, for even carry-on luggage may be weighed, and overweight fees charged. (If this is the case, have someone discreetly take your hand luggage aside when you check in.) Boarding passes are issued with seat numbers, and rows written in Cyrillic! Remember that Russians are quite assertive and can push vigorously to get on the plane which is usually not boarded by row numbers—one general announcement for boarding is made, often just in Russian. If the flight has open seating, do not be last on the plane—the airlines frequently overbook. Consider taking some drinks and snacks along. Airport departure tax is usually included in the price of the ticket.

You can reserve and buy Aeroflot (and other airline) tickets at many major hotels, or go directly to the airline office in town. You can also often reserve and buy tickets on the airline website.

BY TRAIN

Trains are much more fun, efficient and cheaper than flying. The commercial trains between Moscow and St Petersburg are a splendid way to travel. Traveling during daylight hours affords wonderful views of the countryside, or board the sleeper at night and arrive the next morning for a full day of sightseeing.

In 1850, when the Moscow–St Petersburg rail road was being built, Czar Nicholas I drew a straight line on a map to indicate the construction path between the two cities. The story goes that the Czar's finger caused a bump in the ruler line and resulted in a detour in the route, which became known as the 'Czar's Finger.' However, the Ministry of Railways recently straightened this five-kilometer portion of the line.

There are nearly 20 daily trains that run the Moscow–St Petersburg route. Regular trains (that depart both day and overnight) take between 6 and 8 hours (with stops). The high-speed trains—SAPSAN (Peregrine Falcon) now cover the Moscow-St Petersburg route in 4 hours. For long distance train schedules: www.russianrailways.com, www.russianrail.com, www.russiantrains.com and www.rzd.ru.

Since there are numerous train stations in each city (nine in Moscow alone), make sure you know which one you depart from. In Moscow, trains for St Petersburg leave mostly from Leningradsky Vokzal (Leningrad Station). In St Petersburg, they leave from Moskovsky Vokzal (Moscow Station). (The word *vokzal* stems from London's Vauxhall Station.) Large boards listing time schedules and track numbers are posted at each station. Trains always leave on time with a single five-minute warning broadcast before departure—so pay attention!

There are three classes for long-distance travel. Luxury or *lyuks* (SV) has two soft berths to a compartment (and often a personal bathroom); first or *coupé* class has four soft berths; *platskart* has either six hard berths or standard seats (try to avoid the latter for overnight travel). Your ticket will indicate the train, car (*vagon*), compartment (*kupé*) and berth (*myesto*) number. The lower the car number, the closer it is to the front of the train on departure. A personal car attendant (*provodnik*) offers tea, brewed in the car's samovar, and sometimes a boxed meal, and wakes you up in the morning. If there is a compartment radio, remember to turn it off at night, or it may blast you awake at 6am.

If you are traveling on an overnight train and can afford it, try buying the entire compartment to ensure both privacy and safety. If you share the compartment with strangers, secure your valuables and sleep with money, passport, etc. on your person. Reserve a lower berth, where you can place luggage and other valuables in the storage compartment safely underneath. During the night, compartment locks can be opened from the outside. If you are alone, consider securing both locks before retiring by using a cord, belt or necktie to tie around them as an extra precaution. The compartments are not segregated. If there is a problem, the attendant can usually arrange a swap—it is safe traveling alone as a woman. (Carry earplugs in case of snorers!) A minimal fee may be charged for sheets and towels (which you are expected to fold up upon arrival). Tickets are collected at the beginning of the trip and returned at the end.

Even though a dining car is usually available (though often crowded), it is fun to bring along your own food, drink, and spirits to enjoy in your compartment (remember a knife, fork and bottle opener). Also bring clothes to sleep in, slippers and toilet paper. Toilets on most trains are without supplies and never cleaned during trips, thus not always a pleasant experience. In summer months, it can be quite hot as compartment windows are sealed shut; hallway windows can be opened. Porters (*nosilshchiki*) are available, but they may try to charge a foreigner more; negotiate a per bag price before starting out (find out from a local what this is). In stations, always keep a watchful eye on your bags and valuables. Do not let just anyone carry your bag—it may be the last you see of it.

The easiest way to **purchase train tickets** is through your hotel service desk, or an appropriate travel agency. You can also purchase tickets online with a credit card (www.russiantrains.com); you'll need to print out the ticket. Your passport and visa are supposed to be checked with your ticket when boarding the train.

Same day (and advance) tickets can be purchased at the station of departure. Moscow also has rail ticket centers: Central Railway Booking office at 6/11 Maly Kharitonevsky Lane (Metro Chistye Prudy) and at 5 Komsomolskaya Square (and in Leningradsky and Yaroslavsky train stations). Metro Komsomolskaya.

Besides ticket centers located in each of its five train stations, St Petersburg also has a main rail ticket office at 24 Griboyedov Canal (Metro Nevsky Prospekt).

Local commuter trains, known as *prigorodnye* (suburban) or *elektrichka*, serve the suburbs of both cities and some Golden Ring towns. They usually have only hard wooden benches (some have softer first class seats), poor amenities (toilets are dirty), and can be quite crowded on weekends and in summer months. The advantage is that they are cheap and leave frequently. (These trains leave from another area of the train station.) Tickets can be bought the same day at the station of departure, and an ID is not usually required. Make sure you keep your ticket— you may need it to both enter and exit the station turnstiles—this is a measure to catch 'hares', or ticketless passengers.

Take note that many train and plane schedules are still listed throughout the country using Moscow time, which make things confusing. If you are traveling in a time zone other than Moscow's, always check to see what time (Moscow or local) is actually indicated on your ticket.

BY BUS AND COACH

Group tourists are shown around Moscow and St Petersburg by coach. Often the buses are not air-conditioned, but all are heated during winter. If you are an individual traveler, you can sign up through a hotel, local travel agency or street kiosk for city sightseeing excursions. Comfortable coach tours are also offered to Golden Ring towns. Always take notice of your bus number, as parking lots tend to fill quickly. For longer rides bring along some bottled water and snacks. For international bus routes and schedules, see: www.luxexpress.eu.

LOCAL BUSES, TRAMS AND TROLLEYS

Local transportation operates from about 5.30am to 1am and is charged either by a flat rate or distance. The front and back of each vehicle is marked in Russian with its destination, and the number of the route. To find a bus or trolley stop (A for *avtobus* or T for *trolleybus*), look for numbered route signs on sidewalks. For trams, signs hang on wires by the street adjacent to the tram stop or over tramlines in the middle of the road. (The first electric tram was inaugurated in Moscow on April 6, 1899.) As you board, look for a sign near the door that indicates the cost of a ride). Tickets can be bought from the driver, or an attendant who patrols the aisles. You can also pre-purchase transportation cards, called *talony*, on the bus or at many kiosks and metro stations. Special ticket machines are mounted throughout the vehicle where you may have to punch your ticket (newer vehicles have card scanners). A combined bus and Metro card can also be purchased. Inspectors sometimes make spot checks and fine ticketless passengers. If the bus is crowded, try to anticipate your stop and inch towards the door. You may hear a voice behind asking, *Vi Vikhoditye?* (Are you getting off now?). If locals think you are not alighting, they may push by; the *babushka*, especially, are superb shovers! Similarly, if trying to board a crowded bus, you may find yourself pushed from behind and packed in like a sardine. Just make sure the door does not close on you. Long-distance buses have their own terminals within each city. Minibuses or *marshrut* also stop along bus routes. They make fewer stops but charge more.

METRO

The Metro is the fastest and cheapest way to get around Moscow and St Petersburg. More than eight million people ride the Moscow Metro daily. Trains run every 90 seconds during rush hour. Central stations are beautifully decorated with chandeliers and mosaics. Metro stations are easy to spot—entrances on the street are marked with a large M. Even the long escalator rides are great entertainment. Metro maps are posted inside each station. To ride the Metro, first purchase a magnetic-strip card at the underground *kassa* booth. (In St Petersburg, some stations may still use tokens or *zheton*.) Alas, the old Soviet cost of 5 kopeks has risen with inflation, but it is still a flat rate regardless of where you ride to, or with transfers, how long you remain underground.

Insert the card into the turnstile and wait for the green light before taking your ticket and passing through (some turnstiles are still archaic and can shut violently). All station and transfer areas are clearly marked, but often only in Russian. If you do not read Cyrillic, have someone write down the name of your destination. People are always helpful and are glad to point you in the right direction. Even though transferring to another station while underground can be especially confusing, never forget to relish the adventure and marvel at the beauty of the stations. (For more Metro information, see page 134.)

TAXIS

You can order a taxi from the taxi desk located in the lobby of most hotels, or call a taxi to come to a specific location; a minimal service fee may be charged. For telephone numbers/websites of some taxi companies, see the Practical Information section for the relevant city. Advance notice is usually required, but taxis can arrive within minutes if in the area when ordered. Instead of ordering a taxi from the hotel, it may be easier to just go outside and flag one down (the ride is made cheaper by walking a few blocks away from the hotel). There are official and private taxis (which are required to display ID registrations) and private cars. Unlike most other countries, a Russian taxi ride is not as simple as it would seem. Even hailing a taxi can be a problem. Stand with your arm held out, palm slightly down. If a taxi stops, the driver may ask where you want to go before deciding if he wants to take you. If there is no meter, you need to negotiate a price. Be aware that the wealthier you appear, the higher the driver may bid. Often you can bring the price down by saying it is too much and pretending to walk away. Always carry small bills as the driver often says he has no change.

Taxi fees can be higher in the evening. It is wise to find out the average cost of your journey before you start bargaining. (By law you should pay in rubles, but a driver may accept foreign currency.) If the driver seems to take a circuitous route, and the meter is running, ask—the driver may not be trying to cheat you. Often more direct roads may be closed and under construction. If you have an UBER ride-sharing account, check with UBER before you depart, as there are now UBER riders in Moscow and other cities. (www.uber.com to sign up for the APP.)

Hitching is quite common—taxis are not always available and drivers of private cars are often eager to earn some extra cash by picking up paying passengers. Because of recent crime, evaluate the taxi or car before you get in, and never take a ride late at night, especially to an outlying area. If you do not have a good feeling about the driver, do not get in; always use common sense. Never get alone into a vehicle already occupied by two people, or let your taxi stop to take another passenger en route.

CAR HIRE
Many hotels offer a car hire service with a driver, and a guide can also be hired for the day. There are now both Russian and Western car services where automobiles, jeeps and mini-vans can be rented. (You may be asked to present an International Driving Permit with a Russian translation of your license.) If new to the city, it is highly recommended not to drive on your own; public transportation is actually much faster, safer and more convenient. If you do plan on driving, check with your insurance company before leaving home; often Russia is not covered on a policy. If you want to tour an area, many private cars and off-duty taxi-drivers are often open to suggestions, and can be hired for the day to take you around. Make sure to agree on the amount and payment terms beforehand; gasoline costs are usually extra. ALWAYS wear your seatbelt, as most Russians don't.

BEING THERE
HOTELS
Intourist, the old Soviet travel dinosaur, no longer monopolizes the Russian hotel system and the *dezhurnaya*, that hawk-eyed hall attendant, has also gone extinct. From foreign-owned luxury palaces and restored privatized State-run hotels to hip hostels and bed and breakfasts, there is something for everyone's budget. Bohemian suites, moderate motels and bargain beds are available in every area of town. However, it is best to find a location as close to the center as possible; taxis can be expensive and public transportation a time-consuming experience. Many establishments also provide visa and other travel services. Check to see if your hotel provides airport or train station transfers as well. To prevent crime, hotel doormen may ask to view a hotel card before allowing entrance. If you are stopped, state in

English that you are staying in the hotel and have forgotten your card, or wish to eat at the restaurant—once recognized as a foreigner, the guards should let you in.

Hotels in Russia accept rubles, (often foreign currency) and major credit cards. (Remember to check if VAT and city tax charges are included in the quoted room rate.) Many have restaurants and bars (breakfast is often included in the price), business and fitness centers, shops, post offices and service bureaus, which book travel, sightseeing excursions, theater tickets, train reservations, etc. If you cannot afford to stay in a more expensive hotel, you can still use its amenities—spa centers usually offer special day-rates, or have an espresso in the coffee shop while reading the *Herald Tribune* to recharge! Especially during low seasons, bargaining for special rates can be attempted.

COMMUNICATIONS
INTERNATIONAL CALLS

Communication has become substantially easier since the Soviet era when placing an international call could take days. Today there are a number of ways of making an international call. For example, if you have an AT&T or Sprint Express telephone card, dial the appropriate access number and an operator can provide direct service to the US or elsewhere abroad. Special country discount packages can also be bought for one's mobile phone, depending on the carrier.

You can also direct dial to the United States and other countries from a home or business line. First dial 8 and wait for second dial tone, then dial international code 10, and then the country code and phone number.

A telephone service is also available from most major hotels but this can be very expensive. (Always check prices and service charges before calling.) It may be easier and cheaper for somebody to call you from abroad if they know your contact number.

Yet another way is to use the international (*Mezhdunarodny*) phone booths, placed throughout major cities. You can pay with either a credit or phone card (that can be bought at city kiosks and Metro stations). Always check the cost before you call; some may also have a three-minute minimum charge.

Cell phones can be rented in Moscow and St. Petersburg, and if you bring your own mobile phone, SIM cards are easy to buy (make sure your mobile is unlocked). Stores and kiosks have automated tellers that credit units to a purchased telephone card, which get used up depending if a local or international call. You spend units both when dialing out and receiving calls. It is now illegal to use a mobile phone while driving in Russia unless using a hands-free device.

Internet cafés are now found in cities and larger towns and most major hotels provide fax and computer/Internet services.

CALLS WITHIN RUSSIA

One can direct dial most cities in Russia from a hotel, mobile or landline. From a hotel or other landline phone, first dial 8 and wait for a second dial tone. Now dial the city code and then the phone number. If calling someone's local mobile, make sure you know the area code along with the seven-digit number (a mobile can have a completely different area code, as 915, 916 or 926). Small towns can have an area code with more than 3 numbers. Unless marked as such, regular pay phones cannot make city-to-city calls.

LOCAL CALLS

It once cost only two kopeks to make a local call, but now pay phones are operated by pre-paid phone cards, purchased at shops, metro areas or street kiosks. These cards can be used for international, inter-city, and local calls—but you have to call from the correct phone booth. (The trick to remember is to press the button with the speaker symbol when your party answers the phone.) Moscow now has two area codes: 495 and 499. If calling from within the 495 area to a 495 number, you just dial the 7 digit number. If calling to a 499 area code (from 495), dial 499 first and then the number (it is still charged as a local call). If calling from within the 499 area to a 499 number, you *must* dial 499 and the 7-digit number. If using a landline, remember to dial 8 first and wait for a dial tone.

POST AND MAIL

Russia's post office centers take care of postal services and telegrams. Outbound mail to the US and Europe takes about three weeks; inbound mail can take longer. You can also buy postage stamps at most hotels. To send an international or local package, you may have to first show the contents for inspection before wrapping. There are now several express mail services, such as Federal Express and DHL. (See Practical Information sections for locations.) Never send anything of major importance. Notice that addresses are written backwards in Russia with country and zip code first and name last.

MEDIA

The best places to find newspapers and magazines in English are at news shops in major hotels. Some street kiosks and stores also carry foreign literature. Pick up a free copy of the *Moscow* or *St Petersburg Times* in English, distributed through many restaurants, stores and hotels. Listings also give up-to-date information on restaurants, clubs, concerts, theaters, art events, etc. Find them online at: www.themoscowtimes.com and www.sptimes.ru. See also: www.elementmoscow.ru, www.moscownews.ru and www.passportmagazine.ru. A informative website run by English-speaking Expats in Moscow is www.expat.ru.

There are now numerous national and cable TV channels in Moscow and St Petersburg. Compared to Soviet TV (consumed by boring propaganda news and war musicals), contemporary TV is filled with everything from talk and game shows to New Age healers and soap operas. Many foreign films are broadcast in their original language or shown with subtitles. To get a further cultural view, watch some TV during your stay. The video format in Russia is SECAM, which is not compatible to NTSC.

A few Russian radio stations broadcast in English, along with Voice of America and BBC World Service. Some good FM music stations are Moscow's Europa Plus, Ekho Moscovy or Radio Rox.

ADDRESSES

No other place in the world has harder addresses to locate than in Russia. If you are presented with the following address, for example, this is how to decipher it: Ul Tverskaya, Dom (House) 33, Korpus (Block/Bldg) 2, Etazh (Floor) 3, Kvartira (Apartment) 109, Kode 899. Street numbers are often poorly marked. Once you have located (Street/House) #33 Tverskaya Ulitsa (Street), there may now be several different buildings using this one address, which are separated by their *korpus* or block numbers. (One often enters the building from the back.) Once you locate Block 2, look for a list of apartment numbers usually posted on the outside of each building. Make sure your *kvartira* or apartment number is listed; if not, it may be located in a different block. When you enter the security code of 899, the door should open. (If it does not work, you can also usually ring your host from here.) Once inside, proceed up to the third floor or *etazh* and look for *kvartira* apartment 109. (109 does not mean it is on the first floor!) The passage to the apartment may be blocked by yet another door that secures the hallway. Look for the appropriate apartment number by this door and ring the buzzer. Most Russians also have a double door leading into the apartment—so if you knock they may not hear, so ring the bell. Ideally you should make sure somebody knows you are coming so they can be on the look out for you!

Additionally, many apartment block elevators are old and run down and may not be operating; be prepared to walk up. (On a humorous note: during Soviet times, the primo apartment was considered to be on the first floor and not the penthouse. On the first floor, a tenant was assured of getting hot water and not having to rely on the elevator!) One last point concerning addresses: 3-ya 55 Liniya means 55 Third Liniya Street; this also means that there is a First and Second Liniya Street indicated by 1-ya and 2-ya.

ETIQUETTE

Often Russians appear very restrained, formal or downright glum. But there is a dichotomy between their public (where for so many generations they dared not express their true feelings) and private appearances. In informal and private situations or after friendship has been established, the Russian character is charged with emotional warmth, care and humor. They are intensely loyal and willing to help. Arriving in or leaving the country merits great displays of affection, usually with flowers, bear hugs, kisses and even tears of sorrow or joy. If invited to someone's home for dinner, expect elaborate preparations. Russians are some of the most hospitable people in the world. If you do not like drinking too much alcohol, watch out for the endless round of toasts!

The formal use of the patronymic (where the father's first name becomes the child's middle name) has been used for centuries. For example, if Ivan names his son Alexander, he is known as Alexander Ivanovich. His daughter Ludmilla's patronymic becomes Ivanovna. Especially in formal or business dealings, try to remember the person's patronymic (although the formal patronymic is used less by younger generation these days). As in the West, where Robert is shortened to Bob, for example, Russian first names are also shortened once a friendship is established. Call your friend Alexander 'Sasha', Mikhail 'Misha', Ekaterina 'Katya', Tatyana 'Tanya' and Mariya 'Masha', or even use the diminutive form 'Mashenka'.

SUPERSTITIONS AND CUSTOMS

Here are some customs and superstitions that may be useful to remember if you are visiting a Russian home:

- Never shake hands or press something over a doorway or threshold, it can lead to an argument or misunderstanding.
- Never whistle indoors, it will blow your money away.
- Never light a cigarette from a candle, it brings bad luck.
- Bring only an odd number of flowers, even numbers are for funerals.
- Spit three times over your left shoulder to keep from jinxing something (the devil may be lurking there).
- If invited to a Russian home, always try to bring a small gift such as food or drink. (The guest is also supposed to be the first to greet, and not the host.)
- While in a Russian home, expect to remove your shoes and wear the traditional *tap'pechki* (slippers).
- Do not overly admire a household item, it may be gifted to you upon departure.

- When leaving a party, expect one last toast, *na pososhok*—one for the road. (A pososhok is a walking stick.)
- Before departing it is expected to do one last sit down with friends or associates, it is a good luck gesture for your return.
- The presence of a guest is considered an honor, and it is the host who thanks guests for coming.

COMPLAINTS

Even today, rules, regulations and bureaucracy still play a role in Russian life, with many uniformed people enforcing them. People here are not always presumed innocent until proven guilty. When dealing with police or other officials, it is best to be courteous while explaining a situation. For example, police are allowed to ask anyone for their *dokumenty* or documents (it is sufficient to show a xerox copy of your passport). On roads, the *militsia* can randomly pull over vehicles to spot-check the car and registration. If you are pulled over, it does not mean you have done anything wrong. If you are kept waiting, as in restaurants, remember everyone else is waiting too. Be patient and remember that you are in a foreign country; polite humor can often work well. Do not lose your temper, mock or laugh when inappropriate. Should you be arrested, you have the right to immediately contact your embassy or consulate.

A few commonly used words are *nyet* and *nelzya*, which mean 'no' and 'it's forbidden'. The Russian language uses many negations. If people tell you something is forbidden, it may mean that they simply do not know or do not want to take responsibility. Ask elsewhere.

WOMEN AND MINORITIES

There have been reports of some Russian groups, such as skinheads, targeting Asian and African students who are mainly from Vietnam, Laos or the African continent. An attack on a foreign tourist is very rare. Use proper conduct and common sense as you would to ensure your safety in any big city. Do not walk late at night (especially alone) in unfamiliar neighborhoods or get into cars or taxis you are unsure about. (Carry a whistle and flashlight.) Women should avoid dressing too provocatively, so as not to be mistaken for a prostitute. On the other hand, Russian women love to dress up and wear lots of make-up on nights out—so you may feel uncomfortable if under-dressed in an upscale club or restaurant.

The only real hassle can be intoxicated locals who may try to pick up or get a woman's attention. If followed, enter a hotel lobby or restaurant, where guards are usually standing. If uncomfortable with any suitor, just say NYET! Check out the International Woman's Club of Moscow at www.iwcmoscow.ru.

LGBT

In June 2013, Russia passed a contentious anti-gay law that made it a crime 'to propagandize for untraditional sexual relationships to minors,' which exploded in a massive wave of criticism, since the law can be interpreted as it sees fit. One must remember that Russia has never treated homosexuality lightly—Article 121 of the penal code stated that any type of homosexual conduct, even among consenting adults, was punishable by up to five years in prison or a stay in an asylum. It was not repealed until the early 1990's. Even though gay rights have made enormous strides, there is still prejudice, especially among male heterosexuals who have been known to be aggressive. Openly gay behavior on the street is not advisable. Many prominent figures, especially in the art world, are now having the courage to come out and take a stand for gay rights. Gay clubs have opened in both cities, along with organized special 'gay nights' throughout the year. For useful resources: www.english.gay.ru, www.gaytours.ru and www.lesbi.ru. (See Practical Information sections.)

VISITORS WITH DISABILITIES

Sadly, Russia has never paid special attention to its disabled. (It is rare to see a handicapped person or, for that matter, anyone using a wheelchair or crutches.) It is nearly impossible to use public transportation, and there are no street access elevators to get down to a Metro station. Street curbs are not built for wheelchairs. It is really only the new hotels that offer any assistance for disabled people. Some local useful organizations are the Russian Society for the Blind (www.vos.org.ru) and Russian Society for the Deaf (www.vog.deafnet.ru). Some travel companies have now opened to accommodate visitors with disabilities such as Liberty Travel in St Petersburg, www.libertytour.ru.

WEIGHTS AND MEASURES

Russia operates on the metric system for weights and measures. For some useful conversion tables, see page 762.

MAJOR HOLIDAYS

New Year's Day: January 1.

Russian Orthodox Christmas: January 7. (The Orthodox Church still goes by the old calendar, which differs from the Gregorian by 13 days.)

Day of the Defender's of the Fatherland (Army Day): February 23rd (Also celebrated as Father's Day.)

International Women's Day: March 8. (Established after the Second International Conference of Socialist Women in Copenhagen in 1910)

Orthodox Easter (Pas'kha): Falls in April or May (Observance only)

Spring and Labor Holiday/May Day: May 1 and 2. (Even though no longer celebrated as International Workers' Solidarity Day, it still retains a festive nature with parades on Moscow's Red Square and St Petersburg's Palace Square. Much of the country shuts down for the first two weeks in May.)

Victory Day: May 9. (Parades are held at war memorials, such as the Piskarovskoye Cemetery in St Petersburg, to celebrate VE Day, the end of WWII in Europe.)

Russian Independence Day: June 12.

Orthodox Christianity Day: July 28. In 2010, President Medvedev declared this holiday, the *Baptism of Rus*, in honor of Russia's conversion to Christianity in 988.

Solidarity or Unity Day (formerly known as the Day of the Great October Revolution): November 4.

Long before Vladimir Putin took power, Russia celebrated 31 official holidays (*prazd'niki*) and festivals, today there are over 70—about one every five days!

The **Russian Winter Festival** is celebrated from mid-December to mid-January, with special events held throughout Moscow, St Petersburg and Golden Ring towns. In December, cities unveil the *Yolka*; the tradition of Christmas trees came to Russia under Peter the Great. Moscow celebrates the **December Nights Festival**, a month-long art and music event hosted by the Pushkin Museum of Fine Arts.

The week before Lent people celebrate **Maslenitsa** or Butter Week. This stems from an old Pagan tradition of making blini pancakes (representing the sun) to honor the coming of spring, and culminates—in the burning of a scarecrow—to fend off winter for good. In March, Moscow often hosts an International Contemporary Music Festival (www.mosforumfest.ru/en). Fashion week takes place in Moscow in the spring and fall.

In April, Moscow's **Golden Mask Festival** hosts two weeks chocked full of theater, dance and musical performances.

From May 1 to Victory Day on May 9 most of the country is shut down on holiday; cities put on parades and other cultural events. The **Moscow Stars Music Festival** is May 5–13. **St Petersburg Day** is celebrated on May 27.

In June, the **Moscow International Film Festival** is a week-long event, with films shown in theaters around the city (www.moscowfilmfestival.ru). St Petersburg celebrates the **White Nights** (June 21–July 11), with many cultural events throughout the city.

The first weekend in September is celebrated as **City Day** in Moscow with plenty of parades, fireworks and fun. In September, the Moscow **International Marathon** is run through the city. September 8 marks the **Siege of Leningrad Day**—special ceremonies in St Petersburg mark the end of the 900-day siege during WWII.

Other observances are: **Radio Day**, May 7 (to celebrate Alexander Popov, inventor of wireless telegraphy and, as Russians regard, the co-inventor of Radio along with Marconi); **International Day for the Protection of Children**, June 1; **World Environmental Protection Day**, June 5; **Pushkin's Birthday**, June 6; **Day of Youth**, June 27; **International Day of Small Business**, July 1; **Police (GAI) Day**, July 3; **Day of Russia's Military Glory**, July 10 (in commemoration of the Poltava battle in 1709); **Day of Russian Mail**, second Sunday in July; **Navy Day**, last Sunday in July (in St Petersburg the fleet usually parades along the Neva River); **Day of Railway Troops**, August 6; **Day of Russia's First Sea Victory** (by Peter the Great over the Swedes), August 9; **Air Force Day**, August 15; **Russian Flag Day**, August 22; **Russian Cinema Day**, August 27; **Miner's Day**, August 29; **Computer Programmers' Day**, September 13; **Day of Customs Workers**, October 25 and **Mother's Day**, November 30.

Name Days: Many calendar dates have a corresponding name day. Russians love to celebrate their own name day. For example, January 25 is Tatyana's Day, originally a religious feast day commemorating the martyrdom of St Tatyana. On July 24, the name Olga is celebrated; Olga was the widow of Prince Igor and the first person in Kievan Rus to accept Christianity. The poet Anna Akhmatova wrote of her friend, Mikhail Lozinsky whose name day was November 8 (the feast day of the Archangel Michael): *Sunshine, dust-filled yet translucent. Lit the room, a yellow ray. Waking, I knew in an instant; Dearest, this is your name day...*

For Church Holidays and Festivals, see page 737.

FOOD

Russian cooking is both tasty and filling. In addition to the expected borshch and Beef Stroganov, it includes many delectable regional dishes from the other Commonwealth states, such as Uzbekistan, Georgia or the Ukraine.

The traditions of Russian cooking date back to the simple recipes of the peasantry, who filled their hungry stomachs with the abundant supply of potatoes, cabbages, cucumbers, onions and bread. For the cold northern winters, they would pickle the few available vegetables and preserve fruits to make jam. This rather bland diet was pepped up with sour cream, parsley, dill and other dried herbs. In an old Russian saying, peasants described their diet as *Shchi da kasha, Pishcha nasha* (cabbage soup and porridge are our food). The writer Nikolai Gogol gave this description of the Russian peasant's kitchen: 'In the room was the old familiar friend found in every kitchen, namely a samovar and a three-cornered cupboard with cups and teapots, painted eggs hanging on red and blue ribbons in front of the icons, with flat cakes, horseradish and sour cream on the table along with bunches of dried fragrant herbs and a jug of *kvas* [a dark beer made from fermented black bread].'

RED SHIRTS AND BLACK BREAD

*W*e plunged into plebeian Moscow, the world of red-shirted workmen and *cheap frocked women; low vodka shops and bare, roomy traktirs, where the red-shirted workmen assemble each evening to gossip and swallow astonishing quantities of tea, inferior in quality and very, very weak.*

Here was Moscow's social and material contrast to the big houses, with sleeping Dvroniks, and of the silent street of painted house fronts, curtained balconies and all the rest. Though day had not yet dawned for other sections of Moscow, it had long since dawned for the inhabitants of this. Employers of labor in Moscow know nothing of the vexed questions as to eight-hour laws, ten-hour laws, or even laws of twelve. Thousands of red shirts, issuing from the crowded hovels of this quarter, like rats from their hiding places, had scattered over the city long before our arrival on the scene; other thousands were still issuing forth, and streaming along the badly cobbled streets. Under their arms, or in tin pails, were loaves of black rye bread, their food for the day, which would be supplemented at meal times by a salted cucumber, or a slice of melon, from the nearest grocery.

Though Moscow can boast of its electric light as well as gas, it is yet a city of petroleum. Coal is dear, and, in the matter of electric lights and similar innovations from the wide-awake Western world, Moscow is, as ever, doggedly conservative. So repugnant, indeed, to this stronghold of ancient and honourable Muscovite sluggishness, is the necessity of keeping abreast with the spirit of modern improvement, that the houses are not yet even numbered. There are no numbers to the houses in Moscow; only the streets are officially known by name. To find anybody's address, you must repair to the street, and inquire of the policeman or drosky driver, who are the most likely persons to know, for the house belonging to Mr. So-and-so, or in which that gentleman lives. It seems odd that in a country where the authorities deem it necessary to know where to put their hand on any person at a moment's notice, the second city of the empire should be, in 1980, without numbers to its houses.

Thomas Stevens, Through Russia on a Mustang, *1891*

Russians remain proud of these basic foods, which are still their staples today. They will boast that there is no better *khleb* (bread) in the world than a freshly baked loaf of Russian black bread. One Russian word for hospitality is *khlebosolstvo*, formed from the two words *khleb* (bread) and *sol* (salt). It was the custom to present a guest with freshly baked bread, such as *karavai*, lavishly decorated on the top with bits of dough. The guest cut the first slice of bread and dipped it in salt. In old Russia, the toast *Khleb da Sol* meant Bon Appétit!

Medieval Russians first considered beer to be the work of the devil (the word for hops, *xmel*, lies at the root of *pokhmelye*, or hangover). But, Peter the Great acquired a taste for beer while visiting Western Europe; and, in 1718, he issued a decree for the navy and hospitals to brew beer in the "Dutch manner" as a restorative drink. By 1795 Catherine the Great had opened Russia's first public brewery, and soon St Petersburg became the beer capital of Russia.

In 2011, the Russian samovar celebrated its 265th birthday. Stemming from *sam* (self) and *varit* (to boil), the samovar came to represent the warmth of the Russian soul and was even given a place of honor in the household. Samovars were made mainly from copper, silver, platinum and porcelain, and decorated in the style of the times. One made from gold (fashioned as a rooster) won a grand-design prize at the Vienna's World Fair in 1873. Samovars were used to boil up water for the favorite national pastime—drinking a cup of *chai* or hot tea. It was popular to sip tea through a cube of sugar held between the teeth (known as *vpriskusku*) rather than mixing the sugar directly into the tea (*vnakladku*). As Alexander Pushkin wrote, 'Ecstasy is a glass full of tea and a piece of sugar in the mouth.' It was customary, in the 1700s, to pour the hot tea directly into the saucer, from which cooler mouthfuls could be taken. By the 1800s, Russians enjoyed sipping their steaming tea from a tall glass placed in a *podstakan'nik* (metal holder).

The introduction of tea to Russia is said to have been in 1638, when Czar Mikhail Romanov was gifted a foreign herb from the Mongolian Altun Khan. He tried to chew the bitter herb and the Khan's emissary finally had to instruct the court how to brew the tea in hot water. The tea drinking habit caught on and by the turn of the 20th century, Russia's tea consumption ranked second in the world. A recent survey discovered that half of the Russian population enjoys at least five cups of tea a day (prefering *chyorni* or black tea) and 82 percent still prefer loose tea to tea bags. Many artists painted scenes of samovars and tea drinking, such as Boris Kustodiev's *Kupchikha* (Merchant's Wife) *Drinking Tea* (1916) and *Moscow Traktir* (1916), and Kuzma Petrov-Vodkin's *By the Samovar* (1926). (See page 62).

The potato has long been a staple food of most Russian families. Legend has it that Peter the Great brought back the potato (*kartosh'ka*) from Holland and ordered it planted throughout Russia; it was called 'ground apple'. During these times, so many changes were being implemented upon the peasantry that many, particularly Old Believers, refused to eat what they considered the 'devil's apple'. But, by 1840, after the government decreed that peasants had to plant the potato on all common lands, this 'second bread' soon became the staple food for most of the poorer population. During the lean times of revolution and war, potatoes fed entire armies. Since soldiers did not have time to cut and clean them, they would first boil the potato whole and then eat them with the skin. To this day, unpeeled cooked potatoes (with grated cheese, mayonnaise, or minced garlic added) are known as 'Potatoes in Uniform'. Today, Russia is the world's third largest producer of potatoes.

Peter the Great also introduced French cooking to his empire in the 18th century. While the peasantry had access only to the land's crops, the nobility hired its own French chefs, who introduced eating as an art form, often preparing up to ten elaborate courses of delicacies. Eventually, Russian writers ridiculed the monotonous and gluttonous life of the aristocrats, many of whom planned their days around meals. In his novel *Oblomov*, Ivan Goncharov coined the term 'Oblomovism' to characterize the sluggish and decadent life of the Russian gentry. In *Dead Souls*, Nikolai Gogol described a typical meal enjoyed by his main character in the home of an aristocrat:

> *On the table there appeared salmon, pressed caviar, fresh caviar, herrings, smoked tongues and dried sturgeon. Then there was a baked 300-pound sturgeon, a pie stuffed with mushrooms, fried pastries, dumplings cooked in melted butter, and fruit stewed in honey... After drinking glasses of vodka of a dark olive color, the guests had dessert... After the champagne, they uncorked some bottles of cognac, which put still more spirit into them and made the whole party merrier than ever!*

As a Russian saying goes: 'There can never be too much vodka, only not enough!' Vodka has always been the indispensable drink of any class on any occasion. Whether rich or poor, no Russian is abstemious. Anton Chekhov wrote of a group of peasants who, 'on the Feast of the Intercession, seized the chance to drink for three days. They drank their way through fifty rubles of communal funds...one peasant beat his wife and then continued to drink the cap off his head and boots off his feet!' The writer also added: even though 'vodka is colorless...it paints your nose red, and blackens your reputation!'

The year 2013 marked the 615th anniversary of vodka. Genoese monks are credited as the first to come up with the distillation process. They were said to have begun shipping distilled grain spirits (then called *aqua vitae* or water of life) to Lithuania in 1398. Soon after, Russia embraced this new spirit with gusto. The word vodka stems from *voda*, meaning water; *vodka*, means dear or little water. Rye was the favored distilling ingredient, followed by barley, wheat or potatoes. Ivan the

Terrible built the first *kabak* (tavern) for his palace guard in Moscow near the Kremlin, on the Balchug (where the five-star Hotel Baltschug stands today). Czar Alexis (Peter the Great's father) allowed the building of one *kabak* in every town (but three in Moscow), and instituted the famous Law Code of 1649 which decreed that all revenues from vodka sales went directly into royal coffers; this state monopoly lasted over 300 years. Only home brewing, or the making of *samogon*, was permitted without government control. Even today, 100 percent proof amateur spirits are still known as *speert* (spirit) or *samogon*.

Between national consumption and international sales, the income from vodka was enormous. By the late 1800s, nearly 40 percent of all state revenue came from liquor sales alone, and a typical Russian family spent up to 15 percent of its annual income on alcohol. In 1865, it was the famous scientist, Dmitri Mendeleyev (the inventor of the Periodic Tables) who first recommended from his own studies that the human body could best assimilate alcohol in the proportion of 40 percent spirit. It was during this time that a new reform removed the State's monopoly on vodka supplies. Over the next three decades (before the government again took control), Pyotr Smirnov took advantage of the drinking craze and was able to strike it rich with his enterprising new brand of *Smirnov* vodka. By the end of the 19th century there were already over 100 different flavored vodkas sold in Russia. During World War II, Russian soldiers even received a daily commissar's ration of *narkomovskiye sto gram*—an allotted 100 grams (three-and-a-half ounces). (The term Molotov Cocktail was actually coined by the Finns during the Soviet-Finnish War to mock the Minister of Foreign Affairs, Vyacheslav Molotov. During WWII, Soviet soldiers tossed the incendiary device at German tanks, calling them 'bottles with a flammable mixture.' Only later did historians begin calling them *Kokteil Molotova*.) Distilling factories had opened everywhere by the 20th century; the most famous was the Moscow State Warehouse No. 1. Built in 1900 on the banks of the Yauza River over three artesian wells, the factory now produces the *Yuri Dolgoruky* brand and the elite label of *Kristall* vodka—a vodka double-distilled in a process that takes five times longer than ordinary vodka.

A typical Russian breakfast or *zavtrak*, consists of tea, coffee, eggs, *kasha* (hot cereal), cheese, cold meats or sausage and a plentiful supply of bread and butter. Most hotels now offer either a Russian or Continental-style breakfast. A Russian *obyed* (lunch) consists of soup, bread, salad and usually a choice of meat, chicken or fish with potatoes, a pickled vegetable and a sweet dessert of cakes or *morozhnoye* (ice cream). Salads or vegetables include cucumbers, tomatoes, cabbage, beets, potatoes and onions (a Russian 'salad' often does not contain lettuce). *Smetana* (sour cream) is a popular condiment—Russians like it on everything—some even drink a glass for breakfast. *Oozhiin* (dinner) is similar to lunch, except vodka, wine, champagne or cognac will usually be served.

Gone are the days when a tourist searched for hours for something to eat, waited in long lines, or bribed a way into a State-run restaurant. The good news is that both Moscow and St Petersburg are teeming with restaurants, cafés, fast-food centers and food markets. The service has improved so much that it is practically unrecognizable from the old Soviet mediocrity and inefficiency. But, as a sign of the times, prices have also risen. Russians joke that under socialism when they had money, there was nothing to buy; but now with democracy, they have everything at their disposal, but no money to buy it with. First-class restaurants charge the same as they would in New York, Paris or Tokyo. In one private club, I watched as a large table, filled with Russian *biznissmeny*, charged up $5,000 in appetizers alone! (Beware of menus that have no prices.) But there are restaurants to suit every budget, and to locate a place to dine check listings in the Practical Information sections for each city. There are also plenty of restaurant guides available in the city, or just have a local recommend one of their favorite spots. Take a stroll and see what you can find; practically every corner now offers something edible, and there are also plenty of supermarkets that offer all sorts of groceries at reasonable prices.

Hundreds of eating establishments operate throughout both cities—from typical old-style Russian fare to ethnic cuisines from Georgian, Chinese, Japanese and Italian to fast-food and take-out, for any price and palate. (By the way, *bistro* originates from the Russian word *biistra*, meaning fast. During the 1815 Russian occupation of Paris, Cossack soldiers were known to scream out *'biistra, biistra!'* to restaurant waiters; soon the bistro opened—a place where one could get served quickly.) Most establishments in larger cities accept credit cards. Tipping is 10–15 percent (check to make sure a service charge has not already been added to your bill). Many menus are printed in both Russian and English; if you cannot read it, the waiter can usually translate it for you. For more popular places, making a reservation is advisable.

DINING AND DRINKING

The first point to remember when dining out is that most Russians still consider eating out an expensive luxury and enjoy turning dinner into a leisurely, evening-long experience. Many restaurants provide entertainment, so do not expect a fast meal. (Russians can spend a few hours savoring appetizers—if your waiter is not prompt with bringing your entrée, this may only be for a cultural reason.) It is also customary for the waiter to take your entire order, from soup to dessert, at the beginning. In some establishments, different parties may be seated together at the same table, an excellent way to meet locals and other visitors.

Most restaurants (in Cyrillic **Ресторан**, pronounced 'restoran') are open daily from 11am to 11pm, and close for a few hours in the mid-afternoon. Nightclubs can stay open all night and also be expensive. For fast foods other than pizza, burgers or hot dogs, be on the look out for specialty cafés, such as *shashliki* (shish kebabs), *blinnaya* (pancakes), *pelmennaya* (dumplings), *pirozhkovaya* (meat and vegetable pastries) and *morozhnoye* (ice cream and sweets). Try to drink only bottled water and beware of iced drinks, homemade fruit juices and *kompot*, fruit in sugared water, which are often made with the local water.

If invited to a Russian home, expect a large welcome. Russians love hospitality, which means preparing a large spread. If you can, take along a bottle of wine, champagne or vodka. Remember, a Russian toast is followed by another toast and so on. This usually entails knocking back your entire shot of vodka each time! Since toasts can continue throughout the evening (and if you want to be able to stand up in the morning), you may want to consider diluting the vodka with juice or water, or just giving up—to the chagrin of your host. Some popular toasts are: *Za Mir I Druzhbu* (To Peace and Friendship), *Do Dnya* (Bottoms Up) and, the most popular, *Na Zdoroviye* (To Your Health). Gorky, in a memoir about his boyhood on the Volga, wrote, 'people drank for joy and they drank for sorrow; the Russian soul is versatile.'

ON THE MENU

See pages 745–750 for a useful selection of Russian food and drinks vocabulary.) The Russian menu is divided into four sections: *zakuski* (appetizers), *pervoye* (first course), *vtoroye* (second course) and *sladkoe* (dessert). The order is usually taken all together, from appetizer to dessert. *Zakuski* are Russian-style hors d'oeuvres that include fish, cold meats, salads and marinated vegetables.

Ikra is caviar: *krasnaya* (red from salmon) and *chornaya* (black from sturgeon). The sturgeon is one of the oldest fish species known, dating back over 30 million years. Its lifespan is also one of the longest. No sturgeon is worth catching until it is at least seven years old and *beluga* are not considered adult until after 20 years. The best caviar is *zernistaya*, the fresh unpressed variety. The largest roe comes from the *beluga*, a dark gray caviar appreciated for its large grain and fineness of skin, and the most expensive. Caviar from the *sevruga* is the smallest and has the most delicate taste.

Caviar is usually available at Russian restaurants and can be bought in city stores. It has long been considered a health food in Russia. Czar Nicholas II made his children eat the pressed *payushnaya* caviar every morning. Since they all hated the salty taste, their cook solved the problem by spreading it on black bread and adding banana slices. The caviar-banana sandwich became the breakfast rage for many aristocratic families. Russia is still the largest producer of caviar in the world, processing over 1,000 tons per year.

Many varieties of Russian soup are served, more often at lunch than dinner. *Borshch* was originally not made from beets, but from a root similar to parsnips. Only in the 16th century did the traditional red beet soup start being served with a spoonful of sour cream. *Solyanka* is a tomato-based soup with chunks of fish or meat and topped with diced olives and lemon. *Shchi* is a tasty cabbage soup. A soup made from pickled vegetables is *rasolnik*. *Okroshka* is a cold soup made from a *kvas* (weak beer) base.

Russian meals consist of *mya'so* (meat), *kur'iitsa* (chicken) or *rii'ba* (fish). *Bifshtek* is a small fried steak with onions and potatoes. Beef Stroganov is cooked in sour cream and served with fried potatoes. *Kutlyeta po Kiyevski* is Chicken Kiev, stuffed with melted butter; *Kutlyeta po Pajarski* is a chicken cutlet; *Tabak* is a slightly seasoned fried or grilled chicken. The fish served is usually *lososina* (salmon), *osetrina* (sturgeon), *shchuka* (pike) or *seld* (herring). Russians are not big vegetable eaters, but *kapus'ta* (cabbage), *kartosh'ka* (potatoes) and *gribii's smyetan'oi* (mushrooms and sour cream) are always available. Georgian dishes include *khachapuri* (hot bread), *baklazhan* (eggplant), *chakhokhbili* (steamed dumplings) and *tolma* (meat and rice in vine leaves). Desserts include *vareniki* (sweet fruit dumplings topped with sugar), *tort* (cake), *pon'chiki* (sugared donuts) and *morozhnoye* (ice cream).

Chai (tea) comes with every meal. It is always sweet; ask for *biz sak'hera*, for unsweetened tea. Many Russians stir in a spoonful of jam instead of sugar. Coffee is not served as often. Alcoholic drinks consist of *pivo* (beer), *kvas* (weak beer), *shampanskoye* (champagne), *vino* (wine) and vodka. *Kvas* was the second favorite

Russians love to hang out in their kitchens where they drink chai *(tea) and snack on freshly baked* khleb *(bread).*

drink of Russia for centuries. Brewed mainly from rye, it is then spiced with everything from berries to horseradish. *Kvas* trucks used to be found all around the streets selling glasses of the warm fermenting drink for mere kopeks, but nowadays soft drinks seem to be overtaking tradition. Alcoholic drinks are ordered in grams; a shot glass is 50 grams, small glass is 100 grams and a normal bottle consists of 750 grams or three quarters of a liter. The best wine comes from Georgia and the Crimea. There are both *krasnoye* (red) and *beloye* (white) wines. The champagne is generally sweet. The best brandy comes from Armenia—*Armyanski konyak*. *Nalivka* is a fruit liqueur. Vodka is by far the favorite drink and comes in a number of varieties other than Stolichnaya, Moskovskaya or Russkaya. These include *limonnaya* (lemon vodka), *persovka* (with hot peppers), *zubrovka* (infused with cinnamon, lemon and bison grass), *ryabinovka* (made from ash berries), *tminaya* (caraway flavor), *starka* (apple and pear-leaf), *Okhotnichaya* (Hunter's vodka flavored with port, ginger, pepper, cloves, coffee, juniper berries, star anise, orange and lemon peel, and roots of angelica—it was once customary for hunters to toast with it after returning from a kill), and *zveroboy* (animal killer!). One of the strongest and most expensive is *Zolotoye Koltso*, the Golden Ring.

If you see a Russian smile at you, while flicking the middle finger off his thumb into the side of his neck, your invitation to drink (and drink) has arrived. Normally Russians follow a shot of cold pure vodka (it is, of course, sacrilegious to dilute it with any other liquid) with a mouthful of *zakuska* or hors d'oeuvres, such as smoked salmon, caviar, herring, salami or even a slice of hearty Russian *khleb*, bread. Remember, Russians love to follow toast with toast—*dushá v dúshu*—heart to heart (so make sure you eat something while you drink!). They are quite capable of drinking *do beloi goryachki*—into 'a white fever of delirium' and *na brovyakh*—up to their eyebrows. Their equivalent of 'drinking one under the table' is *napeetsya do polozheniya riz*—literally, drinking till one is positioned very low beneath the icon frame. Never forget that Russians have a millennium of drinking in their blood. In 986, Prince Vladimir rejected Islam as the Russian State religion (he chose Byzantine Christianity) because it prohibited the drinking of alcohol. He reputedly said, 'For the people of *Rus*, drinking is joy; we cannot be without it!' Today, Russians drink more spirits than any other nationality—the equivalent of one 80–proof shot a day for every citizen.)

One note of caution when buying liquor, especially vodka, in Russia: these days, many imitations are being passed off on the market, such as homemade *samogon* poured into brand-name vodka bottles. (If it is *samogon*, you will immediately know the difference!) Do not buy vodka from small kiosks or off the street. Check to make sure the seal is secure and the label not suspiciously attached (horizontal glue lines usually mean factory-produced). Many Russians can tell genuine vodka just by the way bubbles move around in the bottle.

SHOPPING

Since the fall of the Soviet Union the country has come an amazingly long way from the previous offering of half-empty shops and foreign-currency only *Beriozka* stores. The market economy, especially in Moscow, is booming, and stores are full of both Russian and Western goods. Pre-perestroika, a traveler had to bring along essential supplies, but today almost anything can be found, from peanut butter to prescription drugs. Not only are there department stores, galleries and boutiques, but the streets are also lined with small shopping kiosks with salespeople hawking everything from T-shirts and videos to condoms and cologne. Specialty shops for antiques, arts and crafts, and other souvenirs also exist for any budget, and flea markets are especially fun for bargain hunters. Supermarkets and farmer's markets abound.

Traditional and popular Russian souvenirs include the *matryoshka* (painted set of nested dolls), *Bogorodskoye* wood carvings, *dymkovo* (earthenware), *gzhel* (blue-white porcelain), amber or malachite jewelry, *khokkhloma* (lacquerware), *platki* (shawls), *shapki* (fur hats), *Vologda* lace, *Zhostovo* trays…art books, balalaikas, samovars and *znachki* (small pins). Painted lacquer boxes vary in style and price according to which Golden Ring town they were made in. The craftsmen of Palekh, for example, use tempera paint to illustrate elongated figures distinguished by the colors red, black and gold. An authentic box takes up to three months to complete, with the smallest details painted using brushes made from squirrel or mink hair. Many (non hand-painted) fakes are pasted with colored decal scenes—check to make sure you have an original before buying.

LOCAL STORES

Some of the store (*magazin*) designations are: *univermag* (large department store), *kommissioniye* (commission or second-hand store), *co-op* (cooperative), *rinok* (farmer's market) and *kiosks*. The opening hours of most local stores vary widely, but they usually have a one-hour afternoon break sometime between 1pm and 3pm, and are shut during holidays. Many of the larger department stores and food stores are open 12 hours a day and also on Sundays. Expect to pay in rubles for your purchases (make sure you carry some smaller notes—changing large bills can be a hassle); many now accept credit cards.

SHOPPING TIPS

If you see something you would really like, buy it! Otherwise, the item will probably be gone by the time you return for it. Remember to take along an empty bag—in places such as farmers' markets, you are expected to provide your own. (Otherwise you will be emptying the strawberries into your own pocket!) It is illegal to take any item made pre-1947 out of the country. Customs officers are especially

The interior of GUM Department Store on Red Square. Built in 1893, it is Russia's largest store and has a large glass roof and ornate bridges that lead to over 200 shops on three levels.

First appearing in Russia in the 1890s, matryoshka *dolls represented peasant girls.
Today they are still painted in traditional Russian dress with* sarafan *jumpers, embroidered
blouses and* kokoshniki *headdresses, and are one of Russia's most popular souvenirs.*

on the look-out for antiques and icons, and will confiscate things at the airport
(even caviar—there is a limit on the amount that can be taken out). When you buy
a more expensive painting or work of art, check to see if you need an exit permit
from the Ministry of Culture. The gallery owner or artist can often help with this.
Always save receipts to show at customs. Beware of the many fakes, especially icons
and lacquer boxes. For more information on shopping and markets, see the listings
in the Practical Information sections of each city.

RUSSIAN LANGUAGE

HISTORY

In the late 9th century, two Greek brothers Methodius and Cyril (both renowned
scholars from Macedonia) converted vernacular Slavic into a written language so
that teachings of Byzantine Orthodoxy could be translated for the Slavs. They
created the Glagolitic alphabet, based on Greek letters with new letters added for
non-Greek sounds; it had 41 letters. Cyrillic descended from the Glagolitic alphabet
in the 12th century and has 33 letters. When Prince Vladimir brought Christian
Orthodoxy into Kievan Rus in the 10th century, Slavonic became the language of the
Church. Church Slavonic, written in the Cyrillic alphabet, remained the literary and
liturgical language of Russia for over seven centuries.

In 1710, Peter the Great simplified Church Cyrillic into the 'civil alphabet' (*grazhdansky shrift*), a written form used in secular books. The two types of writing, the older script of the Church and Peter's revised version, were both employed in Russia up to the time of Lomonosov and the poet Pushkin, who were largely responsible for combining the two into a national language for the Russian people. The alphabet that is used today was further simplified in 1918, right after the October Revolution. Today over 250 million Eurasians use Cyrillic as the official alphabet for their national languages, and Russian is the fifth most widely spoken language in the world.

LETTERS AND WORDS

'I am certain that even now we do not truly know what a magical chorus of poets we possess, that the Russian language is young and supple, that we have only recently begun to write poetry, and that we love and believe in it.' (Anna Akhmatova, 1962)

Since Russian is not a Romance language, it is more difficult to pick up words compared to French or Spanish. Before leaving for your trip, try to spend time learning some of the Cyrillic alphabet, in which there are 33 letters compared to the English 26. Most Russian sounds are similar to English, but are just expressed with a different character symbol. For example, a Russian C is pronounced 's', and W is a 'sh' sound. Thus Masha is spelled Mawa and Sasha spelled Cawa. Once you start to recognize letters of the Russian alphabet, it is easy to sound out familiar words posted on the street, such as МЕТРО (Metro), Кафе (café) and Ресторан (restaurant). Besides, it is fun to walk down the street and decipher many of the signs and shop names, and you will feel much more at ease in the new environment.

Once you can recognize Cyrillic letters, work on Russian vocabulary and phrases. As with learning any new language, first try memorizing a few common words, such as 'hello', 'goodbye' and 'thank you', and to count from one to ten. Granted, even though Russian is not an easy language to learn (there are six cases of declensions compared with four in English—these are nominative, accusative, dative, genitive, instrumental and prepositional—and the nouns and adjectives are all declined differently based on their case in the sentence and their masculine, feminine or neuter forms), you will discover that native speakers appreciate any effort made in using their language and are delighted to help out. Even a few gestures and simple Russian expressions can go a long way and bring smiles to many faces! Purchase an English-Russian dictionary and phrasebook that can be shown to Russian-speaking people when you meet. Before your trip, you may also try one of the numerous Russian language courses for beginners and listen to its audio lessons to get a feel for the pronunciation.

See the Russian Language section on page 739 for a more comprehensive selection of useful everyday vocabulary.

(top) On St Petersburg's Nevsky Prospekt is the popular 19th century food emporium, Yeliseyev's, once known as the Temple of Gluttons. (See Special Topic on Yeliseyev's).
(bottom) Matryushka dolls and other souvenirs for sale near Moscow's Red Square.

GUM Department store on Moscow's Red Square celebrates its 120th anniversary.

Moscow hosts the Miss Universe Pageant.

(opposite page) A sculpture of Peter the Great sits in Peter and Paul Fortress in St Petersburg. The head is an actual cast from the life mask of the Czar, made by Rastrelli in 1719.

(left) Boy plays with a pigeon around one of St Petersburg's many parks.

(below) A wedding takes place in St Petersburg, with a full day of celebration throughout the city.

(right) The St Petersburg
Metro has five lines, which
serve over two million
passengers daily.

(left) The St Petersburg to
Moscow railway line was
opened in 1851 during the
reign of Nicholas I.

The ethereal White Nights of St Petersburg with the Savior Church on Spilled Blood.

On St Petersburg's Potseluyev
Most or Bridge of Kisses, over the
Moika River, amorous couples
pledge their love with engraved
locks.

(left & below) With its many splendid canals, St Petersburg became known as the Venice of the North.

THE CONQUEROR

*A*t ten in the morning of the second of September, Napoleon was standing among his troops on the Poklonny Hill looking at the panorama spread out before him. From the twenty-sixth of August to the second of September, that is from the battle of Borodino to the entry of the French into Moscow, during the whole of that agitating, memorable week, there had been the extraordinary autumn weather that always comes as a surprise, when the sun hangs low and gives more heat than in spring, when everything shines so brightly in the rare clear atmosphere that the eyes smart, when the lungs are strengthened and refreshed by inhaling the aromatic autumn air, when even the nights are warm, and when in those dark warm nights, golden stars startle and delight us continually by falling from the sky.

The view of the strange city with its peculiar architecture, such as he had never seen before, filled Napoleon with the rather envious and uneasy curiosity men feel when they see an alien form of life. By the indefinite signs which, even at a distance, distinguish a living body from a dead one, Napoleon from the Poklonny Hill perceived the throb of life in the town and felt, as it were, the breathing of that great and beautiful body.

Every Russian looking at Moscow feels her to be mother; every foreigner who sees her, even if ignorant of her significance as the mother city, must feel her feminine character, and Napoleon felt it.

"A town captured by the enemy is like a maid who has lost her honor," thought he, and from that point of view he gazed at the oriental beauty he had not seen before. It seemed strange to him that his long-felt wish, which had seemed unattainable, had at last been realized. In the clear morning light he gazed now at the city and now at the plan, considering its details, and the assurance of possessing it agitated and awed him.

Leo Tolstoy, War and Peace, *1869*

Moscow

СТЫ АРХАГГЛ МИХАИЛЪ

For the dreamer and the night-bird

Moscow is dearer than all else in the world.

It is at the hearth, the source

Of everything that the century will live for.

Boris Pasternak

Moscow City Skyline with Moskva (Moscow) River.

Moscow Nights (Podmoskovniye Vechera) is a popular Russian song:
Lazily the river like a silvery stream,
Ripples gently in the moonlight;
And a song fades as in a dream,
In the spell of this Moscow night.

St. Basil's Cathedral,
Red Square, Moscow.

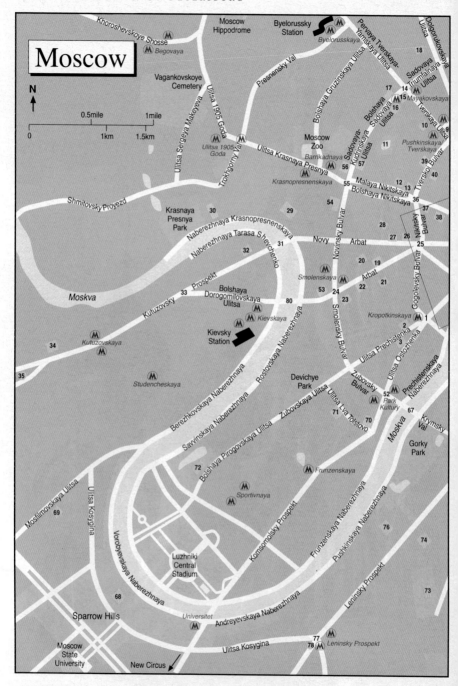

Moscow

N

0.5mile		1mile
0	1km	1.5km

Khoroshevskoye Shosse

Moscow Hippodrome

Byelorussky Station

Byelorusskaya

Begovaya

Vagankovskoye Cemetery

Presnensky Val

Penaya Tverskaya-Yamskaya Ulitsa

Dolgorukovskaya Ulitsa

18

Sadovaya Triumfalnaya Ulitsa

17 14
15 Mayakovskaya
16

Ulitsa Sergeya Makeyeva

Ulitsa 1905 Goda

Ulitsa 1905 Goda

Bolshaya Gruzinskaya Ulitsa

Sadovaya-Kudrinskaya Ulitsa

Bolshaya Sadovaya Ulitsa

Tverskaya Ulitsa

10
9

Moscow Zoo

11

Pushkinskaya/Tverskaya

Troitigorny

Ulitsa Krasnaya Presnya

Barrikadnaya

56   57

Krasnopresnenskaya

55

Malaya Nikitskaya

Bolshaya Nikitskaya

Tverskoi Bulvar

39
40

12
13
36

Shmitovsky Proyezd

Krasnaya Presnya Park

30

Naberezhnaya Krasnopresnenskaya

29

54

Novinsky Bulvar

28

27 26

Nikitsky Bulvar

37

38

25

Naberezhnaya Tarasa Shevchenko

31

Novy   Arbat

32

Smolenskaya

20   19

Arbat

Gogolevsky Bulvar

Moskva

Kutuzovsky Prospekt

33

Bolshaya Dorogomilovskaya Ulitsa

80

Kievskaya

53
24
23
22   21

Smolensky Bulvar

Kropotkinskaya   1

2

3

Ulitsa Prechistenka

34

Kutuzovskaya

Kievsky Station

Studencheskaya

Ulitsa Ostozhenka

Prechistenskaya Naberezhnaya

35

Berezhkovskaya Naberezhnaya

Savvinskaya Naberezhnaya

Rostovskaya Naberezhnaya

Devichye Park

Zubovsky Bulvar

52
Park Kultury

67

71   70

Ulitsa Lva Tolstovo

Zubovskaya Ulitsa

Moskva

Krymsky Val

Gorky Park

72

Bolshaya Pirogovskaya Ulitsa

Frunzenskaya

Frunzenskaya Naberezhnaya

76

74

Mostilmovskaya Ulitsa

Ulitsa Kosygina

69

Sportivnaya

Komsomolsky Prospekt

Pushkinskaya Naberezhnaya

Leninsky Prospekt

73

Vorobyevskaya Naberezhnaya

Luzhniki Central Stadium

68

Sparrow Hills

Universitet

Andreyevskaya Naberezhnaya

Moscow State University

New Circus

Ulitsa Kosygina

77
78   Leninsky Prospekt

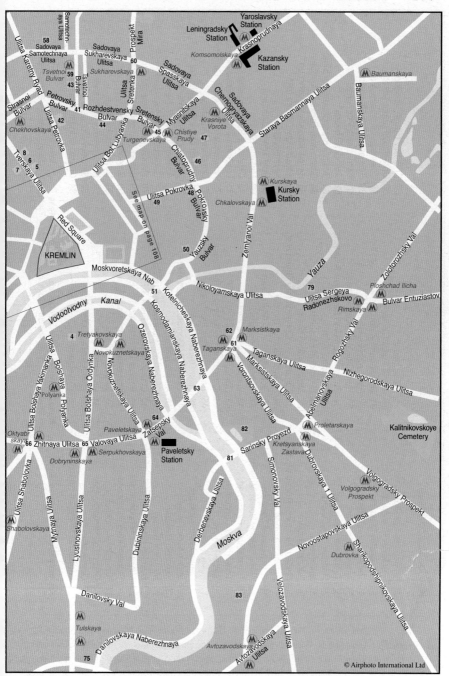

Key for Moscow Map:

1 Kropotkinskaya Ploshchad
2 Alexander Pushkin Museum
3 Leo Tolstoy Museum
4 Tretyakov Art Gallery
5 Aragvi Restaurant
6 Tverskaya Ploshchad
7 Moscow City Council
8 Yeliseyev's
9 Pushkin Square
10 Modern History of Russia Museum
11 Patriarch's Pond
12 Gorky House Museum
13 Alexei Tolstoy House Museum
14 Triumfalnaya Ploshchad
15 Tchaikovsky Concert Hall
16 Satire Theater
17 Pekin Hotel
18 Glinka Music Museum
19 Vakhtangov Theater
20 Skryabin Museum
21 Melnikov House
22 Pushkin House
23 Ministry of Foreign Affairs
24 Smolenskaya Ploshchad
25 Arbatskaya Ploshchad
26 Church of Simon Stylites
27 Dom Knigi
28 Lermontov Memorial House

29 White House
30 World Trade Center
31 Novoarbatsky Most
32 Radisson Royal Hotel
33 Hero City of Moscow Obelisk
34 Battle of Borodino Panorama Museum
35 Triumphal Arch
36 Nikitskaya Ploshchad
37 Mayakovsky Theater
38 Tchaikovsky Conservatory Grand Hall
39 Pushkin Drama Theater
40 Gorky Academic Art Theater
41 Trubnaya Ploshchad
42 Petrovsky Monastery
43 Old Circus Nikulin
44 Convent of the Nativity of the Virgin
45 Turgenevskaya Ploshchad
46 Eisenstein's House
47 Vasnetsov Memorial Apartment
48 Apraksin Mansion
49 Church of Saints Cosmas & Damian
50 Church of Saints Peter & Paul
51 Bolshoi Ustinsky Most
52 Krymskaya Ploshchad
53 Belgrad Hotel
54 US Embassy
55 Kudrinskaya Ploshchad
56 Planetarium

57 Chekhov House Museum
58 Obraztzov Puppet Theater
59 Tsventnoi Tsentralny Mall
60 Sukharevskaya Ploshchad
61 Taganskaya Ploshchad
62 Taganka Theater
63 Bolshoi Krasnokholmsky Most
64 Bakhrushin Theater Museum
65 Serpukhovskaya Ploshchad
66 Kaluzhskaya Ploshchad
67 Krymsky Most
68 Holy Trinity Cathedral
69 Mosfilm Studios
70 Church of St Nicholas at Khamovniki
71 Leo Tolstoy Country Estate Museum
72 Novodevichy Convent & Cemetery
73 Donskoi Monastery
74 Church of the Deposition of the Robe
75 Danilovsky Monastery
76 Academy of Sciences
77 Gagarinskaya Ploshchad
78 Yuri Gagarin Monument
79 Spaso-Andronikov Monastery
80 Borodinsky Most
81 Novospassky Most
82 Novospassky Monastery
83 Simonov Monastery
84 Church of the Intercession in Fili

Key to symbols and Russian terms:

Ⓜ = *Metro Station*
Ulitsa = Street
Bulvar = Boulevard
Ploshchad = Square
Pereulok = Lane
Proyezd = Passage
Most = Bridge
Naberezhnaya = Embankment

(opposite top) The red-brick State Historical Museum on Moscow's Red Square was constructed for Alexander II. When it opened in 1883, the museum contained over 300,000 objects; today it exhibits over 4 million items. In front, stands the Statue of Marshal Georgy Zhukov, a WWII hero, who gazes from his horse over Manezh Square.
(opposite bottom) A scene of the Moscow Kremlin and interior buildings along the Moscow River.

The 15th-century Assumption Cathedral in Moscow's Kremlin was modeled after the cathedral of the same name in the Golden Ring town of Vladimir. To its right stands the imposing Bell Tower of Ivan the Great, built in 1505 and once the tallest structure in Russia.

The 40-ton Emperor Cannon is the world's largest cannon still in existence. Designed in 1586 to protect the Savior's Gate on Red Square, it was never fired—probably because each cannon ball weighed one ton.

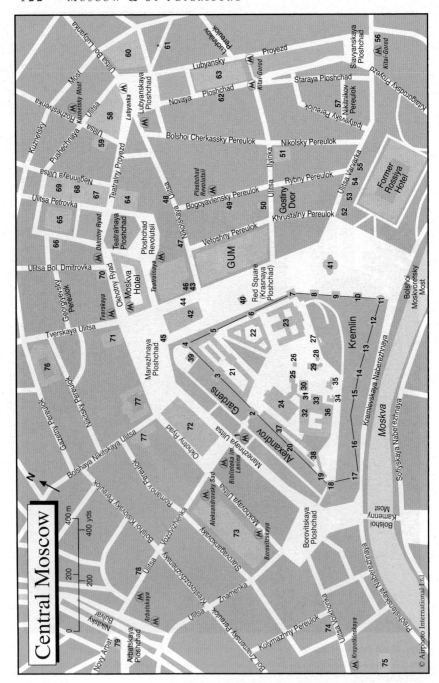

Central Moscow

400 m

400 yds

200

200

0

N

© Airphoto International Ltd

Key for Central Moscow Map:

1 Kutafya Tower
2 Troitskaya (Trinity) Tower
3 Srednaya Arsenalnaya (Middle Arsenal)
4 Corner Arsenal Tower
5 Nikolskaya Tower
6 Senate Tower
7 Spasskaya Tower (Savior)
8 Tsarskaya Tower (Czar)
9 Nabatnaya Tower (Alarm)
10 Konstantino-Yeleninskaya Tower
11 Beklemishevskaya Tower
12 Petrovskaya Tower
13 2-Bezymyannaya Tower (2nd nameless)
14 1-Bezymyannaya Tower (1st nameless)
15 Tainitskaya Tower (Secret)
16 Blagoveshchenskaya Tower (Annunciation)
17 Vodovzvodnaya Tower
18 Borovitskaya Tower
19 Oruzheynaya Tower (Armory)
20 Kommendantskaya Tower (Commandant)
21 Arsenal
22 Senate
23 Presidium and Kremlin Theater
24 Patriarch's Palace
25 Church of the Twelve Apostles
26 Emperor Cannon
27 Kremlin Hill

28 Emperor Bell
29 Ivan the Great's Bell Tower
30 Cathedral of the Assumption
31 Church of the Deposition of the Robe
32 Terem Palace
33 Palace of Facets
34 Cathedral of the Annunciation
35 Cathedral of the Archangel Michael
36 Grand Kremlin Palace
37 Amusement Palace
38 Armory Palace
39 Tomb of the Unknown Soldier
40 Lenin's Mausoleum
41 St Basil's Cathedral
42 Historical Museum
43 Kazan Cathedral
44 Iberian Resurrection Gates
45 Statue of Marshal Georgy Zhukov
46 Old Royal Mint
47 Zaikonospassky Monastery
48 History and Archives Institute
49 Cathedral of Bogoyavlensky
50 St Ilyia Church
51 Moscow Stock Exchange
52 Church of St Varvara
53 Old English Inn
54 Church of St Maximus

55 Znamensky Cathedral
56 Church of All Saints on Kulishki
57 Church of the Holy Trinity in Nikitniki
58 Detsky Mir
59 Savoy Hotel
60 Former KGB Building
61 Mayakovsky Museum
62 Church of St John the Divine "Under the Elm"
63 Polytechnical Museum
64 Metropole Hotel
65 Bolshoi Theater
66 Bolshoi Sister Theater
67 Maly Theater
68 Ararat Park Hyatt Hotel
69 TsUM
70 Dom Soyuzov
71 National Hotel
72 Central Exhibition Hall
73 Russian State Library
74 Pushkin Museum of Fine Arts
75 Cathedral of Christ Our Savior
76 Central Telegraph Building
77 Moscow State University
78 House of Friendship
79 Prague Restaurant

Key to symbols and Russian terms:

Ⓜ = Metro Station
Ulitsa = Street

Bulvar = Boulevard
Ploshchad = Square

Pereulok = Lane
Proyezd = Passage

Most = Bridge
Naberezhnaya = Embankment

*(above and top right) The Kremlin's gilded nine-domed Annunciation Cathedral
was built in 1482 by Ivan the Great. Once the private church of the royal family,
it is now open year-round for visitors.*

(bottom right) Built in 1479, the Assumption Cathedral was formerly the coronation church of the czars. Guarding the czar's doors are frescoes of the archangels Michael and Gabriel, and above them stands a row of bishops. The virgin and child at the top symbolizes the virgin's assumption into heaven to which the cathedral is dedicated.

The Terem Palace was built by Czar Mikhail Romanov to house the children and female relatives of noblewomen. Only the czar's wife, personal confessor and blind storytellers were allowed into the czar's private quarters and royal bedchamber on the top floor.

Two Persian war masks from the
16th-century (above) and a pair of
decorative breastplates,
on display in the Armory Palace.

The Church of St George on Pskov Hill was built in 1657 from donations given by the community of Pskov merchants who were living in Moscow. The golden Byzantine Orthodox crosses mounted on golden onion domes is a Russian design that dates back to the 15th century.

MOSCOW

Come to Moskva!!!
I am hopelessly in love with Moskva.
Whoever gets used to her
Will never leave her.
I will love Moskva forever.

Anton Chekhov

For centuries Moscow has been an inseparable part of the life of Russia. Moscow's history dates back to 1147, when Prince Yuri Dolgoruky established a small outpost on the banks of the Moskva River. The settlement grew into a large and prosperous town, which eventually became the capital of the principality of Moscovy. By the 15th century Moscow was Russia's political, cultural and trade center, and during the reign of Ivan the Great, it became the capital of the Russian Empire. Ivan summoned the greatest Russian and European architects to create a capital so wondrous that 'reality embodied fantasy on an unearthly scale', and soon the city was hailed as the 'New Constantinople'. In the next century Ivan the Terrible was crowned the first czar of all Russia in the magnificent Uspensky Sobor (Assumption Cathedral) inside the Kremlin. The words of an old Russian proverb suggest the power held by the Kremlin: 'There is only God and the center of government, the Kremlin.' People from all over the world flocked to witness the splendors in the capital of the largest empire on earth.

In 1712, after Peter the Great transferred the capital to St Petersburg, Moscow remained a symbol of national pride. Many eminent writers, scientists, artists and musicians, such as Pushkin, Tolstoy, Lomonosov, Repin and Tchaikovsky, lived and worked in Moscow, which never relinquished its political significance, artistic merit and nostalgic charm. Even when Napoleon invaded in 1812, he wrote: 'I had no real conception of the grandeur of the city. It possessed 50 palaces of equal beauty to the Palais d'Elysée furnished in French style with incredible luxuries.' After a terrible fire destroyed Moscow causing Napoleon's retreat, Tolstoy wrote that:

> *It would be difficult to explain what caused the Russians, after the departure of the French in October 1812, to throng to the place that had been known as Moscow; there was left no government, no churches, shrines, riches or houses—yet, it was still the same Moscow it had been in August. All was destroyed, except something intangible, yet powerful and indestructible... Within a year the population of Moscow exceeded what it had been in 1812!*

Moscow symbolized the soul of the empire, and Tolstoy later observed that Moscow remains eternal because 'Russians look at Moscow as if she is their own mother.' The name Moskva is said to derive from the Finnish words *maska ava*, meaning mother bear.

Moscow has also played an important role in the country's political movements: the revolutionary writers Herzen and Belinsky began their activities at Moscow University; student organizations supported many revolutionary ideas, from Chernyshevsky's to Marx's; and Moscow workers backed the Bolsheviks during the October Revolution of 1917 and went on to capture the Kremlin. In 1918, after more than two centuries, Moscow once again became Russia's capital. But this time, the city would govern the world's first socialist state—the Soviet Union. Trotsky, Lenin's main supporter, wrote:

> *...finally all the opposition was overcome, the capital was transferred back to Moscow on March 12, 1918... Driving past Nicholas' palace on the wooden paving, I would occasionally glance over at the Emperor Bell and Emperor Cannon. All the barbarism of Moscow glared at me from the hole in the bell and the mouth of the cannon... The carillon in the Savior's Tower was now altered. Instead of playing 'God Save the Czar', the bells played the 'Internationale', slowly and deliberately, at every quarter hour.*

In 1993, Moscow Mayor Yuri Luzhkov readopted the historic figure of St George as the capital's official coat-of-arms; St George also features on the city's flag. You will notice the dark red shield emblem throughout the city: Georgy Pobedonosets—St George the Victorious, wearing a blue cloak and riding a silver horse, strikes a black dragon with his golden spear. (In 1380, Prince Dmitri Donskoi carried the icon of St George to victory over the invading Mongols, and in 1497, Ivan III had St George's image engraved on Moscow's great seal.) In 2012, Moscow celebrated its 865th anniversary and today is the largest city in the country with a population of 11.5 million.

> *With the beginning of the new century, as if someone waved a magic wand, everything changed. Moscow is overwhelmed with the manic haste of any world capital. Fast money is creating tall buildings, which have seemingly sprung up overnight on every street...*

These words could well have been articulated by any of today's Muscovites, but were in fact written by Boris Pasternak at the beginning of the 20th century. Today, the new Moskva of the 21st century is now not only the center of the Commonwealth, but also the capital of the Russian Federation. And this capital city is the source of the country's industry, politics (the Kremlin remains the seat of government) and culture. With the formation of the Commonwealth of Independent States and the collapse of communist Russia, Moscow is now the hub of an enterprising new metropolis. The last decades of democratic development have created a wealth of business opportunities for the city's entrepreneurs, and the once non-existent advertising sector is now a billion-dollar-a-year industry.

Moscow has taken its place as a burgeoning world capital, and it's time to be truly astonished at the sight of thousands of eating establishments—from Internet coffee cafés and fast-food franchises to the most elegant restaurants in old palaces and ritzy hip hang-outs. However, the opportunities and changes have created many new extremes, unheard of in old Soviet society, but long familiar to the West: from the unemployed to multi-millionaires (Moscow is home to 70 billionaires), the homeless to real-estate moguls, poor borrowers to rich bankers, and destitute pensioners to enterprising youth. Moscow's notorious traffic jams and pollution have risen to global notoriety and real estate prices have now stretched well beyond the reach of the average citizen. As always, a price is paid for a quick transition into a new capitalist society.

In 2007, the short and stocky Yuri Luzhkov, at 70, was sworn in for his fifth and final term as Moscow mayor. No other man in the new era reshaped Moscow like him, and Luzhkov clearly delighted in being the *khozyain* or boss, presiding over the capital's rebirth. Over nearly two decades, the ambitious mayor's construction blitz completely reshaped Moscow's cityscape. But critics argued that his power became so absolute that there was virtually no control over the rapid growth. In front of many mass protests, over 600 historic buildings were torn down to give way for modern hotel, apartment and hi-rise office buildings (while Yuzhkov's wife, Yelena Baturina's construction empire grew in value to $1.5 billion). In addition, many monuments were erected with no public decision-making. Luzhkov has been compared to the brash, dynamic and iron-willed Peter the Great—and Luzhkov allowed the 50-meter tall statue of this Czar, considered an eyesore, placed on an island in the Moscow River. But, the mayor declared "everyone is praising the new Moscow phenomenon. Ancient *Moskva* is transforming into a vibrant modern metropolis and it's common knowledge that today's capital is the most dynamically developing region of the Russian Federation."

In Sept, 2010, after 18 years as mayor, Russia's president abruptly fired Luzhkov, ending the reign of a man who gave the crumbling capital a glamorous face-lift but was much maligned for his bellicose posturing, increasing pro-nationalism campaigns, and staying on vacation while raging forest fires had choked the city only a month before. President Dmitry Medvedev signed a decree relieving the 74-year-old mayor of his duties due to a "loss of confidence." With the sacking, both Medvedev and Putin sent a strong signal that no regional leader is more powerful than them or indispensable. Medvedev then abruptly appointed Luzhkov's deputy, Vladimir Resin, acting mayor, a bureaucrat primarily known for wearing a million-dollar watch.

On October 21, 2010, the Moscow City Duma appointed Sergei Sobyanin Moscow Mayor for five years. But, instead of facing re-election in 2015, Sobyanin decided to game the system—while he was still popular—and resigned in June, 2013, in order to force an early election. A madcap race ensued as the anti-Putin opposition leader, Alexei Navalny, was arrested in July on trumped up embezzlement charges, and was given a five-year sentence, but then he was released. Supposedly, since he was now a convicted felon, Navalny was banned by law from becoming mayor, but officials said his participation was needed to ensure a fair election. Since most media outlets are controlled by the Kremlin, all Mr Navalny could do was to run an aggressive grass-roots campaign; his slogan was, "Change Russia. Start with Moscow!" After the September election, city officials declared that Sobyanin had won with 51.4% of the vote (to 27.4% for Navalny), narrowly clearing the 50% needed to avoid a runoff. Critics complained that the elections were marred by widespread fraud, but Alexei Navalny declared: "Even though we lost, real politics and the opposition have now been born!" Sergei Sobyanin took his place as Moscow Mayor until 2018—when Presidential elections are also scheduled.

The new mayor asserts that there has never been a more exciting time to visit or do business in the nation's capital, and that more than four million people visit Moscow every year. Whether a visitor has a few days or several weeks, there is plenty to do and see. Moscow has over 2500 monuments and historical sites, 50 theaters and concert halls, over 100 museums and 4,500 streets and passages, visited annually by people from 150 countries. Moscow is also rich in history, art and architecture. One of the most memorable experiences of your trip to Russia will be to stand in Red Square and look out on the golden magnificence of the cathedrals and towers of the Kremlin and St Basil's Cathedral.

Other attractions include the Novodevichy Convent, which dates from 1514, and the Andronikov Monastery, which houses the Andrei Rublyov Museum of Old Russian Art, including the famed iconist's masterpieces. Moscow's galleries and museums, such as the Tretyakov Gallery and Pushkin Museum of Fine Art contain collections of Russian and foreign masters. There are also the fascinating side streets to explore—little changed since the time of Ivan the Terrible. The nighttime reflections of the Kremlin's ancient clock tower and golden onion domes on the *Moskva* River bring to mind the lyrics of one of Russia's most popular songs: 'Lazily the river like a silvery stream, ripples gently in the moonlight; and a song fades as in a dream, in the spell of this Moscow night.' Moscow has an eternal enchantment that can be felt in the early light of dawn, in the deepening twilight, on a warm summer's day or in the swirling snows of winter.

ARRIVAL

Most international travelers arrive at Sheremetyevo International Airport, located 29 kilometers (18 miles) northwest of central Moscow, or Domodedovo International Airport, located 42 kilometers (26 miles) to the southeast. The route from Sheremetyevo to the city center winds along the Leningradsky Highway (Leningradskoye Shosse), linking Moscow with St Petersburg. About 23 kilometers (14 miles) from the airport are large antitank obstacles, **The Memorial to the Heroes** who defended the city against the Nazi invasion in 1941; notice how close the Germans came to entering the city. The highway becomes Leningradsky Prospekt at a place that used to mark the outer border of the city. Here the street was lined with summer cottages. The **Church of All Saints** (1683) stands at the beginning of the prospekt at number 73A. Other sights along the route are Peter the Great's Moorish-Gothic-style **Petrovsky Palace**, built in 1775, and the 60,000-seat **Dynamo Sports Complex**. As you approach the center of Moscow, the **Byelorussky Railway Station** is on your right. Trains run from here to destinations in Western and Eastern Europe. This station marks the beginning of one of Moscow's main thoroughfares, **Tverskaya Ulitsa** (Street). A road map of Moscow is made up of a series of rings. The Kremlin and Red Square lie at the center. Six concentric rings circle Red Square, each marking an old boundary of the city, showing its age like a cross-section of a tree.

Centuries ago each ring was fortified by stone, wooden or earthen ramparts, which could only be entered through a special gate. The area around the Kremlin, once known as Kitai-Gorod, formed the original border of the city in the 15th and 16th centuries. Many of the streets and squares in this area carry their original names: Petrovskaya Vorota (Peter's Gate), Kitaisky Proyezd (Kitai Passage), Ulitsa Varvarka (St Barbara Street) and Valovaya Ulitsa (Rampart Street).

The second ring is known as Bulvarnoye Koltso (Boulevard Ring). The city's suburbs were placed beyond this ring in the 17th century. The Sadovoye Koltso (Garden Ring) is the third ring that runs for 16 kilometers (ten miles) around the city. The city's suburbs were placed beyond this ring in the 17th century. (This area is also connected by the Koltso Metro line that stops at various points around the ring.)The fourth ring, which stretches for 40 kilometers (25 miles) around the city, was known as the Kamer-Kollezhsky Rampart; it served as a customs boundary in the 18th and 19th centuries. The fifth ring is the Moscow Ring Road, or MKAD, which winds for 109 kilometers (66 miles) as a multi-highway. Moscow traffic is rated the worst in the world and is non-stop gridlock most of the time. A new freeway, called the Central Ring Road will stretch for 442 kilometers (275 miles) to help ease traffic.

METRO

One of the quickest, easiest and cheapest ways of getting around Moscow is by Metro. It is also the most popular method of transportation—up to nine million people use the Metro daily, more than in New York or London. Construction began in 1931 under Stalin. Many Soviet and foreign architects and engineers spent four years building the deep stations, which served as bomb shelters during World War II. The cost was enormous. In 1934 alone, over 350 million rubles were spent on the metro (compared to 300 million rubles on consumer goods for the entire Soviet Union during the first Five Year Plan).

The first line was opened on May 15, 1935. Today, over 10,000 trains run through twelve major lines and over 190 stations that connect all points of the city. The Metro, with 325 kilometers (200 miles) of track, operates daily from 5.30am to 1am; the trains are frequent, arriving every 60 to 90 seconds during rush hour. (In contrast, St Petersburg's Metro has five lines—a sixth is currently under construction—which run over 100 kilometers (70 miles), and is open from 5:45am to midnight.)

Many of the older stations are beautifully decorated with mosaics, marble, stained glass, statues and chandeliers, and are kept immaculate. An easy tour is to begin at Komsomolskaya and proceed anti-clockwise on the Brown Koltso Ring and get off at Prospekt Mira, Novoslobodskaya, Belorusskaya and Kievskaya. Other interesting ones are: Okhotny Ryad, Teatralnaya and, Mayakovskay, the latter won Grand Prix design awards at the New York International Expositions in 1938 and 1958. Ploshchad Revolutsii, which features 76 bronze statues of workers and revolutionaries, is even on the list of UNESCO's world heritage sites. In 2003, the world's deepest Metro station opened in Moscow—Park Pobedy (Victory Park). The escalators are 125 meters long and the station is 74 meters underground. It was decorated by renowned sculptor Zurab Tsereteli with panels celebrating Russia's victories over Napoleon and the Nazis. The Moscow Metro Museum is at 36 Khamovnichesky Val; above Sportivnaya Metro station (open Thursdays only 9am–4pm;), exit towards the Yunost Hotel and at the top of the escalator go through the passage marked with the blue Militsia sign and continue up to the third floor. Tours of the Metro can also be booked through local travel agencies.

The Metro is easy to use by looking at a map. All the color-coded lines branch out from a central point, and are intersected by the Brown Koltso (Circle) line. Entrances above ground are marked by a large M. Take the long and fast escalators down to the station (stand on right side, as fast runners zoom up/down the left). Maps are located before the turnstiles. From 1935 to 1991, the Metro cost only five kopeks; now the price keeps pace with inflation. By 2000, the Moscow Metro had completely phased out the use of the token, in favor of a Smartcard with a magnetic strip. Buy a card (using Russian currency only) at the ticket booth, *kassa* (касса) or automatic kiosks. Insert or scan the card at one of the turnstile machines; the automatic gates open once the card is registered. (Wait for the green light, or the gates can close right on you!) As of 2015, it is the same fare (R40) for any length trip (whether you make one or more transfers underground), as long as you do not exit out to the street. You can save money by purchasing metro cards for 5 rides or more: 5, 11, 20, 40 or 60 rides (good for 90 days). For unlimited number of rides, a 1-day, 3-day, 7-day, monthly pass, three-month or yearly pass can also be purchased. Also available is a monthly bus/Metro pass. A combo metro/bus ticket (good for 90 minutes) is R50. Each time you pass the card through the turnstiles, an 'M' is stamped on the back, so you can keep track of the number of trips. (The St Petersburg Metro may still use tokens.) See: engl.mosmetro.ru for more information on current prices.

Since many station names are still written only in Russian, ask somebody to write down the name of your destination in Cyrillic. If you have trouble finding your way, show it to the attendant, who usually stands at the entrance, or ask: people are very helpful to strangers and many understand English. The trains can be crowded and commuters push to get to where they are going. Stand near a door as your stop approaches. Maps of the route (in Cyrillic and Roman alphabet) are also posted inside each train car. The loudspeaker announces '*Ostorozhno, dveri zakrivayutsya*' (Look out, the doors are closing), '*Slyeduyushaya stantsiiya ...*' (the next stop is...). The doors open and close automatically. Changing lines at major stations can be confusing. Look for the word Переход (*Perekhod*—Transfer) followed by a list of stations written in Cyrillic (this is usually a blue sign with a stick figure running up the stairs). Try to locate your destination and proceed in that direction to a different train line. If exiting the station locate the sign ВЫХОД В ГОРОД (*Vwykhod v Gorod*—Exit to Town) and take an escalator up to street level.

Even since the fall of Communism, Muscovites still display a proprietary pride in their Metro; it is clean and graffiti-free, with reserved seats at the front of each carriage for the elderly and disabled. Passages to underground stations, once dark and empty, are now teeming with stores, cafés, money changing kiosks, hawkers, beggars and musicians.

RED SQUARE (KRASNAYA PLOSHCHAD)

Most visitors begin their acquaintance with Moscow in Krasnaya Ploshchad, Red Square, the heart of the city. It was first mentioned in 15th-century chronicles as the Veliky Torg, the Great Marketplace and main trading center of the town. From the time of Ivan the Great the square was used as a huge gathering place for public events, markets, fairs and festivals. Many religious processions came through the square led by the czar and patriarch of the Orthodox Church. It was also the scene of political demonstrations and revolts, and the site of public executions. The square received its present name in the 17th century from the old Russian word *krasny*, meaning both red and beautiful. From the Middle Ages it was a popular open-air market and it remained so until GUM, the shopping arcade, was completed in 1893 and the traders moved under cover. The first Victory Parade was held in the square on June 24, 1945.

This magnificent square encompasses an area of over 70,000 square meters (almost 84,000 square yards) and is bounded by the Kremlin walls, St Basil's Cathedral, the Lenin Mausoleum, the Historical Museum and the GUM Department Store.

Today national celebrations are still held here, especially on May Day when it is filled with huge parades and festivities. The closest Metro stop is Okhotny Ryad.

ST BASIL'S CATHEDRAL

Red Square's most famous and eye-catching structure is St Basil's Cathedral. This extraordinary creation was erected by Ivan IV (the Terrible) from 1555 to 1561, to commemorate the annexation to Russia of the Mongol states of Kazan and Astrakhan. Since this occurred on the festival of the Intercession of the Virgin, Ivan named it the Cathedral of the Intercession on the Moat (there used to be a moat around it). The names of the architects were unknown until 1896, when old manuscripts mentioning its construction were found. According to legend, Ivan the Terrible had the two architects, Posnik and Barma, blinded so they could never again create such a beautiful church. However records from 1588, a quarter of a century after the cathedral's completion, indicate that Posnik and Barma built the chapel at the northeast corner of the cathedral, where the holy prophet Basil (Vasily) was buried. Canonized after his death, Basil the Blessed (known as a *Yurodivy*, or 'Fool in Christ'; a *Yurodivy* was a half-wit, thought to have a direct connection to God) died the same year (1552) that many of the Mongol Khanates were captured. Basil had opposed the cruelties of Ivan the Terrible, and since most of the population also despised the czar, the cathedral took on the name of St Basil's after Ivan's death. It was later, in the 17th century, that the church was given its more colorful appearance.

The cathedral is built of brick in traditional Russian style with colorful, asymmetrical, tent-shaped, helmet and onion domes situated over nine chapels, each dedicated to a saint on whose feast day the Russian army won a victory. The interior is filled with 16th- and 17th-century icons and frescoes, and the gallery contains bright wall and ceiling paintings of red, turquoise and yellow flower patterns. Locals often refer to the cathedral as the 'stone flower in Red Square'. The French stabled their horses here in 1812 and Napoleon wanted to blow it up, and later Stalin tried to destroy it after he had demolished the Savior Cathedral. Luckily, both never succeeded.

The interior, now open to the public, has been undergoing a restoration. Inside is a branch of the Historical Museum that traces the history of the cathedral and Ivan IV's campaigns. Under the bell tower (added in the 17th century) is an exhibition room where old sketches and plans trace the architectural history of St Basil's.

The museum is open daily 11am–5pm, except the first Wednesday of the month. In 1991, the cathedral was given back to the Russian Orthodox Church to celebrate Russian New Year and Easter services; Yeltsin attended the first Easter service. On May 24, 2003, Sir Paul McCartney gave his first musical performance in Russia on Red Square. His encore was *Back in the USSR*, the backdrop was the newly-restored St Basil's.

In front of the cathedral stands the bronze **Monument to Minin and Pozharsky**, the first patriotic monument in Moscow built from public funding. It originally stood in the middle of the square. Sculpted by Ivan Martos in 1818, the monument depicts Kozma Minin and Prince Dmitri Pozharsky, whose leadership drove the Polish invaders out of Moscow in 1612. The pedestal inscription reads 'To Citizen Minin and Prince Pozharsky from a grateful Russia 1818.'

Near the monument is **Lobnoye Mesto**, the Place of Skulls. A platform of white stone stood here for more than four centuries, on which public executions were carried out. Church clergymen blessed the crowds and the czar's orders and edicts were also announced from here.

Just east across from St Basil's, on the vast empty lot where the former Rossiya Hotel once stood (torn down in 2006), plans are to create the first new park built in Moscow in over half a century. It was announced in 2013 that a New York firm was the winner of the prestigious design competition. Plans are to divide the Zaryadye Park territory into four zones typical of different parts of Russia: tundra, steppe, forest and marsh. The project, called "wild urbanism," will also involve sleek glass architecture and artificial microclimates, creating an interaction between nature and city.

THE LENIN MAUSOLEUM

By the Kremlin wall on the southwest side of Red Square stands the Lenin Mausoleum. Inside, in a glass sarcophagus, lies Vladimir Ilyich Lenin, who died on January 21, 1924 at 6:50am. Three days after his death, a wooden structure was erected on this spot. Four months later, it was rebuilt and then replaced in 1930 by the granite, marble and black labradorite mausoleum, designed by Alexei Shchusev. 'Lenin' is inscribed in red porphyry. For more than 90 years Russians and foreigners have stood in the line that stretches from the end of Red Square to the mausoleum to view the once idolized revolutionary leader and 'Father of the Soviet Union'. Two guards man the entrance but there is no longer a changing of the guard. Photography is prohibited and cameras are NOT allowed inside—guards carry metal detectors. Any large bags and cameras should be left at the baggage check room across from the Kutafya Tower (opposite the Museum Shop) in the Alexandrov Gardens; one can also try to use the Cloak Room in the History Museum. Once inside, visitors are not allowed to pause for long. The mausoleum is usually open 10am–1pm; closed Mondays, Fridays, and is free of charge. (See Special Topic on Lenin.)

Once in a while some die-hard Communists and Lenin loyalists will gather at the mausoleum to honor the former leader. In 1994, a German executive tried to purchase the body and take it on a world tour with a final resting place in a Cologne museum. Today there is still a movement within the country to remove Lenin's body from the mausoleum and rebury him elsewhere (Lenin had requested to be buried in Petrograd next to his mother). Ironically though, with the new wave of capitalism, Lenin souvenirs are now more popular than ever (sold in many kiosks right off the Square), and Lenin's formaldehyde experts are offering their eternal Lenin Delux preservation techniques for a price of just over a quarter of a million dollars. The square can hold up to 10,000 spectators on national holidays. Atop the mausoleum is a tribune, where the heads of the former Soviet Government and Communist Party once gathered on May and Revolution days to watch the parades.

Behind the mausoleum, separated by a row of silver fir trees, are the remains of many of the country's most honored figures in politics, culture and science, whose ashes lie in urns within the Kremlin walls. They include Lenin's sister and his wife, Sergei Kirov, Maxim Gorky, A K Lunacharsky, the physicist Sergei Korolyov and the cosmonaut Yuri Gagarin. Foreigners include John Reed and William Hayword (USA), Arthur McManus (England), Clara Zetkin and Fritz Heckert (Germany), and Sen Katayama (Japan). There are also the tombstones of previous leaders of the Communist Party: Sverdlov, Dzerzhinsky, Frunze, Kalinin, Voroshilov, Suslov, Brezhnev, Chernenko, Andropov, and Stalin, who was buried next to Lenin in the mausoleum from 1953–61. Nearby are the granite-framed common graves of 500 people who died during the October Revolution of 1917.

THE STATE HISTORICAL MUSEUM

At the opposite end of the square from St Basil's is a red-brick building, decorated with numerous spires and *kokoshniki* gables. This houses the Historical Museum. It was constructed for Alexander II by Vladimir Sherwood between 1878 and 1883 on the site where Moscow University was founded in 1755 by the Russian scientist Mikhail Lomonosov. When it opened in 1883, the museum had over 300,000 objects and was supported by private donations. Today the government museum contains over four million items in 48 halls that house the country's largest archeological collection, along with manuscripts, books, coins, ornaments and works of art from the Stone Age to the present day. These include birch-bark letters, clothing of Ivan the Terrible, Peter the Great's sleigh, Napoleon's saber and the Decree on Peace written by Lenin. An informative exhibit on the War of 1812 was opened to commemorate the 200th anniversary in 2012. The museum is open daily from 10am–6pm; Thursday 11am–9pm; closed Tuesdays.

GUM

Next to the Historical Museum, stretching across the entire northeastern side of Red Square, is the three-story State Universal Store, known as GUM. It is the largest shopping center in Russia, with a total length of 2.5 kilometers (1.5 miles), selling half a million items to almost a quarter of a million Russians and 100,000 foreigners every day. GUM's 120th anniversary was celebrated in 2013. The initials GUM stood for Gosudarstvenny Universalny Magazine, the Government Department Store, until 1990, when the Moscow city government turned it into a joint stock company owned mainly by the employees. The initials now stand for Glavny Universalny Magazine, the Main Department Store.

It was designed in 1893, in neo-Russian style, by Alexander Pomerantsev to replace a market destroyed by one of Napoleon's fires in 1812, as his troops were attempting to occupy Moscow. When it was built it was known as the Upper Trading Stalls. It was a showcase for goods and one of the world's most modern commercial areas, built of steel and concrete with ornate glass roofing and even electrical and heating systems. Today the building has been thoroughly renovated, and over 100 shops, both Russian and foreign, along with numerous cafés, line the first and second floors. The grand ceremonial entrance on Red Square, closed since the Bolshevik Revolution, was reopened in 1992. It is well worth visiting to view the interiors of preserved old-style Russian shops, ornate bridges, ornamental stucco designs and the large glass roof. It is open daily from 10am–10pm.

Exiting GUM at the northwest corner (towards the History Museum) brings you to the **Kazan Cathedral**. The original church was built in 1625 by Prince Pozharsky (whose statue stands in front of St Basil's) in tribute to the Virgin of Kazan icon, whose power was thought to lead Russia in victory over the invading Poles. Stalin had it destroyed in 1936. After the fall of the Soviet Union, private contributions led to the reconstruction of the cathedral. In 1990, a procession led by Boris Yeltsin, the Orthodox Patriarch Alexis II and the Moscow mayor left the Kremlin to lay the foundation stone. The structure was consecrated by the Orthodox Church in 1993. Religious services are conducted (usually Monday at 8pm). Open to visitors from 8am–7pm daily.

Exiting Red Square to the north takes you through the **Iberian Resurrection Gates**. The original main entrance gateway and white towers, first built in 1680, were torn down by Stalin in 1931 to create more room for mass parades and machinery to enter. The gates were reconstructed as a copy of the original in the early 1990s. On the other side of the arch stands the small **Gate Church of the Iberian Virgin**, also rebuilt. It was once customary for the czar to pray here before he entered the Kremlin.

THE ALEXANDROV GARDENS

The entrance to these charming gardens is opposite the Historical Museum at the Kremlin's wrought-iron Corner Arsenal Gate. On your way there take note of the **Statue of Marshal Georgy Zhukov**, a World War II hero, who gazes proudly from his horse onto Manezh Square. The 120th anniversary of Zhukov's birth was celebrated in 2016. The Alexandrov Gardens were laid out on the banks of the Neglinnaya River by Osip Bovet from 1819 to 1822 for Alexander I. They later became Moscow's first public garden. The river was later diverted by a system of pipes to flow beneath the park. An eternal flame burns before the **Tomb of the Unknown Soldier**, who died for his country during World War II. It was unveiled on May 8, 1967, on the eve of Victory Day. Usually every hour, a synchronized ceremony takes place for the changing of the guards.

It is a tradition for newlyweds on their wedding day to lay flowers on the tombstone, on which is inscribed: 'Your name is unknown, your feat immortal. To the fallen 1941–45.' Along the alley in front of the tomb are blocks of red porphyry that hold earth from 'Hero Cities' designated after World War II, including Moscow and St Petersburg. Also in the gardens are a memorial to the War of 1812 and a granite obelisk with the names of the world's great revolutionaries and thinkers. The latter was originally erected in 1913 to commemorate the 300th anniversary of the Romanov dynasty. On Lenin's orders in 1918, the double-headed eagle was replaced by the obelisk. Now, with the spacious underground **Manezh Shopping Mall** located nearby, more people than ever enjoy a promenade within the gardens. The sculptures, fountains and tree-lined paths create a charming spot in the heart of the Russian capital.

The central alley of the Alexandrov Gardens leads to the Troitsky Bridge that approaches the entrance to the Kremlin.

THE KREMLIN

The earth, as we all know, begins at the Kremlin. It is the central point.

Mayakovsky

The Moscow Kremlin, an outstanding monument of Russian history, winds around a steep slope high above the Moskva River, enclosing an area of over 28 hectares (70 acres) next to Red Square. The Russian word *kreml* was once used to describe a fortified stronghold that encased a small town. A Russian town was usually built on a high embankment, surrounded by a river and moat, to protect against invasions. The word *kreml* may originate from the Greek *kremnos*, meaning steep escarpment. The medieval kremlin acted as a fortress around a town filled with palaces, churches, monasteries, wooden peasant houses and markets. The Moscow Kremlin was built between the Moskva River and Neglinka River (the latter now flows underground). The walls are about one kilometer (half a mile) long, up to 19 meters (62 feet) high and 6.5 meters (21 feet) thick, with 20 towers and gates. Over ten churches and palaces lie inside. The Kremlin is open 10am–5pm; closed Thursdays. The closest Metro stations are Okhotny Ryad (for Red Square) and Aleksandrovsky Sad and Borovitskaya (for the Gardens and Kremlin museum entrances).

HISTORY

The Moscow Kremlin has a fascinating eight-century history, and is the oldest historical and architectural feature of Moscow. The first written account of Moscow comes to us from a chronicle of 1147, which describes Prince Yuri ("long-arms") Dolgoruky of Suzdal receiving Grand Prince Svyatoslav on Borovitsky (now Kremlin) Hill. Nine years later, Dolgoruky ordered a fort built on this same hill, which later became his residence. In 1238, the invading Mongols burned the fortress to the ground. By 1326 the Kremlin had been surrounded with thick oak walls and Grand Prince Ivan I had built two stone churches in addition to the existing wooden ones. During this time the metropolitan of Kiev moved the seat of the Orthodox Church from Vladimir to Moscow. In 1367, Prince Dmitri Donskoi replaced the wooden walls with limestone ones to fortify them against cannon attack; Moscow was then referred to as Beli Gorod (White Town). The Mongols invaded again in 1382; they razed everything and killed half the population. Within 15 years the Kremlin walls were rebuilt and the iconists Theophanes the Greek and Andrei Rublyov painted the interior frescoes of the new Cathedral of the Annunciation.

Ivan III (1460–1505) and his son Vasily III were responsible for shaping the Kremlin into its present appearance. When the Mongols no longer posed a threat to the city, the leaders concentrated more on aesthetic than defensive designs. Ivan the Great commissioned well-known Russian and Italian architects to create a magnificent city to reflect the beauty of the 'Third Rome' and the power of the grand prince and church metropolitan. The white stone of the Kremlin was replaced by red-brick walls and towers, and the Assumption and Annunciation cathedrals were rebuilt on a grander scale. During the reign of Ivan IV the architecture took on more fanciful elements and asymmetrical designs with colorful onion domes and tall pyramidal tent roofs, as embodied in St Basil's—a style now termed Old Russian. The Patriarch Nikon barred all tent roofs and ornamental decorations from churches when he took office in 1652, terming the external frills sacrilegious. By 1660 though, the reforms of Nikon had created such schisms in the Church that he was forced to step down. Immediately the old decorative details were again applied to architecture.

Catherine the Great drew up plans to redesign the Kremlin in the new neo-classical style, but they were never carried out. During the War of 1812, Napoleon quartered his troops inside the Kremlin for 35 days. Retreating, he tried to blow it up, but townspeople extinguished the burning fuses, though three towers were destroyed. In the mid-1800s the Kremlin Palace and Armory were built. In 1918, the Soviet Government moved the capital back to Moscow from St Petersburg and made the Kremlin its permanent seat. Lenin signed a decree to protect the works of art and historical monuments and ordered the buildings restored and turned into museums. The Kremlin remains the center of Russian government today.

VIEW FROM RED SQUARE

Ruby-red stars were mounted on the five tallest towers of the Kremlin in 1937, replacing the double-headed eagle. The towers of the Kremlin were named after the icons that used to hang above their gates. The most recognizable tower is the 67-meter-high (220-feet) **Spasskaya (Savior) Clock Tower**, which stands across from St Basil's. It used to serve as the official entrance of the czars, who had to cross a moat over an arched stone bridge to reach the gate. It is now the main entrance of government officials, who pull up in Russian-made black limos or foreign SUVs. (In 1934, a Soviet magazine wrote that the *Zavod imeni Stalina* (Stalin Auto Plant) had begun production on the ZIS-101 automobile, built only for Communist Party bosses, so they could be driven in luxurious, domestically-produced cars. The ZIS-101 was a copy of the American Packard. Later, Stalin was driven around in the ZIS-115; this bullet-proof car weighed 7 tons, and sheets of 6-millimeter steel armor were hidden inside the body panels. Later, after Stalin's death, the auto plant's name changed to Likhacheva, and thus the ZIL was born.)

The Savior Icon once hung above the Spasskaya Gate. Inscriptions in Latin and Old Russian name the Italian Solario as the tower's builder in 1491. In the middle of the 17th century, the Scottish architect Christopher Galloway mounted a clock on its face; this clock was replaced in 1918. Like Big Ben in London, the chimes of the Spasskaya Tower are broadcast over the radio to mark the hour.

The tower behind Lenin's Mausoleum is known as the **Senate Tower**; it stands in front of the Senate building. To the right of the mausoleum stands the **Nikolskaya Tower**, where the Icon of St Nicholas was kept. In 1492, Solario built a corner tower next to a courtyard used by Sobakin Boyars. The Sobakin Tower is now called the **Corner Arsenal Tower**, where munitions were stored.

Gaining Entrance to the Kremlin

A visitor may book a group tour through a hotel (they are conducted in different languages), or a Russian travel agency (as Capital Tours; www.capitaltours.ru). A ticket covers the architectural ensemble of the Kremlin interior, but group tours to the Armory, Diamond Fund and Ivan the Great Bell Tower are sold as separate tickets. To get more information on times and prices, and buy individual tickets online, visit: www.kreml.ru (select English at top of page). The Kremlin is open 10am–5pm; closed Thursdays.

To purchase a ticket in person, go to the Kutafya Tower, located south of the Gardens at the end of the ramp extending from the Kremlin's west wall. This ramp was once a bridge that stretched over the Neglinka River; it's now diverted underground; Deposit any large bags in the Cloak Room down the path and across from the Museum Shop. The ticket windows are at the top of the Kutafya Tower steps (open 9:30am-4:30pm);, and a visitor must go through an X-ray check to get in (bring a copy of your Passport). One can purchase an individual ticket, and there are also more expensive group tours led by a guide at specified times in different languages (meet up at the Excursion Bureau by the Museum Shop). At the Kutafya, you can also buy additional tickets to the Armory; tours begin at 10:00, 12, 14:30 and 16:30. Sessions in the Ivan the Great Bell-Tower are at 10:15, 11:30, 13:45, 15:00 and 16:00 (a ticket to the Bell-Tower also includes entrance to the Kremlin grounds and the museums-churches, but not the Armory). Audio guides are available for rent in the Armory Chamber as well as in other palaces and museums. If you buy a ticket online, you must bring the confirmation print-out to exchange for a ticket. If planning on only visiting the Armory or Diamond Fund, enter through the Borovitsky Tower further down—otherwise proceed along the top of the Kutafya ramp into the Kremlin.

State Kremlin Palace

As you enter the Kremlin through the Kutafya and Trinity towers, the modern Palace of Congresses is on your right. Khrushchev approved the plans for this large steel, glass and marble structure. Built by Mikhail Posokhin, it was completed in 1961 for the 22nd Congress of the Communist Party. When no congresses or international meetings are in session, the State Kremlin Palace is also used for ballet and opera performances. Sunk 15 meters (49 feet) into the ground so as not to tower over the Kremlin, the Palace contains 800 rooms and the auditorium seats 6,000.

THE BROTHERHOOD GRAVE

*L*ate in the night we went through the empty streets and under the Iberian Gate to the great Red Square in front of the Kremlin. The church of Vasili Blazhenny loomed fantastic, its bright colored, convoluted and blazoned cupolas vague in the darkness. There was no sign of any damage.... Along one side of the square the dark towers and walls of the Kremlin stood up. On the high walls flickered redly the light of hidden flames; voices reached us across the immense place, and the sound of picks and shovels. We crossed over.

Mountains of dirt and rock piled high near the base of the wall. Climbing these we looked down into two massive pits, ten or fifteen feet deep and fifty yards long, where hundreds of soldiers and workers were digging in the light of huge fires.

A young soldier spoke to us in German. 'The Brotherhood Grave,' he explained. 'Tomorrow we shall bury here five hundred proletarians who died for the Revolution.'

He took us down into the pit. In frantic haste they swung the picks and shovels, and the earth-mountains grew. No one spoke. Overhead the night was thick with stars, and the ancient Imperial Kremlin wall towered up immeasurably.

'Here in this holy place,' said the student, 'holiest of all Russia, we shall bury our most holy. Here where are the tombs of the Tsars, our Tsar—the People—shall sleep...' His arm was in a sling from the bullet wound gained in the fighting. He looked at it. 'You foreigners look down on us Russians because for so long we tolerated a medieval monarchy,' he said. 'But we saw that the Tsar was not the only tyrant in the world; capitalism was worse, and in all the countries of the world capitalism was Emperor... Russian revolutionary tactics are best...'

As we left, the workers in the pit, exhausted and running with sweat in spite of the cold, began to climb wearily out. Across the Red Square a dark knot of men came hurrying. They swarmed into the pits, picked up the tools and began digging, digging, without a word.

So, all the long night volunteers of the People relieved each other, *never halting in their driving speed, and the cold light of the dawn laid bare the great square, white with snow, and the yawning brown pits of the Brotherhood Grave, quite finished.*

We rose before sunrise, and hurried through the dark streets to Skobeliev Square. In all the great city not a human being could be seen; but there was a faint sound of stirring, far and near, like a deep wind coming. In the pale half-light a little group of men and women were gathered before the Soviet headquarters, with a sheaf of gold-lettered red banners, and the dull red—like blood—of the coffins they carried. These were rude boxes, made of unplaned wood and daubed with crimson, borne high on the shoulders of rough men who marched with tears streaming down their faces, and followed by women who sobbed and screamed, or walked stiffly, with white, dead faces. Some of the coffins were open, the lid carried behind them; others were covered with gilded or silvered cloth, or had a soldier's hat nailed on the top. There were many wreaths of hideous artificial flowers.

All the long day the funeral procession passed, coming in by the Iberian Gate and leaving the square by way of the Nikolskaya, a river of red banners, bearing words of hope and brotherhood and stupendous prophecies, against a background of fifty thousand people—under the eyes of the world's workers and their descendants for ever...

John Reed, Ten Days That Shook the World, 1919

After graduating from Harvard University, Reed traveled to Russia to support the Bolshevik Revolution. He was such an ardent supporter of socialism that Lenin penned the introduction to his book.

THE ARSENAL

The yellow two-story building to the left of the entrance tower was once used as the Arsenal. Peter the Great ordered its construction in 1702 (completed in 1736), but later turned it into a Trophy Museum. Along the front of the arsenal are 875 cannons and other trophies captured from Napoleon's armies in 1812. Plaques on the wall list the names of men killed defending the arsenal during the Revolution and World War II. It now houses the Kremlin Guard.

SENATE BUILDING

Directly in front of the Arsenal stands the three-story triangular building of the former Council of Ministers. Catherine the Great had it built in the classical style by Matvei Kazakov in 1787. After Lenin moved the capital from Petrograd (St Petersburg) to Moscow in 1918, the Soviet Government and the Bolshevik Party took up residence in the building. It's now used by the Senate; the large green dome is topped by the national flag. The plaque on the front wall shows Lenin's portrait and the inscription: 'Lenin lived and worked in this building from March 1918 to May 1923.'

The Central Committee of the Communist Party once met in **Sverdlov Hall**. The hall's 18 Corinthian columns are decorated with copies of bas-reliefs portraying czars and princes (the originals are in the Armory). Lenin's study and flat are in the east wing. Special objects stand on his desk, such as the Monkey Statue presented to him by Armand Hammer in 1921. The study leads to a small four-room apartment that Lenin shared with his wife and younger sister.

Across from the Senate, near the Spasskaya Tower, stand the **Presidium** and **Kremlin Theater**, built between 1932 and 1934. The building has also served as a military school and the former residence of the president of the USSR. To make room for these buildings, Stalin gave permission to tear down the 14th-century Monastery of the Miracles and Ascension Convent, where female members of the royal family lived and were later buried. After the convent was destroyed, the bodies were transferred to the Cathedral of the Archangel Michael. (In the 1980's, excavations in this area discovered two hoards of princely treasure buried before the Mongol sack of Moscow in 1238.) Today, these buildings can only be visited with special permission—they function as the offices of the President of Russia.

PATRIARCH'S PALACE

Opposite the Senate is the four-story Patriarch's Palace and his private chapel, the **Church of the Twelve Apostles** (with the five silver domes), which now house the **Museum of 17th-Century Life and Applied Art** with over 1,000 exhibits. Patriarch Nikon commissioned the palace for himself in 1635. After Nikon banned elaborate decorations on church buildings, he had the architects Konstantinov and Okhlebinin design the structure in simple white Byzantine fashion. The palace was placed near the main cathedral and the Trinity Gate, where clergy formally entered the Kremlin. The vaulted **Krestovskaya Chamber**, the Hall of the Cross, built without a single support beam, was used as a formal reception hall. Every three years the chamber was used for making consecrated oil for the Russian churches. In 1721, Peter the Great gave the palace to the Church Council of the Holy Synod. The museum has an interesting collection of rare manuscripts, coins, jewelry, furniture, fabrics, embroidery and table games. Vestments worn by Patriarch Nikon and the 17th-century golden iconostasis from the Monastery of the Miracles (destroyed to build the Senate) are also on display. The books include an ABC primer written for the son of Peter the Great. Two of the halls are decorated to look like a 17th-century house. Some of the displays in the Church of the Twelve Apostles are wine coffers and ladles, on which Bacchus is carved. These objects belonged to the society of the Highest and Most Jolly and Drunken Council, founded by Peter the Great to make fun of (non-progressive) Church rituals. Recent restoration discoveries revealed a highly complex knot of staircases and hidden cubbyholes that linked together several wings of the palace and thus made it possible to access any part of the building without going outside.

EMPEROR CANNON

Beside the Church of the Twelve Apostles is the 40-ton Emperor Cannon. Its 890mm bore (35 inch caliber) makes it the world's largest cannon still in existence. It was cast in 1586 by Andrei Chokhov and never fired. (The largest was smelted at an arms factory in Perm in the 1530s and used to defend Russia against the Tartars; it was fired over 300 times.) A likeness of Fedor I is on the barrel. The decorative iron cannon balls (weighing one ton each) were cast in the 19th century.

Across from the cannon in the southeastern corner of the Kremlin lie the **Tainitsky (Secret) Gardens**. Winter fairs are held here for children during New Year celebrations. A statue of Lenin used to stand on the highest spot, known as **Kremlin Hill**, but was removed in 1997 (see picture on page 600). Nearby is the **Cosmos Oak**, which cosmonaut Yuri Gagarin planted on April 14, 1961. This vantage point affords a good view of the Kremlin and Spasskaya Tower. The **Tsarskaya (Czar's) Tower** stands to the right and is decorated with white-stone designs and a weather-vane. A wooden deck used to stand on top of the tower, from which Ivan the Terrible supposedly watched executions in Red Square. The next tower is the **Nabatnaya (Alarm) Tower**; the bell that used to hang here is on display in the Armory Museum. Farther to the south is the **Konstantino-Yeleninskaya Tower**, which honors St Constantine and St Helen. In earlier days it was also referred to as the Torture Tower, since it housed a torture chamber. The corner tower is called **Moskvoretskaya**, built in 1487 by Marco Ruffo. It was known as Beklemischevskaya, named after Ivan

Beklemisch, whose home stood next to it in the 16th century; his spirit is said to have haunted it. The Mongols broke through this tower to enter the Kremlin in the 17th century.

EMPEROR BELL

The largest bell in the world stands on a stone pedestal by the Secret Gardens. The bell is six meters (20 feet) high and weighs 210 tons. The surface bears portraits of czars and icons. It was designed in 1733 by Ivan Matorin and his son Mikhail for the empress Anna Ivanova, and took two years to cast. An 11.5-ton fragment broke off during the fire of 1737, when water was thrown on it. After the fire the bell was returned to its casting pit, where it lay for a century. The architect Montferrand raised the bell in 1836. It has never been rung.

The square between the Spasskaya Tower and the bell was known as Ivan's Square, along which government offices were located. Here criminals were flogged and officials read the czar's new decrees.

BELL TOWER

Behind the Emperor Bell stands the three-tiered Bell Tower of Ivan the Great. Built between 1505 and 1508, the tower contains 32 bells that hang in the arches of each section, the largest of which is the Uspensky (Assumption) Bell, weighing 70 tons; it traditionally rang three times to announce the death of a czar. The Old Slavonic inscription around the gilded dome notes that it was added to the belfry in 1600 by Boris Godunov. This was once the tallest structure (81 meters, 266 feet) in Moscow and was used as a belfry, church and watchtower. When the enemy was sighted, the bells signaled a warning. The upper tent-roof section, built in the 17th century, was rebuilt after Napoleon partially blew it up. Climb the 137 steps to the upper gallery for a superb panoramic view from what was the city's highest vantage point for 300 years. An exhibition hall and multimedia presentation is on the ground floor, which features the architectural history of the Kremlin complex. Note that a separate entrance ticket is needed that includes the walk to the top view tower. (The price of the Bell-Tower ticket includes admission to the Kremlin grounds and the museums-churches, but not he Armory.)

CATHEDRAL OF THE ASSUMPTION

In front of the bell tower stands the Kremlin's main church, the Assumption Cathedral or Uspensky Sobor. It faces the center of Cathedral Square, the oldest square in Moscow, built in the early 14th century. In 1475, Ivan the Great chose the Italian architect Aristotle Fioravante to design the church. He modeled it on the Cathedral of the Assumption in the Golden Ring town of Vladimir (see page 353).

This church, also known as the Cathedral of the Dormition of the Virgin, was built on the site of a stone church of the same name first constructed by Ivan I in

1326. For two centuries this national shrine stood as a model for all Russian church architecture. Within its walls czars and patriarchs were crowned. It also served as the burial place for Moscow metropolitans and patriarchs.

Combining Italian Renaissance and Byzantine traditions, the cathedral is built from white limestone and brick with *zakomara* rounded arches, narrow-windowed drums and five gilded onion domes. The ornamental doorways are covered with frescoes painted on sheet copper; the southern entrance is especially interesting, decorated with 20 biblical scenes in gold and black lacquer.

The spacious interior, lit by 12 chandeliers, is covered with exquisite frescoes and icons that date back to 1481. The artists Dionysius, Timofei, Yarets and Kon wove together the themes of heaven and the unity of Russia's principalities, symbolizing the 'Third Rome'. Some of these can still be seen over the altar screen. The northern and southern walls depict the life of the Blessed Virgin. In 1642, more than 100 masters spent a year repainting the church, following the designs of the older wall paintings. These 17th-century frescoes were restored after the Revolution. Frescoes were painted in colors prepared from local clays and minerals mixed with water and bound by using egg-yolk and vegetable glues. Russian frescoes were painted by artists applying colors onto the still wet plaster. Sometimes others were executed in the Italian tempera manner—painting done on dry plaster. This cathedral contains both types of frescoes. (See Special Topic on page 337.)

The elaborate five-tier **iconostasis** (altar screen) dates from 1652. Its upper rows were painted by monks from the Trinity-Sergius Monastery in Sergiyev Posad in the late 1600s. The silver frames were added in 1881. To the right of the royal gates are two 12th-century icons from Novgorod: St George and the Savior Enthroned. A 15th-century Rublyov-school copy of the country's protectress, the Virgin of Vladimir, also lies to the left. The original, painted in 12th-century Byzantium, was first hung in Kiev. In 1155, Grand Prince Andrei Bogolyubsky carried it to Vladimir to save it from the invading Mongols. Later, in 1395, Grand Prince Vasily I, son of Dmitry Donskoi, brought it to Moscow and placed it in the original Assumption Church. After the Revolution, it was placed in the Tretyakov Gallery. The icons, *Savior of the Fiery Eye*, the *Trinity*, and the *Dormition of the Virgin*, were specially commissioned for the cathedral in the 14th and 15th centuries. Napoleon's armies used the Cathedral as a stable and some of the icons as firewood; troops also tried to carry off 295 kg of gold and five tons of silver, but most of it was recovered; the central chandelier, Harvest, was cast from silver recaptured from the retreating troops.

The Church Metropolitan Peter (cofounder of the cathedral) and his successor are buried in the southern chapel. The 15th-century fresco *Forty Martyrs of Sebaste* separates the chapel from the main altar. Other metropolitans and patriarchs are buried along the northern and southern walls and in underground crypts.

Metropolitan Iov is buried in a special mausoleum, above which hangs the icon of Metropolitan Peter, the first Moscow metropolitan. The gilded sarcophagus of Patriarch Hermogenes (1606–12) stands in the southwest corner covered by a small canopy. During the Polish invasion Hermogenes was imprisoned and starved to death. (In 1589, a Metropolitan was elevated to a Patriarchate.) After Patriarch Adrian, Peter the Great abolished the position and established the Holy Synod. The patriarch seat remained vacant until 1917. In 1991, Patriarch Alexei was voted in by Church elections. Only after 1991 was the Russian Orthodox Church, headed by the patriarch, allowed to govern itself again.

Ivan the Terrible's carved wooden throne stands to the left of the southern entrance. Made in 1551, it is known as the **Throne of the Monomakhs**. It is elaborately decorated with carvings representing the transfer of imperial power from the Byzantine Emperor Monomakh to the Grand Prince Vladimir Monomakh (1113–25), who married the emperor's sister. The Patriarch's throne can be found by the southeast pier; the clergy sat upon the elevated stone that is decorated with carved flowers. The *Last Judgment* is painted over the western portal. Traditionally the congregation exited through the church's western door. The final theme portrayed was the Last Judgment as a reminder to people to work on salvation in the outside world.

In October 1989, for the first time in over 70 years, the Soviet Government under Gorbachev allowed a Russian Orthodox service to be conducted within the cathedral. This was a significant act of tolerance, since only three decades earlier Khrushchev had over 10,000 churches closed.

In 2006, a ceremonial changing of the guard was created for Cathedral Square on Saturdays at noon from April to October. The Presidential regiment, on foot and on horseback, are dressed in uniforms styled after 1913 czarist times, and the choreography is accompanied by flutes and drums played by the presidential orchestra, which has played in the Kremlin since 1938. If here on a Saturday, it is well worth viewing!

CHURCH OF THE DEPOSITION OF THE ROBE

To the west of the Assumption Cathedral is the smaller single-domed Church of the Deposition of the Virgin's Robe, built by Pskov craftsmen from 1484 to 1485. It once served as the private chapel of the patriarch and was linked by a small bridge to his palace. It later became a court chapel in 1653. The iconostasis was executed by Nazari Istomin in 1627. The interior wall frescoes, some dating back to 1644, are devoted to the Blessed Virgin. The northern gallery displays an exhibition of wooden handicrafts.

TEREM PALACE

In the small courtyard west of the church are the Terem Palace and the **Golden Palace of the Czarina**, which served as the reception site for czarinas in the 16th century. The Terem Palace resembles a fairy-tale creation with its checkerboard roof and 11 golden turrets. It housed the children and female relatives of noblewomen, and was built for Czar Mikhail Romanov, whose private chambers on the fourth floor were later occupied by his son Alexei. At this time, women and their daughters were secluded in a *terem* (the word is derived from the Greek word *teremnon*, meaning 'special quarters'). Many State functions took place here and in the **Hall of the Cross**. The czar received petitions from the population in the Golden Throne Room. Only the czar's wife, personal confessor and blind storytellers were allowed into the private chapel and Royal Bedchamber, which is whimsically decorated. All the chapels of the Terem were united under one roof in 1681, including the churches of the Resurrection, Crucifixion, Savior and St Catherine.

The adjoining Golden Palace of the Czarina at the eastern end was built in 1526 by Boris Godunov for his sister Irina, who was married to Czar Fedor I. This was her own private reception hall. When Fedor died, Irina refused the throne (the last son of Ivan the Terrible had died earlier in an epileptic attack); her brother Boris Godunov became the first elected czar. Admission to the Terem is by special permission only.

PALACE OF FACETS

Facing the bell tower and on the west side of Cathedral Square, is the two-story Renaissance-style Palace of Facets, one of Moscow's oldest civic buildings, constructed by Ruffo and Solario between 1487 and 1491. It took its name from the elaborate stone facets decorating its exterior. State assemblies and receptions were held here— Ivan the Terrible celebrated his victory over Kazan in 1532 in this palace, and Peter the Great celebrated here after defeating the Swedes at Poltava in 1709. After Ivan III, all wives including the crowned czarinas were barred from attending State ceremonies and receptions in the Hall of Facets; a small look-out room was built above the western wall, from which the women could secretly watch the proceedings. The **Red Staircase**, which led from the Assumption Cathedral to the palace's southern wall, was reconstructed in 1994; it had been destroyed in the 1930s under Stalin. Peter acquired his dislike of Moscow when the Streltsy (palace guards) revolted in 1682, and the future czar (then only aged ten) witnessed the murder of family members who were hurled off this staircase onto sharpened pikes below. In 1812, Napoleon also watched his attempted burning of Moscow from here. Today the Hall is used for State occasions. Entrance to the Palace of Facets is by special permission only. Both this and the Terem Palace have recently undergone a 300-million-dollar renovation.

CATHEDRAL OF THE ANNUNCIATION

This white-stoned cathedral, with its nine gilded domes, and jasper floors (a gift from a Persian shah), stands directly south of the Palace of Facets. It was built from 1484 to 1489 by Pskov craftsmen, commissioned by Ivan the Great, as the private chapel of the czars. (It is on the site of the first wood and stone church built in 1397 by Grand Prince Vasily; the ground floor is the oldest surviving construction of the Kremlin.) After a fire destroyed it in 1547, Ivan the Terrible rebuilt the cathedral in 1564 with six additional golden domes and four chapels that included the Archangel Gabriel Chapel. After Ivan's fourth marriage, the Orthodox Church barred him from entering a church, so he had this chapel built through which he could view services. In 1572, a new porch, known as the Steps of Ivan the Terrible, was also added to the southeast corner. In 2001, a late 15th-century Moscow-school copy of the *Virgin of Vladimir* icon was returned from the Tretyakov Gallery to the Chapel of St Nicholas-the-Miracle-Worker, where it originally hung. The three stars on the veil symbolize virginity, while the robed child represents Christ Emmanuel. Distinguishing it from the 12th-century Byzantine original are the placement of the hands, the tilt of the head and the direction of the Virgin Mary's gaze. (See Special Topic on The Russian Icon on page 337.)

Inside, frescoes that date back to 1508 include themes from the Book of Revelation, Moscovy princes and Byzantine emperors. Portraits of Greek philosophers and poets, such as Plato, Homer, Aristotle, Virgil, and Socrates, holding scrolls upon which are written their sayings, can also be found on the pillars and in the galleries. Old chronicles state that several tiers of the iconostatis, dating back to 1405, were painted by Theophanes the Greek (from left to right, on the largest right-hand deesis row are: *The Virgin, Christ Enthroned, St John the Baptist, Archangel Gabriel, Apostle Paul* and *St John Chrysostom*). Prokhor of Gorodets and Andrei Rubylov also painted icons on the second and third tiers, including Rublyov's *The Annunciation* and the *Archangel Michael*. The lovely iconostasis frame is made out of repoussé gilt bronze, and the Heavenly Gates, leading to the altar, are of chased silver. The multi-tiered chandeliers date back to the 17th century. The first clock in Moscow was supposedly hung beside the cathedral at the prince's court in 1404. (Exhibits are often held in the basement hall of the Cathedral, and sessions are held every hour that begin at 10:15am.)

CATHEDRAL OF THE ARCHANGEL MICHAEL

The third main cathedral of the Kremlin is the five-domed Cathedral of the Archangel Michael (1505–08), which served as the burial place of the czars; the Archangel Michael was considered the guardian of Moscow princes. It stands directly east across from the Annunciation Cathedral. Ivan the Great commissioned the Italian architect Alevisio Novi to rebuild the church that stood here. Novi combined the styles of Old Russian and Italian Renaissance; notice the traits of a Venetian palazzo. The surviving frescos date from 1652 and depict aspects of Russian life. A large iconostasis (1680) is filled with 15th- to 17th-century icons, including the *Archangel Michael* by Rublyov. Nearly 50 sarcophagi line the walls of the cathedral, containing grand princes and czars and some of their sons. All czars and Moscovy princes were buried here up to the 18th century (except for Boris Godunov whose body lies in Sergiyev Posad). White tombstones give their names in Old Slavonic. The first grand prince to be buried here was Ivan I in 1341, who built the original church. After Peter the Great moved the capital to St Petersburg, the czars were buried in the Peter and Paul Fortress, except for Peter II, who died in Moscow.

Russian Czarinas were traditionally buried in the Monastery of the Ascension, which was destroyed in 1928. At that time, museum workers manually moved over 40 tons of stone sarcophaguses to basement chambers here. In 2009, a ceremony was held that transferred the remains of the only grand princess to have been canonized—Dmitri Donskoi's wife, Yevdokia, from the underground chamber to the sacraium in the cathedral.

Behind the cathedral stands **Petrovskaya (Peter's) Tower**, named after the first Moscow metropolitan. The fourth unadorned tower from the corner is the **Tainitskaya (Secret) Tower**, which had an underground passage to the Moskva River. The next one over is the **Blagoveshchenskaya (Annunciation) Tower**, which contained the Annunciation Icon. The round corner tower is called the **Vodovzvodnaya, the Water-Drawing Tower** (1633), in which water was raised from the river to an aqueduct that led inside. This is Russia's first pressurized system; it was used for pumping water to the royal palaces and gardens.

GRAND KREMLIN PALACE

Built from 1838 to 1849, the Grand Palace, behind the Annunciation Cathedral, was the Moscow residence of the imperial family. Nicholas I commissioned Konstantin Thon to erect it on the site of the former Grand Prince Palace. There are 700 rooms and five elaborate reception halls; two of these, along the southern wall overlooking the river, were combined to form the Meeting Hall of the Russian Federation. The long gold and white St George Hall has 18 columns decorated with statues of victory. The walls are lined with marble plaques bearing the names of heroes awarded the Order of St George (introduced by Catherine the Great) for service and courage. The six bronze chandeliers hold over 3,000 light bulbs.

This hall is now used for special State receptions and ceremonies; cosmonaut Yuri Gagarin received the Golden Star Hero Award here in 1961. The **Hall of St Catherine** served as the Empress' Throne Room. In October 1994, Britain's Queen Elizabeth II made her first visit to Russia (her grandfather called Nicholas II 'Cousin Nicky') where she met with Boris Yeltsin in the gold and cream splendor of this hall.

The Hall of Vladimir connected the Palace of Facets, the Golden Palace of the Czarina and the Terem Palace. The ground floor rooms used to contain the imperial family's bedchambers. Entrance is by special permission only.

AMUSEMENT PALACE

The Poteshny (Amusement) Palace, situated along the west wall behind the Terem Palace, was acquired in 1652 by Czar Alexei Mikhailovich (father of Peter the Great), who turned the building into a residence for his father-in-law, the Boyar Ilya Miloslavsky. When he died, Alexei I eventually turned this Baroque palace into the court's first theater. Recent restorations discovered carved friezes on the façades, including mermaids and an equestrian competition with riders dressed in European clothes; these are the only palace interiors from the second half of the 17th century to have survived. Later, Stalin lived here with his wife and two children. (They married in 1918 when Stalin was 39 and Nadezhda only 17.) When his wife Nadezhda committed suicide in November 1932 (disillusioned with her husband's ways), the children were moved to other quarters, and Stalin lived separately in another Kremlin apartment.

ARMORY PALACE

The Oruzheinaya Palata (Armory Palace) is the oldest museum in the country which houses one of the greatest collections of its kind in the world. In 1485, Grand Prince Vasily III, son of Ivan the Great, constructed a special stone building on the edge of the Kremlin grounds to house the royal family's growing collection of valuables. It also contained the czar's workshops and a place to store armor and weapons. In the late 1600s Peter the Great converted it into a museum to house the art treasures of the Kremlin. The present building, designed and erected between 1844–1851 by Konstantin Thon, has nine exhibition halls that trace the history of the Kremlin and the Russian State. It also houses a magnificent collection of Western European decorative and applied art from the 12th to 19th centuries.

Hall I (Halls I–IV are on the first floor) has displays of gold and silver from the 12th to 17th centuries, including jewelry, chalices (one belonging to Yuri Dolgoruky), bowls, watches and the Ryazan Treasure collection. Hall II contains a collection of 18th- to 20th-century jewelry, including a fabulous collection of Fabergé eggs. The Czar and Czarina traditionally exchanged Fabergé gifts at Easter. Most famous is a silver egg whose surface is engraved with a map of the Trans-Siberian Railway. The surprise inside the egg is a gold model of a train with a platinum engine, windows of crystal, and a tiny ruby headlamp, made to commemorate the completion of the railway from Moscow to Vladivostok. Hall III showcases Asian and Western European arms and armor. Hall IV exhibits a huge collection of Russian armor, the sabers of Minin and Pozharsky, and the iron helmet of Yaroslavl the Wise, father of Alexander Nevsky.

Hall V (**Halls V–IX are on the ground floor**) is filled with gold and silver objects gifted by visiting ambassadors to the tsars. Among the display is the "Olympic Service" of china presented to Alexander I by Napoléon after the signing of the Treaty of Tilsit in 1807. **Hall VI** has a collection of precious fabrics, vestments, and coronation dresses of Elizabeth I and Alexandra (wife of Nicholas II), worn in 1896, as the last of the Romanov Empresses. The silver wedding gown, worn by Catherine II in 1762, is embroidered with imperial eagles and accentuates her once tiny waistline. The elaborate robe, presented to the Church Metropolitan by Catherine the Great, contains over 150,000 semiprecious stones. A silk *sakkos* vestment was embroidered for Patriarch Nikon in 1654; it consists of so many pearls and precious stones that it weighs over 22 kilograms (50 pounds)! **Hall VII** is known as the **Throne and Crown Room** and contains ancient royal regalia. The oldest throne, carved from ivory, belonged to Ivan the Terrible. A Persian shah presented Boris Godunov with a throne encrusted with 2,000 precious stones in 1604, and the throne of Alexei Romanov contains over 1,000 diamonds. The most interesting is the **Double Throne** used by Peter the Great and his half-brother Ivan, when they were proclaimed joint czars. Peter's older half-sister Sophia acted as regent (from 1682–89), and used to sit in a secret compartment in the throne behind young Peter to advise him on what to say. The **Crown of Monomakh**, decorated with precious stones and sable (first worn by Grand Prince Vladimir Monomakh in 1113), was used by all grand princes and czars until Peter the Great. **Hall VIII** contains saddles, bridles and other equestrian gear from the 16th to 18th centuries. **Hall IX** is the **Carriage Room**, containing the world's largest collection of carriages dating back to Boris Godunov. The most elaborate is the Parisian Bourinhall coronation carriage presented to Elizabeth I, daughter of Peter the Great, by Count Razumovsky in which she rode from St Petersburg to Moscow (pulled by 23 horses) for her coronation. The carved gilt wood is made to represent the sea and breaking waves, and the paintings on the panels are by François Boucher. The most absurd is the miniature coach made in 1675 for young Peter the Great; it was pulled by ponies, and dwarves served as coachmen.

The Diamond Fund Exhibit is a collection of the crown jewels and precious gems. These include the Orlov Diamond (189 carats) that Count Orlov bought for his mistress, Catherine the Great. Catherine the Great's coronation crown is covered with pearls and 4,936 diamonds. A new section of the Armory displays gifts to the former USSR and Russia from foreign countries (open 10am–1pm and 2pm–5pm; a separate entrance ticket is necessary).

THE MAN IN THE WINDOW

*T*he building stands behind the high red-brick wall known to the entire world. There are many windows in that building, but one was distinguished from all the others because it was lit twenty-four hours a day. Those who gathered in the evening on the broad square in front of the red-brick wall would crane their necks, strain their eyes to the point of tears, and say excitedly to one another: "Look, over there, the window's lit. He's not sleeping. He's working. He's thinking about us."

If someone came from the provinces to this city or had to stop over while in transit, he'd be informed that it was obligatory to visit that famous square and look and see whether that window was lit. Upon returning home, the fortunate provincial would deliver authoritative reports, both at closed meetings and at those open to the public, that yes, the window was lit, and judging by all appearances, he truly never slept and was continually thinking about them.

Naturally, even back then, there were certain people who abused the trust of their collectives. Instead of going to look at that window, they'd race around to all the stores, wherever there was anything for sale. But, upon their return, they, too, would report that the window was lit, and just try and tell them otherwise.

The window, of course, was lit. But the person who was said never to sleep was never at that window. A dummy made of gutta-percha, built by the finest craftsmen, stood in for him. That dummy had been so skillfully constructed that unless you actually touched it there was nothing to indicate that it wasn't alive. Its hand held a curved pipe of English manufacture, which had a special mechanism that puffed out tobacco smoke at pre-determined intervals. As far as the original himself was concerned, he only smoked his pipe when there were people around, and his moustache was of the paste-on variety. He lived in another room, in which there were not only no windows but not even any doors. That room could only be reached through a crawl-hole in his safe, which had doors both in the front and in the rear and which stood in the room that was officially his.

He loved this secret room where he could be himself and not smoke a pipe or wear that moustache; where he could live simply and modestly, in keeping with the room's furnishings—an iron bed, a striped mattress stuffed with straw, a washbasin containing warm water, and an old gramophone, together with a collection of records which he personally had marked—good, average, remarkable, trash.

There in that room he spent the finest hours of his life in peace and quiet; there, hidden from everyone, he would sometimes sleep with the old cleaning woman who crawled in every morning through the safe with her bucket and broom. He would call her over to him, she would set her broom in the corner in business-like fashion, give herself to him, and then return to her cleaning. In all the years, he had not exchanged a single word with her and was not even absolutely certain whether it was the same old woman or a different one every time.

One strange incident occurred. The old woman began rolling her eyes and moving her lips soundlessly.

"What's the matter with you?"

"I was just thinking," the old woman said with a serene smile. "My niece is coming to visit, my brother's daughter. I've got to fix some eats for her, but all I've got is three roubles. So it's either spend two roubles on millet and one on butter, or two on butter and one on millet."

This peasant sagacity touched him deeply. He wrote a note to the storehouse ordering that the old woman be issued as much miller and butter as she needed. The old woman, no fool, did not take the note to the storehouse but to the Museum of Revolution, where she sold it for enough money to buy herself a little house near Moscow and a cow; she quit her job, and rumor has it that to this day she's still bringing in milk to sell at Tishinsky market.

Vladimir Voinovich, A Circle of Friends, 1969

Vladimir Voinovich, who turned 80 in 2012, is one of Russia's greatest satirists. His other works include Life and Extraordinary Adventures of Private Ivan Chonkin, Ivankiad and the comic masterpiece Moscow 2042.

OLD MOSCOW

The area to the east of the Kremlin is known as **Kitai-Gorod**. *Kitai* is derived from either the Mongolian word for central or the Old Russian *kiti* meaning bundle of stakes as these protective palisades surrounded the area. *Gorod* is the Russian word for town. (In modern Russian, *Kitai* means China.) Foreign settlements were later established in this area. In the 14th century the central town was surrounded by a protective earthen rampart and served as the central *posad* (market and trade area), where merchants and townspeople lived. Beyond the rampart lay the forest. Later Ivan the Terrible constructed larger fortified stone walls. The original area of Kitai-Gorod (which formed Moscow's second ring) stretched in the form of a horseshoe from the History Museum on Red Square, along the back of GUM Department Store, and east down to the banks of the Moskva River. On each side of GUM are the small streets of Nikolskaya and Ilyinka.

On the opposite side of the square, the Iberian Gates (Iverskiye Vorota) served as the main entrance to Red Square. The Chapel of the Iberian Mother of God once stood atop the gates and contained the Virgin of Iver Icon, said to possess miraculous powers. The gates were also the access route from Kitai-Gorod (China Town) to the Beli Gorod (White Town). Before setting out on long journeys, Muscovites also stopped here to pray.

NIKOLSKAYA ULITSA (STREET)

This street, which begins at the northeastern corner of Red Square, runs along the side of GUM, and ends at Lubyanskaya Square. It is now a pedestrian walkway, and closed to traffic. After the Revolution until 1991, its name was 25th of October Street, commemorating the first day of the 1917 Revolution. In the 17th century the area was nicknamed the Street of Enlightenment; Moscow's first learning academy, printing yard and bookshops lined the passage. The street was originally named after the nearby Nikolsky Monastery.

The first corner building as you leave the square was the Governor's Office, where the writer Alexander Radishchev was held before his exile to Siberia (by Catherine the Great) in 1790. His book, *A Journey from St Petersburg to Moscow*, described the terrible conditions of serfdom. Behind the Kazan Cathedral stands the **Old Royal Mint** inside the small courtyard. An inscription on the gates shows it was built by Peter the Great in 1697. When he later moved the Mint to St Petersburg, the vice-governor had his office here.

Down the street from the Royal Mint, at number 7–9, are several buildings that remain from the **Zaikonospassky Monastery** founded by Boris Godunov in the early 1600s. The name means 'Icon of our Savior'; the monastery used to make and sell icons. The red and white **Savior's Church** was built in 1661. The church and adjoining buildings housed the **Slavic-Greek-Latin Academy**, Moscow's first and largest academy for higher education, which operated from 1687 to 1814. Among the first students were the poet Kantemir, the architect Bazhenov and Mikhail Lomonosov (1711–65), who became a renowned poet, historian and educator. Known as the 'Father of Russian Science', Lomonosov established Moscow University under Empress Elizabeth in 1755. (See also St Petersburg pages 482 and 519.) After 1814, it was part of the Trinity Monastery of St Sergius.

At number 15 was the first Printing Yard, now the History and Archives Institute. Ivan the Terrible brought the first printing press to Russia in 1553. Still hanging on the Gothic-style aquamarine and white building are the emblems of the old printing yard, a lion and unicorn, together with a sundial, mounted in 1814. The thick black gates lead to the colorfully tiled **Building of the Old Proofreader**, where Ivan Fedorov spent a year printing Russia's first book. Ivan the Terrible visited Fedorov daily until *The Acts of the Apostles* (now in the State Public Library) was completed on March 1, 1564. The first Russian newspaper, *Vedomosti*, was printed here on December 16th 1702. The present building was constructed in 1814 and was used as the printing center for the Holy Synod, the council established by Peter the Great that regulated church affairs.

At number 19 was the **Slavyansky Bazaar**, one of Moscow's oldest and most popular hotels (it later closed due to fire damage). When the restaurant opened in the 1870's, it became a popular meeting place for Moscow merchants who negotiated deals over the delicious *blini* pancakes. The hotel was also a favorite hangout of Anton Chekhov when he lived in Moscow. (The hotel appeared in Chekhov's short story, The Lady with the Lapdog.) On June 22, 1897, the playwright and theater critic Vladimir Nemirovich-Danchenko met with actor Konstantin Stanislavsky (the creator of the Stanislavky Method). They sat and talked about the dire state of Moscow theater. While drinking and eating, over the course of 18 hours, they hammered out plans for the creation of the legendary Moscow Art Theater, which later staged Chekhov's plays.

Opposite the Printing House is the former **Chizhov Coach Exchange**. The Chizhov family hired out horse-drawn carriages and carts as taxis. The Coach Exchange was popular year-round, when Moscow streets were either muddy or frozen. In winter Muscovites could hire a Chizhov troika, or sled (see excerpt from Nikolai Gogol's *Dead Souls* on page 240 for a wonderful description of a troika ride). Next door is the one-domed **Church of the Dormition**.

The small passage known as **Tretyakovsky Proyezd** links Nikolskaya Street with Okhotny Ryad. The wealthy merchant Sergei Tretyakov (who established the Tretyakov Gallery) knocked this passage through the Kitai-Gorod wall in 1871 to gain quick access to the banks along Okhotny Ryad. It is now known as Moscow's

Fifth Avenue, with stores from Tiffany to Gucci. At its front entrance stands the **Monument to Ivan Fedorov** (1510–83), the first Russian printer. (See page 57.)

Halfway down Nikolskaya Street, take a right on Ilyinka Proyezd. Near the corner, on Bogoyavlensky Pereulok, stands the red-brick 17th-century Baroque-style **Cathedral of Bogoyavlensky** (Epiphany), once part of a monastery established in 1296 by Prince Daniil (son of Alexander Nevsky) in order to protect inhabitants of the then unwalled city. The cathedral stands on the site of Moscow's first stone church, built by Ivan I in the early 14th century. Many of the sculptures that were in the church are now on display in the Donskoi Monastery. The wealthy Boyar Golitsyn family had their burial vaults here until the mid-18th century; they were transferred to the Donskoi Monastery outside the city when a cholera epidemic prohibited burial in the city center.

The pharmacy shop at number 21 is over a century old. The first pharmacy, for members of the czar's family, was set up in the Kremlin by Ivan the Terrible in 1581. Beginning in the 1600s, pharmacies sold medicinal herbs in Moscow. Many of the herbs were grown in the area of what is now the Alexandrov Gardens near the Kremlin. The first public pharmacies opened in 1721.

ULITSA ILYINKA (ILYINKA STREET)

Ilyinka Proyezd (Passage) leads into this street, which begins on Red Square and continues past the southeast side of GUM. It was once the main thoroughfare of Kitai-Gorod. In 1497, Ivan the Great gave a parcel of land on this street to 500 Novgorod merchant families to establish the Moscow-Novgorod Trade Exchange, at a time when Novgorod was still independent of Moscovy. The wealthy merchants erected **St Ilyia Church**, recognizable by its single dome and *zakomara* gabled arches. From 1935 to 1991 this street was named after the popular revolutionary figure Kuibyshev. The passage was once the busy thoroughfare of Moscow's bank and financial district. At number 6 the classical building of the **Moscow Stock Exchange** or Birzha (1838), with its large Ionic columns, once again bustles with commercial activity.

The wealthy merchant Pavel Riabushinsky commissioned Fedor Shekhtel to build the Riabushinsky Bank in 1904. Shekhtel also designed the nearby Moscow Merchants Building in 1909. Riabushinsky was a highly respected spokesman for the merchant class and chairman of the Moscow Stock Exchange.

As Ilyinka Passage continues across the street of the same name, it becomes Ribny Pereulok (Fish Lane), where many food stalls were once set up. From 1795 to 1805 the Italian architect Giacomo Quarenghi, the favorite architect of Catherine the Great, built the Old Merchant Arcade, **Gostiny Dvor,** in Neo-Classical style, which occupied an entire block. This Corinthian-columned white structure now serves as a shopping plaza.

ULITSA VARVARKA (VARVARKA STREET)

Ribny Pereulok leads into Ulitsa Varvarka. Nearby are the remains of the 16th-century brick rampart walls that surrounded Kitai-Gorod; this wall was over 2.5 kilometers (one and a half miles) long and six meters (20 feet) high. One entered Kitai-Gorod through the Vladimirsky Gates; all that remains today is a red gate built in 1871. After the Revolution until 1991 the street was known as Razin, named after Stenka Razin, a popular Cossack rebel who was executed in Red Square in 1671.

This area used to lie beyond the old marketplace on the outer fringes of Red Square. In Old Russian *zaryadi* means 'beyond the trading stalls'. The large **Rossiya Hotel** (once the world's largest hotel), which had been located behind St Basil's Cathedral since 1967, was demolished in 2006. The large Zaryadye Park is planned for this 30-acre site.

The salmon and white **Church of St Varvara** (Barbara) stands at the beginning of the street, which is named after this saint. The 16th-century church was rebuilt in the 18th century by the architect Matvei Kazakov. (Services are held here.) This passage once stretched from the Kremlin, along the old trade route, to the towns of Vladimir and Kolomna. Prince Dmitri Donskoi used this route to return home after his victorious battle with the Mongols in the Battle of Kulikovo in 1380.

The small cube-shaped and five-domed **Church of St Maxim** stands nearby. Built in 1698 by Novgorod merchants, it held the remains of St Maxim, an ascetic prophet who died in 1433. It now houses branches of the Society for Environmental Protection and the Nobility League Art Salon, which sells souvenirs to do with the last royal family.

Between these two churches, at 4 Varvarka, is the **Old English Court**, a white-washed house with tiny irregularly placed windows and a steep wooden roof. It originally belonged to a wealthy Russian merchant until, in 1556, Ivan the Terrible presented it to Sir Richard Chancellor, an English merchant who began trade relationships with Russia. It was the first official residence of a Western power in Moscow, and up until 1649 it remained the English trading and ambassadorial office in the capital. Ivan IV even proposed marriage to Queen Elizabeth I, but she declined and instead offered Ivan asylum in England whenever he might need it. Each room in the Museum is devoted to a particular aspect of Anglo-Russian trade. Because of its unique acoustics the Main Hall is used for concerts of early music played on Renaissance and Baroque instruments. It is open 11am–6pm, closed Mondays and the last Friday of each month. (Often closed for renovation.)

Up the street, at number 8, is the **Znamensky Cathedral**, built in the 1684, all that remains of the Nunnery of Our Lady of the Sign. It now houses a small concert hall (with 250 seats), a chapel (which holds services), and an icon workshop. At number 12 is the **Church of St George on Pskov Hill**. The colorful church, with red walls and a blue belfry (1818), was erected by Pskov merchants in 1657. Open daily 11am–7pm.

Near the Cathedral, at number 10, is the **House of Boyars Romanov**. Built in 1547, it's the oldest surviving private house in Moscow. It is now a branch of the State History Museum (also known as the Zaryadye Museum) that has displays of life from 17th-century Boyardom (Nobility). The rich Boyar Nikita Zakharin had his home in the center of Kitai-Gorod. Nikita's sister, Anastasia, was married to Ivan the Terrible. Nikita's grandson Mikhail, born in the house, was later elected to the throne in 1613 and began the 300-year reign of the Romanov dynasty. The house has operated as a museum since 1859 and is furnished to look like an early noble household. Open 10am–5pm, closed Tuesdays and the first Monday of each month.

The street ends at Slavyanskaya Square. Heading south on Kitaigorodsky Proyezd, by the Moskva River, is the **Church of the Conception of St Anne-in-the-Corner**. The church stood at the corner of the Kitai-Gorod wall and was named after the Virgin's mother, St Anne. The barren wife of Grand Prince Vasily III, Solomonia (whom he later divorced), often prayed here.

KITAI-GOROD

Varvarka Street leads east to Slavyanskaya Square and the Kitai-Gorod Metro station. Kitai-Gorod .(China Town) is where the foreign merchants used to live. Following the Bolshevik Revolution, the area was known as Nogin Square, after the revolutionary figure Viktor Nogin. In 1991 it reverted to its original name. The **Church of All Saints on Kulishki** stands on the south side of the square.

After Prince Dmitri Donskoi defeated the Mongols at Kulikovo in 1380, he erected a wooden church on the *kulishki*, marshy land. It was replaced by the stone church in the 16th century, which has been restored. To the left of the church are the gray buildings of the **Delovoy Dvor**, the business chambers. Built in 1913, they were used for the business operations of the city.

Near the square are the **Ilyinsky Gardens**, with a monument to the Russian Grenadiers who died in the Battle of Plevna against Turkey in 1877. Along the small side street called Staraya (Old) Ploshchad, are buildings that were once used by the Central Committee of the Communist Party. A few minutes' walk west, at 3 Nikitnikov Pereulok, is a 'jewel of merchant architecture', the Byzantine five-domed **Church of the Holy Trinity in Nikitniki**. In 1620, Mikhail Romanov hired a wealthy merchant from Yaroslavl, Grigory Nikitnikov, to work in the financial administration; and, he later became the only merchant authorized to trade with China. Nikitnikov named the street after himself, and later (with all his profits from importing tea and silk) built this Onion-domed church (1635–53) on the site of the wooden Church of St Nikita (his family saint), which later burnt down. The oldest icon is St Nikita, which Nikitnikov supposedly rescued from the burning church. The icon of the Trinity can be found on the iconostasis, carved in 1640. There are many unique frescoes and wood carvings on the walls.

The burial chapel of the Nikitnikovs lies to the right of the altar (Grigory was the first merchant to be buried inside a Russian Orthodox Church). Part of the church now functions as the **Museum of 17th-Century Architecture and Painting**. Open 10am–5pm, 12–7pm Wednesdays and Thursdays; closed Tuesdays. Church services are also held here.

Nearby, Staraya Ploshchad (Old Square) becomes Solyanka Ulitsa (Street). *Sol* means salt, and the old saltyards were along this street in the 17th century. At this time the area was considered the countryside of Moscow; Ivan the Great had a summer palace near the Convent of St John. Farther up the street is the **Church of St Vladimir-in-the-Old Gardens**. Solyanka intersects with Arkhipova Ulitsa, named after the artist who lived here in 1900. Many middle-class artisans lived in this part of the city. The **Moscow Choral Synagogue** is at 8 Bolshaya Spasoglinishhevsky Pereulok. The building went up in 1891, but did not open for another 15 years because the Moscow governor had expelled Jews from the city. But, it remained open after the Revolution. Today, it is the most important temple for Moscow's estimated 200,000 Jews. The synagogue serves kosher food in its café 'Na Gorke' on the first floor. The complex is open to the public 10am–6pm except on Saturdays and Jewish holidays.

THE OLD MARX PROSPEKT

In 1991, Prospekt Marxa, the city's busiest avenue, was officially divided into three different streets. From Lubyanka Square to Teatralnaya Square, it is Teatralny Proyezd (past the Bolshoi Theater). From Teatralnaya Square to Pushkinskaya Street it is Okhotny Ryad (which leads from the Bolshoi Theater to Tverskaya Street and the National Hotel). The rest of the thoroughfare that runs alongside the Kremlin is now called Mokhovaya Street.

LUBYANSKAYA PLOSHCHAD (LUBYANKA SQUARE)

Teatralny Proyezd (Theater Passage) begins at this square, where a bronze statue of Felix Dzerzhinsky (1877–1926), a prominent revolutionary leader and founder of the Cheka (the All Russia Extraordinary Commission for Combating Counter-Revolution, Sabotage and Speculation), once stood in the center (earlier called Dzerzhinsky Square). The "Iron-Felix" statue was pulled down by crowds on the night of August 22, 1991, after the attempted coup. (It now stands in the Park of the Fallen Heroes on the grounds of the State Art Gallery near Gorky Park.) Various graffiti, coup memorabilia and an occasional Orthodox cross decorate the pedestal, which now commemorates all those killed by the KGB. For a century a charming fountain of cherubs, designed by Giovanni Vitali, had stood in the center of the square; in 1932, it was moved to the Academy of Sciences on Leninsky Prospekt. The Dzerzhinsky Monument was erected in its place 26 years later. (There is a current movement to bring back the statue to its original place.) In 1991, the square was given back its historical name of Lubyanka. In the 15th century, new settlers from Novgorod named the area Lubyanitsa, after a place in their native city. On the southeastern side of the square is the great stone from the northern Solovetsky Islands in the White Sea (where the infamous 1930s Solovki gulag camp was located); it was laid in October 1990 by the Memorial Society, and it bears an inscription as a **Memorial to the Victims of the Soviet Period.**

The Lubyanka Metro station exits on to the square. Original Kitai-Gorod walls were demolished to provide room for the Metro station, designed by Nikolai Ladovsky and opened in 1937. The large department store on one corner is **Detsky Mir** (Children's World), built in 1957, the largest children's store in Russia. More than half a million shoppers visit daily. Behind it is the **Savoy Hotel.** To the north, the street becomes Ulitsa Bolshaya Lubyanka.

Standing on the northeast side of Lubyanka Square is the infamous former **KGB Building**, constructed in the early 1900s as the headquarters of the Rossiya Insurance firm. It was built on the site of the Royal Secret Dispatch Office, where a dreadful prison was kept in the cellars during the reign of Catherine the Great. After the Revolution, Dzerzhinsky took the building over to house his Cheka police. In the 1930s the building was reconstructed; a new façade was erected, two floors were added and a massive underground prison complex, known as the Lubyanka, was built in the original cellars. (Under Stalin, in five years alone, the secret police or NKVD—People's Commissariat of Internal Affairs—executed over one million people. They also created the labor camp system.) In 1954, after the secret execution of Beria, Khrushchev founded the Committee for State Security—the KGB—to establish party control over the secret police after Stalin. At its height, the KGB employed an estimated 400,000 people.

On the left stands another (gray and black) KGB structure, built in 1980, and reputed to have many floors hidden underground. When the Communist Party was banned, the KGB tried to improve its image and even held a Miss KGB contest.

With the fall of the Communist government, the organization of the KGB was disbanded; it was split into separate agencies, headed by the Federal Security Service or FSB (*Federalnaya Sluzhba Bezopasnosti*). It is now forbidden to use substances (such as poisoned umbrella tips) that could damage human health or to blackmail people into cooperation. In a decree, Boris Yeltsin harshly spelled out every acronym that the secret police had used since the Bolshevik Revolution 'The system of the organs of the Cheka OGPU-NKVD-MGB-KGB-MB turned out not to be reformable.' (The OGPU was formed in 1922; NKVD in 1934; NKGB in 1943; MGB in 1946; and the KGB in 1953.) The original Cheka underwent nearly 20 name changes since 1919.

Today the agencies have been paralyzed with budget cuts and reorganizations, (At one point, in the 1990's, a paper shortage in the country forced agents to type reports on the back of old documents.) It is now not only difficult to recruit foreigners as (secret) Russian agents, but native Russians as well. The American CIA and FBI were even called in to help revamp their computer systems. The goal of building Communism and the Great Motherland has been usurped by capitalist ideology, and the brightest no longer consider it prestigious to work for intelligence; registration at the Andropov Red Banner Institute, which trains intelligence recruits, has dropped by more than 75 percent. With Vladimir Putin, an ex-KGB agent, in office, many are still suspicious of where the intelligence organizations are heading.

Three interesting museums are nearby the square. The **Mayakovsky Museum** is on the corner of Myasnitskaya Ulitsa and Lubyansky Proyezd. The popular poet Vladimir Mayakovsky (1893–1930) lived at this address for over a decade, but then, disillusioned with socialism, committed suicide here in April 1930. Many of his works and personal items are on display. Films of Mayakovsky are also shown, along with recordings of him reading his work. The museum is open 10am–5pm, 1pm–8pm Thursdays (when literary readings are held in the evening); closed Wednesdays. (In 2013, the museum closed for a two-year renovation.)

At 12 Novaya Ploshchad (New Square) is the Church of St John the Divine 'Under the Elm', built in 1825; it was recently returned to the Russian Orthodox Church. It used to house the **History of Moscow Museum**, which moved to 2 Zubovsky Blvd in 2013.

Opposite, at 3/4 Novaya Ploshchad, is the **Polytechnical Museum**. Opened in 1872, it was one of Moscow's first museums. The current building, completed in 1907, has 60 halls containing over 170,000 items that trace the history of Russian science, technology and industry. In the basement is a fabulous collection of old Russian automobiles; the first Russian car was the Pobeda (Victory), manufactured after World War II. Henry Ford also exported his cars to Moscow (through Armand Hammer) until Lenin's death in 1924.The third floor exhibit traces the history of Russian Animation. On the top floor is an interesting collection of Russian space capsules and an exhibition on the life of the first Soviet cosmonaut Yuri Gagarin. The library has over three million volumes.

The Polytechnical building (through the years built in three different styles) was also a popular center for local meetings; writers such as Akhmatova, Gorky and Mayakovsky gave readings here, and Lenin often presented lectures. In 1967, the longest telepathic experiment in history took place between the museum and Leningrad. The sender Yuri Kamensky sent telepathic messages from here to the psychic receiver Karl Nikolayev at Leningrad University. From the 1950s until the 1980s, the Soviets vigorously studied parapsychology and aspects of psychic warfare. Today the Central Hall is run by the Znaniye (Knowledge) Society, and lectures and readings are still staged. The museum is open from 10am–6pm; closed Mondays. (It is closed for extensive renovation through 2016.)

TEATRALNAYA PLOSHCHAD (THEATER SQUARE)

The main section of the old Prospekt Marxa opens onto Teatralnaya Ploshchad (Theater Square). From 1919 until 1991 it was known as Sverdlov Square, after the first president of Soviet Russia, Yakov Sverdlov (1885–1919). The statue of Karl Marx, inscribed with the words 'Workers of All Countries Unite!' stands in the middle of the square. The Metro station is Teatralnaya. From Theater Square to Red Square, the street is now known as Okhotny Ryad (Hunter's Row—the street once led to the countryside and a popular hunting ground).

On the corner, at 1/4 Teatralny Proezd, is one of Moscow's finest and most expensive hotels, the **Metropol**. In the late 1880s, the Chelyshy Hotel stood on this spot. The Chelyshev family sold it to the St Petersburg Insurance Society for over one million rubles and the company then rebuilt the site, renaming the hotel Metropol, the Greek word for 'mother-city.' The head of the Society was Savva Mamontov, a Russian railroad tycoon and art patron who, in 1899, chose to stage a design contest for the building's façade. At first, the Russian Lev Kekushev was deemed the winner for his 'style-moderne.' But Mamontov pushed for a design by William Walcott, who had a more innovative approach with his art-nouveau design, entitled 'Woman's Head.'

The first cornerstone of the hotel was laid in November 1898. After a disastrous fire ruined construction in December 1901, the hotel was finally completed in early 1905. Newspapers called it the 'Tower of Babylon of the 20th Century.' Costing over seven million rubles to build, it had hot water, electric elevators and even a state-of-the-art ventilation system. The mosaic panels and classical friezes were designed by Russian artists such as Alexander Golovin and Nikolai Andreev (*The Four Seasons*) on the fourth floor, and Mikhail Vrubel on the exterior of the western façade. Vrubel's famous Art-Nouveau mural, *Princess of Dreams*, tells the story of a knight who falls in love with a beautiful princess and embarks across an ocean of soaring waves to find her. During the voyage, he falls ill and is near death when Princess Melisande finds him. As she embraces him, he dies in her arms, but a miracle takes place, and beauty triumphs in the world. The hotel proved an enormous success. Fyodor Shalyapin sung here and many other famous artists, writers and musicians had work residences in the hotel. Rasputin even once had his headquarters here. In 1918, the Bolsheviks re-appropriated the hotel to become the Second House of Soviets. In 2012, the Moscow City government sold the hotel in auction (as part of its privatization program) to the Azimut hotel chain for $275 million.

For nearly a century, the hotel has hosted thousands of international VIPs. Mstislav Rostropovich met his wife, Galina Vishnevskaya, in the restaurant, and in an irony of fate both John F Kennedy and Lee Harvey Oswald stayed at the hotel at different times. From 1986–91, the hotel was closed to transform its 370 rooms into the city's first five-star hotel. Inside are restaurants, bars and coffee shops, some with excellent all-you-can-eat breakfast and lunch buffets. Facing the hotel to the right are walls of the 16th-century Kitai-Gorod.

The magnificent **Theater Square** hosts two of Moscow's most prominent theaters—the Bolshoi (Big) and Maly (Small). The Bolshoi was originally known as the Petrovsky Theater as it stood on Petrovka Street. It was originally founded by Catherine the Great, who gave Prince Urusov permission to open his private theater to the public in 1776; it staged mostly performances of comic operas and ballets, but later burnt down in 1805. In 1819, a competition was won by Andrei Mikhailov, along with Osip Bovet, who wanted to bring the grandeur of St Petersburg to Moscow with the design of a front façade, decorated by a massive eight-columned portico and an alabaster statue of Apollo's chariot. On January 6, 1825, the opening ceremony for the new Petrovsky Theater took place—as it was much bigger than its predecessor, it was known as the Big (Bolshoi) Petrovsky Theater. After yet another fire in 1853, the Bolshoi was rebuilt in Neo-classical style by Alberto Kavos, and opened to coincide with Alexander II's coronation in 1856. The six-tiered (including the *galyorka* upper gallery) gold and crimson auditorium accommodated over 2000 people, and the chandelier was made from 13,000 pieces of cut glass. The Portico is crowned by the famous four bronze horses pulling the chariot of Apollo, patron of the art, and is the work of sculptor Peter Klodt. The theater premiered compositions by Tchaikovsky, Glinka, Mussorgsky and Rimsky-Korsakov. The last performance at the Imperial Bolshoi Theater took place on February 28, 1917. And on 13 March the State Bolshoi Theater opened its doors to the public.

After nearly nine decades, the stately building, reflecting the crumbling of old Soviet society, was rewarded with a mammoth renovation in 2005 that was to take six years and eventually balloon in cost (with many tales of scandal and corruption) to over $1.5 billion. The Bolshoi re-opened on October 28, 2011 for its 236th season.

For more information on the theater and ticketing, see www.bolshoi.ru/en. Tickets can also be purchased at the Theaters' Box Offices. The Historic Stage Box Office is open noon–8pm; closed 4pm–6pm. (To prevent scalping, passports are necessary to present at the box office and at the door.) The Bolshoi also offers tours in English: on Mondays and Fridays at 12:30pm, a visitor can take a one-hour guided tour. Tickets can be purchased on the day of the tour at the ticket office (door #12) in the Historic Building of the Theater. Chamber concerts are also held in the Beethoven Hall.

The cream-colored theater, now steadied on 7,000 new pilings, has been restored to its ornate czarist-era glory, with embroidered silk tapestries, replicated spruce panels and a magnificently restored Apollo and Muses ceiling piece; five kilos of gold leaf were used to coat the interior of the grand hall. A factory was found which could duplicate the only two remaining Villeory & Boch floor tiles, and another that matched a swatch of original upholstery, taking three years to weave 820 yards of new cloth. The main chandelier, weighing 2.3 tons, is made of 260 kilograms of crystal and coated with 300 grams of gold leaf.

From 1955, for fifty years, Fyodor Fydorovsky's famous gold 'Soviet' curtain, bearing the state symbols of the USSR, reigned supreme at the Theater. Now replaced, the immense curtain, newly designed with the Russian imperial crest, weighs more than a ton due to all the golden thread used to embroider it. In addition, all the communist insignias, including the Hammer and Sickle that once hung above the royal balcony, have been taken off and replaced with the Russian Imperial symbol of the two-headed eagle and the initials NA for Nicholas Alexandrovich, the last Romanov czar.

The legendary and largely lost original acoustics have also been restored with a dynamic new hydraulic stage and an enlarged orchestra pit that holds up to 130 musicians. Spaces beneath the theater—including an underground concert hall for rehearsals and chamber concerts, and additional rooms that store the company's 30,000 costumes and set pieces—all together double the theater's original size.

The Bolshoi's new 'Sister Theater,' standing directly across the street, had its grand opening in September 2002 (after six years of construction) and premiered a new production of Rimsky-Korsakov's *The Snow Maiden*. Schedule of performances and ticket sales are at: www.bolshoi.ru/en. The New Stage building has its own Box Office, open 11am–7pm; closed 2pm–3pm.

After all the corruption complaints throughout the six-year restoration process, a new scandal resonated when, in January, 2013, a masked assailant splashed sulphuric acid onto the face of Sergei Filin near his home. (A former principal dancer, Filin had been the Bolshoi's Artistic Director since 2011.) In December, 2013, a Moscow court sentenced Pavel Dmitrichenko, a former Bolshoi soloist, to six years in a penal colony for ordering the attack that nearly blinded Filin. Reasons for the attack included corruption within the company.

Across Petrovka Street from the Bolshoi is the pale-yellow **Maly Drama Theater**. At its entrance stands the statue of Alexander Ostrovsky (1823–86), the outstanding Russian playwright. The theater is nicknamed the Ostrovsky House. Many classic Russian plays are staged here. Nearby is the Central Children's Theater, formed in 1921. Across the street from the Maly is the old Mostorg, or Moscow Trade. In 1907, when the building was completed, it housed the English department store Muir and Murrilies.

Before continuing along the avenue, some old and interesting side streets off Theater Square merit exploration.

ULITSA PETROVKA (PETROVKA STREET)

Ulitsa Petrovka is a small side street that begins in front of the Maly Theater. The street has long been a popular shopping district with stores selling *podarki* (gifts), *bukinisti* (secondhand books) and *almazi* (diamonds). Next to the Maly, at number 2, is the gray four-story neo-Gothic-style building that houses TsUM, the **Central Universal Store**, open daily 9am–8pm; till 6pm Sundays. At number 10 is **Petrovsky Passazh**, a popular shopping arcade. The Society of World Art had its first exhibition at number 15, displaying the work of Alexander Benois. The writer Anton Chekhov lived at number 19 for several years. (He also lived by the Garden Ring, at 6 Sadovaya-Kudrinskaya, now the Chekhov House Museum, see pages 242/278.)

At Petrovka 16 is the **Gulag History Museum**; walk through the barbed-wire courtyard, surrounded by pictures of past political prisoners. It is dedicated to the GULAG—an acronym for the Main Administration of Corrective Labor Camps. As told by Alexander Solzhenitsyn in his book *The Gulag Archipelago*, more than 20 million people passed through these horrific labor camps during the peak years from 1929–1953. (Many camps continued to operate through 1991.) The Museum recounts the terrors of prison life and acts as a memorial to its many victims.

At number 25 (nearer the Chekhovskaya Metro), is the capital's first **Museum of Contemporary Art**, housed in an old 18th-century building, where the Dolgoruky princes resided for 50 years. Opened in 1999 by artist Zurab Tsereteli, it displays both Russian and international paintings, graphics and sculptures, including many from Tsereteli's own private collection, which include works by Chagall, Kandinsky, Picasso and Dali. Open 12–8pm; Thursdays 1pm–9pm.

The **Literary Museum**, at number 28, traces the history of Russian and Soviet literature with over 700,000 items. It is located in the Naryshkin chambers of the Vyosko-Petrovsky Monastery. Open 11am–6pm; closed Sundays.

Three centuries ago, the passage was named after the **Monastery of St Peter-on-the-Hill**, which also served as a protective stronghold and entrance to the town. (It is situated right on the corner of Petrovka and Petrovsky Bulvar; open daily 8am–8pm.) The monastery was built by Prince Dmitri Donskoi to honor the Mongol defeat in the Battle of Kulikovo in 1380. In 1682, the future Peter the Great escaped to the monastery with his mother, Natalya Naryshkina, during the bloody Streltsy revolts. Today it serves as the Patriarch's Department for Religious Education and contains three churches. The **Church of the Virgin Icon of Bogolyubovo** (1685) was built over the graves of Ivan and Afanasy Naryshkin, killed in 1682 by the Streltsy. The octagonal-drum and helmet-domed **Cathedral of Metropolitan Peter** was reconstructed between 1514 and 1517. The baroque-style Refectory **Church of**

Sergius Radonezhsky (founder of Sergiyev Posad Monastery) was commissioned by Peter the Great at the beginning of his reign in 1690; religious services are held here.

A **Monument to Wit** was erected in 2002 on the nearby boulevard; shaped as a stone pyramid fountain, each side represents the different moods of man. Before it stands a bronze statue dedicated to Moscow's most beloved clown, Yuri Nikulin, who died in 1997. The **Hermitage Gardens**, north of the boulevard, at 3 Karetny Ryad, have been here for over a century; open daily 9am–11pm. The **Maly Concert Hall** is located in the gardens.

KUZNETSKY MOST

Ulitsa Petrovka leads to Kuznetsky Most (Blacksmith's Bridge), a small lane intersecting it. As far back as the 15th century, the area was the popular residence of Moscow's blacksmiths, who lived along the banks of the Neglinka River, which at the time flowed through here.

Almost every building along this steep passage has a fascinating story related to it. It became a highly respected shopping district in the 19th century; items were stamped with 'Bought in Kuznetsky Most'. At number 9 was an ornate and popular restaurant called Yar, which Pushkin and Tolstoy mention in their writings. It was famous for its Gypsy dancers and drunken revelry; Rasputin was thrown out of the restaurant after he got involved in a brawl. Tolstoy listened to one of the world's first phonographs in the music shop that was at number 12, and he wrote of Anna Karenina shopping at Gautier's at number 20. The House of Fashion and many airline agencies are also located along this narrow street.

ULITSA NEGLINNAYA (NEGLINKA STREET)

Kuznetsky Most intersects Ulitsa Neglinnaya, which runs parallel to and east of Petrovka Street to Trubnaya Ploshchad (Square) on the Boulevard Ring. This street also sprang up alongside the banks of the Neglinka River, where many popular shops were located. *Neglinnaya* means without clay. Catherine the Great ordered that the river be diverted underground. In the 19th century, it was redirected to a larger aqueduct where it now flows underground to the Moskva River.

The revolutionary Nikolai Schmit had his furniture store at the corner of Kuznetsky Most. The Moorish-style building of the **Sandunovskiye (Sanduny) Baths** at number 14 was frequented by Chekhov. This is one of the grandest banya in town. The building was bought by the actor Sila Sandunov, who turned it into sauna baths in 1896. The banya is still a marbled and gilded extravaganza where one can steam, sweat and swim; open 9am–9pm; Sat/Sun 8am-9pm; closed Tuesdays from 9am–2pm. www.sanduny.ru. Another popular banya is the **Presnya Banya** at 7 Stolyarny Pereulok. Open 8am–8pm; Tuesdays noon-8pm; near Ulitsa 1905 Goda Metro station. Try to bring along your own towel, but buy a bunch of birch leaves usually sold seasonally outside; Russians love to swat each other with these while sweating! (See Special Banya Topic on page 438 and page 727 on Practical Information listings.)

OKHOTNY RYAD

The continuation of the Prospekt from Theater Square to the Kremlin is now known as Okhotny Ryad (Hunter's Lane) the name of the old local markets. The main markets of Moscow spread from here to Red Square.

At the western end of the street once stood the **Moskva Hotel**, built in constructivist and Stalinist-empire style between 1932 and 1935. The top left of the building's façade was different from the right. In the 1930s, when the architect designed two different fronts for the hotel, the story goes he asked Stalin, 'Which one do you like best?' 'Da (Yes),' replied Stalin. Afraid to question the Soviet leader again, the architect built the structure asymmetrically, including both designs. A new five-star hotel Four Seasons Moskva, built according to the initial 1930s' plans of Soviet architects Shchusev, Saveliev and Stapran, is currently underway. Next to it is a small archeology museum, situated in a 7-meter deep pavilion, that exhibits artifacts unearthed during nearby excavations.

Across from the Hotel is **Dom Soyuzov** (House of Trade Unions) on the corner of Dmitrovka and Tverskaya streets, at number 10. Built in 1784 in Russian classical style by Matvei Kazakov, it used to be the Noble's Club. Its Hall of Columns and October Hall hosted social functions. In 1856, Alexander II addressed the nobility on his desire to abolish serfdom, and the playwright George Bernard Shaw was even honored here on his 75th birthday in 1931. Also past leaders such as Lenin, Stalin and Brezhnev lay in state here before their burials. Next door is the City Duma or Parliament building.

Located in front of the hotel, in Manezh Square, is the 350-million-dollar **Okhotny Ryad Underground Shopping Complex**, which was opened in 1997. Spot the stained-glass domes and proceed down the bronze-banistered stairwell into the new commercial heart of Moscow. The three-story underground atrium, complete with indoor fountain, holds 86 shops, 26 restaurants, banks,and an Internet café; open daily 10am–10pm. The closest Metro station is Okhotny Ryad.

Crossing the prospekt, via the underpass, brings you out in front of the grandly restored five-star **Hotel National**. Opened in 1903 (the cornerstone was laid on June 15th 1900), it is still one of Moscow's finest hotels, with 202 rooms and 56 suites. Immediately after the Revolution, the House of Soviets expropriated the hotel and turned it into the House of Soviets No.1. Lenin stayed in Suite 107; his green desk is still preserved in this room. Other Bolshevik leaders, such as Dzerzhinsky, Sverdlov and Stalin also lived here. In 1931, the building was returned to its hotel status. From 1991–95, the National was completely restored to its original design and decoration.

MOKHOVAYA ULITSA (STREET)

Running south from the Hotel National to the end of the prospekt at Borovitskaya Ploshchad is Mokhovaya (Moss-Grown) Street. In the center, in Manezhnaya Ploshchad (Square), stood the Manège, the former imperial riding school. Built in 1817 to commemorate Russia's victory over Napoleon, the 7,500-square-meter building later served as the country's largest exhibition hall. Designed by Osip Bovet, the city's general architect who helped rebuild the city after the Great Fire of 1812, the building was considered innovative for its system of wooden girders, which allowed the roof to stand unsupported by internal walls. After a fire destroyed the structure, in 2004, the mayor had it rebuilt; today the **Manège Exhibition Center** hosts exhibitions and fashion shows. At number 6 is the former mansion of Prince Shakhovsky, built in 1821. (It used to house the Kalinin Museum during Soviet times.)

On the corner of Bolshaya Nikitskaya Ulitsa, stands one of the oldest buildings of Moscow University, recognizable by its columned portico and small dome. It was built in classical style, between 1786 and 1793 by Matvei Kazakov. A statue of Lomonosov (1711–65), who founded the university (along with Ivan Shuvalov) in 1755, stands in the courtyard. Next door a newer building dating from 1836 now houses the Student Union. In the courtyard are two statues of graduates, Nikolai Ogarev and Alexander Herzen.

Mokhovaya ends a few minutes' walk farther down by the **Russian State Library** (formerly the Lenin Library), the largest library in Russia with 36 million books. Between 1784 and 1786, the former governor of Siberia, Pyotr Pashkov, built his Neoclassical mansion (to designs by Vasily Bazhenov) with beautiful exotic gardens filled with peacocks that wandered the hills around the western wall of the Kremlin. It is still referred to as the **Pashkov Dom** and stands on the corner of Mokhovaya and Znamenka streets. Later in 1861, the building housed the famous Rumyantsev collection of over one million books and manuscripts. When Lenin died in 1924, it was renamed the Lenin Library. When the Metro was built in the 1940s, many books were moved into the larger building next door. In 1993, its name was changed once again after extensive restoration. For Moscow's 850th Birthday in 1997, a 3.7-meter-high bronze statue of Russian novelist Fyodor Dostoeyevsky (1821–1881) was unveiled. Sculpted by Mikhail Posokhin, there was quite a local stir over the $1 million price tag. The closest metro station is Biblioteka Imeni Lenina.

VOLKHONKA AND PRECHISTENKA STREETS

Ulitsa Volkhonka begins at the Kremlin's Borovitsky Tower and runs into Ulitsa Prechistenka at the Boulevard Ring. The **Pushkin Museum of Fine Arts** is at 12 Volkhonka, and is a highly recommended stop during your visit. The Neoclassical-style building was constructed in 1898 by Roman Klein to house a collection of fine art. The museum was initially named after Alexander III, but renamed after Pushkin during the poet's centenary year in 1937. After the Revolution, paintings belonging to two great collectors, Sergei Shchukin (1854–1937) and Ivan Morozov (1871–1921) were nationalized by the State. By 1914, Shchukin had more than 220 French impressionist artworks displayed at his house, the former Trubetskoi Mansion in Moscow. Rooms were filled with Matisse, Gauguin, Cézanne and Picasso. In his mansion at 21 Prechistenka Street, Morozov exhibited more than 100 impressionist paintings and 450 other works by Russian artists, including Marc Chagall. They both fled the country after the Revolution and, until 1948, their paintings were exhibited at Morozov's Mansion, known as the Museum of Western Art. After Stalin closed the mansion, their collections were kept in storage in the Pushkin Museum. Only after Stalin's death in 1953 were the paintings gradually put back on display. Today the museum boasts one of the world's largest collections of ancient, classical, Oriental and Western European art, with over half a million works. (In 2013, the renowned British architect Norman Foster resigned from the $670-million renovation and expansion project of the museum. A design competition is planned to elect another architect.) Open 10am–7pm; Thursdays 10am–9pm; closed Mondays. Metro Kropotkinskaya. www.arts-museum.ru.

The museum has also expanded to include the **Museum of Private Collections**, located next door at number 10, in the green and white palace. This was once the palace of the aristocratic Golitsyn family, and Catherine the Great stayed here during her coronation in 1762. Today its three floors and 23 halls exhibit more than 1500 works of art from private collections, many donated to the state. Open 11am–7pm; Thursdays 11am–9pm; closed Mondays and Tuesdays. At number 13 is the **Glazunov Gallery**, housed in an Empire-style mansion. Its three floors exhibit the artist's many huge and fanciful paintings of historical and biblical events. His most famous is 'Eternal Russia.' Open 11am–6pm; closed Mondays.

Behind the museums, at 3/5 Maly Znamensky Lane, is the **Roerich Museum** (open 11am–7pm; closed Mondays), with paintings by artist Nikolai Roerich (1874–1947), an avid Buddhist and mystic. He traveled extensively throughout the Himalayas, India, Tibet, and Mongolia, and created more than 7,000 paintings which are on display in Moscow's Tretyakov Gallery and Oriental Art Museum, and other major museums around the world. Roerich traveled across America in the early 1920s and founded a museum in New York which still operates today on West 107th Street in Manhattan. In 2006, in a Sotheby's auction, Roerich's 'Lao-tze' fetched $2.2 million, the most-ever for a Roerich work.

Standing beside Kropotkinskaya Ploshchad (Square) is the magnificent and newly reconstructed **Cathedral of Christ Our Savior**. Its history is both long and unbelievably tragic. Founded in honor of the famous Russian victory over Napoleon, it took 45 years to build, but only one day to destroy. Alexander I stipulated that the cathedral was to express the scale of the czar's gratitude to Christ for the country's protection, and selected the site on the bank of the Moscow river. But it was not until 1830, under the rule of Nicholas I, that serious planning began. Designed by Konstantin Thon, the czar's favorite architect, its construction then continued through the reigns of yet two more rulers. Alexander III was present during its consecration on May 26, 1883. With a capacity of 15,000, the cathedral was the country's largest and most lavishly decorated shrine, symbolizing the glory of the Russian empire. The cathedral was over 30 stories high, bedecked with over half a ton of gold, and its walls made from 40 million bricks, Altai marble and Finnish granite. The gigantic roof cupola was composed of 176 tons of copper, topped by a cross three stories high. Fourteen bells hung in the four belfries, one weighing 27 tons. The central iconostasis was decorated with bejeweled icons, which reflected thousands of beeswax candles. Hundreds of frescoes were painted along the upper stories, and the lower portion was covered with 177 marble plates, each engraved with particular places, dates and heroes of the battles of Russian armies. This enormous shrine dedicated to the Son of God stood for 48 years—three years longer than it took to build.

Then, in 1931, to perpetuate the glory of the Soviet regime, Stalin decided to build his own glorified House of Soviets and selected the cathedral as its site. (Imagine if Mussolini had ordered St Peter's Basilica in Rome to be razed.) On July 18, 1931, workmen began removing thousands of priceless artifacts; they had four months to complete their assignment. (During this time, ten million would starve to death in the Ukraine, and Stalin started his first purges and labor camps.) Then began the demolition. Finally, on December 5, 1931, after one last detonation, a huge smoking mountain of rubble was all that remained of this wondrous accomplishment.

The final blueprints of 1933 had the planned House of Soviets higher than any American skyscraper at 420 meters (1,380 feet), topped with a 70-meter (230-foot) statue of Lenin (taller than the Statue of Liberty)—130 stories in all. The monument to Socialism was to look like an enormous multitiered wedding cake. But it turned out, ironically, that the swampy mound of floating bedrock could not support the proposed building. Stalin died in 1953, and in the end it was Khrushchev in 1959 who ordered a pit dug for a swimming pool utilizing the bemired foundation (by then a garbage dump), all that remained of the demolished cathedral. Until 1994 this remained the Moskva Open-Air Pool Complex. With the fall of the Soviet Union, the new government allocated nearly 360 million, underwritten by private donations and nongovernmental funds, to construct a near-replica of the original cathedral. It opened in 1997 after only two years of construction.

The interior walls are bedecked in white marble and covered with many golden icons. A gallery in the lower church holds a souvenir shop and an exhibit of the reconstruction process; open daily 10am–6pm. With a group tour, an elevator ride to the roof is given with a panoramic view of the city. The cathedral is open daily 8am–8pm. It stands near the Kropotkinskaya Metro station.

The feminist punk rock group, Pussy Riot, garnered much publicity, when in February, 2012, they were arrested while performing a political protest "prayer" within the Cathedral. They turned the performance into a music video entitled "Punk Prayer—Mother of God, Chase Putin Away!" Six months later, two members were convicted of "hooliganism motivated by religious hatred," and each was sentenced to two years imprisonment. Putin stated that the band had "undermined the moral foundations of the nation and got what they deserved." After serving 21 months, the two women were released on December 23, 2013 after the State Duma approved an amnesty (shortly before the Sochi Olympics).

A few areas behind the Kremlin and Cathedral are worth exploring. Head south from the Kremlin Alexandrov Gardens (or east along the river from behind the Cathedral), and across the Luzhkov Bridge (that spans a canal in the Moscow River) to a small Island, where the area has been nicknamed the "Trees of Love." A newlywed couple began the tradition by placing a padlock on the bridge's railing to symbolize the permanence of their union, and then threw the key into the river below. Within a few weeks time, the railings were covered with hundreds of locks, but the city, considering them graffiti, cut them off. But, then in response to the popularity, the city allowed scores of trees made of steel to be put up along the entire street upon which the newlyweds were allowed to place their locks. Each tree contains hundreds of locks, both old and new, and in many sizes, with inscriptions of the couples' names and wedding dates.

Directly behind the Cathedral, cross the pedestrian Patriarshy Most (Patriarch's Bridge) over the river; it has spectacular views of the city, both day and night. It leads over to Bersenevskaya Embankment to the hip and vibrant **Krasny Oktyabr** or Red October District. The warehouses once housed Russia's oldest candy factory, Okyabr (October). Originally, the factory was owned by French businessman, Adolphe Siu, who built it in 1844, and it provided the Russian court with cakes and candies until the 1917 Revolution. After the factory was nationalized, the red-brick facilities continued to produce chocolate for the Soviets. After privatization and a multi-million dollar facelift, the energetic district brings to mind the industrial glamor of London's Dockyards or New York's Tribeca area. The enormous factory complex, which occupies the westernmost part of Bolotny (Marshy) Island, is now chock full of restaurants, bars, cafés, hotels, shops, loft spaces and an array of swinging nightclubs, considered Moscow's Party Mecca. Proceeds from Bar Strelka (Spit of the Island) help fund the Strelka Institute for Media, Architecture and Design with an adjoining outdoor amphitheater. Art Akademiya boasts the largest bar-stand in Europe (it's also a club and art gallery), and the Lumière Brothers Gallery has outstanding photographic exhibits. Even *SNOB* magazine has its headquarters in the heart of the Red October complex. (For a list of restaurants and nightclubs, see Moscow Practical Information Section.)

Further south, across the river from the cathedral, looms the controversial bronze monument **Statue of Peter the Great**, erected in 1998 on an island near the Krymsky Bridge at a cost of $20 million. Then mayor Yuri Luzhkov hired Georgian-born Zurab Tsereteli (many nicknamed him the mayor's court sculptor) to create a statue in honor of the Russian navy's 300th anniversary. The 50-meter-high (164 feet) statue depicts Peter the Great in Roman attire standing on the prow of a sailing frigate. (Ironically, Peter hated Moscow and moved to St. Petersburg.) Shortly after the monument's unveiling a few critics tried to blow it up; seven bombs planted in the base of the monument were discovered and diffused. Yeltsin even called it a 'colossal eyesore,' and in 2009 it was voted one of the world's ugliest monuments.

A recipient of the prestigious Lenin Prize, Tsereteli (who turned 80 in 2014) was awarded the entire former West German Embassy (at 15 Bolshaya Gruzinskaya Street) by then Mayor Luzhkov as his private home and studio-museum. A prolific artist, he helped design the Okhotny Ryad Underground Shopping Mall and the Cathedral of Christ Our Savior. His works can also be viewed worldwide. His 39-foot-high sculpture, *Good Defeats Evil*, stands outside the United Nations Building in New York, a 1990 gift from the former Soviet Union.

From the Revolution until 1991, Prechistenka Street was called Kropotkinskaya (the Metro station still is), named after the revolutionary scholar, Pyotr Kropotkin (1842–1921), who lived nearby at 26 Kropotkinsky Lane. For centuries the street had been known as Prechistenka (Holy), after the Icon of the Holy Virgin kept in Novodevichy Convent. Many aristocratic families built their residences along this street. In the 18th and 19th centuries the area was one of the most fashionable places to live in Moscow. At number 10 lived Count Mikhail Orlov, a descendant of Catherine the Great's lover, Grigory. Note the outside plaque commemorating the Jewish Committee, which worked diligently for the Russian war effort against the Germans. They were later arrested and sent off to gulags by Stalin in 1952.The poets Zhukovsky and Davydov also lived on this street at number 17. At 9 Mansurovsky Pereulok (near the Palace of Fine Arts), in the yellow wooden house, another writer, Mikhail Bulgakov (1891–1940) lived for a while in the basement apartment. It is here that, in his famous novel *The Master and Margarita*, the master catches a glimpse of Margarita. (See Patriarch's Pond section on page 198 for more on where Bulgakov also lived.)

The mansion at 12 Prechistenka Street was built by Afanasy Grigorev. It now houses the **Alexander Pushkin Museum**, containing over 80,000 items connected with the celebrated poet. It also exhibits everything connected to his tragic dual, including his death mask and the pen with which he wrote his last poem. Open

10am–6pm, closed Mondays and last Friday of the month. Another Museum is at 53 Arbat where Pushkin briefly lived with his new bride, Natalia Gancharova.

Across the street, at number 11, is the **Leo Tolstoy Museum**, which includes a collection of the beloved writer's manuscripts, book editions, literature on his life, a documentary ('Tolstoy Alive') and recordings of his voice. At the entrance is a portrait of Tolstoy by Ilya Repin, painted only a year before the writer's death. Open 10am–5pm; closed Mondays.

In 1862, Leo Tolstoy (known as Lev Tolstoy in Russian) married Sofya Andreyevna with whom he fathered 13 children. Between 1863 and 1869 he wrote *War and Peace* (his wife hand-copied it seven times), and between 1874 and 1876 *Anna Karenina*. Two years later, Tolstoy published *Confession*, views on his newly embraced Christian moralities and commitment to individual rights and nonviolence (he even received interested letters from Mahatma Gandhi). The **Tolstoy Estate Museum**, where Tolstoy lived from 1882 to 1901, is at 21 Ulitsa Lva Tolstovo (Leo Tolstoy Street); open 10am–5pm; closed Mondays. Metro Park Kultury. (See also Yasnaya Polyana, page 282.)

The building that houses the **Russian Academy for Arts** and **Zurab Tsereteli Arts Gallery**, at number 19–21, was once the residence of Prince Dolgorukov. In 1998, a statue honoring Vasily Surikov (1848–1936) was placed in front of the academy to honor the 150th anniversary of the artist's birth, and an entire gallery of busts of outstanding Russian artists have joined Surikov. Open noon–7pm; closed Mondays. See: www.tsereteli.ru and eng.rah.ru, Prechistenka Street ends at the Garden Ring by a statue of Engels.

Walking east on the Garden Ring, at 2 Zubovsky Boulevard is the **Museum of the History of Moscow**, founded in 1896, which is housed in the buildings of the former **Provisions Warehouses**; the structures were designed by Stasov, and built by Shestakov in 1829–35. It has photographic displays of early Kremlin settlements to World War II reconstructions, and archeological finds (many from the early 1990s Kremlin Manezh Square excavations for the underground shopping center). The gallery has paintings and prints for sale. Open 10am–8pm; Thursdays 11am–9pm; closed Mondays.

The next street south of Prechistenka, running parallel, is Ostozhenka, one of Moscow's oldest streets dating from the 16th century. In those times, meadows of haystacks or *ostozhye* covered the area. During the era of Ivan the Terrible, many noble families lived in this area; and the side lanes or *pereulok* still carry their names, such as Lopukhinsky, Khilkov and Yeropkinsky. Walking east down from the Garden Ring, the three buildings of the former Provisions Warehouses still stand. The structures were designed by Stasov, and built by Shestakov in 1829–35. By the Park Kultury Metro (one of city's first stations) is the Diplomatic Academy of

Russia's Foreign Ministry, once a lyceum school. At number 49 is the empire-style mansion once owned by noblemen (the coat of arms is of the Loshakovsky-Vzevolzhky families), and later by the revolutionary, Bakunin. Whenever the writer Ivan Turgenev (*Fathers and Sons*) visited Moscow, he stayed at the gray-blue wooden dacha at number 37 with his mother, Varvara Petrovna. Here the writer observed scenes that he later described in his famous story *Mumu* about a deaf-mute janitor who drowned his dog *Mumu* on the orders of his eccentric and cruel landlady (based on his mother). This tiny structure is affectionately known as the *Mumu* House. Across the street, at number 38, is a classical palace, designed by architect Kazakov. It once belonged to General Yeropkin, who was famous for his many luxurious parties and banquets; the young Alexander Pushkin even attended a ball here. In 1806, it was bought by the Merchants' Society, and future author Goncharov (*Oblomov*) studied here in 1822–30. Today, the building houses the Moscow State Linguistic University. The mansion, at number 21, was built in 1901 in Art Nouveau style by the architect Kekushev for his family. A big lion once adorned the front façade. Located back off the street are the remains of the **Zachatyevsky (Conception) Nunnery**, founded in 1584. The interior ensemble and Church of St Anne were demolished during Stalinist times. The outside walls and Above-the-Gate Church (1696) have survived. The area is under restoration, and some nuns now live in the convent. Turning down 2nd Obydensky Lane towards the river brings the visitor to the **Church of Elijah Obydenny**, constructed in one day (*obydenny*), and later rebuilt in 1702. The Church is famous for never having closed down, not even during wars or purges. The 17th-century icons *Savior Not Made By Hands* and *The Icon of Our Lady of Kazan*, both painted by Simon Ushakov, still hang in the church's interior. Continue to 3rd Obydensky Lane onto Soymonovsky Passage, which leads to the **Pertsov House** at 1 Kursovoy Lane. It was built in 1901 (to the drawings of Malyutin—creator of the Matryoshka doll), for P. Pertsov, a notable collector and entrepreneur. The fairy-tale house has decorative panels of colored majolica depicting mythical characters, such as Yarilo (Sun), Serin birds, dragons and stars. It is now the home to the Russian Diplomatic Corps (GlavUpDK) who have meticulously restored the site.

Jump on the Metro and travel east across the river to Tretyakovskaya station. At number 10 Lavrushinsky Pereulok is the newly renovated **State Tretyakov Gallery**, which turned 160 in 2016. In 1856, the Moscow merchants, Pavel and Sergei Tretyakov, avid art patrons, began to collect works of Russian artists. In 1892, after the death of his brother, Pavel Mikhailovich founded Russia's first public museum of national art and donated their collection of 3,500 paintings, drawings & sculptures to the city. The Tretyakovs also helped fund the artists of the *Peredvizhniki* (Itinerants) Movement of realist artists, and purchased works by Kramskoi, Perov and Repin. After Pavel's death in 1898, the Tretyakov mansion was transformed into the museum. Today, the gallery houses one of the world's largest Russian and Soviet art collections from the 12th to the 20th centuries with well over 170,000 works displayed in over 60 rooms. These include the famous 12th-century Byzantine icon Virgin of Vladimir, Rublyov's *Old Testament Trinity* icon, Ilya Repin's *Ivan the Terrible and His Son*, Vasily Surikov's *Morning of the Execution of the Streltsy*, and the largest painting in the gallery, Alexander Ivanov's *The Coming of Christ*. The shop inside has a collection of guidebooks, art posters and postcards for sale. It is open 10am–6pm; Thursdays/Fridays 10am–9pm; closed Mondays, www.tretyakovgallery.ru/en.

A new branch of the museum has opened at 10 Krymsky Val; it is known as the **New Tretyakov Gallery**, which showcases the Russian avant-garde with pieces by Gancharova, Malevich, Kandinsky and Chagall. This is opposite Gorky Park near Oktyabrskaya Metro station. Behind the gallery is the **Art Muzeon Sculpture Park** with outdoor contemporary and historical pieces. It is also nicknamed the Park of the Fallen Heroes, for in the back stand statues of former Soviet icons, as Stalin, Dzerzhinsky, Sverdlov, Kalinin, Lenin, etc. (They were rounded up from around the city and put out to pasture here.) The park is open 10am–9pm.

This area is still known as Zamoskvarechiye—Across the Moskva River. A few blocks east of the Tretyakov Gallery is Bolshaya Ordynka Ulitsa. The medieval name stems from *orda*, which refers to the Mongol Golden Horde. This route once led to the Khan's southern headquarters. Moscow once boasted over 500 churches, and today the city's largest concentration of churches (over 15) is located within this small area. The **Church of the Virgin of All Sorrows**, at 20 Bolshaya Ordynka, dates from 1790. When the church was destroyed in the fire of 1812 (which destroyed 80 percent of the city), Osip Bovet designed a new one with a yellow rotunda in empire style in 1836; the Icon of the Virgin is in the left chapel. Orthodox services are held on Sunday mornings.

At 17 Bolshaya Ordynka is the **Anna Akhmatova Museum**, where the famous poet stayed during her visits to Moscow from Leningrad. (See Special Topic, page 675.)

At number 34 Bolshaya Ordynka is the **Convent of Saints Martha and Mary**, built by the sister of Empress Alexandra in 1908. After her husband Grand Prince Sergei was assassinated, the Grand Duchess Yelizaveta decided to retire to a convent of her own creation. The main Church of the Virgin Intercession was built by architect Alexei Shchusev in 1912, who later designed Lenin's mausoleum on Red Square. The interior frescoes were painted by Mikhail Nesterov; an icon restoration workshop is still on the grounds. After the Revolution Yelizaveta Fedorovna, along with other Romanov family members, was exiled to the Urals. In 1918 they were murdered by Bolsheviks in Alapaevsk (they were thrown down an old mine shaft and grenades were thrown in after them) a day after the royal family's execution in nearby Yekaterinburg. In 1992, the convent reopened in a nearby building.

At number 39 Bolshaya Ordynka a small church now houses the **Art Moderne Gallery** with exhibits by contemporary artists (closed Mondays). The **Church of St Catherine**, at number 60, was also reconstructed after a fire. Catherine the Great had Karl Blank build this church on the original site in 1767. One block west, at number 10 Shchetininsky Pereulok, look for the **Tropinin Museum and Moscow Artists of His Time** (open 10am–6pm, Thursdays noon–8pm, closed Tuesdays and Wednesdays). It houses works by 18th-century serf-artist, Vasily Tropinin, as well as other painters who studied at the Academy of Arts. Exhibits include landscape portraits and watercolors of old Moscow. Other churches can be found along the neighboring streets of Pyatnitskaya (numbers 4, 26, 51) and Vtoroy Kadashovsky, where at number 2 stands the five-domed Moscow Baroque **Church of the Resurrection**, built between 1687 and 1713, and funded by donations made from neighborhood weavers.

One block east, at 9 Malaya Ordynka Ulitsa and behind the whitewashed five-domed **Church of St Nicholas in Pyzhi** (built in 1670), is the **Ostrovsky House Museum** (open 12–7pm; Saturdays 1pm–9pm; closed Mondays/Tuesdays and the last Friday of the month), where one of Russia's best-known playwrights was born on March 31, 1823. The small wooden house is filled with photographs and pictures that document Moscow's theatrical history, especially from the Maly Theater where Alexander Ostrovsky worked from 1853 until his death in 1886. A statue of him stands outside the theater. Further east, on the corner of Novokuznetskaya and Vishnyakovsky streets stands the **Church of St Nicholas the Blacksmith** (1681). Rebuilt in the 19th century, it is known as St Nicholas of the Miracles because of its wonder-working icons; many people continue to faithfully pray before them. Running south, Novokuznetskaya ends at the Garden Ring and **Paveletsky Railway Station**, where trains lead to the Ukraine and lower Volga regions.

During their brief marriage in 1922, the famous American ballet dancer Isadora Duncan and her husband, Russian writer Sergei Yesenin (he spoke no English, she no Russian) lived nearby at 24 Bolshoi Strochenovsk; the house is now the **Yesenin Museum**. Yesenin, yet another poet who became disillusioned with socialism, committed suicide by hanging himself in 1925, aged 30. He penned his final words in his own blood, 'In this life, there's nothing new in dying.' Isadora was strangled two years later in the south of France when her long scarf wrapped itself around the wheel of the car she was driving. Open 10am–6pm; Wed/Thurs 1pm–9pm; closed Mondays and last Friday of each month. Audio guides in English are available. Metro Paveletskaya.

FABERGÉ

In 1842, during the reign of Nicholas I, Gustav Fabergé founded the first Fabergé workshop in St Petersburg. His son Peter Carl later extended the French family business to the cities of Moscow, Kiev, Odessa and London. These workshops produced a wealth of exquisite jewelry, clocks, cut glass, and other decorative objects made from gold, silver and semiprecious stones.

For over a century Fabergé crafted unique art objects for the imperial court. Master craftsmen like Mikhail Perkhin, Erik Kollin, Henrik Wigström and Julius Rappoport had their own Fabergé workshops and sometimes spent years designing and crafting a single piece of art.

The fabulous Fabergé eggs were a favorite gift presented by the Romanov family and other members of the aristocracy. The first Fabergé Easter egg was commissioned in 1885 by Alexander III. When Carl Fabergé proposed creating an Easter gift for the Empress Maria Fedorovna, the czar ordered an egg containing a special surprise. On Easter morning, the empress broke open what appeared to be an ordinary egg, but inside, a gold yolk contained a solid gold chick with a replica of the imperial crown and a tiny ruby egg. (The crown and egg are now lost.) The empress was so delighted by the egg that the czar ordered one to be delivered to the court each Easter. Alexander's son Nicholas II continued the Fabergé tradition and ordered two eggs each Easter, one each for his wife and mother.

On Easter morning 1895, Nicholas gave his mother a Fabergé egg decorated with diamonds, emeralds and a star sapphire. Hand painted miniatures depicting Danish scenes known to the dowager empress (the former Princess Dagmar of Denmark) were hidden inside what became known as the Danish Egg. By 1896, the year of the coronation of Nicholas II, virtually all the State's royal gifts came from Fabergé . (At the height of the firm's success, Fabergé had four shops in Russia, one in London, over 500 employees, and an additional catalog business). In 1900, Fabergé presented the imperial family with a silver egg that contained a golden replica of the Trans-Siberian Railway. The surface of the egg is engraved with a map of the route. The compartment windows are made of crystal, and the

headlamp on the locomotive is a ruby. Every detail is correct down to the destination boards and the labels on special compartments reserved for passengers. The train actually moves and can be wound with a tiny golden key. It is now kept in the Kremlin Armory.

The last work by Mikhail Evlampiyevich Perkhin (who died in 1903) was an egg composed of clover leaves and stems, constructed of diamonds and rubies. In 1909, Wigström and Nikolai made a crystal egg with two pear-shaped pendants set at each end. The interior contained a gold model of the royal yacht *Standart*, set inside a turbulent sea of rock crystal.

In 1911, eggs were presented for the royals' 15th anniversary. Alexandra received an egg decorated with scenes of the coronation, and the dowager empress was presented with an orange tree egg complete with a golden feathered bird that sang at the press of a button. Another egg is designed to look like a vase in rock crystal (which appears to be filled with water) with a pansy decoration. By pressing a button on the stem, its petals flowered revealing miniature portraits of Nicholas II's children.

When the Russian Exhibition was held in Moscow in 1882, Carl Fabergé received the Gold Medal (in 1887, a Moscow workshop was opened on Kuznetsky Most); later, in 1900, at the Exposition Universelle in Paris, he won the Grand Prix award along with the Legion of Honor. By 1915, there were more than 150,000 Fabergé pieces in circulation around the world; and by 1917 Fabergé had created 54 Imperial Eggs; today 47 survive. Forced to close the company after the Revolution, Carl Fabergé fled Russia and died in Switzerland in 1920. Today, one of the most extensive Fabergé collections in the world can be seen at the Armory Museum in the Moscow Kremlin.

In 2004, oils and metals magnate, Viktor Vekselberg, paid $100 million to a private collector for nine Fabergé eggs. After a $30 million renovation at St Peterburg's Shuvalov Palace, perched on the banks of the Fontanka River, it now houses this famous Fabergé collection. For its 250th anniversary in 2014, the Hermitage Museum in St Petersburg also opened its own exhibit of Fabergé jewelry pieces and sketches.

In 1908, Henrik Wigström made a nephrite egg whose interior was a model of Tsarskoye Selo's Alexander Palace in St Petersburg. The surface of the egg is encrusted with elegant gold garlands, decorated by miniature portraits in frames made out of small diamonds.

(left) Peter Klodt sculpted the four bronze horses that crown the roof; they pull the chariot of Apollo, patron of the arts.

(bottom) The Bolshoi Theater stands on Moscow's Theater Square. Built in 1824 to stage performances of opera and ballet, it premiered compositions by some of Russia's greatest composers.

(opposite top) In Moscow's Church of the Holy Trinity women donate their time to polish the golden iconostasis in preparation for an Orthodox service.

(opposite bottom) Standing in Moscow's Lubyanka Square is the infamous former KGB building, used by Felix Dzerzhinsky to house the Cheka police after the Revolution. (His statue, which stood in the middle of the square, was pulled down by crowds on the evening of the August, 1991, attempted coup.) With the collapse of the Soviet Union, the KGB was disbanded; today, the building is still occupied by current Intelligence Services.

Master icon painter Andrei Rublyov painted the Apostle Paul in the early 15th century. Its elongated proportions make the three-meter-long figure look slender and weightless. The blue lapis lazuli was a favorite color used by Rublyov. In 1918 it was discovered in a shed in the town of Zvenigorod where it once hung within the Assumption Cathedral's iconostasis. It now hangs in Moscow's Tretyakov Gallery.

Statue of the famous writer Alexander Pushkin (1799–1837) which stands on Moscow's Pushkin Square.

Modern graffiti art on Malaya Bronnaya Ulitsa in the Patriarch's Pond district. Since this was the home of Mikhail Bulgakov, who wrote the famous novel The Master and Margarita, *the colorful mural is entitled* Margarita *and depicts scenes from the story.*

(top) Moscow's original Cathedral of Christ Our Savior was built by Alexander I to commemorate Russia's 1812 victory over Napoleon. It was the country's largest and most lavishly decorated cathedral, which took 45 years to build. In 1931, Stalin ordered it razed to the ground. With the fall of the Soviet Union, the government allocated funds to construct a near-replica of the original cathedral, opened in 1997.

(bottom) From Moscow's Byelorussky Railway Station, opened in 1870, trains journey to points west in Europe. Additional local elektrichki trains run to the suburban areas of Borodino and Zvenigorod. Moscow has nine major train stations within the city.

Children of the Arbat, *a novel by Anatoly Rybakov (1911–1998), is the first book in a tetralogy on the lives of a group of friends and their families who live in the Arbat district of Moscow in the 1930's just prior to Stalin's Great Purges. The author himself suffered through these times, and his characters also experience the many political repressions.*

Today, the Old Arbat is one of the most popular shopping areas in Moscow. Everything from antikvariant *antique stores and portrait painters to ethnic restaurants and McDonald's are found along this bustling pedestrian thoroughfare.*

(above) Moscow's old Arbat district, an area dating back to the 15th century, is, today, one of the most popular meeting and shopping spots in the capital. The one-kilometer long cobbled pedestrian thoroughfare is filled with shops, cafes, theaters and galleries.

(right) A youthful audience gathered at a rock 'n' roll concert in Moscow's Gorky Park.

TVERSKAYA ULITSA

In the 18th century, Tverskaya Ulitsa was the main street of the city; today it is still one of the busiest in Moscow. The passage was named Tverskaya because it led to the old Russian town of Tver 256 kilometers (160 miles) north; from there it continued on to St Petersburg. From 1932 until 1990, the street was called Gorky, after Maxim Gorky, a famous writer during the Stalinist period. In 1990, the Moscow City Council voted to restore the street's old name. From the Kremlin to the Garden Ring, the thoroughfare is known as Tverskaya, and from the Garden Ring to Byelorussky Train Station it is called Tverskaya-Yamskaya (in the 17th century the Yamskaya Sloboda, or settlement, appeared outside the city's ramparts). From the train station it becomes Leningradsky Prospekt, which leads to Sheremetyevo International Airport.

In prerevolutionary days the street, once winding and narrow, was known for its fashionable shops, luxurious hotels and grandiose aristocratic mansions. The first Moscow trams ran along this street, and the first movie theater opened here. In 1932 (after being renamed Gorky), the thoroughfare was reshaped and widened, and now retains little of its former appearance.

It takes about an hour and a half to stroll the length of Tverskaya Street. You can also ride the Metro to various stops along it—Pushkinskaya, Mayakovskaya and Byelorusskaya—to shorten the time.

Tverskaya Street begins in front of Red Square at the **Manezhnaya Ploshchad**, known as the 50th Anniversary of the October Revolution Square from 1967 to 1990. The czar had his riding school, the *manège*, in this area. Okhotny Ryad Metro station is at the beginning of the street. On the corner is the elegant **National Hotel** with a splendid view of Red Square. Lenin lived here during the Revolution. In March 2002, developers began demolition of Moscow's 30-year-old Intourist Hotel, at number 3, and replaced the 22-story building with the 11-story **Ritz-Carlton**. Since the 1990s new shops have opened all along Tverskaya, including foreign clothing and cosmetic outlets, along with many other Russian stores.

Continuing along the street is the **Yermolova Drama Theater**, named after a famous stage actress, Maria Yermolova. Founded in 1925, the theater moved into the present building at number 5 in 1946. The Meyerhold Theater occupied the building from 1931 to 1938. At number 9 is a small branch of the Moscow Museum of Modern Art. **The Central Telegraph Building**, with its globe and digital clock, is on the corner of Gazetny Pereulok. The building, designed by Ilya Rerberg in 1927, is a post office and filled with numerous cafés.

Across the street at 3 Kamergersky Pereulok is the **MKhAT Moscow Art Theater** (today known as the Chekhov Moscow Artistic Academic Theater). Established by Stanislavsky and Nemirovich-Danchenko in 1897, it revolutionized theater throughout Europe. Stanislavsky wrote: "We declared war on all the conventionalities of the theater" and the "actors had to act like in real life." Here Stanislavsky practiced his 'method-acting' and staged many plays by Chekhov Gorky, Ibsen and Hauptmann. After Chekov's *The Seagull* premiered, the bird was put on the outside of the building as its emblem. Plays such as *The Three Sisters*, *The Cherry Orchard*, *The Lower Depths*, *Anna Karenina* and *Resurrection* marked a new epoch in the theater. In 1987, the building was reconstructed and now seats 2,000. Next door at 3A is the Moscow Arts Museum, founded in 1923.

In 2008, the **Prokofiev Museum** opened at no. 6 where the famous composer, Sergei Sergeyevich (1891–1953), lived from 1947–53. In the winter of 1946–1947, he finished work on Symphony No. 6 in E-flat minor, but in early 1948, the Union of Soviet Composers issued commands (via Stalin) that Prokofiev's music (among others) be banned from concert halls. (Most of his music was not performed in the Soviet Union until 1957.) Famous works include *Peter and the Wolf*, *Romeo and Juliet* and *Cinderella*. Open 11am–7pm, Sunday noon–6pm; Thursday noon–9pm; closed Mondays, Tuesdays, and last Wednesday of month. The pedestrian Kamerkersky Lane has a lively sidewalk scene, filled with cafés and restaurants.

The Aragvi Restaurant (on the site of the old Dresden Hotel, a favorite of Turgenev and Chekhov), specializing in Georgian cuisine, is on the next corner at Stoleshnikov and 6 Tverskaya. At the location since 1938, the historic building recently underwent extensive restoration. After the Arbat, Stoleshnikov became Moscow's second pedestrian lane. Craftsmen embroidered tablecloths for the czar's court in this lane over 300 years ago (stoleshnik means tablecloth in Old Russian).

At an early age, the famous writer, Vladimir Gilyarovsky (1853–1935) ran away from home to experience adventure and real life (at one time, he even worked as a *burkak*—a man who pulled boats by rope up the Volga). He eventually became a journalist (known as the 'King of Reporters'), who wrote about the common people. His real-life stories (as investigating Moscow's Khitrov market, one of the city's most criminally-infested areas) became best-selling thrillers. Gilyarovsky also wrote the popular *Moscow and the Muscovites* (1924); he lived across the street at number 9 for over half a century. The Stoleshniki Café, at number 6, is decorated in Old-Russian style. It is affectionately known as U Gilyarovskovo (At Gilyarovsky's) in tribute to the popular writer who was a regular here. Two rooms have been renovated in the café's 17th-century cellars: the Reporter's and Moscow and Muscovites halls. Here Gilyarovsky medals are awarded annually to the writers of the best articles about Moscow. At number 11, the pastry shop still uses old-fashioned ovens built into the walls, and has some of the best cakes in the city. The lane leads to Petrovka Street, a popular shopping area.

Stoleshnikov also leads to the octagonal-drum and small-cupola **Church of Saints Cosmas and Damian** (patron saints of blacksmiths), rebuilt in stone in 1626. Once a factory, it is now slowly being restored.

The southern side street Bryusov Pereulok leads to the terracotta-yellow **Church of the Resurrection** on Yeliseyevsky Lane. The church is said to have been built on the spot where Mikhail Romanov welcomed his father's return in 1619 after Polish imprisonment. It was reconstructed in 1629, and the church even remained open during Soviet years. Its interior is filled with icons, including a 16th-century copy of the Virgin of Kazan (believed responsible for the Russian 1613 victory over the Poles) and the icon of St George, the symbol of the city.

Tverskaya Ploshchad (Square) is marked by the equestrian **Statue of Yuri Dolgoruky**, founder of Moscow. It was erected in 1954 to mark the 800th anniversary of the city. Directly across the street stands the large red-brick and white-columned **Moscow City Council**, the city's legislature (and Mayor's office).The architect Matvei Kazakov designed the building as the residence for the first governor-general, appointed by Catherine the Great in 1782. Two of Moscow's governors were Prince Dmitri Golitsyn (1820–44), who paved the streets and installed water pipes, and Vladimir Dolgorukov, a descendant of Yuri Dolgoruky. In 1946, the building was moved back 14 meters (46 feet) and two more stories were added.

Further up Tverskaya is the Tsentralnaya Hotel at number 10, built in 1911 as the Hotel Lux. In the same building is the most famous bakery in Moscow, known as Filippov's, operating here for over a century. Next door is another popular food store, Gastronom Number 1, which recently reverted to its original name of **Yeliseyev's** (see Special Topic on page 595). Beautiful white sculptures and garlands line the shop front, and the gilded interior is filled with stained glass and colorful displays. It is worth a visit just to see the interior. At 14 Tverskaya is the **Ostrovsky Humanitarian Museum**, open 10am–6pm, Thursdays 1pm–9pm; closed Mondays and last Friday of month. Nikolai Ostrovsky (1904–1936) wrote *How the Steel Was Tempered*, and lived here from 1935 to 1936 (at the end of his life, he was blind, but continued to write). The collection is of the 200-year history of the house, including the Soviet author's books, photographs and letters. The Museum also focuses on the creativity of people with restricted abilities. Artistic expositions, evening concerts and literary salons often take place here as well.

Down the southern side street, at 6 Leontevsky Pereulok, is the **Stanislavsky Memorial Museum**, open 11am–6pm, Wednesdays/Fridays noon–7pm; closed Mondays and Tuesdays. The theater director lived here from 1922 until his death in 1938. On display are the living quarters of Stanislavsky and his wife, the opera hall and collections of books, costumes and theatrical props. The ballroom was converted into a theater; the first production was Tchaikovsky's *Evgeny Onegin*. A museum to Stanislavsky's partner, **Nemirovich-Danchenko** (1858–1943), is located nearby at 5 Glinishchevsky Pereulok, where he lived for the last five years of his life. Open 11am–5:30pm; closed Mondays and Tuesdays. At no 7 Leontevsky is the **Matryoshka Museum**, which exhibits Russian national crafts and showcases the history of Matryoshka or nesting dolls. The centrepiece is a 1m-high matryoshka with 50 dolls inside; souvenirs are for sale. In 1900, the building was bought by art patron Savva Morozov specifically to house a museum of folk art. Open 10am–6pm; closed Saturdays and Sundays. At 17 Tverskaya is the **Konenkov Memorial Studio**, open 11am–6pm; closed Mondays and Tuesdays. It displays marble, bronze and wooden statues by famous sculptor Sergei Konenkov (1874–1971), who lived and worked here from 1947 until his death.

As Tverskaya crosses the Boulevard Ring, it opens into **Pushkin Square** (Pushkinskaya Ploshchad). In the 16th century the stone walls of the Beli Gorod (White Town) stretched around what is now the Boulevard Ring; they were torn down in the 18th century. The Strastnoi Convent used to stand on what is now Pushkin Square—the square was originally called Strastnaya (until 1931), after the Convent of the Passion of Our Lord. The convent was demolished in the 1930s and in its place was built the Rossiya Movie Theater and the Izvestia news building. In the center of the square stands the **Statue of Alexander Pushkin**, by the sculptor Alexander Opekulin. It was erected in 1880 with funds donated by the public. Pushkin lived over a third of his life in Moscow, where he predicted, 'Word of me shall spread across the Russian land.' Dostoevsky laid a wreath on the statue at its unveiling. Today it is always covered with flowers and is a popular spot for open-air readings and political rallies. In 1999, to celebrate the 200th anniversary of Pushkin's birth, over 100 historical locations connected with the poet's life and work were restored throughout the city. Under the square are the three Metro stations: Tverskaya, Pushkinskaya and Chekhovskaya.

Behind the square is the 3,000-seat Pushkinsky Cinema, built in 1961 for the 2nd International Moscow Film Festival. The venue is now a complex for staging musicals. Walking up Malaya Dmitrovka Ulitsa (behind *Izvestia*) leads to the white-green tent-roofed **Church of Nativity of Our Lady in Putniki**, built between 1649 and 1652. Legend has it that a noblewoman gave birth in her carriage as she passed this spot and later commissioned a church to honor the Nativity. When it burned down, Czar Alexei I donated money to have it rebuilt, along with a chapel dedicated to the icon that prevented fires, Our Lady of the Burning Bush, which is in the chapel. Behind it was once a rest house where travelers or *putniki* stayed.

Across the street from Pushkin Square is the world's largest and busiest **McDonald's** fast-food outlet, with 800 seats, 27 cash registers and 250 employees serving up to 50,000 people a day (open daily 8am–midnight). When the restaurant opened, Russians automatically stood in the longest queue—in Russia a longer queue was indicative of better quality merchandise. Brochures had to be distributed explaining that each queue gave the same service and food. As part of an agreement with the Moscow City Council, McDonald's was required to purchase or produce its raw materials in Russia, resulting in a vast production and distribution complex on the outskirts of the city. After decades of waiting hours in long lines, the country enthusiastically embraced fast food.

To give an idea of the extent of business enterprise developing in the early 1990s, there was even a black market for hamburgers. Entrepreneurs would stand in line for hours to purchase eight Big Macs each (the maximum allowed per person), eat one, and then sell the rest at a huge profit to those not willing to wait. They earned more in one day than a physicist did in a month. Today black-market burgers are bust and the long lines gone, but the grounds surrounding the restaurant are still a popular meeting place.

On McDonald's yellow-brick building can be seen a small bust in tribute to Soviet cinema star Lyubov Orlova (1902–1975), who was a film cultural icon in the 1930s and 40s. In 1936, she received a State prize for her role in *Circus* as US circus artist Marion Dixon. But it was her role as the postwoman, Dunya, in the comedy *Volga-Volga* in 1938 (one of Stalin's favorite films), that made her a star. Her last apartment was in this building.

The **Contemporary History Museum** is at 21 Tverskaya (formerly known as the Revolution Museum until 1992). This mansion was built for Count Razumovsky in 1780 by the architect Manelas. In 1832, it was rebuilt by Adam Menelaws after a fire, and was bought by the Angliisky (English) Club, formed in 1772 by a group of foreigners residing in Moscow. The club's members (all men) were made up of Russian aristocratic intellectuals and included the best minds in politics, science, art and literature. One member of the wealthy Morozov family gambled away one million rubles in a single evening. Tolstoy once lost 1,000 rubles in a card game in the 'infernal' room. Pushkin wrote of the club in his long poem *Evgeny Onegin*. When Tatiana arrived in Moscow, Evgeny described 'the two frivolous-looking lions' at the gates. The last bolshoi gala at the club was a banquet thrown for Nicholas II to celebrate the 300th anniversary of the Romanov dynasty in 1913. The museum, opened in 1924, exhibits over a million items from the 1905 and 1917 revolutions and the 1991 coup attempt. The highlight is the collection of propaganda posters. The gun outside was used to shell the White Guards in 1917. Also on display here is a tram that burned during the 1991 attempted coup. The museum is open

10am–6pm, Thursday noon–9pm, Sat/Sun 11am–7pm; closed Mondays, and last Friday of month. For more info: eng.sovr.ru Next to the museum, at number 23, is the **Stanislavsky & Nemirovich-Danchenko Drama Theater**. Metro Chekhovskaya.

THE PRESNYA AREA AND PATRIARCH'S POND—BULGAKOV'S HAUNT

Turn west off Tverskaya by McDonald's and head along Bolshaya Bronnaya Ulitsa. This leads to Malaya Bronnaya—turn right and at number 30 you will find Patriarch's Pond, one of the oldest and most charming residential areas of Moscow. This land was once known as Patriarskaya Sloboda, the Russian Orthodox patriarch's land in the 17th and 18th centuries. The pond was dug to provide the dining tables with plenty of fish. Later, it was occupied by artisans—the bronnaya (armorers) and the *kozia* (wool spinners). The writer Mikhail Bulgakov (1891–1940) set his well-known masterpiece *The Master and Margarita*, in this neighborhood. (The novel begins with "...at the hour of sunset, on a hot spring day, two citizens appeared in the Patriarch's ponds park...") Completed in 1938, and about the Devil's influence on corrupt Soviet authorities, it was not allowed published until 1966.

Between 1921 and 1924, Bulgakov, who was voted by Russians as one of their most influential 20th-century writers, lived just around the corner in a communal apartment at number 10 Bolshaya Sadovaya Ulitsa—in the beige building, now the **Bulgakov Museum**. (He describes in his novel, 'it was painted cream, and stood on the ring boulevard behind a ragged garden fenced off from the pavement by a wrought-iron railing.') It is nicknamed the "Odd Flat," where in *The Master and Margarita*, Woland took up residence with his court. (Bulgakov's third wife, Yelena Shilovskaya, was the inspiration for Margarita.) Go left at the back of the yard and notice the graffiti written by fans on the stairwell—a memorial to the writer who died in disgrace in 1940 and was described in the *Soviet Encyclopedia* as a 'slanderer of Soviet reality'. A black cat hangs in the courtyard. The museum displays personal items, posters and other illustrations of his work. Readings and concerts are often held in the space. Open 1pm–11pm. www.dombulgakova.ru. A monument to the author and his characters stands near the pond. A popular TV Mini-series version of The Master and Margarita was made in 2005 and aired throughout the country.

A **Monument to Ivan Krylov** (1769–1844), a popular children's fabulist, stands in the square. In winter, there is ice-skating and in summer boating. Across the street from the pond, at number 28, the Café Margarita is lined with bookshelves and often hosts live music in the evenings.The **Moscow Drama Theater** is at 4 Malaya Bronnaya. Formed in 1950, the theater seats 850.

In 2002, at the intersection of Bolshaya and Malaya Bronnaya streets, a monument to Russia's famous Jewish writer Sholom Aleichem (nom de plume of Sholom Rabinovich) was unveiled. The column of the statue features some of the favorite characters from his novel Errant Stars (basis for the musical *Fiddler on the Roof*). The **Lyubavicheskaya Synogogue** is at no. 6 Bolshaya Bronnaya.

The southern end of Bolshaya Bronnaya intersects with Ulitsa Spiridonovka, and at number 7 is the newly restored **Morozov Mansion**, a magnificent structure with an incredible history. In April 1893, Zinaida Morozova, wife of prominent businessman Savva Morozov, bought this nobility compound in the upmarket section of the old Arbat. Savva, grandson of a serf-peasant, became a millionaire textile merchant and popular patron of the arts. (Morozov funded Stanislavsky's Moscow Arts Theater.) The Morozovs commissioned the famous architect Fyodor Shekhtel to redesign their house in medieval Gothic style, completed in 1898. The attention to detail is astounding—gargoyles, griffins, stone carvings and cast-iron railings decorate the exterior. For the interior, Mikhail Vrubel created enormous stained-glass windows. Pavel Schmidt contributed hand-carved wooden staircases and furniture, and great sandstone fireplaces and crystal chandeliers came from the Zakharov and Postnikov workshops. Savva Morozov, a member of the Old Believer sect, backed the socialists. He even hid revolutionaries within the many corners of his home and secretly funded Lenin's newspaper *Iskra* (The Spark). After the bloody consequences of the 1905 Revolution, Savva Morozov could no longer live with the conflicts—bouts of industrial strikes in his factories coupled with his promotion of reforms—he committed suicide by shooting himself in the head.

In 1909 his wife sold the house to Mikhail Riabushinsky, who added art works by artist Konstantin Bogarevsky. The Riabushinsky family was forced to flee to America in 1918. Under Stalin, the mansion became the People's Commissariat for Foreign Affairs. In 1995, a large fire broke out, and many parts of the structure were severely damaged. For two years the Russian diplomatic firm UpDK painstakingly restored the entire building. Today it serves as the House of Receptions for the Ministry of Foreign Affairs.

At no 4 is the **Icon House on Spiridonovka** that contains a collection of over 2000 pieces of iconography, some part of a collection of the last Czar, Nicholas II. Often evening concerts are held here. Open noon–10pm; closed Mondays. (For more information on the Museum of Russian Icons near the Taganskaya Metro, see www.russikona.ru/en.)

Continuing south down Spiridonovka leads to Malaya Nikitskaya and the **Gorky House Museum** at number 6. Maxim Gorky (1868–1936), known as the 'Father of Soviet Literature', lived here for five years before his death. It was Stalin who gave Gorky this house as a meeting place for the union of writers and artists, but the writer felt uncomfortable here, 'like a bird in a golden cage'. The writer's real name was Alexei Maximovich Peshkov; he later adopted the pen name Gorky (meaning bitter). Orphaned in childhood, Maxim was put to work at the age of 11, and attempted suicide eight years later in 1887. He became widely known after writing his 1899 Sketches and Stories, and the poem *Song of the Stormy Petrel* in 1901, and followed with the plays *The Lower Depths* (centered in Moscow's destitute Myasnitskaya or Butcher area) and *Summer Folk*. In 1906, to avoid post-revolution crackdowns (he had already been exiled to Siberia in 1901), Gorky journeyed to the United States supported by Mark Twain. While there, he wrote his most famous work, *Mother*, the first example of socialist realist literature. Although it is suspected he was poisoned on Stalin's orders, the dictator still honored Gorky by placing his ashes in the Kremlin wall.

In 1902, the architect Shekhtel was commissioned by a member of the Riabushinsky banking dynasty, Stepan Pavlovich, to design the house in art-nouveau style; it was completed four years later. Encompassing style-moderne themes of nature and fluidity, the mansion was given stained-glass windows, a glass roof and flowered bas-reliefs. The exquisite staircase resembles a giant crashing wave, which spills out onto the parquet floors. Today the library has over 10,000 volumes and the parlor looks as it did when Gorky lived here. A superb collection of carved ivory is in the bedroom, and many of the writer's books and letters are on display. The museum is open 11am–5:30pm; closed Mondays, Tuesdays, and last Thursday of the month. (The Gorky Literary Museum is at 25 Povarskaya Ulitsa, near Arbatskaya Metro station.)

Next to the Gorky House, at 2/6 Spiridonovka, is the **Alexei Tolstoy House Museum**. This is not the Leo Tolstoy of *War and Peace*, but a distant relative. This Tolstoy wrote *Ivan the Terrible, Peter the Great*, and the well-known trilogy about the Revolution, *The Road to Calvary*, completed in 1941; a year later it was awarded the Stalin Prize. His granddaughter Tatyana Tolstaya is a well-recognized contemporary author. Currently entrance is permitted only with reserved visits.

On the other side of Gorky House stands the white Empire-style **Church of the Grand Ascension**, on the western side of Nikitskiye Vorota Square. It was here in February 1831 that Alexander Pushkin married Natalia Goncharova (who later was the cause of the St Petersburg duel in which Pushkin was killed). It is said that during the ceremony a crucifix fell from a wall and candles mysteriously blew out; an omen not taken lightly. The church, still in the process of being restored, is open for worship. At 12 Malaya Nikitskaya stands the 18th-century classical **Bobrinsky Mansion**, originally built by the Dolgoruky family and inhabited by Catherine the Great's illegitimate son with Grigory Orlov. Bobrinsky's descendants lived here up until the Revolution.

TVERSKAYA-YAMSKAYA ULITSA

At the intersection of Tverskaya and the Sadovoye Koltso (Garden Ring) is **Triumfalnaya Ploshchad**. In the 18th century the square was marked by triumphal arches used to welcome czars and returning victorious armies. Often the square has been closed due to demonstrations by regular protests held on the 31st of each month. Known as Strategy-31 (named after Article 31 of the Russian Constitution which allows free assembly), protest groups often gather to draw attention to the crackdown on civil liberties. Banners herald, "Free Political Protestors, "Russia Without Putin!"

On the corner of the square stands a large building with ten columns—the **Tchaikovsky Concert Hall** (built for Meyerhold's Theater in the 1930s), where orchestras and dance ensembles perform. The Moscow Stars and Winter Festivals also take place here. The Mayakovskaya Metro station is in front of the Hall. Directly behind it, at number 2, is the circular-domed building of the **Satire Theater**, founded in 1924, whose productions have ranged from *The Cherry Orchard* to the *Three-Penny Opera*. Across the street is the **Peking Hotel**, housing the very first Chinese restaurant in Moscow.

A statue of the poet Vladimir Mayakovsky (1893–1930) stands in the square at Mayakovskaya Metro station. At number 43 is the House of Children's Books, and at number 46 the Exhibition Hall of Artist Unions. A ten-minute walk northeast to 4 Ulitsa Fadeyeva is the **Glinka Museum of Musical Culture**, opened in 1943. The museum, named after the famous composer Mikhail Glinka, has a large collection of musical instruments (over 3,000 pieces), rare recordings and unique manuscripts of famous composers, such as Tchaikovsky, Shostakovich and Glinka himself; open 11am–7pm; Thursday noon–9pm; Sunday 11am–6pm; closed Mondays.

Three streets east around the Ring, at 3 Delegatskaya Ulitsa, is the **Museum of Decorative and Folk Art** with unique displays (over 40,000 pieces) of centuries-old Russian, applied art, wood work, pottery, porcelain, rare books, toys, samovars, and traditional handicrafts. It also exhibits an impressive collection of *Palekh* hand-painted boxes. Open 10am–6pm; Thursday 10am–9pm, Saturday 11am–7pm; closed Tuesdays, and last Monday of the month. Visit: www.vmdpni.ru.

Tverskaya-Yamskaya Street ends at Byelorusskaya Ploshchad, also called Zastava (Gate) Square, which was the old site of the Kamer-Kollezhsky gates on the road to Tver. At the center of the square is a **Monument to Maxim Gorky** (1868–1935), erected in 1951. Trains from the **Byelorussky Railway Station**, opened in 1870, journey to points west, including Warsaw, Berlin, Paris and London. The Byelorusskaya Metro station is in front. Here Tverskaya-Yamskaya Street turns into Leningradsky Prospekt, which runs all the way to Sheremetyevo International airport. The **Museum of Russian Impressionism**, devoted solely to the history of Russian Impressionism and founded by private collector Boris Mints, is located on the site of the former Bolshevik Factory, a significant city landmark. Founded in 1855 as a confectionary factory by Adolf Sioux, a French industrialist, it was the first building in Moscow to have electric light. From Belorusskaya Metro, walk 10 minutes northwest towards Tverskaya and the Hippodrome to the prominent four-hectare site facing Leningradsky Prospekt.

Along Begovaya Ulitsa (Running Street) is the **Moscow Hippodrome**, a race course. It was built a century ago in Empire style and frequented by the Russian aristocracy. Equestrian sports were very popular in Czarist Russia. By 1905, over 2,000 horses were competing in over 50 hippodromes, and the total prize money reached the sum of 3 million rubles, equal to the value of two tons of gold. Today, the Hippodrome is open three or four times weekly, drawing up to 20,000 people for the nine daily races. It annually hosts the International President's Cup equestrian tournament. During off hours, horses can be hired. In nearby Begovaya Lane, find the small archway designed by Klodt, who also crafted the famous horse sculptures on St Petersburg's Anichkov bridge. A little farther up, at 32 Leningradsky, the **Romany Gypsy Theater** opened in 1931. Seating over 800, the theater focuses on gypsy national culture. The **Moscow Chamber Musical Theater** is at 71 Leningradsky Prospekt.

Two blocks north and two blocks east from the Novoslobodskaya Metro station, at 19 Obratsova St, is the **Jewish Museum of Tolerance**, run by the Moscow Jewish community, making use of all the converted wide-open interiors for its exhibits of Jewish life in Moscow from Czarist to contemporary times; with memorial galleries, a library and media room, store and café. (The large space, once a Soviet-era bus depot, was designed in 1926 by constructionist architect Konstantin Melnikov.) Open noon–10pm, Friday 10am–3pm; closed Saturdays. www.jewish-museum.ru/en.

About another kilometer walk east is the **Central Museum of the Armed Forces**, on 2 Sovyetskoi Armii Ulitsa, which covers the history of the Soviet and Russian military since 1917. Over 800,000 items are on display. Open 10am–5pm; closed Mondays and Tuesdays. From here you can take the Metro or a bus to return to the city center.

ULITSA VOZDVIZHENKA AND NOVY (NEW) ARBAT

In 1991, Kalinin Prospekt was divided into two different streets. Vozdvizhenka Street (the name stems from the 16th-century Krestovozdvizhensky or Church of the Exaltation) runs from the Kremlin's Kutafya Tower (by the Alexandrov Gardens) to Arbatskaya Ploshchad (Arbat Square). Novy Arbat begins at Arbat Square and continues to the Novoarbatsky Most (Bridge). Here Novy Arbat becomes Kutuzovsky Prospekt and later the Minsk Highway.

The old route was known as Novodvizhenskaya; it stretched from the Kremlin to the outer walls of the city. A new thoroughfare was built along this former road and from 1963 to 1991 it was named Kalinin, after a leader of the Communist Party, Mikhail Kalinin. The old section of the prospekt runs from the Kremlin to the Boulevard Ring, where the more modern part begins.

The road starts by a large gray building off Mokhovaya—the Russian State Library (see page 172). At number 5 is the **Shchusev Architectural Museum** exhibiting the history of Russian architecture. The museum was founded in 1935 and the collection contains over a million items; open 11am–7pm, Thursdays 1pm–9pm; closed Mondays. The first part of the street still contains a few 18th-century buildings. At number 7 is the former **Monastery of the Holy Cross**. The house at number 9 belonged to Tolstoy's grandfather, Count Volkonsky, upon whom he based a character in *War and Peace*. At the corner of Romanov Pereulok is an early 18th-century mansion that belonged to a member of the wealthy Sheremetyev family. Across the street at number 5 is an old mansion of the Tolyzin estate, built by Kazakov. Many prominent Soviet officials also lived along this street, such as Frunze, Voroshilov, Kosygin and Khrushchev. The nearest Metro station is Alexandrovsky Sad.

At number 16 is the white, medieval former mansion of the merchant Arseny Morozov who, in 1899, hired his friend, the designer Mazyrin, to model his residence after a 16th-century Moorish castle they had seen while visiting Portugal; each room was decorated in a different style from Greek to English Gothic. After the Revolution it was turned over to the Union of Anarchists. In 1959, it became the **House of Friendship**, where delegations of foreign friendship societies meet. Nearby, the eight-story building with one turret was built in the 1920s as the first Soviet skyscraper in constructivist style. Near the Arbatskaya Metro station, on the square, is a **Monument to Nikolai Gogol**, standing in front of the house where the writer lived.

STARY (OLD) ARBAT

On the southwest corner of Arbat Square is the Prague Restaurant, marking the entrance to one of the city's oldest sections, the **Arbat**. Long ago the Arbat Gates led into Moscow. *Arbad* is an old Russian word meaning beyond the town walls. Alternatively, some believe the word could stem from the Mongol word *arba*, a sack to collect tributes; the ancient 'Arab' settlements ("rabat" meaning suburban outskirts); or the Latin *arbutum*, cherry, because of the cherry orchards that were once in the area. There is one other proposed origin: a creek named Chertory, the Devil's Creek, once meandered or 'hunchbacked' through the vicinity, which was quite damp and boggy. When a small one-kopek candle started a fire in the All Saints Church and burnt it and the rest of Moscow to the ground in 1365, many thought the area cursed. The Russian word *khorbaty* means hunchbacked place.

The area was first mentioned in 15th-century chronicles. It lay along the Smolensk Road, making it a busy trade center. Many court artisans lived here in the 16th century; in the 19th century many wealthy and educated people chose to live in the Arbat. Today the street is a cobbled pedestrian thoroughfare about one kilometer (two-thirds of a mile) long, and one of the most popular meeting and shopping spots in Moscow. Along with its shops, cafés, art galleries, concert and theater halls and a museum tracing the history of the area, are portrait painters, performance artists and even demonstrators. It is also a frequent site for festivals and carnivals. At its eastern end, notice the **Wall of Friendship and Peace**, composed of hundreds of individually painted tiles. Chekhov once said that 'the Arbat is one of the most pleasant spots on Earth'. It is definitely worth a stroll.

The colorful buildings lining the pedestrian mall and its side streets have a rich and romantic history. Many poems, songs and novels, such as Anatoly Rybakov's *Children of the Arbat*, have been written about this area. The czar's stablemen once lived along Starokonivshenny (Old Stable) Lane. An old church stood on the corner of Spasopeskovsky Pereulok (Savior-on-the-Sand Lane). Other small streets have the names Serebryany (Silversmith), Plotnikov (Carpenter) and Kalashny (Pastrycook). After a leisurely stroll, you will better understand the lyrics to a popular song: 'Oy, Arbat, a whole lifetime is not enough to travel through your length!'

At 7 Arbat is the Literary Café, a favorite of both Mayakovsky and Isadora Duncan's husband, the Russian poet Yesenin, in the 1920s. The niece of Tolstoy, Countess Obolenskaya, lived at number 9; it is now an antique store. Several other *antikvariant*, souvenir shops and book stores are located along the street. After passing the 1,000-seat **Vakhtangov Theater** (founded in 1921), at number 26, turn right up Bolshoi Nikolopeskovsky Pereulok. At number 11 is the **Scriabin Museum**, home of the famous Russian composer and pianist from 1912 to 1915. Here Alexander Nikolayevich composed his Eighth, Ninth and Tenth Sonatas, Two

Dances "Garlands," "the Dark Flame" Composition 73 and Five Preludes Composition 74. His concert programs, photographs and books are on display, along with recordings of his music; each year the Museum hosts a competition to award scholarships to young musicians. Concerts of classical and contemporary music are held here as well as recitals and readings. Open 10am–4pm, Wed/Fri noon–6pm; closed Mondays, Tuesdays, and last Friday of the month.

Walking a few short blocks west to Spasopeskovsky Pereulok leads to the **Spaso House**, residence of the US ambassador (since 1933); it was originally built in neo-Empire style by banker Vtorov in 1913. (It was also the scene of Satan's Ball in Bulgakov's *Master and Margarita*.) Along this street notice the Church of the Savior-on-the-Sand, built in 1711, and currently under restoration. The artist Polenov depicted its bell tower in his famous painting "Moscow Courtyard".

Crossing the Arbat, continue a block south down to 10 Krivoarbatsky Pereulok and the **Melnikov House**. In 1927–29, the avant-garde architect Konstantin Melnikov built this house in constructivist style for his family, and lived here until his death in 1974. (Melnikov designed Lenin's glass sarcophagus.) The exterior consists of two honeycombed concrete cylinders cut into each other and connected by hexagonal windows, and the inside stories are linked by a spiral staircase. Today, the Russian Avant-garde Heritage Preservation Foundation is attempting to preserve the masterpiece and establish a Melnikov House Museum. www.melnikovhouse.org. One block further south leads to the **Herzen Museum** at 27 Pereulok Sivtsev Vrazhek (*vrazhek* means gully—once the River Sivtsev ran through a gully in this location). The writer Alexander Herzen (1812–70) lived here in this Empire-style building from 1843 to 1846. Here he wrote *Dr Krupov, Magpie and the Thief* and his famous novel *Who is to Blame?* For these revolutionary views he was exiled in 1847. From London, Herzen wrote his radical political magazine *Kolokol* (The Bell) and smuggled copies into Russia. His *Letters on Nature*, according to Lenin, put him alongside 'the most prominent thinkers of his time'. (Herzen was born in the house at 25 Tverskoi Boulevard.) The museum is open 11am–6pm, Thursday 2pm–8pm; closed Mondays, and last day of month.

At 53 Arbat is the blue and white stucco **Pushkin House Museum**. Here, in this Empire-style mansion, in 1831, the famous writer lived with his new bride Natalia Goncharova. (Across the street is a gilded statue of the couple by Zurab Tsereteli.) Exhibits are on his marriage and Moscow activities. (Tchaikovsky also lived here in 1875.) Open 11am–6pm, Thursday noon–9pm; closed Mondays, Tuesdays, and last Friday of the month. In connection with the 200th anniversary of Alexander Pushkin's birth in 1999, the city created a 'Pushkin Path' that leads from this house to the Pushkin Museum on Prechistenka Street. Digital copies of its vast collection can be viewed online at: www.russianprints.ru and www.britishprints.ru.

Another native of the Arbat was popular poet and singer Bulat Okudzhava, who coined the word *arbatstvo* or the Arbat spirit. "The Arbat to me is not just a street. It is a place that embodies Moscow and Russia." In the 1960's, like Bob Dylan, Okudzhava inspired a whole new movement in songwriting and folk singing. A monument in tribute to Okudzhava was put up on the corner of Plotnikov Lane, next to the house where the poet was born.

The Arbat ends at the Garden Ring Road and Smolenskaya Ploshchad where one of Stalin's seven Gothic skyscrapers stands, now the MID or Ministry of Foreign Affairs.

NOVY ARBAT

The avenue from Arbat Square on the Boulevard Ring to the Novoarbatsky Bridge is known as Novy (New) Arbat, the main western thoroughfare of the city. The shops and flats in this area were built during Khrushchev's regime in the 1960s; and were designed by Moscow's chief architect Mikhail Posokhin. Across the street from the Prague Restaurant (one of the oldest in Moscow) is the **Church of Simon Stylites** with colorful *kokoshniki* gables. It was here in 1801 that Prince Nikolai Sheremetyev married serf-actress Praskovia Zhemchugova-Kovalyova. Theirs is one of Russia's most romantic love stories. She, a daughter of a serf blacksmith, worked as an actress on the Sheremetyev estate in Kuskovo. They fell in love in 1789 and ten years later Nikolai granted her freedom. Sadly, two years after the marriage, Praskovia died in childbirth. Today the church has an exhibition hall, and is open for worship.

Heading north, down the side street behind the church, leads to the **Lermontov Memorial House-Museum** at 2 Malaya Molchanovka. Mikhail Lermontov (1814–41) lived here with his grandmother from 1829 to 1832, and while studying at Moscow University, wrote about 100 poems and plays. He is best known for the 1840 prose-novel *A Hero of Our Time*; the main character Grigory Pechorin is one of the great romantic heroes in modern literature. For a poem criticizing the court's connivance in the death of Pushkin, Lermontov was exiled to the Caucasus by Nicholas I. Like Pushkin, Lermontov also died in a duel—over a trivial quarrel with a fellow infantry officer—he was shot through the heart on July 15, 1841. Open 11am–4pm, Wed/Fri 2pm–5pm; closed Mondays and Tuesdays. (The museum may be closed for on-going restoration.)

Next to the church, at 8 Novy Arbat, is **Dom Knigi** (House of Books), the city's largest bookstore (open 9am–11pm; weekends 10am–11pm). Here books, posters, and even antiques and icons are for sale. On the same side of the street is the **Oktyabr Cinema** at number 24. It is one of the largest multiplex cinemas in Russia, with 11 auditoriums and seats 3,000.

A series of shops and cafés line the left side of Novy Arbat. On the second floor of number 19 is the **Irish House**, where you can find most Western food products and the **Shamrock Bar**. The block ends at the 2,000-seat Metelitsa entertainment complex (open 24 hours, with loud music and floor shows).

Novy Arbat crosses the Garden Ring at Novinsky Bulvar (Boulevard) and ends at the river. The **White House** or Beli Dom, once headquarters of the Russian Parliament, stands to the right. It was the famous scene of two coup attempts. In August 1991, a number of conservative plotters tried to overthrow the Gorbachev government while he was vacationing in the Crimea. Boris Yeltsin, who became the nation's hero, climbed atop a tank in front of the building and rallied thousands of demonstrators to oppose the coup's collaborators. The events of these days led to the fall of the Soviet Union four months later. Then two years later, in September 1993, after Yeltsin suspended the constitution for three months, Parliament mutinied and Yeltsin's deputy, Alexander Rutskoi, declared himself 'acting president'. For eleven days, Rutskoi and his 300-member unofficial entourage took control of the White House until army tanks shelled them into submission. After the building's restoration, the Moscow patriarch came by and blessed it. Today it is officially called the House of Government of the Russian Federation, and the Prime Minister has an office here.

Further west, on the same side of the river, is the **World Trade Center (WTC)** and the Crowne Plaza Moscow Hotel; the complex was originally built with the help of Armand Hammer. Looming in the distance are the steel and glass structures of the new international business center. The large twin-tower skyscrapers are known as the **City of Capitals**, symbolizing Moscow and St Petersburg. The "Moscow Tower" was the tallest in Europe with a height of 302 meters (990 feet) until the construction of the The Shard in London exceeded its height in January 2012. Then, in November, 2012, the Moscow Mercury City Tower overtook The Shard as Europe's tallest building at 339 meters (1112 feet). The Empire skyscraper offers a 40-minute tour and a spectacular panoramic view from the 58th floor. Open weeknights 6pm–10pm or on weekends from 11am–10pm; sign up online at smotricity.ru. The closest metro is Vystavochnaya.

KUTUZOVSKY PROSPEKT

After crossing the Novoarbatsky Bridge, Novy Arbat becomes Kutuzovsky Prospekt, named after the Russian General Mikhail Kutuzov (1745–1813), who fought against Napoleon. The building on the right with the star-spire is the Radisson Royal Hotel (formerly the Ukraine Hotel). This was the last of Stalin's 'seven sisters' skyscrapers to be built. On the next corner south of the hotel is the **Hero City of Moscow Obelisk**. Troops left from this point in 1941 to fight the advancing German army.

The obelisk stands at the junction with Bolshaya Dorogomilovskaya, along which stands the **Kievsky Railway Station** (with a Metro station). Kievsky, which celebrates its 100th anniversary in 2018, was once the largest station in Europe (this honor is now held by Moscow's Kazansky Station), and is still considered the city's most beautiful. Designed in Byzantine-revival style by Rerberg and Shukhov, it is flanked by a 51-meter (167-foot) high clock-tower. The train terminal handles up to 35,000 passengers a day.

A five-minute walk from Kutuzovskaya Metro station is the large circular building at number 38 Kutuzovsky—the **Battle of Borodino Panorama Museum**, open 10am–6pm, Thursday 1pm–9pm; closed Fridays and last Thursday of the month. The 68 cannons in front were captured from Napoleon. In 1912, to commemorate the 100th anniversary of the war, Franz Roubaud was commissioned to paint scenes of the Battle of Borodino, which took place on August 26, 1812 (September 7 on the new calendar). The large 360-degree mural (115 meters long and 15 meters high) is displayed in the museum, constructed in 1962 to honor the 150th anniversary. Behind is the Kutuzov Hut. Here on September 1, 1812, as the French invaded Moscow, Kutuzov and the Military Council decided to abandon the city. The actual site of the Battle of Borodino is about 120 kilometers (75 miles) outside of Moscow (see Borodino in Vicinity of Moscow section, page 270).

The prospekt ends at the **Triumphal Arch** in **Victory Square** (Ploshchad Pobedy), designed by Osip Bovet in 1829 to honor Russia's victory in the War of 1812. It originally stood in front of the Byelorussky Train Station and was reconstructed on this spot in 1968, when Tverskaya Street was widened. It is decorated with the coats-of-arms of Russia's provinces. Here on Poklonnaya Hill, Napoleon waited for Moscow's citizens to bow to him and relinquish the keys to the city. From the hill is a magnificent view of Moscow—Anton Chekhov once said, 'Those who want to understand Russia should look at Moscow from Poklonnaya Hill.' Between Kutuzovskaya Metro station and the arch is the **Statue of Mikhail Kutuzov** by Nikolas Tomsky and an obelisk that marks the common graves of 300 men who died in the War of 1812.

Ride the metro to Park Pobedy, the world's deepest metro station at 80 meters
• (262-feet) underground, with two mosaics by Tsereteli that depict events from the
War of 1812 and WWII. Today, Park Pobedy or Victory Park is a huge memorial
complex commemorating the sacrifice of the Great Patriotic War or WWII. The
huge obelisk, designed by Tsereteli, is topped with a sculpture of St George slaying
a dragon; every 10cm represents one day of war. Across from the Obelisk is the
Museum of the Great Patriotic War with its two impressive rooms, Hall of Glory
and Hall of Remembrance and Sorrow. Open 10am–8pm; closed Mondays and last
Thursday of month. The **Memorial Synagogue at Poklonnaya Hill** is a memorial to
both Holocaust victims and persecuted Russian Jewry. Tours only with a museum
guide.

About 1.5 kilometers north of the museum is the **Church of the Intercession in
Fili.** From Fili Metro station, walk five minutes north to number 6 Novozavodskaya
and the red and white baroque-tiered towers come into view. Built between 1690–93
by Peter the Great's uncle, the boyar Lev Naryshkin (in honor of his slain brothers,
killed in the 1682 uprising); it is a superb example of 'Naryshkin-style' architecture—
using non-traditional proportions and white-stone fretwork. The upper-story
summer Church of the Savior (open May 15 to Oct 15) has a magnificent golden
iconostasis with icons painted by renowned artists, Kirill Ulanov and Karp Zolotarev.
The lower, winter church is open daily 11am–6pm, closed Tuesdays and Wednesdays.

Just outside the MKAD highway west of Moscow is the upscale street known as
Rublyovka, residence of choice for the mega-rich; both Putin and Medvedev have
homes here. The Barvikha Luxury Village contains many swanky shops from
Armani to Lamborghini. Near Myakinino Metro station, towards the north end of
the light blue Filevskaya line, is **Crocus City,** built by developer, Aras Agalarev. Here
are more upscale malls, and the popular concert hall, named after Azerbaijani singer,
Muslim Magomaev, which hosts major international artists (from Elton John to
Sting). The Miss Universe Pageant took place here in 2013. Not far from here is the
Moscow Indoor Ski and Snowboard Center; open year-round and rents warm
jackets and equipment.

From here, Kutuzovsky Prospekt becomes the Mozhaiskoye Chausee, the Minsk
Highway, which leads south to the city of Minsk in Byelorussia.

MOSCOW BURNING

N arye at lunch next day—the Moscow Chief of Police, Schetchinsky by name. Before we had been more than 10 minutes at table a wild-looking police officer rushed in unannounced and uttered one word—"Pajare!"— "Quick!" The Chief of Police sprang from his seat while Narychkine and Jenny, with one voice, exclaimed: "A fire? Where?" A fire is no rare event in Moscow and is always a serious matter, for of the 11,000 houses in the centre of Moscow only 3,500 are of stone, the rest are of wood. Just as St. Petersburg counts its disasters in floods, Moscow numbers the fires that have reduced great stretches of the city to ashes, the most terrible being, of course in 1812, when barely 6,000 buildings remained standing.

I was seized with a sudden urge to see this fire for myself.

"Can I come with you?" I begged the Chief of Police.

"If you promise not to delay me a single second."

I seized my hat as we ran together to the door. His troika, with its three mettlesome black horses, was waiting. We jumped in and shot off like lightning while the messenger, already in the saddle, spurred his own mount and led the way. I had no conception of how fast a troika can move behind three galloping horses, and for a moment I could not even draw breath. Dust from the macadamised country road billowed up in clouds above our heads; then, as we skimmed over the pointed cobbles of Moscow's streets, sparks struck by our flying hooves fell around us like rain and clung desperately to the iron strut while the Chief of Police yelled: "Faster! Faster!"

As soon as we left Petrovsky Park we could see smoke hanging like an umbrella—fortunately there was no wind. In the town there were dense crowds, but the messenger, riding a horse's length ahead, cleared a path for us, using his knout on any bystanders who did not move fast enough to please him, and we passed between ranks of people like lightning between clouds. Every moment I feared that someone would be run over, but by some miracle no one was even touched and five minutes later we were facing the fire, our horses trembling, their legs folding beneath them. A whole island of houses was burning fiercely. By good fortune the road in front of it was fifteen or twenty yards wide, but on every other side only narrow alleys separated it from neighbouring dwellings. Into one of these alleys rushed M. Schetchinsky, I at his heels. He urged me back—in vain. "Then hold fast to my sword-belt," he cried, "and don't let go!" For several seconds I was in the midst of flames and thought I would suffocate. My very lungs seemed on fire as I gasped for breath. Luckily another alley led off to our right. the Chief of Police ran into it, I followed and we both sank on a baulk of timber. "You've lost your hat," he laughed. "D'you feel inclined to go back for it?"

"God! No! Let it lie! All I want is a drink."

At a gesture from my companion a woman standing by went back in to her house and brought out a pitcher of water. Never did the finest wine taste so good! As I drank, we heard a rumble like thunder. The fire-engines had arrived!

Moscow's Fire Service is very well organised, and each of the 21 districts has its own engines. A man is stationed on the highest tower in the area, on the watch day and night, and at the first sign of fire he sets in motion a system of globes to indicate exactly where smoke is rising. So the engines arrive without losing a second, as they did on this occasion, but the fire was quicker still. It had started in the courtyard of an inn, where a carter had carelessly lit a cigar near a heap of straw. I looked into that courtyard. It was an inferno!

To my amazement, M. Schetchinsky directed the hoses not on the fire itself but on the roofs of the nearby houses. He explained that there could be no hope of saving the houses that were actually burning, but if the sheets of iron on neighbouring rooftops could be prevented from getting red hot there might be a chance of saving the homes they covered.

The only source of water in the district was 300 yards away, and soon the engines were racing to it to refill their tanks. "Why don't the people make a chain?" I asked.

"What is that?"

"In France, everyone in the street would volunteer to pass along buckets of water so that the engines could go on pumping."

"That's a very good idea! I can see how useful that would be. But we have no law to make people do that."

"Nor have we, but everyone rushes to lend a hand. When the Théâtre Italien caught fire I saw princes working in the chain."

"My dear M. Dumas," said the Chief of Police, "that's your French fraternity in action. The people of Russia haven't reached that stage yet."

"What about the firemen?"

"They are under orders. Go and see how they are working and tell me what you think of them."

They were indeed working desperately hard. They had climbed into the attics of the nearby houses and with hatchets and levers, their left hands protected by gloves, they were trying to dislodge the metal roofing sheets, but they were too late. Smoke was already pouring from the top storey of the corner house and its roof glowed red. Still the men persisted like soldiers attacking an enemy position. They were really wonderful, quite unlike our French firemen who attack the destructive element on their own initiative, each finding his own way to conquer the flames. No! Theirs was a passive obedience, complete and unquestioning. If their chief had said "Jump in the fire!" they would have done so with the same devotion to duty, though they well knew that it meant certain death to no purpose.

Brave? Yes, indeed, and bravery in action is always inspiring to see. But I was the only one to appreciate it. Three or four thousand people stood there watching, but they showed not the slightest concern at this great devastation, no sign of admiration for the courage of the firemen. In France there would have been cries of horror, encouragement, applause, pity, despair, but here—nothing! Complete silence, not of consternation but of utter indifference, and I realised the profound truth of M. Schetchinsky's comment that as yet the Russians have no conception of fraternity as we know it, no idea of brotherhood between man and his fellows. God! How many revolutions must a people endure before they can reach our level of understanding?

Alexandre Dumas, Adventures in Czarist Russia, 1960

THE BOULEVARD RING

During the 16th and 17th centuries, the stone walls of the Beli Gorod (White Town) stretched around the area now known as the Boulevard Ring. During the 'Time of Troubles' at the end of the 17th century, Boris Godunov fortified the walls and built 37 towers and gates. By 1800 the walls were taken down and the area was planted with trees and gardens, divided by a series of small connected boulevards. Ten *bulvari* make up the Bulvarnoye Koltso, the Boulevard Ring, actually a horseshoe shape that begins in the southwest off Prechistenka Street and circles around to the back of St. Basil's Cathedral on the other side of the Kremlin. Some of the squares still bear the name of the old gate towers. Frequent buses run around the ring, stopping off at each intersecting boulevard.

THE TEN BOULEVARDS

The first bears the name of the writer Nikolai Gogol. **Gogolevsky Bulvar** stretches from the Cathedral of Christ Our Savior to Arbat Square. It was known as the Immaculate Virgin Boulevard (Prechistensky Bulvar) until 1924; the first square is still called Prechistenskiye Vorota (Gates) with the Kropotkinskaya Metro station nearby. The right side of the street is lined with mansions dating back to the 1800s. In the 19th century the aristocratic Naryshkin family had their estate at number ten. At number 14 is the Central Chess Club. Chess is popular in Russia and the country has produced many world champions. In 1994, Anatoly Karpov set a world record by becoming the first international chess player to win 100 tournaments.

The next square is Arbatskaya, which leads into the Old Arbat district (see page 204). A side street leading to the Kremlin is Znamenka, which dates back to the 13th century. It means 'the sign', taking its name at the time from the Church of the Virgin Icon. In the 17th century the czar's apothecary was nearby; medicinal herbs were planted on Vagankovsky Hill.

Nikitsky Bulvar extends from Novy Arbat to Bolshaya Nikitskaya Ulitsa. Until 1992, it was named after the famous Russian army commander Alexander Suvorov, who lived at the end of the thoroughfare. The Nikitskiye Gates used to stand at the junction square of the boulevard and Bolshaya Nikitskaya Ulitsa, which is named Nikitskaya Ploshchad after a monastery that was in the area. For four years, Gogol lived at number 7, now the **Gogol Memorial House** Increasingly despondent in his later years, Gogol burned the second volume of his novel Dead Souls in the house fireplace, and died here in 1852. A reading room contains his works, and literary events and concerts often take place here. A monument to Nikolai Gogol, upon which characters from his books are depicted, stands in front. Open noon–7pm, Thursdays 2pm–9pm, Sat/Sun noon–5pm; closed Tuesdays and last day of month. Metro Arbatskaya. For more info on the history of the mansion and museum: www.dom.gogolya.ru/en.

At number 8 is the The Union of Journalists, opened in 1920. The General Lunin House, at number 12, was built by Gilliardi in Russian-Empire style with eight Corinthian columns (1818–22). It is now the **Oriental Art Museum**, open daily 11am–8pm, Thursdays noon–9pm; closed Mondays. The three floors of the museum exhibit works spanning the entire Asian continent, with Siberian shaman artifacts and works by Nikolai Roerich (1874–1946), who studied and traveled in the Himalayas. www.orientmuseum.ru.

Bolshaya Nikitskaya extends from the Kremlin's Manezhnaya Square to the Boulevard Ring. In the 15th century, this was the route to the town of Novgorod. At number 19 is the **Mayakovsky Theater**, home to Meyerhold's Theater of the Revolution in the 1920s. (Meyerhold was later arrested in the 1930s and died in prison.) At number 13 is the **Tchaikovsky Conservatory**, the country's largest music school. The conservatory was founded in 1866 by Nikolai Rubinstein. (His brother Anton founded the St Petersburg Conservatory in 1862.) Tchaikovsky taught here and pupils included Rachmaninov, Scriabin and Khachaturian. The building also has two concert halls. The International Tchaikovsky Competition is held here every four years (the next one is in 2015); the four competitive disciplines are in piano, violin, cello and voice (male and female singers). A statue of Tchaikovsky stands in front (sculpted by Vera Mukhina in 1954). Notice the musical notes on the cast-iron railings—they come from the famous opus *Glory to the Russian People* from the Glinka opera *Ivan Susanin*. This was once the mid-18th century Moscow home of Princess Ekaterina Vorontsova-Dashkova, a close friend of Catherine the Great's; the czarina made her head of the Russian Academy of Arts and Sciences in 1783.

Nearby, at number 12 Gazetny Pereulok (Lane) is the **Menschikov Mansion**. Popular architect Matvei Kazakov designed the blue and white portico residence for Prince Sergei Menschikov (grandson of Alexander, Peter the Great's prime minister). It was restored after the great 1812 fire in Empire style.

Back on Bolshaya Nikitskaya, at number 6, is the **Zoological Museum**. Founded in 1791 as a natural history project of Moscow University, it is one of Moscow's oldest museums. It was opened to the public in 1805; the present building was completed in 1902. The museum has a collection of over 10,000 species of animal, bird, fish and insect from around the world. Open 10am–5pm; closed Mondays and last Tuesday of month.

Tverskoi Bulvar begins with the Monument to Kliment Timiryazev, a prominent Russian botanist. Built in 1796, it is the oldest boulevard on the ring, and was once a very fashionable promenade. Pushkin, Turgenev and Tolstoy all mentioned the Tverskoi in their writings. At number 11, where the famous Russian actress, Maria Yermolova, lived during the last half of her life, is now the **Yermolova House Museum**. Yermolova (1853–1928) was the first person in the Soviet era to be awarded the title of 'Peoples' Artist'. The theater hosts a salon where small concerts are also performed. The museum is open 12–7pm; Thursday 1pm–9pm; closed Tuesdays and last Friday of the month. At number 23 is the **Pushkin Drama Theater**, and across the street the **Gorky Theater**, built in 1973. The Literary Institute, at number 25, was started by Maxim Gorky in 1933. (The revolutionary Alexander Herzen was born in this building in 1812.) Tverskoi ends at Pushkin Square and the Pushkinskaya Metro station.

The Strastnoi (Passion) Monastery used to be in the area of the **Strastnoi Bulvar**, which begins with the Statue of Pushkin. On Pushkin's birthday, June 6, many people crowd the square to honor the poet. Chekhovskaya Metro station is closest to the square. Strastnoi is one of the shortest and widest parts of the Boulevard Ring. It was Catherine the Great who ordered the city's original walls taken down from around the ring area. The city's Catherine Hospital, with its 12 Ionic columns, is at number 15. It was originally built by Matvei Kazakov as a palace for the Gagarin princes, and later housed the English Club from 1802 to 1812.

About one and a half kilometers (one mile) to the north at 2 Ulitsa Dostoevskovo is the **Dostoevsky Apartment Museum**, where the pensive writer lived from 1823–37. The events surrounding this ground floor apartment would greatly affect his later writings—Fyodor's father worked as a surgeon at the Hospital for the Poor next door; his mother contracted consumption and died here. Their windows also faced onto a route that prisoners took on their way to Siberia. The three rooms are open 11am–6pm, Wed/Thurs 1pm–8pm; closed Mondays and last day of the month. Metro Novoslobodskaya.

The Petrovskiye Gates used to stand at what is now the beginning of **Petrovsky Bulvar**, which runs from Ulitsa Petrovka to Trubnaya Ploshchad. It is one of the few areas on the ring whose appearance has hardly changed since the 1800s. Some buildings still remain from the 14th century, such as the **Petrovsky (St Peter's) Monastery**, which still stands on the Neglinnaya River (see Ulitsa Petrovka on page 169). Trubnaya originates from the Russian word *truba*, meaning pipe; the river was diverted through a pipe under this square. Many of the old mansions on this boulevard were converted into hospitals and schools after the Revolution. At the end of Petrovsky stands the building of the former Hermitage Hotel; its restaurant was once the most popular in Moscow—Turgenev, Dostoevsky and Tchaikovsky all ate here. After the Revolution it became the House of the Collective Farmer and today is a theater. At 3 Karetny Ryad (Carriage Row) are the **Hermitage Gardens**. In this lovely setting, the **Novaya Opera** (New Opera) stages many Russian classics. At number 5 is the **Eisenstein Film Library**, a cultural center with books and magazines on art and movies; its cinema also screens many domestic and international films.

Branching off north from Petrovsky is Tsvetnoi Bulvar, named after the flower (*tsveti*) market that used to be here. At number 13 is the **Old Circus**, also known as *Tsirk Nikulina na Tsvetnom Bulvare* or *Nikulin's* Circus on Tsvetnoi Bulvar. It was originally established by Salamonsky for his private circus, the first in Moscow. After the Revolution it was turned into the State Circus. In the late 1980s a new circus was built on the site to match the original building. The 'new' Old Circus was reopened in 1989 under private management. When Russia's most beloved clown, Yuri Nikulin (who also managed this circus), died in 1997, it was named after him; a bronze **Statue of Nikulin** stands out front. Tickets can be purchased at the Circus box office or online at www.circusnikulin.ru. Some kiosks on the street and in the nearby Tsvetnoi Bulvar Metro station also sell tickets.. Make sure you buy tickets for the Old Circus (Stary Tsirk) since the New Circus (Novy Tsirk) is near Moscow University. (In summer tent circuses are set up in Gorky and Izmailovo parks.) Heading left coming out of the circus leads to the old Tsvetnoi Central Market area, now an upscale shopping mall. Continue along the street to the salmon-colored church on the hill. In the courtyard behind the church is the Troitskaya Kniga shop that sells a large variety of religious items (including icons) at discounted prices.

Rozhdestvensky (Nativity) Bulvar ends at Ulitsa Sretenka, a popular shopping area. On the south side are the 14th-century walls of the **Convent of the Nativity of the Virgin**. It was founded in 1386 by the wife of Prince Andrei Serpukhovsky, son of Ivan I, as a place for unmarried women and widows to take refuge. The Church of St John Chrysostom was built in the mid-17th century. The white single-domed Cathedral of the Nativity (1501–05) houses the Icon of the Virgin, which hangs on the left of the iconostasis. Closed in 1922, it was returned to the Church as a monastery in 1992. On the corner of the boulevard and Sretenka Street stands the **Printer's Assumption Church**, built with money donated by printers who lived in the area.

The **Statue to Nadezhda Krupskaya** (1869–1939), Lenin's wife, marks the beginning of **Sretensky Bulvar**, the shortest boulevard with a length of 215 meters (705 feet). The Old Russian word *vstreteniye* means meeting. In 1395, the Vladimir Icon of the Mother of God was brought to Moscow and was met here at the gate of the White Town on its way to the Kremlin. Lining the sides of the boulevard are early 20th-century homes, distinguished by their original façades. In 1885, Moscow named its first public library, located here, after the writer Turgenev. The boulevard ends on Turgenevskaya Ploshchad with a Metro station of the same name.

A **Statue of Griboyedov** (1795–1829), a Russian writer, marks the beginning of **Chistoprudny Bulvar**. Its name, Clear Pond, comes from the pond at its center, which offers boating and ice-skating in winter. (The Rachka River was diverted underground.) To the right, in Arkhangelsky Pereulok, one can make out the tower of the Church of the Archangel Gabriel. Prince Alexander Menschikov ordered it built on his estate in 1707, and he wanted it to be taller than the Kremlin's Ivan the Great Bell Tower. In 1723, the archangel at the top was struck by lightning, so the tower then had to settle as the second largest structure in Moscow. It was rebuilt in 1780 without the spire, and today it is topped by a golden cupola and known as the **Menschikov Tower**. Next door is the 19th-century neo-Gothic **Church of St Fyodor Stratilit**, used as a winter church. The Sovremennik (Contemporary) Theater (called the Moscow Workers' Theater of the Prolekult in the 1930s) is at number 19. It was originally built as a cinema in 1914. Nearby at 23 Ulitsa Makarenko lived the renowned master of Russian cinema, Sergei Eisenstein. (See Special Topic on page 220.)

Pokrovsky (Intercession) Bulvar begins at Ulitsa Pokrovka. The 18th-century buildings to the east used to serve as the Pokrovsky barracks. The highly decorative rococo-style house at number 14 was known as the **Chest of Drawers**. Built in 1766, the façade is decorated with many strange beasts and birds. Ulitsa Pokrovka is distinguished by many well-preserved old churches and aristocratic residences. North of the ring, at number 22, is the baroque-style **Apraksin Mansion**, built in 1766. At the south corner of Pokrovka and Armyansky Pereulok stands the classical-style **Church of Saints Cosmas and Damian**, built between 1791–93 by Matvei Kazakov. A Colonel Khlebnikov commissioned the church, and also lived across the street in the palace located behind what is now the Belarus Embassy. Another palace, at 11 Pokrovka, was built in 1790 by Prince Ivan Gagarin, a famous naval captain. Stroll down Armyansky Lane to find the Armenian Embassy at number 2. The wealthy Armenian businessman Lazar Lazaryan came to Moscow from Persia during the reign of Catherine the Great and built this residence. The Lazaryan family later bequeathed the buildings to the Armenian community.

Across the street at number 3 is an old 17th-century manor house, which now houses the **Lights of Moscow Museum** with exhibits on the history of Moscow's street lighting from 1730 to present day. Open 11am–6pm, Thursdays 11am–8pm; closed weekends. The city's first kerosene lamps were installed on Tverskaya Street in 1861 (prior to this oil and alcohol-burning street lamps were used), which were soon followed by new gas lights around 1865. In 1883, the invention of electric lights (known as Yablochka's 'electric candle') was put to use during the coronation of Alexander III. The square of the Cathedral of Christ the Savior was lit by these special arc lights. Filament lamps soon followed. The last gas lamp was removed from Moscow in 1932, marking the end of an era—imagine, prior to the 18th century, Moscow was draped in winter darkness for over 15 hours a day!

Yauzsky Bulvar is the last and narrowest section of the Boulevard Ring. This ends by Yauzsky Gate Square, where the Yauza River joins the Moskva River. A few 18th-century mansions remain in this area. Branching off to Petropavlovsky

Pereulok brings you to the 18th-century baroque **Church of Saints Peter and Paul**. The 17th-century **Trinity Church** is located to the south in Serebryanichesky Pereulok (Silversmiths' Lane), named after the jewelers' quarter. Across the river lies Moscow's old Zayauzye district, once home to artisans and tailors. Continuing along the banks of the Moskva, past another of Stalin's Gothic skyscrapers, leads you to the back of the Kremlin. One of the best views of the Kremlin is from the **Bolshoi Kamenny Most** (Large Stone Bridge), first constructed in 1692 and rebuilt in 1936.

The czars often took Pokrovsky Boulevard to their estate in **Izmailovo**, now a popular 3,000-acre park in the northeastern part of the city. The estate, situated on the artificial Silver Island, dates back to the 14th century and was the property of the Romanovs. Later Peter the Great staged mock battle maneuvers in Silver Pond. The 17th-century baroque-style Churches of the Nativity and Protecting Veil survive along with some of the gates and three-tiered bridges. The park has gone through a major transformation, and not only is the **Izmailovo Flea Market** well worth a visit, but the area is also chocked full of shops, restaurants, museums and monuments, all contained within a 'mock' kremlin, complete with whitewashed walls and towers, made to look like an old Russian settlement. In summer, there are amusement rides and a tent circus, and ice-skating in winter. It's a good 20-minute walk north (past the Izmailovo Hotel complex) from the Partizanskaya Metro Station (to 73 Izmailovsky Hwy); open 10am–8pm. The numerous trade rows in the Vernisage and Flea Market are laden with every imaginable souvenir: arts, handicrafts, antiques, icons, carpets, old Soviet paraphernalia ...bargaining is a necessity. (Beware of fake icons and antiques, and pickpockets!) Note: the best days for the Flea Market are Friday, *Saturday and Sunday. The **Vodka History Museum** has three rooms that trace the history of vodka—sample the vodka in the attached tavern; open 10am–6pm. There is also a **Toy Museum** and **Museum of Russian Costume and Culture**. The **Church of St Nicholas** is the tallest wooden church in Russia. To reach the old estate, head southeast across the river onto the moated island.

A short walk from the Semyonovskaya Metro stop is the **Nikolsky Old Believers' Commune**. In 1652, the newly appointed Patriarch Nikon sought to reform the Church and remove any traditions from the service that did not follow the original Byzantine beliefs. Many people felt these reforms as an attack on the true Russian Church they had come to honor. Thus, a great schism broke out between Nikon's Orthodoxy and the groups who called themselves the Old Believers. They were even ready to go into exile for the sake of continuing to cross themselves with two fingers instead of with the newly prescribed three. The schism so weakened the independence and wealth of the Church that, after Nikon's death, Peter the Great placed the Church under the governing control of the Holy Synod. When Catherine the Great in 1771 granted Russia's citizens freedom to worship as they pleased, many Old Believers returned to Moscow from as far away as Siberia and continued to live together in community compounds. They still maintain old forms of Orthodox worship, such as the wearing of beards. The Old Believers established this residence in 1790; the red and white Gothic-style **Intercession Church** was soon filled with valuable icons and other works of art contributed by wealthy patrons. In the 1800s many aristocratic families such as the Riabushinskys and Morozovs belonged to the Old Believers' sect and are buried in the **Rogozhskoye Cemetery** located by the **Church of St Nicholas**. The compound is open 9am–6pm, usually closed on Mondays. (Women are advised to wear skirts and headscarves.)

Another two Metro stops toward the city is Baumanskaya. Outside on the building to the right is a mosaic that depicts scenes from the Nyemyetskaya Sloboda or German Quarter where, in the 16th and 17th centuries, most foreigners were required to live outside the city walls (so as not to so easily spread Western ideas to the population). It was in this area that Peter the Great was first introduced to his lover Anna Mons by his Swiss friend Franz Lefort, after whom the nearby prison, Lefortovo, is named. A few minutes walk away is the **Yelokhovsky Cathedral**, at 15 Spartakovskaya Ulitsa. From 1943 to 1988 the complex was the seat of the Russian Patriarchy when it was then transferred to Danilovsky Monastery. The five-domed aquamarine structure, also known as the Church of the Epiphany, was rebuilt between 1837 and 1845 in an eclectic style. The poet Pushkin was baptized in the earlier church. The interior is filled with golden iconostases, and a few Church Patriarchs are buried in the chapel; Patriarch Alexei, who died in 1971, is buried in front of the main iconostasis. Open daily 8am–8pm with services held.

THE GARDEN RING (SADOVOYE KOLTSO)

After much of Moscow burned in the great fire of 1812 (80 percent of the city and over 7,000 buildings were destroyed), it was decided to tear down all the old earthen ramparts and in their place build a circular road around the city. Anyone who had a house along the ring was required to plant a *sad* (garden); thus the thoroughfare was named Sadovoye Koltso (Garden Ring). It is Moscow's widest avenue, stretching for 16 kilometers (ten miles) around the city, with the Kremlin's Bell Tower at its midpoint. It is less than two kilometers (just over one mile) from the Boulevard Ring. Each of the 16 squares and streets that make up this ring has a garden in their name, such as Big Garden and Sloping Garden. Buses, trolleys and the Koltso Ring Metro circle the route. Along the way, 18th- and 19th-century mansions and old manor houses are interspersed among the modern buildings.

Beginning by the river, near the Park Kultury Metro station and Gorky Park, is Krymskaya Ploshchad (Crimean Square), surrounded by very old classically designed provisional warehouses, built by Stasov between 1832 and 1835.

THE RUSSIAN CINEMA

In May 1996, Russia celebrated the centennial of the first movies ever shown in the country. The first motion picture or Cinématographe-Lumière in Russia was shown in St Petersburg on May 4, 1896, at the Aquarium Gardens (now St Petersburg Film Studios). Three weeks later it also opened at Moscow's Hermitage Pleasure Garden. (The first Cinéma, created by the Lumière brothers, had been shown in Paris on December 28, 1895.) In May 1896, the coronation of the last czar, Nicholas II, was filmed at the Kremlin and Red Square by a team of Parisian filmmakers; the motion picture they produced is regarded as the world's first newsreel. Russia's first feature film, *Stenka Razin* (a popular Russian hero who led a cossack uprising in 1670), premiered on October 15, 1908, and was seven and a half minutes long. Even at this time Russian films were censored by the czar; thus the subject matter focused mainly on mystical dramas or historical costume pieces, such as *The Death of Ivan the Terrible*. The most popular film of 1915 was *Song of Triumphant Love* with silent film legend, Vera Kholodnaya. Opening in Moscow on October 24, 1917 (and for only one day), *The Silent Ornaments of Life* was about the lives of aristocrat Prince Obolensky and two of his sweethearts. By the next day the Bolshevik Revolution had changed the course of history, along with the future of Russian cinema.

The world's first film school opened in the budding Soviet Union, and the new government recognized the propaganda value of filmmaking, turning out films such as *Tractor Driver*, *The Song of Russia* and *Volga-Volga*. In 1923, film student Lev Kuleshov incorporated his 'Kuleshov technique'—the first pioneering montage effects—in his film *The Strange Adventures of Mr West in the Land of the Bolsheviks*, a satire about an American visitor to Russia. Even after the Revolution, Russia put forth some of the world's most memorable cinematic classics: Pudovkin's *Mother* (1925), Donskoi's *Gorky's Childhood* (1938) and Dovzhenko's *Earth* (1930) were at the core of the silent cinema. Vertov's *The Sixth Part of the World* (1926) and *Man with a Movie Camera* (1929) became the forerunner to cinéma vérité.

The master of the Golden Age of Russian Cinema was Sergei Mikhailovich Eisenstein, born in 1898 to a Jewish family in Riga, Latvia. In 1914 he moved to Petrograd in order to study architecture and civil engineering. When his authoritarian father joined the White forces in 1918, Sergei rebelled by serving in the Red Army where he studied arts and theater and worked as a poster artist in the psychological action division. By 1920 he was attending classes with leading stage director Vsevolod Meyerhold and working with avant-garde theater groups. As part of a theater production, Eisenstein made his first film in 1923, called *Glumov's*

Diary, a five-minute interlude for a play by Alexander Ostrovsky. A year later he followed with his first feature, *Strike*, a criticism of czarist times. Here, the filmmaker created his own form of dramatic montage effects called shocks.

Eisenstein settled in Moscow's Chistoprudny District and lived at 23 Makareno Street, near the Sovremennik Theater. By the age of 27, Sergei had created one of his masterpieces, *Battleship Potemkin*, about the 1905 revolutionary events and mutiny of the battleship crew which culminated in the famous massacre scene on the Odessa steps. (At the Brussels Exhibition in 1958, this classic was voted the Best Film of All Time by a jury of film critics.) *Oktober* was made to celebrate the tenth anniversary of the 1917 Revolution. Supported completely by the government, *Oktober* became the Soviet Union's first film epic; thousands of extras and nearly 50,000 meters of film were used. But upon completion so many political changes had occurred that Eisenstein had to re-edit the film. When it premiered on March 14, 1928, the new version was only 2,800 meters long. A year later, the first sound-film theater (at 72 Nevsky Prospekt) was opened in Leningrad on October 5, 1929.

In 1930, Eisenstein traveled to Europe and then America where he lived in Hollywood, met Charlie Chaplin and pitched ideas to Paramount Film Studios. American novelist Upton Sinclair offered to help finance Eisenstein's movie about Mexico, *Que Viva Mexico*. In 1932, when Sinclair's wealthy wife broke off their deal with Eisenstein, the director was forced to stop filming with only one episode remaining. (The first version of the Mexican film was edited in 1954, and finally reconstructed in 1979.) After returning to Moscow and suffering the strict confines of Soviet-Realism, Eisenstein suffered a nervous breakdown. For the next few years he was only allowed to make *agitkas*, or propaganda films. Then, after his first sound-speaking film, *Bezhin Meadow*, Eisenstein followed with his brilliant classic, *Alexander Nevsky*, (with Russian star Nikolai Cherkasov as Nevsky), about the Russian hero who, in 1240, defeated invading Teutonic knights. (The famous battle on the ice was shot outside Moscow in summer with artificial snow and ice.) Luckily Stalin liked the film (released in 1938 on the eve of World War II), with its anti-German tones and dramatic musical score by Prokofiev. Eisenstein fell back into favor and received the Order of Lenin. But, over the next three years (a period of Stalin's anti-Semitic stances and ruthless purges), Eisenstein was once again forbidden to practice his craft.

Finally, in 1942, the gifted filmmaker was permitted by ministers Zhdanov and Molotov to begin production on *Ivan the Terrible*, a three-part film epic. (Stalin felt a kinship with Ivan the Terrible and his Opritchniki police forces.) Part one was to be about Ivan IV's rise to power and proclamation as the first czar of all Russia. Filmed during the war years at a special studio in Central Asia, the movie was a triumphant success when it opened on January 16, 1945, and Eisenstein was awarded the Stalin Prize. But later, during the filming of part two, *The Boyars' Plot* (the last sequence was shot in color with Agfa film confiscated from the Germans at the end of the war), the mercurial Stalin staged vicious attacks and forbade the release of the film, demanding reshoots (the picture was not to be screened publicly until 1958). Under terrific strain, Eisenstein died of a heart attack on February 9, 1948, at the age of 50. Stalin allowed him to be buried in Moscow's Novodevichy Cemetery with honors. In 1998 Russia celebrated the centenary of his birth.

After World War II, one of the few themes that could pass by the censor boards of Goskino (Government controlled cinema) was that of the patriotic military. The best films of this genre usually involved the adventures of a hero struggling within the larger context of battle. Other popular films included Mikhail Kalatozov's *And the Cranes are Flying* (1957, winner of the Grand Prix at Cannes); Sergei Bondarchuk's *This Man's Destiny* (1959); Grigory Chukhrai's *Ballad of a Soldier* (1959); Naum Birman's *Chronicle of the Nose-diving Bombardier* (1968); Anorei Smirnov's *Belorussky Railway Station* (1971); Aleksei Gherman's *The Great Patriotic War* (1965) and Andrei Tarkovsky's *Ivan's Childhood* which won the Grand Prix at the Venetian Film Festival in 1962. (Tarkovsky went on to make many other classics

The giant of Soviet cinema, Sergei Eisenstein, wrote, produced, directed and edited many film classics. He wrote in his A History of the Close Up *(1942– 46): 'A branch of lilac. White. Double. In lush green of the leaves... it becomes the first childhood impression I can recollect. A close up!'*

such as *The Passion According to Andrei Rublyov* (1966), *Solaris, The Mirror* and *Nostalgia*. His last film *The Sacrifice* was shot in 1985.)

During the mid-1980s, another war film, *A Battlefield Romance* by Pyotr Todorovsky, was nominated for an Oscar (Best Foreign Film). It was only after perestroika that Todorovsky's next film, *Encore, Encore*, was permitted to paint a depressing portrait of Soviet military life. In 2004, his *In the Constellation of Taurus* was set in 1942 in the outskirts of Stalinigrad. Todorovsky's son, Valery, also a filmmaker, directed the hits *Love* (1992), *Moscow Nights* (1995), and the cult film *The Country of the Deaf*, examining life in modern Russia against the backdrop of a Mafia gang. One of the last successful war genre films was Sergei Bodrov's 1997 *Prisoner of the Caucasus,* a realistic portrayal of the war in Chechnya—as a reinterpretation of the short story by Tolstoy, and Alexander Rogozhkin's *Kukushka* (Cuckoo) set in August, 1944, when Finland signed an armistice agreement with the Soviet Union. In 2006, Dmitry Meskiev's wartime film *Svoit* (Ours), set in 1941, won a Russian Oscar for 'Best Film'. Fyodor Bondarchuk's Stalingrad (2013), about one of the bloodiest battles of WWII, was the first Russian film produced with IMAX 3-D technology.

Voted "Russian Viewers Most Loved Film" was *White Sun of the Desert* made in 1969 by maverick film director Vladimir Motyl (it was then considered "ideologically shaky" with its Western-style plot lines). The movie is about the adventures of Red Army officer, Fyodor Sukhov, who is trying to return home across Central Asia's Turkestan territories after the Civil War. In addition to the popular song, "Your Nobility Mrs Luck" by Bulat Okudzhava, the customs officer in the movie utters one of Russian cinema's most famous lines: "I take no bribes. *Za derzhavu obidno*—I just feel sorry for the country." (Former general, Alexander Lebed, who ran against Yeltsin for President in 1996, entitled his autobiography, *I Feel Sorry for the Country*.) The movie was Russia's first mega-hit, seen by over 100 million people within the first year of its release. When Brezhnev made a trip to the United States, he brought *White Sun* as one of Russia's five best classics to be shown at Carnegie Hall. For over 25 years Russian cosmonauts have made it a ritual to view the film before launching into space, and during the Soyuz-Apollo flight a video of White Sun was taken for the participating American astronauts to watch.

After the fall of the Soviet Union, long-banned films were released to packed houses, including Tengiz Abuladze's *Repentence* (about Stalinist horrors); Alexander Askoldov's *The Commissar*; Alexei German's *My Friend Ivan Lapshin*; and Panfilov's *Tema*, whose hero (a censored writer forced to work as a gravedigger to earn a living) utters the memorable line, 'Death is living in a country where one cannot practice the craft that gives one life!'

Once the film censor board was disbanded, scores of realistic films flowed from the studios: *Is It Easy to Be Young?*; *Solovki Power* (about Stalin's Siberian prison island) and *The Humiliated and the Offended* (a dramatized version of Dostoevsky's classic novel with Nastasia Kinsky as the heroine). Other popular films included *Little Vera*, a candid portrayal of a young woman and her family in a small industrial town. Andrei Konchalovsky shot *The Inner Circle*, about Stalin's projectionist, and Yevtushenko made *Stalin's Funeral*. Konchalovsky's half-brother, Nikita Mikhalkov won a 1995 Best Foreign Film Oscar for *Burnt by the Sun*. His other films include *Oblomov* (after a novel by Ivan Goncharov), *Urga*, *Black Eyes* (with Marcello Mastroanni) *The Barber of Siberia* and "12". Five other Russian films have also won an Academy Award for Best Foreign Film: the first was *Route of the German Troops* (1942); Mark Donskoi's *Rainbow* (1944); Sergei Bondarchuk's *War and Peace* (1968; nearly ten hours long, it took six years to film, using over 100,000 soldiers from the Soviet army who were mobilized to re-enact the battle of Borodino); the Soviet-Japanese production directed by Akiro Kurosawa, *Dersu Uzala* (1976); and Vladimir Menshov's *Moscow Does Not Believe in Tears* (1981). Foreign ventures also came to Russia to produce such feature and television projects as *The Russia House*, *The Saint* and *Rasputin*. In 2002, Konchalovsky's *House of Fools* won the Grand Jury Prize at the Venice Film Festival. It is based on the true story of a psychiatric hospital located near the border during the 1996 Chechen war with Russia.

Another 2002 phenomenon was Alexander Sokurov's *Russian Ark*. This 90-minute film was the first ever full-length feature ever shot in one single, uninterrupted take. The story has actors traveling through history as it unwinds through the vast halls of the Czar's Winter Palace and Hermitage Museum. It took eight months of rehearsal to prepare 2,000 actors and extras, three live orchestras and 22 assistant directors. The movie was shot in winter—there was only one shooting day and four hours of existing light. It's a must-see, and now is available with English subtitles.

Today, Russia's young directors and producers are forging a new film industry for the 21st century. In 2003, *The Return*, about the harrowing reunion of a father and his sons after a 10-year absence, won Venice Film Festival's top prize by first-time director, Andrei Zvyagintsev. *The Stroll*, a love triangle between three young Russians as they walk through the streets of St Petersburg, opened Moscow's International Film Festival. In Aleksei Balabanov's stylish gangster film, *Brother*, the former Leningrad becomes a lawless frontier town in the post-Soviet era. *Bumer*, the tale of four friends on the run in a stolen BMW, broke Russian box office records. The colorful slang or *fenya* spoken by the characters, along with the slick editing techniques and hip soundtrack from St Petersburg rocker, Sergei Shnurov, labeled the young director, Pyotr Buslov, the Russian Quentin Tarantino. In 2006, the sequel to the 2004 blockbuster *Night Watch* was released. In *Day Watch* (Dnyevnoi Dozor), the main character spends his evenings fighting witches and vampires on the streets of Moscow, while trying to manage the balance between the forces of Dark and Light. The trilogy is based on material by the popular Russian fantasy writer Sergei Lukyanenko. *The Stroll* (*Progulka*, 2003) is a delightful film in which three close friends encounter different situations on the streets of St Petersburg

Many new films and TV productions are also based on previously banned Soviet literature. In 2005, the 10-part TV miniseries of Mikhail Bulgakov's *The Master and Margarita*, directed by Vladimir Bortko, debuted with a quarter of the Russian population tuning in. (In Pskov, the book quickly disappeared from all bookstore shelves.) In 2006, another TV mini-series, *The First Circle*, based on the famous book about Russian *gulags* by Alexander Solzhenitsyn, was directed by Gleb Panfilov; it starred Dmitry Pevtsov in the role of Innokenty Volodin. Other films include *Notes from the Underground*, based on Dostoevsky's novel, depicting a more modern reflection of the nameless 19th-century St Petersburg clerk, and *His Wife's Diary*, the story of an intricate love triangle involving Nobel Prize winning Russian author, Ivan Bunin and his young lover, the poet Galina Plotnikova. It vied for an Oscar nomination for 'Best Foreign Film.' Every year, both Moscow and St Petersburg host a popular International Film Festival. The last Russian movie to win a Golden George in Moscow (St George is the patron saint of the city) was *Pete on the Way to Heaven* in 2009.

Here is a list of 20 Must See Russian Films (each is available with English subtitles): *Aelita*, by Yakov Protazanov (1924); *Battleship Potemkin*, by Sergei Eisenstein (1925); *The Circus*, by Grigory Alexandrov (1936); *The Fall of Berlin*, by Mikhail Chiaureil (1949); *The Cranes are Flying*, by Mikhail Kalatozov (1957); *Andrei Rublyov*, by Andrei Tarkovsky (1966); *Diamond Arm*, by Leonid Gaidai (1968); *White Sun of the Desert*, by Vladimir Motyl (1970); *Belorussky Train Station*, by Andrei Smirnov (1970); *Gentlemen of Fortune*, by Alexander Sery (1972); *17 Moments of Spring*, by Tatyana Lyuznova (1973); *Irony of Fate*, by Eldar Ryazanov (1975); *Slave of Love*, by Nikita Mikhailkov (1976); *Mimino*, by Georgi Daneliya (1977); *The Ascent*, by Larisa Shepitko (1977); *An Ordinary Miracle*, by Mark Zakharov (1978); *Moscow Does Not Believe in Tears*, by Vladimir Menshov (1979); *Repentance*, by Tengiz Abuladze (1984); *Brother*, by Alexei Balabanov (1997); *Siberiade* and *Gloss*, by Andrei Konchalovsky (2007).

Virtually no visitor returns from Russia without a painted wooden souvenir reflecting 17th-century 'Khokloma' folk art. Originating in the Golden Ring village of Khokloma, its tradition is based on poetic floral and geometrical patterns and a rich variety of lacquered colors. After the 1889 Paris Exhibition, the art became recognized around the world.

View of the Kremlin from the Moskva River. In the center stands the Bell Tower of Ivan the Great and the golden-domed Assumption Cathedral. The eleven small golden turrets on the left belong to the Terem Palace, and the polished silver domes on the right grace the Church of the Twelve Apostles, now housing an art museum.

Novodevichy Convent was built in 1524 by Vasily III, and became part of the city's outer defensive ring. In 1598, Boris Godunov was crowned czar in the five-domed Smolensk Cathedral.

A large variety of items are for sale at the popular weekend Izmailovsky Flea Market, including contemporary cartoons and old religious icons.

(opposite page) Zakomara gold trim decorates the plain walls of a small chapel in Moscow's Novodevichy Convent.

The author at the Russian Circus.

In Russia, the performing arts had become so popular by the 17th century that Peter the Great (1689–1725) built entertainment spots all around his new capital of St Petersburg, and even permitted women to perform. Peter especially loved the shuti, or jokesters, and court functions frequently included theatrical spectacles. Fireworks were set off in the Summer Gardens, and the Swan Canal had a tiny boat for Peter's favorite court jester.

THE RUSSIAN CIRCUS

'Oh, how I love the circus,' bellows Alexander Frish, a charismatic and eccentric clown, who has been clowning around in the Russian Circus for over 20 years. Frish believes that 'the circus is the universal language of joy and laughter that lets us all become children again'.

The Russian Circus is a world of vibrant artistry, precision and grace. Throughout the country the circus is a highly respected art form taken as seriously as classical ballet. During the time of the Soviet Union, the circus was one of the country's most popular forms of entertainment, and half the population attended at least one circus performance a year. At its height in the early 1990's, there were over 70 permanent circus buildings (more than in the rest of the world combined) spread across the country. Today, RosGosTsirk, the Russian State Circus, oversees the many circuses throughout Russia; each year performances are staged to audiences of over 10 million. Spectators are truly astounded by the levels of artistry that take place within the traditional one-ring theater.

The early traditions of the circus go back over three centuries. The first formalized circus was created in England in 1770 by an ex-cavalry officer and showman named Philip Astley. It consisted mostly of trick riding, rope dancers, tumblers and jugglers, staged within a circular ring. In 1793, one of Astley's horsemen and later competitor Charles Hughes introduced this novel form of entertainment to Russia, with a private circus for Catherine the Great in the Royal Palace at St Petersburg. (In the same year, Hughes' pupil John Bill Ricketts introduced modern circus to American audiences in Philadelphia.)

Russia's first permanent circus building was built in St Petersburg in 1877 by Gaetano Ciniselli, an equestrian entrepreneur from Milan. The Ciniselli Circus was the center of performance activitity up to the Revolution, and this classic building still houses today's St Petersburg Circus. The second oldest circus was the Old Circus in Moscow (a new Old Circus has been built on the site where the original once stood). Moscow also boasts the New Circus and summer tent circuses.

(main picture) The Zapashny family is considered a circus dynasty after performing with elephants and tigers for four generations; (above right) the circus always has a variety of acts, such as this bird act performed by a female Lilliputian; (right) a poster shows the face of a young Alexander Popov, known as the Sunshine Clown, one of Russia's most famous clowns; (left) Popov (in blue jacket) as he is today. After performing in the circus for over 60 years, he prefers to continue working. 'What happens,' he reflects, 'is that a fine speck of sawdust enters your bloodstream and stays there for life.' (far left) the audience discovers that circus magic never ends.

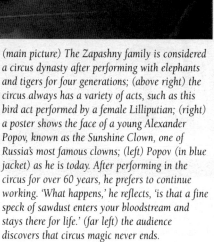

Russia's first permanent circus building was built in St Petersburg along the Fontanka Canal in 1877 by Gaetano Ciniselli, an entrepreneur from Milan, Italy. The Ciniselli Circus was the center of popular performance activities right up to the 1917 Revolution. Today, it still functions as the Bolshoi Circus, and its museum contains over 100,000 historical items. www.circus.spb.ru.

Nowhere in Europe were circus performers as politically active as in turn-of-the-century Russia. The circus became a sort of political sanctuary where sketches depicting the tumultuous state of Russia were tolerated. The clowns, especially, took every opportunity to satirize the czars, landowners and merchants. Many of the performers participated in active demonstrations with organized parades through the cities. Lunacharksy, the head of the Circus House that organized performers, encouraged their participation: 'Here it will be possible to have fiery revolutionary speeches, declarative couplets and clowns doing caricatures on enemy forces.' The artists performed on small flatbed stages that were rolled through the streets of Moscow. Vladimir Durov, with trained animals, joined the merry cavalcade, as did the most popular clown of the era, Vitaly Lazarenko, on stilts! Taking up the Bolshevik cause, the acts were now catalysts for social reform. The circus had become a political hotbed.

The poet Mayakovsky wrote for the circus. In one of his most famous skits, Moscow Burning, he wrote: 'Proud of the year 1917/Don't forget about 1905/A year of undying glory and fame/When the dream of the land came alive.../Comrade Circus, where's your grin?/Here's a sight to tickle us/Look and see who's trotting in/The Dynasty of Czar Nicholas !!!'

During these years of intellectual and political intensity, some of Russia's finest writers and directors, such as Gorky, Chekhov and Stanislavsky, turned their attention to the circus. In one of his short stories, Maxim Gorky wrote: 'Everything I see in the arena blends into something triumphant, where skill and strength celebrate their victory over mortal danger.' Later, even Lenin took time off from the Revolution to nationalize the circus—on September 22, 1919, the world's first government circus began its operations.

In order to provide a consistently high standard of training in the circus arts, the government founded the first professional circus school in 1927. Today at scores of circus schools throughout the country, students train for up to four years, studying all facets of circus life. During the final year, the student creates his own act and utilizes the services of circus producers, directors and choreographers. Once approved by a circus board, the performer's professional career begins.

Sadly, on August 21, 1997, the heart of Russia's most beloved clown, Yuri Nikulin, stopped beating. He had performed in the circus for over 30 years and had acted as the director of the Old Circus since 1984. Nikulin always tried to overcome hard times with the help of humor. He had accumulated more than 10,000 jokes since he started collecting them in 1936, which filled two volumes of his books Anekdoti I & II. The circus has been renamed Nikulin's Circus on Tvsetnoi Bulvar. He is buried in Novodevichy Cemetery where there is a bronze sculpture of him sitting on the edge of a circus arena with his favorite dog.

'Laughter is beneficial to the human body,' he wrote. 'When smiling, giggling, bursting into laughter (until you drop) a person, without even suspecting it, keeps himself healthy.'

The emblem of the Russian Circus depicts a circus performer reaching for the stars. The language of the circus is without words, as beauty, courage and skill bridge the gap between generations and nationalities. The circus is the universal language of the heart. While in Moscow visit the Nikulin Old Circus on Tsvetnoy Bulvar, or the Bolshoi New Circus on Vernadsky Prospekt. In St Petersburg, the Bolshoi Circus on Fontanka is undergoing renovation to restore it to its 19th-century grandeur. This circus also houses the first museum dedicated to circus arts, which opened in 1928 and now showcases more than 100,000 items. Check out: www.circopedia.org for more information on Russian circuses..

(opposite) The famous Flying Cranes trapeze act, produced by Vilen Golovko, chalk up before a performance. Considered one of the finest aerial acts of our time, the ten flyers rehearsed more than five years together before a single performance was given. They combined extraordinary trapeze and acrobatic skills and performed a breathtaking aerial ballet to classical music. The act was first inspired by a Russian song commemorating the spirits of the fallen soldiers who turn into white cranes and fly away, their souls released to heaven. The sole female performer, Lena Golovko, played the last of the fallen cranes, who is courageously rescued so that peace may prevail. "When I appear.. My soul is in it," After performing for more than 20 years, a new generation of Flying Cranes continues its soaring magic throughout the world.

THE TROIKA RIDE

Selifan sat up and, flicking the dappled-grey on the back with his whip a few times and making him set off at a trot, then flourishing the whip over all the three horses, he cried out in a thin, sing-song voice: 'Gee-up!' The horses roused themselves and pulled the light carriage along as though it were a feather. All Selifan did was to wave his whip and keep shouting: 'Gee-up, gee-up, gee-up!', bouncing smoothly on the box, while the troika flew up and down the hillocks scattered all along the highway that sloped imperceptibly downhill. Chichikov only smiled as he bounced lightly on his leather cushion, for he was very fond of fast driving. And what Russian does not love fast driving? How could his soul, which is so eager to whirl round and round, to forget everything in a mad carouse, to exclaim sometimes, 'To hell with it all!'—how could his soul not love it? How not love it when there is something wonderful and magical about it? It is as if some unseen force has caught you up on its wing and you yourself fly and everything with you flies also; milestones fly past, merchants on the coachman's seat of their covered wagons fly to meet you, on each side of you the forest flies past with its dark rows of firs and pines, with the thudding of axes and the cawing of crows; the whole road flies goodness only knows where into the receding distance; and there is something terrible in this rapid flashing by of objects which are lost to sight before you are able to discern them properly, and only the sky over your head and the light clouds and the moon appearing and disappearing through them seem motionless. Oh, you troika, you bird of a troika, who invented you? You could only have been born among a high-spirited people in a land that does not like doing things by halves, but has spread in a vast smooth plain over half the world, and you may count the milestones till your eyes are dizzy. And there is nothing ingenious, one would think, about this travelling contraption. It is not held together by iron screws, but has been fitted up in haste with only an axe and chisel by some resourceful Yaroslav peasant. The driver wears no German top-boots: he has a beard and mittens, and sits upon goodness only knows what; but he has only to stand up and crack his whip and start up a song, and the horses rush like a whirlwind, the spokes of the wheels become one smooth revolving disc, only the road quivers and the pedestrian cries out as he stops in alarm, and the troika dashes on and on! And very soon all that can be seen in the distance is the dust whirling through the air.

Nikolai Gogol, Dead Souls, 1842

Zubovsky Bulvar ends at Zubovsky Square, near Devichye Park (Maiden's Field) where carnivals were held and maidens danced to Russian folk tunes. To the north, Prechistenka Street leads to the Kremlin. The area between the Boulevard and Garden rings was once an aristocratic residential district; many old mansions are still in the area. Bolshaya Pirogovskaya (named after Nikolai Pirogov, a renowned surgeon) leads southwest to Novodevichy Monastery. Many of Moscow's clinics and research institutes are located in this area. At number 18 Zubovsky Bulvar is the former estate of the wealthy merchant Morozov.

On **Smolensky Bulvar** (formerly called Sennaya, the Haymarket) is the tall Ministry of Foreign Affairs (MID), one of Stalin's seven skyscrapers. The Hotel Belgrad is at number 8.

Novinsky Bulvar begins at Smolenskaya Ploshchad. The great singer Fyodor Shalyapin (1873–1938) lived at number 25 from 1910 to 1922; it is now the **Shalyapin House Museum**. Open Tues/Sat 10am-6pm, Wed/Thurs 11:30am-7pm, Sunday 10am-4:30pm; closed Mondays/Fridays, and last day of each month (www. shalyapin-museum.org). Fyodor wrote in his autobiography *Pages From My Life* that his childhood was a mixture of beatings, poverty and hunger. At the age of 17, he was taken under the wing of Tbilisi Imperial Theater artist Dmitry Usatov to learn the art of singing. He would soon perform operas in St Petersburg and Nizhny Novgorod where he met Savva Mamontov, who later became his patron. After marrying the ballerina Iola Tornagi, Shalyapin (1873–1938) began the 1896 Moscow operatic season as Susanin in *A Life for the Czar*. By training his incredible basso voice, utilizing expressive gestures, exerting strong stage control and using dramatic face make-up, Shalyapin was attracting the attention of the West by the end of the century. After performing on stages of the Paris Grand Opera and La Scala in Milan, he also continued to tour throughout Russia and played every role imaginable. Later, severely disillusioned with the new Soviet regime, Shalyapin left Russia on July 29, 1922, on a foreign tour which lasted 16 years, until the singer's death. In his other book *The Mask and The Soul* Shalyapin wrote that he was a free man and wanted to live freely; he could not adapt his art to the confines of Soviet realism. Many decades later, upon the request of Shalyapin's five children, their father's remains were transferred from Batignoles Cemetery in Paris and reburied, on October 29, 1984, in Moscow's Novodevichy Cemetery (see page 249).

The boulevard ends at Kudrinskaya Ploshchad, named after the local village of Kudrino. Up until 1992, it was called Vosstaniya (Uprising) Square, named after the heavy fighting that took place here during the revolutions of 1905 and 1917. The US Embassy is just south of the square at 19–21 Novinsky Bulvar.

Povarskaya Ulitsa, heading southeast from the square, was once one of the most fashionable areas of the city. It was named centuries ago, when the czar's servants and cooks lived in this area; *povarskaya* means cook. (Over 150 court cooks were employed to prepare 3,000 daily dishes for royalty and guests.) Other side streets were Khlebny (Bread), Nozhevoy (Knife), and Chashechny (Cup). The two lanes Skaterny (Tablecloth) and Stolovoy (Table) still branch off the street. In *War and Peace*, Tolstoy described the Rostov's estate at 52 Povarskaya Ulitsa, where there is now a statue of Tolstoy; it is now the Russian Writer's Club. The **Gorky Literary Museum** at number 25, recognizable by the statue of Gorky at the front, chronicles the life of the Russian writer who lived here before his departure abroad in 1921. It is open 10am–5pm, 12–7pm Wednesdays and Fridays; closed weekends and first Thursday of month. (Metro Barrikadnaya) Gorky also spent his last years (1931–36) in a house on the neighboring street of Malaya Nikitskaya, at number 6, which is also a museum. (See page 199.)

On the other side of Kudrinskaya Ploshchad is Barrikadnaya Ulitsa with a Metro station of the same name. The Planetarium and Zoo are in the area. In May 1996 the **Moscow Zoo** was reopened after major reconstruction designed by Zurab Tsereteli; open daily 10am–7pm (winter 10am–5pm; closed Mondays). Check out the nocturnal animal exhibit; by day the black lighting creates nighttime prowling activities. The zoo first opened in 1864 and is one of the oldest in the world with a collection of over 5,000 animals. Barrikadnaya leads into Krasnaya Presnya, once a working-class district and the scene of many revolutionary battles. Nearby, at number 4 Bolshoi Predtechensky Pereulok is the **Krasnaya Presnya Museum**, which traces the history of the area and revolutions in Russia up to the present day. Open 10am–5pm; closed Mondays.

The famous writer Anton Chekhov lived from 1886 to 1890 along the next boulevard, **Sadovaya-Kudrinskaya**, in the small red house at number 6. It is now the **Chekhov House Museum**. Open 11am–6pm, Wed/Fri 2pm–8pm closed Mondays and last day of month. Anton Chekhov (1860–1904)was not born into nobility; his grandfather had, only a generation before, purchased the family's freedom from serfdom. In 1876 the family moved to Moscow. By 1879 Chekhov had entered the Moscow University medical school and supported the family by writing humorous fiction. During his first seven years of literary activity, he published over 400 stories, novellas and sketches, and in 1883 received the Pushkin Prize in Literature. His first full-length play *The Seagull* failed miserably in its 1896 St Petersburg première. However, two years later, under the guidance of Stanislavsky at the Moscow Arts Theater, the production was a triumphant success. The company took the image of a seagull as its symbol, and Chekhov became, in the words of Stanislavsky, 'the soul of the Moscow Arts Theater'. He followed with *Uncle Vanya* in 1899, and while in

Yalta wrote *The Three Sisters* (1901) and *The Cherry Orchard* (1903). In 1901, he married Olga Knipper, a leading actress with the Moscow Arts Theater. One room in the house is dedicated to his time at his country estate in Melikhovo, south of Moscow. "My estate's not much but the surroundings are magnificent." Here he lived from 1892–1899, and wrote some of his most celebrated plays. Anton Chekhov died of tuberculosis on July 2, 1904, at the age of 44. Both Chekhov and Stanislavsky are buried in Moscow's Novodevichy Cemetery (see page 249 and 278).

The new stellar **Moscow Planetarium**, reopened at 5 Sadovaya-Kudrinskaya, is well worth a visit. The Big Star Hall, with its 25-meter silver roof dome, projects both full dome Planetarium and Universarium shows. In the small Star Hall, visitors can enjoy a ride to Saturn, and the 4-D movie theater utilizes special effects with sounds and movements. The facility also includes the Space Exploration Hall, the interactive Lunarium, the Urania Museum, and the outdoor Sky Park, which is both an observatory and open-air museum (open May-Sept). A meal can be had at the Retro Café and Telescope Restaurant. Open 9am–9pm, weekends 10am–10pm; closed Tuesdays. www.planetarium-moscow.ru/en.

Bolshaya Sadovaya Ulitsa (Great Garden Street) once had a triumphal arch through which troops returned to Moscow. The next boulevard, **Sadovaya-Triumfalnaya Ulitsa** is followed by **Sadovaya Karetnaya** and then **Sadovaya-Samotechnaya Ulitsa**. At number 3 is the **Obraztzov Puppet Theater**, founded in 1931, and named after its founder. The puppet clock on the front of the building has 12 little houses with a tiny rooster on top; every hour, one house opens. At noon, all the boxes open, each with an animal puppet dancing to a Russian folk song.

The next street east is Olympiisky Prospekt which, after a few blocks north, intersects at Durova Street (walk west or take Tram 7 from Prospekt Mira Metro). Here, at 4 Durova, is the famous **Durov Animal Theater**, which celebrated its 100th anniversary in 2012. Founded by the great clown and animal trainer Vladimir Durov, it is still run today by his octogenarian great-granddaughter Natalia. (Durov was the first to train animals by rewarding instead of punishing them.) The theater has a big and small stage, and also a museum that charts the theater's history of the Durov Circus Dynasty. The theater and its acts are a genuine treat, particularly for younger children. (See Special Topic on the Russian Circus, page 233.)

Branching off to the south is Tsvetnoi (Flower) Bulvar, with the Nikulin Old Circus near the Tsvetnoi Bulvar Metro station. At nearby 5 Pushkarev Lane is the **M'ARS (M'ARC) Contemporary Art Center**, with halls exhibiting the works of top contemporary artists; a café and club are in the basement. Open noon–8pm; closed Mondays.

The next street and square returned to their original names of **Sukharevskaya** in 1992; they are named after Sukharov, a popular commander of the czar's Streltsy guards who were quartered here. After the Revolution the street and square were called Kolkhoznaya (Collective Farm). Peter the Great opened Russia's first navigational school in the center of the square where the Sukharov Tower had stood.

Several blocks north, off Meschanskaya, at 13 Vasnetsova Lane, is the **Vasnetsov Museum**, open 10am–5pm, closed Mondays/Tuesdays and last Thursday of month (Metro Sukharevskaya). A contemporary of the painter Ilya Repin, Vasnetsov exhibited in the *Peredvizhniki* or Society for Traveling Art Exhibitions, and enjoyed painting themes of Old Russia, filled with mystical and fairy-tale subjects. (His paintings can be also found in the Tretyakov Gallery.) The attic studio contains many of his *Baba Yaga* fairy-tale motifs. Victor Vasnetsov (1848–1926) lived in this log house, which he designed himself, for more than 30 years. The museum of his artist brother, Apollinary (1856–1933), is at 6 Furmanny Lane, near Metro Chistiye Prudy.

Prospekt Mira (Peace Prospekt) leads north to the **All-Russian Exhibition Center** (see page 255). Prospekt Mira's original name was Meshchanskaya Sloboda, Commoners' Quarters; immigrant settlements were concentrated here. At 5 Prospekt Mira is the Perlov House, the former home of an old tea merchant family of the same name. At number 18 is the **Wedding Palace**, an 18th-century structure designed by Bazhenov. At number 26 are the **Aptekarsky Botanical Gardens**, the city's oldest gardens, and started by Peter the Great as medicinal gardens for the court. Today they are still filled with medicinal herbs, along with thousands of types of trees and bushes. Also near the Prospekt Mira Metro station is the Olympic Sports Complex, built in the late 1970s.

Returning to the Garden Ring, the next square, **Lermontovskaya**, is named after the Russian poet Mikhail Lermontov, who was born in a house near the square on October 3, 1814; a plaque on a building marks where the house once stood. The plaque is inscribed with Lermontov's words: 'Moscow, Moscow, I love you deeply as a son, passionately and tenderly.' (The Lermontov Museum is at 2 Malaya Molchanovka St.) The square was known as Krasniye Vorota (Red Gate) because red gates once marked the entrance to the square. The Metro station was given this name.

Zemlyanoi Val (Earthen Rampart) is the longest street on the ring, once named after the pilot Valeri Chakalov, who made the first nonstop flight over the North Pole from the USSR to America in 1936. At numbers 14 to 16 lived the poet Marshak, the violinist Oistrach and composer Prokofiev. (The Prokofiev Museum is at 6 Kamergersky Lane.) Tchaikovsky once lived at number 47. At number 57 is the **Sakharov Museum**, opened in 1996, with exhibits on the life and works of the

Nobel prize-winning physicist and dissident during the Soviet period. The museum is dedicated to the legacy of Andrei Sakharov (1921–89), and chronicles the political repression of Soviet citizens; it regularly showcases events on human rights. In 2003, while exhibiting paintings and sculptures, entitled 'Caution! Religion', members of a Russian Orthodox Church entered the hall and defaced many of the provocative works with spray paint, terming them 'sacrilegious'. The perpetrators were arrested, but later the State Duma passed a resolution condemning the museum's organizers. One artist expressed that "...we have freedom of speech and religion in our Constitution, but do they only exist on paper?" Open 11am–7pm; closed Mondays.

Behind the Kursky Railway Station is an 18th-century stone mansion, the Naidyonov Estate. Gilliardi and Grigorev built the estate, whose gardens stretch down to the Yauza River. The region north of the river is known as **Basmanny** and south as **Taganka**. After crossing the Yauza River, the ring reaches Taganskaya Ploshchad (with a Metro station of the same name), where the popular avant-garde **Theater Taganka** is located. After its establishment in 1963, the Taganka, under the direction of Yuri Lyubimov, became one of Moscow's most beloved theaters. After staging such provocative plays as The Master and Margarita, and later Crime and Punishment in London (where he openly criticized Soviet leadership), Lyubimov was forced into Western exile 1984. He returned to Russia in 1989, and for the next 20 years continued to direct award-winning theater. In June 2011, the actors refused to rehearse unless they were first paid. Incensed, Lyubimov paid the money and then dramatically left the theater for good. He died in 2014 at age 97.

A few blocks west of the Metro stop, at 5-y Koteinichesky, is **Bunker-42 on Taganka**, a facility that housed a Cold War command post meant to serve as the city's communication center during a nuclear attack. A visitor travels by elevator 60 meters (192 feet) underground to explore the four secret chambers. (Admission by appointment only.) Nearby, at 3 Ulitsa Goncharnaya is the **Russian Icon Museum**, which contains the private collection of Mikhail Abramov, a businessman and art patron. The space exhibits more than 4,000 pieces of Russian and Eastern Christian art, with more than 600 icons on display. Open 11am–7pm; closed Wednesdays. www.russikona.ru/en. Not far away, at 4-y Syromyatnichesky Lane, is the **Winzavod Art Complex**, home to many of Moscow's most prestigious galleries, a design studio, and other boutiques and gift shops.

The **Vysotsky Museum and Cultural Center** is located north of the square at 3 Nizny Tangansky Tipik, off Verkhnaya Radishchevskaya Street; open 11am–5.30pm, closed Sundays and Mondays. Besides a museum on his life, the space also presents musical concerts as well as other theater and dance performances. Known as the 'Russian Hamlet with a guitar,' the Moscow-born Vladimir Vysotsky (1938–1980) was one of Russia's most talented and popular bards. His songs defined the realities and hardships of Soviet times (he was barred by the government from officially recording them). He also achieved fame by acting in feature films and, at the Taganka Theater, he played such roles as Shakespeare's Hamlet and Brecht's Galileo. When Vysotsky died at the age of 42 (presumably of a heart attack—nothing was announced in the Soviet press), over 300,000 people followed his coffin from Taganka Square to Vagankovo Cemetery, where a bronze statue of his likeness stands over his grave. (In 1995, a second statue of him was unveiled at the intersection of Petrovka Street and Strastnoi Bulvar.) A few days before his death he wrote a poem for his wife Marina Vlady:

I'm half my age—a little way past forty.
I'm living thanks to God and you, my wife.
I have a lot to sing to the Almighty.
I have my songs to justify my life.

Across the Bolshoi Krasnokholmsky Most (Bridge) that spans the Moskva River and just off Zatsepsky Val, our next stop on the Garden Ring is the **Bakhrushin Theater Museum**, a Neo-Gothic mansion at 31 Ulitsa Bakhrushina. Established by merchant Alexei Bakhrushin in 1894, the museum displays over 200,000 items, which illustrate the history of Russian theater and ballet from the classics to avant-garde. The basement floor is dedicated to the opera singer Fyodor Shalyapin and the art patron Savva Mamontov. Open 12–7pm; closed Tuesdays and last Monday of each month. Nearby is the Paveletskaya Metro station.

Serpukhovskaya Ploshchad was, until 1992, named Dobryninskaya Square after the 1917 revolutionary. The next square, Kaluzhskaya, leads to the entrance of **Gorky Park** (see page 251), with two large Ferris wheels. Across from the park, at 10–14 Krymsky Val, is the **Tretyakov Gallery** (see page 178). Krymsky Val (Crimean Rampart) is the last section of the ring. It crosses the Moskva River by way of the Krymsky suspension bridge. Back, on an island in the river, the controversial **Statue of Peter the Great** can be seen (see page 176).

When strolling along the Garden or Boulevard rings, pay attention to the traffic. Even 150 years ago, Nikolai Gogol wrote: 'What Russian doesn't like fast driving?' (See Literary Excerpt on page 240.) And this is just as true today. Traffic accidents have multiplied; cars often use sidewalks as passing lanes and headlights are not normally used at night. Many *yama* (potholes) are left unrepaired, so that getting splashed while walking, with rain and mud during a rainfall is likely. In 1986, there were only 650,000 cars on the road in Moscow; today there are over three million.

SPARROW HILLS (VOROBYOVIYE GORY)

Sparrow Hills are situated in the southwestern part of the city; they were given this name in the 15th century. From 1935 to 1992, the area was referred to as Lenin Hills. Peter I and Catherine the Great had their country palaces in this area, and today many dachas, or country homes, are still situated here. It remains a favorite place for recreational activities like hiking, picnicking, swimming in summer, and ice-skating, sledding and skiing in winter. This spot is the highest point in Moscow and provides one of the most spectacular views of the city. The Metro to Universitet, passes the Sparrow Hills station, which goes above ground, and crosses the Moskva River. After leaving the Metro, stand and face the river; in good weather even the golden domes of the Kremlin are visible. It is customary for wedding parties to have photographs taken at this spot.

In the opposite direction you can see a massive 36-story building. This is Lomonosov University, more widely known as **Moscow University**, founded in 1755 by Russian scientist Mikhail Lomonosov. This university building was erected between 1949 and 1953 on the highest point of Sparrow Hills by Stalin, who had six other similar Gothic-style skyscrapers built throughout the city. (In 2001, the centenary of architect Dmitry Tchechulin's birth was celebrated. He was appointed Stalin's chief architect in 1945 and designed Moscow's seven *vysotki* skyscrapers. He also designed several metro stations, the Tchaikovsky Concert Hall, Pekin Hotel and Rossiya Hotel (now torn down); and, in 1980, one year before his death, he completed his last work, the White House.) This is the tallest of the seven at 240 meters (787 feet). A golden star in the shape of ears of corn crown the top of the university's main tower. It is the largest university in Russia; the campus comprises 40 buildings, including sports centers, an observatory, botanical gardens and a park. The Gorky Library has over six million volumes. Gorbachev graduated from Moscow University with a degree in law, and his wife, Raisa, with a degree in Leninist philosophy. Recently Moscow University became independent from the Ministry of Education. Within the campus stands the green-domed **Trinity Church**, built in 1811 and open for worship. (The University is closed to visitors.)

A few blocks to the east, at 24 Vernadsky Prospekt, is the large circular building of the **Bolshoi Moscow State Circus** or New Circus (seats 3400), built under the reign of Leonid Brezhnev; it opened its doors on April 30, 1971. Its ring has four interchangeable floors that can be switched in less than five minutes. One is the regular ring, another a special ring for magicians, and the others are a pool for the aquatic circus and a rink for ice ballet. The Universitet Metro station is directly behind the New Circus. (The other main circus of Moscow is the **Stary Tsirk** (Old Circus) at 13 Tsvetnoi Bulvar. www.bolshoicircus.ru.

In front of the New Circus is the former Moscow Palace of Young Pioneers, sometimes still referred to as **Pioneerland**. This is a large club and recreational center for children. Before the Communist Party lost its supreme power in 1991, children who belonged to the Communist Youth Organization were known as Young Pioneers. Older members belonged to the Young Komsomol League. During the last years of Communist rule, there were over 25 million Young Pioneers, and over 39 million in the Komsomol. The 400 rooms in the palace include clubs, laboratories and workshops. It also has its own concert hall, sports stadium, gardens and even an artificial lake for learning how to row and sail. **The Statue of Malchish-Kibalchish**, a character from a popular children's book, marks the entrance to the palace. On the corner is the **Children's Music Theater**. A monument to the theater's musical director, Natalya Satz (1909–93) was unveiled in 2000; her father, Ilya Satz, scored the famous ballet *Bluebird*.

Along Mosfilmovskaya Ulitsa, at number 1, is **Mosfilm Studios**, dating from 1927. Here worked many of the great Russian film directors like Pudovkin, Dovzhenko, Eisenstein and Tarkovsky. The studio now offers a 90-minute tour (reserve in English) of the complex (at 3pm Tues/Wed/Thurs), which includes costume exhibits, old vehicles and equipment, as the camera used by Eisenstein to film *Battleship Potemkin*. (See Special Topic on Russian Cinema.) www.mosfilm.ru/eng.

Across the river from Sparrow Hills are the white buildings of the **Luzhniki Central Stadium** (the largest in Moscow). The complex consists of the stadium (seating 100,000), the Sport Palace, the swimming and tennis stadiums, the Friendship Hall and the Museum of Physical Culture. Many events of the Moscow 1980 Olympics were held here. The Olympic Village was built behind the University on Lomonosov Prospekt. Glancing to the left of the stadium, you can make out the golden domes of the **Novodevichy Convent**.

Beyond the stadium, at 2 Lev Tolstoy Street (Ulitsa Lva Tolstovo), is the five-domed and colorfully tiled **Church of St Nicholas at Khamovniki**, built between 1676–1682; the interior contains many beautiful icons and frescoes; services are held. In the past, weavers lived in the area and their guild paid for the construction of this church; the old Russian word for weavers is *khamovniki*. A copy of the Virgin Icon Helper of all Sinners (credited for working a few miracles) rests in the iconostasis left of the royal gates; to the right is an Icon of St Nicholas. Farther along the street, at number 10, the whitewashed building with the steep roof was once the Weaver's Guild House, where textiles were woven.

Also along this street, at number 21, is the 18-room **Tolstoy Country Estate Museum** where the writer lived in winter from 1882 to 1901, the year he was excommunicated from the Orthodox Church. After this act by the Holy Synod, Tolstoy moved permanently to his estate at Yasnaya Polyana (see page 282). A few of the works he wrote at his study while living in this house are *Power of Darkness*, *The Death of Ivan Ilyich*, *The Kreutzer Sonata* and *Resurrection*. In the bedroom is a small desk where his wife, Sofia Andreevna, meticulously hand copied his manuscripts. The upstairs piano was played by such greats as Rachmaninoff and Rimsky-Korsakov. When in this room, ask to hear the recording of Tolstoy greeting a group of schoolchildren, followed by a piano composition written and played by him. The 100th anniversary of his death was celebrated in 2010. Open 10am–6pm, Thursday noon–8pm; closed Mondays and last Friday of month. (Metro Park Kultury) Tolstoy's family would often stop by the beer factory next door, which has been brewing for over a century! (Another Tolstoy Museum is located at Ulitsa Prechistenka, see page 172.)

NOVODEVICHY CONVENT
From Universitet Metro station, take the train towards Bol. Pirogovskaya across the river to Sportivnaya and get off in front of the stadium. Walking a short distance to the northwest brings you to one of the oldest religious complexes in the city, **Novodevichy (New Maiden) Convent**, a baroque-style complex of 15 buildings and 16 gilded domes dating from the 16th and 17th centuries. Grand Prince Vasily III founded the convent in 1514 to commemorate the capture of Smolensk from Lithuania, which had controlled the area for over a century (the convent was built on the road to Smolensk). It was also one in a group of fortified monasteries that surrounded Moscow. Novodevichy served mainly as a religious retreat for Russian noblewomen. Peter the Great banished his half-sister Sophia and first wife Evdokia to the convent and forced them to wear the veil. (Many noblemen, as a form of divorce, forced their wives into a convent in order to remarry.) Boris Godunov was crowned here in 1598. Napoleon tried to blow up the convent before he fled the city, but a nun pulled out the fuses. The convent was converted into a museum in 1922.

The white-stone five-tiered **Virgin of Smolensk Cathedral** (1524) was the convent's first stone building and lies at its center. It was dedicated to the Virgin of Smolensk, a much-revered 16th-century icon, and modeled on the Kremlin's Uspensky Cathedral. Many 16th-century interior frescoes portray the life of Vasily III (the father of Ivan the Terrible). A copy of the Icon of Our Lady of Smolenskaya hangs over the altar, and many icons were painted by Simon Ushakov. Peter's half-sister Sophia donated the beautiful gilded five-tiered iconostasis in 1685; its wooden columns, decorated with climbing grapevines, are made out of whole tree trunks. Ivan the Terrible's daughter Anna, Sophia and Evdokia are some of the noblewomen in the south nave burial vault.

The red and white baroque **Transfiguration Gate Church** (1687–9) stands above the main north entrance. To its right (west) are the two-story **Lopukhina Chambers**, where Peter the Great's first wife Evdokia Lopukhina lived. The next building along the wall, in front of the **Pond Tower**, houses **Sophia's Chambers**. Sophia's chamber-prison is where Peter the Great incarcerated his half-sister (until her death) when he deposed her as regent and took the throne at the age of 17. To further punish Sophia for leading the 1689 Streltsy revolt against him, the legend goes, Peter ordered dead bodies of revolt members strung up outside her cell. The **Miloslavsky Chambers** are named after Sophia's sister, Maria Miloslavskaya, who also lived here until her death. The **Gate Church of the Intercession** (1688) tops the southern entrance, and west of the cathedral is the **Church of the Assumption** (1687), which has been open for worship for over three centuries (a choir sings during Sunday services). Behind it is the 16th-century **Church of St Ambrose**. Next to the church, along the southern wall, stands the small **Irina Godunova Palace**, where Irina Godunova lived out her last days. (It now displays religious artwork.) Irina was the sister of Boris Godunov and the wife of Fyodor I. When the czar died in 1598, Irina refused the throne and her brother Boris was elected ruler during the Time of Troubles. Other structures include the **Refectory Church** (1685–87), the six-tiered 72-meter (236-feet) high octagonal baroque **Bell Tower** (1690) (then one of the tallest towers in the city), small exhibit halls and nun's residences (in 1994, Novodevichy was permitted its first resident nun since 1922).

Many distinguished Russian personalities are buried in Novodevichy's **two cemeteries**. Within the convent's grounds are the graves of princes, wealthy merchants, clergymen and war heroes. Behind the southern wall (the entrance is on the east side), the 19th- and 20th-century cemetery has been the burial site of many of Russia's most prominent statesmen, artists and scientists. These include Bulgakov, Chekhov, Eisenstein, Gogol, Khrushchev, Mayakovsky, Prokofiev, Scriabin, Serov, Shalyapin, Shostakovich, Stanislavsky, Stalin's wife Nadezhda Alliluyeva (who committed suicide in 1932), and Boris Yeltsin, who died in 2007. The beloved clown Yuri Nikulin, who directed the Old Circus, was buried here in 1997. A monument was erected over his grave in 2000; the sculpture, by Alexander Rukavishnikv, is of Nikulin sitting on the edge of a circus arena next to his favorite dog. Raisa Gorbacheva, the wife of Mikhail Gorbachev, who died of leukemia in 1999 aged 67, is also buried in the cemetery. A bronze monument was unveiled on the first anniversary of her death. A map of the graves can be bought at the entrance kiosk. The complex is open 10am–5.30pm, grounds 8am–8pm; closed Tuesdays and first Monday of month. This is a functioning monastery, dress appropriately.

Nearby, at 4 Novodevichy Pereulok, is **Restaurant U-Pirosmani** with delicious Georgian food and paintings on the wall by famous Georgian painter Pirosmani, along with other artists.

GORKY PARK

Gorky Park, stretching 3 kilometers along the river, lies a few minutes walk over the Moskva River from Park Kultury Metro station in the Frunze district. It can also be reached from the other side of the river from Oktyabrskaya Metro station. A large archway marks the entrance to the park. Named after popular Soviet writer Maxim Gorky, the area was commissioned as a Park of Culture and Rest in the 1920s. In 2011, it was redeveloped by a group funded by Russian billionaire, Roman Abramovich. The original pavilions from the 1920's have been restored, and today there are restaurants, boats and bicycles for hire, and the Zelyoni (Green) open-air theater. In summer the park is teeming with strollers, performance artists and circus performers of the tent circus. In winter the popular ice-skating rink (there are skates for rent) is in operation (made famous by the book *Gorky Park*), along with cross-country skiing. The park is open daily 10am–10pm.

Prominent Russian art collector and entrepreneur, Dasha Zhukova (and partner Roman Abramovich) opened the **Garage Center for Contemporary Art** inside the Park. This massive art and cultural center is aimed at showcasing contemporary and avant-garde Russian and foreign art. The center was first housed in a large temporary pavilion (located by Pioneer Pond, turn left after the Central entrance), designed by Japanese architect Shigeru Ban, with the exterior lined with huge cardboard-like tubes. A new large permanent two-story building, designed by Dutch architect Rem Koolhaas, known as **Garage Gorky Park**, includes exhibition galleries, a creative center for children, auditorium, offices, an Art Book Shop and Garage Café. (The center will also be expanding into the neighboring Hexagon Pavilion once renovation is complete.) A satellite edition of Garage Center is planned for New Holland Island in St Petersburg as well. Open 11am–9pm, Fri/Sat/Sun until 10pm, garageccc.com/en

Also in the park are the Neskuchny Sadi (Not-Boring Pleasure Gardens), originally part of the Trubetskoi Estate and later bought by Nicholas I in 1826; it is now used by the Academy of Sciences. The estate is part of the Main Botanical Gardens (with a collection of over 16,000 varieties of roses) that stretch as far as the river.

DONSKOI MONASTERY

South of Gorky Park, and a 10-minute walk from the Shabolovskaya Metro station, is the Donskoi Monastery. Heading west along Donskaya Street leads directly to the monastery walls. This monastery, with its 12 towers and seven churches, were founded by Czar Fyodor I and Boris Godunov in 1591, on the site of the Russian army's line of defense against the invading Mongols. It was believed that the Donskaya Virgin Icon protected the city, the same icon that Prince Donskoi took for protection against the invading Tartars during the divisive 1380 Battle of Kulikovo near the River Don. Legend has that, in 1591, the Tatar Khan Kazy-Girey retreated from Moscow without a fight after the Icon showered him with arrows in a dream. (The monasteries were also connected by protective earthen ramparts, today's Garden Ring.) By the 18th century, this monastery was one of the most prosperous in all of Russia and owned over 7,000 serfs. After the Revolution, the Donskoi Monastery was opened to the public as a government architectural museum. In the early 1990s the complex was returned to the Orthodox Church and is now a working monastery.

The red and white **Old Cathedral of the Donskaya Virgin** (1591) was the first building of the monastery. (This was one of the few churches allowed to conduct services throughout the Soviet period.) The cube roof and onion domes are topped with golden half-moon crosses that symbolize the Christian victory over Islam. A copy of the Donskaya Virgin Icon is on the eight-tiered iconostasis; the original is in the Tretyakov Gallery. Patriarch Tikhon, who was appointed the head of the Orthodox Church on the eve of the October 1917 Revolution, is buried in a marble tomb at the southern wall.

The Naryshkin baroque-style **New Cathedral of the Donskaya Virgin** was commissioned by Peter the Great's half-sister Sophia in 1684. The Italian artist Antonio Claudio painted the interior frescoes between 1782 and 1785. At the southwestern corner of the monastery is the classical **Church of the Archangel Michael**, built between 1806 and 1809. The church served as a memorial chapel for the Golitsyn family. Mikhail Golitsyn (1681–1764) was Peter the Great's star general who began his career as a service drummer. Fourteen Golitsyns are buried here, including Dmitri and his wife Natalia, who is the subject of Pushkin's novel *Queen of Spades*. (When a plague in 1771 banned burials in central Moscow, many of the nobility were buried here.) Some of the other notable people buried in the cemetery are Turgenev, the architect Bovet, and Zhukovsky, the father of Russian aviation. Other baroque buildings include the **Tikhvin Gate Church** (1713) over the north gate, the Abbot's residence, a bell tower and the 20th-century **Church of St Seraphim**. The monastery is still undergoing restoration work, but is an active institution with a publishing house and a studio for icon restoration. Outside the gates is the Church of Rizpolozhenie, whose priests also conduct mass in the Old Cathedral on Sundays and holidays. Grounds are open 7:30am–7pm.

At 20 Donskaya Ulitsa is the Moscow baroque **Church of the Deposition of the Lord's Robe**, built in 1701. The Church is filled with splendid cherubs and contains a copy of the Icon of the Deposition of the Lord's Robe under a gilded canopy. In 1625, an envoy of a Persian shah presented Czar Mikhail Romanov and the Patriarch Filaret with a fragment of Jesus' robe. Filaret had an icon painted and declared a new Church holiday. The icon shows the Czar and Filaret placing the gold box, containing the piece of cloth, on the altar of the Kremlin's Uspensky Cathedral. The original icon is now in the Tretyakov Gallery.

A 10-minute walk northeast of the monastery (east of Shabalovka St), at 42/44 Mytnaya, stands the historic 160-meter (525-foot) **Shukhov Radio Tower**. In need of better radio communications in Moscow during the Civil War, the military hired Vladimir Shukhov in 1920 to construct a tower on top of a high piece of land in the city. Shukhov designed a unique steel free-standing hyperboloid structure that used four times less metal than the Eiffel Tower. For its time it was an engineering marvel and to this day skyscrapers and towers are designed around the same diagrid and hyberbolic principles. The Tower was in use until 2002, and often seen in the opening montages of many TV shows. Today funds are being raised for its restoration.

DANILOVSKY MONASTERY
The Danilovsky Monastery, off Danilovsky Val, is a 5-minute walk northeast of Tulskaya Metro station. The grounds are open daily 7am–7pm. It was founded in 1276 by Prince Daniil, the youngest son of Alexander Nevsky, and the only Moscow prince to be canonized by the Russian Church. The monastery's thick white walls served as part of the southern defenses of the city. During Stalin's rule the monastery was closed and later served as an orphanage, electronics factory and juvenile prison. Restoration work began in 1983 when the government returned the complex to the Orthodox Church. Two years later the buildings were reconsecrated for religious use. In 1988, to celebrate the Millennium of the Baptism of Rus, Patriarch Pimen chose Holy Danilov Monastery for the celebrations. During this time, the Danilovsky Monastery complex replaced Sergiyev Posad as the church's spiritual and administrative center. It is now the official residency of the Patriarch of all Russia.

Standing over the monastery entrance is the pink and white **Belfry Chapel of St Simon Stylites** (1730). The 18 bells were sold abroad in 1930, narrowly escaping a melt down during the country's anti-religion campaigns; they were bought by American industrialist Charles Crane, who donated the bells to Harvard University. The largest of the bells, Bolshoi (or Mother Earth Bell), weighs 13 tons and has a 317-kilo (700-lb) clapper. In 2008, the bells were returned to the Monastery, thanks to Viktor Vekselberg, famous for also buying back and returning Fabergé eggs to Russia. The university accepted replicas in exchange, which were custom-made in Voronezh.

The whitewashed **Cathedral of the Holy Fathers of the Seven Ecumenical Councils**, situated along the eastern wall, was built by Ivan the Terrible in 1565 on the original site of St Daniil's church. St Daniil is buried here within a golden coffin, and a few of the 17th-century frescoes remain. Services are held daily from 10am–5pm. Inside, at ground level, is the **Church of the Protecting Veil**, added in the 17th century, and at the northern end is a Chapel to St Daniil; its tabernacle is said to contain holy relics of the saint. The largest structure in the complex is the yellow **Trinity Cathedral**, designed in Moscow Neo-classical style by Osip Bovet in 1833. At the far end of the grounds is the **Patriarch's Official Residence**. Against the north wall is the 13th-century Armenian carved stone cross or *khachkar*, a gift from the Armenian church. The monastery also has an icon-painting workshop.

The Moscow Patriarch even has its own hotel on the southern grounds at 5 Starodanilovsky Lane. The modern-style **Danilovsky Hotel Complex** has a restaurant, café and bar, and even a swimming pool.

Leninsky Prospekt runs past the Donskoi Monastery and leads out of the city and into Moscow's modern southwestern district, which consists mostly of residential housing. Beginning at Oktyabrskaya Metro station the prospekt passes the **Academy of Sciences**, formerly Neskuchny Castle, and Gagarinskaya Ploshchad (Gagarin Square). The square (at Leninsky Prospekt Metro station) features a titanium **Monument of Yuri Gagarin**, who made the first manned space flight. At the base of the monument is a replica of the space capsule Vostok (East) in which Gagarin traveled on April 12, 1961. (Gagarin, trained as a test pilot, died in a plane crash in 1968; his ashes lie in the Kremlin Wall in Red Square.) This square used to mark the city limits in the 1950s. The prospekt continues past many department stores to the **Lumumba People's Friendship University**, founded in 1960, and today has over 20,000 students from around the world. (Patrice Lumumba was one of the key activists of the African peoples' fight for independence.) The prospekt eventually becomes the Kievsky Highway and ends at **Vnukovo Airport**.

SPASO-ANDRONIKOV MONASTERY

This monastery, at 10 Andronevskaya Ploshchad, is situated along the Yauza River, a tributary of the Moskva, in the eastern part of the city, a five-minute walk from Ploshchad Ilicha Metro station. It was founded in 1359 by the Metropolitan Alexei during the reign of Prince Donskoi and has quite an interesting history. After Alexei was confirmed by the Byzantine Patriarch in Constantinople in 1353, a heavy storm occurred at sea during his return journey. Alexei promised God that if he should live he would build a monastery dedicated to the saint whose feast day was celebrated on the day of his safe arrival in Moscow. Alexei returned on August 16, the Savior Day, or Vernicle. When the Mongol Khan suddenly summoned Alexei to help his ailing wife in the south, the metropolitan appointed Andronik, a monk at Sergiyev Posad's Trinity-Sergius Monastery, to oversee the complex's construction in his absence. The monastery was named the Spaso-Andronikov after the Savior and its first abbot. It later became the stronghold of the Old Believers.

This is the oldest architectural complex in Moscow after the Kremlin. The white helmet-domed **Cathedral of the Savior**, with its cluster of *kokoshniki* gables, was built between 1420 and 1427, and is considered the oldest building in Moscow. The master Iconist, Andrei Rublyov, who also trained as a monk at the Trinity-Sergius Monastery, painted many of the interior frescoes. (It was here that Rublyov painted his famous Old Testament Trinity icon, now in the Tretyakov Gallery.) Rublyov is said to be buried somewhere in the grounds of the monastery. The baroque **Church of the Archangel Michael** (1691–1739) was commissioned by Ustinia Lopukhina in 1694 to celebrate the birth of her grandson Alexei, son of Peter the Great, and her daughter Evdokia. Peter later banished Evdokia to Novodevichy Monastery (a form of divorce in those days) and the Lopukhinas to Siberia. The church is now an icon restoration studio.

The **Andrei Rublyov Museum of Old Russian Art**, opened in 1960, is housed in three separate buildings in the monastery. They are located immediately beyond the main gate. The former Seminary Building contains many 15th- and early 16th-century icons by Rublyov and his students (mostly copies of the originals). Some of the icons include St Sergius, St George, John the Baptist and the Almighty Savior. Many of the icons found in the Monks' Quarters (behind the Savior Cathedral) were painted in Moscow, Rostov, Tver and Novgorod from the 13th to 17th centuries. Nearby is a new Exhibition Hall of mainly 17th- and 18th-century icons that include Our Lady of Tikhvin. There are also displays of other paintings, sculpture, embroidery, old books and chronicles. The museum complex is open 11am–6pm, Thursday 2pm–9pm; closed Wednesdays and last Friday of each month. Andrei Tarkovsky filmed many of the scenes for his well-known film *Andrei Rublyov* here at the complex.

ALL-RUSSIAN EXHIBITION CENTER

A utopian exhibition of Soviet agricultural and collectivization achievements was first planned by Stalin, and opened on the site in 1939. A larger complex, named the Exhibition of Economic Achievements or VDNKh, opened in 1956, just a few days before the 20th Communist Party Congress (that denounced Stalin's personality cult). Nearly 100,000 objects, representing the latest in Soviet achievements in science, industry, transport, building and culture were exhibited in 300 buildings and 80 pavilions which spread out over an area of 220 hectares (545 acres). Each of the 15 republics had its own pavilion, and others included the Atomic Energy, Agriculture and Culture Pavilions. Now called the All-Russian Exhibition Center (VVC), this huge park is situated on the opposite side of the street from the **Kosmos Hotel** at the end of Prospekt Mira, near VDNKh Metro station. Enter through the main entrance at the Arch. Grounds are open from 9am-10pm and most pavilions from 10am–7pm. At the entrance once stood the 24-meter high Soviet-realist Monument to the Worker and Collective-Farm Girl, which was sculpted between 1935 and 1937 by Vera Mukhina, who created it for the Soviet Pavilion at the

Exhibition Universelle in Paris. It stood here from 1937 until 2003, when it was removed and took seven years (and about $30 million) to restore. Its new home is in a pavilion that also houses a cinema and museum. In 1998, a Hollywood firm offered to purchase the statue (it has long been a symbol of Mosfilm Studios, as the lion is to MGM), but the government refused the sale. Another of Mukhina's works, the brigade sculpture, *We Demand Peace*, was also restored and moved to the Tretyakov's Art Muzeon Park. Mukhina is also known as the designer of the *granyony staken*—the 12-sided glass tumbler created for the working class. They were used throughout the country from *stolovayas* (cafeterias) to *kommunalkas* (communal-living flats); and, by the mid 1980s, half a billion were being produced, costing 7 kopeks each.

The main pavilion that used to house the "The Triumph of Lenin's Socialist Ideas" is now ironically filled with capitalist consumerism, and shops are full of kitschy items and electronics for sale. The large 'Friendship of Nations Fountain' (which has dried up) includes golden statues of women dancing in a ring. The restored pavilions are now mostly used as exhibition centers and shopping outlets.

The first monument that comes to view is the 96-meter high (315-feet) titanium **Sputnik Rocket**—the first Sputnik satellite was launched on October 4, 1957. (Imagine, in a little more than 50 years, there are today nearly 3,000 satellites orbiting the earth!) At the base of the Sputnik rocket is the **Cosmonautics Memorial Museum**, open 10am–7pm, closed Mondays. The museum focuses on the history of space exploration and includes the first Soviet rocket engine, a moon-rover, cool space propaganda posters and an exhibit on Yuri Gagarin to honor the 50th anniversary of his 1961 space flight. The 27-year-old Gargarin, who stood at just 1.57 m (5 ft 2 in), squeezed into the small pod of the Vostok spacecraft and was launched on April 12, 1961 as the first man into space; his historic flight from launch to landing lasted 108 minutes. (Ten months later, the first American, John Glenn, would orbit the earth.) Gagarin tragically died seven years later when his fighter jet crashed. Every year, celebrations take place around the world on April 12th, known as 'Yuri's Night' to commemorate the dawning of space exploration.

At the end of the park, stands a replica of the **Vostok Rocket** that carried Gagarin into space. The rocket looms in front of the former **Kosmos Pavilion**, where a display once honored Konstantin Tsiolkovsky, the father of the Russian space program. He invented the first wind tunnel and outlined the principle of the reactor rocket; he once said, 'This planet is the cradle of the human mind, but one cannot spend one's life in a cradle.' After Sputnik's launch in 1957, the three dogs Laika, Belka and Strelka had their own space rides (Belka and Strelka returned to earth). Lunik-2 landed on the moon in 1959. The first woman in space, Valentina Tereshkova, orbited the earth on June 16, 1963. On March 18, 1965, Alexei Leonov made the first spacewalk. By 1975, the first joint US–USSR space mission, Soyuz–Apollo, had been undertaken. MIR, the first space station was launched into orbit on February 19, 1986. The cosmonaut, Valery Polyakov, holds the world record for the longest time spent by an individual in space at 437 days/18 hours, completed during 1994–95. Then in February 2001, after 15 years in space (it was originally designed to last for only five), the Mir was allowed to leave its orbit—the government could no longer afford to fund it. The 136-ton Mir's planned destruction marked the end of the world's longest running space-station which orbited the earth nearly 100,000 times, hosted more than 100 people and survived more than 1,500 breakdowns.

Later, in 2001, a Russian Soyuz space capsule and two cosmonauts took the world's first space tourist for a visit to the first International Space Station. The American tycoon, Dennis Tito, trained at Star City outside Moscow and paid a reported $20 million for the eight-day trip. In 2003 the first ever marriage from space took place when Russian cosmonaut Yuri Malenchenko married his sweetheart on earth, taking their vows via a live video link from the international space station.

OSTANKINO

Not far from VDNKh Metro station, at 5 Pervaya Ostankinskaya Street, is the **Ostankino Palace** (walk west from the station, cross the intersection and take tram number 7 or 11 west to the last stop). It was built by serf-architect Pavel Argunov between 1792 and 1797 as the summer residence of Count Nikolai Sheremetyev on the grounds of the family's estate. The pink and white classical palace was built of wood, but painted to resemble bricks and stone. Interesting rooms are the Blue Room, Egyptian Ballroom, Italian Reception Room, the Picture Gallery and Theater, which had over 200 serf actors, dancers and musicians. The palace also houses the Museum of Serf Art. The beautiful serf-actress Praskovia Zhemchugova-Kovalyova later became the count's wife (see page 276). The red-brick Trinity Church (1678) adjoins the palace. A beautiful English-landscaped park and gardens are also on the grounds, and a theater often holds summer evening concerts. The Park is open 11am–8pm; closed Mondays and Tuesdays. (The Palace has recently been closed for restoration.)

The 540-meter (1771-foot) high **Ostankino TV Tower** looms nearby at Akademinika Korolyova Street. The tower, which surpassed the Empire State Building as the world's tallest freestanding structure when it was built in 1967, closed after a fire in 2000. In 2007, the restored tower was reopened with a glass-floored observation deck and a rotating restaurant called *Sedmoye Nebo* (Seventh Heaven), which first started serving in 1969. Open 10am–8.00pm; closed Mondays.

DOWN THE MOSKVA RIVER

The Moskva River is 500 kilometers (300 miles) long, of which 77 kilometers (48 miles) wind their way through Moscow. Fourteen road bridges cross the river. Boat cruises leave at regular intervals (April to October) from various locations on both sides of the river; one of the popular embarkation points is at the crystal pedestrian bridge near the Kievsky Railway Station—take the Metro to Kievskaya. (The boat pier is by the Evropeisky Shopping center and Crystal Bridge.) The cruise lasts about 90 minutes, and runs from Kievsky down river to Novospassky Bridge and monastery. The *Rocket* hydrofoils also leave from beside Gorky Park and the Bolshoi Ustinsky Most where the Yauza and Moskva rivers meet. At any stop along the route, once you disembark, that is the end of the journey (or buy a full day pass for unlimited rides). Some sites along the way are the Kremlin, Cathedral of Christ the Savior, Novodevichy Monastery, Sparrow Hills, Moscow University, Gorky Park, Ostankino TV Tower, and many estates, palaces and churches. Boats leaving from the same piers also run westward to Kuntsevo-Krylatskoye in Fili-Kuntsevo Park, with a river beach and the swimming island of Serebryany Bor. This trip lasts about an hour. There are many types of cruises offered—check with a travel agency or at your hotel for other options.

From Kievsky Pier, the cruise ends at the **Novospassky Monastery**, founded in the 15th century by Ivan the Great (nearest Metro is Proletarskaya; open daily 7am–7pm). The 17th-century **Cathedral of the Transfiguration of the Savior**, built by the Romanov family as a vision of the Kremlin's Assumption Cathedral, became the burial site of the czar's relatives; masters from the Kremlin armory painted the inner vaults. The Romanov family tree, which dates back to the Viking prince Rurik, climbs one wall. The bell tower, gates and stone walls also date from the 17th-century. Today the New Monastery of the Savior is again a working monastery. Also lying on the banks of the Moskva River is the 17th-century **Krutitskoye Metropolitans' Residence** (*krutitsy* are small hills). When the church lost its place in the Kremlin in the 16th century, the Ecclesiastic Residence was built here (the residence of the Patriarch is now at the Danilovsky Monastery). The **Simonov Monastery** was founded in the 14th century by the nephew of St Sergius of Radonezh, and named Simonov, after a nobleman who had donated the land. It was built as a defensive fortress to protect the southern end of Moscow from the invading Mongols. Today, only a few buildings and a church remain. Another architectural ensemble is the **St Andrew Monastery** with a 17th-century Church painted like a peacock's tail. Founded by Fyodor Rtishchev, a cultural advisor to Czar Alexis (father of Peter the Great), the monastery set up Moscow's first school, and the monks also translated books from foreign languages. Today, it houses the Library of the Synod, the central repository of the Russian Orthodox Church.

VICINITY OF MOSCOW

Strewn throughout the Moscow suburbs are the beloved dacha or 'country homes'. From czarist through Stalinist times, the *dacha* was a privilege granted for loyalty or special service. (The name derives from the verb *dat*—"to give".) Later, ordinary Russians began to build their own modest country houses, often from scrounged materials. These suburban retreats into nature were enjoyed as a re-connection to the Russian soul. In warmer months, families gathered wild mushrooms and berries in the forest, grew potatoes, tomatoes and cucumbers in their small garden plots, and socialized with neighboring *dachniki*.

Today, a whole new breed of country home, the *"kottedzhi"* is evolving with the richer "New Russians," who are changing the landscape of suburbia into gated communities. Many wealthy are now building luxury country palaces, surrounded by high brick fortress walls; and, understandably, the regular dacha dwellers are upset with the change. Today, it is now common to see million-dollar mansions go up next door to wooden shacks. A new trend is also developing where country-club settlements have everything from community swimming pools to kindergartens. In the new prestigious locations around Rublyovo-Uspenskoye or Dmitrovskoye Highways and Serebreny Bor, huge houses can rent from $5,000 up to even $50,000 per month. The market for the simple traditional Russian *dacha* is giving way to new symbols of affluence and excess.

In the 18th- and 19th-centuries, the privileged classes of Russia also built their summer residences in the countryside around Moscow. Many of these palaces and parks have been preserved and converted into museums. Here are 14 spots that can easily be reached by Metro, train or inexpensive *elektrichka* (surburban train), bus or car. There are also group excursions (day or overnight) to some of these areas; check at the Service Bureau in your hotel or a local travel agency for more information.

Usually travel distances less than 2–3 hours are serviced by the *prigorodny* or surburban trains, known as *eletrichki*. At the train station, there is a separate *Prigorodny Zal* (Пригородным Зал), which sells local tickets (buy the ticket before you depart). (The posted time-tables are also separate from the long-distance schedules.) Make sure to ask for the location of the departure platform. These are slow trains, and have a single-class hard seat. Most stations now have electronic ticket readers. Keep the ticket! It may be checked on the train. When you arrive, you may also need to scan it again to exit the station. Upon arrival, it is advised to first check on returning times of trains to Moscow before you set off.

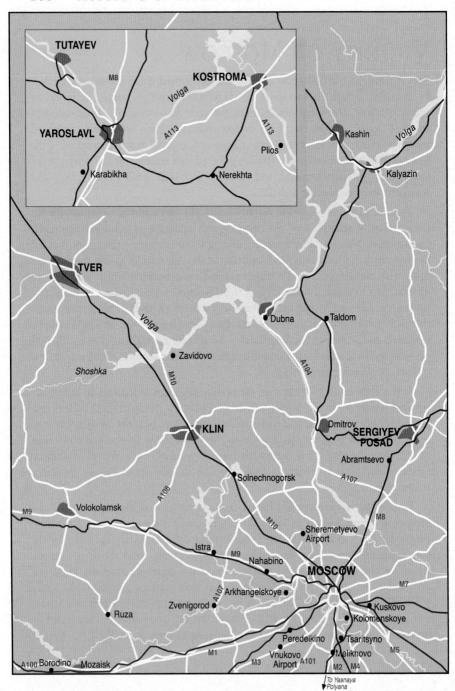

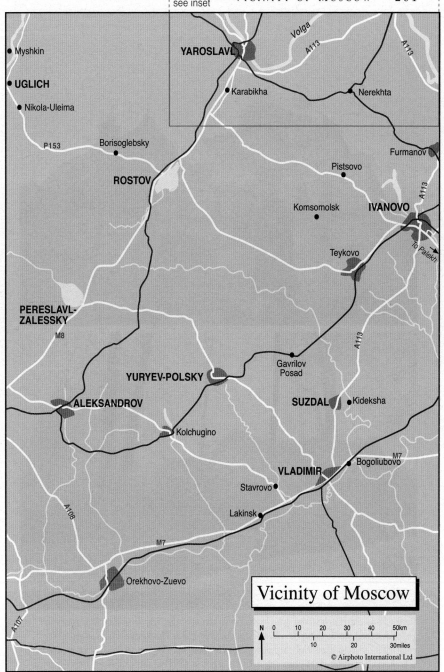

Vicinity of Moscow

© Airphoto International Ltd

(top) Church Patriarch Nikon, who began construction of the New Jerusalem Monastery in 1656, designed the site after the churches in the Holy Land. The Resurrection Cathedral is modeled after Jerusalem's Holy Sepulcher Church. (bottom) The famous Russian composer, Peter Tchaikovsky lived for eight years (up until his death in 1893) in this charming timber-framed house in the quaint town of Klin. Here he scored many of his most popular works, such as The Nutcracker and Sleeping Beauty.

In the town of Istra, west of Moscow, an old 17th-century church is exhibited in the Museum of Wooden Architecture, surrounded by beryoza or birch trees.

(above) Today, the Kolomenskoye Museum Preserve, outside Moscow, is a four-square kilometer open-air museum of 16th-and 17th-century architecture which includes many elaborately decorated Russian Orthodox churches. The area was used by Peter the Great and Ivan the Terrible as their country estates.

The Kuskovo Mansion (1769–75), faced with white stone, has the initials PS (for the owner Peter Sheremetyev) carved above the front door. The estate has its own small church with a colorful iconostasis.

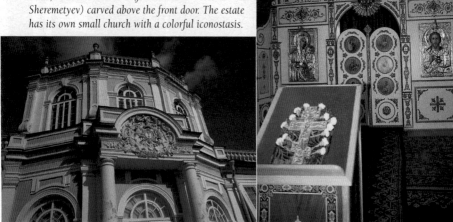

When the wealthy merchant, Peter Sheremetyev, married a Romanov princess in 1743, he built a lavish summer estate at Kuskovo, nicknamed the Moscow Versailles. They lived in this pink and white mansion, which now houses a collection of 18th-century Russian art. On the estate grounds are other colorful pavilions, cottages and theaters.

At the Persian walnut desk, inherited from his father, Tolstoy penned his novels Anna Karenina and War and Peace (see Literary Excerpt on page 112).

(opposite top & left) The great Russian writer Count Leo Tolstoy was born at Yasnaya Polyana, south of Moscow, in 1828. He inherited the estate in 1847 and lived and worked here for more than 60 years. Today this 19th-century estate is known as the Leo Tolstoy Museum where everything of the writer's has been preserved, including the 22,000 tome library and study. (see www.ypmuseum.ru).

(below) Zvenigord, founded in 1339, later became the powerful religious center of Czar Alexei, father of Peter the Great. Today, the picturesque town, situated on a hill that overlooks the Moscow River, is known as Moscow's Switzerland. The operating monastery contains numerous old churches and buildings, many of which are historical museums.

ABRAMTSEVO ESTATE MUSEUM (Абрамцево)

The **Abramtsevo Estate Museum** is located along the M8 Yaroslavskoye Highway (a few kilometers past the 61km signpost) near the town of Sergiyev Posad, about 60 kilometers (37 miles) northeast of Moscow. (Signs to Abramtsevo and Khotkovo mark the turn-off, and continue over the railway tracks.) Local buses run to and from Sergiyev Posad, or it is about a 90-minute journey by train from Yaroslavsky Railway Station (Komsomolskaya metro). Trains run every half hour to Sergiyev Posad or Alexandrov; check that it stops at Abramsevo. (At Abramtsevo, cross the tracks and behind the tent-shaped archway in the middle of the platform find a flight of steps that lead down to a woodland path. This route will take you all the way to the museum.The estate will appear on the right, on 1 Museynaya St—about a 20-minute walk from the station.) If driving, try the Russkaya Skazka Restaurant at 43 Yaroslavskoye Highway. Otherwise bring food from Moscow for a picnic lunch; there is a small café next to the museum.

Chronicles dating back to the 16th-century remark on the region's *obramok* or forested hills flanked by a river. The name of the area became Obramkovo and later in the 18th-century it was softened to Abramtsevo. In 1843, the Russian writer Sergei Aksakov bought the country estate (built in the 1770s); over the next 15 years, it was frequented by many prominent writers, such as Gogol, Tyutchev and Turgenev. Here Gogol gave a reading of the first chapter from his second volume of *Dead Souls*, which he later burned at his home in Moscow. (His portrait hangs on the wall of the central mansion.) The writer Ivan Turgenev often came here to hunt and was mentioned in Aksakov's popular *Hunting Almanac*. In 1847, Aksakov wrote his famous book, *Notes on Fishing*. In 1870, the railway, textile baron and art patron, Savva Mamontov, bought the estate and turned it into a popular meeting place and artist colony. Art, theater, writing, carpentry and pottery workshops were conducted, and Serov, Repin, Vrubel, Shalyapin (who made his debut in the theater) and Stanislavsky all lived and worked here. In the **Manor House**, Serov's famous portrait *The Girl with Peaches* (1887) hangs in the dining room (the original can be found in the Tretyakov Gallery); it is of Mamontov's daughter Vera, who is buried on the estate. Also gracing the walls are Repin's portraits of Mamontov and his wife Elizaveta. The traditional long timber-framed house with fancy lacework gable was said to be the model for Chekhov's manor house in *The Cherry Orchard*. Mamontov also opened a school for peasant children and taught their parents traditional folk crafts.

Standing in the park, the white **Church of the Savior-Not-Made-By-Hands** was designed by artist Viktor Vasnetsov and built in 1882. It was based on the Novgorod 12th-century-style Church of the Savior in Nereditsa. Repin, Polenov and Vasnetsov painted the interior icons. In 1886, Valentin Serov painted the lovely *Winter in Abramtsevo* and *The Church*. The ceramic tiles that decorate the exterior were produced at the estate's own ceramic workshop. In 1891, a small chapel was added to the northern side to commemorate the tragic death of Mamontov's son, Andrei. Both Mamontov, who shot himself shortly after the Revolution in 1918, and his son are buried here. Vasnetsov also dreamed up the *Izbush'kha na Kur'nikh Nozhkakh'* (Hut on Chicken Legs), the headquarters of the witch Baba Yaga in a popular Russian fairy tale, a must see on the property!

The countryside, filled with birch groves, colorful gardens and woods, greatly inspired the landscape artist Isaac Levitan, who often visited the estate. Abramtsevo is now a museum and displays the rooms as used by Aksakov and Mamontov. Paintings and other art executed on the estate, including many by Vrubel, are exhibited in the art studio. Another neo-classical building exhibits works by the avant-garde 'Knave of Artists' group and pieces by later artists, such as Vera Mukhina; in the 1930's many lived nearby at the Artist's Village on the banks of the Vorya River. The museum is open from 10am–6pm Apr–Sept, 10am–4pm Oct–Mar; closed Mon/Tues and last Thursday of the month. www.abramtsevo.net/eng.

If the weather is pleasant, take a stroll about a kilometer north to the village of **Khotkovo** (or ride the train to the Khotkovo stop), at 23 Kooperativnaya St, where the Pokovsky (Protector of the Veil) Convent was founded in 1308 (and destroyed in the 17th century during the Time of Troubles and later restored in the 18th-century). The recently restored **Cathedral of the Intercession** holds the remains of the parents of St Sergius who founded the monastery at Sergiyev Posad. Across the street from the Convent's southern gate is the **Arts and Crafts Museum**, dedicated to the art of woodcarving. Abramtsevo artist, Vasily Vornoskov (1876–1940), developed the special style known as Abramtsevo-Kudrino. The museum exhibits works by Vornoskov and other contemporary artists. Operating hours are the same as Abramtsevo.

ARKHANGELSKOYE ESTATE MUSEUM (Архангельское)

This museum lies in the village of Arkhangelskoye, 16 kilometers (ten miles) west of Moscow. Take the M9 Volokolamskoye Highway and then the left road toward Petrovo-Dalniye. The closest Metro station is Tushinskaya; exit station right, turn right around the corner, and take bus 549 (about eight stops). It lets you off across the street from the museum entrance. The grand estate is situated along the banks of the Moskva River and took 40 years to complete. Prince Golitsyn originally founded the estate at the end of the 18th-century. The mansion and park were designed in French style by the architect Chevalier de Huerne and built by serf craftsmen. In 1810, the estate passed into the hands of the wealthy landowner Prince Yusupov (a descendant of one of the Khans—not the one who killed Rasputin) who was the director of the Hermitage Museum and Imperial Theater. He turned the classical palace into his own personal art museum. Today the palace contains works by such artists as Boucher, Hubert Robert, Roslin and Van Dyck and the Italian master, Tiepolo. As rumor has it, the palace once contained the portraits of each of Yusupov's 300 mistresses. The rooms and halls are beautifully decorated with antique furniture (many pieces were owned by Marie Antoinette and Madame Pompadour), marble sculptures, tapestries, porcelain and chandeliers; much of the china and glassware was produced on the estate. The oldest structure is the **Church of the Archangel Michael** (1667); the **Holy Gates** link it with the estate. The **Colonnade**, originally built on the eastern side as the Yusupov Mausoleum (but never completed), now hosts a small museum and musical concerts. The estate is surrounded on three sides by a multi-level Italian-style park, lined with classical sculptures, arbors, and pavilions that include the **Tea House** and **Caprice Hall**. The **Temple to Catherine the Great** depicts her as Themis, Goddess of Justice. There is also a **Monument to Pushkin** who enjoyed visiting the grounds.

Just west of the gardens is the wooden Serf Theater, exhibiting theatrical and original set designs by Pietro Gottardo Gonzaga. Built in 1819 by the serf-architect Ivanov, the theater, which seated 400, had one of the largest companies of serf actors in Russia. The park grounds are open 10am–8pm, and the museums 10:00am–5pm; weekends 10am–6pm; closed Mon/Tues and last Wed of the month. www.arkhangelskoe.ru/eng. A local restaurant is the **Russkaya Izba** (Russian Cottage), fashioned after Russian peasant rooms. The cooking is Old Russian; the menu offers bear meat and venison along with kvas, mead and tea served from a bubbling samovar. Open daily noon–10pm at 1 Naberezhnaya St, in Ilyinskoye village. As an additional dining choice, try the **Arkhangelskoye Restaurant**, located across from the estate's main entrance, open noon to midnight. It has Russian and European dishes and wines, and a dining terrace is open in summer months (live music Thurs–Sun after 7pm).

BORODINO (Бородино)

Borodino, site of the most famous battle in the War of 1812, lies on the M1 Moscow –Minsk road, 120 kilometers (75 miles) southwest of Moscow. (By car, at 95-km, past the Outer Ring, take the Mozhaisk turn off. It's 5km north to Mozhaisk, then another 13km west to Borodino.) *Elektrichka* commuter trains run from Moscow's Byelorussky Train Station and take about two hours (You can also travel to Mozhaisk and take a taxi to Borodino.) The Preserve is spread over 100-sq-km, so driving a car opens up a visit to far more sites. If coming by train, you can walk several kilometers along the main road from the station to the main museum with stops along the way that include Semyonskoye (battle central) and the monastery. The train station also contains a small Borodino exhibit; open 9am–4:30pm; closed Sun/Mon. For more information and a map of the battlefield, see: www.borodino.ru.

In the late spring of 1812, Napoleon led his massive army of more than half a million men into Russia. Presented with no other option but a bloodbath, the generals of Alexander I's armies ordered a humiliating retreat. But, in August, the Czar appointed 67-year-old Prince Mikhail Kutuzov as commander-in-chief to stop Napoleon invading Moscow. On August 26 (new calendar Sept 7), 1812, the Russians took on the French at Borodino. Napoleon's army numbered over 135,000 soldiers with 600 guns and the Russians, 150,000 soldiers with 640 guns. Remarkably, after 15 hours of fighting (and 80,000 dead from both sides), Napoleon was forced to retreat, and the Battle of Borodino marked the turning point of the war. (Kutuzov remarked that 'this was the bloodiest combat ever seen in modern times.') Kutuzov's generals, including Barclay de Tolly, wanted to stage another battle with Napoleon before Moscow, but Kutuzov wanted to save his armies from yet another bloody encounter. He argued, 'Moscow will be the sponge that will suck him in.' Meeting no resistance, Napoleon's remaining troops entered the gates of Moscow on September 2 at Poklonnaya Gora (Hill of Greeting) and waited for a formal surrender. No one arrived and the French found Moscow nearly deserted. As Napoleon slowly marched towards the Kremlin, immense fires (set purposely by the Muscovites) broke out throughout the city; eventually over 80 percent of Moscow would burn to the ground. By mid-October, with winter approaching and no supplies at hand, Napoleon was forced to abandon Moscow and undertake a long march home during one of the worst winters on record. When he finally released his army only 25,000 Frenchmen remained alive. To celebrate Russia's triumphant victory, Alexander I ordered the Cathedral of Christ the Savior built in Moscow 'in the name of the fatherland to express our thanks and gratitude to all our loyal subjects, true sons of Russia.'

The entire area is known as the **Borodino War and History Museum and Reserve**, which encompasses the many battle sites and memorials. In 1912, to mark the battle's 100th anniversary, 34 monuments were erected throughout the battlefields. The polished granite obelisk crowned by a bronze eagle is dedicated to Field Marshal Kutuzov. Leo Tolstoy visited the battlefield in 1876 while writing *War and Peace*. Midway between the train station and museum is **Semyonovskoye**, the area of the most intense battles. Here, General Bagration's Second Army was obliterated by French troops. (In front of the museum on the hilltop is **Bagration's Tomb**.) Several kilometers to the west, an obelisk mark's the spot of Napoleon's headquarters; in the town of Gorki to the north, Kutuzov's headquarters are marked by one as well. Other memorials commemorate World War II battles that took place here in 1941. Every year, during the first Sunday in September, the anniversary is celebrated by a Borodino Field Day, when the battle is actually reenacted. People playing the French and Russian soldiers dress in period uniforms, cannons roar and smoke rises from the battlefield. A religious ceremony is held after the battle to give thanks for Napoleon's defeat. The 200th anniversary had a grand celebration in 2012.

Filmmaker Sergei Bondarchuk's four-part nine-hour epic *War and Peace* (1966–67) was Russia's longest and most expensive film ever made. Taking five years to produce, it encompassed some of the most spectacular battle scenes ever seen on film. During the recreated Battle of Borodino over 120,000 extras were used from the Soviet army. Five museums are in the area, including the **Borodino Military History Museum**; which is a good starting point—the diorama gives a big picture of the battle scenes, and other exhibits showcase uniforms, weapons and other items. The museums are open 10am–6pm (Apr–Oct), 9am–4:30pm (Nov–March); closed Mon/Tues and last Friday of the month. (Another Battle of Borodino Museum is in Moscow at 38 Kutuzovsky Prospekt, by the Triumphal Arch, see page 208.)

If you have time for a local side-trip while in Borodino, visit the **Spaso Borodinsky** (Savior Borodino) **Convent** in the Village of Tuchkovo. It was established by Margarita Tuchkova, widow of the famous General Alexander Tuchkov, who died in Borodino defending positions against the French. In 1820, Alexander I donated 10,000 rubles for Margarita (she was of the noble Naryshkin family) to construct a church in honor of her husband and those who fell in battle. Inside the church is a marble cross inscribed with the words, 'Remember, O Lord, in Thy Kingdom, Alexander, killed in battle.' Later, Margarita moved to Borodino from Moscow and became a nun in 1840. Czar Nicholas I made further donations to the site and was present at the convent's consecration. Up until her death in 1852, Margarita (now Mother Superior Maria) provided shelter to homeless, abused and elderly women. Until 1917 it was the model for all other convents across the country. In a twist of fate, when the Nazis invaded during WWII the buildings were used as a concentration camp. In the 1990s, the convent underwent massive renovation work and today the churches and refectory (with its splendid iconostasis) are open to the public. The convent was renown for its beautifully sewn icons, where women embroidered on silk, satin and velvet, with gold and silver threads. It also houses the exhibit "Leo Tolstoy and the Battle of Borodino", with some of the author's original draft notes made on the battlefield. An *elektrichka* train runs from Borodino to the nearby Tuchkovo stop. Open 10am–5pm; closed Mondays.

ISTRA RIVER MUSEUM OF WOODEN ARCHITECTURE AND ETHNOGRAPHY (Истра)

The museum is located 56 kilometers (35 miles) west of Moscow, along the M9 or Volokolamskoye Highway. *Elektrichka* trains run from Moscow's Rizhsky Railway Station (the Prigorodniye *kassa* and trains are at the very end of the building) and take about an hour. The **Museum of Wooden Architecture**, in the Gethsemane Park along the Istra River, contains a 17th-century wooden church and farmstead, cottages, granaries and windmills brought in from nearby areas as well as the original meditation house of Nikon. Both Istra and the New Jerusalem Monastery grounds are open 10am–5pm; closed Sundays and Mondays.

The Novoyarusalimsky or **New Jerusalem Monastery** (now returned to the Orthodox Church) is situated a few kilometers to the west of Istra (one train stop further, then by Bus no. 22, or a 20-minute walk). Patriarch Nikon, who caused the great Orthodox schism, began construction of the monastery in 1656, designing the site after the grounds and churches in the Holy Land. (Ironically, he was later stripped of his position by the czar and exiled here until his death in 1681.) During World War II the Germans blew up the grounds, but today much has been restored. The **Resurrection Cathedral** (1656–85) is modeled after Jerusalem's Holy Sepulcher Church, and the surrounding fortress walls represent the city of Jerusalem with its Zion and Damascus Towers. Many parts of the cathedral are named after the Stations of the Cross, and are extensively covered by tiles and colorful plasterwork. The most intriguing spot is the **Golgotha Chapel** where an artificial fissure (representing the earthquake that shook the world when Christ died) cuts across a 17th-century wooden iconostasis with figures of the crucifixion. Nikon is buried beneath in the Chapel of St John the Baptist. A collection of Russian paintings, icons, furniture and porcelain and military uniforms is on display in the refectory and other buildings, including the Nativity Church, behind the cathedral. In 2009, Russian President Dmitry Medvedev signed a decree that allocated government funds for further restoration work on the New Jerusalem Monastery.

KLIN (Клин)

The Russian town of Klin, founded on the banks of the Sestra River (a tributary of the Volga) in 1318, is located 85 kilometers (53 miles) northwest of Moscow along the M10 Highway. *Elektrichka* trains run from Leningradsky Train Station on the way to Tver, and take about two hours. Continue to Tchaikovsky's House by Bus 5. Get off at Bolnitsa (hospital). The museum is across the street at 48 Tchaikovsky. The **Tchaikovsky Memorial House** is open 10am–6pm, closed Wed/Thurs and last Monday of the month. www.tchaikovsky-house-museum.ru.

The town was the ancestral home of the Romanov dynasty; today only two Naryshkin baroque-style churches remain of the monastery. In the 19th century, it was the center of ornament making; and today, a town museum exhibits over 2000 items, including historical Christmas tree ornaments. Klin is more widely known as the home of the renowned Russian composer Peter (Pyotr) Tchaikovsky (1840–93). The composer who said, 'I find no words to express how much I need the charm and quiet of the Russian countryside', bought the estate in 1885. (Tchaikovsky also yearned for peaceful isolation after the public rebuffed him for his homosexuality, and a number of friends had criticized some of his earlier works.) In the gray-green timber-framed house, at 48 Tchaikovsky Street, the composer went on to score some of his most popular works: the ballets *The Nutcracker* and *Sleeping Beauty*, and his Fifth and Sixth Symphonies. Not long after the première of his *Pathétique* (Sixth) Symphony in St Petersburg, Tchaikovsky died, on November 6, of cholera after ignoring a warning not to drink the water during an epidemic. (Some consider he committed suicide.) Pyotr's brother, Modest, transformed the house into a museum. Inside the dacha, portraits of famous musicians hang in the living room, along with a photographic picture of Tchaikovsky's father in the study; the library, with original scores and letters, contains over 2000 books. On his birthday, May 7, and day of his death, November 6, winners of the Moscow Tchaikovsky International Competition and other virtuosi play works on his Becker grand piano. Concerts are also given year-round in a hall on the grounds.

For the first Tchaikovsky International Competition (held in March 1958 and chaired by Dmitri Shostakovich), the surprise winner of the Gold Medal (this was the height of the Cold War under Khrushchev) was a 23-year-old Julliard-trained pianist named Van Cliburn, a tall blonde Texan, who flawlessly performed Rachmaninov's Third Piano Concerto and Tchaikovsky's Piano Concerto No. 1. The Russian pianist, Lev Vlasenko, came second. Van Cliburn won the sum of $6,000 (25,000 rubles) and was honored with a ticker tape parade in New York City. On his 60th birthday in 1994, Van Cliburn performed with the Moscow Philharmonic in Los Angeles; he died in 2013. Today, the Tchaikovsky Competition, held every four years in Moscow, continues to rank among the most prestigious in the world.

The **Tchaikovsky Memorial House** and estate-museum is open 10am–6pm (ticket *kassa* closes at 5pm); closed Wednesdays, Thursdays and the last Monday of each month.

KOLOMENSKOYE MUSEUM PRESERVE (Коломенское)

This large preserve is situated about ten kilometers (six miles) southeast of Moscow on the banks of the Moskva River, at 39 Andropova Street. It is well worth taking a day's excursion to the outer suburbs for a visit. Drive south of the city along the Kashirskoye Highway or take the Metro to the Kolomenskaya (accent on 'lo') station; it is only about a ten-minute walk from there. Head east along Novinki Street and then south on Bolshaya which turns into Shtatnaya Sloboda and leads to the northern entrance gate. In summer, some Moscow River cruises also stop at the ferry landing by the eastern gate. Kolomenskoye was once the country estate of numerous Russian princes and czars, including Ivan the Terrible and Peter the Great. The name of the area dates from the 13th-century, when villagers fleeing

Mongol attacks on the town of Kolomna settled here. Some of the oldest trees in Moscow can be found in the preserve, many over 400 years old.

The area is now a four-square-kilometer open-air museum of 16th- and 17th-century architecture. Visitors enter the park through the northern, whitewashed **Savior Gate**, which stands on the grounds that were once Czar Alexei's orchards.

The czar (father of Peter the Great) was passionate about hunting, and also helped train falcons; more than 300 birds of prey and 100,000 doves were said to have been on his estate. Between 1666 and 1667, a large wooden palace known as the **Jewel-Box**, complete with 270 rooms, 3,000 windows of glittering mica, and elaborate *kokoshniki* gables was constructed. It was hailed by many as the "eighth wonder of the world." The czar's throne was flanked with a pair of large gilded lions who could roar and roll their eyes with a pull on a hidden mechanism. In 1768, Catherine the Great had the palace torn down and a new one built near the Ascension Church. In 2010, after the Moscow government invested over a billion rubles to rebuild the destroyed complex (based on archival documents and floor plans), the **Alexei Mikhailovich Palace**, with its 24 magnificently reconstructed chambers, was reopened to the public. The royal palace was originally joined by a passageway to the 17th-century baroque-style **Church of the Kazan Virgin**; it stands on the left as you walk through the gates. A copy of the famous icon of the Virgin of Kazan is located in the main iconostasis. (After the Revolution the original icon disappeared.) Today the church is a busy place of worship, and services are held daily.

On the south side of the complex, rising high on the banks of the river stands the tent-shaped and elaborately decorated **Ascension Church**. The brick structure was built in 1532 to celebrate the birth of Vasily III's first son, Ivan the Terrible. The building was also the highest structure in all of Moscow at 60 meters (197 feet) and served as a watchtower. It was the first church to reproduce the design of wooden churches in brick and it is believed to be the forerunner to St Basil's Cathedral, built a quarter of a century later. From an upper window Ivan the Terrible could observe his soldiers fighting the invading Mongols. Alongside stands the 16th-century **St George Bell Tower**, all that remains of the Church of St George the Victorious. Other structures of interest are the Dyakovskaya Church, the water tower (which brought water up from the river), a Siberian watch tower (1631) and a gatehouse whose clock has been working since the time of Peter the Great. A museum housing religious and royal artifacts is situated within the eastern **Palace Gatehouse**, built in 1673. Of particular interest is the replica of Czar Alexei's wooden palace, made by the carver Smirnov in the 19th century. The **Stable Yard** building includes a coach house, a smithy and a hayloft. Follow the wooden steps southwest through the forest to the fived-domed **Church of St John the Baptist**, built in 1529, thought modeled on Moscow's St Basil's Cathedral.

From the 1930s to 1950s, monuments of Russian architecture were brought to the park from different regions of the country. These buildings, located on the northwestern side of the park, in the older palace area, now exhibit 16th- to 19th-century Russian applied and decorative art, including collections of paintings, ceramics, woodcarvings and clocks. **Peter the Great's** cabin is in this area; he lived in the six-room cottage in 1702, while supervising the building of his navy in the northern city of Arkhangelsk. It is a favorite area for picnics, shaded by oaks, elms and poplars; one of the ancient oak trees is thought to date back to the 14th century and the rule of Ivan I. Russian film director Sergei Eisenstein also shot some of the famous scenes of his film *Ivan the Terrible* here at Kolomenskoye. The museums are open 10am–6pm; closed Mondays. Each year a festival of Sacred Music takes place in the Ascension Church and, around the last Sunday in May, there is a parade to celebrate Peter the Great's birthday. Every year in February/March, during the *Maslenitsa* (Butter Week) holiday, a huge festival takes place on the grounds, where *blini* pancakes are served to celebrate the return of spring. For more info, see: http://mgomz.com/.

KUSKOVO PALACE MUSEUM (КУСКОВО)

This estate-museum is located within the city limits, 12 kilometers (7 miles) to the southeast and can be easily reached from the Ryazansky Prospekt Metro station. From the station, it is a 20-minute walk or short bus ride (six stops on bus number 133) to 2 Yunost Street. The lands of Kuskovo were in the Sheremetyev family since the early 17th century. (Boris Sheremetyev fought with Peter the Great against the Swedes in the Battle of Poltava in 1709.) The Sheremetyevs were incredibly wealthy with over three million acres of land holdings and 200,000 serfs. (Today, Moscow's main airport, built on land that belonged to their estates, has the Sheremetyev family name.) When Boris' son, Count Pyotr Borisovich, married the Romanov princess Varvara Cherkassova in 1743, they decided to built a summer estate at Kuskovo, where as many as 30,000 guests could be entertained in a single day; it was soon nicknamed the Moscow Versailles. The pink and white wooden **Mansion** (1769–75) was designed by Karl Blank and serf-architects Alexei Mironov and Fyodor Argunov. It is faced with white stone and decorated with parquet floors, antique furniture, embroidered tapestries and crystal chandeliers; notice the carved initials PS over the front door. The mansion also houses an excellent collection of 18th-century Russian art; Catherine the Great's portrait hangs in the Raspberry Drawing Room and the White Ball Hall is decorated with rich bucolic scenes painted by Sheremetyev serfs. A museum shop is located in the palace basement.

Exiting the palace, and walking in a counter-clockwise direction, leads to the Estate **Church** (1739) and **Bell tower** (1792) and then on to the large **Kitchen** wing and **Coach House**; in front stands the **Grotto**, where five small pink-white **menagerie** pavilions are situated around the pond. (Sheremetyev loved to stage mock military battles on the lake for his friends.) Above them stands the white **Italian House** (1755), which displays a collection of 18th-century paintings and sculpture. Walking up past the wooden-framed **Bird Pavillion** brings you to the famous **Open-Air Theater** (1763), where the celebrated company of Sheremetyev serf-actors performed weekly plays. One of the most popular actresses was Praskovia Zhemchugova-Kovalyova (1768–1803), the daughter of a serf blacksmith. In 1789, when she caught the eye of Nikolai Sheremetyev, son of Pyotr, one of Russia's most romantic love stories developed. Creating a major scandal, Nikolai granted her freedom in 1798, and went on to marry the commoner in 1801. To get away from increasing social gossip, they moved to a palace at Ostankino (see page 257). Sadly, Praskovia died two years later of consumption after giving birth to a son; in the neighboring **Orangerie**, a small display tells their love story. The **Ceramics Museum** contains the world's largest collection of ceramics, mosaics and glassware—with over 30,000 pieces from ancient times to the present. Continuing around brings you to the **Manager's House** (1810) and the **Large Stone Conservatory** (1763). Walking down through the **Sculptures in the Park** (over 50 are placed throughout the grounds), leads past the yellow, neoclassical **Hermitage**, designed by Karl Blank in 1765, the brick-façade **Dutch Cottage** (1749), and the brick and wooden-tiered **Swiss House**, built in 1864 by Nikolai Benois. In summer, the palace stages music festivals and concerts in the Hall of Mirrors.

The estate and museums are open 10am–6pm April to October, 10am–4pm Nov–March; closed Mon/Tues and last Wednesday of month. www.kuskovo.ru/en.

In the vicinity, at 6 Topolyovaya Alley in Kuzminki Park, is the country estate of the Stroganovs (and later Golitsyn family), known as **Kuzminki**. Grigory Stroganov (1656–1715) was the first owner, who hired celebrated architects Kozakov, Bazhenov and the Gilyardi family to create the estate buildings. In 1716, at the request of Maria Stroganova, the wooden **Church of the Vlakhernskaya Virgin** was built. In 2000, a museum opened in the **Kuzminki Country Estate**, with exhibits on 18th/19th-century nobility estate life. It's a lovely stroll through the parks and around the four connecting ponds; in winter one can ice skate and go ice fishing, and bicycling and sailing in summer. (Metro Kuzmiki or by car MKAD 12km.) Open 10am–6pm; closed Mondays.

MELIKHOVO (МЕЛИХОВО)

The Melikhovo Estate, located 50 km (30 miles) south of Moscow, is where the renowned writer Anton Chekhov lived from 1892–1899, and penned more than 40 works, including *The Seagull* (1895) and *Uncle Vanya* (1896). The **Chekhov House-Museum** exhibits more than 18,000 items, including his literary works and personal items. (Open 10am–5pm; closed Mondays and last Friday of month). As a practicing doctor, who famously described 'medicine as my wife and literature as my mistress,' Chekhov saw patients in his study; during the 1892 cholera epidemic, he was responsible for the care of 26 villages. He also helped establish several new schools; one destitute teacher he knew is thought to have inspired the character Medvedenko in *The Seagull*. In May, 1899, after the success of *The Seagull* at the Moscow Arts Theater, Chekhov invited its leading actress Olga Knipper to Melikhovo; they married in May, 1901. 'My estate is not much, but the surroundings are magnificent!', he declared.' Besides the museum, visitors can wander about the grounds and peek into the 18th-century wooden church. (Around 1927, the estate was destroyed, but later the house and guesthouse were reconstructed.) After Chekhov's health declined due to tuberculosis, the writer sold the estate and moved to a warmer climate in Yalta, Crimea; he died July 15, 1904 at age 44.

In May, the museum hosts *Melikhovo Spring*, a week-long theater festival. Here, international groups perform many of Chekhov's plays. *Elektricki* trains frequently depart from Kursky Train Stain (surburban kiosks are below the main level), and take 90 minutes to reach the town of Chekhov (in the Kursky direction). From here, Bus 25 makes the 20-minute run to Melikhovo almost every hour. (While in Chekhov, the Chekhov Museum of Letters is at 4a Chekhov St.)

MOSCOW COUNTRY CLUB (Нахабино)

The 142-hectare (350-acre) Moscow Country Club, at Nahabino, with Russia's first 18-hole championship golf course, is located about 30 kilometers (18 miles) northwest of Moscow in the Krasnogorsk district (a 40-minute drive from the city center along the M9 Volokolamskoye Highway (by the 31 kilometer marker) or by *elektrichki* train from Moscow's Rizhsky Railway Station. Designed by renowned California golf architect Robert Trent Jones II, the course is rated as one of the top ten golf courses in Europe and has an 18-hole, 6,735-meter (7,000-plus-yard) par-72 championship course. The club is owned by GlavUpDK, Russia's Diplomatic Service.

The golf course construction began in 1987, and took over six years to complete. The first Russian Golf Association was established in 1992; and, a year later, Moscow held its first Golf Open Championship at Nahabino. In September 1996, the club hosted Russia's first international golf tournament as part of the PGA European Challenge Tour, with 100 tour-ranked members, including 20 professionals from 26 countries; ten of the participants were Russian, playing for the first time on home soil.

It took over two decades to negotiate and build Russia's first golf course. The first joint venture planning began in 1974 between Robert Trent Jones Senior and Junior, Armand Hammer and GlavUpDK. Many interruptions (some serious, others wildly amusing) occurred during periods of the Brezhnev stagnation and Afghanistan War.

When Trent Jones II submitted some of his first course plans to the US Commerce Department (a mandatory requirement when doing business in Russia at the time), the US Defense Department wanted to immediately halt the progress when they noticed that 'bunkers' had been incorporated into the design! (Later, while building the course in Moscow, Jones' employees actually came across foxholes, dug during World War II as protection against invading Germans.) Russia has come a long way—no golf terminology existed in their language: 'Fore' started out as *Ostarozhno* or 'Look Out!' Today the Reds on the greens include many Russian children who come as part of school curriculums to practice their golf swing. There are also numerous junior and amateur tournaments.

On the grounds, there is also a driving range, practice greens, and a clubhouse with restaurant and bars, and a pro-shop, complete with locker room facilities and a computerized golf simulator. The club has a hotel complex and conference center, a multi-million dollar spa and sports club with an indoor pool, tennis, squash, basketball, gymnasium, aerobics and fitness training. Outside, there is also a lakeside beach area, water sports, boating and fishing. Individual luxury homes, modeled on 18th-century wooden dachas, are arranged around a central garden area. In colder months one can try cross-country skiing, snowmobiling, and winter golf. Spa and golf facilities are available for non-members. www.moscowcountryclub.ru/en.

On a drive west towards Nahabino, looming over the birch forests, a giant 12-story-high fiberglass **Pyramid** comes into view. Alexander Golod, a Ukrainian ex-defense contractor spent millions building pyramids throughout the former Soviet Union for he believes they are capable of 'changing physical and psychological conditions.' People flock to this New Age Monastery to quietly sit inside and take in the pyramid's energy. Three glass balls in the middle of the floor represent geography, topography and astronomy. The shop sells energized crystals and water, and you can have your aura read. Free admission to the good vibrations.

PEREDELKINO (Переделкино)

Take an *elektrichka* train from Moscow's Kievsky Railway Station for the half-hour ride southwest to Peredelkino in the Solntsevo district. From the station, either take a bus to the end of Pavelyenko Street, or walk 20 minutes to the village. (If driving, take the Mozhaiskoye Highway to the Minskoye Highway and at the 21-km signpost, turn left for Peredelkino.) For decades the Soviet Government granted the Writers' Union land in this area to build resident dachas for their members. Peredelkino became a name synonymous with a writers' and artists' colony. Even Anna Akhmatova and Alexander Solzhenitsyn lived here at one time; the latter lived in a spare room of a writer friend after he had smuggled out The *Gulag Archipelago* to the West. (After Solzhenitsyn died in 2008, the government ironically changed the name of Moscow's Big Communist St to Alexander Solzhenitsyn St.)

Above the railway station stands the 15th-century **Church of the Transfiguration**, whose interior is decorated with a multitude of saints and a fine iconostasis. Follow the path right across the square which brings you to Pasternak's grave (the headstone bears his profile), bordered by three pines and usually covered with flowers. Other prominent writers are also buried in the cemetery. It is a lovely place to stroll, and nice spot for a picnic. Nordic skiing and ice fishing are also possible in winter months.

Continuing down the hill, head up the road for half a kilometer to reach the Museum Homes of Pasternak and Chukovsky (Pasternak's home, at 3 Pavlenko St, is signposted down a lane to the right, and Chukovsky's to the left).

At his dacha, Russian writer Boris Pasternak (1890–1960) wrote his famous novel, *Dr Zhivago*—for this book the disillusioned writer was expelled from the Writers' Union and forced to decline his 1958 Nobel prize. The home, where the author died in 1960, is now the **Pasternak House Museum**; the exterior is said to resemble the prow of a ship. Open 10am–5pm; closed Mondays and last Tuesday of month. The 1965 film adaptation of *Dr Zhivago* is one of the highest grossing films of all times; in 2006, Mosfilm produced an epic eight-hour television miniseries based on the book.

Pasternak wrote of Moscow:
> *For the dreamer and the night-bird*
> *Moscow is dearer than all else in the world.*
> *It is at the hearth, the source*
> *Of everything that the century will live for.*

Nearby is the **Chukovsky House-Museum**, home of celebrated children's writer, Korney Chukovsky, who wrote *Doctor Ayboliit*, based on Dr Doolittle stories. Outside the dacha is a tree decorated with shoes, in tribute to one of his popular tales. (Group visits only). If looking for a place to dine, the Deti Solntsa (Children of the Sun) Restaurant is at 4 Pokodina St in the Writers' House of Creativity. The Dacha atmosphere makes it a lovely place to eat and relax.

TSARITSYNO (Царицыно)

Tsaritsyno Estate lies 21 kilometers (13 miles) south of Moscow at 1 Dolskaya Street. To get here, drive via the Kashirskoye Highway or take the Zamoskvoretskaya Liniya to Orekhovo Metro station. (Note the line splits at Kashirskaya. If coming from the city center, make sure the destination posted on the front of the train reads Krasnogvardeiskaya/Promzona, not Kakhovskaya.) Once there, head west, about a ten-minute walk to the park. The grounds are open daily from 6am to midnight.

In the 16th-century Irina, wife of Czar Fyodor Ioannovich, lived at her country estate here and had the Tsaritsyno (Czarina) ponds dug. Later it was the favorite of the Golitsyn princes; in 1712, Peter the Great presented the estate to a Moldovan count.

After Catherine the Great remodeled the Winter Palace and Hermitage in St Petersburg, she turned her attention to Moscow. In 1775, she bought this estate in the wooded countryside, complete with a palace and miniature opera house. It was known as Chornaya Gryaz (Black Mud); Catherine renamed it Tsaritsyno. Her architect Vasily Bazhenov was commissioned to transform the main building into a Moorish-Gothic-style palace, and the 6,200 acres into English-style formal gardens. After ten years of work, Catherine came down from St Petersburg to inspect it. She commanded that all work be stopped and the main palace torn down. In 1786, Bazhenov's pupil and main rival, Matvei Kazakov, was asked to redesign the property; these are the buildings we see today. Some speculate that Catherine had the original palace torn down because she had had it constructed in two parts—one for herself and one for her son Paul—connected by a common corridor. After a decade, however, she had come to abhor her son, who held equal contempt for her, so she no longer wanted anything to do with him. She also came to dislike the Freemasons and hated all freemasonry motifs. The rebuilding was halted at the resumption of the Turkish wars and stopped altogether upon her death in 1796.

Intended as the main entrance to the palace, the **Figurny Bridge** (with stone Maltese crosses—motifs of the Freemasons) separates Tsaritsyno's two lakes. The main building, through the **Grapevine Entrance** gates, looks more like a cathedral than a palace. Its windows are broken and the roof is crumbling—in the 19th century, a local factory needed roofing materials and raided the roof. At one time it was also used for mountaineering training, and crampon holes can still be seen in the walls. The **Palace** has never been lived in and has stood empty for more than two centuries.

The palace is bordered by the **Bakery** (Khlebny Dom) and the **Small Palace** (Maly Dvoretz). Next door is the restored **Opera House** with a small exhibit of porcelain, sculptures and paintings; musical concerts are also held here. The path in front of the palace leads to the octagonal **Octahedron** and a church originally constructed in 1765. The strange deserted buildings are fun to explore, and strolling around the grounds is a delight; bring a picnic. Boats are available for hire in summer. In winter it is fun to ice-skate, sled or cross-country ski in the area (you need to bring your own equipment). The Palace and Bakery exhibits are open from 11am–6pm, Sat 11am–8pm, Sun 11am–7pm; closed Mondays. The Orangerie complex is open 11am–6pm; closed Mondays and Tuesdays.

In 1988, the Russian Church was allowed to build a church in the town of Tsaritsyno to commemorate the Millennium of the Baptism of Rus; it was the first church allowed built in Moscow during the Soviet era. **The Museum of History, Architecture, Art and Nature** is open 11am–5pm; weekends 11am–6pm; closed Mondays and Tuesdays. Concerts are usually held on Saturday and Sunday.

To dine, try the **Usadba (Country Estate)** at 10 Polskaya Ulitsa, with live music some evenings. It is located in an elegant old mansion built by Catherine the Great; open daily noon–midnight.

YASNAYA POLYANA (Ясная Поляна)

The town lies some 200 kilometers (125 miles) south of Moscow along the M2 Simferopolskoye Highway. A high-speed train now runs between Moscow and Tula that takes less than three hours. Other suburban trains (four hours) also depart Moscow's Kursky Station for Tula. From the Tula station, it is 15 km to the museum. Because of the difficulty of public transport, it is advised to take a taxi. A group excursion can also be booked in Moscow.

The great Russian writer, Count Lev (Leo) Nikolayevich Tolstoy, was born in Yasnaya Polyana (Clear Glade) on August 28, 1828, and lived and worked here for over 60 years; he inherited the property in 1847. Everything on the estate, situated in a pastoral setting of birch forests and orchards, has been preserved as he left it—his living room (Tolstoy was born on the leather sofa), library (with 22,000 volumes), and parlor (where his wife Sonya Andreyevna meticulously copied his manuscripts). On the Persian walnut desk in the study, Tolstoy wrote *Anna Karenina* (*1873–77*), chapters of *The Resurrection*, and *War and Peace* (1863–69). Sonya claimed to have copied the entire manuscript—more than 3000 pages—seven times, when not busy bearing his 13 children (only eight survived to adulthood). Portraits by Ilya Repin and Valentin Serov decorate the walls. Today the manor house functions as the **Tolstoy House Museum**. It is said that Tolstoy wrote on average 50 pages a day, including diaries and correspondence, the equivalent of half of *War and*

Peace every year for sixty years. The Preshpekt Café is by the museum entrance. The writer also opened a school for local peasant children, and this now houses the **Literary Museum**. Peasants and other followers would gather outside under the Tree of the Poor to ask his advice.

The 445-hectare (1,100-acre) Yasnaya Polyana was the main source of creative inspiration for Tolstoy, and the location is reflected in many of his works. Here he wanted to create a miniature of Russian society. Tolstoy wrote: 'It is difficult for me to imagine Russia without my Yasnaya Polyana.' By 1885, Tolstoy had eschewed his position as an aristocrat and adopted a more austere life style. He became a vegetarian, gave up tobacco, enjoyed wearing simple peasant attire and worked in the fields alongside his serfs. He also railed against private property and all forms of violence. Tolstoy developed his own philosophy of Christianity so potent that, in 1901, the Russian Church excommunicated him (and he remains excommunicated today). His views caused a major schism within his family as well. (A translated book of Sonya's recollections, *The Diaries of Sophia Tolstoy*, was published in 1985.)

On October 28, 1910, at the age of 82, Tolstoy decided to renounce his possessions and family, and left the estate with his youngest daughter, Alexandra, and his doctor to embark on a journey. When they arrived at Astapovo Railway Station almost 320 kilometers (200 miles) away, Tolstoy was stricken with influenza. The great writer died in the station master's hut on November 7; his last words were said to be: 'Search, always go on searching...' The 2009 film, *The Last Station*, based on the tempestuous last months of Tolstoy's life, stars Christopher Plummer and Helen Mirren, and was produced by Andrei Konchalovsky; it is based on the novel of the same name by Jay Parini. In 2010, the centenary of Tolstoy's death was celebrated at the estate.

Three years after the death of his mother, when Lev was 5, his 10-year-old brother, Nikolai, proudly created the Ant Brotherhood and claimed to have discovered "the way for all men to... become continuously happy." Nikolai said that he wrote the answer to the secret of garnering earthly happiness on a green stick, which he buried at the edge of a gorge on the family estate. Tolstoy spent much of his life searching for the secret of happiness for all mankind. Upon his death, in accordance with his wishes, he was buried at the spot where his brother had assured him contained the green stick. A short walk down a well-worn path leads to Tolstoy's simple grave—a small mound of earth with no headstone. Tolstoy's wife, and then his daughters, managed the estate until 1956, when it was placed under Soviet control. Today, Tolstoy's great-great grandson Vladimir I. Tolstoy (over 200 descendants are scattered around six countries) presides over the daily management. Visit www.ypmuseum.ru for more detailed information on the museums and estate.

The grounds are open April 1–Oct 1 from 9am–8pm; Nov 1–March 31 9am–5pm; closed Mondays. From April to November admission to the memorial buildings is only by guided tour from 9:30am to 3:30pm (also closed last Tuesday of month). For a tour in English, it is advised to book in advance at vtv@tgk.tolstoy.ru (otherwise with no advance booking, you can join a Russian tour to get in; English audio guides are available). **The Yasnaya Polyana Hotel** is 2 km from the estate with the Country Estate Restaurant.

ZAVIDOVO (Завидово)

At the confluence of the Volga and Shoshka rivers, 120 kilometers (74 miles) northwest of Moscow (off the M10 Highway north of Klin) is the resort village of Zavidovo, The year-round resort has hotel and cottage accommodation, a golf course, health spa, swimming pool and shooting range. Sports include tennis, squash, horse riding, windsurfing, water skiing and other water activities. In winter there is even skiing, skating and ice fishing. From here an excursion to nearby Klin can easily be made. www.zavidovo.ru/eng.

Thirty kilometers further north along the Volga from Zavidovo is the city of **Tver**, (formerly Kalinin), famed site of the 1327 rebellion against the Mongol Horde and one of Moscow's chief rivals during the time of Ivan I. Since it was on the Moscow–St Petersburg road, Catherine the Great popularized the destination by resting here on route. With many museums, old churches and markets, Tver is another interesting area to explore on a day trip from Zavidovo or Klin. Trains leave from Moscow's Leningradsky Station and take under three hours. From Tver, there are daily trains to St Petersburg and buses to Novgorod.

ZVENIGOROD (Звенигород)

Zvenigorod lies about 50 kilometers (30 miles) west of Moscow along the M1/A105/A107 routes. *Elektrichka* trains also run from Moscow's Byelorussky Railway Station and take less than 90 minutes. At Zvenigorod, Bus 23 runs to the museum complex; get off by the **Alexander Nevsky Church**, built in memory of Alexander III in 1898.

In the small square along Moskovskaya St is the **Anton Chekhov Monument**, who stands with his dog. After graduating from Moscow University in the summer of 1884, the young doctor found work at the local hospital, which is now named after him; he later wrote the short story *Ward 6* about a doctor who goes mad. Walk downhill to Ulitsa Frunze, which runs alongside the river and leads to a staircase up the hill to the town's ancient center.

Zvenigorod, standing atop a hill that overlooks the Moskva River and founded in 1339, is known as Moscow's Switzerland. The heart of the town, known as "Gurodok" (citadel) is a former earthen fortress. Up in the hills stands the

14th-century single-domed **Cathedral of the Assumption** (Sobor na Gorodke), built by the son of Dmitri Donskoi; the interior walls contain fragments of frescoes painted by Andrei Rublyov. To reach the ancient monastery, continue down the road for about 15 minutes. St. Savva of Sotorzhi, a disciple of St Sergius, began construction on the **Monastery of Savva-Storozhevsky** at the end of the 14th century, and was buried here in 1407. It became the favorite religious retreat of Czar Alexei in the mid-17th century; his white palace is situated across from the cathedral's porch. Over the centuries the monastery grew to one of the richest and most powerful in Russia. Monks led a local revolution against the Bolsheviks in 1918; but a year later the new government shut down the monastery. It was returned to the Orthodox Church in 1985.

The 15th-century **Cathedral of the Nativity**, decorated with *kokoshniki* and stone carvings, is open for religious services. The interior iconostasis towers from floor to ceiling. Next to the multi-tiered bell tower (which you can climb) is the **Transfiguration Church**. The 17th-century **Trinity Church** is nearby with the attached Kazan Refectory. It was here that one of Russia's greatest film directors, Andrei Tarkovsky, staged much of his classic film on the life of the famous icon painter Andrei Rublyov, whose icons were discovered within the church in 1918 (These include the *Savior, Apostle Paul* and *Archangel Michael*, now exhibited in Moscow's Tretyakov Gallery). Lining the left-hand wall of the fortress is the red and white **Czaritsa's Chambers**, used by the Polish wife of Czar Alexei, and later Ivan the Terrible's. On the outside porch, notice the carved double- and single-headed eagles, emblems of Russian and Polish rulers. The **History Museum** is now located within the chambers, and another museum, exhibiting paintings, ceramics and wood carvings by local contemporary artists, is in the nearby two-story monks' quarters. Museums are open 10am–5pm; closed Mondays. Stop in the monastery's popular bakery for fresh *kvas* and *medovukha* (honey mead) and pastries. Women should don headscarves and long skirts, which are provided at the church entrance.

Hundreds of pilgrims congregate every weekend at Savvinsky Skit, an ancient cave downhill from the monastery where Saint Savva is said to have kept vigil. The cave is now considered a holy place, and pilgrims flock to kiss the rock. The sloping hill offers a stunning view of the surrounding landscape.

In summer, have a picnic by the Moscow River and even a swim. To reach the train station, return to the Alexander Nevsky Church and wait at the Bani stop; all passing buses head toward the station.

THE OLD ARISTOCRACY

Wealth was measured in those times by the number of "souls" which a landed proprietor owned. So many "souls" meant so many male serfs: women did not count. My father, who owned nearly twelve hundred souls, in three different provinces, and who had, in addition to his peasants' holdings, large tracts of land which were cultivated by these peasants, was accounted a rich man. He lived up to his reputation, which meant that his house was open to any number of visitors, and that he kept a very large household.

We were a family of eight, occasionally ten or twelve; but fifty servants at Moscow, and half as many more in the country, were considered not one too many. Four coachmen to attend a dozen horses, three cooks for the masters and two more for the servants, a dozen men to wait upon us at dinner-time (one man, plate in hand, standing behind each person seated at the table), and girls innumerable in the maid-servants' room—how could anyone do with less than this?

Besides, the ambition of every landed proprietor was that everything required for his household should be made at home by his own men.

"How nicely your piano is always tuned! I suppose Herr Schimmel must be your tuner?" perhaps a visitor would remark.

To be able to answer, "I have my own piano-tuner," was in those times the correct thing.

"What a beautiful pastry!" the guests would exclaim, when a work of art, composed of ices and pastry, appeared toward the end of the dinner. "Confess, prince, that it comes from Tremblé" (the fashionable pastry cook).

"It is by my own confectioner, a pupil of Tremblé, whom I have allowed to show what he can do," was a reply which elicited general admiration.

As soon as the children of the servants attained the age of ten, they were sent as apprentices to the fashionable shops, where they were obliged to spend five or seven years chiefly in sweeping, in receiving an incredible number of thrashings, and in running about town on errands of all sorts. I must own that few of them became masters of their respective arts. The tailors and the shoemakers were found only skillful enough to make clothes or shoes for the servants, and when a really good pastry was required for a dinner-party it was ordered at Tremblé's, while our own confectioner was beating the drum in the music band.

That band was another of my father's ambitions, and almost every one of his male servants, in addition to other accomplishments, was a bass-viol or a clarinet in the band. Makar, the piano-tuner, alias under-butler, was also a flautist; Andrei, the tailor, played the French horn; the confectioner was first put to beat the drum, but misused his instrument to such a deafening degree that a tremendous trumpet was bought for him, in the hope that his lungs would not have the power to make the same noise as his hands; when, however, this last hope had to be abandoned, he was set to be a soldier. As to "spotted Tikhon", in addition to his numerous functions in the household as lamp-cleaner, floor-polisher, and footman, he made himself useful in the band—today as trombone, tomorrow as bassoon, and occasionally as second violin...

Dancing-parties were not infrequent, to say nothing of obligatory balls every winter. Father's way, in such cases, was to have everything done in good style, whatever the expense. But at the same time such niggardliness was practised in our house in daily life that if I were to recount it, I should be accused of exaggeration. However, in the Old Equerries' Quarter such a mode of life only raised my father in public esteem. "The old prince," it was said, "seems to be sharp over money at home; but knows how a nobleman ought to live."

Prince Peter Kropotkin, Memoirs of a Revolutionist, 1899

THE GOLDEN RING (ZOLOTOYE KOLTSO)

The ancient towns of the Golden Ring, built between the 11th and 17th centuries, are the cradles of Russian culture. During Russia's early history, the two most important cities were Kiev in the south and Novgorod in the north. They were both situated in what is now western Russia and lay along important commerce routes to the Black and Baltic seas. The settlements that sprang up along the trade routes between these two cities prospered and grew into large towns of major political and religious importance. From the 11th to 15th centuries, the towns of Rostov, Yaroslavl, Vladimir and Suzdal became capitals of the northern principalities, and Sergiyev Posad served as the center of Russian Orthodoxy. In the 12th-century Moscow was established as a small protective outpost of the Rostov-Suzdal principality. By the 16th century Moscow had grown so big and affluent that it was named the capital of the Russian Empire. These prominent towns that lay in a circle to the northeast of Moscow became known as the Golden Ring. Each town is a living chronicle documenting many centuries in the history of old Russia.

THE RUSSIAN TOWN

Up to the end of the 18th century, a typical Russian town consisted of a kremlin, a protective fortress surrounding the site. Watchtowers were built in strategic points along the kremlin wall and contained vaulted carriageways, which served as the gates to the city. The timber town within the kremlin contained the governmental and administrative offices. The boyars, or noble class, had homes here too that were used only in time of war—otherwise they lived outside the town on their own country estates, where the peasants or serfs worked the land. The *posad* (earth town) was the settlement of traders and craftsmen. The *posad* also contained the *rinoks*—the markets and bazaars, as well as the storage houses for the town. The merchants and boyars used their wealth to help build the churches and commissioned artists to paint elaborate frescoes and icons. The number of churches and monasteries mirrored the prosperity of the town. The rest of the townspeople lived in settlements known as the *slobody* around the kremlin. The historical nucleus and heart of the town was known as the *strelka*. The regions were separated into principalities with their own governing princes. A ruler of the united principalities was known as the grand prince and later czar. The head of the Orthodox Church was called the metropolitan and later patriarch.

The Golden Ring area provides an excellent opportunity to view typical Russian towns, which are still surrounded by ancient kremlins, churches and monasteries. The towns of Rostov, Vladimir, Suzdal and Pereslavl-Zalessky retain much of their original layouts. Outside Suzdal and Kostroma are open-air architectural museums—

entire wooden villages built to typify old Russian life. All the towns of the Golden Ring have been well restored, and many of the buildings are now museums that trace the history of the area that was the center of the Golden Age of Rus.

RELIGION AND THE CHURCH

Before Prince Vladimir introduced Byzantine Christianity to the Kievan principality in AD 988, Russia was a pagan state; the people of Rus worshipped numerous gods. Festivals were held according to the seasons, planting and harvest cycles, and life passages. Special offerings of eggs, wheat and honey were presented to the gods of water, soil and sun. Carved figures of mermaids and suns adorned the roofs of houses. When Prince Vladimir married the sister of the Byzantine Emperor and introduced Christianity, Russia was finally united under one God and Kiev became the center of the Orthodox Church. (According to the Primary Chronicle—the first recorded history of Kievan Rus, written by monks in the eleventh century—emissaries of Vladimir's, whom he had dispersed on a fact-finding mission to locate the 'true faith', were so enamored with the capital of Byzantium that they exclaimed, "We knew not whether we were in heaven or on earth, for surely there is no such splendor or beauty anywhere else".) But it took almost a century to convert the many pagan areas, especially in the north. Early church architecture (11th-century) was based on the Byzantine cube-shaped building with one low rounded cupola on the roof bearing an Orthodox cross facing east. The domes gradually evolved into helmet drums on tent-shaped roofs. In the 17th century Patriarch Nikon banned the tent-shaped roof because it appeared too similar to the design of Western Lutheran churches. Thus the onion-shaped dome (also more suitable for the heavy snowfalls) became the distinctive design of the Orthodox Church. Nikon also decreed the assembly of five domes (instead of the usual one); the central higher dome symbolized 'the seat of the Lord', while the four lower ones, the four evangelists. The next two centuries witnessed classical and baroque influences, and the onion domes became much more elaborately shaped and decorated. During your tour of the Golden Ring, try dating the churches by the shapes of their domes.

The outer walls of churches were divided into three sections by protruding vertical strips, which indicated the position of the piers inside. Several centuries later churches had expanded considerably and were built from white stone or brick instead of wood. (Unfortunately, many of the wooden buildings did not survive and stone churches were built on their original sites.) The main body of the church was tiered into different levels and adjoined by chapels, galleries and porches. A large tent-shaped bell tower usually dominated one side.

During the two and a half centuries of Mongol occupation (beginning in the mid-13th century), Russia was cut off from any outside influence. Monasteries united the Russian people and acted as shelters and fortresses against attacks. They became the educational centers and housed the historical manuscripts which monks wrote on birch-bark parchment. During this period Russian church architecture developed a unique style. Some distinctive features were the decorative *zakomara*, semicircular arches that lined the tops of the outer walls where they joined the roof. The *trapeza* porch was built outside the western entrance of the church and other carved designs were copied from the decorations on peasant houses. Elaborate carved gables around doors, windows and archways were called *kokoshniki*, named after the large headdresses worn by young married women. Through the years, even though the architecture took on European classical, Gothic and baroque elements, the designs always retained a distinctive Russian flair. Each entrance of the kremlin had its own Gate Church. The most elaborate stood by the Holy Gates, the main entrance to the town. Many cathedrals took years to build and twin churches were also a common sight—one was used in winter and the other, more elaborate, for summer services and festivals.

The interior of the church was highly decorated with frescoes. Images of Christ were painted inside the central dome, surrounded by angels. Beneath the dome came the pictures of saints, apostles and prophets. Images of the patron saint of the church might appear on the pillars. Special religious scenes and the earthly life of Christ or the Virgin Mary were depicted on the walls and vaults. The Transfiguration was usually painted on the east wall by the altar and scenes from the Last Judgment and Old Testament were illustrated on the west wall, where people would exit the church. The iconostasis was an elaborate tiered structure, filled with icons that stretched behind the altar from the floor toward the ceiling. The top tiers held Christ, the middle the saints and prophets, and the lower tiers were reserved for scenes from church history.

Fresco painting was a highly respected skill and many master craftsmen, such as Andrei Rublyov and Daniil Chorny, produced beautiful works of art. The plaster was applied to the wall of the church and then artists would sketch the main outline of the fresco right onto the damp plaster. The master supervised the work and filled in the more intricate and important parts of the composition, while the apprentices added the background detail.

The building of elaborate churches and painting of exquisite frescoes and icons reached its zenith in the prosperous towns of the Golden Ring. Even cathedrals in the Moscow Kremlin were copied from church designs that originated in Rostov, Vladimir and Suzdal. Today these churches and works of art stand as monuments to an extraordinary era of Russian history.

RELIGION AFTER THE REVOLUTION

For nearly 1,000 years the Russian Orthodox Church dominated the life of Russia and, as Tolstoy observed, for most of the Russian people 'faith was the force of life'. (A popular slogan of czarist times was "Orthodoxy, Autocracy, Nationhood!") But after the 1917 Revolution, when Marx proclaimed that 'religion is the opium of the masses,' all churches were closed to religious use and their property confiscated and redistributed by the government. Trotsky scathingly condemned the superstitious, backward Russia of 'icons and cockroaches,' and Lenin denounced religion as 'spiritual booze in which the slaves of capital drown their human image.' In 1918, there were 50,000 Russian Orthodox priests in the Soviet Union; by 1935, there were just 500. By the time of Stalin's purges in the 1930s, the capital had lost over a third of its glorious churches, and less than 100 still functioned officially in the entire Soviet Union. Churches were turned into swimming pools, ice-skating rinks, and atheist museums. Moscow's Danilovsky Monastery was used as a prison, and the Church of St Nicholas became a gas station.

In 1988, the Millennium of Russian Christianity was officially celebrated throughout the former Soviet Union, and government decrees provided a new legal status for the Orthodox Church and other religions. The Russian Orthodox Church remained headed by the patriarch and assisted by the Holy Synod, whose seats are in Sergiyev Posad and Moscow respectively. But the government continued to control and dictate the moves of the Church, while the topic of religion was discussed in meetings of the Supreme Soviet. Positive signs of increased religious tolerance and freedom slowly emerged and a small number of churches were eventually given back for religious use.

During the period of perestroika, the process of renewal of Soviet society brought about major changes in the relations between Church and State and believers and nonbelievers. On April 29, 1988, the eve of the Millennium of Russian Orthodoxy, Gorbachev received the Patriarch of Moscow and All Russia and members of the Synod in the Yekaterinsky Hall in the Kremlin. Gorbachev stated: 'Believers are Soviet people; they are workers and patriots and they have a full right to adequately express their convictions. The reforms of perestroika and glasnost concern them also without any limitations.' On October 13, 1989, a Thanksgiving Service was held in the Kremlin's Assumption Cathedral, the first service to take place there in 71 years. (The last Mass held there had been at Easter in 1918.) The government also returned the Danilovsky Monastery which became the seat of the Orthodox Church in Moscow. In 1988 alone some 900 buildings were returned to the Church, and religious figures were even elected to the Congress of Peoples' Deputies. On December 1, 1989, Gorbachev became the first Soviet leader to set foot in the Vatican.

One well-respected St Petersburg rector of the Orthodox Church and city seminary (who was allowed to visit Rome for an audience with the Pope during perestroika) remarked, 'I am an optimist. People are not only interested in bettering themselves economically, but also morally and spiritually. The powers of the Communist State could never extend to the soul. And in these uncertain times, we would like to help the new generation find its way.'

Since the collapse of the Soviet Union, the Patriarch of All Russia is now the head of the Russian Orthodox Church and the Church is separate from the State. Since the establishment of Christianity in Russia, the form of Church leadership has changed several times. The Church was headed by a metropolitan from 988 to 1589, and then by a patriarch until 1721. Peter the Great then dissolved the seat of the patriarch and created a governing Church body known as the Holy Synod, a group of 11 of the highest-ranking priests. (When Peter the Great returned from his travels to Western Europe, he changed New Year's Day from September 1—a legacy of the Byzantine Empire—to January 1 (as used in the West). He adopted the *Anno Domini* calendar (and renounced the *Anno Mundi*); thus January 1, 7208 become January 1, 1700.) In November 1917, the Bolshevik government decided to restore the patriarchate—that is, leadership by one supreme individual rather than by a collective body. The Bolsheviks also adopted the Gregorian calendar, 13 days ahead of the former Julian calendar. (In Soviet times, this is why the October Revolution holiday was celebrated in November.)

In 1992, Boris Yeltsin became the first Russian leader since the 1917 Bolshevik Revolution to attend Easter ceremonies in an Orthodox Church. Yeltsin, who was baptized, told Patriarch Alexei, 'It is time for Russia to return to her strong religious heritage.' On November 4, 1993, Yeltsin attended the consecration of the newly restored Kazan Cathedral in Red Square. During the siege of the White House, the Patriarch was called in to help arbitrate between the hard-liners and Yeltsin. Another battle was also being waged: to determine whether the government, museums or the Church owned the religious art. In 1993, Yeltsin signed orders to transfer two famous icons by Andrei Rublyov in the Tretyakov Gallery back to the Orthodox Church.

After the fall of the Soviet Union more than 10,000 churches were reopened for religious activities. Today the Orthodox Church claims 80 million followers, or more than half of Russia's population. St Petersburg has over 30 places of worship and Moscow supports over 130 active churches. More people, especially the younger generation, are attending religious services and being baptized. Ever since the 11th-century Orthodox Russians have worshiped in the same way. There are no pews, and the congregation remains standing throughout the long service.

The priest, bedecked in heavy embroidered vestments while gently swinging incense censers, leads the worshippers through the familiar liturgy. Theological seminaries are training monks and priests, and Church charity organizations are now permitted to help the new classes of homeless, poor and unemployed. The Russian Orthodox Church has also embraced the capitalist spirit. Many churches have their own shops, and priests are earning money blessing everything from businesses and apartments to cars, bars and casinos (Orthodox priests have even been invited to sprinkle holy water on new surface-to-air missiles.)

With Moscow's new 360-million-dollar Cathedral of Christ Our Savior (rebuilt on the spot where Stalin destroyed the old one), the Orthodox Church and its patriarch find themselves back at the apogee of political power in the new Russia. During the presidency of Boris Yeltsin a strong partnership, which had not existed for centuries, was formed between the Orthodox Church and the Russian State. While State officials attended Christmas and Easter services, the Patriarch was invited to the Kremlin to attend secular ceremonies and treaty signings.

In 1997, to fully cement its dominance, the Orthodox Church sponsored a bill in an attempt to restrict all other faiths in the country. Patriarch Alexei II commented: 'A law on religion is needed to protect Russians from destructive pseudo-religious cults, and foreign false missionaries.' (Ironically, Communists also supported the bill.) On September 26, 1997, Yeltsin signed the Freedom of Conscience and Religious Association Acts, which state that only those churches that collaborated with the regime during 1917–91 are recognized by the Russian Government; others may still pray and worship, but only in their homes. (Any religious denomination that had failed to secure a new registration was effectively banned from practicing in Russia.) Today, clashes continue between post-Soviet Church conservatives, members of other religious groups and State reformists. In 2003 a Russian Orthodox priest was defrocked for marrying two men in the Church's first gay marriage.

Additionally, in 1997, the Council of Archbishops of the Russian Orthodox Church bestowed sainthood on metropolitans Pyotr and Sarafim, and Archbishop Faddei, who were subjected to repression by Stalin in 1937. Even though an official St Petersburg burial was permitted for Czar Nicholas II and his family (in July 1998), the Chairman of the Holy Synod refrained from canonizing them; although, in 2000, Nicholas and Alexandra were beatified by the Church. Vladimir Putin, a former KGB agent who now wears a cross and goes to church, said: 'Orthodoxy has always had a special role in shaping our statehood, our culture and our morals.' Although two-thirds of Russians consider themselves Orthodox, only 4 percent (according to opinion polls) say they look to religion as a source of morals—most identify with the church out of nationalism.

In 2009, over 700 priests and monks gathered in Moscow's Christ the Savior Cathedral to vote for the first patriarch since the fall of the Soviet Union. As the tabulation board proclaimed the result, bells rang loudly in the Cathedral and throughout the nearby Kremlin. Elected as the 16th Patriarch of Moscow and All Russia was 62-year-old Kirill I, a native of St Petersburg, and the interim leader after the death of Alexei II. One newspaper editor remarked, 'Today the Orthodox Church is not only a spiritual but also a tremendous social force in Russia.' In 2010, President Medvedev signed a law making July 28 a state holiday to mark the country's conversion to Orthodox Christianity in AD 988.

Today, after all the transitions, most religious (minority) groups are enjoying a period of openness. There are one and a half million officially registered Jews (given as their nationality), two million Roman Catholics, five million Uniates (Catholics of Eastern Rite), 800 Protestant congregations, two million Lutherans and over one million Baptists. An estimated 20 million persons are of the Islamic faith, or about one in seven Russians. There are also over a million Buddhists and two million Old Believers, a sect resulting from the 1666 schism of the Orthodox Church. No matter what ecclesiastical precedence is established, it is well worth recognizing that as Russia heads into the 21st century, such religious tolerance within her lands has not been known since the era of Peter the Great.

GETTING THERE

Many travel organizations (both international and local) offer package tours specifically to Golden Ring destinations. Once you are in Russia, a hotel service desk or local agency can also suggest excursions along the Golden Ring route. (See Travel Agencies and Tour Companies in Moscow Practical Information section.) Some places, like Sergiyev Posad or Alexandrov, can be visited as a day trip from Moscow.

The Golden Ring area is easily accessible to independent travelers by car, train or bus, though planning and patience is needed. (It is also possible to fly to some towns.) Pre-plan an itinerary by finding out the best routes to each location. If not journeying by car, check train and bus schedules in advance (trains depart from different Moscow stations). For long-distance train schedules, see www.russianrails. com or www.russianrailways.com (tickets can be purchased online, but you need to print out the e-ticket.) The easiest and least expensive way to the nearest towns, such as Sergiyev Posad and Alexandrov, is by taking an *elektrichka* commuter train—with no reserved seats and sold on day of departure. You will need the ticket to both enter and *exit* the station. (Dress warmly in winter as many of these trains are not heated.) Regular train routes have daily departures to other cities as Vladimir and Yaroslavl. (Long distance and *elektrichka prigorodnye* (surburban) trains depart from separate areas in the station, and tickets are bought at different kiosks.) Long-distance buses to most Golden Ring areas also run from Moscow's northeast

Shchyolkovsky Station. The best way is to spend several days on the road and combine a few towns during the tour. It is always better to go during weekdays, when trains and towns are less crowded, especially in summer. Today, many more hotels, restaurants and supermarkets have opened, but it is always a good idea to bring along some bottled water and snacks. Internet cafés have popped up in most towns as well. A more detailed description on how to get to each Golden Ring location and where to stay is provided under each individual listing. Check out the websites: www.waytorussia.net or www.booking.com for hotel listings in the Golden Ring area. There are now a wide variety of places to stay: from 4-star complexes (with pools and saunas) to inexpensive hotels, guestrooms (in private homes) and hostels; most include breakfast. Many can now be reserved and paid for online with a credit card. Most towns have places that rent out bikes, a great way to explore the area.

The towns of the Golden Ring are a majestic mirror of Russia's past grandeur. The monasteries and churches are beautifully preserved, and their frescoes and icons have been painstakingly restored. Many of the churches hold religious services which you are welcome to attend. (Do not wear shorts or sleeveless shirts; men should remove hats, and women cover their heads.) Other religious buildings have been converted into museums that house the art and historical artifacts of the region.

A splendid skyline of golden-domed churches, tent-shaped towers, ornamental belfries, picturesque old wooden buildings and rolling countryside dotted with birch trees greets you—as it did the visitor more than seven centuries ago.

SERGIYEV POSAD Сергиев Посад
CENTER OF RUSSIAN ORTHODOXY

A 75-kilometer (46-mile) ride northeast of Moscow leads to Sergiyev Posad, the most popular town on the Golden Ring route. As soon as the road leaves Moscow, it winds back in time through dense forests of spruce and birch, past old wooden dachas, country homes and farms, and eventually opens onto a magical view upon which fairy tales are based.

You can drive via the M8 Yaroslavskoye Highway (a continuation of Prospekt Mira) or take an express train from Moscow's Yaroslavsky Railway Station (Komsomolskaya Metro) to Yaroslavl, which departs twice daily, and stops an hour later in Sergiyev Posad (these tickets are bought at the long-distance kiosk). Departing every half hour are the inexpensive *elektrichka* surburban trains; the journey to Sergiyev Posad takes about ninety minutes. Departure times are listed on boards in front of the station. Buy your ticket at a suburban *kassa* booth; usually, only same-day tickets are sold. Get on the train early to secure a window seat, as it is open seating on the *elektrichka*. (Keep the ticket for exiting the station!) Once arriving, remember to check on return times of trains to Moscow. From near Moscow's VDNKh metro station, Bus 388 departs about every half hour for Sergiyev Posad from about 8:30am–7:30pm, and takes 70 minutes. Once in Sergiyev Posad, buses depart for other towns along the Golden Ring route as well. To call, the area code is 496.

Upon arrival, head west a few hundred meters and then turn right onto Krasnoi Armii Prospekt, the main street. It is only about a 15-minute walk to the complex; you will spot the bell tower and main entrance up on the west side.

If you are driving, the **Russkaya Skazka** (Russian Fairytale) Restaurant is by the 43-kilometer marker on the M8 (Yaroslavskoye) Highway from Moscow. This unique wood-carved restaurant offers hearty appetizers, soups and stews. Across the street from the monastery, at 134 Krasnoi Armii, is the **Russky Dvorik**, (Russian Dacha) Restaurant which serves traditional dishes such as *pelmeni* and *blini*. Nearby, at 138, is the **Art Café San Marino**, a lively cellar café with frequent jazz concerts. You can also bring food with you (or buy snacks at the local market) and have a picnic by the pond or river (and a McDonalds is in town). Hotels in the area include the **Old Monastery Hotel** (Staraya Hotel Lavra) at 133 Krasnoi Armii (www. lavrahotel.ru) and the less expensive red-brick **Hotel Ascension** (Voznesenskaya). Other hotels along Krasnoi Armii are the **Mini Hotel Center** at 158, and the **Posadsky Hotel** at 171. Located nearby are the **Central Hotel** (Tsentralnaya) at 2 Ovrazhny Pereulok (Lane), and the **Imperial Village Hotel** at 14/2 Mitkina St. These can all be reserved through www.Booking.com.

A small fee is charged at the front kiosk to enter the monastery grounds, camera and video permits cost extra. Tours of the complex are also available with a private guide. Shops on the premises sell souvenirs, books, art works and religious items. The grounds are open 7am–9pm daily, and museums from 10am–5pm; closed Mondays. Some churches are not open to the public on weekends. www.stsl.ru.

HISTORY

In the early 14th century two brothers, Bartholomaeus and Stefan, built a small wooden church and monastic retreat in the forests of Radonezh (lands inherited from their father, a pious Rostov boyar). Varfolomei took his monastic vows as Sergius and founded his own monastery, dedicated to the Trinity, in 1345—St Sergius would one day be named the patron saint of all Russia. Sergius and his pupils went on to establish 50 other monasteries across northeastern Russia that also acted as educational centers and regional strongholds during the Mongol occupations. Seventy of St Sergius' disciples attained sainthood.

Legend has, that in 1380, Grand Prince Dmitri Donskoi and his armies were blessed before battle by Sergius Radonezhsky. Outnumbered four to one, they defeated Khan Mamai's horde—the first major Mongol defeat in over a century. (In 1914, the artist Viktor Vasnetsov painted the famous work: *The Duel of Monk Alexander Peresvet against the Tatar Champion Chelubei*.) At the monastery, one of St Sergius' pupils, the famous iconist Andrei Rublyov (see Special Topic on page 337), painted the *Old Testament Trinity* (now in Moscow's Tretyakov Gallery) to commemorate this famous battle at Kulikovo on the Don. After the victory, Moscow princes and rich boyars contributed heavily to the establishment of the Troitse-Sergiyev Lavra (Trinity Monastery of St Sergius) until it became not only the wealthiest in all Russia, but also the most revered pilgrimage shrine in Muscovy.

The thick kremlin walls were built around the monastery in 1540 during the reign of Ivan the Terrible to protect it from attack. A half-century later, the *lavra* (large monastery) withstood a 16-month siege by Polish forces; it was protected by over 3,000 monks. The complex was such an important center for the Russian people that its fall would have meant the end of Rus; the monastery remained an important fortress that defended Moscow well into the 17th-century. Eleven octagonal towers were built into the walls as key defense points. The most famous, the northeast tower, is known as the Utichya (Duck) Tower; the duck atop its spire symbolizes Peter the Great's hunting expeditions in Sergiyev Posad. (He also enjoyed taking shots at the ducks swimming in the pond below.) The place also played an important cultural role; the manuscript-writing and color miniature painting sections date back to the 15th-century.

After his death in 1392, Sergius was later canonized in 1452; he is buried in the Holy Trinity Cathedral on the monastery grounds. In 2012, the Orthodox Church celebrated the 620th anniversary of St Sergius' passing. Each year special church processions are held, especially during St Sergius Day (October 8) and Holy Trinity Days, New Year's and Easter holidays. Today the Trinity-Sergius Monastery is the largest lavra run by the Orthodox Church, with over 100 monks. (A *Lavra* is the highest rank of an Orthodox monastery, and there are only four in all of Russia.) The monastery remains a place of devoted pilgrimage, and believers from all over the country continue to pay homage to 'the saint and guardian of the Russian land'.

In 1930, the town's name of Sergiyev Posad (Settlement of Sergius) was changed to Zagorsk, after the revolutionary Vladimir Zagorsk. The monastery was closed down and converted into a State museum by Lenin in 1920 and during the Stalinist era it lost most of its wealth and power. The town officially reverted back to its original name of Sergiyev Posad in 1990, when the monastery was also returned to the Orthodox Church. Sergiyev Posad has a population of over 100,000, but receives nearly a million visitors a year.

The art of carving wooden toys has long been a tradition here; the first toys were made and distributed by St Sergius to the children of the town. Many painters, sculptors and folk artists trace their heritage back to the 17th-century, when the first toy and craft workshops were set up in the town. The shop to the left as you pass through the main gates sells many locally made wooden toys.

SIGHTS

The parking square, near the main gates of the monastery complex, looks out over many ancient settlements that dot the landscape and the large kremlin citadel that houses priceless relics of old Russian architecture. Enter the main gates at the eastern entrance; paintings of the Holy Pilgrims depict the life of Sergius Radonezhsky, the 14th-century monk who established the Trinity Monastery of St Sergius. The small **Gate Church of St John the Baptist**, built in 1693 by the wealthy and princely Stroganov family, stands over the main or Holy Uspensky Gates. It now functions as a confessional for Orthodox pilgrims.

The first large structure that catches the eye is the monastery's main **Assumption Cathedral** (Uspensky Sobor). This blue and gold-starred, five-domed church with elegant sloping *zakomara* archways was consecrated in 1585 to commemorate Ivan the Terrible's defeat of the Mongols in the Asian territory of Astrakhan. Yaroslavl artists, whose names are inscribed on the west wall, painted the interior frescoes in 1684. The iconostasis contains the *Last Supper*, a painting by the 17th-century master icon-artist Simon Ushakov. The burial chambers of the Godunov family (Boris Godunov was czar from 1598 to 1605) are located in the northwestern corner. Its design resembles the Kremlin's Uspensky Cathedral. By the south wall is the Sergius Church (1686–92), and the first oak coffin of St Sergius is preserved here. Under the cathedral is the crypt where Patriarchs Alexis I (1970) and Pimen (1990) are buried. Many of these churches are open for worship and conduct services throughout the day. Respectfully dressed visitors are welcome. Photography without flash is usually permitted, but you may need to buy a permit.

The brightly painted **Chapel-over-the-Well**, located outside by the cathedral's west wall, was built in Naryshkin cube-shaped, octagonal-style at the end of the 17th-century. Legend has it that when St Sergius touched a stick to the earth here, a well miraculously appeared, and a blind monk was the first to be healed by the holy water. Near the riverbank stands the **Sergius Well Chapel**. It was customary for small chapels to be built over sacred springs; today, pilgrims still bring bottles to fill with holy water.

Directly beyond the cathedral, standing in the complex center, is the five-tiered turquoise and white baroque **Bell Tower** (88 meters/288 feet high), designed by Prince Ukhtomsky (1740–70) and Rastrelli. Topped with a gilded dome in the form

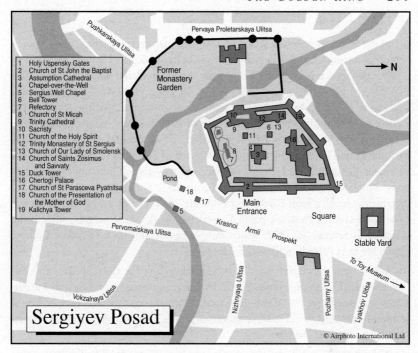

1   Holy Uspensky Gates
2   Church of St John the Baptist
3   Assumption Cathedral
4   Chapel-over-the-Well
5   Sergius Well Chapel
6   Bell Tower
7   Refectory
8   Church of St Micah
9   Trinity Cathedral
10 Sacristy
11 Church of the Holy Spirit
12 Trinity Monastery of St Sergius
13 Church of Our Lady of Smolensk
14 Church of Saints Zosimus
       and Savvaty
15 Duck Tower
16 Chertogi Palace
17 Church of St Parasceva Pyatnitsa
18 Church of the Presentation of
       the Mother of God
19 Kalichya Tower

Sergiyev Posad

© Airphoto International Ltd

of a crown, it once held 40 bells; the largest weighed 65 tons. The chiming clock of
the tower dates back to 1905.

Head past the cathedral to the southern end of the complex. A stroll in this
direction to the Refectory may lead past long-bearded monks dressed in the
traditional black robes and *klobuki* tall hats. The **Refectory Church of St Sergius**,
rebuilt in 1686, is painted in colorful checkerboard patterns of red, blue, green and
yellow. It has a large open gallery with 19th-century paintings and wide staircases,
and is decorated with carved columns and gables. In times past, pilgrims gathered
here to dine on feast days. (The building is usually closed outside of morning
service, except for guided tours.) The pink building just beyond the refectory is the
metropolitan's residence.

The small chapel at the end of the hall has a carved iconostasis by the altar and
a beautiful red jasper inlaid floor. Another quaint church, standing next to the
Refectory, is the **Church of St Micah**. In 1379, St Sergius' cell attendant, Micah,
witnessed the appearance of the Blessed Mary promising prosperity for the
monastery. In 1734, this church was built to hold the relics of St Micah.

Near the Refectory, in the southwestern corner, is the oldest building in the
monastery, the one-domed **Trinity Cathedral**, which Abbot Nikon erected over the

site of the original Church of St Sergius in 1422. Pilgrims still visit the remains of St Sergius of Radonezh, which lie in a silver sarcophagus, donated by Ivan the Terrible; a memorial service is conducted here daily. An embroidered portrait of St Sergius that covered his coffin is now preserved in the History and Art Museum, a short walk away. In 1425, Andrei Rublyov and Daniil Chorny painted the icons on the cathedral's iconostasis, which include a copy of Rublyov's *Holy Testament Trinity* (the original is now in Moscow's Tretyakov Gallery). The cathedral contains 42 works by Rublyov and is joined by the smaller **Church of St Nikon** (1548), Sergius' first successor. Behind the Cathedral is the **Sacristy**, now a small museum that exhibits early Russian applied art (14th–17th centuries), and includes collections of metalwork, jewelry, icon covers and exquisite embroideries or 'needle paintings'. (The artist Mikhail Nesterov painted a series of works on St Sergius, such as the Youth of St Sergius, in 1897, which now hangs in Moscow's Tretyakov Gallery; others are in St Petersburg's Russian Museum.)

Across from the cathedral is the slender **Church of the Holy Spirit** with a tall bell tower under its dome built in 1476 by Pskov stonemasons. Prominent Russian saints are buried here: St Maxim the Greek (1556), a translator of church books; St Innocenti of Moscow (1879), a missionary; and Church metropolitans Platon (1812) and Philaret (1867).

Behind this church in the northwest corner stands the **Trinity-Sergius Monastery**, one of the most important monuments of medieval Russia. The Metropolitan's House, vestry and adjoining monastery buildings now house the **Art Museum** and **Treasury** (Museum of Ancient Russian Art). These museums, which display gifts in the order presented to the monastery, contain one of Russia's richest collections of early religious art. The exhibits on two floors include icons from the 14th to 19th centuries, and portraits, chalices, china, costumes, crowns, furniture, handicrafts, latticework, tapestries and vestments from the 14th to 20th centuries. The art museum also has the original 15th-century gates from the iconostasis of the cathedral; open 10am–5pm, closed Mondays. In front of the museum is the **Church of Our Lady of Smolensk** (1745–53) with a blue baroque-style rotunda. In 1730, a pious psalm reader who suffered from paralysis was allegedly healed after praying to the Icon of the Mother of Smolenskaya.

The monastery also served as the town's hospital and school. Next to the museum is the red-brick and yellow-and-white sandstone hospital building with the adjoining white tent-roofed **Church of Saints Zosimus and Savvaty** (1635). Behind the church, climb up the **Kalichya Tower** for a splendid view of the complex and town (usually open in summer months).

In the northeastern corner, behind the Duck Tower, is the colorfully painted and tiled **Chertogi Palace**, built at the end of the 17th-century for Czar Alexei, who often came to Sergiyev Posad with an entourage of over 500 people. One of the ceilings in the palace is covered with paintings that honor his son's (Peter the Great) victories in battle. It now houses the Moscow Theological Academy and Seminary. Founded in 1742, it has over 1,000 students today.

Exiting through the main gate, turn right and walk southwest toward the **Kelarskiye Ponds**, situated beyond the southeastern Pyatnitskaya Tower. There you may find artists sketching and people strolling among the old garden walls. Two churches built in 1547 stand outside the walls—the **Church of St Paraskeva Pyatnitsa** and the **Church of the Presentation of the Mother of God**, nearest the pond. The Zolotoye Koltso (Golden Ring) Restaurant is only a few minutes' walk away.

The craft of wood carving remains alive in Sergiyev Posad. The famous *matryoshka*, the nest of carved dolls, has its origins here. First appearing in Russia in the 1890s, the *matryona* doll was later called by its diminutive form, *matryoshka*, representing peasant girls. The dolls were carved from wood and painted in traditional Russian dress, with *sarafan* jumpers, embroidered blouses and *kokoshniki* headdresses. Up to 24 smaller dolls could be nested within the largest, including Russian lads or fairy-tale figures. The doll first attained popularity at the 1900 World Exposition in Paris.

Today, there are even Putin *matryoshki* (containing past leaders back to Lenin and Nicholas II) as well as dolls representing other foreign leaders. In 2000, a Matryoshka Museum (marking the centenary of the doll) opened in the Moscow Folk Art Museum near the Arbat. Its largest doll stands one-meter high and houses 50 smaller ones inside. Another popular Russian folk art—Zhostovo trays—celebrated its 185th anniversary in 2011. Artists paint designs on metal trays, which are then coated with several coats of lacquer.

The history of toys and folk art can be viewed in the large red-brick **Toy Museum**, at 123 Krasnoi Armii Prospekt. There are displays of over 30,000 toys dating back to the Bronze Age and include many unique matryoshka dolls. A special souvenir section sells carved wooden dolls, boxes, trays and jewelry. Open 10am–5pm, closed Mondays, Tuesdays and last Friday of the month.

ALEKSANDROV Александров
RESIDENCE OF IVAN THE TERRIBLE ON THE GRAY RIVER

From Moscow, you can travel here directly (120 kilometers/74 miles north) and inexpensively by *elektrichka* train, which depart hourly from Moscow's Yaroslavsky Railway Station (Komsomolskaya Metro) and take about two and a half hours. You can also travel by train from Sergiyev Posad in less than an hour. (An express train and a few regular trains to Yaroslavl stop in Aleksandrov; these tickets are bought at the long-distance kiosk). Bus 676 departs three times daily for Aleksandrov by

Moscow's VDNKh metro station. By car, take the M8 past Sergiyev Posad and then turn east (at Dvoriki) on the P75. (It is possible to cover both towns in one day.) The old town is about a ten-minute ride from Aleksandrov Railway Station. (Inside the station, departure times are posted for both Moscow and Sergiyev Posad.) When exiting the station, walk directly across the street to the bus stop. Take bus number 7 (facing the station, travel right) five stops to 'Museum'. The bus will pass the main square with a statue of Lenin, cross the Gray River and climb up a hill. You will see the old kremlin on your left. The Aleksandrov Hotel is at 59 Revolutsii St and the nearby **Larsen Hotel** at 1 Koroleva St.

If you have time, it is a pleasant half-hour walk through town back to the train station. A number of cafés dot the path, along with markets selling bread, fruit and drinks. The museum town is open 9am-5pm (Friday till 4pm) and closed on Mondays. A small gift shop is located inside the entrance gates on the left.

The **Aleksandrovskaya Sloboda**, packed full of grim history, was once the residence of Ivan the Terrible for 17 years (1564–1581) and headquarters to his police army of ruthless *oprichniki*. (After the suspicious deaths of his wife and first son, Ivan abandoned Moscow for Aleksandrov.) It is from here that Ivan launched his reign of terror over Russia and kept its citizens in the grip of fear. Ivan married six more times in Aleksandrov. (Of his wives, five died mysteriously and one was sent off to a nunnery.) The most unfortunate, Martha Sobakina, whose story is depicted in Rimsky-Korsakov's *The Bride of the Tsar*, lasted a mere two weeks. By 1569, Ivan the Terrible had become so paranoid about plots against his life that he proposed marriage to England's Queen Elizabeth I, regarding her as an ideal ally. (England and Moscovy had developed trade relations ten years earlier.) Even though she spurned his offer of marriage, Elizabeth agreed to offer Ivan asylum should he ever need it.

The oldest buildings are the (nonfunctioning) convent and white-rectangular one-domed **Trinity Cathedral** that women helped build in the early 15th-century. The interior walls are decorated with the Icon of the Virgin Mary, said to be her real portrait from first-century Rome. After Ivan's army sacked Novgorod in 1570 (suspicious of the town's betrayal during a war with Poland, his troops slaughtered 35,000 of its citizens), he brought the golden oak doors from the Hagia Sophia Cathedral to adorn the Trinity's entrance. A covered gallery surrounds the cathedral which contains several coffins of white limestone.

Each morning Ivan climbed the nearby tent-shaped **Bell Tower** with its three-tiered layers of arched *kokoshniki*; he enjoyed ringing the bells and giving morning sermons. (When Philip, the head of the Moscow Church, criticized the abuses of Ivan the Terrible, he was convicted of sorcery and executed.) Adjacent to the bell tower are residential quarters which later housed Marfa, the stepsister of Peter the

Great (who forced her to become a nun); she was exiled here between 1698 and 1707. Two daughters of Czar Alexei, Peter's father, are buried in the Church of the Purification.

Opposite the bell tower stands Ivan IV's personal church, the red brick and green tent-roof **Church of the Intercession**. It was in the adjoining palace (later destroyed by invading Poles) that Ivan the Terrible committed his last and most atrocious crime—the murder of his own son. The son became enraged one night when finding Ivan in his bedroom with his wife whose dress was in 'slight disarray'. The ensuing fight between father and son ended in Ivan the Terrible beating his son to death with a cane. The czar was so horrified by what he had done that he left Aleksandrov and returned to govern from Moscow, where he died a few years later. (When in Moscow's Tretyakov Gallery, note the famous painting by Ilya Repin, *Ivan the Terrible and His Son—16 November 1581*, the date of the murder.)

PERESLAVL-ZALESSKY Переславль-Залесский
IMPORTANT OUTPOST OF MOSCOVY

The tranquil town of Pereslavl-Zalessky, which celebrated its 865th anniversary in 2017, is situated on a hilltop by the southeastern shores of Lake Pleshcheyevo, about 56 kilometers (35 miles) northeast of Sergiyev Posad. Approaching Pereslavl from the road, pleasantly scented by the surrounding groves of pine and birch, you have an enchanting view of the shimmering azure waters of the lake, three old monasteries on the side of the road, and golden crosses on top of painted onion domes that loom up from sprawling green fields dusted with blue and yellow wildflowers. Young boys wave at passersby as they fish in the lake with long reed poles. The River Trubezh meanders through the old earthen kremlin that winds around the center of town. These ramparts date back over eight centuries. One of Russia's most ancient towns, Pereslavl-Zalessky (today with 45,000 residents) is a charming place, scattered with well-preserved churches and monasteries that once numbered over 50. Take a pleasant walk along the dirt roads and imagine that Peter the Great may have traversed the same footpaths before you. **The Pereslavl History and Art Preserve** operates from May to September 10am–6pm and October to April 10am–5pm; closed Mondays. On the last Tuesday of each month, the museum is open 10am–2pm. (In winter, some churches may be closed.)

With no train station, the easiest way is to visit by car; it is about a two-and-a-half hour drive north on the M8 and R74 from Moscow. Inexpensive buses run from Moscow's *Schyolkovskaya* bus station (metro station same name at end of Arbatsko northeast line) with frequent departures to Pereslavl (2.5 hours direct) and most other Golden Ring towns. In addition, many buses destined for Rostov Veliky or Yaroslavl stop in Pereslavl enroute; those marked 'SP' make a stop in Sergiyev Posad.

Daily buses also run between Sergiyev Posad and Pereslavl (an hour ride), Rostov (one-and-a-half hours) and Yaroslavl (three hours). Return buses to Moscow from these locations are also frequent.

The bus station in Pereslavl is located two kilometers southwest of town. Once there, catch local bus number 1 to the stop 'Museum'. To dine, try the Skazka (Fairytale) restaurant set in a lovely old wooden building near the town center. Inside the Kremlin, on Sovietskaya Street, the Blini Café also has Russian fare. Pinocchio Pizzeria is on Ulitsa Svobodi, The area code for Pereslavl–Zalessky is 48535.

Hotel **Zapadnaya** (West), opened in 2002, is located on the bank of the Trubezh River in the historical center of town at 1A Pleshcheyevskaya St. (www.westhotel. ru). The large Soviet-style **Hotel Pereslavl** is centrally located north of the river at 27 Rostovskaya Street (www.hotelpereslavl.ru). Additional hotels are the **Art Hotel**, located at 45 Bolshaya Protechnaya St, **Royal Palace** at 158 Moskovskaya St, and the **Komfort Hotel** at 2 Severny Pereulok (Lane).

The **Botik Tourist & Camping Complex** is situated down the path from the Botik Museum on the bank of the Lake near Veskovo Village. It offers wooden cabins, camping areas, a sauna and beach. The Botik Café, designed in the shape of a boat, serves traditional Russian food. Driving into Pereslavl from Moscow, in Krest Village, is the **Lesnaya Skazka Hotel** ('A Forest Tale').

HISTORY

Pereslavl-Zalessky's long and fascinating history can be traced back to the year 1152, when Prince Yuri Dolgoruky (who founded Moscow five years earlier) fortified the small village of Kleschchin on the banks of the Trubezh and renamed it Pereslavl after an old Kievan town. Situated in an area on the *zalasye* (beyond the dense woods of Moscow), it became known as Pereslavl-Zalessky. The area was an important outpost of Moscow; Prince Alexander Nevsky set out from Pereslavl to win his decisive battle against the Swedes in 1240. Since the town also lay on important White Sea trade routes, it quickly prospered. By 1302 Pereslavl had grown large enough to be annexed to the principality of Moscovy.

SIGHTS

Ivan the Terrible later consolidated Pereslavl, along with the nearby village of Aleksandrov, into a strategic military outpost and headquarters for his *oprichniki* bodyguards. In 1688, the young Peter I came here from Moscow to build his first *poteshny* (amusement) boats on Lake Pleshcheyevo. It was in a small shed near the lake that Peter discovered a wrecked English boat, which he learned to sail against the wind. In 1692, Peter paraded these boats (forerunners of the Russian fleet) before members of the Moscow court. One of them, the *Fortuna*, can be found in the

Botik Museum, which lies about three kilometers (two miles) from Pereslavl, by the south bank of the lake near the village of Veskovo. Other relics from the Russian flotilla are also displayed here. Two large anchors mark the entrance and a monument to Peter the Great by Campioni stands nearby. Open May to Sept 10am–6pm and Oct to April 10am–5pm; closed Mondays.

An easy way to get to the Botik Museum is by taking the narrow-gauge train that leaves three times daily from the bus station on Kardovskaya St, just north of the Goritsky Monastery. It departs at 9am, 1pm and 4.30pm daily and returns from the museum at 12.30pm, 4pm and 8.30pm. The single-track train also continues all around the lake to Kupan.

Make your way to the central Krasnaya Ploshchad (Red Square). The small grassy hills around you are the remains of the town's 12th-century earthen protective walls. In front of the **Statue of Alexander Nevsky** (who was born in Pereslavl) is the white stone **Cathedral of the Transfiguration**, the oldest architectural monument in northeastern Russia. Yuri Dolgoruky himself laid the foundations of this church, which was completed by his son, Andrei Bogolyubsky (Lover of God), in 1157. This refined structure with its one massive fringed dome became the burial place for the local princes. Each side of the cathedral is decorated with simple friezes. The *zakomara*, the semicircular rounded shape of the upper walls, distinguish the Russian style from the original simpler cube-shaped Byzantine design. Frescoes and icons from inside the cathedral, like the 14th-century *Transfiguration* by Theophanes the Greek and Yuri Dolgoruky's silver chalice, are now in Moscow's Tretyakov Gallery and Kremlin Armory. The other frescoes were executed during the cathedral's restoration in 1894. Across from the cathedral is the **Church of St Peter the Metropolitan**. Built in 1585 (with a 19th-century bell tower), the octagonal frame is topped with a long white tent-shaped roof. This design in stone and brick was copied from the traditional Russian log-cabin churches of the north.

In the distance, north across the river, is the **Church of St Semion** (1771). Between this church and the Lenin Monument on Svoboda Ulitsa are the early 19th-century shopping arcades, Gostiny Dvor. Religious services are held at the **Church of the Intercession** on Pleshcheyevskaya Ulitsa.

Take a leisurely stroll towards the river and follow it westwards down to the lake. Scattered along the paths are brightly painted wooden dachas with carved windows covered by lace curtains. Children can be found playing outside with their kittens or a *babushka* hauling water from the well. A *dedushka* may be picking apples and wild strawberries or carving a small toy for his grandchildren out of wood. Stop for a chat; it is amazing how far a few common words can go—an invitation for tea may soon follow. At the point where the Trubezh flows into the lake stands the **Church of the Forty Saints** (1781) on Ribnaya Sloboda, the old fish quarter. With

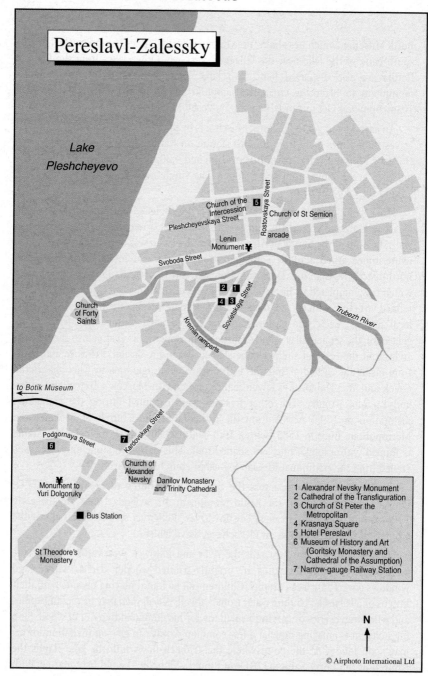

Pereslavl-Zalessky

Lake
Pleshcheyevo

Church of the
Intercession
Pleshcheyevskaya Street

Rostovskaya Street

5

Church of St Semion

Lenin
Monument ¥

arcade

Svoboda Street

2 1

4 3

Sovietskaya Street

Church
of Forty
Saints

Kremlin ramparts

Trubezh River

to Botik Museum

Kardovskaya Street

Podgornaya Street

6

7

Church of
Alexander
Nevsky   Danilov Monastery
and Trinity Cathedral

¥
Monument to
Yuri Dolgoruky

■ Bus Station

St Theodore's
Monastery

1 Alexander Nevsky Monument
2 Cathedral of the Transfiguration
3 Church of St Peter the
    Metropolitan
4 Krasnaya Square
5 Hotel Pereslavl
6 Museum of History and Art
    (Goritsky Monastery and
    Cathedral of the Assumption)
7 Narrow-gauge Railway Station

N

© Airphoto International Ltd

a little bargaining or a smile, get a row boat for the lake or go out with the fishermen. On a warm day, it is a perfect place for a picnic; you may even want to take a dip.

In the town center, at 11 Sovetskaya St, is the **Museum of Flat Irons**, housed in an old merchant house. It exhibits an interesting collection of over 200 irons (weighing 10 grams to 10 kilos) and other household items. Open daily 10am–6pm. The owner has also created the nearby **Museum of Teapots**, situated in a wooden *izba* (log house); closed Mondays and Tuesdays. Situated 15 km outside of town on the way to Uglich, in the village of Talitsy, is the **Steam Engine Museum**, a large depot filled with steam locomotives, old train engines, section cars, and even an old Stalin-era limousine, the bottom reconfigured to ride the rails. Open 10am–6pm; closed Mondays and Tuesdays. Here you can also take a short trip on the narrow-gauge railway, first laid down in 1930.

At the southern end of town, you may have glimpsed a number of monasteries and chapels if you arrived from Sergiyev Posad. The four monasteries lining the southern road into Pereslavl also acted as protective strongholds, guarding the town from invasions. The one farthest away is the **Convent of St Theodore**, six and a half kilometers (four miles) south on Kardovskaya Street. Ivan the Terrible built this convent and the **Chapel of St Theodore** to honor his wife Anastasia, who gave birth to their first son, Fedor (Theodore), in 1557. Ivan often stopped at the shrine to pray when he visited his bodyguard army residing in Pereslavl-Zalessky.

About a kilometer closer to town is the memorial **Church of Alexander Nevsky** (1778). A few minutes' walk from this church, set in a woody rustic setting, is the **Danilov Monastery**. A few buildings remain of this 16th-century structure. The **Trinity Cathedral** was commissioned by Grand Prince Vasily III in 1532. The single-domed cathedral, with 17th-century frescoes by renowned Kostroma artists Nikitin and Savin, was built by Rostov architect Grigory Borisov in honor of Vasily's son, Ivan the Terrible. The Abbot Daniel, who founded the monastery in 1508, was in charge of the cathedral's construction and present at Ivan's christening. The smaller **Church of All Saints** was built in 1687 by Prince Bariatinsky, who later became a monk (Ephriam) at the monastery and was buried near the south wall. Other surviving structures are the two-story Refectory (1695) and the large tent-roofed bell tower (1689), whose bell is now in the Moscow Kremlin's Ivan the Great Bell Tower.

On the west side of the road, behind the **Monument to Yuri Dolgoruky**, is the **Goritsky Monastery**, surrounded by a large red brick kremlin. On the hilltop, a cluster of sparkling onion domes rise up from inside the fortified walls. The monastery is now the **Museum of History and Art** (open 10am–5pm; closed Tuesdays). The monastery, founded during the reign of Ivan I in the 14th century (rebuilt in the 18th), is a fine example of medieval architecture with its octagonal towers, large cube-shaped walls and ornamental stone entrance gates. The tiny white gate-church next to the gatekeeper's lodge was once known as the 'casket studded with precious stones', for it was richly decorated with gilded carvings and colorful tiles. The large seven-domed **Cathedral of the Assumption** was built in 1757. The exquisite golden-framed and figured iconostasis, designed by Karl Blank, was carved and painted by the same team of artists who decorated the churches in the Moscow Kremlin.

The monastery, with 47 rooms filled with local treasures, is now one of the largest regional museums in Russia. The rooms include a unique collection of ancient Russian art, sculptures and rare books. The museum also exhibits the plaster face mask of Peter the Great by Rastrelli (1719) and Falconet's original model of the Bronze Horseman. The elaborately carved wooden gates from the Church of the Presentation won the Gold Medal at the 1867 Paris World Exhibition. May 2nd is a town holiday, Museum Day, at the Goritsky Monastery.

Heading north toward Rostov and Yaroslavl, you will find the last monument structure of Pereslavl-Zalessky, the 12th-century **Monastery of St Nicetas**, encased in a long white-bricked kremlin. In 1561, Ivan the Terrible added stone buildings and the five-domed cathedral. He intended to convert the monastery into the headquarters of his *oprichniki*, but later transferred their residence to the village of Aleksandrov.

ROSTOV VELIKY Ростов Великий
THE WEALTHY ECCLESIASTICAL CENTER OF EARLY CHRISTIANITY

Approaching Rostov on the road from Moscow (54 kilometers/34 miles north of Pereslavl-Zalessky), the visitor is greeted with a breathtaking view of silvery aspen domes, white-stone churches and high kremlin towers. Rostov is one of Russia's most ancient towns and has stood along the picturesque banks of Lake Nero for more than 11 centuries. It was once called 'a reflection of heaven on earth'. Named after Prince Rosta, a powerful governing lord, the town was mentioned in chronicles as far back as AD 862. Rostov's size and splendor grew to equal the two great towns of Novgorod and Kiev. By the 12th-century Rostov took on the title of *Veliky* (the Great) and became the capital of the Russian north. Rostov later came under the jurisdiction of Moscow and lost its importance as a cultural center by the end of the 18th century.

Today Rostov is the district center of the Yaroslavl region, and considered a historical preserve, heralding the glory of old Russian art and architecture. The town, with a population of about 32,000, has been restored to much of its original grandeur after a tornado destroyed many of the buildings in 1953. The oldest section of the town, set by the lake, is still surrounded by low earthen walls built around 1630. Rostov proudly celebrated its 1150 anniversary in 2012.

Rostov is about an hour's drive on the M8, north of Pereslavl-Zalessky. Trains depart from Moscow's Yaroslavl Station (Metro Komsomolskaya). Long distance trains on the way to Yaroslavl also stop in Rostov (taking between three and four hours). Or take the local *elektricka* surburban train which leave regularly; you may need to change trains at Aleksandrov. (Regular and *Elektricka* trains also run between Rostov and Yaroslavl.) Various bus routes from Moscow's Shchyolkovsky station (in the northeast, by metro stop of same name) also make runs and transit stops at Rostov (about 5 hours). Note that in winter some of Rostov's churches may be closed. The area code for Rostov is 48536.

The main bus station is right in town. Once there, the local bus number 6 runs the one and-a-half kilometers between the station and the town center along Lunacharskaya Street. In 2006, Rostov's first 3-star **Hotel Moscovsky Trakt** opened on 29a Okruzhnayta St. The **Selivanov Hotel** is down the street at number 5. Inside the Kremlin, near the east gate, is the **Hotel Dom na Pogrebakh**. The former servants' quarters have been turned into a basic 17-room hotel with shared bathrooms and a café. Inside the refectory is the Trepeznaya Palata Restaurant and a few blocks west of the Kremlin is the Traktir na Pokrovskoy, both serving traditional Russian food. In a Kremlin courtyard, at 4 Kammeny Most, is the Georgian eatery, Café Alaverdy. The Restauran Teremok, at 9 Moravskaya St, serves delicious soups and *blini* with caviar; an outdoor market is located across the street. **Russkoe Podvorye Hotel** is at 9 Marshala Alexeeva St with a restaurant offering a medieval menu. **Pleshanov's Manor** is at 34 Leninskaya St. The inexpensive **Khors Guesthouse**, on the waterfront at 30 Podozerka St, is run by an artist and his mother in two independent parts of their house. Another section is an enamel museum (www.booking.com/hotel/ru/khors.html).

HISTORY

Rostov Veliky was one of the wealthiest towns in all Russia and the most important trade center between Kiev and the White Sea. Rostov became not only the capital of its own principality, but also the northern ecclesiastical center of early Christianity and the seat of the Orthodox Church. In the 17th-century the metropolitans Jonah and Ion Sisoyevich built a large number of magnificent cathedrals and church residences, decorated with the Byzantine influence of icons and frescoes. The many religious shrines of a Russian town symbolized its wealth and status. Unlike other Russian towns, the Rostov kremlin was not originally built as a protective fortress, but served as a decorative feature that surrounded the palace of the metropolitan. Also the main cathedral stood outside the kremlin walls and not in the town's center.

SIGHTS

The kremlin itself, built in 1670, has 11 rounded towers and encompasses an area of about five acres. At the west gate is the **Church of St John-the-Divine** (1683), whose interior paintings depict the life of this saint. The five-domed **Church of the Resurrection** (1670) at the northern gates is designed with intricate white-stone patterns and the classic Russian *zakomara*, forming the 24 slopes of the roof. The towers on either side of both churches are made from aspen, and sparkle with a silken sheen. Stone iconostasis (instead of traditional wooden ones) inside both churches are decorated with beautiful frescoes painted by the artists Nikitin and Savin from the Golden Ring town of Kostroma. The Church of the Resurrection stands over the Holy Gates, so named because the metropolitan passed through them on the way from his residence inside the kremlin to the main cathedral.

Situated between the north and west gates stands the colorful **Church of the Icon of the Mother of God Hodegetria**, built after the death of Jonah in 1690 by the new Metropolitan Josephat. Its exterior is covered by trompe l'oeil diamond rustication, imported from Italy. Inside is a small exhibition of church vestments.

The first stone of the massive **Cathedral of the Assumption** was laid by Prince Andrei Bogolyubsky (son of Yuri Dolgoruky who founded Moscow) in 1162. Bogolyubsky (Lover of God) ruled the Russian north from Rostov. The 11th-century Vladimir Virgin hangs to the left of the Holy Doors. A few of the 12th-century frescoes have survived, along with the original lion mask handles that guard the western doors. Rostov frescoes were known for their soft color combinations of turquoise, blue, yellow and white. Five large aspen-hewn onion domes and beautiful white-stone friezes decorate the outside of the structure. The four-tiered **Bell Tower** (1687), standing alongside the Assumption Cathedral, was the most famous in all Russia. Bells played an important role in the life of Russian towns. The 13 bells (the heaviest, the Sysoi, weighs 32 tons), usually rung on the half hour and full hour, can be heard 15 miles away.

Other churches include the one-domed **Church of the Savior-on-the-Marketplace** (1690) that is located a few blocks north of the cathedral; it is now the town library. In the northeast corner stands the single-domed **Church of St Isodore the Blessed** (1566), built during the reign of Ivan the Terrible. Directly behind this church, on the other side of the earthen walls, stands the **Church of St Nicholas-in-the-Field** (1830) on Gogol Street. This is one of the few places in town open for religious services. At the eastern end, within the ramparts, is the **Church of the Nativity**. Gostiny Dvor (Traders' Row) marks the town's center. This long yellow arcade, with its many carved white archways, is still the shopping and market district of Rostov. The southeast part of the kremlin is made up of 17th-century civic buildings and the cube-shaped, single-domed **Church of the Savior-in-the-Vestibule** (1675), whose interior is made up of stone arcades that rest on thick gilded columns; it served as the house chapel of the metropolitan's residence. The walls and stone altar iconostasis are decorated with exquisite frescoes painted by local master artists, and the chandelier and candelabra are also from the 17th-century.

The large complex along the southwestern end is the **Metropolitan's Palace** (1680), containing the highly decorated Otdatochnaya Hall; here people gathered to pay their respects to the metropolitan. The White Chambers were built for the prince, and later, visiting czars. The Red Chambers accommodated other church and civil dignitaries. This complex of buildings now houses the **Rostov Museum Preserve of Art and Architecture**. The chambers are filled with collections of icons, wood carvings and enamels from the 14th to 20th centuries. Of particular interest is the 15th-century Icon of the Archangel Michael, the carved limestone cross (1458) of the prince's scribe, and the 15th-century wooden figure of St George the Victorious.

Rostov enamels (known as *finift*), produced here since the 12th-century, were famous throughout Russia. The art originated in Byzantium and the name stems from the Greek word meaning colorful and shiny. Craftsmen painted miniature icons, personal portraits, and other decorative enamels for church books and clergy robes. The complex process of enamel making involves oxidizing different metals to create an assortment of colors: copper produces green and blue; iron, yellow and orange; and gold mixed with tin oxidizes into a rich ruby-red. Rostov's factory has been open since the 18th-century and the local craftsmen still produce elegant enamel jewelry, ornaments and small paintings that are sold in stores throughout Russia. Museums are open 10am–5pm and tickets can be bought at the west gate. One can enter the kremlin grounds at any time from the east gate.

Heading west out of the kremlin brings you to the small three-domed **Church of the Savior-on-the-Sands**. This is all that has survived of a monastery built by Princess Maria, whose husband was killed by invading Mongols in the 13th-century. Princess Maria and other noblewomen of Rostov chronicled many of the events of medieval Russia. During the 17th-century the library of Countess Irina Musina-Pushkina was one of the largest in Russia.

On the banks of **Lake Nero**, west of the Kremlin, are the 17th-century remains of **St Jacob's Monastery of Our Savior** (founded in 1389); the original walls are still standing. The Immaculate Conception Cathedral (1686) and Church of St Demetrius (1800) are designed in the Russian classical style.

Along the lake, at 16 Tolstovsky Embankment, is the **House of Crafts** where visitors can try their hand in making dolls, bark shoes, clay whistles, Easter eggs and other traditional souvenirs. Open 10am–6pm.

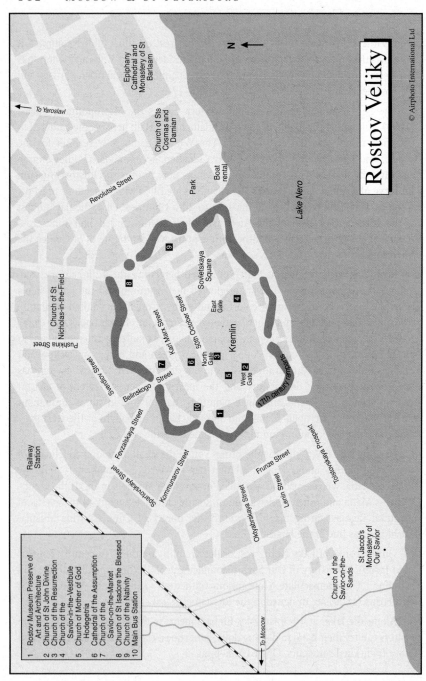

© Airphoto International Ltd

Rostov Veliky

N

To Yaroslavl

To Moscow

Lake Nero

Epiphany Cathedral and Monastery of St Barlaam

Church of Sts Cosmas and Damian

Revolutsia Street

Park

Boat rental

Church of St Nicholas-in-the-Field

Pushkina Street

Sverdov Street

Belinskogo Street

Karl Marx Street

50th October Street

Sovietskaya Square

North Gate

East Gate

West Gate

Kremlin

17th century ramparts

Fevralskaya Street

Spartovskaya Street

Kommunarov Street

Frunze Street

Oktyabrskaya Street

Lenin Street

Tolstoskaya Prospekt

Railway Station

Church of the Savior-on-the-Sands

St Jacob's Monastery of Our Savior

8

9

7

6

3

5

2

4

10

1

1 Rostov Museum Preserve of Art and Architecture
2 Church of St John Divine
3 Church of the Resurrection
4 Church of the Savior-in-the-Vestibule
5 Church of Mother of God Hodegetria
6 Cathedral of the Assumption
7 Church of the Savior-on-the-Market
8 Church of St Isadore the Blessed
9 Church of the Nativity
10 Main Bus Station

For a different perspective, board the **Zarya Ferry** for a cruise around Lake Nero. The hour-long trip leaves from the Pier near the west gate of the kremlin and runs along the monasteries. May–Sept—11am–6pm. Boats can also be rented in the park.

Along the shores of the lake at the eastern end of town is the **Church of Saints Cosmas and Damian** (1775). Next to this small church stands the larger five-domed **Epiphany Cathedral** (1553), the oldest standing building in Rostov, and part of the **Monastery of St Barlaam** (Abraham); this is one of the oldest surviving monasteries in Russia, dating back to the 11th-century.

Outside Rostov, in the northwestern suburbs of the village of Bogoslov, is the lovely red **Church of St John upon Ishnya**, one of the last wooden churches left in the region. It stands on the River Ishnya and legend has that it miraculously appeared from the lake and was washed up on the shores of its present location. It is open for visits and closed on Wednesdays.

VICINITY OF ROSTOV VELIKY

About 20 kilometers (12 miles) northwest of Rostov Veliky (on road P153), lies the **Borisoglebsky Fortress-Monastery**. Built in the early 14th century, it was later surrounded by a kremlin during the reign of Boris Godunov to protect it from Polish invasions. Surrounded on three sides by the River Ustye, the fourth was once protected by a moat. The fortifications were as strong as those of Moscow's Kremlin; the walls were 12 meters (40 feet) high and over three meters (ten feet) thick and had 14 observation towers. (The towers were placed the distance of an arrow's flight apart.) The walls also had stone arches that held cannon and archer posts, and the two gateways were fortified with heavy oak and iron doors.

The famous Rostov architect Grigory Borisov built the single-domed **Cathedral of Saints Boris and Gleb** in 1524, and had it decorated with colorful tiles, gables and frescoes. Boris and Gleb, sons of Prince Vladimir (who introduced Christianity to Russia in AD 988), were the first saints of Russia. As political and religious turmoil swept Kiev, they passively accepted their deaths without fighting, believing in Christ's redemption.

Borisov also built the five-domed **Gate Church of St Sergius** (1545); each narrow window is topped by cylinder-shaped *kokoshniki*. Other buildings inside the monastery grounds include the **Church of the Annunciation** (1526), Refectory, Head Monk's Residence, Dormitory Quarters, Treasury and Wafer Bakery (which once contained a dungeon), all designed by Borisov. The **Church of the Purification** stands over the Water Gates on the north side. The three-tiered bell tower (1680) was the last structure built, with the **Church of St John** on the ground floor.

RUSSIAN BELLS

Bells were first introduced to Russia from Byzantium in the 10th century. By the 14th century, Russia began to cast its own bells, and they played a prominent role in Russian town life. They chimed the hours, sounded alarms, tolled for funerals, heralded special announcements and summoned parishioners to worship. Russian bells do not swing when rung; only the interior clappers hang free. This affords the bell ringers more control over the intensity and rhythmic patterns, especially when playing together with other bells. By the 17th-century, bell ringing was a profession (150 bell ringers were employed in the Moscow Kremlin alone), and 100-ton bells (as the Czar Bell, today on display in the Moscow Kremlin) could be cast.

By the early 19th century, over 200 bells hung across Moscow. But, on December 6, 1929, the new Soviet government issued Decree No. 118, which forbade bell ringing, and ordered that all bells be removed from church towers; many of these were sadly melted down to make anything from cauldrons to tractors. The Rostov Bells survived because the Rostov Museum director wrote to the Minister of Culture, Anatoly Lunacharsky (a street is named after him), asking to protect them. Even though the historical bells remained intact, they hung silent until the 1960s when the government allowed them featured in a recording. Today, bell founding and ringing is experiencing a new Renaissance in the Golden Ring area, and every year in Yaroslavl contemporary casters present their works.

NIKOLA-ULEIMA Никола-Улейма

About 60 kilometers (37 miles) west of Borisoglebsky, along the P153, lies the quaint **Monastery of St Nicholas-on-the-Uleima**. Founded in 1400 as a lookout post, it was one of the bloodiest sites of the attempted Polish invasions of Moscovy. The monks and village inhabitants fought to their deaths trying to resist the enemy; during the last battle the monastery burnt to the ground. Later, in 1675, the five-domed **Cathedral of St Nicholas** was reconstructed on the old foundation, and the helmet-domed **Church of the Presentation-in-the-Temple** restored. Later, a refectory and bell tower were added next to the *kokoshniki*-gabled walls. White birch and dark-green lime trees surround the monastery, and its towers are covered with ornamental shapes and colorful pilaster panels.

UGLICH ON THE VOLGA Углич

Only 18 kilometers (11 miles) west of Nikola-Uleima along the P153 road is the town of Uglich, with a population of 40,000. Trains also stop here on their way to Rybinsk; they depart from Moscow's Savelovsky Railway Station, and take six to seven hours. Buses also run from Rostov. The best place to stay is at the **Volgskaya Riveria Hotel** at 8 Uspensky Square, and the **Hotel Uspenskaya** is down the street at number 3. The **Moskva Hotel**, at 3 Ostrovsky St, is situated on the banks of the Volga River.

In the 16th century the seventh wife of Ivan the Terrible, Maria Nagaya, was banished here to live in a palace within the kremlin walls. Later, Dmitri, the youngest son of Ivan the Terrible, was found dead in the palace garden on May 15, 1591; many believed he was killed by assassins sent by Boris Godunov. Alexander Pushkin wrote of the event in his epic poem *Boris Godunov*.

The **Church of St Demetrius-on-the-Blood** (1630) was built over the spot where Dmitri was murdered. It was replaced in 1692 by a more elaborate red-and-white stone and five-domed church which now functions as a museum. All that remains of the czarina's court is the two-story stone **Palace of Czarevich Dmitri**, built in the 15th-century by Prince Andrei Bolshoi. Later, after a feud with his brother Grand Prince Ivan III, Andrei died in prison. The palace walls are decorated with bands of brick terracotta, and the tent roofs with sheets of weathered copper. It now houses a small museum. Outside the kremlin stands the five-domed **Church of St John the Baptist** (1689–1700) with an adjoining octagonal bell tower, made famous by the painting by Russian artist Nikolai Roerich.

Across the street stands the **Monastery of the Resurrection**, ordered built in 1674 by Metropolitan Jonah of Rostov. The enclave is made up of a cathedral, bell tower, refectory and the **Church of Our Lady of Smolensk**. The neighboring **Monastery of St Alexis** is the oldest in Uglich and founded in 1371 by Alexis, Metropolitan of All Russia. It was burnt to the ground during Polish and Lithuanian invasions, and rebuilt in the 1620s. Next to the two-story Refectory stands the slender triple-spired **Church of the Virgin Dormition** (1628). This church, nicknamed the *Divnaya* (Wondrous), has long remained dear to the people of Uglich. A few surviving secular structures are also of interest: the two-story wooden **Voronin House**, once owned by the Mekhov family, has a tile stove that is still located on the ground floor. The two-story 18th-century stone houses of the Kalashnikov family (a member of the family invented the famous rifle of the same name) and Ovsiannikov merchants are located nearby.

In 1999, Uglich opened the **Library of Russian Vodka**, where visitors can sample different brands and browse books on vodka; and in 2001, well-known sculptor Ernst Neizvestny was commissioned to create a monument to Russian vodka for the town. Folk legend has it that the town's name is derived from the phrase, *Tut zhgli ugli* (here they burned coals). Charcoal is an essential element for filtering fine vodkas. In town, one can also visit a varied collection of other museums: the **Puppet Museum**, **Museum of Prison Art**, and the **Museum of Russian Superstition**.

VICINITY OF UGLICH

A short drive to the northwest, crossing the Volga River (along the top of a hydroelectric dam), brings the visitor to the quaint town of **Myshkin**, with a population of just 6,000. Legend has it, that a prince, after a hunting expedition, fell asleep here and dreamt of a mouse—thus, the name Myshkin, derived from *mysh*, the Russian word for 'mouse'. Across from the **Mouse Museum**, is the **Ethnographic Museum**, which exhibits everything from ancient pagan decorations to machinery from Stalin's First Five Year Plan. Another interesting place to visit is the **Museum of Pyotr Smirnov**, born in a nearby village. The museum displays the history of Smirnov vodka production and contains other old 19th-century glass and bottles. The brothers Smirnov also built homes designed with fancy carved façades, which are still found throughout this little gem of a town.

YAROSLAVL Ярославль
JEWEL ON THE VOLGA

The English writer and adventurer Robert Byron wrote of his first visit to Yaroslavl in the early 1930s:

> While Veliki Novgorod retains something of the character of early Russia before the Tartar invasion, the monuments of Yaroslavl commemorate the expansion of commerce that marked the 17th-century... The English built a shipyard here; Dutch, Germans, French and Spaniards followed them. Great prosperity came to the town, and found expression in a series of churches whose spacious proportions and richness of architectural decoration had no rival in the Russia of their time.

Today Yaroslavl is still an important commercial center and regional capital with a population of 600,000 people. Lying 280 kilometers (175 miles) northeast of Moscow on the M8 Highway, it occupies the land on both sides of the Volga at its confluence with the River Kotorosl. Yaroslavl, the oldest city on the Volga, celebrated its millennium in 2010. A monument commemorating its 975th anniversary was placed in the city center in 1985. The seven-ton Ice Age boulder was unearthed on the site of the strelka and the inscription reads: 'On this spot in 1010 Yaroslavl the Wise founded Yaroslavl.' Another statue, dedicated to Yaroslavl the Wise and unveiled by Yeltsin in 1983, has him holding a piece of the town's kremlin while gazing toward Moscow. The oldest part of town, located at the confluence of the two rivers, contains many grandiose monasteries, churches, bell towers and residences erected by prosperous merchants. (In 2005, Yaroslavl's historic district was added to UNESCO's World Heritage List.) Outside of town is the Estate-Museum of 19th century writer, Nikolai Nekrasov, and the Cosmos Museum, dedicated to the first Soviet woman cosmonaut, Valentina Tereshkova.

Nearly 20 trains depart daily for Yaroslavl from Moscow's Yaroslavsky Train Station (Komsomolskaya Metro); the journey takes between three and four hours (depending on the number of stops). (See www.russianrailways.com or www. russianrail.com for schedules and ticket purchase.) Buses run from Moscow's Central Shchyolkovsky Station and take five-and-a-half hours. From Yaroslavl, buses and trains also depart for other Golden Ring locations, or routes farther east into the Urals or north to St Petersburg. *Elektrichka* suburban trains run regularly between Yaroslavl, Rostov Veliky and Sergiyev Posad. (Yaroslavl has two train stations. The main one being Yaroslavl Glavny, on the north side of the river, and then Yaroslavl Moskovsky on the southern side, where the bus station is located). The area code for Yaroslavl is 485.

In summer months, a hydrofoil departs five days a week for Kostroma (two hours) and on to Plyos (one hour) from the River Station at 2a Volzhskaya Embankment. (Boats also run from both towns to Yaroslavl.) Check at the station for current times of departure; tickets are on sale about 30 minutes before departure, but on weekends, people start to queue hours before.

As the largest city of the region, many hotels and eateries are scattered about the area. The 4-star **Ring Premiere Hotel**, located at 55 Svoboda St, has over 100 rooms, a restaurant and pub. The 4-star **Hotel Ibis** is in the town center at 2 Pervomaisky Lane; across the street is the Golden Bear Café. Down the street at number 55 is the 3-star **Alyosha Popovich Dvor Hotel**. A few other 3-star hotels are the **Kotorosl** at 87 Bolshaya Okyabrskaya St near the main train station; the **Yubileynaya Hotel**, conveniently located near the monastery on the west bank of the river at 26 Korotoslnaya Embankment (at number 55 is the 4-star **SK Royal Hotel**), the **St George Hotel** at 10 Moskovsky Prospekt, the **Ioann Vasiliyevich** at 34 Revolutsionnaya and the **Kuptsov Dom** at 21 Trefoleva St. Along the Volzhskaya Embankment (on the Volga), at number 2, is the **Volzhskaya Zhemchuzhina Hotel**, near the Bashnya Arsenal. Many hotels can be reserved on the website www. booking.com.

HISTORY

The bear was long worshipped by pagan inhabitants as a sacred animal. Another legend provides the story of Prince Yaroslavl the Wise (978–1054 AD) who wrestled a bear on the banks of the river and won. On the city's coat-of-arms a bear stands on his hind legs and holds a gold pole-ax, representing the endurance of the Yaroslavl spirit. In the ninth century a small trade outpost arose on the right bank of the Volga River and became known as *Medvezhny Ugol* (Bear Corner), forming the northern border of the Rostov region. When Kievan Grand Prince Yaroslav the Wise visited the settlement in 1010 (to baptize the Pagan heathens), its name was changed to honor him. It grew as large as Rostov; an early chronicle entry stated that in one great fire 17 churches burned to the ground. By the 13th century Yaroslavl had become the capital of its own principality along the Volga and remained politically independent for another 250 years.

The hordes of the Mongol Khan Batu invaded in 1238 and destroyed a great part of the city. In 1463, when Prince Alexander handed over his ancestral lands to Ivan III, the Grand Prince of Moscow, Yaroslavl was finally annexed to the Moscovy principality. For a short time Yaroslavl regained its political importance when it was made the temporary capital during the Time of Troubles from 1598 to 1613.

The city reached the height of its prosperity in the 17th-century when it became known for its handicrafts. Located along important trade routes, merchants journeyed from as far away as England and the Netherlands to purchase leather goods, silverware, wood carvings and fabrics. Because craftsmen treated skins with bark to improve the leather quality (pounding the oak bark), the region was nicknamed Tolchkovaya (*toloch* in Russian means 'pound'). At one time, one-sixth of Russia's most prosperous merchant families lived in Yaroslavl, which was the second most populated city in the country. These families, in turn, put their wealth back into the city. By the middle of the 17th-century, more than 30 new churches had been built. During this time the city became an architectural chronicle etched in stone on a scale unmatched anywhere else in Russia. Yaroslavl was also Moscow's Volga port until the Moscow–Volga canal was built in 1937.

The *burlaki* (barge haulers) were a common sight, as portrayed in Repin's famous *Barge Haulers on the Volga*. (See page 326.) Merchants would travel along the Volga and Kotorosl rivers to Rostov, and then along a system of rivers and dry land (*volokoi*), on to Vladimir. In 1795, Count Musin-Pushkin discovered in the Savior Monastery the famous 12th-century chronicle *The Lay of Igor's Host*. This text was based on the fighting campaigns of Prince Igor of Novgorod who, in the words of the chronicle, 'did not let loose ten falcons on a flock of swans, but laid down his own wizard fingers on living strings, which themselves throbbed out praises....' Later Borodin composed the opera *Prince Igor* based on this chronicle.

Today there are over 300 historical sites listed in the city, and R38 billion was poured into the city to renovate and build for the 1000th year jubilee. Joint ventures have been established, and Burlington, Vermont was even named Yaroslavl's sister city. A local foundation has financed the re-creation of a whole pedestrian street to look like old Rus, with everything from coach inns and trading stalls to craft workshops and eating houses. If you look at the 1000 Ruble note, on front is an image of Yaroslav the Wise, and on back is Yaroslavl's Church of St John the Baptist with its adjoining 7-tiered bell tower—symbols of ancient Rus.

THE FIREBIRD

*O*nce upon a time, a very long time ago, there was a beautiful girl named Marushka, who was orphaned at an early age. This maiden was capable of embroidering the most beautiful and exquisite patterns on cloths and silks; no one, on all the earth, could match her talents.

Word of her marvelous works spread far and wide, and merchants from all over the world sought Marushka, trying to lure her off to their kingdoms. 'Come away with us,' they pleaded, 'riches and fame will surely be yours.' Marushka always replied, 'I shall never leave the village where I was born. But if you indeed find my work beautiful, then I will sell it to you. If you don't have the money, you can repay me whenever you can. I get my pleasure from the work itself; the money I distribute throughout my village.'

Even though the merchants would leave the village without Marushka, they spread their stories of her incredible talent across the world. The tales finally reached the ears of Kaschei the Immortal, the most wicked of the sorcerers. Kaschei was immediately curious and enraged to think that such beauty existed somewhere that he had never seen. He learned too that Marushka was quite beautiful herself, so he turned himself into the handsomest of princes and flew out over the mountains, oceans, and almost impassable birch forests until he found Marushka's village.

'Where is the maiden who embroiders the most exquisite of patterns?' He was led to her very door, as the villagers were used to the many visitors. When Marushka answered the door herself, the disguised sorcerer asked to see all the needlework and tapestry that she had ready to show. Marushka fetched all her shirts and sashes, towels and trousers, handkerchiefs and hats. Kaschei could hardly contain his delight.

Marushka said, 'My lord, I hope my work pleases you. Anything that meets your fancy is yours to keep. If you don't have the money, you needn't pay me. My happiness comes from your delight.'

Although the great Kaschei could not believe that this girl could fashion things even better than he, he was also taken by her beauty and kindness. He decided that if he could not make such things himself, then he most possess her and take her home to his kingdom.

'Come away with me, and I will make you my queen. You shall live in my palace, all the fruits of my kingdom shall be yours, your clothes shall be covered with jewels, and birds of paradise will sing you to sleep every night. You shall even have your own chamber, containing the most exotic of threads and materials, where you will embroider for me and my kingdom.'

Marushka listened quietly to all this, then she softly replied, 'I couldn't ever leave this village where my parents are buried, where I was born. Here my heart shall always be. There is nothing sweeter than the fields and woods and neighbors of my own village. I must give my embroidery to anyone who receives joy from my work. I could never embroider for you alone.'

The Great Kaschei had never been refused, nor had he ever failed to bewitch a mere girl. Furious, his face suddenly changed from that of the handsome prince to his very own, dark and raging. At this sight, Marushka gasped and tried to flee the room. But it was too late.

'Because you will not leave your village and come to be my queen, because you dared to refuse the Great Kaschei, from this moment on I cast a spell on you. You shall be a bird! I shall make sure that you fly far, far away and never see your village again!'

As he spoke these terrible words, the beautiful Marushka turned into a magnificent, flaming red firebird. In the same moment, the Great Kaschei turned himself into a great black falcon, who swooped down on the firebird, grasping her in his enormous claws. He carried her high into the clouds so she would never return to her birthplace.

Marushka knew that she had to leave something behind. As the great falcon carried her through the sky, the firebird began to shed her flaming plumage. Soon, feather after feather floated down, dusting her beloved homeland. A

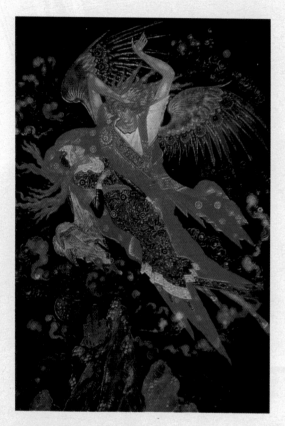

rainbow of colors dotted the meadows and forests; and by the time the falcon had reached its own kingdom, all her feathers had fallen, leaving a shimmering trail right back to her cottage.

Even though the firebird died, all her magical feathers continued to live forever. The firebird's feathers carried their own spell: All those who loved and honored beauty in themselves and others, as Marushka, and who sought to create beauty for others, without expecting anything in return, would always be able to see the firebird's feathers.

With the new era of religious freedom, many artists practice the trade of fresco restoration and also paint religious art for the many new churches now under construction.

A monk stops to chat with a member of his congregation in front of the Assumption Cathedral in Sergiyev Posad, one of the major centers of the Russian Orthodox Church.

(left top) *The 18th-century baroque bell tower in Sergiyev Posad.*

(left) *The Chapel-over-the-Well in Sergiyev Posad. It is customary for pilgrims to fill bottles with holy water to take home.*

(above) One of the most outstanding collections of Russian church architecture is to be found in the town of Sergiyev Posad. A monk walks toward the bell tower; beyond stands the blue 18th-century Church of Our Lady of Smolensk. On the left is the Church of Saints Zosimus and Savvaty and in the background stands the Pilgrim Tower, part of the monastery walls.

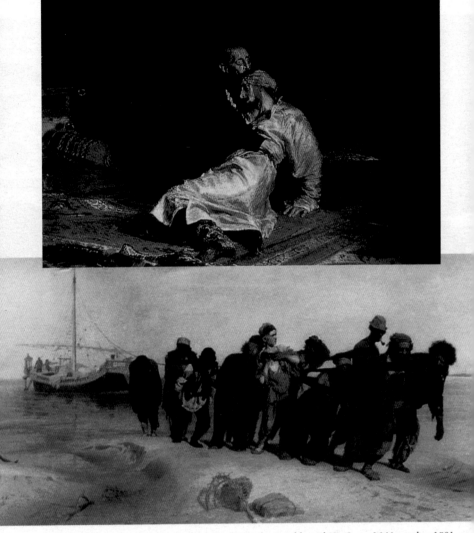

(top) *In 1885, realist artist Ilya Repin painted* Ivan the Terrible and His Son—16 November 1581. *On this date, in Alexandrov, Ivan the Terrible killed his son in a fit of jealous rage. The painting now hangs in Moscow's Tretyakov Gallery.* (bottom) Barge Haulers on the Volga *was completed by Ilya Repin in 1873, shortly after he graduated from St Petersburg's Art Academy. Besides portraying the brutal reality of hard physical labor, the artist also symbolizes the spiritual strength of man which cannot be broken. The painting now hangs in St Petersburg's Russian Museum.*

(opposite page) *Inside Kostroma's Museum of Old Wooden Architecture stands the weathered Church of the Virgin, built in 1552;* (inset) *The 17th-century Church of St John-the-Divine in Rostov Veliky with its aspen-shingled domes.*

The massive bell cote inside the kremlin at Rostov Veliky. Its 13 large bells can be heard 15 miles away. In ancient times bells played a significant role in village life—sounding as a fire alarm, calling the town to battle, summoning the congregation to church or celebrating a joyous occasion.

Most all the towns in the Golden Ring contain elaborately decorated Russian-Orthodox churches with zakomara semi-circular arches and carved kokoshniki gables, topped with colorful onion domes—a magnificent sight even on a bleak winter's afternoon.

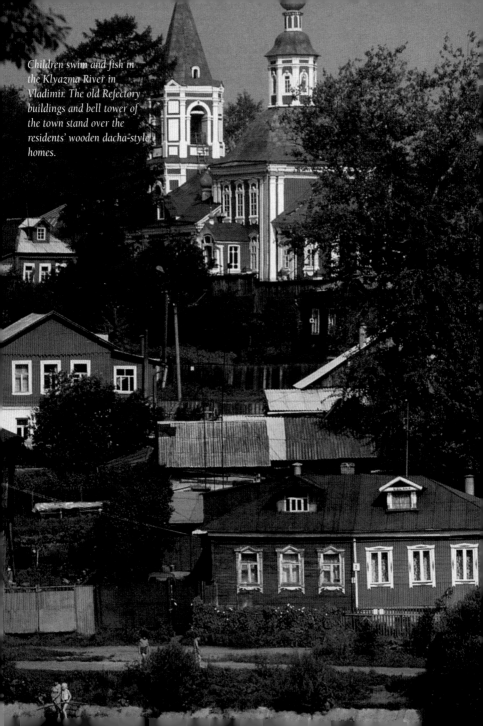

Children swim and fish in the Klyazma River in Vladimir. The old Refectory buildings and bell tower of the town stand over the residents' wooden dacha-style homes.

(top) Residents of Suzdal sell their homegrown vegetables at the local market. Most people living outside the bigger cities grow their own potatoes, cabbage, tomatoes and other vegetables in small garden plots by their homes out of economic necessity. (bottom) The Cathedral of St Demetrius in Vladimir, built by Vsevolod III in the 12th-century. More than 1,300 bas-reliefs decorate its outer walls.

Besides churches, Suzdal is full of historic residential architecture. Children play after school by the elaborately decorated 18th-century wooden house that once belonged to an influential merchant named Bibanov.

The Virgin of Vladimir is one of Andrei Rublyov's most beautiful icons. Painted in the early 15th-century for the Assumption Cathedral in Vladimir and based on the Byzantine Virgin of Eleousa, it can be seen today in the Vladimir-Suzdal Museum of History and Art.

The 15th-century icon by Andrei Rublyov known as the Old Testament Trinity *is one of the greatest masterpieces of Old Russian art. Painted for his teacher St Sergius, it once hung as the central icon in Sergiyev Posad's Trinity Cathedral. The three angels represent the harmony of the Father, Son and Holy Spirit. It now hangs in Moscow's Tretyakov Gallery.*

THE RUSSIAN ICON

The ancient art of icon painting has been a part of Russian life for over 11 centuries and is still being passed on to future generations. The core of this art portrays spiritual and aesthetic ideals, as well as historical events and lifestyles of Old Russia. Soon after Prince Vladimir introduced Christianity in AD 988, Byzantium's art and religious customs were quickly absorbed into Russian culture. The word *icona*, in Russian, stems from the Greek *eikon*, meaning holy image; icons portrayed the likenesses of Christ, the Virgin, saints and martyrs.

Byzantine art dissipated greatly during the Mongol invasions in the mid-13th-century, when artistic styles transcended their Byzantine heritage. During Russia's long period of isolation (two and a half centuries of Mongol occupation), several unique types of icon painting were established. The main schools were the Novgorod, Pskov, Moscow and Central Russian. Each retained some of the original elements of color and design from early Byzantium, while adding their own distinctive flair.

The purpose of the icon was to bring spiritual power to light. The icon's own light and color mirrored the sacred qualities of the celestial world. In addition, the icon's impersonation of the divine and earthly planes was based on a hierarchy of colors: the tops were white, purple and gold, which symbolized divine light, purity, salvation and love. Blue and green, the earthy colors, represented heaven, joy and hope; and red portrayed the Holy Spirit's flame, the passions of Christ, and the burning fire of faith and martyrdom. The treachery of Judas was symbolized in yellow. Black was derived from Russia's old folk beliefs: the gloom of the underworld and the emptiness of the nonbeliever; the icon educated the viewer how to overcome this chaos and darkness. Many monks fasted for several days before starting work on an icon, chanted prayers, and wholeheartedly believed in the moral and educational powers of their creations.

The Novgorod school mainly used a symmetrical design and painted in bold and simple outlines using red, white, and black—with a style similar to folklore traditions. The iconographers of Pskov, one of the last remaining regions to be annexed to Moscovy, developed a more dynamic style, using dramatic color schemes of gold, green, red and yellow. The Central Russian school was greatly affected by Moscow and Novgorod, but used blue as its dominant color combined with yellow and white. This style was centered in the Golden Ring towns of Rostov, Pereslavl-Zalessky, Palekh, Yaroslavl, Vladimir and Suzdal.

Icons were painted on panels of wood with tempera paints. Designs were initially sketched with chalk or charcoal and then filled in with colors. First glazes, then a varnish of linseed oil were applied to the completed work. But, after about 80 years, the linseed oil darkened the icon, at which time another artist usually painted over the original design. With some icons, this process was repeated many times. Today, restorers can remove paint layer by layer to recreate many of the original portraits. These efforts have been especially concentrated in churches in Moscow and the Golden Ring area.

Icons were at the center of Old Russian art and kept in churches, chapels and homes. Later the iconostasis, a number of icons layered together on wooden or stone tiers, were painted as well. This allowed Christ, the Virgin and numerous saints to be brought together as one entity. Icons played an essential role in people's lives; they were given a place of honor in the homes and thought to possess healing powers. The 16th-century icon of the Kazan Virgin was believed to have saved Moscow residents from the plague. Icons were also placed along roads, at the entrances to gates and towers and were even carried on poles high above troops as they entered military campaigns.

By the beginning of the 15th-century, Andrei Rublyov was recognized as the Church's foremost artist. The master lived in Moscow, establishing it as the new center of icon painting. No one is quite sure of the year of Rublyov's birth, but his name became a symbol for the highest values in Old Russian art; he eventually painted for all the grand princes of Moscovy. His innovative style, luminous colors, symbolic images, and rhythmical lines had a profound effect on the other schools. In his later life Rublyov became a monk, lived at the Spaso-Andronikov Monastery in Moscow, and painted frescoes in the Cathedral of Our Savior. He died in 1430.

Rublyov's technique was asymmetrical in form, and his colorful images possessed a narrative and harmonious tone. He meticulously individualized his portraits and gave each figure a life of its own. Instead of the simple Novgorod outline, Rublyov's personages were enveloped with character and movement. Rublyov also used the circle as a symbol for the unity of life, and angels and saints were portrayed in real-life scenes on earth, surrounded by rocks, trees and animals. Allegorical symbols were introduced: Christ wore purple robes; the golden chalice contained a calf's head; and angels held trumpets or swords. Dark and somber colors gave way to vibrant greens, blues and yellows. Attention was paid to background; gems and metal were even added to create a more multidimensional setting.

Both Theophanes, Greek leader of the Novgorod school during the late 14th-century, and Rublyov painted frescoes and the iconostasis in the Moscow Kremlin's Annunciation Cathedral. Rublyov and Daniil Chorny painted in Vladimir's Assumption Cathedral, where many of the icons and frescoes are still visible today. In the Trinity-Sergius Monastery, Rublyov portrayed the famous religious figure of Old Russia—St Sergius who blessed Dmitry Donskoi before the decisive Battle of Kulikova, where Donskoi destroyed the Mongol-Tatar yoke in 1380. For once, icons not only symbolized God, but also the awesome events of human life. The saint's blessing (as portrayed in the Old Testament Trinity) symbolized Russian's desire for freedom and unity; the Eucharist served as a metaphor to sacrifice in battle and the chalice hope, faith and the common bond of the Russian people.

Many of Rublyov's works were lost through the centuries, destroyed in fires or painted over. But, some of his works, such as the Virgin of Vladimir, can still be found in the Vladimir-Suzdal Museum; the Archangel Michael, the Savior, Apostle Paul and the Old Testament Trinity can be viewed in the Tretyakov Gallery in Moscow. Other copies are exhibited at the Rublyov Museum in the Spaso-Andronikov Monastery. When British travel author, Robert Byron, made his first visit to Moscow and viewed Rublyov's icons, he professed: in Rublyov's masterpieces 'live the eternal sorrows, joys, and the whole destiny of man. Such pictures bring tears to the eye and peace to the soul'.

The genius of Andrei Rublyov can be compared to that of other major artists of Renaissance Europe, such as Giotto and Raphael. He was so revered that a century after his death, the Church Council decreed that Rublyov's icons were merited as the true standard of artistic Orthodoxy. It was Rublyov's desire in life to help lead the world out of medieval darkness and despair and back into realms of beauty, harmony and love. By capturing infinite goodness on a simple and timeless icon, Andrei Rublyov achieved his own immortality and will always live in the hearts of those who view his work. The renowned Soviet film director, Andrei Tarkovsky, made a classic film on the life of Andrei Rublyov.

By the 17th-century, Western European art had greatly influenced Russian religious painting. The icons became smaller and more intricate, decorated with jewels and cloisonné enamels and mosaics. With the reforms of Peter the Great (in the early 18th-century) and the subsequent Westernization of Russian society, the popularity of icon painting made a sharp decline. It took several centuries before an interest returned to the old icon masterpieces; the first to be restored was Rublyov's Old Testament Trinity. A leading exhibition of restored medieval icons took place in Russia in 1913; many artists, such as Henri Matisse and Kazimir Malevich were greatly influenced by their beauty. Sadly, during the Communist era, icon painting was banned altogether, and the art of painting lacquered wooden boxes and dolls replaced religious art. Thousands of icons were burnt and destroyed, and many more stolen, smuggled or sold to the West.

Today restoration and icon painting schools are being revived in Russia, and the art of *spiski*, making copies of old icons, is flourishing. Most major monasteries (particularly in Sergiyev Posad) now have their own icon workshops. Many of these incorporate old-style techniques: the icons are painted atop wooden boards which are covered with *levki*, a mixture of linen oil, chalk, glue, bones and sturgeon skin. The color blue, for example, is made by crushing lapis lazuli, and the pigments are then mixed with eggs and water. It usually takes up to three months to create an average icon; generally students paint the nature scenes, architecture and clothing, while the most experienced artists design the faces, hands and feet. The Moscow Icons Workshop is considered one of the best in Russia; one of their most recent creations was the iconostasis for St Nicholas Church on Bersenevskaya Embankment. One private Russian company even presented Boris Yeltsin with the icon Boris and Gleb (based on the original). Boris and Gleb are patron saints of Russia as well as being the names of Yeltsin's grandsons.

SIGHTS

A tour of Yaroslavl, known as the Florence of Russia, begins at the oldest part of town, the *strelka* (arrow or spit of land), lying along the west bank of the Volga, where the Kotorosl empties into it. The Bear Ravine, now Peace Boulevard, once separated the timber town from the *posad*, earth town. The kremlin grounds are open 8am–8pm from May to September, and 9am–6pm from October to April. Note: many of the churches are closed Mondays and Tuesdays, and the main cathedral on Tuesdays and Wednesdays. During bad weather, many of the churches may close.

By the Kotorosl, on Bogoyavlenskaya Ploshchad (Square), is the oldest surviving structure in Yaroslavl, the **Transfiguration of Our Savior Monastery**, founded at the end of the 12th-century. Northern Russia's first school of higher education was set up here, and the monastery library contained a huge collection of Russian and Greek literature. It also grew into a large feudal power—by the end of the 16th century the monastery was one of the strongest fortresses in the northern states, with a permanent garrison of its own Streltsy, musketeer marksmen, to protect it. The white kremlin walls that dominate the town center were fortified to three meters (ten feet) thick in 1621. During an attack, the defenders would pour boiling water or hot tar on their enemies.

The Holy Gates of the monastery were built at the southern entrance in 1516. The archway frescoes include details from the Apocalypse. The 16th-century **bell tower** (in 1991, the museum mounted 18 ancient bells found in a storage area) stands in front of the gates; climb up to the observation platform along its upper tier for a breathtaking panorama view of the city.

The monastery's gold-domed **Cathedral of the Transfiguration of the Savior** (1506) was one of the wealthiest churches in Russia. The frescoes that cover the entire interior are the oldest wall paintings in Yaroslavl. The fresco of the *Last Judgment*, painted in 1564, is on the west wall; the east side contains scenes of the *Transfiguration and Adoration of the Virgin*. It served as the burial chamber for the Yaroslavl princes. The vestry exhibits icons and old vestments that were used during church rituals and services. Open 10am–5pm; closed Tuesdays, Wednesdays and when it rains.

Behind the bell-clock tower are two buildings, the Refectory and Chambers of the Father Superior and Monks, which now house branches of the **Yaroslavl Museums of Art, History and Architecture**. The museums are open daily 10am –6pm; closed Mondays and the first Wednesday of each month. (In winter the museum closes an hour earlier.) The Refectory exhibits the history of the Yaroslavl region up to the present day. The monk cells contain collections of Old Russian art, including icons, folk art, manuscripts, costumes, armor and jewelry. Here also is the

Museum of The Lay of Igor's Host. The story of this famous epic, along with ancient birch-bark documents and early printed books, is on display. Twelve years after Count Musin-Pushkin discovered the epic and other old rare manuscripts in the monastery library, the great fire of Moscow, during Napoleon's invasion, destroyed all the originals. **The Church of the Yaroslavl Miracle Workers** (1827), at the southern end of the cathedral, is the museum's cinema and lecture hall.

The red brick and blue five-domed **Church of the Epiphany** (1684) stands on the square behind the monastery. It is festively decorated with *kokoshniki* and glazed colored tiles, a tradition of Yaroslavl church architecture. The interior is a rich tapestry of frescoes illustrating the life of Christ, painted by Yaroslavl artists in 1692; notice that the faces of the saints appear decidedly more human than in earlier decades. It also has an impressive gilded seven-tiered iconostasis. The church is open 9am–4pm; closed Mondays and Tuesdays.

One popular holiday takes place twelve days after Orthodox Christmas— between January 18 and 19, when Orthodox believers gather on the banks of the Volga and Kotorosl rivers to take part in the ritual of cleansing and blessing of the waters for Epiphany (*Kresheniye*), a celebration of divinity taking flesh in Christ. Residents make holes in the ice in the shape of crosses; and, by tradition, one must fully dunk underwater three times, along with crossing oneself three times; the water is believed to alleviate physical and spiritual illness. If you don't want to jump into the icy waters, priests also hand out holy water to take with to bless the corners of the home.

Crossing the square and walking up Pervomaiskaya Ulitsa (away from the Volga) leads to the early 19th-century **Central Bazaar.** Today this area is still a busy shopping district. A short walk behind the walls of the arcade brings you to the Znamenskaya (Sign) Tower of the kremlin. Towers in Russia were usually named after the icon that was displayed over their entrance. This tower once held the icon known as Sign of the Mother of God.

On Volkov Square is the **Volkov Drama Theater,** founded by Fyodor Volkov who opened Russia's first professional public theater in 1750; he formed his own drama company in 1748, and it was the first to stage *Hamlet* in Russia. In 1870, the first train ran from Yaroslavl to Moscow; and, in 1900, Russia's first trolley was put into service here.

At the end of Ushinskov Ulitsa is a Statue of Lenin on Krasnaya Ploshchad (Red Square). Circle back toward the Volga, heading south on Sovietskaya Ulitsa until it intersects with Sovietskaya Ploshchad (Soviet Square). Dominating the town's main square is the **Church of Elijah the Prophet,** now a Museum of Architecture. In memory of Yaroslav the Wise's victory over wrestling the bear (which occurred on August 2, name day of Prophet Elijah), the prince ordered a church built here in

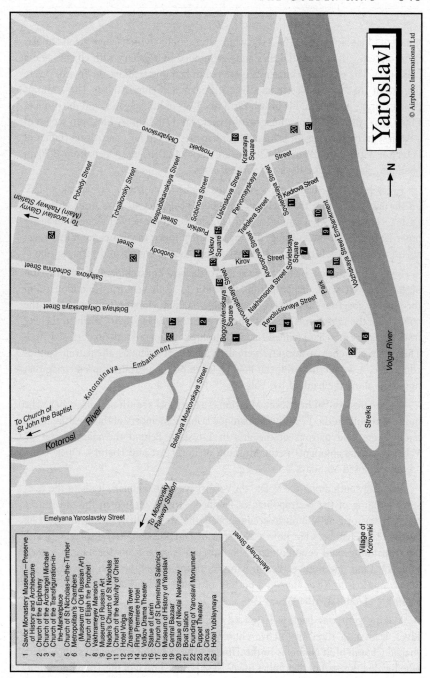

© Airphoto International Ltd

Yaroslavl

N →

1 Savior Monastery Museum—Preserve
   of History and Architecture
2 Church of the Epiphany
3 Church of the Archangel Michael
4 Church of the Transfiguration-in-
   the-Marketplace
5 Church of St Nicholas-in-the-Timber
6 Metropolitan's Chambers
   (Museum of Old Russian Art)
7 Church of Elijah the Prophet
8 Vakhrameyev Mansion
9 Museum of Russian Art
10 Nadei's Church of St Nicholas
11 Church of the Nativity of Christ
12 Hotel Volga
13 Znamenskaya Tower
14 Ring Premiere Hotel
15 Volkov Drama Theater
16 Statue of Lenin
17 Church of St Demetrius Salonica
18 Museum of History of Yaroslavl
19 Central Bazaar
20 Statue of Nikolai Nekrasov
21 Boat Station
22 Founding of Yaroslavl Monument
23 Puppet Theater
24 Circus
25 Hotel Yubileynaya

Pobedy Street
Tchaikovsky Street
Okryabrskovo Prospekt
Republikanskaya Street
Sobinova Street
Ushinskova Street
Krasnaya Square
Street
Pushkin Street
Svobody Street
Street
Bolshaya Oktyabrskaya Street
Salykova Street
Schedrina Street
Pervomayskaya Street
Trefoleva Street
Sovietskaya Street
Kedrova Street
Volkov Square
Kirov Street
Andropova Street
Sovietskaya Square
Nakhimsona Street
Vozhhskaya Street Embankment
Revolusionaya Street
Park
Bogoyavlenskaya Square
Peromalskaya Street
Volga River
Strelka
Village of Korovniki
Kotorosinaya   Embankment
Kotorosl   River
To Church of
St John the Baptist
Bolshaya Moskovskaya Street
Melnichya Street
Emelyana Yaroslavsky Street
To Moscovsky
Railway Station
To Yaroslavl Glavny
(Main) Railway Station

honor of Elijah. Rebuilt in 1647, the white-stone church with its large green cupolas is decorated with ornamental tiles and surrounded by a gallery with chapels and a bell tower. The wooden iconostasis is carved in baroque fashion; the frescoes were painted in 1680 by the Kostroma artists Sila Savin and Gury Nikitin. These murals depict Christ's ascension, his life on earth, the lives of his Apostles, and the prophet Elijah. The walls also depict images from everyday 17th century life, even scenes of a harvest and other peasant labors. Prayer benches carved for Czar Alexei (father of Peter the Great) and Patriarch Nikon are also found inside. Open from 8:30am –6:30pm; closed Wednesdays and when it rains.

Every year on the main square, residents celebrate *Maslenitsa*, which takes place on the last day before the beginning of Lent (Lent lasts 40 days until Orthodox Easter.) Traditional *blini* pancakes and *baranki* bagels are served along with many other festivities. In the evening, out on the Volga River, the Scarecrow Zima is set ablaze to make way for Vesna. (In Russian *zima* means 'winter' and vesna 'spring.')

Behind this church, by the Volga at 23 Volzhskaya Embankment, is the **Museum of Russian Art** with displays from the 18th to 20th centuries and housed in the former governor's residence. Open 10am–5:00pm; closed Mondays. Across the street from the museum is **Nadei's Church of St Nicholas** (1620), a gift to the city from a wealthy merchant named Nadei Sveteshnikov. Open 10am–5pm; closed Wed/ Thurs. Ten churches in Yaroslavl were dedicated to St Nicholas, the patron saint of commerce. A wonderful stroll can now be taken on the pedestrian promenade that now runs along the bank of the Volga.

The impressive **Vakhrameyev Mansion** is a few blocks south near the water. The house was built in the 1780s in the baroque fashion. Members of this wealthy noble family were avid patrons of the arts in Yaroslavl. Behind the mansion (at 17 Volzhskaya Embankment) is the **Museum of Local Art and History**. Open 10am –5.00pm; closed Mondays.

Walking south along the Volga, on Volzhskaya Embankment, leads to the two-story building of the Metropolitan's Chambers (1690), located in the old timber town. It was originally built to accommodate the Metropolitan of Rostov when he visited. The chambers are now a **Museum of Old Russian Art**, displaying many icons, paintings and ceramic tiles. The museum is open from 10am–6pm; closed Mondays (and one hour earlier in winter). Of interest is the icon *The Lay of the Bloody Battle with Khan Mamai*, a portrait of Count Musin-Pushkin, and a bronze sculpture of Yaroslavl the Wise.

Making your way back west toward the Savior Monastery, along the Kotorosl River, leads past three distinctive churches. The first is the simple white cube-shaped **Church of St Nicholas-in-the-Timber** (1695), built by the local shipbuilders who lived in this part of the timber town. Next is the **Church of the Transfiguration-**

in-the-Market-Place (1672). It was built from funds collected by townspeople in the old marketplace of the original earth town, where the local merchants and artisans lived. In the summer of 1693, 22 Yaroslavl artists helped paint the interior frescoes. The red brick **Church of the Archangel Michael** (1658), directly across from the monastery, stands on the site of a former palace. It once marked the boundary between the kremlin and the marketplace and is filled with brightly colored frescoes painted by local Yaroslavl artists in 1730.

In the village of Tolchkovo (in the southwestern part of the city) is the picturesque 15-domed Church of St John the Baptist (1671), located at 69 Kotorosl Embankment. (Its image is on the 1000 Ruble note.) The city was divided into *sloboda* districts depending on the trade or craft, and each often competed to build the most beautiful church. Thus the residents of the Tolchkovaya (Leather-making) Sloboda decided to construct a church like never seen before. The five green domes with a tulip-shaped dome in the middle, gold crosses and ornamental tiles are prime examples of the architecture of the Golden Age of Yaroslavl. (The use of different shaped and sized stone give the walls the appearance of lace.) In 1694, 15 masters from around Russia painted the frescoes and icons that adorn every part of the interior. The baroque-style iconostasis was carved in 1701. The complex also includes a 45-meter (135-foot) seven-tiered bell tower. The church is open 10am–5pm; closed Mondays and Tuesdays.

At dawn on the Summer Solstice pagan believers would bathe nearby in the Kotorosl River. Later, when these customs were replaced with Orthodox ones, the river was tied to the Feast Day of John the Baptist—now celebrated as Ivan Kupala Day (*kupatcya* is the Russian word for 'bathing').

Just south of the confluence of the Kotorosl with the Volga (at 2 Port Embankment), is a delightful architectural ensemble in the **Village of Korovniki**. (From the Savior Monastery, it is a kilometer walk, or ride two stops on bus number 4; you can also rent a rowboat). The most impressive structure is the five-domed red brick **Church of St John Chrysostom** (1649), used as the summer church. Its tent-shaped, 37-meter (100-foot) bell tower is known as the Candle of Yaroslavl. The **Church of Our Lady of Vladimir** (1669) was used as the winter church. (During the Soviet era, when the structures were used as a salt warehouse, many of the frescoes were lost.) Other buildings of interest are the **Church of St Nicholas-the-Wet** and its 'twin' winter **Church of Our Lady of Tikhvin**. The Korovnikova Sloboda was built in 1654, and its churches decorated with colored ceramic tiles and faceted tent-shaped roofs and bell towers.

If you have time, take a ride along the Volga; in summer, boats leave from a pier at the end of Pervomaiskaya Ulitsa. The trip to Dolmatovo takes about half an hour. For a longer excursion, try the 35-minute (8-km) ride to the **Village of Tolga** (on the Konstantinovo route), where one can explore and picnic in the area. (Long-distance cruise ships also stop in Yaroslavl on their way to Moscow or Astrakhan. These ships are rarely full, and tickets can often be bought at short notice.)

The legend goes that early in the 14th century, the Bishop of Rostov was returning home along the Volga. One night, as he camped on the right bank of the river, the Bishop was awakened by a mysterious bright light from the opposite bank. A bridge of light spanned the river and, as the Bishop walked across, he saw an image of the Mother of God holding the Christ child in her arms; in all the wonder, he left his staff on the left bank. In the morning, when people gathered around the site, they found an Icon with the Image of the Mother of God next to the staff. Within a day, a church was built on the spot, and later became the main church of the Tolga Convent. To this day, the Icon is the city's most important religious artifact.

The **Tolga Convent** and **Tolchkovo Church** have been beautifully restored with funds donated by city and local firms, and are once again active. The structures are highly decorated with ornamental bricks, terracotta and colorfully glazed tiles. On Tugova Hill, to the left of the village, looms the single-domed **Church of St Paraskeva**, built over the mass grave of Yaroslavl warriors who were killed in battle against the invading Mongols. To its right stands the **Church of St Theodore**, the **Church of St Nicholas Pensky**, and beyond another **Church of St Nicholas-at-Melenki**.

For an evening's entertainment go to the **Yaroslavl Circus** (located at 69 Svobody Ultisa across from Truda Square). The Puppet Theatre is at 25 Svobody. Each summer, beginning on August 1st, the Yaroslavl Sunsets Music Festival is held, which usually opens with the overture to Borodin's *Prince Igor*.

VICINITY OF YAROSLAVL

On the Uglich Highway, 29 kilometers (18 miles) southwest of Yaroslavl, is the **Cosmos Museum**, dedicated to Valentina Tereshkova the first female cosmonaut. In 2000, Tereshkova was honored as a 'Woman of the Century.' She was born on March 6th 1937 to a family of communal farmers. Soviet leader Nikita Khrushchev picked her (from among four final candidates) to be the first woman in space. Tereshkova's first space flight was on June 16th 1963 on board Vostok-6. It lasted 70 hours and 41 minutes and she orbited the earth 48 times. 'It is I, Chaika [Seagull],' she radioed back after reaching orbit. From then on she was known as 'Our Chaika' by fellow Russians. The museum, near the house where she was born in the village of Nikulskoye, displays her space capsule and the history of Soviet space travel. The museum is open 9:30am–4:30pm; closed Mondays and Tuesdays.

About 16 kilometers (10 miles) south from Yaroslavl, along the Moscow–Yaroslavl M8 Highway, is the **Nekrasov Estate Museum** in the village of Karabikha. The famous Russian writer Nikolai Nekrasov (1821–78) stayed on the estate in summer months; it retains much of its former appearance. Among his works is the satire *Who is Happy in Russia?* His poems and other works are on display. The museum is open 10am–5pm; closed Mondays and Tuesdays. Each summer there is a Nekrasov Poetry Festival at Karabikha.

TUTAYEV ON THE VOLGA Тутаев

About 40 kilometers (25 miles) northwest of Yaroslavl, on the way to Rybinsk (along the P151 road) is the village of Tutayev. *Elektrichka* trains also travel here from Yaroslavl. If you have time, and enjoy viewing historical architectural sites, it is a pleasant short trip along the Volga to this quaint town.

In the 13th century when Prince Roman (great-grandson of Grand Prince 'Big Nest' Vsevolod) was granted lands in this area, the village district became known as Romanov-Borisoglebsk. On opposite banks of the Volga, the prince constructed two fortified towns with ramparts and a moat. The prince's troops lived in Romanov, while the townspeople congregated in Borisoglebsk, on the right bank. It was not until 1921 that the town's name was changed to Tutayev, in honor of a Red Army hero.

In the 1670s the five-domed **Cathedral of the Resurrection** was built on the foundations of an older 12th-century church and embellished with a tent-shaped bell tower, elaborate porches and ornamental brickwork and tiling. Yaroslavl artists painted the 17th-century interior frescoes. *The Tower of Babel*, *The Last Judgment*, and *Tortures of Hell* attest to their love of biblical scenes.

Along the left bank, six other churches and their tent-shaped bell towers rise above the maple and birch sprinkled countryside. The oldest is the **Cathedral of the Exaltation of the Cross**, standing on the town's old ramparts. Further up river are the **Spaso-Arkhangelskaya Church**, the **Church of the Virgin of Kazan** (on the hillside), and the **Church of the Intercession**, all built in the early 18th-century.

KOSTROMA Кострома

Kostroma, 76 kilometers (47 miles) northeast of Yaroslavl, can be reached by the A113 road.   Trains run to/from from Yaroslavl (taking between two and three hours), and from Rostov Veliky as well. A few overnight trains (six hours, fifteen minutes) depart from Moscow's Yaroslavsky Train Station. Buses make more frequent departures from Moscow's Shchyolkovsky Terminal (taking between eight and nine hours). Buses also depart from here for other Golden Ring towns. From the train station take Trolley number 2; it takes 15 minutes to the town center. It is a 20-minute bus ride along Kineshemskoye Highway to the center from the main Bus station. The area code for Kostroma is 4942.

From Pier 1, a hydrofoil departs in summer months five days a week to/from Yaroslavl (two hours) and Plyos (one hour). Check at the station for current times of departure; tickets go on sale about 30 minutes before departure, but on weekends, people start to queue hours before.

The moderately-priced **Kostroma Hotel**, at 120 Sovietskaya is on the south bank of the Volga (request a room on the river side with balcony). On the same street, at number 29, is the inexpensive, comfortable **Mush Guesthouse**. The **Hotel Stary Dvor** is down the street at number 6. The **Snegurochka** (Snow Maiden) is at 38 Lagernaya St and **Shelestoff Hotel** at 1 Kommunarov. The **Volga Hotel** is located about two kilometers east of town at 1 Yunosheskayay St. (Check out listings on www.booking.com.)

Kostroma, with a population of 268,000, is the only city in Russia which has retained the original layout of its town center; it was founded by Yuri Dolgoruky in the 12th-century. Reconstructed in the early 18th-century, it is one of the country's finest examples of Russian classic design; no two houses are alike. In 1994, rock star Boris Grebenshchikov's band Aquarium released the album called 'Kostroma Mon Amour.'

Once a bustling trade center known as the Flax Capital of the North, Kostroma (pronounced with last syllable accented) supplied Russia and Europe with the finest of sailing cloth. The emblem of this picturesque town set along the confluence of the Kostroma and Volga Rivers depicts a small boat on silvery waters with sails billowing in the wind. The central mercantile square was situated on the north banks of the Volga. The Krasniye (Beautiful) and Bolshiye (Large) stalls were connected by covered galleries where fabrics and other goods were sold. Today the modernized **Arcade** still houses the town's markets and stores. In the center of these stands the **Monument to Ivan Susanin** on the town's central square of the same name. Susanin was a local peasant hero who saved the first Romanov czar from a Polish assassination attempt. A popular patriotic opera, *Ivan Susanin*, was later written in his honor by Mikhail Glinka. After a 1773 fire, Catherine the Great had the Susaninskaya Square rebuilt and today it still appears as if it were the original, complete with fire tower, former military jail, and town hall. The **Borschchov Mansion** (home of the general who fought in the War of 1812), the largest of the older residential buildings, is now a courthouse.

North from the square, at 5–7 Pavlovskaya Ulitsa, is the **Art Museum**, originally built in 1913 to honor 300 years of Romonov rule. Today, it has a small exhibit of 16th- to 19th-century Russian art. A few minutes walk west along Ulitsa Simanovskovo brings you to the recently restored **Monastery of the Epiphany**. The monastery's cathedral is the town's main functioning church. Inside can be found the "Icon of the Fyodorovsky Virgin", said to have worked miracles for Alexander Nevsky.

The real gem of the area is the **Ipatyevsky Monastery**, located west of town on the opposite side of the Kostroma River. It was founded in the 14th century by the Zernov Boyars, ancestors of the Godunovs. This large structure is enclosed by a white-brick kremlin and topped by green tent-shaped domes. Later the relatives of Boris Godunov built the monastery's golden-domed **Trinity Cathedral**. While Boris Godunov was czar (1598–1605), the Ipatyevsky Monastery became the wealthiest in the country, containing over 100 icons. The Godunov family had its own mansion (the rose-colored building with the small windows) within the monastery, and most family members were buried in the cathedral. The monastery was continually ravaged by internal strife, blackened by Polish invasions, and captured by the second False Dmitri in 1605, who claimed the throne of the Russian Empire. Later the Romanovs who, like the Godunovs, were powerful feudal lords in Kostroma, got the young Mikhail elected czar after the Time of Troubles. In 1613, Mikhail Romanov left the monastery to be crowned in the Moscow Kremlin. In 2006, Britain's Prince Michael of Kent (who is related to the Romanov Dynasty) presented a new eight-ton, brass bell to the cathedral. Today the famous **Ipatyevsky Chronicles** are displayed here; this valuable document, found in the monastery's archives, traces the fascinating history of ancient Rus. Right next to the monastery, at 3a Beregovaya Street, is the small wooden hotel **Ipatyevskaya Sloboda**, with seven cozy guest rooms.

The **Church of St John the Divine** (1687), which functioned as the winter church, stands nearby. From the monastery's five-tiered bell tower, there is a pleasing view of the countryside and the **Museum of Old Wooden Architecture**, open daily to the public. Intricately carved old wooden buildings gathered from nearby villages include the **Church of the Virgin** (1552), a typical peasant dwelling, a windmill and a bathhouse.

Other churches on the north bank of the Volga are the **Church of the Transfiguration** (1685), **Church of St Elijah-at-the-Gorodishche** (1683–85) and the beautiful hilltop **Church of the Prophet Elijah**.

The beautiful **Church of the Resurrection-on-the-Debre** is situated on the eastern outskirts of town. In 1652, the merchant Kiril Isakov built this elaborate red brick and green-domed church from money found in a shipment of English dyes. When informed of the discovery of gold pieces, the London company told Isakov to keep the money for 'charitable deeds'. Some of the bas-reliefs on the outside of the church illustrate the British lion and unicorn. The towering five-domed church has a gallery running along the sides; at the northwestern end is the **Chapel of Three Bishops**, with a magnificently carved iconostasis. The gates of the church are surrounded by ornamental *kokoshniki*, and the interior is ornately decorated with frescoes and icons from the 15th-century.

VICINITY OF KOSTROMA

The areas in and around Kostroma were well known in Moscovy for their production of gold and silver ornaments, and the major jewelry workshops were situated in the village of **Krasnoye-on-the-Volga**. The Godunov family once owned the Krasnoye lands. The oldest building in the village is the white-stone and octagon-shaped **Cathedral of the Epiphany** (1592). Its helmet drum, tented roof (the tent-shape style became popular in the early 16th century), long gallery, side chapels and decorative *kokoshniki* patterns are similar to Moscow's St Basil's Cathedral, built three decades earlier.

Situated 63 kilometers (38 miles) southeast of Kostroma is the small enchanting town of **Plyos**. In summer, boats make the trip along the Volga from Yaroslavl and Kostroma. Local buses also run from Kostroma. The son of Dmitri Donskoi, Vasily I, founded the village in 1410 as a stronghold and lookout point from the area's *plyos*, the straight part of a river between its bends. The fortress protected the region from the Mongols, who had already conquered the Kingdoms of Kazan and Astrakhan further down the Volga. The lovely white five-domed **Church of the Resurrection**, built in the 18th-century, stands on a bluff overlooking the water. One of Russia's finest landscape artists, Isaak Levitan, loved to spend his summers here. He painted the famous *Golden Plyos in the Evening*, one of Anton Chekhov's favorites. The **Levitan House Museum** is situated in the eastern part of town, across the Shokhonka River. Here are exhibited some works by Levitan and other local artists. Open 10am–5pm, closed Mondays.

IVANOVO Иваново

Ivanovo, an industrial and regional center 288 kilometers (180 miles) northeast of Moscow (and 80 kilometers/50 miles south of Kostroma), began as a small village on the right bank of the River Uvod. Trains run here from Yaroslavl, as well as from Moscow's Yaroslavsky Station. Buses also run from Moscow's Shchyolkovskoye station (six and a half hours), and from Vladimir (three hours), Yaroslavl and Kostroma (two hours). To drive, take the A113 south from Kostroma, or the M7 from Moscow then the A113 north from Vladimir. The Ivanovo area code is 4932. The River Talka crosses the town; both the Talka and Uvod flow into the River Klyazma, a tributary of the Moskva. The village of Voznesensk on the left bank was annexed by Ivanovo in 1871. In 1561, a chronicle mentioned that Ivan the Terrible presented the village of Ivanovo to a powerful princely family. When two centuries later an Ivanovo princess married a Sheremetyev, the town passed over to this powerful aristocratic family. In 1710, Peter the Great ordered weaving mills and printing factories built here. Soon the town grew into a major textile and commercial center with little religious significance. Ivanovo calico was famous worldwide; by the mid-1800s, the town was known as the Russian Manchester. Today almost 20 percent of the country's cloth is produced in this city of 400,000 people. Ivanovo is nicknamed the City of Brides—since 80 percent of textile workers are women, many men come here to look for a wife.

Ivanovo participated actively in the revolutionary campaigns and was called the Third Proletarian Capital after Moscow and the former Leningrad. Major strikes were held in the city. In 1897, 14,000 workers held a strike against the appalling conditions in the factories. A 1905 strike, with over 80,000 participants, was headed by the famous Bolshevik leader Mikhail Frunze, who established the town's first Workers' Soviet which provided assistance to the strikers and their families during the three-month protest.

Compared to other Golden Ring towns, Ivanovo is relatively new and modern, with only a few places of particular interest. On Lenin Prospekt, the **Ivanovo Museums of Art and History** portray the city's historical events and display collections of textiles, old printing blocks and other traditional folk arts. Off Kuznetsov Street is the **Museum-Study of Mikhail Frunze**. On Smirnov Street is the 17th-century **Shudrovskaya Chapel**; on nearby Sadovaya Street stands the large red-bricked **House Museum of the Ivanovo-Voznesensk City Council**. Other locations of interest in the city are the circus, puppet theater, a 17th-century wooden church and **Stepanov Park**, with an open-air theater and boats for hire.

PALEKH Палех

This village lies 48 kilometers (30 miles) east of Ivanovo and is famous for its colorfully painted lacquer boxes. Drive east along the P152/80, or local buses run here from Ivanovo, Vladimir or Suzdal. After the Revolution when icon production was halted, it became popular to paint small miniatures on lacquer papier-mâché boxes, which combined the art of ancient Russian painting with the local folk crafts. Ivan Golivko (1886–1937), the Master of Palekh Folk Art, created many beautiful lacquer scenes drawn from traditional Russian fairy tales, folk epics and songs; he sometimes lined the box interiors with Russian poetry. The **Museum of Palekh Art** displays a magnificent collection of painted boxes and other lacquer art by the folk artists of Palekh. These include works by the master Golivko, who established a shop of ancient folk art in 1924. This included a wide assortment of objects: wooden toys, porcelain, glass and jewelry boxes. The most popular became the lacquered papier-mâché boxes. The **Timber House of Golivko** where he lived and worked, is also open to the public.

The painter, Pavel Korin (1892–1967) was born in Palekh, and his family house, a typical wooden *izba*, hosts a museum dedicated to this gifted artist. Korin often featured Palekh in his watercolors, and later amassed one of the largest collections of icons in Soviet Russia. He also worked as the head of restoration at Moscow's Pushkin Museum of Fine Arts.

Traditionally the Palekh box was fashioned from birch wood or linden and varnished black on the outside, with a red interior and gold highlights. (This trinity of colors has a meaning: the word red, *krasny*, also signifies beauty, black symbolizes the mystery and sorrows of life, and gold represents the spirit's eternal glory.) The artists used special tempura (egg-based) paints and made fine brushes from squirrels' tails.

Today, fine layers of papier-mâché (slow-cooked for up to three months) are applied to the wood, followed by several coats of clear lacquer. Then the outline of the painting is sketched on with white paint. It can then take up to a year for an artist to paint a more complex design. Upon completion, between seven and 12 more coats of lacquer must be applied, and each one dried and polished to achieve the perfect finish. The top can be further decorated with gold, silver and mother-of-pearl. A wolf's tooth was once used to fine polish the decorative colors. Besides Palekh, three other nearby villages also developed their own schools of Russian lacquer art, including Kholui and Mstyora.

The third, Fedoskino, located north of Moscow, also has its own specialty school, where students train up to five years. It was first established in 1798, when the merchant Korobov began to produce snuff boxes. He was the first in Russia to produce boxes of papier-mâché, a process he discovered in Germany. The artists became known for their snow and troika scenes, and village landscapes with girls in traditional costumes. The paintings are also characterized by an underlay of gold leaf or mother of pearl, which adds an iridescent glow.

Beware when purchasing a lacquer box. A recent survey in Moscow found that over 90 percent of the so-called lacquer miniatures were not genuine. (There are less than 2,000 qualified artists trained in this tradition, so many boxes sold are not high quality.) Stores often tout authenticity, but sell replicas at inflated prices (and count on the ignorance of the buyer). Check out the smoothness of the lacquer; if pimple dots bubble along the surface, it's not an original. Often, on cheaper boxes, the design is a decal lacquered on, not an original painting. If interested in purchasing an expensive box, buy only from a reputable dealer. Ultimately, let your eye be the best judge.

The 17th-century **Cathedral of the Exaltation of the Holy Cross**, now a museum, stands in the town center. A plaque on the outside of the west wall shows the builder to be Master Yegor Dubov. Local craftsmen carved and painted the magnificent golden baroque-style iconostasis inside the church, bedecked with nearly 50 icons from floor to ceiling. In front stands a near life-size sculpture of Christ on the cross, with a large intricate chandelier hanging above. The Czar Gates were brought from a church in the town of Uglich. For centuries before the Revolution the highly respected Palekh artists were sent all over Russia to paint beautiful icons and frescoes in the Central Russian style.

Today the artists of Palekh carry on the traditions of lacquer design and over 250 craftsmen are employed at the Palekh Art Studio. Palekh lacquerware and jewelry are widely sold throughout Russia and the world. One of the most popular motifs is the Firebird, a well-known Russian folk tale. The writer Maxim Gorky, who often asked Golivko to illustrate his texts, wrote: 'The masters of Palekh carry on the icon painting traditions through their boxes... and with these beautiful achievements, win the admiration of all who see them.'

VLADIMIR Владимир
THE CENTER OF THE GOLDEN AGE OF RUS

Vladimir, with a population of 350,000, lies 178 kilometers (110 miles) northeast of Moscow. A journey here takes you through cultivated countryside dotted with farms that raise corn and livestock. The same rural scenes of farmers, dressed in embroidered peasant shirts with wide leather belts and *valenki* (black felt boots), plowing the fertile land were painted by Russian artists such as Kramskoi, Vrubel and Repin over a century ago. It is recommended to spend a day or two in Vladimir and then travel on to Suzdal.

By car, take the M7 Highway. Long-distance trains frequently depart from Moscow's Kursky and Yaroslavsky train stations and take between two and three hours. The express Sapsan from Kursky station to Nizhny Novgorod stops in Vladimir after 1.45 hours (www.russianrail.com). Direct and transit buses also run to Vladimir from Moscow's northeast Shchyolkovsky bus terminal and take between three and four hours. Privately run buses also leave regularly from Kursky and Kazansky train stations, but only depart once they fill up. From Vladimir, buses also depart for other Golden Ring towns as Suzdal, Ivanovo and Yaroslavl. Both train and bus stations are located in the southeast section of Vladimir, on Vokzalnaya St (within walking distance of the center), and trolley buses cover all main routes about town. The area code for Vladimir is 4922. For more information on Vladimir see: www.vladimir-russia.info.

Two hotels located on the town's main street of Bolshaya Moskovskaya are the **Hotel Vladimir** at number 74 (www.vladimir-hotel.ru), and the **U Zolotykh Vorot** at number 15. At number 19 is the Salmon and Coffee café with European and Japanese-style dishes The **Guinness Pub** is at number 67 with television screens tuned into soccer and hockey games. Set in a mansion-style building, **Vladimirsky Dvorik** mini-hotel is just 250 meters from the Kremlin at 12 Ul Podbelskovo. At the west end is the largest hotel in town, the 15-story **Amaks Zolotoye Koltso** (Golden Ring) at 27 Chaikovskaya. The **Monomakh Hotel** is at 20 Gogol St (www.monomahhotel.ru), and the **Rus Hotel** at 14 Gagarin St. The 4-star art-nouveau style **Park Hotel Voznesenskaya Sloboda** (at 14b Voznesenskaya) is perched on a hill, about a kilometer outside town, with spectacular valley views and the popular Krucha restaurant (www.vsloboda.ru). A lively place to dine is at the rustic log-hewn **Traktir Cottage Restaurant** at 1a Letneperevozinskaya (near the Golden Gates), serving Russian fare with an open terrace in summer and live music at night Thursday to Saturday. Many hotels can be reserved at www.booking.com.

After visiting Vladimir, spend the next day in the ancient town of Suzdal, only 16 miles (26 kilometers) to the north. The historic village of Bogolyubovo and the Church-of-the-Intercession on the River Nerl are situated between these two cities.

HISTORY

Even though Vladimir is now the administrative head of the region, it is still one of the best preserved centers of 12th- and 13th-century Old Russian architecture. Eight centuries ago Vladimir was the most powerful town of ancient Rus. Located on the banks of the Klyazma River, a small tributary of the Volga, Vladimir was an important stop on the trade routes between Europe and Asia. Greeks from Constantinople, Vikings from the north, Bulgars from the Volga and Central Asian merchants all journeyed through the Vladimir-Suzdal principality.

In the late 11th century, Vsevolod, one son of Kievan Grand Prince Yaroslavl the Wise, began to settle the area of Vladimir in northeastern Rus after numerous hostile tribes began attacking Kiev. At this time many Russians began to migrate northward; and this exodus is described in one of Russia's earliest epic chronicles, *The Lay of Igor's Host*. With the death of his father, Vsevolod became the most powerful prince in the land. He built a small fortress near the village of Suzdal on the road from Kiev; and, later, his son established a trading settlement around the fort, and built the first stone church. The town was later named after Vladimir Monomakh who ruled from 1113–1125. After Monomakh's death, the Kievan states in the south began to lose their political and economic importance. Later under the rule of Monomakh's son, Yuri Dolgoruky, the northern territories began to flourish. Vladimir grew so large and prosperous that it became the capital of northern Rus by the middle of the 12th-century.

Dolgoruky's heir Andrei Bogolyubsky decided to rule Russia from a more centralized and peaceful area. After the death of his father in 1157, he transferred the throne of the grand prince from Kiev to Vladimir; a vision of the Blessed Virgin directed him to do so. Bogolyubsky (Lover of God) left Kiev under the protection of a holy icon, Our Lady of Vladimir, said to have been painted by St Luke from Constantinople. This revered icon became the sacred palladium of the Vladimir region; the prince even took it on his military campaigns. As the protectorate of the city, it became the symbol of divine intervention and power of the grand princes, and now hangs in Moscow's Tretyakov Gallery.

Prince Andrei brought in master artists and craftsmen to recreate the splendors of Kiev in the new town of Vladimir. A crowned lion carrying a cross was the town's coat-of-arms. Under his brother Vsevolod III (who ruled from 1177 to 1212) the Vladimir-Suzdal principality, with Vladimir as its capital, reached the zenith of its political power.

When the Mongol Tartars invaded in 1238, Vladimir, like many other towns in Russia, suffered extensive damage. A Novgorod chronicle described the Mongol invasion: 'The Tartars struck the town with their wall-battering weapons; they released endless streams of arrows. The prince saw their fierce battle axes, took fright (because of his youth), and fled forth from the town with his group of men, carrying many gifts and hoping to save his life. Batu Khan [son of Genghis], like a wild beast, did not spare him, but ordered that he be slaughtered before him, and then he slew the rest of the town. When the bishop, with the princess and her children, fled into the church [the Assumption Cathedral], the godless one commanded it to be set on fire. Thus, they surrendered their souls to God.'

For a brief time, Vladimir retained the seat of the Church Metropolitan, and the grand princes were still crowned in the town's Assumption Cathedral. But eventually the princes began governing Russia through the Khans (until the Tartar yoke was broken in 1480). In 1328, Grand Prince Ivan I transferred his residence from Vladimir to Moscow and shortly thereafter Vladimir was annexed to the principality of Moscovy. When Moscow became the capital of the country in the 16th century, Vladimir's importance slowly declined; by 1668, the population numbered only 990. After the Revolution the city grew with industrialization and, during the Soviet era, became a large producer of electrical machinery. Today, many of Vladimir's architectural sites are on the UNESCO World Heritage List.

SIGHTS

To enter the old part of town along the river, pass through the **Golden Gates** (the only surviving gates of the city), built in 1158 by Prince Bogolyubsky, who modeled them after the Golden Gates of Kiev. The oak doors of the now white gates were once covered with gilded copper; the golden-domed structure on top was the Church of the Deposition of the Robe. These gates were used as a defense fortification for the western part of town and also served as a triumphal arch— Alexander Nevsky, Dmitri Donskoi in 1380 and troops on their way to fight Napoleon in the Battle of Borodino in 1812—all passed through the arch. The gates were damaged many times through the years, and were reconstructed in the 18th-century. Today the Golden Gates house the local **Military Historical Museum**, open 10am–5pm; closed Thursdays. Next to the Gates, in the red brick building (housed in the former Old Believer's Trinity Church) and the fire observation tower,

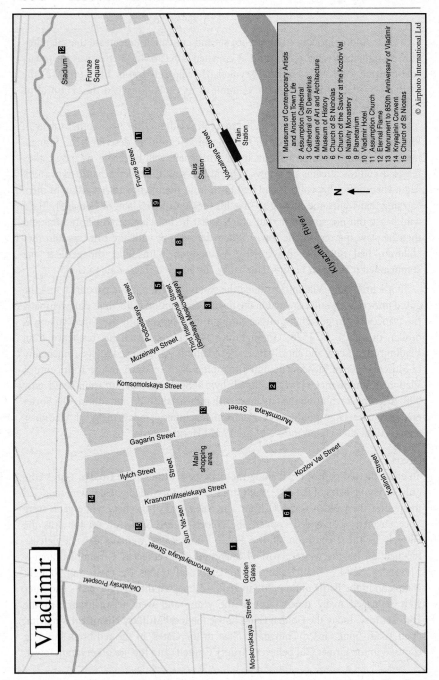

Vladimir

Oktyabrsky Prospekt

Moskovskaya Street

Golden Gates

Pervomayskaya Street

Sun Yat-sen Street

Krasnomilitseiskaya Street

Main shopping area

Ilyich Street

Gagarin Street

Komsomolskaya Street

Muzeinaya Street

Podbelskaya Street

Third International Street (Bolshaya Moskovskaya)

Kozlov Val Street

Muromskaya Street

Kalinin Street

Frunze Street

Vokzalnaya Street

Bus Station

Train Station

Klyazma River

Frunze Square

Stadium

N ←

© Airphoto International Ltd

1   Museums of Contemporary Artists
    and Ancient Town Life
2   Assumption Cathedral
3   Cathedral of St Demetrius
4   Museum of Art and Architecture
5   Museum of History
6   Church of St Nicholas
7   Church of the Savior at the Kozlov Val
8   Nativity Monastery
9   Planetarium
10 Vladimir Hotel
11 Assumption Church
12 Eternal Flame
13 Monument to 850th Anniversary of Vladimir
14 Knyaginin Convent
15 Church of St Nicetas

are the **Museums of Crystal, Lacquer and Embroidery**, which feature the crafts of nearby towns. The basement shop sells crystals and other crafts. Open 10am–4pm; closed Tuesdays.

During and after the reigns of Catherine the Great, Vladimir became best known for the 'Road of Tears,' called Vladimirka, along which an innumerable stream of prisoners were marched into exile from Moscow to Siberia. The town was also used as a transit prison during the Stalin era.

One block south of the Golden Gates are the simple white **Church of St Nicholas** and the **Church of the Savior at the Kozlov Val**, both built in the late 17th century. Climb the Kozlov Tower for a great view of the city. Nearer the water is the **Church of St Nicholas-at-Galeya**, with a tent-shaped bell tower, and built by a wealthy citizen of Vladimir in the early 18th-century.

The oldest buildings of the city were constructed on the hills by the water, which served as a defense. As you walk through the gates a cluster of golden-domed white churches come into view. In 1158, Andrei Bogolyubsky brought in master craftsmen from all over Russia and Europe to build the triple-domed Uspensky Sobor, the **Assumption Cathedral**. Built to rival Kiev's St Sophia, the cathedral was decorated with gold, silver and precious stones. It was the tallest building in all of Rus. Filled with frescoes and icons, the iconostasis was also the largest of its kind in Russia. A tenth of the grand prince's revenue was contributed to the upkeep of the cathedral. After much of it was destroyed by fire in 1185 (along with 33 other churches), Prince Vsevolod III had it rebuilt with five domes. Since the original walls were encased within a larger structure, the cathedral doubled in size, with an area for a congregation of 4,000 people. The Italian architect Fioravante later used it as his model for the Moscow Kremlin's own Assumption Cathedral. After more fires blackened the walls, the famous iconists Andrei Rublyov and Daniil Chorny were sent to restore the interior in 1408 and painted over 300 square meters (3,200 square feet) of wall space; frescoes from the 12th and 13th centuries are still evident on the western and northern walls. Rublyov's and Chorny's frescoes, including scenes from the Last Judgment, decorate two vaults beneath the choir gallery and the altar pillars. Rublyov's famed icon of the Virgin of Vladimir that once hung by the altar was transferred to Moscow's Assumption Cathedral in 1380; it is now in the Vladimir-Suzdal Museum of History and Art (see picture on page 335). A replica now hangs here.

This cathedral was one of the most revered churches in Russia; all the Vladimir and Moscow grand princes were crowned inside it—up to Ivan III, in 1460. It was also the main center of the Church Metropolitan through the 14th-century. The Assumption Cathedral was the burial place of the princes of Vladimir, including Andrei Bogolyubsky and Vsevolod III. The three-story belfry was built in 1810. It is open 7am–8pm, but only between 1.30pm–4.30pm for tourists; closed Mondays. Mass is celebrated on Saturday evenings, Sundays and Orthodox feast days. Visitors are welcome in respectful attire. Flash photography is not permitted.

A short walk northeast of the cathedral is one of the most splendid examples of Old Russian architecture, the **Cathedral of St Demetrius** (1193–97). Vsevolod III built this as his court church and his palace once stood nearby. The cathedral, with its one large helmet drum, was named after 'Big Nest' Vsevolod's patron saint (St Demetrius of Thessaloniki) and newborn son Dmitri. (Vsevolod was nicknamed 'Big Nest' because of his large family of 12 children.) It is built from blocks of white limestone and decorated with intricate *kokoshniki* along the doorways and arches. Over 1,300 bas-reliefs cover the outer walls: decorative beasts, birds, griffins, saints, prophets, the labors of Hercules and many elaborate floral patterns all glorify the might of Vladimir. The friezes of King David and Alexander the Great symbolize Vsevolod's cunning military exploits. At the top of the left section of the northern façade is Prince Vsevolod seated on the throne with his young son; the other sons are bowing to their father. The interior frescoes date back to the 12th-century. In 1834, Nicholas I ordered the cathedral restored; it is now part of the local museum complex. Preservation experts still battle the ongoing effects of town pollution on the limestone.

Across from this cathedral is the **Vladimir Museum of Art and Architecture**, housed in the grand 18th-century court chambers, known as the *Palaty* with displays of old religious paintings, manuscripts and architectural designs (there is also a children's museum). Open 10am–5pm; closed Mondays. The **Museum of History** is directly across the street at 64 Bolshaya Moskovskaya where a rich collection of artifacts, archeological materials, old fabrics, weapons, princely possessions and the white-stone tomb of Alexander Nevsky are on display. Open 10am–5pm; closed Tuesdays.

At the eastern end of Bolshaya Moskovskaya is the **Nativity Monastery** (1191–96), one of Russia's most important religious complexes until the end of the 16th century; it was closed in 1744. Alexander Nevsky was buried here in 1263. Peter the Great later transferred his remains to St Petersburg in 1724.

Next to the Vladimir Hotel (down the street from the Planetarium on Frunze Street) is the brick and five-domed **Assumption Church** (1644), built from donations given by rich local merchants. At the end of the street is the Eternal Flame, commemorating the soldiers who lost their lives during World War II. Down the street from the Golden Gates is the city's main shopping district, the *Torgoviye Ryady* or Merchant Stalls. Across the street is the **Monument to the 850th Anniversary of Vladimir**.

Stroll north along Gagarin Street and look out over the old section of Vladimir. In the distance are many old squat wooden houses with long sloping roofs and stone floors. Many of the town's inhabitants have lived in these homes for generations. The people enjoy a simple town life. During the day you may see residents hanging out laundry, perhaps painting lattice work around their windows a pastel blue-green, chopping wood, or gathering fruits and mushrooms. The children enjoy having their pictures taken. Bring a few souvenirs from home to trade.

West from the end of Gagarin Street is the **Knyaginin (Princess) Convent**, founded by the wife of Vsevolod III, Maria Shvarnovna, in 1200. The grand princesses of the court were buried in the convent's **Assumption Cathedral**, rebuilt in the 16th century. The cathedral's three-tiered walls are lined with fancy *zakomara* and topped with a single helmet drum. In 1648, Moscow artists painted the colorful interior frescoes. The north and south walls depict the life of the Virgin Mary, and the west wall shows scenes from the Last Judgment. Paintings of Vladimir princesses, portrayed as saints, are on the southwest side, and the pillars recount the lives of the grand princes. The cathedral is the only remaining building of the convent complex and now houses a restoration organization. Near the convent stands the **Church of St Nicetas** (1762). This green and white, three-tiered baroque church was built by the merchant Semion Lazarev. The interior is divided into three separate churches on each floor, and restored in 1970. In front of this church is a Bust of the writer Nikolai Gogol (1809–1852). Pervomaiskaya Street winds south back to the Golden Gates.

At the end of the day, you may stop at the rustic log-hewn **Traktir Restaurant** for an enjoyable meal of the local cuisine.

VICINITY OF VLADIMIR

The quaint village of **Bogolyubovo** lies ten kilometers (six miles) northeast of Vladimir. Take Trolley number 1 east from Vladimir and get off at Khimzavod. Then walk along the main road for a few minutes to the bus stop, where you can catch a marshrutka mini-bus to Bogolyubovo (second stop). One legend says that when Prince Andrei was traveling from Kiev to Vladimir, carrying the sacred icon of Our Lady of Vladimir, his horses stopped on a large hill and would move no farther. At this junction, by the confluence of the Klyazma and Nerl rivers, Andrei decided to build a fortress and royal residence. He named the town Bogolyubovo (Loved by God) and took the name of Bogolyubsky; he was canonized by the Church in 1702. Supposedly, after the Virgin appeared to him in a dream, he built the white-stone blue-domed **Nativity of the Virgin Church**. This cathedral was still standing in the 18th century, but when one father superior decided to renovate it in 1722 by adding more windows, the cathedral collapsed; it was rebuilt in 1751. On the staircase tower are pictures depicting the death of Andrei Bogolyubsky—assassinated by jealous nobles in this tower in 1174. The coffins of his assassins were said to be buried in the surrounding marshes and their wailing cries heard at night. Near the road is the **Bell Tower** and Assumption Cathedral, built in 1866, Only a few of the 12th-century palace walls remain, of which chronicles relate: 'it was hard to look at all the gold.'

About a kilometer southeast of Bogolyubovo on the River Nerl is the graceful **Church of the Intercession-on-the-Nerl**, built during the Golden Age of Vladimir architecture. Standing alone in the green summer meadows or snowy winter landscape, it is reflected in the quiet waters of the river that is filled with delicate lilies. It has come down from legend that Andrei built this church in 1164 to celebrate his victory over the Volga Bulgars. The Virgin of the Intercession was thought to have protected the rulers of Vladimir. With the building of this church, Andrei proclaimed a new Church holiday, the Feast of the Intercession. To get here from Bogolyubovo, walk to the end of Vokzalnaya St, cross the railway tracks, and then follow the path a kilometer across the field to the church.

YURYEV-POLSKY Юрьев-Польский

About 65 kilometers (40 miles) northwest of Vladimir (situated halfway to Pereslavl-Zalessky along the P74 road) lies the old town of Yuryev-Polsky. Trains also stop here on the way from Ivanovo. Prince Yuri Dolgoruky founded Yuryev-Polsky in 1152, and named it after himself. Since two other Russian towns were already named Yuryev, Dolgoruky added Polsky, meaning 'Yury's town among the fields'. At the confluence of the Koloksha and Gza rivers, Dolgoruky had a fortress built, complete with moat and rampart walls that stood over six meters (20 feet) high; for a short period the town became the capital of Dolgoruky's principality. During the next several centuries Yuryev-Polsky was taken over by invading Lithuanians and Mongols, and never again regained its status and power. The original Holy Gates had four separate entrances, two for pedestrians and two for carriages. The **Monastery of the Archangel Michael** (1250) was reconstructed at the end of the 17th-century. The **Cathedral of the Archangel Michael** and tent-shaped bell tower are decorated with green-glazed tiles. The town's greatest treasure is the limestone **Cathedral of St George** (1234), modeled after Vladimir's Cathedral of St Demetrius. The elegant helmet-shaped dome survived a partial collapse of the walls in the 15th-century. Today carved scenes and floral designs are still visible on some of the greenish-yellow walls. Figures include St George—patron saint of Dolgoruky, lions with tails in shapes of trees, masks and emblems, and the fairy-tale bird, Sirin. Burial vaults and the tomb of Grand Prince Svyatoslav (13th-century) are situated in the northwest corner.

SUZDAL Суздаль

Suzdal is a pleasant half-hour journey from Vladimir (26 kilometers/16 miles north along the A113 road) through open fields dotted with hay stacks and mounds of dark rich soil. There are no trains to Suzdal. It's easiest to take a train or bus to Vladimir and then a local bus, which run every half hour to Suzdal. The bus station is located two kilometers east of the town center on Vasilevskaya St. (Buses usually run through the town's central square on their way to the station; ask the driver to stop and let you out.) The area code for Suzdal is 49231. Vladimir was the younger rival of Suzdal which, along with Rostov Veliky, was founded a full century earlier. The town was settled along the banks of the Kamenka River, which empties into the Nerl a few miles downstream. Over 100 examples of Old Russian architecture (in a space of only nine square kilometers/three and a half square miles) attract a half million visitors each year to this remarkable medieval museum, designated a UNESCO World Heritage Site. (Suzdal is not only famous for its churches, but also for its cucumbers. The annual Cucumber Festival occurs here every summer, along with the Festival of Crafts.)

The first view of Suzdal from the road encompasses towering silhouettes of gleaming domes and pinkish walls atop Poklonnaya Hill, rising up amidst green patches of woods and gardens. It is as though time has stopped in this enchanting place—a perfection of spatial harmony. Today Suzdal is a quiet town of 10,000 people with no industrial enterprises. Crop and orchard farming are the main occupations of the residents who still live in the predominant *izba* (wooden houses). The scenic town is a popular site for film making. The American production of *Peter the Great* used Suzdal as one of its locations.

Traveling along the Golden Ring route, you may have noticed that the distances between towns are similar. When these towns were settled, one unit of length was measured by how much ground a team of horses could cover in 24 hours. Most towns were laid out about one post-unit apart. So the distance between Moscow and Pereslavl-Zalessky, Pereslavl and Rostov, or Rostov and Yaroslavl could easily be covered in one day. Distances in medieval Russia were measured by these units; thus the traveler knew how many days it took to arrive at his destination—from Moscow to Suzdal took about three days.

Suzdal offers many unique places in which to stay overnight and all are comfortable with a wide selection of prices; many offer bike rentals. (For a listing of hotels, see www.booking.com or www.suzdaltravel.com) The 4-star **Best Western Art Hotel Nikolaevsky Posad**, on 138 Ul Lenina, is located in its own private surroundings with pool and sauna. At 45 is **Pushkarskaya Sloboda**, consisting of 19th-century log cabins in the setting of a Russian village (www.pushkarka.ru), and the mini hotel **Cherry Garden** is at number 10. The 4-star **Hotel Kremlovsky**, a five

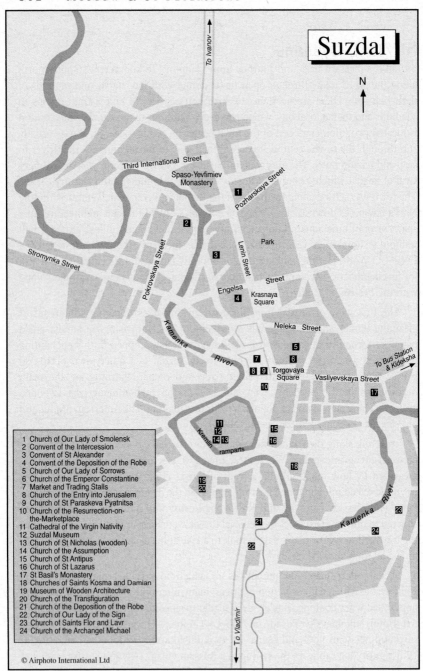

Suzdal

N

To Ivanov

Third International Street

Spaso-Yevfimiev Monastery

Pozharskaya Street

Park

Stromynka Street

Pokrovskaya Street

Lenin Street

Street

Engelsa

Krasnaya Square

Neleka   Street

Kamenka

River

Torgovaya Square

Vasliyevskaya Street

To Bus Station & Kideksha

Kremlin

ramparts

Kamenka   River

To Vladimir

1 Church of Our Lady of Smolensk
2 Convent of the Intercession
3 Convent of St Alexander
4 Convent of the Deposition of the Robe
5 Church of Our Lady of Sorrows
6 Church of the Emperor Constantine
7 Market and Trading Stalls
8 Church of the Entry into Jerusalem
9 Church of St Paraskeva Pyatnitsa
10 Church of the Resurrection-on-
     the-Marketplace
11 Cathedral of the Virgin Nativity
12 Suzdal Museum
13 Church of St Nicholas (wooden)
14 Church of the Assumption
15 Church of St Antipus
16 Church of St Lazarus
17 St Basil's Monastery
18 Churches of Saints Kosma and Damian
19 Museum of Wooden Architecture
20 Church of the Transfiguration
21 Church of the Deposition of the Robe
22 Church of Our Lady of the Sign
23 Church of Saints Flor and Lavr
24 Church of the Archangel Michael

minute walk from the Kremlin, is at 5 Ulitsa Tolstovo. **Petrov Dom** is a private guesthouse in a wooden dacha-style house on a quiet street at 18 Per. Engelsa Lane, off of Engels St. (www.petrovdom.ru). Centrally located at 34 Slobodskaya Street is the stylish **Dom Kuptsa Likhonina**, a cozy bed-and-breakfast with 7 rooms in a 17th-century merchant house. At 2a Torgovaya Square is the 35-room **Sokol Hotel**. **Godzillas Hostel**, at 32 Naberezhnaya (Embankment) St, has a fully-equipped kitchen, sauna and bikes for rent. (www.godzillashostel.com).

The **Pokrovskaya Hotel** offers moderately-priced 19th-century log cabins near the grounds of the Pokrovsky Monastery (on Pokrovskaya St). Nearby, at 35a Pokrovskaya, is the **Traktir Kuchkova Guest House** which offers 17 types of apartment-style rooms. Within the complex of the Convent of the Deposition of the Robe, at 9 Kommunalny Gorodok, is the inexpensive **Hotel Rizopolozhenskaya**. Down the street, at number 73, is the Kharchevnya Café which offers tasty Russian food at reasonable prices.

Two hotels are situated on Korovniki Street, (at the north end of the river near the St Euthymius Monastery)—the large Soviet-style **GTK** (Main Tourist Komplex), with hundreds of basic rooms; rents bicycles and skis, and the **Heliopark Suzdal** is down the street at 14b which also has different types of wooden-dacha lakeside *banya* (saunas) for rental.

HISTORY

The area of Suzdalia was first mentioned in chronicles in 1024, when Kievan Grand Prince Yaroslavl the Wise came to suppress the rebellions. By 1096 a small kremlin had been built around the settlement, which one chronicle already described as a town. As Suzdal grew, princes and rich nobles from Kiev settled here, bringing with them spiritual representatives from the Church, who introduced Christianity to the region. The town slowly gained in prominence; Grand Prince Yuri Dolgoruky named it the capital of the northern provinces in 1125. From Suzdal, the seat of his royal residence, he went on to establish the small settlement of Moscow in 1147. His son Andrei Bogolyubsky transferred the capital to Vladimir in 1157.

After the Kievan states crumbled in the 12th-century Suzdal, along with Rostov Veliky, became the religious center of medieval Rus. The princes and boyars donated vast sums of money to build splendid churches and monasteries; by the 14th century Suzdal had over 70 churches, 15 monasteries, 400 dwellings and a famous school of icon painting. No other place in all of Russia had such a high proportion of religious buildings. The crest of Suzdal was a white falcon wearing a prince's crown. Since the town itself was not situated along important trade routes, the monks (and not the merchants) grew in wealth from the large donations to the monasteries. The Church eventually took over the fertile lands and controlled the serf-peasants.

Suzdal was invaded many times, first by Mongols in 1238, then by Lithuanians and Poles. After the Mongol occupation no new stone buildings were erected until well into the 16th century. Suzdal was annexed to Moscovy in the late 14th-century and as a result lost its political importance, but remained a religious center.

In the early 17th-century, the Russian state collapsed and Polish troops occupied Moscow. One of Suzdal's most famous residents, Prince Dmitri Pozharsky (a Suzdal street is named after him), organized an army to beat back the foreign invaders. Today a monument to Pozharsky (along with merchant Kuzma Minin) stands on Red Square in front of St Basil's Cathedral.

During the 1700s Peter the Great's reforms undermined ecclesiastical power and the Church in Suzdal lost much of its land and wealth. Churches and monasteries were mainly used to house religious fanatics and political prisoners. In addition, many barren or unpopular wives were forced to take the veil and exiled to Suzdal's convents. By the end of the 19th century only 6,000 residents remained, and one account described Suzdal as 'a town of churches, bell towers, old folk legends and tombstones'. On a bright note, because Suzdal had become so insignificant, a railroad was never built through it; the result was that no industrialization ever came to Suzdal, and thus the town's rural character and historic architecture was preserved. The local historian Voronin wrote: "The future of Suzdal lies in its past...in carefully preserving itself for future generations." Today with a population of over 12,000, this enthralling poetic spot has been restored to the majesty of its former days. As one 13th-century chronicler observed: "Oh, most radiant and bountiful, how wondrous art thou with thy beauty vast."

SIGHTS

Approaching Suzdal from Vladimir, as horse coaches once did, two churches are passed on the right before crossing the Kamenka River. These are the summer **Church of Our Lady of the Sign** (1749) and the winter **Church of the Deposition of the Robe** (1777).

As you cross the river, down along the northeastern embankment stands the charming **Church of Saints Kosma and Damian** (1725), built by the local blacksmiths to honor their patron saints. (Many local artisans built their own churches.) Across the river are several other churches, constructed between the 16th and 18th centuries, with money raised by local tanners.

Further along Lenin Street, stands the simple red and white **Church of St Lazurus**. Built in 1667 by the townspeople, it is the oldest of the *posad* churches. The slender helmet-domed winter **Church of St Antipus** stands next to it and according to local lore, a toothache can be healed here. Just walk around the church, and chew on each of the four corners!

The old kremlin can be sighted along the southwestern side of Lenin Street. The present-day 1.4 kilometer long *kreml* was protected on three sides by the river; along the eastern wall ran a large moat, now the main street. Remnants of the 11th-century earthen walls are still evident today. These ramparts are topped with wooden walls and towers.

A tour of Suzdal begins on the east bank of the river, where much of the old architecture is clustered. Take a moment to gaze out over the fertile plains and meandering waters of the river. The rich arable land in this area first attracted settlers seeking greater freedoms from Novgorod, where pagan priests were still leading uprisings against Kievan attempts to Christianize and feudalize the northern lands. In Old Russian, *suzdal* meant to give judgment or justice. Today several streets still carry the names of Slavic pagan gods, such as Kupala, Netyoka and Yarunova.

The 13th-century **Korsunsky Gates** lead to the main cathedral and are covered with Byzantine patterns; religious scenes from the New Testament were engraved and etched with acid on copper sheets and then gilded.

Prince Vladimir Monomakh laid the first stone of the town's main **Cathedral of the Virgin Nativity** at the beginning of the 12th-century. In 1528, Grand Prince Vasily III of Moscow reconstructed it from brick and white stone and surmounted it with five helmet-shaped domes. In 1748, the onion domes were altered to the present blue and gold-star pattern.

The southern doors, surrounded by elaborate stone decorations, were the official entrance of the princes. Lions, carved along the portals, were emblems of the princes of Vladimir. The carved female faces symbolize the Virgin Mary, whose nativity is celebrated. The southern and western doors (1230–33) are made of gilded copper and depict scenes from the life of St George, the patron saint of both Prince Georgi and his grandfather Yuri Dolgoruky.

Early 13th-century frescoes of saints and other ornamental floral patterns are still visible in the vestry; most of the other murals and frescoes are from the 17th-century. Tombs of early bishops and princes from as far back as 1023 are also found inside. The burial vaults of the early princesses are near the west wall. The octagonal bell tower was built in 1635 by order of Czar Mikhail Romanov and repaired in 1967. Old Slavonic letters correspond to numbers on the face of the clock.

The impressive whitewashed **Archbishop's Palace**, now the **Suzdal History Museum**, was built next to the cathedral on the bank of the Kamenka between the 15th and 18th centuries. The main chamber of the palace, the large Cross Hall, held important meetings and banquets. In the 17th-century this *krestovaya* (cross-vaulted) chamber was considered one of the most elegant rooms in Russia. The museum contains collections of ancient art and traces the evolution of architecture in the Suzdal region.

Enter the palace chamber through the western entrance. In the center stands a long wooden table, covered with a rich red cloth, once used by the archbishop and his clergy. An 18th-century tiled stove stands in one corner. The walls are decorated with many 15th- and 16th-century icons. Suzdal developed its own school of icon painting in the early 13th-century. Its use of lyrical flowing outlines, detailed facial qualities and soft designs in red and gold were later adopted by the Moscow school, headed by Andrei Rublyov. Both the Moscow Tretyakov Gallery and the St Petersburg Russian Museum include Suzdal icons among their exhibits.

Pass through the gateway to the left of the palace to reach another art section of the museum. Here are more displays of icons, paintings, sculptures, ivory carvings, embroideries and other crafts. Buildings in this complex are open 10am–5pm, closed Tuesdays.

For a lunch break, try dining at the **Trapeznaya Restaurant**, located in the Refectory of the Archbishop's Palace. Sample the splendors of ancient Suzdalian monastic cooking—the local fish soup and home-brewed mead are especially tasty. Also try the *medovukha*, an alcoholic beverage combined with honey that is made only in Suzdal. According to local legend, the recipe was developed by Suzdal's St. Euthymius in the 14th-century. For centuries, it was the most popular drink in Russia; but, during the reign of Peter the Great, vodka finally eclipsed it as the beverage of choice. A visitor can sample up to 10 varieties of *medovukha* in the **Graf Suvorov Mead Tasting Hall** located inside the Trading Rows arcade.

In front of the palace is the wooden **Church of St Nicholas** (1766). It represents one of the oldest types of Old Russian wooden architecture and is built from logs into a square frame with a long sloping roof. The early architects used only an ax, chisel and plane to build these designs. No nails were needed; the logs were held together by wooden pegs and filled with moss. The church was transferred from the village of Glotovo in 1960. Beside it, in lovely contrast, stands the red-and-white-trimmed **Church of the Assumption** (1732), with its green rounded roof and horseshoe *kokoshniki*.

The long trading stalls near Torgovaya (Merchant) Square, built in 1806, mark the center of town. During holidays the grounds were opened to fairs and exhibitions and were filled with jolly jesters, merry-go-rounds and craft booths. Horses were tied up along the arcade. Today, the colonnade has numerous stores and outdoor markets where townspeople congregate, especially around midday. Pick up a charming picnic basket made from native willow branches. They are sold at the entrance of the Museum of Wooden Architecture.

Along the western side of the arcade, by the riverbank, is the lovely whitewashed summer **Church of the Entry into Jerusalem** (1707). The winter **Church of Paraskeva Pyatnitsa** (1772), with its half-dome drum and gilded cross, stands next to it.

Near the southern corner of the Torgoviye Ryady (Trade Rows) stands the **Church of the Resurrection-on-the-Marketplace** (1720), a large white-brick cube crowned with an onion dome on a tall drum. It is now a branch of the Suzdal Museum, with exhibits of architectural decorations, wooden carvings and colorful tiles used to adorn buildings in the 17th and 18th centuries. Behind it stands the more modest winter **Church of Our Lady of Kazan**.

Across the street on the northeastern side of Torgovaya Square are two other sets of church complexes. Not only did the number of churches in a town symbolize its wealth, but it was also customary in medieval Russia to build twin churches. This added even more to the cluster of religious structures. These twin churches usually stood in close proximity to each other—one cool, high-vaulted and richly decorated was used only in summer, the other, simpler and smaller, held the congregation in winter.

The white summer **Church of the Emperor Constantine** (1707), with elaborate *kokoshniki* designs and bell tower, is located nearest the square (a functioning church today). The five, slender drum domes are a unique feature of Suzdalian architecture. The neo-classical rotunda was later added to the western façade. The plainer white-bricked **Church of Our Lady of Sorrows** (1787), with a green-glazed tent roof, was used in winter.

Suzdal had the largest monasteries and convents in the region, which served as protective citadels for the citizens during times of war. These institutions, besides being religious, became the educational centers of the town as well. Husbands could also force their wives to take the veil as a quick way to divorce. Fathers would also place daughters in a convent until they were married.

North along Lenin Street, west from Krasnaya Ploshchad (Red Square), is the **Convent of the Deposition of the Robe**, founded by Bishop John of Rostov in 1207. The convent's **Deposition Cathedral** was built in 1560 by Ivan Shigonia-Podzhogin, a rich boyar who had served Vasily III. The real gems of the ensemble are the white **Holy Gates** (1688), flanked by two red and white octagonal tent-roofed towers that are decorated with colored glazed tiles. The citizens of Suzdal erected the 72-meter (236-foot) neo-classical **Bell Tower** in 1813 to commemorate Napoleon's defeat; it remains the largest structure in the town with lovely views from the top. An art restoration school is located nearby at 106 Lenin Street. Over 100 university-age students from across the country come here to learn how to restore historical works of art. A visitor can drop by to observe the teachers and pupils restoring icons, frescoes and paintings. The school celebrated its 35th anniversary in 2016.

Walking a few blocks northwest brings you to the red brick **Convent of St Alexander**, originally founded in 1240 in honor of Prince Alexander Nevsky, who defeated the Swedes on the Neva River that same year. (It was later burned down by invading Poles.) In 1682, the **Ascension Cathedral**, with its five small onion domes, was constructed from funds donated by Peter the Great's mother, Natalya Naryshkina. The convent closed in 1764, but the ensemble remains open to the public.

Nestled by the park, a few blocks northeast, is the elegant **Church of Our Lady of Smolensk** (1696). Directly across the street, in the area of the former *posad*, is the 18th-century, gabled-roof, tailor's **House of Nikita Pustosviat**. It is now a domestic museum with displays of furniture and utensils from the 17th to 19th centuries. The rooms represent a typical peasant hut. Across from the *pechka* (stove), over which the eldest member of the family slept, was the *krasnaya ugol* (beautiful corner) where the family icons were kept. Usually the *gornitsa* (living area) comprised one or two rooms. Here were found a few beds, chairs, tables and a clothes chest. The kitchen was situated in the corner nearest to the *kamin* (fireplace or stove). A small storage house was also built into the hut. It is open 10am–4pm; closed Mondays.

Dominating the northeast bank of the river is Suzdal's largest architectural complex, the **Spaso-Yevfimievsky Monastery** (Savior Monastery of St Euthymius). A Suzdal prince founded it in 1350 to protect the town's northern entrance. Over the next few centuries, the monastery continued to receive funding from czars and noble families until it grew into a massive fortress enclosed by a one-and-a-half-kilometer-long kremlin. Of the 12 towers, the southern 23-meter-high decorative Vkhodnaya was used as a watchtower; it is used as the entrance today. In front of this tower is the 17th-century **Church of the Annunciation-over-the-Gates**, with an exhibit on the hero Dmitri Pozharsky (1578–1642). The monks eventually owned vast amounts of land and their monastery became the wealthiest in the region. By the 17th-century the complex controlled over 10,000 serfs. Today, film companies often use the high red brick walls to double as Moscow's Kremlin. The complex is open 10am–6pm; closed Mondays.

The centerpiece of the complex is the **Cathedral of the Transfiguration**, built in 1594. Both exterior and interior 17th-century frescoes, painted by masters from Kostroma, depict the history of the monastery. The tomb of Prince Dmitri Pozharsky, hero of the 1612 Polish war, is beside the altar at the east wall; a monument to him, standing outside the cathedral, is inscribed: 'To Dmitri Mikhailovsky 1578–1642.' Adjoining the cathedral is a small chapel that stands over the grave of the Abbot Yevfim. A particular treat is to listen to the ringing of the bells in the adjacent **Bell Tower**. On the hour, the bell-ringer ascends the tower and performs a ten-minute concert. It sounds like an entire bell choir, but it is just one individual tugging on the multitude of ropes that hold the clappers.

The **Assumption Church** (1526) on the west side was added to the chambers of the Archimandrite for his private use. It was decorated with *kokoshniki* and a large tent-shaped dome. The Kostroma artists Nikitin and Savin painted the frescoes on the southern and western walls. On the other side of the bell tower, the monk cells on the first floor now contain an exhibit of icons and local folk art. The prison at the northern end was built by Catherine the Great in 1766 for religious dissidents; it now houses an exhibit on the prison's history. Many members of the Decembrist group, who staged a revolt against the government in 1825, were interned here as political prisoners. (The writer Lev Tolstoy was almost imprisoned here after being excommunicated by the church.) Next door is the old hospital and **St Nicholas Church** (1669), now a museum of Russian applied art and church gold treasures.

The large complex across the river on Pokrovskaya St is the **Convent of the Intercession**, built by Prince Andrei in 1364. Prince Vasily III commissioned the convent's churches in 1510 as supplication for the birth of a male heir. The polygonal bell tower, rebuilt in the 17th-century, is one of the earliest examples of a brick tower and conical roof design. The white three-domed **Cathedral of the Intercession** served as the burial place for Suzdal noblewomen. Eventually, in 1525, Vasily exiled his wife Solomonia Saburova to the convent; he wanted to divorce her on grounds that she was barren. The metropolitan granted Vasily his divorce and sent Solomonia to the Pokrovsky (Intercession) Convent to live out her life as a nun. Vasily then married a Polish girl named Elena Glinskaya. Some time later news reached Moscow that Solomonia had given birth to a son. Fearing for her son's life, Solomonia hid him with friends and then staged a fake burial. For centuries this tale was regarded only as legend, but in 1934 a small casket was unearthed beside Solomonia's tomb (she died in 1594). There was no skeleton, only a stuffed silk shirt embroidered with pearls. The small white tomb and pieces of clothing are on display in the Suzdal Museum. Ivan the Terrible (son of Elena Glinskaya) also sent his wife Anna to this convent in 1575. Peter the Great even exiled his first wife Evdokia Lopukhina here in 1698. The convent buildings have been returned to the Orthodox Church; there is also a hotel residence and restaurant in the complex. A museum of the convent's history is open 9.30am–4:30pm, closed Tuesdays and Wednesdays. For a splendid panoramic view of Suzdal, climb the bank of the river in front of the convent.

At the southern end of town, on the west bank of the Kamenka on Pushkarskaya Street (a 10-minute walk from the Kremlin), is the **Suzdal Museum of Wooden Architecture**. Old wooden village structures have been brought in from all around the Vladimir-Suzdal region and reassembled at this location on Dmitriyevskaya Hill to give an idea of old peasant life in a typical Russian village. For nearly 250 years, beginning in 1238, not a single stone building was erected. Using the simplest of tools, structures were created without the use of iron or nails. (Unfortunately, none of these survive today.) The outstanding wooden **Church of the Transfiguration** (1756), was assembled by old methods, and brought in from the neighboring village of Kozlyatyevo. This open-air museum consists of other log-built churches covered with aspen-shingled roofs, residential houses, windmills, barns and bathhouses. Open May–October, 9.30am–7pm, closed Tuesdays.

At the end of the day take a walk along the river as the sun sets over the town. Young boys can be seen swimming and fishing in the warmer months or skating in winter. Many small side streets are filled with the local wooden dachas, covered with elaborate wood carvings and latticework. Ask your driver to stop by the **House of Merchant Bibanov**, the most lavishly decorated house in town. If you are lucky, a pink full moon will rise above the magical display of gabled roofs and towers, to signal an end to the delightful Suzdalian day.

VICINITY OF SUZDAL

Four kilometers east of Suzdal is the small **Village of Kideksha**. In 1015, according to chronicles, the brothers Boris and Gleb, sons of the Kievan Prince Vladimir who brought Christianity to Russia, had a meeting here where the Kamenka River empties into the Nerl. (They were later assassinated by their elder brother Svyatopolk who, in turn, was later murdered by a fourth brother, Yaroslav). Boris and Gleb, who died defending the Christian faith, became Russia's first saints. In 1152, Prince Yuri Dolgoruky (who founded Moscow in 1147) chose to build his country estate on this spot. Dolgoruky also erected the simple white-stone **Church of Saints Boris and Gleb**, where his son Boris and daughter-in-law Maria are buried. The winter **Church of St Stephan** was erected in the 18th-century. On the road to Kideksha are the remains of the **St Basil Monastery**, the fifth monastery complex of Suzdal; only a small cathedral and church remain standing.

THE TRANS-SIBERIAN RAILWAY

Although today Russia has one of the world's largest rail networks and arguably the most famous of train journeys—the Trans-Siberian—for years it actually lagged behind the railway systems of other European powers. Fourteen years after George Stephenson began building his railway in England from Stockton to Darlington, and eight years after the engineer's locomotive *Rocket*, was built, Czar Nicholas I opened Russia's first railroad. The Tsarskoye Selo to St Petersburg line was inaugurated on October 30th 1837, and was 30.5 kilometers (18 miles) long. It was succeeded by additional tracks including a St Petersburg to Moscow service in 1851. It took over a year and a half to build the 647-kilometer- (388-mile-) long route between the two cities, one of the straightest railway lines in the world. It took the first train more than 20 hours to cover the distance, where today the new high-speed SAPSAN train takes only four hours.

Russia's transport and military supply service was shown to be woefully inadequate in 1854 when British, French and Turkish armies inflicted a humiliating defeat on the country in the Crimean War. More Russian troops died on the freezing march to the Crimea and from disease than perished in battle.

The first proposal of a steam railway through Siberia by the American Perry McDonough Collins in 1857 was rejected. But soon after, the reform-minded Czar Alexander II instituted programs of modernization, often inspired by military campaigns, which included railway building. The St Petersburg to Warsaw line was initiated in 1861; a decade later the rails reached the Volga. At the time of his death in 1881, Russia had 22,500 kilometers (14,000 miles) of track.

Construction of the Trans-Siberian Railroad was ordered by Alexander III and on May 31, 1891, his son Nicholas laid the foundation stone. By 1898 it linked Chelyabinsk in the Ural Mountains to Irkutsk. The last leg to the Pacific port of Vladivostok was finally completed in 1916. At Lake Baikal (until track was laid around the south of it) a ferry carried passengers across in summer, and in winter they were pulled across the frozen lake on horse sleighs to the next depot—or track was laid across the ice; it would take over five hours to cross the 48-kilometer (30-mile) wide lake.

The railroads held enormous economic and strategic importance for the country. The Trans-Caspian line to Central Asia was part of a military campaign to conquer the territory. As the rails snaked their way from the Baltic Sea through the rolling heartland of Russia and on across the Siberian wilderness and the deserts of Uzbekistan and Kazakhstan, markets and trade opened up almost overnight. The railways were responsible for Russia's first speculative boom. In the 1890s the population of Siberia was just 5 million, today it is over 40 million people (27% of Russia's population).

Today the Commonwealth of Independent State's network carries some 11 million travelers every day on some 233,300 kilometers (145,000 miles) of rails. (There are 85,000 kilometers/53,000 miles of railroads in Russia, carrying over 1 billion passengers a year.) Thanks to Lenin's prognosis that Communism was Soviet power plus the electrification of the whole country, nearly half the rail network is now electrified while the rest runs on diesel. (Steam engine production ceased in 1956.) The most heavily used route is between Moscow and St Petersburg.

In 2005, the Ministry of Transportation completed the 10,000 (6,250-mile) Trans-Siberian Highway, the first road to completely stretch across all of Russia. To commemorate the event, the Expedition Trophy Car Rally was held in a race across Siberia, from Murmansk to Vladivosotok, and the grand prize was 10 kilos of gold. The race is planned annually in February/March.

The Cyrillic on this Trans-Siberian dining car reads RESTORAN and illustrates how a little time spent learning the Cyrillic alphabet can help visitors understand and pronounce many simple words and street names.

The year 2016, marks the 100th anniversary of the completion of the Trans-Siberian Railroad—one of the world's greatest travel adventures. The main section of the railroad stretches approximately 8,000 kilometers (5,000 miles) from Moscow to Beijing, or 9,342 kilometers (5,805 miles) to Vladivostok.

Trans-Siberian trains have both 1st and 2nd class carriages. First class has two berths one over another with a private shower/washroom. Second class, with four soft berths, shares a hall toilet/washroom. (Cheaper third class hard berths are also available, but not recommended.) Meals are not included in the price of a ticket; the train has a restaurant car. When the train crosses the border between Mongolia/China or Russia/Manchuria, the wheels of the train are changed to a smaller gauge—the whole process takes a few hours. Custom inspections at borders can take many hours. Most nationalities need a Chinese visa, and some a Mongolian transit visa. One can coordinate getting off at certain city stops along the route, but make sure you have a continuing ticket, as space is often booked far in advance. See www.transsiberianexpress.net, www.waytorussia.net and www.russiantrains.com for schedules, prices and making reservations.

Note that on Russian trains the timetable often runs according to Moscow time, but local time often applies to stations and dining cars. Beijing time is the same as Ulan Bator, Mongolia, but four hours ahead of Moscow in summer, and five hours in winter. Vladivostok is 7 hours ahead of Moscow.

Travelers on the Trans-Siberian should always pack basic foods, snacks and drinks, including bottled water and alcohol if so desired. Items such as bread and sweets can be bought at stations along the way. The Russian restaurant car has a tasty enough menu but a limited supply as time goes by. Other handy items to have are earplugs, a Swiss army knife, instant soup, coffee, tea and milk creamer, a large mug, bowl and utensils, Thermos flask, toilet paper, tissues and a Russian phrase book. Hot water is available from each wagon's titan-samovar usually located at the end of the hallway. Dress appropriately for the season and pack lounging clothes. Bring along plenty of reading material; an IPOD with music can also help pass the time.

(Ticket prices may vary, depending on whether bought in Moscow, Beijing or from a Western ticket agency, and on the time of year. Trans-Siberian packages can also include a night or two in Moscow with hotel accommodation, and additional stops in Novosibirsk and Irkutsk. Various travel companies even offer private rail car tours along Trans-Siberian routes, as aboard the Golden Eagle

(*Zolotoy Oryol*) Express, with gold and silver class accommodations: See GW Travel (www.goldeneagleluxurytrains.com) and Geographic Expeditions, who also offer other Siberia adventures (www.geoex.com).

Note: All the following trains depart and arrive at Moscow's Yaroslavsky Train Station.

There are a number of **Trans-Mongolian** trains that cross Mongolia to China. The **Moscow to Beijing** train 0043 departs Moscow at 9:35pm and arrives in Beijing at 2:04pm, taking 5 days, 16 hours and 29 minutes (and makes a stop in Ulan Bator). Train 0033 departs Beijing at 8:05am and arrives in Moscow at 1:58pm, five days later.

The **Moscow to Mongolia** train 006 operates on Wednesdays and Thursdays every second week between Moscow and Ulan Bator and takes four days. Both leave from Moscow at 21:35pm and arrive at 6:40am.

The **Trans-Manchurian** train runs from Moscow through Manchuria (and Harbin) to Beijing. Train 020 leaves Moscow at 11:45pm and arrives in Beijing at 5:46am six days later. Train 019 departs Beijing at 11pm and arrives in Moscow at 5:58pm taking six days as well.

The **Trans-Siberian** train runs from **Moscow to Vladivostok** and makes stops in many Siberian cities as Nizhny Novgorod, Perm, Ekaterinburg, Omsk, Novosibirsk, Krasnoyarsk, Irkutsk, Ulan Ude, Chita and Khabarovsk.

The **Rossiya** Train 002 departs Moscow at 1:50pm and arrives in Vladivostok at 1:10pm six days later. Train 001 departs Vladivostok at 4:25am and arrives in Moscow at 5:52am. (There is a shower compartment that can be used by all 2nd class passengers; and Carriage 6 is equipped for handicapped people.)

Train 100 departs Moscow at 12:35 am and arrives in Vladivostok at 7:13pm almost seven days later. Train 099 returns from Vladivostok at 6:42pm and arrives in Moscow at 11:03am. Only second and third class carriages are usually available. This train makes 120 stops along the 9300-km (5800-mile) route (taking an extra 20 hours more than the above Rossiya).

A separate branch of the Trans-Siberian is known as the BAM (Baikal Amur Main Line). This railway, running through northeastern Siberia, was completed (for about 60 billion dollars) in 1990 as part of Brezhnev's Fifteen-Year Plan. The task was monumental—seven large tunnels and 2,400 bridges were built across 3,200 kilometers (2,000 miles) of permafrost (the ten-mile-long Severomuisk tunnel was not completed until 2001). Earthquakes, mud flows and avalanches continue to pose additional hazards. There is nothing much but endless *taiga* to see on the journey; the route was mainly built to stimulate timber, coal and oil production and increase industrial transport. The line begins at Tayshet (slightly west of Irkutsk), continues north to Bratsk (along the Angara River), across the northern end of Lake Baikal (at Severobaikalsk), on to Tynda and Komsolmolsk-na-Amure (north of Khabarovsk), and terminates at Imperatorskaya (formerly Sovyetskaya) Gavan on the Pacific.

From Vladivostok on the Pacific Ocean, a ferry service operates to Niigata, Japan from May to September. Air connections also run between Khabarovsk and Vladivostok throughout the year. There is a ferry between Sakhalin Island and Hokkaido. You can also stop overnight or spend a few days in Siberian cities, such as Novosibirsk or Irkutsk on Lake Baikal. (If you do get off along the way, make sure you have already prebooked the continuation of your journey.)

Popular connection destinations to the West include: Berlin, which can be reached from Moscow in 24 hours; Budapest (34 hours) and Helsinki (15 hours). If you are a real train fanatic, you can extend the journey all the way to Paris, London or beyond on the East-West Express via Berlin.

HISTORY OF THE RAILWAY GAUGE

The United States has the same track gauge (distance between the rails) as England, as British expatriates built the first American railroads. The first rail lines were actually designed by the same people who built the earlier tramways; they incorporated the same gauge on the rail roads. And the tramways were built as the same width between two covered-wagons wheels. The wagon wheel standard dates all the way back to the chariots of Imperial Rome, which were designed wide enough to fit two horses. Thus, the U.S. standard railroad gauge of 4 feet 8.5 inches (1435mm) is derived from the original specifications of a Roman chariot.

In the 19th-century, Russia chose a broader gauge (1520mm) than what the European or American railways were using. It is widely believed that the choice was made for military reasons, and to prevent foreign invaders from using the Russian railway system.

See Recommended Reading (page 751) for details of specific books on the Trans-Siberian Railway.

MOSCOW PRACTICAL INFORMATION

TELEPHONE NUMBERS
Country Code for Russia (7)

Moscow Tourist Information Center
4 Ilyinka Street; Gostiny Dvor; www.moscow-city.ru.

CITY CODES

Aleksandrov	(49244)	Moscow	(495) or (499)	Tula	(4872)
Borodino	(49638)	Novgorod	(81622)	Tver	(4822)
Gatchina	(81371)	Pereslavl Zalessky	(48535)	Uglich	(48532)
Istra	(49631)	Pskov	(8112)	Vladimir	(4922)
Ivanovo	(4932)	Rostov Veliky	(48536)	Yaroslavl	(4852)
Klin	(49624)	Sergiyev Posad	(496)	Zvenigorod	(49632)
Kostroma	(4942)	St Petersburg	(812)		
Kaluga	(4842)	Suzdal	(49231)		

(Note that some Golden Ring towns are Moscow time plus one hour.)

EMERGENCY SERVICES
International Crisis Line   8 926-113-3373
Free English speaking service for foreigners in distress (8am–11pm)

Fire	01	Police	02	Ambulance	03

TAXIS
Order a taxi by phone or online. The Dispatcher or driver will ring you back with the license number of the car. (May take up to 60 minutes.) Set price for distance (or time) and airports.

Central Taxi Bureau (495) 627-0000 www.6270000.ru

City Taxi (495) 225-9225/740-3777 www.citytaxi.ru

Taxi Blues (495) 925 5115 www.taxi-blues.ru

Detskoye Taxi (495) 765-1180 www.detskoetaxi.ru (has smoke-free cars and children car seats)

Diligence Taxi (495) 419-3524 www.the-taxi.ru

New Yellow Taxi (495) 940-8888 www.nyt.ru

Taxi Bistro (499) 685-1300 www.taxopark.ru

Moscow now has UBER service. www.uber.com. The app, Yandex Taxi, is a similar service to UBER for taxis in the area. Taxi.yandex.ru

EXPRESS MAIL/POST

DHL, 7 Tverskaya St (Central Telegraph). Tel. (495) 956-1000; www.dhl.ru. (DHL has over 40 Moscow locations and can arrange pickups.)

Federal Express, 1 Sokolnichesky Val (Metro Rizhskaya). Tel. (495) 788-8881 (Also contained in Mail Boxs Etc. and Kwik Kopy centers) www.fedex.com/ru.

City Express, 1a 1st Varshavsky Lane. (495) 792-3232. www.cityexpress.ru.

United Parcel Service, International Trade Center, 12 Krasnopresenskaya Emb, Ent 6, Floor 10, Office 1003. Tel. (495) 258-2267, www.ups.com. (Also located in many Mail Boxes Etc centers.)

USEFUL PUBLICATIONS IN ENGLISH

The best places to find English newspapers and magazines are at hotels, restaurants, newsstands or central kiosks about town.

Moscow News is published in Russian and English. www.themoscownews.com.

The *Moscow Times* (www.themoscowtimes.com) is distributed daily and, together with the *Moscow Times Weekly,* provide current local and international news, along with listings of theater events, concerts, movies, and reviews of restaurants and other shows.

Expat, www.expat.ru has a wealth of city information.

Passport Magazine can be found at www.passportmagazine.ru.

Pravda newspaper is at english.pravda.ru/.

The trendy magazine *SNOB* is online at www.snob.ru.

The *Moscow Tribune* and The *Russia Journal* magazines also offer news and entertainment guides, published daily.

Moscow Magazine (monthly) is in English and Russian, with a city guide and information on restaurants, shops and museums.

Traveller's Yellow Pages: www.infoservices.com.

Where in Moscow Magazine (monthly) provides information for consumers and details of many cultural events. www.where.ru.

MEDICAL

Most top-end hotels have quick access to a nurse or doctor. In case of major medical emergencies, contact a clinic below or an embassy; you may need to arrange for evacuation to a foreign hospital. If you have a preexisting condition, consider purchasing travel medical insurance before departing; a medical evacuation can be very costly.

American Medical Center, 26 Prospekt Mira, bldg. 6 (entrance from Grokholsky Pereulok), Metro Prospekt Mira. Can be contacted 24 hours a day. It has a full range of medical specialists (with lab tests and dentists) along with a pharmacy, ambulance service; house calls; medical evacuations can be arranged. Tel. (495) 933-7700. (Accepts health insurance from international providers.) www.amcenters.com.

European Medical Center, 5 Spiridonevsky Lane, Bldg 2. Metro Pushkinskaya. Open 24 hours; whole range of medical services. Tel. (495) 933-6655, www.emcmos.ru.

Botkin Hospital is the best Russian facility in Moscow. 5 2nd Botkinsky Proezd. Tel. (495) 945-0045, www.botkinmoscow.ru.

The 24-hour **Pharmacy** chain **36.6** has many branches located throughout the city, including at 25 Tverskaya, 1/13 Pokrovka and 15 Novy Arbat, www.366.ru.

DENTAL

The **American Medical Center** listed above has a dental clinc.

American Russian Dental Center, 21a Sadovaya-Kudrinskaya. Metro Barrikadnaya. Also provides emergency care. Tel. (495) 797-9759, www.ardc.ru.

American Dental Clinic, 5 1st Tverskaya-Yamskaya. Full dental services. Tel. (495) 730-4334, www.americandental.ru.

European Dental Care, 6 1st Nikoloschepovsky Per. Metro Smolenskaya. Full dental services and 24 hour dental emergencies, including night and weekend. Tel. (495) 933-0002.

US Dental Care, 7/5 Bolshaya Dmitrovka. Metro Okhotny Ryad. Tel. (495) 933-8686, www.usdentalcare.com.

EMBASSIES

This is a partial listing of foreign embassies in Moscow, open Monday through Friday and closed on weekends. For a visa, call first to find out department hours and locations—the visa department may be in a separate location.

Australia, 10A/2 Podkolokolny Lane. Tel. (495) 956-6070. www.russia.embassy.gov.au. Open 9am–5pm; Visa Dept Mon/Wed/Fri 9am–11am.

Austria, 1 Starokonyushenny Lane. Metro Kropotkinskaya. Tel. (495) 780-6066.

Belgium, 7 Malaya Molchanovka. Metro Arbatskaya. Tel. (495) 780-0331.

Bulgaria, 66 Mosfilmovksya. Metro Kievskaya. Tel. (499) 143-9022.

Canada, 23 Starokonyushenny Lane. Metro Kropotkinskaya. Tel. (495) 925-6000, www.canadainternational.gc.ca.

China, 6 Druzhbi. Metro Universitet. Tel. (499) 783-0867, ru.china-embassy.org.

Czech Republic, 12/14 Yuliusa Fuchika. Metro Mayakovskaya. Tel. (495) 276-0703/0719.

Denmark, 9 Prechistensky Lane. Metro Kropotkinskaya. Tel. (495) 642-6800/6801.

Estonia, 5 Malaya Kislovsky Lane. Metro Arbatskaya. Tel. (495) 737-3640/3648, www.estemb.ru.

Finland, 15/17 Kropotkinskaya Lane. Metro Park Kultury. Tel. (495) 787-4174.

France, 45 Bolshaya Yakimanka. Metro Okyabrskaya. Tel. (495) 937-1500/1577, www.ambafrance-ru.org.

Germany, 56 Mosfilmovskaya. Tel. (495) 937-9500. Metro Universitet/Kievskaya (Bus 119 or trolleybus 34 from metro.)

India, 6–8 Ulitsa Vorontsovo Polye. Metro Kitai-Gorod. Tel. (495) 783-7535, www.indianembassy.ru.

Ireland, 5 Grokholsky Lane. Metro Prospekt Mira. Tel. (495) 937-5900/5911. www.embassyofireland.ru.

Israel, 56 Bolshaya Ordynka. Metro Tretyakovskaya. Tel. (495) 660-2700.

Italy, 5 Denezhny Lane. Metro Smolenskaya. Tel. (495) 796-9691.

Japan, 27 Grokholsky Lane. Tel. (495) 229-2520, www.ru.emb-japan.go.jp

Latvia, 3 Chapligina. Metro Turgenskaya. Tel. (495) 232-9743/9760.

Lithuania, 10 Borisoglebsky Lane. Metro Arbatskaya. Tel. (495) 785-8605.

Mexico, 4 Bol. Levshinsky Lane. Metro Kropotkinskaya. Tel. (495) 695-3167/3139

Mongolia, 11 Borisoglebsky Lane. Metro Arbatskaya. Tel. (495) 690-6792. (Consular section at 7/1 Spasopeskovsky Lane, Metro Smolenskaya), www.mongolianembassy.ru.

Netherlands, 6 Kalashny Lane. Metro Arbatskaya. Tel. (495) 797-2900, www.netherlands-embassy.ru.

New Zealand, 44 Povarskaya. Metro Barrikadnaya. Tel. (495) 956-3579. (Consular dept. Tel. 956-2642), www.nzembassy.com/russia.

Norway, 7 Povarskaya. Metro Arbatskaya. Tel. (499) 951-1000/1050, www.norvegia.ru.

Poland, 4 Klimashkina. Metro Belorusskaya. Tel. (495) 231-1500.

Slovak Republic, 17/19 Yuliusa Fuchika. Metro Belorusskaya.
Tel. (495) 956-4920/4922.

Spain, 50/8 Bol. Nikitskaya. Metro Arbatskaya. Tel. (495) 202-2657/690-3002.

South Africa, 1 Granatny Lane. Tel. (495) 926-1177.

Sweden, 60 Mosfilmovskaya. Metro Universitet.
Tel. (495) 937-9200), www.swedenabroad.com.

Switzerland, 2/5 Ogorodnoi Slobody. Metro Turgenevskaya.
Tel. (495) 258-3830 (Consular dept. 258-3838).

Thailand, 9 Bol. Spasskaya Ul. Tel. (495) 608-0856. Metro Sukharevskaya.

United Kingdom, 10 Smolenskaya Emb. Metro Smolenskaya.
Tel. (495) 956-7200, www.greatbritain.ru.

United States, 8 Deviatinsky Lane. Metro Barrikadnaya.
Tel. (495) 728-5000. moscow.usembassy.ru. The Consular Section is at 21 Novinsky
Bulvar. Tel. (495) 745-3388.

CIS EMBASSIES

A foreign visitor may now need a visa to the following areas:

Armenia, 2 Armyansky Lane. Metro Kitai-Gorod. Tel. (495) 624-1269/1441.

Azerbaijan, 16 Leontevsky Lane. Metro Pushkinskaya. Tel. (495) 629-4332.

Belarus, 17/6 Maroseika. Metro Kitai-Gorod.
Tel. (495) 777-6644, www.embassybel.ru.

Georgia, 6 Maly Rizhsky Lane. Metro Arbatskaya. Tel. (495) 691-2136.

Kazakhstan, 3a Chistoprudny Bul. Metro Chistiye Prudy.
Tel. (495) 627-1811/1838, www.kazembassy.ru.

Kyrgyzstan, 64 Bolshaya Ordynka. Metro Dobrinskaya. Tel. (499) 237-4882.

Moldova, 18 Kuznetsky Most. Metro Kuznetsky Most. Tel. (495) 926-1773.

Tajikistan, 13 Granatny Lane. Metro Barrikadnaya. Tel. (495) 690-3846/4186.

Turkmenistan, 22 Filippovsky Lane. Metro Arbatskaya. Tel. (495) 691-6593.

Ukraine, 18 Leontevsky Lane. Metro Pushkinskaya. Tel. (495) 629-9742/3542.

Uzbekistan, 12 Pogorelsky Lane. Metro Polyanka. Tel. (499) 230-0078.

AIRPORTS

Moscow has three main airports: Sheremetyevo (SVO), Domodedovo (DME) and Vnukovo (VKO).

Sheremetyevo (www.svo.aero/en) is located 28 km (18 miles) northwest of the city. The new $300 million Sheremetyevo International Airport currently has four operating passenger terminals: A, C are the North Terminals (A is used for business and private aviation), and D, E, F the South Terminals. Terminal D is the hub for Aeroflot and its SkyTeam partners.

To get into the city: **Aeroexpress** trains (from Terminals D, E, F) currently run every half hour to/from Belorussky Train Station from 5:30am to 11pm; the journey takes 35 minutes. (A shuttle bus runs to the Rail Terminal from Terminals B and C) On some airlines, you can check in your luggage at the AeroExpress train station terminal no later than two hours before departure. For more information: **www.aeroexpress.ru/en.**

If you have little luggage, cheaper buses and *marshrut* mini-bus shuttles also run from Sheremetyevo airport to Rechnoi Vokzal or Planernaya metro stations. (Mini-bus fixed route 949 and regular bus 851 run to Rechnoi Vokzal, and mini-bus 948 and bus 817 to Planernaya.) There are also night buses that run every 30 minutes between 1am and 5:30am and the route is north to south through the city, with stops in the center at Pushkin Square and Kropotkinskaya metro; the final stop is Yugo-Zapadnaya metro station.

Domodedovo (www.domodedovo.ru/en) is located 42 km (26 miles) south of town. From Domodedovo, the **Aeroexpress** runs to/from Paveletsky Train Station from 6am to 11:30pm and takes 45 minutes. From the airport, shuttles and mini buses also go to Domodedovo Metro station.

Vnukovo (www.vnukovo.ru) is located 28 km (17 miles) southwest of the center.

From Vnukovo, **Aeroexpress** trains run to/from Kievsky Train Station from 6am to 11pm and take 40 minutes. Buses also run to/from Yugo-Zapadnaya metro station.

Each airport has official taxis; order one from the dispatch desk for a set price depending on the area of your destination. (To book a taxi in advance, see Taxi Listing). Check with your hotel, many can arrange airport pick-ups for a fee. In addition, you can pre-book rides from travel agencies, such as www.enjoymoscow.com. Moscow also has car services such as Uber.

Remember that traffic in Moscow is horrendous, especially during rush hour; allow ample time to get to the airport!

AIRLINES

Aeroflot, Tel. (495) 223-5555 or 8-800-444-5555; www.aeroflot.com. There are many city branch offices, with central offices at 10 Arbat, Tel. (495) 500-7595; 20 Petrovka, Tel. 621-5131; and 3 Kuznetsky Most, Tel. 621-9293. Open 9am–8:30pm, Sun 9am–4:30pm.

Air China, 11/1 Lubyansky Proezd. Tel. (495) 230-0080, www.airchina.com.

Air France, 1 Mytnaya. Metro Okyabrskaya. Tel. (495) 937-3839, www.airfrance.ru.

Air India, 7 Kirovy Val. Metro Okyabrskaya. Tel. (495) 236-4440 ,www.airindia.com.

Alitalia, 1 Mytnaya. Metro Okyatbrskaya. Tel. (495) 221-1130, www.alitalia.com.

American Airlines, 20 Sadovaya Kudrinskaya, Metro Barrikadnaya. Tel. (495) 234-4074/75, www.aa.com.

Austrian Airlines, 2 Trubnaya Sq. Tel. (495) 995-0995, www.austrianairlines.ru.

British Airways, 4 4th Lesnoi Per. (5th floor) Metro Belorusskaya. Tel. (495) 363-2525, www.britishairways.com.

Cathay Pacific, 40/2 Prechistenka. Metro Park Kultury. Tel. (495) 980-0708, www.cathaypacific.com.

Delta Airlines, 11 Gogolevsky Bulvar, (2nd floor). Metro Kropotkinskaya. Tel. (495) 937-9090, www.delta.com.

El Al Isreal Airlines, 20 Sadovaya-Kudrinksaya. Metro Barrikadnaya. Tel. (495) 215-2464, www.elal.com.

Emirates, 2 Tsvetnoi Bulvar. Metro Trubnaya. Tel. 8-800-555-1919 or (499) 918-6240, www.emirates.com.

Finnair, 7 Kropotkinsky Lane. Metro Park Kultury. Tel. (495) 933-0056, www.finnair.com.

JAL Japan Airlines, 61/2 Bolshaya Gruzinskaya. Metro Belorusskaya. Tel. (495) 234-5930, www.jal-europe.com.

KLM Royal Dutch Airlines, 1 Mytnaya. Metro Okyabrskaya. Tel. (495) 258-3600, www.klm.com.

Korean Air, 4 4th Lesnoi Lane (8th floor) Metro Belorusskaya. Tel. (495) 725-2727, www.koreanair.com.

LOT Polish Airlines, 14 Olimpiisky Pr. Metro Dostoevskaya. Tel. (495) 937-5922, www.lot.com.

Lufthansa, Domodedovo and Vnukovo airports. Tel. (495) 980-9999, www.lufthansa.ru.

MIAT Mongolian Airlines, 7/1 Spasopeskovsky Lane. Metro Smolenskaya. Tel. (499) 241-1052, (495) 578-8319, www.miat.com.

OrenAir, www.orenair.ru.

Quantas, 20 Sadovaya-Kudrinakaya. Metro Barrikadnaya.
Tel. (495) 234-4074/75, www.quantas.com.

Qatar Airways, 29 Serebryanicheskaya Emb. Metro Kurskaya.
Tel. (495) 981-0077, www.qatarairways.com.

S7, 30/16 Tsvetnoi Bul. Metro Tsvetnoi Bulvar. Tel. (495) 624-0203, www.s7.ru.

SAS, 7 Korovii Val. Metro Dobryninskaya. Tel. (495) 961-3060, www.scandinavian.net.

Singapore Airlines, 14 Olympiisky Pr. Metro Dostoevskaya.
Tel. (495) 775-3087, www.singaporeair.com.

South African Airways, 14 Olympiisky Pr. Metro Dostoevskaya.
Tel. (495) 937-5953, www.flysaa.com.

Swissair, Tel. (495) 937-7767, www.swiss.com.

Thai Airways, 12 Trubnaya. Metro Trubnaya.
Tel. (495) 647-1082, www.thai-airways.ru.

Transaero, 11a Zubovsky Bul. Metro Park Kultury.
Tel. (495) 788-8080, www.transaero.ru.

Turkish Airlines, 7/5 Bolshaya Dmitrovka. Metro Okhotny Ryad.
Tel. (495) 775-0849, www.turkishairlines.com.tr.

Ural Airlines, 7/1 Soimonovsky Proezd. Metro Kropotkinskaya.
Tel. (495) 777-5188, www.uralairlines.ru.

RAILWAYS

See **Getting Around** section for more details on train travel and buying tickets. The Central Railway Booking offices are at 6/11 Maly Kharitonevsky Lane (Metro Chistiye Prudy), and 5 Komsomolskaya Square (and in Leningradsky and Yaroslavsky train stations). Informative websites with train routes and schedules are: www.raileurope.com and www.trainsrussia.com. Tickets can also be reserved and purchased online (you need to print out the E-ticket). Websites include: www.russiantrains.com and www.russianrailways.com. (Besides longer overnight trains, there are the daily SAPSAN high-speed trains to St Petersburg that depart from Leningradsky Station.) Aeroexpress trains run daily to/from the three main airports. www.aeroexpress.ru.

Belorussky, 7 Tverskaya Zastava Sq. www.belorusskiy.info. Trains to northern and western Europe, such as Berlin, Geneva, Madrid, Vilnius, Smolensk, Brest, Minsk, Prague and Warsaw. *Elektrichka* run to suburbs of Borodino and Zvenigorod. (Aeroexpress trains to Sheremetyevo Airport; see airport listing above.) Metro Belorusskaya.

Kazansky, 2 Komsomolskaya Sq. Trains to/from Kazan and points southeast as Nizhny Novgorod, and further east to the Ural mountains and Siberia. Metro Komsomolskaya.

Kievsky, 2 Kievsky Vokzal Sq. Trains to the Ukraine and Eastern Europe. (Aeroexpress trains run to Vnukovo Airport; see airport listing above.) Metro Kievskaya.

Kursky, 29 Zemlyanoi Val. Trains to south and southwest (to Vladimir) Azerbaijan, Crimea and Caucasus. Metro Kurskaya.

Leningradsky, 3 Komsomolskaya Pl. Trains to St Petersburg, Murmansk, Finland, Novgorod, Pskov and Estonia. Metro Komsomolskaya.

Paveletsky, 1 Paveletskaya Sq. Trains to east and southeast, Volgograd region. (Aeroexpress trains run to Domodedovo Airport; see airport listing above.) Metro Paveletskaya.

Rizhsky, 2 Rizhsky Vokzal. Trains to Baltic areas. *Elektrichka* suburban trains to Istra and New Jerusalem. Metro Rizhskaya.

Savelovsky, Savelosky Vokzal. Trains to Uglich and Rybinsk areas. Metro Savelovskaya.

Yaroslavsky, 5 Komsomolskaya Sq. Trains to the Far East. The Trans-Siberian departs daily. *Elektrichka* also run to Sergiyev Posad and Aleksandrov in the Golden Ring area. Trains also stop at Vladimir and Yaroslavl. Metro Komsomolskaya.

ACCOMMODATION

Moscow has one of the world's most expensive average hotel rates. But, the good news is that the city now has far more choices—from five-star luxury, mid-range and mini-hotels to hostels, homestays and apartment rentals.

One can select a hotel based on location, cost, service and style. Before booking, find out what extras and amenities are included, such as breakfast, private bath, visa support, and airport/town center transportation. Ask if the 18 percent VAT and city tax are already included in the price. What is the closest Metro station? Cheaper hotels can be situated far from the city center; you may consider booking a slightly more expensive yet more centrally located hotel to save time and money on travel within the city. Ask for a room without street noise or the best view available. Most all accommodations now accept credit cards. It is highly advisable to make a reservation as far in advance as possible; rates are the highest in summer months (but weekend rates are often considerably cheaper than weekday). Today, most hotels have their own online web sites (where you can reserve a room), and take a closer look at pictures of the rooms and what the accommodation has to offer—many also offer promotional online discounts. (Many hotel reviews are now up on Trip

Advisor.) Upon check-in you will be asked for your visa and passport for registration. (Always keep a copy of both.) Other sites where you can book your stay online: www.moscow-hotels.com, www.allrussianhotels.com, and www.booking.com.

AIRPORT ACCOMMODATION

Most hotels can be reserved through www.booking.com or www.hotels.ru.

SHEREMETYEVO AIRPORT

Atlanta Sheremetyevo Hotel, 36/7 Tsentralanaya. Reduced rates for 6- and 12-hour layovers. Free shuttle service to/from airport. www.atlantahotel.ru.

Novotel is a 4-star hotel, located 200 meters from Sheremetyevo Airport with over 400 rooms, fitness center and pool. Free shuttle services. www.novotel.com.

Sheraton Airport Hotel, 28B Mezhdunarodny Hwy. www.starwoodhotels.com.

Aerostar Hotel Moscow is located about a half hour's drive from Sheremetyevo at 37 Leningradsky Prospekt, situated between Metro stations Dynamo and Aeroport. www.aerostar.ru/en.

Holiday Inn Vinogradovo, 171 Dmitrovskoye Hwy. This four-star hotel, built in 1998, has over 150 rooms and transfer service to the airport and downtown. Only a 20-minute drive from/to Sheremetyevo airport. www.holidayinn.com.

DOMODEDYEVO AIRPORT

Aerotel Domodedovo is less than a kilometer away with free shuttle bus to/from Domodedovo airport. www.airhotel.ru.

Ramada Moscow is 5 km from the airport at 1B Ilushina St. Transportation to/from the airport. www.ramadamoscow-domodedovo.com.

VNUKOVO AIRPORT

Hotel Ekipag, is less than a kilometer from Vnukovo Airport at 13 1st Reisovaya St.

Uninn Hotel is a five-minute drive from the airport. Free airport shuttle.

Inside Transit Hotel is a cheaper option, 10 km from the airport, at 2G Poselok Rumayantsevo, 6th floor.

DELUXE—FIVE STAR

Most luxury hotels provide visa invitation services and airport transportation. The complex contains restaurants, bars, fitness, business and bank-exchange centers, and all the other amenities usually associated with luxury hotels. The following average from $300 a night and up with more expensive suites. Many have special weekend rates.

Alrosa on Kazachy is a small 16-room boutique hotel set in an old-fashioned setting within the heart of the historical Zamoskvorchiye District south of the Moskva river near the Polyanka metro. www.alrosa-hotels.ru.

Ararat Park Hyatt, located in the center near the Bolshoi Theater, at 4 Neglinnaya St, has over 200 spacious rooms (including 16 suites), fitness center and indoor pool, a Sushi Bar, and the Conservatory Lounge has great views of Theater Square. Metro Lubyanka. www.moscow.park.hyatt.com.

Baltschug Kempinski, 1 Balchug, is behind St Basil's Cathedral by the Moskva River, (The hotel dates back to 1898—the area was once known as the *balchug*, a Tartar word meaning muddy. In 1552, Ivan the Terrible had the first *tabak* or tavern built in this area.) Completely reconstructed in 1992, it has 230 high-ceiling rooms, spectacular views of the Kremlin, and indoor pool and luxury spa. Sunday brunch is popular with live jazz and an extravagant buffet. Metro Tretyakovskaya. www. kempinskimoscow.com.

The Kempinski Nikolskaya, at 22 Nikolskaya St, overlooks the famous Lubyanka Square in the heart of the city, near the Bolshoi Theater. The hotel's 19th-century Art-Deco style mimics the former grand times when the building functioned as the residence of Count Orlov-Davydov.

Four Seasons Hotel Moskva is situated on Manezhnaya Square at 2 Okhotny Ryad right by Red Square. The first Constructionist-style Hotel Moskva opened in 1935, and was built as one of the city's finest hotels. The story goes that when one of the architects presented Stalin with two designs from which to select, Stalin just said "Da!" Afraid to question further, the hotel was built in two different styles. The old hotel was demolished in 2004 for a modern reproduction that was opened in 2014. www.fourseasons.com/moscow.

Golden Apple is Moscow's first Boutique Hotel, located in an 8-story 19th-century historical building at 11 Malaya Dmitrovka near the Hermitage Gardens and Pushkinskaya Metro. www.goldenapple.ru.

InterContinental Tverskaya, 22 Tverskaya. With over 200 rooms, 19 suites, restaurant and luxury spa and fitness center, many rooms also have magnificent views over the city center. www.ihg.com.

Marriott Grand Hotel, at 26 Tverskaya, boasts 386 luxurious rooms, an indoor pool and spa, and a rooftop patio, just minutes from Red Square. Metro Mayakovskaya. www.marriotthotels.com.

Marriott Royal Aurora Hotel, 11/20 Petrovka, located just a block from the Bolshoi Theater. It has 230 rooms, a basement pool, and even offers butler service. Metro Teatralnaya. (There are also other, less expensive, Marriott Hotel locations in the city.) www.mariotthotels.com.

Metropol Hotel, originally built in 1901 by a British architect in style-moderne and decorated with ceramic friezes by Vrubel (Rasputin even had gatherings here), it was completely restored in 1990. At 1/4 Teatralny Proezd (near the Bolshoi Theater), it is decorated with antiques and paintings and has over 350 rooms, restaurants (one with a famous stained-glass ceiling), bars, and an indoor swimming pool. Offers a popular Sunday brunch. Metro Teatralnaya. www.metropol-moscow.ru.

National Hotel, built in 1903 in art-nouveau style, it is located directly across from Red Square and reopened (after four years of reconstruction) in 1995 after an $80 million transformation. Check out the historic exterior mosaic-façade. (Lenin lived in Room 107 after moving the capital back to Moscow in 1918.) It has 202 rooms (some museums in themselves), an indoor heated rooftop pool, and spectacular vistas of Red Square. Metro Okhotny Ryad. www.national.ru.

Ritz-Carlton Hotel, 3–5 Tverskaya, opened in 2007 (on site of former Intourist Hotel), right off Red Square. This 11-storey hotel has 334 large guest rooms with bathrooms even finished with Siberian marble from the Altai. It has a roof-top lounge, luxury spa and indoor pool. www.ritzcarlton.com.

Sheraton Palace Hotel, 19 1st Tverskaya-Yamskaya (a five-minute drive from the Kremlin), it has over 200 rooms and a marble mosaic of Moscow in the lobby; Metro Belorusskaya. www.sheraton.com or www.starwoodhotels.com.

Swissôtel Krasnye Holmy, 52 Kosmodamlanskaya Emb. Situated in the metallic Riverside skyscraper complex overlooking the Moscow River three kilometers from the Kremlin, off the Garden Ring, between the Obvodny Canal and the River. Superb views from the City Space Bar on the 34th floor. Metro Paveletskaya. www. swissotel.com.

TOP END FOUR AND FIVE STAR

These hotels offer all the amenities of high-end hotels. Prices start at about $200 per night.

Akvarel Hotel is a 23-room boutique hotel situated on the historic Stoleshnikov Lane, at 12/3, near Chekhovskaya metro. www.hotelakvarel.ru.

Artel, has a terrific location at 3 Teatralny Proezd tucked behind the Bolshoi Theater. Artists created the decorations for the graffiti-covered walls in the rooms and lobby. Take note that the funky popular music club, Masterskaya, is one floor below, an eatery by day with live music at night. www.artelhotel-moscow.ru.

Bentley Hotel is a mini-hotel with a dozen brightly-decorated rooms, and the top-floor American-style diner, Frendy's. Located in the historic Kitai-Gorod area at 28 Pokrovka. www.bentleyhotel.ru.

Crowne Plaza Hotel, located in the World Trade Center complex, it is situated across from the Moskva River and the White House. With over 700 rooms (including 149 special Club Rooms with panoramic city views), pool and fitness center, and many restaurants and cafés, it is located at 12 Krasnopresnenskaya Emb. Metro Vystavochnaya. www.hotel.wtcmoscow.ru.

Golden Ring Swiss Diamond, at 5 Smolenskaya near the White House, has over 240 rooms and a panorama restaurant with great views of the city. Metro Smolenskaya. www.hotel-goldenring.ru.

Hilton Moscow Leningradskaya is situated in the shortest of the iconic Stalinist skyscrapers at 21/40 Kalanchevskaya on Komsomolsky Square near three main train stations. Formerly the old Leningradskaya Hotel, Hilton performed a major upgrade in 2008. www.hilton.com.

Hotel Savoy, formerly known as the Hotel Berlin, built in 1912, was fully restored in 1989 with 70 rooms, a health club and pool. Centrall located near the Bolshoi Theater at 3 Rozhdestvenka. Metro Kuznetsky Most. www.savoy.ru.

Katerina Hotel, with Scandinavian management, is located at 6/1 Shluzovaya Emb., a few minutes walk from the Paveletskaya train and metro station. www.katerinahotels.com.

Kebur Palace is an 80-room boutique hotel two km from the Kremlin at 32 Ostozhenka St with a pool, sauna, and live piano music in the lobby at night. Metro Kropotkinskaya. The landmark Georgian restaurant, Tiflis (Tbilisi) is also located here for fine dining. www.keburpalace.ru.

Kitai-Gorod is a cosy mini-hotel at 25 Lubyansky Proezd in the old part of town, only a 15-minute walk to the Kremlin, near Kitai-Gorod metro. www.otel-kg.ru.

Korston Hotel is located on Sparrow Hills not far from Moscow University at 15 Kosygina St and Vorobyovy Gory (Sparrow Hills) metro. It is situated in an entertainment complex with numerous bars and bowling. www.korston.ru.

Marco Polo Presnya Hotel, at 9 Spiridonevsky Lane, is situated in the quiet Patriarch's Pond area, not far from Red Square. Metro Pushkinskaya. www.marco-polo-presnja-hotel.com.

Radisson Royal, built in 1957 as the Hotel Ukraine, it is located in one of Stalin's Seven skyscraper buildings. Renovated and reopened in 2010, it has over 500 rooms on 29 floors, and centrally located on the banks of the Moskva River at 2/1 Kutuzovsky Prospekt. Year-round river cruises with ice-breaker boats in winter. The Radisson Slavyanskaya is at 2 Europe Square. Metro Kievskaya. www.ukraina-hotel.ru or www.radisson.com.

Red (Zarya) Dawn is a stylish boutique hotel located at 3/10 Bersenevksy Lane (Bldg 8) on the waterfront in the trendy Red October factory district, center to some of Moscow's hottest clubs and nightlife. Nearest metro Kropotkinskaya. www.red-zarya.ru.

Sretenskaya Hotel is a mini-hotel at 15 Sretenka St, about a 20-minute walk north of Red Square, with a fitness center, sauna and pool. Near metro Sukharevskaya www.hotel-sretenskaya.ru.

MID-RANGE
These hotels average around $100 and up per night.

Art Hotel, 2 3rd Peshchnaya. A quiet hotel on the edge of a park, the art-gallery owner has covered the walls in contemporary Russian art. A 20-minute car ride north of the Kremlin. Metro Sokol. www.arthotel.ru.

Arbat Hotel at 12 Plotnikov Lane, is on a quiet street just steps from the Old Arbat district. Metro Smolenskaya. arbat.president-hotel.ru.

Basilica Hotel is a gem of a hotel that is located on the grounds of the 18th-century Church of the Silver Trinity in the historical Kitai Gorod area just a 20-minute walk from Red Square. A hostel is also located in the same building (see listing under hostels). Metro Kitai-Gorod. www.basilicahotel.ru.

Boulevard Hotel is on the Boulevard Ring at 1 Sretenka near metro Chistiye Prudy. Situated on the 2nd floor of an old classical building, this mini-hotel has period furnishings and offers special weekend rates. www.bulvar-sr.ru.

Brighton, 29 Petrovsko-Razumovsky Lane, a quiet hotel next to the Petrovsky Park with ten comfortable rooms, located in the northern part of town. Includes a pool, sauna, health club and restaurant. Metro Dynamo. www.brh.ru.

Budapest Hotel, 2/18 Petrovskiye Linii. A 19th-century building transformed into an elegant hotel with a central location behind the Bolshoi Theater and Petrovka shopping area; it has over 100 rooms and a popular tavern. Metro Teatralnaya. www.hotel-budapest.ru.

Club 27, 27 Malaya Nikitskaya, is a mini-hotel that exudes old Victorian charms. Metro Pushkinskaya. www.club27.ru.

Danilovskaya Hotel is situated in the 12th-century Danilovsky Monastery complex (at 5 Bol Starodanilovsky Lane) and run by the Orthodox Church. The modern five-story hotel has over 100 rooms, a pool and two Finnish saunas. Metro Tulskaya. www.danilovsky.ru.

East–West Hotel, 14/4 Tverskoi Bulvar. Set in a charming 19th-century mansion, the small 26-room hotel sits in a quiet garden behind the boulevard. It's a 15-minute stroll to downtown and the Kremlin. Metro Tverskaya; www.hotel-east-west.ru.

Karetny Dvor is a small boutique hotel located in a renovated 19th-century "Carriage House" near the Hermitgage Gardens on the Boulevard Ring at 5 Karetny Lane on the 5th floor. Metro Tsvetnoi Bulvar. www.kdvorhel.ru.

Novotel, 2 Presnenskaya Emb. stands amongst the skyscrapers of the Moscow Business District. Metro Mezhdunarodnaya. www.novotel-moscow-city.com. (Another Novotel is at 23 Novoslobodskaya) www.accorhotels.com.

Pekin, this hotel is located within a Gothic-style building, built in the 1950's, that towers over Triumfalnaya Square; it has over 240 rooms, a pool, sauna, and the first Chinese restaurant in town. The very raucous Radio City Bar is on the ground floor. 5/1 Bol Sadovaya Ul. near Metro Mayakovskaya. www.hotelpeking.ru.

Petrovka Loft is a stylish 10-room mini-hotel centrally located at 17/2 Petrovka. Metro Teatralnaya. www.petrovkalofthotelmoscow.com.

Sovietsky Hotel, 32/2 Leningradsky Prospekt near Metro Belorusskaya. This hotel is a throw back to the Soviet era with its gilded hammer & sickles, grand staircases and chandeliers. The legendary Yar Restaurant is complete with Russian-style food and costumed dancing girls (be sure to make advance reservations) www.sovietsky.ru.

Sverchkov-8 is a cosy 11-room mini-hotel at the same address as the name near Chistiye Prudy metro. www.sverchkov-8.ru.

BUDGET HOTELS

These average $30–$80 for single/double, and offer comfortable accommodation (if a little more spartan). Check to find out what amenities are included, such as television or air conditioning. Some offer cheaper room rates for shared hallway bathroom, and there may be different classes of rooms, such as standard, upgraded or even semi-lux. Note the location, for it can be situated far from the center or not close to a Metro station. Many hostels below also offer single or double rooms.

Belgrade Hotel, at 8 Smolenskaya, this hotel is centrally located within a post Soviet block opposite Arbat St and the (MID) Foreign Ministry building, with 434 rooms, five restaurants, and a business center. Metro Smolenskaya. www.hotel-belgrad.ru.

Bulgakov Hotel is centrally located at 49 Arbat St. The building also houses a popular hostel (see Home From Home). www.bulgakovhotel.com. The same owners also run the **A La Russe Hotel** at 5 Voznesensky St. (bldg. 5), a 10-minute walk to the Kremlin. www.hotelalaruss.com (www.moshotels.com).

Godzillas Urban Jungle Lodge started with a hostel (see below) and opened this mini-hotel, with 13 rooms, at 21 Pokrovka near Chistiye Prudy Metro. (The entrance is on Belgorodsky Proezd) www.godzillashostel.com.

Sputnik, 38 Leninsky Prospekt, this basic Soviet-style hotel is about four kms southwest of the town center near Sparrow Hills and Moscow University. The delicious on-site Darbar Restaurant offers great Indian cuisine. Metro Leninsky Prospekt. www.hotelsputnik.ru.

Suharevka Hotel is a mini-hotel, along with a hostel, on the Garden Ring. Singles, doubles, triples and an 8-bed dorm room. Located at 16/18 Bolshaya Suharevskaya on the 4th floor near metro Suharevskaya. www.suharevkahotel.ru.

Varshava (Warsaw) Hotel, at 2 Leninsky Prospket. Opened in 1960, this has 122 renovated rooms and a restaurant. Located by the Okyabrskaya Metro on the southern end of the Garden ring. www.hotelwarsaw.ru.

Yunost, at 34 Khamovnichesky Val (near Novodevichy Convent), this Soviet-style hotel has 200 rooms, upgraded 'Euro-class' doubles, and a restaurant. Metro Sportivnaya. www.hotelyunost.com.

Zolotoi Kolos, 15/3 Yaroslavsky. With 390 rooms, it's located near VDNKh metro.

HOSTELS

For each hostel, advance bookings are recommended—reservations can be made on the website (most hostels have female-only dorm rooms). Many provide visa support and other travel services.

Check: www.airbnb.com, www.hostelbookers.com and www.hostelz.com for more listings.

Basilica Hostel has a lovely, quiet location on the grounds of the Church of the Silver Trinity in Kitai-Gorod, just a 20-minute walk to the Kremlin. Four and six-bed dorm rooms, kitchen and lounge area. www.sweetmoscow.com. The building also contains the Basilica Hotel. www.basilicahotel.ru.

Chocolate Hostel is near Pushkinskaya metro at 15 Degtyarny Lane (Apt 4). Bring some chocolate from home to add to their collection. Provides twins, 3,6 and 10 bed dorm rooms, and a fully-equipped kitchen and bike rentals. www.chocohostel.com.

Comrade Hostel is in the historical Kitai-Gorod area near the Kremlin at 11 Maroseika St. Metro Kitai-Gorod. (Entrance is through the courtyard, at number 3, on the third floor) Offers singles and doubles with shared bathrooms and 6 (female only) and 8 bed dorms. www.comradehostel.com.

Home From Home (Hotel and Hostel Bulgakov) is centrally located at 49 Arbat (enter from Plotnikov Lane, entrance 2) with dorm rooms that accommodate up to 50 people. Private en-suite rooms are also available in the Bulgakov Hotel in the building. Metro Smolenkaya. www.home-fromhome.com and wwwbulgakovhotel.com.

Hostel Sherstone, 8 Gostinichny Proezd, bldg 1 (a five-minute walk from Vladykino Metro). It has 100+ beds, with singles/doubles and dorms. It is a 15-minute metro ride to the center of town. www.sherstone.ru.

Godzillas Hostel, 6 Bolshoi Karetny. Metro Tsvetnoi Bulvar. One of the largest and most centrally located hostels in Moscow, set up in a pre-revolutionary building near Pushkin Square. With nearly 100 beds spread out over four floors, it has both female and mixed dorms and singles/doubles. Bathroom facilities are on each floor, with three kitchens and a living room with satellite television. Also provides airport/train transfers. (There is also a hostel in Suzdal.) www.godzillashostel.com.

Napolean Hostel is named so because supposedly Napolean stayed in the building during his 1812 occupation of Moscow. Located in Kitai-Gorod at 2 Maly Zlatoustinsky Lane on the 4th floor. Offers 6, 8 and 10 bed dorm rooms (some female only) with a kitchen and common room. www.napoleonhostel.ru.

Trans-Siberian Hostel is located in the Kitai-Gorod area, a 10-minute walk from Kurskaya Metro. Good bargains for the double and triple room, along with the 4, 8 and 10 bed dorm rooms. A communal kitchen space and train-themed décor! www.tshostel.com.

APARTMENTS AND SHORT TERM RENTALS
For a visitor, it is also worth considering renting an apartment for a short-term stay while in town. They can be cheaper than a hotel (especially if others split the cost), and offer more space and amenities—equipped with kitchen and laundry facilities, cable television, wireless internet access, etc. Many also provide airport pick-up and visa support. A few websites that offer rental services are: www.moscowsuites.com, www.enjoymoscow.com, www.hofa.ru, www.airbnb.com and www.moscow4rent.com. (For long-term rentals, check www.expat.ru, www.redtape.ru or work with a realtor, such as City Realty at www.cityrealityrussia.com and Penny Lane at rent.realtor.ru.)

HOMESTAYS AND BED & BREAKFASTS
Several international organizations can book homestays in Russian apartments. (A two-night minimum stay may be required, and there can be discounts for longer stays.) This usually includes a private room within the family apartment, breakfast (sometimes other meals), use of a shared bathroom and kitchen. The host family is usually English-speaking and the apartment and family pre-approved by a Russian host organization. Plus, the added advantage is that you are able to experience the life of a typical Russian family and have conversations about their opinions and lifestyles. Check to find out what the price includes: how many meals/day, city walking tours guided by host, city transfers, etc. Many of these homestays can now be pre-booked through an overseas travel agency (working with a corresponding Russian agency), which can also provide visa and other travel support. (Extra fees may be charged for these services.) Never wait till the last minute to book these homestays.

HOFA (Host Families Association), established in 1991, HOFA offers a full choice of budget accommodation: homestays, apartment rentals and hotel reservations for guests in more than 60 cities in Russia. They also can provide visa sponsorship and assistance, transportation transfers, travel information, bookings, and city-guided tours (walking or with car/driver), even Russian language lessons. www.hofa.ru. Another popular site for Bed and Breakfasts is www.airbnb.com.

DINING

Today Moscow is filled with thousands of eating establishments—from cafés and fast-food outlets to the most elegant and elaborate restaurants in old palaces and plush new hotels. (There are more than 8,000 bars scattered throughout the city!) Aside from classic Russian dishes (see the Menu vocabulary on page 745), hundreds of ethnic restaurants serving Armenian to Vietnamese have sprung up which have live music or variety shows, and serve wine, beer and other alcoholic beverages. (Many also offer discount business luncheons and happy hour specials.) Every type of dish imaginable is offered, as well as matching prices, which vary from the very cheap to amazingly expensive. The larger hotels have their own restaurants, bars and cafés. For many popular and upscale establishments, reservations are recommended. Besides payment in Russian rubles, most now accept credit cards. (If the menu prices are marked 'Y.E.' this means 'conventional units' or US dollars/ Euros, but payment is in rubles or by credit card.) The standard for tipping in Moscow is 10%, but sometimes the service charge is included in the bill. Most restaurants are open noon to midnight, and later on weekends. (Check individual websites for more information on the menu, prices and location.)

The average price per person without beverage is indicated by the symbols: $—up to $15, $$—$16--$35, $$$—$36-$50, $$$$—$51 and much higher.

AFRICAN
Addis-Abba $$, 6/1 Zemlyanoi Val. Has tasty Ethiopian food, which you can eat with your hands! Metro Kurskaya.

AMERICAN
American Bar and Grill $$, 59 Zemlyonoi Val. Wild West atmosphere with American burgers, spicy chicken wings, and lots of cold beer. Metro Taganskaya. Another branch is at 2 1st Tverskaya Yamskaya. Metro Mayakovskaya.

Chicago Prime Steakhouse $$$, 8a Strasnoi Bulvar. Grilled Prime-grade steaks and seafood. Metro Chekhovskaya. www.chicagoprime.ru.

Hard Rock Café $$, 44 Arbat. On two floors with TV screens. Metro Smolenskaya. www.hardrockcafe.ru.

City Grill $$, 2/30 Sadovaya Triumfalnaya. New York and Philadelphia fare, with sandwiches and fries. Metro Mayakovskaya. www.citygrill.ru.

Louisiana Steakhouse $$$, 30/4 Pyatniskaya. Setting is a 19th-century saloon, serving generous portions of grilled steak from Black Angus to filet mignon. Extensive wine and beer list. Metro Tretyakovskaya. www.lusiana.ru.

Planet (Gollivud) Hollywood $$, 23b Krasnaya Presnya. US chain serving American food. Happy hour every afternoon with half-price food. Metro Krasnopresnenskaya.

Starlight Diner $$, 16a Bol Sadovaya. American diner with everything from milkshakes to grilled cheese sandwiches, and breakfasts all day. Jukebox plays Retro music. Open 24 hours. Metro Mayakovskaya. (Three other locations in the city) www.starlite.ru.

T.G.I. Friday's $$, 18/2 Tverskaya (at eleven other locations). Delicious steaks, burgers, sandwiches. Cold beer and cocktails. Metro Pushkinskaya. www.tgifridays.ru.

ARMENIAN

ArArAt $$,119 Prospekt Mira (in All-Russian Exhibition Center, Bldg 68). The restaurant is on the second floor, with a hall for tasting Armenian cognacs on the first. Metro VDNKh. www.restoranararat.ru.

Café Ararat $$$$, 4 Neglinnaya in Ararat Park Hotel. Superb food with vintage Armenian brandies and wine. Also has a summer dining terrace. Metro Kuznetsky Most.

Noyev Kovcheg (Noah's Ark) $$$$, 9 Maly Ivanovsky. Situated in a 19th-century mansion, the menu offers over 120 Caucasian dishes and a large cognac selection. Live music. Metro Kitai-Gorod www.noevkovcheg.ru.

AZERBAIJANI

Farkhad $$, 4 Bolshaya Marfinskaya. Oriental decor and live music. Metro Vladykino.

Barashka $$$, 20/1 Petrovka. Created by renowned restaurateur Arkady Novikov, the interior is minimalistic with bright accents of lemon jars; the menu offers grilled meats, hearty stews and delectable lamb for which the restaurant is named. Metro Kuznetsky Most. Another branch is located at 21/1 Novy Arbat. Metro Smolenskaya. www.novikovgroup.ru.

Karyetny Dvor (Carriage House) $$, 52 Povarskaya, is one of the oldest restaurants of Azeri cooking; very tasty food. Metro Barrikadnaya.

Zafferano $$$, 8 Novinsky Bul (inside Lotta Center). Lovely view of Novy Arbat from the windows. Metro Smolenskaya. www.zafferanorest.ru.

BAKERIES

Moscow has bread and bakery stores on practically every street corner—freshly baked goods abound. A must is trying the traditional Russian brown or black bread. To order in Russian: *khleb* is bread; *baton* (oval white loaf); *bely kirpich* (white brick loaf); *chorny kirpich* (dark brick loaf); *tort* (sweet cake); *bulochki* (sweet rolls). **Baltisky Khleb** (Baltic Bread), 3/10 Malaya Dmitrovka, has huge selection of breads, cakes and pies near Pushkin Square. Open 10am-11pm. The **French Bakery** is at 3 Boyarsky Per. Mon–Sat 8am–8pm; metro Krasniye Vorota. **Le Pain Quotidien** is a popular international chain with nine outlets in town. Baked goods and organic menu of breakfasts and other food. www.lpq.ru. The **Volkonsky** Café-bakery has four outlets in town with delicious baked goods and other main dishes and salads. www.wolkonsky.com. **Upside Down Cake Company**, 76 Bol Gruzinakaya, is filled with everything from cakes and cupcakes to sorbet and many blends of tea. Metro Belorusskaya.

The confectioner shop, **A Korkunov**, at 13/16 Bol Lubyanka is chocked full of homemade chocolate and candies. **Art Lebedev Café**, at 35 Bol. Nikitskaya (Metro Barrikadnaya) is owned by designer, Artemy Lebedev, and is a trendy café offering many baked cakes and other sweets. **Confael Chocolate**, at 12 Nikitsky Bulvar (Metro Arbatskaya), is filled with all kinds of mouth-watering chocolate; sample them in the café. **Gogol-Mogol** lets you indulge in French pastries; even the front door is painted with a cake recipe in French, 6 Gagarinsky Lane, Metro Kropotkinskaya. The **Magazin Chai-Kofe** (Tea & Coffee Store), at number 19 Myasnitskaya (Metro Turgenevskaya), is in the old Perlov Tea House, built in 1894 and decorated in the style of a Chinese Pagoda.

BARS AND PUBS

Bar Denis Simachev \$\$\$, 12/2 Stoleshnikov Lane. This fashion designer has opened a restaurant/bar on the ground floor of his Moscow boutique. In summer, sit out on the terrace, drink a mojito, and watch all the fashionistas strut by. Evening DJ's, dancing and lots of beautiful people. Open 24 hours. Metro Okhotny Ryad. www.denissimachev.ru.

Bar Strelka \$\$, 14 Bersenevskaya Emb. On the roof deck of the Design Institute in the hip Red October factory district, this bar has cool cocktails and delicious tapas, and is frequented by a mix of local artists. A block away is Dome, its name inspired by the view of the great Savior Cathedral. Aside from a bar/café, it also has a cinema-lounge with an in-house theater with couch seating.

Art Akademiya \$\$\$, 6 Bersenevskaya Another popular spot in the Red October District, it boasts the largest bar stand in Europe with 3,000 square feet of art, alcohol and food in this hybrid restaurant, gallery and nightspot. Closest metro Kropotkinskaya.

Chesterfield Café $$, 19/1 Novy Arbat. American pub with TV Sports screens, live bands, salsa nights. Metro Arbatskaya. www.chester-bar.ru.

Churchill's $$, 66 Leningradsky Pr. British-style pub with Sunday evening concerts. Metro Aeroport www.churchillpub66.ru.

City Space $$$, 52 Kosmodamianskaya Emb (in Swissôtel, 34th fl) Drink a cocktail with an absolutely stunning 360-degree view of the city. Open 5pm–3am. Metro Paveletskaya. www.cityspacebar.com.

Dissident Vinoteca $$, 25 Nikolskaya (Nautilus 5th fl). This wine bar offers over 200 kinds of wine by the glass, along with a selection of hors d'oevres. Metro Lubyanka. www.dissident.msk.ru.

Dream Bar $$$, 17/1 Myasnitskaya. Dreamy interior with comfy sofas and a large list of cocktails. Offers Molecular Mixology—your drink may come surrounded by meringue and fruit foam. Open 24 hours. Metro Chistiye Prudy. www.dreambar.ru.

Free Bar $$, 21/1 Pokrovka, Opened by Dmitri Sokolov and dedicated to 50's–60's America with Tex-Mex food and a large seletion of whiskeys and bourbon. Open 24 hours. Metro Chistiye Prudy. www.free-bar.ru.

Glavpivtorg $$, (Main Beer Restaurant), 5 Bol. Lubyanka. Serves beer brewed on-site and tasty Russian fare. Metro Kuznetsky Most. www.glavpivtorg.ru.

Help $$, 27 1st Tverskaya-Yamskaya, tasty food and lots of alcoholic offerings. Open 24 hours. Metro Belorusskaya. www.helpbar.ru.

John Bull Pub $$$, 9 Karmanitsky Lane (Metro Smolenskaya) and 25/1 Krasnaya Presnya (Metro 1905 Goda). Cozy British-style pub with extensive menu.

Kruzhka (Glass of Beer) $, inexpensive beer hang-out with multiple locations. www.kruzhka.ru.

Luch, $$$ 27/1 Bol. Pirogovskay. High ceilings and a 30-meter bar with a large cocktail, whiskey and wine list. The menu offers Asian food. Metro Sportivnaya www.luchbar.ru.

Maximilian's Braueri $$, 15 Novy Arbat. Authentic Bavarian brew-house with live music. Metro Arbatskaya.

Monks & Nuns $$, 3/18 Sivtsev Vrazhek. A great Belgian beer cellar with tasty Belgian and Russian food. Metro Kropotkinskaya.

Progressive Daddy & Daddy's Terrace $$, 6/2 Bersenevskaya Emb. Red October District. Located on the top floor of the factory, this bar-restaurant has one of the best views in the city, especially of the Savior Cathedral. Metro Kropotkinskaya. www.progressivedaddy.ru.

Real McCoy, $$, 1 Kudrinskaya Sq, Two-for-one happy hour; Tex-Mex food and dancing at night. Live jazz or rock in the evenings from 9pm Wed–Sun. Open 24 hours. Metro Barrikadnaya. www.mccoy.ru.

Rosie O'Grady's, 5/1 Prospket Mira. Authentic Irish pub, Guinness and Irish food, along with fish n' chips to Oriental. Metro Prospekt Mira. www.rosie.ru.

Silver's Irish Pub, 5/6 Nikitsky Lane. Running since 1997, popular pub with lots of Guinness, satisfying food and hangover breakfasts. www.silverspub.com.

Tema Bar $$$, 5/2 Potapovsky Lane. Open 24 hours. Huge cocktail list (with over 20 varieties of martinis) music at night. Metro Chistiye Prudy. www.temabar.ru.

Tinkoff $$, 11 Protochny Per. Oleg Tinkoff started Moscow's first microbrewery. Different beers are brewed on site according to old family recipes. Restaurant. Metro Smolenskaya www.tinkoff.ru.

Vision on Novy Arbat $$$, 11/1Novy Arbat. Menu offers over 200 cocktails and the huge windows allow for great views of Novy Arbat. Open 11am–2am and weekends till 6am. Metro Arbatskaya. www.vision-moscow.ru.

Vision on Yakimanka $$$, 22 Bol. Yakimanka. As its branch on Novy Arbat. Metro Polyanka.

SUNDAY BRUNCH
Most upscale hotels offer superb Sunday brunches with live music from 12:30–4:30pm. The **Ararat Park Hotel** in its Park Restaurant offers everything from fresh oysters to Kamchatka crab legs. The **Baltschug Hotel** serves a smorgasbord brunch with live music, as do the **Marriott Grand** and **Sheraton Palace Hotels**. The main dining hall in the **Metropolel Hotel** (under a magnificent stained-glass roof) has a great spread and live jazz ensemble. The Amadeus Restaurant in the **Radisson Slavyanskaya** has everything from smoked salmon to French pastries.

BYELORUSSIAN
Belaya Rus $$, 14 Bol. Nikitskaya. Offers European and Byelorussian cuisine, as yummy potato pancakes. Metro Aleksandrovsky Sad www.belayarus.ru.

CARIBBEAN
Aruba $$, 4 Narodnaya. Delicious Cuban food. Metro Taganskaya. www.arubabar.ru.

Barbudos $$, 24 Bol. Tatarskaya. Caribe Island fare. Metro Novokuznetskaya. www.barbudos.ru.

Caribe $$, 18/18 Pokrovka. Delicious Caribbean meals. Metro Chistiye Prudy. www.caribeclub.ru.

Caribius Café $$, 4/3 Strastnoi Bulvar, Tasty Caribbean fare. Metro Pushkinskaya. www.caribius.ru.

Che $$ 10/2 Nikolskaya. This restaurant-club, decorated in the style of the Cuban revolution, has Cuban-Mexican food, lots of cocktail choices and Cuban cigars. Evenings bring in DJ's, dancing and live music. Open 24 hours. www.clubche.ru.

Old Havana $$$$, 28/1 Talalikhina, Cuban appetizers, soups and delicious seafood dishes. Lengthy cocktail list and hand-rolled Cuban cigars. Music, dancing and free dance master classes on Thursday. Open 24 hours. Metro Volgogradsky Prospekt. www.old-havana.ru.

CHINESE

China Club $$$$, 21 Krasina. Another super chic restaurant by the Novikov group. Colonial-style interior and exquisite cuisine. Metro Mayakovskaya. www.novikovgroup.ru.

Dim Sum $$, 3 Smolenskaya Sq. Shanghai cooks, offering over 40 dishes. Metro Smolenskaya.

Djun Go $$$, 24 Tverskaya. Delicious 'imperial' dishes from Guangzhou Province. Metro Mayakovskaya. www.djungo.ru.

Druzhba (Friendship), 4 Novoslobodskaya (bottom floor of Shopping Center), hot and spicy Sichuan cuisine; menu boasts over 180 dishes. Metro Novoslobodskaya. www.drugba.ru.

Drevny Kitai $$$, 5/6 Kamergersky Lane, 'Ancient China' interior is decorated with red paper lanterns and Ming vases. Metro Okhotny Ryad. www.old-china.ru.

Dynasty $$$, 29 Zubovsky Bulvar. Speciality is Shanghai cuisine. Metro Park Kultury. www.china-dynasty.ru.

Five Spice $$$, 3/18 Sivtsev Vrazhek Lane. Serves Chinese as well as Tandoori dishes. Metro Kropotkinskaya. www.5spice.ru.

Hepin $$, 56 Prospekt Mira, Delicious inexpensive Chinese food. Metro Prospekt Mira.

Ki Ka Ku $$$, 28/30 Begovaya. Chinese food and buffet, sushi, and Karaoke bar. Metro Begovaya. www.kikaku.ru.

Peking Duck $$, 24/1 Tverskaya. House special is, of course, delicious Peking Duck! Not only Chinese dishes, but Japanese and Thai as well. (Six other branches in town) Metro Mayakovskaya. www.ytka.ru (Utka is Russian for duck).

Shatush $$$$, 17 Gogolevsky Bulvar, Superb food, elegant décor, wide, selection of cocktails and gourmet teas. Metro Kropotkinskaya. www.shatush.ru.

Silk, 29/1 $$$, Tverskaya-Yamskaya. Traditional Chinese food by Beijing chef, and many tea choices. Open 11am–5am. Metro Belorusskaya. Metro Mayakovskaya. www.spicy-thai.ru.

Tan $$$, 13/1 Oruzheiny Lane. Culinary recipes of both China and Tibet. Tea rituals and other eclectic touches, such as tarot card readings and Syrian hookahs. Metro Mayakovskaya. www.restorantan.ru.

Turandot $$$$, 26/5 Tverskoi Bulvar. Meticulously planned, this 'palace' took six years to build, and the lush interior can almost be compared to rooms in the Winter Palace. Outstanding Asian and European cuisine. Metro Tverskaya. www.turandotpalace.ru.

EUROPEAN

Amsterdam $$$, 4 Ilyinka (inside Gostinny Dvor). Dutch and European cooking. Metro Okhotny Ryad. www.amsterdam-restaurant.ru.

Andreas $$$, 12 Kutuzovsky Pr. Delicious grilled meat and fish. Live concerts in the evening, and a summer veranda. Metro Kievskaya. www.andreasbar.ru.

ArteFAQ $$, 32 Dmitrovskaya. A cool Bohemian-club restaurant with a second floor bar. Often hosts literary readings and concerts. Metro Tverskaya. www.artefaq.ru.

Delicatessen $$, 20/2 Sadovaya-Karetnaya, From pizza and pasta to salads and steak tartar; closed Mondays. Metro Tsvetnoi Bulvar.

Dodo $$$, 21/2 Petrovka. A creative blend of French, Italian and Asian cuisines. Open 10am–midnight and Fri/Sat 10am–6am. Metro Chekhovskaya.

Dyed Pikhto $$, 37 Myasnitskaya. Set in a woodcutter's cottage with an open fireplace. Tasty European food and a lovely summer veranda. Metro Chistiye Prudy.

Filial $$, 3/1 Krivokoleny Lane. Inexpensive European-style restaurant near Lubyanka metro. www.filialmoscow.com.

Filimonova & Yankel Fish House $$$, 23 Tverskaya. Offers ten varieties of fish grilled, baked or fried to your liking. (Lobster and crab in season) Metro Pushkinskaya.

La Maree $$$$, 28 Petrovka. The place in town to go for seafood with over 100 sorts cooked in any way or style. Guest can also compose their own dish. Metro Pushkinskaya. www.lamaree.ru.

Los Bandidos $$$$, 7 Bol Ordyka. Replica of the restaurant from the Spanish town of Puerto Banus, it serves superior Spanish cuisine with an extensive wine list. Outdoor seating in summer. Metro Tretyakovskaya.

Malenka $, 1/2 Solyanka, Inexpensive European fare with both a buffet and regular menu. Metro Kitai-Gorod. www.melenka.ru.

Porto Malteste $$$, 21 Pravdy. Specializes in fish with more than 25 entrée selections. Metro Belorusskaya. Another location is at 8 Bol. Spasskaya. www.portomaltese.ru.

Propaganda, $$, 2 Bol Zlatoustinsky Lane. This popular restaurant opened more than decade ago and is still going strong. Red-brick warehouse with DJ's and dancing at night. Metro Lubyanka. www.propagandamoscow.ru/en.

Restoran Fresh $$, 21 Petrovka. Offers simple and healthy foods, along with freshly squeezed juices.

Scandinavia $$$$, 7 Maly Palashevsky Lane. Superb upscale Scandinavian/Swedish food and smorgasbord. Metro Pushkinskaya. www.scandinavia.ru.

Sirena $$$$, 15 Bol Spasskaya. Arkady Novikov opened this as his first restaurant in 1992. Specializing in fresh seafood, much of which is fished out of the aquarium tanks in front of your very eyes. Metro Sukharevskaya. www.novikovgroup.ru.

Syrnaya Dyrka (Cheese Hole) $$$, 15 Bolshoi Cherkassky in the heart of Kitai-Gorod. Known for its Swiss cheese dishes from fondue and quiche to other European selections. Metro Kitai-Gorod. Another branch is at 6/20 Pokrovsky Bulvar. www.sdyrka.ru.

Tapa $$$, 20/2 Trubnaya. One of Moscow's first tapas bars is on the first floor. The second and third floors (with Sports screens) offer other Spanish dishes and wines.

Vkus (Taste) $$$, 13/1 1st Tverskaya-Yamskaya. Cosy setting and tasty European-style food. Metro Mayakovskaya. www.cafevkus.ru.

EASTERN EUROPEAN
Baba Marta $$$, 8 Gogolevsky Bulvar. Tasty Bulgarian national dishes in a quiet atmosphere. Metro Kropotkinskaya. www.babamarta.ru.

Budvar $$$, 33 Kotelnicheskaya Emb. Czech/European dishes and draft beer. Metro Tanganskaya. www.budwar.ru.

Code 011 $$, 3a Kozhevnichesky Vrazhek (011 is a Belgrade telephone code) The second floor has a classic Serbian restaurant, and the first a beer bar. Metro Paveletskaya. www.code011.ru.

Kolkovna $$$, 34/1 Petrovka. Classic Czech dishes with two sorts of beer. Metro Tverskaya.

Pilsner $$, 1 1st Tverskaya-Yamskaya. Czech food with great beers. Metro Mayakovskaya. Another branch is at 15/16 Pokrovka. Metro Chistiye Prudy.

Praga, 2 Arbat. One of Moscow's oldest restaurants. Praga restaurant pastry chef, Vladimir Guralnik, invented the now-famous dessert, Ptichye Moloko or Bird's Milk Tort (a biscuit-type soufflé cake). Metro Arbatskaya. www.praga.ru.

FRENCH

Bouillabaisse $$$$, 37 Leninsky Pr. Serves the world-famous soup from Marseille, along with other seafood dishes. Metro Leninsky Prospekt. www.buyabes.ru.

Café De Ville $$, 24 Sadovaya-Samotechnaya. French bistro atmosphere. Metro Tsvetnoi Bulvar. www.cafe-deville.ru.

Carré Blanc (White Square) $$$$, 19/2 Seleznyovsky. Set in a 19th-century manor, the restaurant is named after Malevich's famous artwork with artfully-prepared French food. The manor also contains a bistro with cheaper selections. Metro Novoslobodskaya. www.carreblanc.ru.

Chez Geraldine $$, at 27/2 Ostozhenka is open 24 hours. Near Metro Kropotkinskaya. www.geraldine.ru.

Creperie de Paris $, has three branches in town, including at 2/3 2nd Tverskaya-Yamskaya. Metro Mayakovskaya. www.creperie.ru.

Jean-Jacques $$, 12 Nikitsky Bulvar. Cosy café with French dishes, fresh baking and wine. Metro Arbatskaya. Three other locations; open 24 hours (closed 6am–8am). www.jan-jak.com.

Maison Café $$$, 12/8 Savsinskaya Emb. Set in a 19th-century building, this gastronomic French restaurant is filled with large windows, candles and oo la la glamor. Metro Kievskaya. www.maisoncafe.ru.

Maison Vatel $$$, 14/1 Komsomolsky Pr. Named after the French chef, Francois Vatel, this cosy French bistro lists the daily specials on blackboards. Metro Park Kultury. www.maisonvatel.ru.

Nostalgie $$$, 12a Chistoprudny Bul. Good French food and live music. Metro Chistiye Prudy. www.nostalgie.ru.

Parisienne $$$$, 31 Leningradsky Pr. Decorated to look like a French street, with a model of the Eiffel Tower Metro Dynamo. www.parisiene.ru.

Ragout $$$, 69 Bol. Gruzinskaya. Brunches on Sunday 1pm–4pm. Metro Belorusskaya. www.caferagut.ru.

GEORGIAN

Georgian specialities include: *shashlik* (shish kebab), *lavash* (bread), *khachapuri* (bread and melted cheese), *chebureki* (thin fried bread with a meat filling), *khinkali* (large steamed dumplings), *tsatsivi* (cold chicken in walnut sauce), *piti* (lamb and potato soup), *kharcho* (spicy meat soup), *lobio* (spicy beans), *baklazhany* (eggplant stuffed with nuts), and *gutap* (stuffed crepes).

Glamour $$$, 2/3 Merzlyankovsky Lane. Superb Georgian food and wine; live music every evening. Metro Arbatskaya.

Dukhan Alaverdi $$, 32/4 Nizhegorodskaya. Classic Georgian food for a reasonable price set in a traditional rustic interior. Metro Taganskaya. Another branch is at 23/25 Gruzinsky Val. Metro Belorusskaya.

Genatsvale on Arbat $$$, 11/2 Novy Arbat. Georgian food on three floors and set in a picturesque setting. Yummy shashliks. Metro Arbatsksya. A quieter version of Genatsvale is located at 12/1 Ostozhenka. Metro Kropotkinskaya. http://restoran-genatsvale.ru.

Guriya $$, 7/3 Komsomolsky Pr. A favorite among the locals, so you know it's good. Metro Park Kultury.

Kabanchik $$$, 27/1 Ul Krasina. Traditional fare, especially grilled meat dishes. Metro Belorusskaya. www.restoran-kabanchik.ru.

Kavkazskaya Plennitsa $$$$, 36 Prospekt Mira. Opened in 1998, and named after a popular Yuri Nikulin (famous Russian clown) movie, entitled *Prisoner of the Caucasus* (also a novel by Lermontov). Large selection of soup to shashlik, Georgian wines with music in the evenings. Run by the Novikov Group. Metro Prospekt Mira. www.novikovgroup.ru.

Khachapuri $$$, 10 Bol. Gnezdnikovsky Lane. Offers all the Georgian favorites for a moderate price. Metro Pushkinskaya.

Prince Bagration $$$, 58/1 Plyushchikha. Set in an old manor-style surrounding, with a wine cellar, garden and lovely summer terrace. Metro Park Kultury. www.knyazbagration.ru.

Pirosmani's $$$, 4 Novodevichy Proezd. Traditional and tasty Georgian fare in a Tbilisi setting with artwork by Georgian artist, Pirosmani. Lovely view of Novodevichy Monastery. Metro Sportivnaya. www.upirosmani.ru.

Sam Prishyol $$$, 76a Pr. Vernadskovo. Extensive menu and live music in the evenings. Metro Pr. Vernadskovo.

Sakhli $$$, 6/1 Bol Karetny Lane. Metro Tsvetnoi Bulvar. www.sakhli.ru.

Suliko $$$. 7 Yermolaevsky Lane in Patriarch's Pond area. Traditional Georgian recipes and music. Metro Maykovskaya. Another restaurant is at 42/2 Bol. Polyanka near Metro Polyanka. www.suliko.ru.

INDIAN

Ajanta $$$$, 23/1 Mal. Gruzinsky. Situated in a palace atmosphere, serving Indian vegetarian and meat dishes. Metro Ulitsa 1905 Goda. www.ajanta.ru.

Aroma $$ 20/30 Krzhizhanovskovo. Tasty Indian food for a reasonable price. Metro Profsoyuznaya. www.aromamoscow.ru.

Darbar $$, 38 Leninsky Pr (Hotel Sputnik). One of Moscow's best Indian restaurants with Indian chef, located south of the city center. Live music at night. Metro

Leninsky Prospekt. www.darbar.ru.

Maharaja $$$, 1 Starosadsky Lane. Moscow's oldest Indian restaurant serving up delicious traditional dishes as Tandoori and kebabs. Metro Kitai-Gorod. www.maharaja.ru.

Put Yogi $$, 43/3 Pyatnitskaya, Vegetarian café in the Yoga Center. Metro Tretyakovskaya. www.omyoga.ru.

Vasantha $$$, 14 Neglinnaya. Sri Lankan born Chef Vasantha was US President Bill Clinton's personal cook for four years. Metro Kuznetsky Most.

ITALIAN AND MEDITERRANEAN
Popular bistro chains serving Italian pizzas and pastas are **Acadamy** (www.academiya.ru), **Il Patio** (www.ilpatio.ru), **Mi Piace** (www.mipiace.ru) **Papa Johns**, **Pronto** (www.bistro-pronto.ru) and **Vapiano**.

Accenti $$$, 7 Kropotkinsky Lane. Located in three separate halls, with a lovely summer terrace. Everything is delicious from appetizers to dessert. Metro Park Kultury. www.accenti.ru.

Adriatico $$$, 3 Blagoveshchensky Lane. Offers over 190 dishes and an impressive wine list. Metro Mayakovskaya. www.adriatico.ru.

Bocconcino $$$, 7/1 Strastnoi Bulvar. Neopolitan menu with more than 20 types of pizza and great desserts. Metro Tverskaya. www.bocconcino.ru.

Bontempi, $$$$ 12 Bersenevskaya Emb in the Red October Factory District. For classic *cucina italiana* it is the restaurant of Lombardy-born chef, Valentino Bontempi. Metro Kropotkinskaya. www.bontempirest.ru.

Capri $$$, 7 Ak Sakharova Pr. Homemade Italian food and 18 kinds of pizzas. Metro Turgenevskaya. www.restokapri.ru.

Cheese $$$$, 16/2 Sad Samotechnaya. Mediterranean selections with 20 cheeses on the menu. Metro Tsvetnoi Bulvar. www.novikovgroup.ru.

Da Cicco Trattoria $$, 13/12 Profsoyuznaya. Family-style tavern with tasty Italian fare, pizzas and desserts. Metro Profsoyuznaya. www.cicco.ru.

Discreet Pleasures of the Bourgoisie $$, 24 Bol Lubyanka. Serving Italian food 24 hours a day. Metro Trubnaya. www.bourjousia.ru.

Dorian Gray $$$, 6/1 Kadashevskaya Emb. Homemade pasta and good seafood dishes and tiramisu. Metro Tretyakovskaya. www.doriangray.ru.

La Cipolla d'Oro $$$, 39 Ul Gilyarovskovo, A proud winner of Best Italian restaurant abroad, it serves delicious Italian classics. Metro Prospekt Mira. www.cipolla.ru.

Lemoncello $$$, 32/1 Bol. Serpukhovskaya. Tasty Italian dishes. Metro Serpukhovskaya. www.lemoncello-restoran.ru.

Mario's $$$$, 17 Klimashkina,. One of the city's top Italian restaurants with beautiful summer garden dining. Metro Barrikadnaya.

Pasta and Basta $$, 4 Sretensky Bulvar (open 24 hours) this restaurant specializes in pasta with over 20 types. Metro Chistiye Prudy. www.pastaandbasta.ru.

Peperoni $$$, 17 Petrovka. Arkady Novikov's Italian restaurant, with a take away shop next door. Metro Trubnaya. www.novikovgroup.ru.

Piccolino $$, 11 Kolobovsky Lane. An inexpensive and cosy Italian trattoria. Metro Trubnaya.

Pinocchio $$$$, 4/2 Kutuzovsky. An upscale trattoria housed in a Neo-Classical-style dining room that serves delicious Italian cuisine and wines. Metro Kutuzovskaya (several other locations). www.pinocchio-rest.ru.

Produckty $$ (Products), 5 Bersenevsky Lane in Bldg 1, located in the Red October Factory complex, serves up Italian food with affordable prices.

Roberto $$$, 20 Rozhdestvensky Bulvar. Italian chef with truly tasty and authentic dishes. Metro Chistiye Prudy.

Semplice $$, 6 Chaplygina. Fresh pasta and pizza. Metro Chistiye Prudy. www.semplice.ru.

Settebello $$$, 3 Sadovaya-Samotechnaya (in Puppet Theatre), Mediterranean specialities from imported Italian ingredients. DJ's Friday/Saturday. Metro Tsvetnoi Bulvar. www.settebello.ru.

Spago $$, 1 Bol Zlatoustinsky Per. Wide-range of exotic Italian fare. Metro Lubyanka.

Truffel $$$, 12/27 Gnezdnikovsky Lane. Truffle can be added to any of the superb Italian dishes. Metro Tverskaya.

Venezia $$, 4/3 Strastnoi Bulvar. Tasty Italian fare. Metro Pushskinskaya. Another location is at 17 Shabolovka. www.trattoria-venezia.ru.

JAPANESE
Moscow is a city of fanatics for Sushi Bars, and numerous chains have opened about town, such as: **Dai Sushi** (www.daisushi.ru), **Gin-notaki** (www.gin-notaki.ru), **More Sushi** (www.moresushi.ru), **Planet Sushi** (www.planetsushi.ru), **Take** (www.takesushi.ru), **Tanuki** (www.tanuki.ru), **Yakitoria** (www.yakitoriya.ru) and **Yaposha** (www.yaposha.com).

Bamboo Bar $$$, 8/1 Presnenskaya Emb. From Japanese sushi to Chinese dim sum with other Asian fare. Large selection of sake and other cocktails. Metro Vystavochnaya.

Not Far East $$$$, Another of Novikov's special restaurants, the interior was designed by Japanese designers. Impressive dishes include Kamchatka King crab. Metro Pushkinskaya. www.novikovgroup.ru.

Kyoto $$$$, 14 Strasvoi Bulvar. High-quality Japanese cuisine in luxurious surroundings. Metro Chekhovskaya. www.kyotorest.ru.

Nobu $$$$, 20/1 Bol. Dmitriovskaya. The restaurant was personally opened by Chef Nobuyuki Matsukhisa and Robert de Niro. Perfect for Japanese gourmands. Metro Pushkinskaya.

Seiji $$$$, 5/2 Komsomolsky Pr. Chef Seiji Kusano has fish delivered straight from Japan several times a week. Delicious Kobe steaks as well. Metro Park Kultury. www. seiji.ru.

Tokyo Table $$, 4/3 Strastnoi Bulvar. Japanese café, open from 8am (serves breakfast) until midnight. Metro Chekhovskaya. www.tokyotable.ru.

Yoko $$$$, 5 Soimonovsky Proezd. The Restaurant (owned by Arkady Novikov), with views of the Cathedral of Christ Our Savior, flies in fish twice a week from the Tokyo auction market. Metro Kropotkinskaya. www.novikovgroup.ru.

JEWISH
Chagall $$, 47/3 Bol. Nikitskaya (inside the Jewish Community Center) Certified kosher by Moscow Rabbinical Court. Metro Barrikadnaya. www.chagall.ru.

Hummus $$, 19/9 Novosuschevsky Lane. Metro Marina Roshcha. www.thehummus.ru.

Jerusalem $$, 6 Bol. Bronnaya (by Synagogue). Tasty Kosher food. Metro Pushkinskaya. www.bronnaya.ru.

Yona Meat Restaurant $$, 5a 2nd Vysheslavtsev Lane (In Jewish Community Center) Metro Novoslobodskaya. www.mjcc.ru.

KOREAN
Koryo $$ 11 Ordzhonikidze, bldg 9. First North Korean restaurant in Moscow with a Pyongyang television feed up on its Sony TV. From kimchi and dumplings to *Pyongyang naegmyeon*—buckwheat noodles in a cold broth of meat, egg and chili paste, it offers both classic and spicy, along with sushi and sashimi. A quote by Kim Jong II is "Before a dish can be placed on the menu, one must first gather its ingredients." Savor the wisdom and the food. Metro Leninsky Prospekt.

MEXICAN
La Cantina $$$, 5 Tverskaya. One of the oldest Tex-Mex restaurants in the city, with bar and music in the evenings. Metro Okhotny Ryad. www.lacantina.ru.

Muchachos $$, 28 Komsomolsky Pr (in MDM Bldg) Great burritos, even for breakfast! Metro Fruzenskaya. www.muchachos.ru.

Pancho Villa $$$, 52 Bol Yakimanka. Whips up everything from burritos and fajitas to margaritas. Club and Latin music in the evenings. Metro Oktyabrskaya. www.panchovilla.ru.

Sombrero $$, 51a Bol Polyanka. Traditional Mexican food and cocktails. Metro Polyanka. www.sombrero.su.

MOROCCAN

Kasbar $$$ 53/6 Ostozhenka. Metro Park Kultury. www.kasbar.ru.

Ketama $$$, 5/6 Bol Dmitrovka. A two-level café with cosy seating; relax with delicious Moroccan food. Open 24 hours. Metro Okhotny Ryad. www.dvg.ru.

Marocana $$$, 1/15 Kotelnicheskaya Emb. Great specialities with couscous, tapas, hookahs and even Moroccan tea. Metro Taganskaya. www.marocana.ru.

Marrakesh $$$, 4/3 Strasnoit Bulvar. Arabian and Eastern favorites with Belly-dancing on weekends. Metro Pushkinskaya.

NEAR AND MIDDLE EASTERN

Al Andaluz $$, 13/16 Bol. Lubyanka. Lebanese food with an Arabic-style interior. Metro Lubyanka. www.al-andaluz.ru.

Bash na Bash $$, 4/2 Maroseika; Metro Kitai-Gorod. www.bashnabash.ru.

Damas $$$$ is nearby at 8 Maroseika. An Arabic restaurant with excellent Syrian, Lebanese and Italian dishes as well. www.damas-rest.ru.

Eastern Room $$, 3 Smolenskaya Sq (2nd Passage) Blend of Arabic, Indian and Asian fare with, of course, hookahs and belly dancing on Tue–Sat. Metro Smolenskaya.

Farsi $$, 2/1 Kutuzovsky Pr. Metro Kievskaya.

Gandhara $$$, 15/7 Rochdelskaya. The only Pakistani Restaurant in town that serves up meat, seafood and vegetarian dishes with traditional spices and curries. Metro Ul 1905 Goda. www.gandhara.ru.

Shafran $$$, 12/9 Spiridonyevsky Per. Near Patriarch Pond, the menu includes falafel, hummus, kebabs, Lebanese wines. Metro Pushkinskaya. www.restoran-shafran.ru.

Sindbad $$ 14 Nikitsky Bulvar. Delicious Lebanese cooking for a reasonable price. Metro Pushkinskaya. www.sindbad.ru.

Za Barkhanami (Behind the Sand Dunes) $$$ 3 Nizhny Kiselny Lane. Metro Kuznetsky Most. www.zabarhanami.ru.

RUSSIAN

The inexpensive **Yolki-Palki** restaurant chain with 40 branches in the city, serves Russian-style home cooking that includes soups, starters, snacks and main courses. www.elki-palki.ru. Another popular chain is Moo Moo (www.cafemumu.ru).

Art Klumba $$ is on the grounds of ArtPlay on the Yauza River with inexpensive yummy Russian cooking. Metro Chkalovskaya.

Bochka $$$$, 2 Ul 1905 Goda. Delicious Russian food prepared on a grill and served in a wood and brick-style medieval tavern. Metro Ul 1905 Goda. www.vbochke.ru.

Central House of Writers (**TsDL**) $$$$, 50 Povarskaya. In 1889 a countess had this elaborate dwelling built and today the restaurant serves recipes that are over 200 years old; specialties include Czar Nicholas Salmon, Quail Golitsyn and Veal Orlov. Metro Barrikadnaya. www.cdlrestaurant.ru or www.cdlart.ru.

Chaika (**Seagull**) $$$$, 7 Marksistskaya. An opportunity to experience unique 'molecular' dishes and cocktails—everything is a gastronomic artistic creation. Tasty breakfasts too. Open 10am–midnight. Metro Taganskaya. www.chaika-café.ru.

Count Orlov $$$$, 2 2nd Verkhny Mikhailovsky. This restored 18th-century manor, surrounded by a park and fountain, was once a residence of Count Orlov, a favorite of Catherine the Great. The three floors have restaurants where Russian and European dishes are served. Metro Shabolovskaya. www.graforlov.ru.

Dacha on Pokrovka $$, 18 Pokrovsky Bulvar. Contained within three rooms of an old-style mansion, the dacha serves delicious Russian home-cooked choices. Metro Kitai-Gorod.

Expeditsiya (**Expedition**) $$$ 6 Pevchesky Lane. Siberian restaurant with an adventurous décor and helicopter as a centerpiece. Unique Siberian cuisine such as Baikal fish soup, polar partridge, reindeer meat, Venison Stroganov, and cold alcoholic infusions. The complex also has its own Banya (sauna) and shop of adventure goods. Metro Kitai-Gorod. www.expedicia.ru.

Galereya Khudozhnikov (**Artists' Gallery**) $$$, 19 Prechistenka. Located inside the Tsereteli Gallery of the well-known Russian artist and sculptor. The menu is Russian with European fushion. Metro Kropotkinskaya. www.gal-h.ru.

Godunov $$$$, 5/1 Teatralnaya Sq. Set inside the refectory of the former Zaikonospassky Monastery that dates back to the reign of Boris Godunov, the three halls are decorated like Boyar chambers with arched ceilings. Dishes are cooked according to ancient culinary recipes, and live Russian music is performed in the evenings. Metro Teatralnaya. www.godunov.net.

Grand Imperial $$$$, 9/5 Gagarinsky Per. Located in the old mansion of Prince Kurakin, with elegantly-prepared Russian cuisine. Metro Kropotkinskaya. www.grandimperial.ru.

Kitchen $$, 16/16 Pokrovka. Tasty Russian fare. Metro Chistiye Prudy. www.kitchencafe.ru.

Kitezh, 23/10 Petrovka. Set in a 17th-century interior near the St Peter Monastery, the menu offers classic Russian fare as prepared in the days of old. Interestingly, Kitezh was a legendary town that could magically disappear from the enemy at the sound of a bell. Metro Pushkinskaya.

Kvartira (Apartment) 44 $$, 22/2 Bol Nikitskaya. Cosy Soviet-style apartment now converted into a cosy bar and restaurant with delicious European food with an Italian flare, and jazz and piano music some evenings at 10pm. Metro Biblioteka Imeni Lenina. Another location is at 24/8 Mal. Yakimanka. Metro Polyanka. www.kv44.ru.

Kvas $$$, 29 Sadovaya-Chernogryazskaya. Situated in a pre-revolutionary setting and surrounded by photographs of old Moscow, the menu offers home-style Russian cooking, along with alcoholic infusions and kvas brewed on the premises. Metro Krasniye Vorota.

Lucien $$$, 65/1 Gilyarovskovo. Set in a noble interior, many dishes are made from 19th-century recipes; it also creates a splendid tea ceremony with a samovar heated on coals. Metro Prospekt Mira. www.lucienrest.ru.

Margarita's $$, 28/2 Malaya Bronnaya across the street from Patriarch's Pond. Good Russian food with live music in the evenings. Metro Pushkinskaya. www.cafe-margarita.ru.

Mari Vanna $$, 10 Spiridonovsky Lane. Ring the doorbell at No. 10, and enter this cosy home environment complete with bookcases and a television airing B/W old Soviet movies. Serving delicious Russian home cooking. Metro Pushkinskaya. www.marivanna.ru. Reservations are needed to enter!

Neglinny Verkh $$, 9/10 Kuznetsky Most. Tasty Russian food. Metro Kuznetsky Most. www.nverh.ru.

Oblomov $$$$, 1st 5 Monetchikovsky Lane. Named after the aristocratic hero of the 19th-century novel by Ivan Goncharov, it also offers set-priced meals of seven different courses and flavored vodkas. Metro Paveletskaya.

Oblomov in Presnya $$$, 2 1905 Goda St. Set in the style of a 19th-century country estate, it has a wide selection of traditional Russian food. Metro 1905 Goda. www.tabanton.ru.

Pavilion $$$, 7 Bol. Patriarshy Lane. Located in the old Boathouse by the pond with Russian food and vodkas. Open noon–5am. Metro Mayakovskaya. www.restsindikat.com.

Pelmeshka $, 8/1 Nikolskaya, A cafeteria that serves a variety of juicy *pelmeni*, dumplings with different fillings. Metro Pl Revolutsii. Down the street, at no 5, is Drova, a cheap self-service stolovaya with an all-you-can-eat buffet.

Petrovich Club $$$, 24/3 Myasnitskaya. Bar-club retro restaurant with artwork by cartoonist Andrei Bilzh. The menu is ladled with funny Soviet Propaganda. Quite popular, better make a reservation. (Open 1pm–5am) Metro Chistiye Prudy. www.club-petrovich.ru.

Petrov Vodkin $$$$, 3/7 Pokrovka. Moscow's first real vodka restaurant with more than 300 varieties; traditional Russian food, live piano and gypsy music in the eveninga. Metro Kitai-Gorod.

Pokrovskiye Vorota $$, 19 Pokrovka. Named after a popular film, this Soviet-style restaurant serves up delicious typical Russian dishes, and homemade kvas. Metro Kitai-Gorod. www.pokrovskievorota.ru.

Pushkin $$$$, 26 Tverskoi Bul. Flagship restaurant of Andrei Dellos and styled in the atmosphere of Imperial Russa. The second and third floors serve the restaurant; the first floor Chemist Hall is less expensive; summer roof terrace. Open 24 hours. Metro Tverskaya. www.cafe-pushkin.ru.

Razgulyai $$$ (Merrymaking), 11 Spartakovskaya. Named after an ancient square from the 17th century, this eating house has hearty Russian food with rooms decorated with traditional *gzhel* pottery and khokloma lacquerware. The poet Pushkin was christened at the church next door. Metro Baumanskaya.

Seven Fridays (Sem Pyatnits) $$$, 6 Vorontsovskaya. Traditional Russian cuisine in atmospheric setting. Metro Taganskaya.

Stolovaya 57 $$, on the third floor of GUM Dept Store on Red Square. An old-style cafeteria with inexpensive tasty Russian food. Metro Pl. Revolyutsii. www.gum.ru.

Sudar $$$, 36/2 Kutuzovsky Pr. Traditional Russian cuisine in an elegant setting. Metro Kutuzovskaya. www.sudar.ru.

Varvary $$$$, 8a Strasnoi Bulvar. Created by Anatoly Kumm, who calls his establishment a gastronomic theater! From 7:30pm–9pm, the guest experiences a very elegant affair with the transformation of 16 dishes around a theme which changes each season. Advance booking necessary and a set price per person (over $200). For all those non-molecular enthusiasts there is also an Italian menu. Metro Tverskaya. www.anatolykomm.com.

Vodka Bar $$$, 18b Leo Tolstoy St. Russian dishes and extensive vodka list. Metro Park Kultury. www.vodkabar.ru.

Yar $$$$, 32/2 Leningradsky Pr. (in Sovietsky Hotel). Founded in 1862, this legendary restaurant hosted Pushkin, Chekhov, Shalyapin and even Rasputin. Russian and European cuisine with evening variety shows. Metro Belorusskaya.

SOUTH AMERICAN

Brazilliero $$,10 Arbat. Brazilian food. Metro Arbatskaya. www.braziliero.ru.

El Gaucho $$$$, With three locations, offers delicious Argentina fare, with steaks and ribs cooked on an open fire grill, and served with the best of Argentine wines. Waiters are dressed in costume to reflect the Gaucho cowboy. www.elgaucho.ru.

Navarros $$$, 23/4 Shmitovsky Proezd. Peruvian specialities. Metro Ulitsa 1905 Goda. www.navarros.ru.

TATAR

Idel $$, 8 Tatarsky Lane. The only wild Tatar place in town. Metro Novoslobodskaya. www.cafeidel.ru.

THAI

Baan Thai $$, 11 B. Dorogomilovskaya. Thai food, curries, vegetarian dishes and sushi. Metro Kievskaya. www.baanthai.ru.

Buddha Bar $$$, 2 Tsvetnoi Bulvar, Chic interiors and fushion-style cuisine as Thai prawns and sesame tuna. Trendy DJs play at night. Metro Tsvetnoi Bulvar.

Shanti $$$, 2/1 Myasnitsky Proezd. Thai and Vietnamese with a tapas bar and special chutney menu. Metro Krasniye Vorota. www.shanti.ru.

TIBETAN

Tibet Himalaya Restaurant $$, 10 Nikolskaya. Metro Lubyanka.

Shangshung $$, 19 Pokrovka. A cosy restaurant that serves Tibetan-style food. Metro Kitai-Gorod.

UKRAINIAN

Shinok $$$$, 2 Ulitsa 1905 Goda. Ukrainian-themed restaurant (a *shinok* is a roadside tavern) with a staged farmyard in the center. House special is *varenki* boiled dumplings. Sat/Sun have an all-you-can-eat brunch from 1pm–6pm. Open 24 hours. Metro Ulitsa 1905 Goda. www.shinok.ru.

Taras Bulba Korchma $$, an inexpensive chain of Ukrainian restaurants (15 locations) with a large choice of dishes and flavored vodkas. Decor designed to resemble a traditional *hata* or single-room country home. www.tarasbulba.ru.

Uvaga $$$ 9 Arbat. Traditional Ukrainian fare in three halls. Metro Arbatskaya. www.uvaga.tv.

UZBEK

An inexpensive restaurant chain is **Chaihona No 1** (Tea Room No 1) with Uzbek cooking, comfy sofas, hookah pipes and DJ sets. www.chaihona.com.

Beloye Solntse Pustiny $$$, (named after the Soviet film, *White Sun of the Desert*), 29 Neglinnaya. Uzbek cuisine and wines. Evening gypsy entertainment. Metro Tsvetnoi Bulvar. www.bsp-rest.ru.

Dzhon-Dzholi, 21 Ul Tverskaya. The dining room is an open kitchen where chefs prepare all the Uzbeki favorites. Metro Pushkinskaya.

Khodzha Nasreddin v Kivye (named after a Bukhara folk tale) $$$, 10 Pokrovka. The first hall is modeled on a square in Khiva and the second on a harem. Uzbek dishes with nightly belly dancing. Metro Kitai-Gorod. www.nasreddinhiva.ru.

Kishmish, 28 Novy Arbat. (kishmish is a dried grape or raisin) Decorated as an Uzbek *chaikhona* or teahouse, it serves tasty *shashlik* kebabs and *plov* with a great salad bar. Metro Smolenskaya.

Navoi $$$, 25 Universitetskaya Pr. Uzbeki chef with traditional and delicious national dishes. Metro Kievskaya. www.restaurant-navoi.ru.

Sherbert $$$, 32 Sretenka, feast on Uzbek specialities, while smoking a hookah and watching a belly dance show. Open 24 hours. Metro Sukharevskaya. (Two other locations) www.scherbet.ru.

Utskuduk (Under an Open Sky), 6 Vorontsovskaya. Cozy, airy restaurant where diners lounge on plush pillows while eating tasty Uzbek dishes. Metro Taganskaya.

Vostochny Kvartal (Eastern Quarter), 45/24 Arbat, Well-known Uzbek-style restaurant on the trendy Arbat. Metro Smolenskaya.

Uzbekistan $$$$, 29/14 Neglinnaya. As one of the city's oldest restaurants (opened in 1957), it has an exotic interior with plush cushions, along with hookah pipes and evening belly dancing. The kitchen makes its own chutneys, jams and other sweets. Open noon–3am. Metro Teatralnaya. www.uzbek-rest.ru.

VEGETARIAN

Avocado $$, 12/2 Chistoprudy Bulvar All organic vegetarian dishes with soups and salads and lots of avocado. Special oxygen cocktails. Open 10am–11pm. Metro Chistiye Prudy.

Fresh $$, 11 Bol Dmitrovka, Food prepared with no animal products; fresh food, salads, and fruit & vegetable juices. Metro Teatralnaya. www.freshrestaurant.ru.

Jagannath $$, 11 Kuznetsky Most. All vegetarian dishes and big salad bar with an Indian-themed décor and attached health food shop. Daily 11am–11pm. Metro Kuznetsky Most.

Sok $$, 15 Lavrushinsky Lane, vegetarian and vegan options with other soup, salad, pasta choices and freshly-squeezed *Sok* or juices. Metro Tretyakovskaya.

VIETNAMESE

The inexpensive **Vietcafe** restaurant chain has a large menu of Vietnamese dishes, a good bar list and DJ playing in the evenings. www.vietcafe.ru.

Fragant River $, 11 Tokmakov Lane. This traditional Vietnamese Restaurant also offers delicacies such as frog legs and rattle-snake liqueur. Metro Baumanksaya.

SHOPPING

Shopping in Moscow is now like any other large city. Everything from mega malls, shopping centers and boutique stores to supermarkets, farmer's markets and smaller kiosks are scattered throughout the city. Most are open from 9/10am to 8/9pm, and close earlier on Sunday. Since many places do not provide bags (or a *paket* can be bought for a few rubles), always take some type of carrying bag along for purchases. Bring small bills, for often the seller will not have change. Some stores require you to check in large bags at the front with a security guard before entering. At markets make sure you understand if the price is per kilo or item; these areas also tend to be crowded, so beware of pickpockets. In theory, anything over 100 years old cannot be taken out of the country. Before purchasing an antique always check to see if you are allowed to take it out over the border—particularly icons, artwork and samovars; otherwise it could be confiscated at customs upon departure. (Beware of fake icons, artwork and lacquer boxes.) In theory, anything 'art like' that looks like it was made before 1941 may need special permission to leave the country. It can be assessed at *RosOkhranKultura* at 7/2 Kitaigorodsky Pr. (Metro Kitai-Gorod). Bring the item (or a photo of it) and your receipt. Custom officials will issue a receipt for tax paid (permission to exit), which you show to customs on your way out of Russia.

Russian policy on **caviar** purchase has changed, and they now take the Endangered Species of sturgeons very seriously. Be aware that black caviar (sturgeon caviar) is now under very tight legal controls, and it is not recommended to buy it. Red caviar (salmon caviar) on the other hand is completely legal to purchase (there is a limit on how much one can exit the country with) and is just as delicious.

ART GALLERIES

Moscow is booming with a plethora of art galleries, studio and exhibition space and centers for contemporary art. The Moscow Times (www.themoscowtimes.com) carries a listing of current exhibits. Most galleries are closed on Mondays.

GARAGE CENTER FOR CONTEMPORARY CULTURE in Gorky Park at 9/45 Krymsky Val (Metro Park Kultury) Founded by entrepreneur Dasha Zhukova, this large art and cultural center is aimed at showcasing contemporary and avant-garde Russian and foreign art. The center was first housed in a large temporary pavilion (located by Pioneer Pond, turn left after the Central entrance), designed by Japanese architect Shigeru Ban, and made out of huge cardboard-like tubes. A new larger permanent two-story building, designed by Dutch architect Rem Koolhaus, known as **Garage Gorky Park**, includes exhibition galleries, a creative center for children, auditorium, offices, an Art Book Shop and Garage Café. (The center will also be expanding into the neighboring Hexagon Pavilion once renovation is complete.) Open 11am–9pm, Fri/Sat/Sun until 10pm, garageccc.com/en.

RED OCTOBER FACTORY DISTRICT (across the river bridge from Savior Cathedral, metro Kropotkinskaya.) **Lumiére Brothers Photo Gallery** 3/4 Bolotnaya Emb. (A second branch is at 10 Krymsky Val, Metro Oktyabrskaya.) Focuses on Soviet art and photographs from 1920–1950, and also exhibits contemporary Russian photographers. www.lumiere.ru. In the same area is the **Pobeda Gallery** (www.pobedagallery.com) and **Igor Kormyshev Gallery**.

WINZAVOD CENTER FOR CONTEMPORARY ART, 6 Syromyatnichesky Lane (Metro Kurskaya). Formerly a wine-bottling factory, the area has been converted into exhibition and studio space for Russian artists and is home to Moscow's most prestigious galleries. The complex also includes a design studio, and other shops, boutiques and cafés. Galleries include:

Aidan Gallery, founded by Azerbaijani artist, Aidan Salakhova. www.aidangallery.ru/en.

Marat Guelman's Gallery, an exhibition of works of contemporary Russian artists, along with performance art. www.guelman.ru.

XL Gallery has exhibits of Russian and foreign contemporary art. http://xlgallery.artinfo.ru/.

VinkoRajic (or Regina) Gallery, 6/1 4th Syromyantnichesky Lane. A collection of modern art work, this gallery is also known for its often shocking art performances. www.regina.ru.

ArtPlay on Yauza, near Winzavod, at 10 Nizhnaya Syromyatnichesky, occupies the complex of the former Manometer factory. Mainly a design center with furniture showrooms and antique stores, there are also rotating art exhibits, and the Art Clumba Café. Metro Okyabrskaya. www.artplay.ru.

Arielio Galery, 1 Manezhnaya Square. One of the city's largest exhibition halls, it hosts everything from art and photo works to fashion shows. Okhotny Ryad www.manegemoscow.ru.

Burganov House, 15 Bol Afansyevsky Lane. Comprised of several houses connected by courtyards, the space houses the art and sculptures of well-known artist Alexander Burganov; often the art and craft is going on around the displays. Metro Kropotkinskaya. www.burganov.ru.

Dom Gallery, 24 Bol. Ovchinnikovsky Lane. On the second floor of Club Dom, this gallery has rotating exhibits and installations. Metro Novokuznetskaya. www.dom. com.ru/gallery.

Dktkeekf Gallery, 3/3 Georgievsky Lane. The New Manège oftens hosts temporary exhibits of contemporary art and photography. Metro Teatralnaya. www.new-manege.ru.

Ekaterina Cultural Foundation, 21/5 Kuznetsky Most. Hosts a variety of exhibitions. Metro Lubyanka. www.mamm-mdf.ru/en.

Fabrika at 18 Parevedonovsky Lane, exhibits contemporary Russian and foreign art, with lectures and creative workshops. Metro Baumankskaya. www.proektfabrika.ru.

Glazunov Gallery, 13 Volkhanka. Opposite the Pushkin Museum, this mansion-museum houses the work of artist, Ilya Glazunov, famous for his enormous and colorful paintings that portray all types of events (including fanciful to political commentary) from Russian history, such as *Eternal Russia* and *Mystery of the 20th Century*. www.glazunov.ru.

G3Visas Gallery, 10/2 Bol. Sadovaya. Fine Art Gallery that exhibits artists from the 1960's through today. Metro Mayakovskaya.

Moscow Museum of Modern Art, 25 Petrovka. Housed in an 18th-century merchant's home, the space was converted into Moscow's first Contemporary Art Museum by renowned artist and sculptor, Zurab Tsereteli. With an impressive collection of 20th-century paintings, avant-garde art and sculptures, it also features contemporary artists. Sculpture garden in the courtyard. Metro Tverskaya. An additional branch of the museum is at 17 Yermolaevsky Lane. Metro Mayakovskaya. www.mmoma.ru/en.

M'ARS Contemporary Art Center, 5 Pushkarev Lane. This space contains ten exhibition halls, and a club. Metro Tsvetnoi Bulvar. www.marsgallery.ru.

Mulimedia Art Museum, 16 Ostozhenka. Formerly the House of Photography, this modern gallery is now an archive of historic and contemporary photography. The facility also hosts work by Soviet and contemporary artists. Metro Kropotkinskaya. www.mdf.ru or www.mamm-mdf.ru.

Naschokina Gallery, 12 Vorotnikovsky Land. Metro Mayakovskaya. www.domnaschokina.ru.

NikzTtbbzz Gallery, 10 Krymsky Val. Aside from the main space of the Tretyakov Gallery, there is also a permanent exhibition of the Tretyakov on Krymsky Val on 'Art of the 20th Century.' From Abstract to Soviet Propaganda, this is a rich collection of masterpieces from futurists Goncharova, Popova, Petrov-Vodkin and Chagall to such works as ' White Square on White' by suprematist, Kasimir Malevich and 'Improvisations' by expressionist Vassily Kandinsky. Metro Oktyabrskaya. www.

tretyakovgallery.ru. (See also Lumiére Gallery.) **Central House of Artists** (ЦДХ) is also located at 10 Krymsky Val, and contains studios, galleries and exhibition spaces with paintings and prints for sale. www.cha.ru.

PhotoSoyuz Gallery, 5 Pokrovka. Features work by modern Russian photographers. **Metro Kitai-Gorod**. www.photounion.ru.

Tsereteli Gallery of Fine Arts, 19 Prechistenka. Housed in the 18th-century Dolgoruky mansion, this gallery displays Zurab Tsereteli's primitive-style paintings and many sculptures. Metro Kropotkinskaya. www.tsereteli.ru. Next door is the **Russian Art Academy** which hosts temporary exhibits of Russian and foreign artists.

Tsereteli Studio Museum, 15 Bol. Gruzinskaya Studio space of the artist that exhibits his sketches, paintings, enamel art, small-scale models of his monuments, along with many sculptures in the courtyard (including Putin in his judo outfit). Metro Belarusskaya. www.mmoma.ru.

Zverevsky Center of Contemporary Art, 29/4 Novoryazanskaya. Exhibits and installation works by contemporary Russian artists. Metro Baumanskaya. www. zverevcenter.ru.

Near the Zverevsky Center, at 18 Perevedonovsky Lane, is **Proekt Fabrika** an art venue and functioning glass factory, along with architectural firms, a film studio and publishing house. The Aktovy Hall hosts dance, theatre and music performances each evening. www.proektfabrika.ru and www.aktzal.ru.

BOOKSTORES
(In English and other foreign languages)
Atlas, 9/10 Kuznetsky Most, Metro Kuznetsky Most. A large collection of maps of every area of Russia.

Biblio-Globus, 6/5 Myasnitskaya Street. Metro Lubyanka. www.biblio-globus.ru.

Bookhunter, 9 Krivokolenny Lane. Metro Chistiye Prudy. www.bookhunter.ru.

Britannica Book, 7 Bol Tartarskaya. Metro Novokuznetskaya. www.britannia-elt.ru.

Dom Knigi (House of Books), 8 Novy Arbat. Metro Arbatskaya.

House of Foreign Literature, 18/7 Kuznetsky Most. Metro Kuznetsky Most. www. mdk-arbat.ru.

Molodaya Gvardiya, 28 Bol. Polyanka. Metro Polyanka. www.bookmg.ru.

Moskva, 8 Tverskaya. Metro Tverskaya. www.moscowbooks.ru.

Respublika has four locations in town. (10 1st Tverskaya Yamskaya; Metro Mayakovsky). It is a book, music and gift shop all rolled into one, with a café too. www.respublica.ru.

DEPARTMENT STORES

Moscow is now packed with mega malls, shopping centers and department stores. The following are the largest and most popular, and centrally located. Most are open daily from 10am to 9/10pm. Many stores accept credit cards.

Berlin House, 5 Petrovka. Metro Teatralnaya.

Detski Mir (Children's World), 2 Teatralny Square. Metro Lubyanka. Renovated in 2008, the art deco building is a Moscow landmark. Stores, a multiplex theater and family entertainment zone.

Evropeisky (European) Shopping Center, 1 Kiev Square, Metro Kievskaya. One of the world's largest shopping centers, it has hundreds of stores and restaurants, along with a supermarket, movie theater, and an ice-skating rink.

Gostiny Dvor (Trading Rows), 4 Ilyinka, Metro Pl. Revolutsii (near Red Square). This 18th-century classic building housed the merchant stores, and is today made up of scores of shops and cafés.

GUM (State Department Store), 3 Red Square. Metro Okhotny Ryad. Two floors of shops, specialized boutiques and cafés. www.gum.ru.

Kursk Shopping Complex, Zemlyanoi Val. Metro Kurskaya, next to Kursk railway station. (Six floors, ten-screen cinema complex, 20-lane bowling alley, and food court.)

Okhotny Ryad (three-level underground shopping mall) on 1 Manezh Square in front of Red Square. Metro Okhotny Ryad. Stores, food courts and a 24-hour Time Online internet café. www.ox-r.ru.

Petrovsky Passazh, 10 Petrovka. Metro Kuznetsky Most.

Trading House Moscow, 31 Kutuzvosky Pr. Metro Kutuzvosky.

Tretakovsky Passazh, located next to Metropol Hotel on Teatralny Proyezd. Moscow's Rodeo Drive Shopping District (Armani, Gucci, Brioni). Metro Tretyakovskaya.

TsUM (Central Department Store), 2 Petrovka, Metro Teatralnaya.Filled with lots of designer labels and a café on the top floor. www.tsum.ru.

FASHION

Russian Fashion designers have garnered international recognition.

Alena Akhmadullina Boutique, 10/2 Nikolskaya. The St Petersburg designer gained international renown when designing an outfit for Angelina Jolie in the film *Wanted*. Designs around Russian themes. Metro Lubyanka. www.alenaakhmadullina.ru.

Art Lebedev Café, at 35 Bol. Nikitskaya (Metro Barrikadnaya) is owned by designer, Artemy Lebedev, and is a cool café offering many baked cakes and other sweets.

Chapurin Boutique, 21 Savinskaya Emb. Igor Chapurin began his career designing costumes for the theater; today his creative clothing is for both men and women, with even a children's line. www.chapurin.com.

Masha Tsigal Showroom, 1 Yauzskaya. Bright casual clothing that includes sweatshirts and T-shirts. Metro Kitai-Gorod.

Odensya Dlya Schastya (Dress for Happiness), 31 Pokrovka. This boutique carries fashions by a few unique designers, such as Oleg Biryukov. Metro Kurskaya.

Russkiya Ulitsa (Russian Street), 8/1 Bersenevskaya Emb (in the hip Red October district). This boutique stocks clothing and accessories from more than 50 up-and-coming Russian designers. Metro Kropotkinskaya. www.russian-street.ru.

Simachyov Boutique, 12/2 Stoleshnikov Lane, Metro Chekhovskaya. Denis Simachyov is known for his wild and creative styles inspired by diverse themes, from Russian sailors to gypsy nomads. The space also has a popular bar. www. denissimachev.com.

Valentin Yudashkin Boutique, 19 Kutuzovsky. One of Russia's best known designers, this classy boutique is also a showroom for his latest fashions. (His clothes are on display at the Louvre and the Met!) Metro Kievskaya. www. yudashkin.com.

FOOD STORE

Yeliseeyev's, 14 Tverskaya. Metro Pushkinskaya. See Special Topic on Yeliseyev's on page 595.

GIFTS AND SOUVENIRS

Many souvenir shops and kiosks are located throughout the city. Stroll down the Arbat, Izmailovsky market, or the Manege underground mall by Red Square. Tverskaya Street and the lanes around Kuznetsky Most are also good for souvenir browsing where you can find *matryoshka* dolls, hand-painted boxes, lacquerware, pottery, samovars and other handicraft items.

ARBAT runs along Stary Arbat, a pedestrian street. Good for souvenir shopping. **Skazka** (Fairy Tale) is at number 51 with lots of hand-painted dolls, toys and other handicrafts. Metro Smolenskaya. At numbers 11 and 25 are stores **Russkiye Chasovye Traditsii** (Russian Watch Tradition) that sells many brands of Russian watches. **Bukle**, at number 27, is the casual ware collection of Ludmilla Mezentseva, called Vereteno. At number 31 is **Embroidery and Lace**, and at number 49 is the **Army Store**.

Artefact Gallery, 30 Prechistenka, Metro Kropotkinskaya. Near the Academy of Art, this art mall houses a few dozen galleries where one can purchase paintings, sculptures, pottery, etc.

Dom Farfora (House of China) 17 1st Tverskaya-Yamskaya, Metro Belorusskaya. (Open 10am–9pm) With a wide variety of china, including tea sets. Down the street, at number 28, is **Karpov Chess** with hand-made chess sets.

Dom Knigi (House of Books), 8 Novy Arbat. Metro Arbatskaya. Has everything from books, calendars and postcards to a wide assortment of souvenirs.

Ikony Podarki, 17 Bol. Lubyanka, Metro Lubyanka. By the Vladimirsky Cathedral, this gift shop sells a wide variety of icons and other souvenirs. (Many churches have their own small shops.)

Jewelry: K Fabergé, 20 Kuznetsky Most. Owned by the granddaughter of the jeweler to the Czars, this lovely boutique contains unique jewelry, crystal, china and ceramic eggs. Metro Kuznetsky Most. www.moonstone.ru.

Vladimir Mikhailov is at 10 Nikolskaya, Metro Lubyanka. Expensive jewelry made from gems that include religious themes, icons and easter eggs.

Khudozheztvenny (Art) Salon, 12 Petrovka, Metro Chekhovskaya. (Open 11am–10pm). An artists' cooperative, this salon is filled with handicrafts, jewelry and paintings.

Ministerstvo Podarkov (Ministery of Gifts), 12/27 Maly Gnezdnikovsky Lane. Metro Pushkinskaya. (11am–9pm) The space contains artists' cooperatives where you can find many cool and clever gifts. Other outlets are at 7/9 Smolensky Bulvar, called the **Buro Nahodok**, (Metro Park Kultury) and **Podarky, Dekor & Podarky** at 28/2 Mal. Bronnaya (Mero Mayakovskyaya).

Russian Gift, 2 Zorge St, Metro Polezhaevskaya. (Open 10am–8pm) The complex is dedicated to preserving Russian folk tradition, and thousands of handicraft products are on display. www.russiangifts.ru.

Salon Podarkov (Gift Salon), 5 Myasnitskaya, Metro Lubyanka. (Open 11am–7pm; closed Sunday) This salon is an indoor gift market with dozens of individual stalls that sell every souvenir product imaginable, from arts and crafts to jewelry, linen and folk toys. (If you don't have time to journey out to Izmailovo Market, this is the place to shop.)

MARKETS OR *RINOK*

The markets are open daily from about 8am–6pm; Sun 8am–4pm. A better selection is usually found in the mornings, and on weekends. Here people sell fresh fruit and vegetables, flowers and other interesting wares. Bring a few empty bags to carry your purchases in. Beware of pickpockets and hustlers at the crowded markets.

Cheryomushkinsky Rinok, 1 Lomonovsky Prospekt, Metro Universitet. Along with food and plants, this market also sells homemade crafts. Metro Universitet.

Danilovsky Rinok, 74 Mytnaya; Metro Tulskaya. Produce, honey, meat, fish and flea market.

Dorogomilovsky Rinok, 10 Mozhaisky Val; Metro Kievskaya. Large food market that spills out around Kievsky Train Station.

Izmailvosky Rinok, Metro Izmailovsky Park. The **Izmailovsky Market** is best on weekends with a large selection of old items from icons to coins, and many handicraft products; great for gift and souvenir shopping. Metro Izmailovsky Park. (See page 218.)

Palashevsky (Fish Market), 3a Sytinsky. Metro Puskinskaya. Fresh and frozen fish, and caviar. Another place to buy fresh fish is the **Eldorado Market** at 1/3 Bol. Polyanka (metro Polyanka) which offers 40 types of fish; it also has a restaurant. Open 24 hours.

Tishinsky Rinok, Tishinskaya Square at 50 Bol. Gruzinskaya Street; Metro Belorusskaya. This is one of Moscow's oldest markets, rebuilt in 1996. It is now housed in a 3-story contemporary pyramid-shaped building. Next to the Western supermarket on the first floor are spaces for over 200 private vendors who sell everything from *tvorog* (cottage cheese) to pickles and preserves, along with meat, fish, fruit and flowers.

MUSIC

Check out **Transylvania** at 6/1 Tverskaya; metro Teatralnaya. A black metal door leads down to the shop, filled with room after room of CD's of different music genres. Sample Russian Rock songs, and pick up the latest Rock groups here.

Gorbushka Shopping Center, 8 Barklaya St. Metro Bagrationovskaya (near Fili). Open 10am–9pm. Located in a former furniture store, this large space sells music CD's and film DVD's on the second floor (many pirated) for cheap, along with other electronics.

MUSEUMS

Today Moscow has well over a hundred museums. Many ticket *kassa* close 30–60 minutes before actual closing time. Beware of duel pricing: a foreigner in Russia can still pay from double to five times more than locals at cultural sites such as museums and theaters. (One can try to have a Russian buy the ticket, but entrance guards are sharp at recognizing foreigners.) A photography/video permit is usually an extra fee. Showing an international Student ID (ISIC) may receive up to a 50 percent discount on the ticket price (as well as for Senior citizens). For museums in the Vicinity of Moscow and Golden Ring areas, see individual town locations. www.russianmuseums.info.

Airforce Museum located in Monino, 38 kms (24 miles) along the Gorky Hwy from

Moscow; Russia's largest aviation museum which functioned as an air base from 1932–1956. Open 9:30am–5pm (closed 1:30–2:15pm) and Sat 9am–2pm; closed Wed/Sun. www.moninoaviation.com.

Accordion Museum, 18 2nd Tverskaya-Yamskaya. Open 10am–5pm, Thursday 10am– 9pm, Wed/Sun 10am–6pm; closed Monday and last Friday of month. (Every third Sunday of month museum free). www.mosmuseumm.ru.

Andrei Bely Museum, 55 Arbat. Open 10am–6pm, Thursday noon–9pm; closed Mon/Tue and last Friday of month. Metro Smolenskaya.

Andrei Rublyov Museum of Old Russian Art, Spaso-Andronikov Monastery, 10 Andronevskaya Square. Open 11am–6pm, Thursday 2pm–9pm; closed Wednesday and last Friday of month. Metro Ploshchad Ilicha. www.rublev-museum.ru.

Armed Forces Central Museum, 2 Sovyetskoi Armii. Open 10am–5pm; closed Monday/Tuesday. Metro Novoslobodskaya. www.cmaf.ru.

Arkhangelskoye Estate Museum, Metro Tushkinskaya. Park is open 10am–6pm, Exhibitions 10am–5pm (Sat/Sun until 6pm); closed Mon/Tue and last Wed of month. www.arhangelskoe.su.

Bakhrushin Theater Museum, 31/12 Bakhrushina. Open 12–7pm, Thursday 1pm–9pm; closed Monday and last Friday of month (in summer, closed Mon/Tue). Metro Paveletskay.

Battle of 1812 Borodino Museum and **Kutuzov Hut**, 38 Kutuzovsky Pr. Open 10am–6pm, Thursday 10am–9pm; closed Friday and last Thursday of month. (Every third Sunday of month museum free). Metro Kutuzovskaya. www.1812panorama.ru/english.

Boyar Romanov House Museum, 10 Varvarka. Open 10am–5pm, Thursday 11am–6pm; closed Tuesday. Metro Kitai-Gorod.

Brothers Lumière Center of Photography, 3/1 Bolotnaya Emb. Open noon–9pm, Sat/Sun 11am–9pm; closed Monday. www.lumiere.ru.

Bulgakov House Theater, 10 Bol Sadovaya (thru Arch, Apt 50). Open 1pm–11pm, Fri/Sat 1pm–1am. Metro Mayakovskaya. www.dombulgakova.ru.

Chambers of Old English Yard, 4a Varvarka. Open 10am–6pm, Thursday 1pm–6pm; closed Monday and last Friday of month. Metro Kitai-Gorod. (Occasionally closed for restoration.)

Chekhov House Museum, 6 Sadovaya-Kudrinskaya. Open 11am–6pm, Wednesday/ Friday 2pm–8pm; closed Sun/Mon and last Friday of month. Metro Barrikadnaya. www.my-chekhov.com (For the Chekhov Museum in Melikhovo, www.chekhov-melikovo.com.)

Contemporary History of Russia Museum, 21 Tverskaya. Open 10am–6pm, Thursday noon–9pm, Sat/Sun 11am–7pm; closed Monday. Metro Tverskaya. www.sovr.ru.

Cosmonauts Memorial Museum, 111 Prospekt Mira. Open 10am–6pm; closed Monday and last Friday of month. Metro VDNKh.

Decorative and Folk Art Museum, 3 Delegatskaya. Open 10am–6pm, Thursday 10am–9pm, Saturday 11am–7pm, Sunday 10am–6pm; closed Tuesday and last Monday of month. Metro Tsvetnoi Bulvar. www.vmdpni.ru.

Dostoevsky Memorial-Apartment, 2 Dostoevskovo. Open 11am–6pm, Wed/Thur 1pm–8pm; closed Monday and last day of month. Metro Novoslobodskaya.

Folk Graphics Museum, 10 Maly Golovin Lane. Open 10am–5pm, Thur 2pm–9pm, Sat/Sun noon–5pm; closed Monday. Metro Sukharevskaya. www.russianlubok.ru.

Gogol House, 7a Nikitsky Bulvar. Open noon–7pm, Thursday 2pm–9pm, Sat/Sun noon–5pm; closed Tuesday and last day of month. Metro Arbatskaya. www.domgogolya.ru.

Glinka Music Culture Museum, 4 Fadeeva. Open 11am–7pm, Thursday noon–9pm, Sunday 11am–6pm; closed Monday and last day of month. Metro Mayakovskaya. www.glinka.museum.

Golubkina Museum, 12 Bol Lyovshinsky Lane. Open noon–7pm, Sat/Sun 10am–5pm; closed Monday and Tuesday. Metro Park Kultury.

Gorky (Ryabushinsky) House Museum, 6 Malaya Nikitskaya. Open 10am–5pm, Wed/Fri noon–7pm; closed Mon/Tue and last Friday of month. Metro Arbatskaya.

Gulag History Museum, 16 Petrovka. Open 11am–7pm, Thursday noon–9pm; closed Monday and last Friday of month. Metro Kuznetsky Most. www.gmig.ru.

Herzen Memorial House, 27 Sivtsev Vrazhek Lane. Open 11am–6pm, Thursday 2pm–8pm; closed Monday and last day of month. Metro Kropotkinskaya.

Historical State Museum, 1/2 Red Sq. Open 10am–6pm, Thursday 11am–8pm; closed Tuesday. Metro Okhotny Ryad. www.shm.ru.

History of Moscow Museum, 12 Novaya Sq. Open 10am–6pm, Wed/Fri 11am–7pm; Thursday 1pm–8pm; closed Monday. Metro Kitai-Gorod/Lubyanka.

Icon House, 4 Spiridonovka. Open noon–10pm (with evening concerts). Metro Tverskaya. www.dom-ikony.ru.

Icon Museum, 3 Goncharnaya Emb. Open 11am–7pm; closed Wednesday. Metro Taganskaya. Free admission. www.russikona.ru/en.

Jewish Museum and Tolerance Center, 11 Obraztsova (Bldg. 1a). Open noon–10pm, Friday 10am–3pm; closed Saturday. Metro Savyolovskaya. www.jewish-museum.ru.

Krasnya Presnya Museum, 4 Bolshoi Predtechensky Lane. Open 10am–6pm, Thursday noon–9pm, Sat/Sun 11am–7pm; closed Monday. Metro Krasnopresnenskaya.

Kremlin Museums Red Square, open 10am–5pm (ticket office 9:30am–4.30pm); closed Thursday. www.kreml.ru/en (tickets can be purchased online).

Lermontov Memorial House, 2 Malaya Molchanovki. Open 1pm–5pm, Wed/Fri 2–6pm; closed Monday and Tuesday. Metro Arbatskaya (occasionally closed for renovation.)

Lights of Moscow Museum, 3–5 Armyansky Lane. Open 10am–6pm, Thursday 11am–8pm; closed Sat/Sun. Metro Kitai-Gorod.

Literary Museum, 28 Petrovka. Open 11am–6pm, Thursday 2pm-8pm; closed Monday. Metro Chekhovskaya.

Matryoshka Museum, 7 Leontevsky Lane. Open 11am–6pm (until 5pm on Friday); closed Sun/Mon. Metro Arbatskaya.

Mayakovsky Museum, 3 Lubyansky Proyezd. Open 10am–5pm, Thursday 1–8pm; closed Wednesday and last Friday of month. Metro Lubyanka.

Meyerhold House Museum, 12/11 Bryusov Lane (Apt 11). Open noon–6pm; closed Mon/Tue and last Friday of month. Metro Okhotny Ryad.

Museum of Moscow, 2 Zubovsky Bulvar. Open 10am–8pm, Thursday 11am–9pm, Sat/Sun 10am–8pm; closed Monday and last Friday of month. Metro Park Kultury. www.mosmuseum.ru.

Museum of Modern Art, 25 Petrovka. Open noon–8pm, Thursday 1pm–9pm; closed every third Monday of month. Metro Chekhovskaya. (Other branches at 10 Gogolevsky Bulvar, metro Kropotkinskaya; 17 Yermolayevsky Lane, Metro Mayakovskaya; 9 Tverskoi, Metro Tverskaya.) Every third Sunday museum is free. www.mmoma.ru/en.

Museum of Private Collections (branch of Pushkin Museum), 14 Volkhonka. Open 12–7pm, Thur/Fri 11am–9pm; closed Mon/Tue. Metro Kropotkinskaya. www.artprivatecollections.ru.

Museum of Russian Impressionism, on site of former Bolshevik Factory, Leningradsky Prospekt; 10 minute walk from Belorusskaya Metro northwest towards Tverskaya and the Hippodrome. Sponsored by private collector, Boris Mints, the museum is due to open in 2015.

Nemirovich-Danchenko Memorial Apartment, 5/7 Glinishchevsky Lane (Ent 5, Fl 3, Apt 52). Open 11am–5:30pm; closed Mon/Tue. Metro Okhotny Ryad. www.mxat.ru/museum.

Novodevichy Convent, 1 Novodevichy Proezd. Open 10am–6pm. Closed Tuesday and first Monday of month. Cemetery open daily 9am–6pm. Metro Sportivnaya.

Operetta Theater Museum, 6 Bolshaya Dmitrovka (inside Operetta Theater). Metro Okhotny Ryad.

Oriental Art Museum, 12 Nikitsky Bul. Open 11am–8pm, Thursday noon–9pm; closed Monday. Metro Arbatskaya. www.orientmuseum.ru.

Ostrovsky Museum Center (author Nikolai Alexeeyevich), 14 Tverskaya. Open 11am–7pm, Thursday 1pm–9pm; closed Monday. Metro Pushkinskaya.

Ostrovsky Memorial House (playwright Alexander Nikolayevich), 9 Malaya Ordynka. Open noon–7pm, Thursday 1pm–9pm; closed Mon/Tue and last Friday of month. Metro Tretyakovskaya.

Paleontology Museum, 123 Profsoyuznayal. Open 10am–6pm; closed Mon/Tue. Metro Tyoply Stan. www.paleo.ru.

Panorama View from the Empire skyscraper in Moscow City. View from the 58th floor and a 40-minute tour of the building. Daily weeknight 6pm–10pm or on weekend from 11am–10pm. Sign up online at smotricity.ru. Metro Vystavochnaya.

Planetarium, 5 Sadovaya-Kudrinskaya. Open 10am–9pm. Closed Tuesday. Metro Barrikadnaya. www.planetarium-moscow.ru.

Polytechnical Museum, 3 Novaya Sq. Metro Lubyanka. www.polymus.ru/en (may be closed for reconstruction).

Prokofiev Museum, 6 Kamergersky Lane. Open 11am–7pm, Thursday noon–9pm, Sunday 11am–6pm. Closed Mon/Tue and last Wed of month. Metro Teatralnaya.

Pushkin Memorial Apartment, 53 Arbat. Open 10am–6pm, Thursday noon–9pm; closed Mon/Tue and last Friday of month. (Every third Sunday of month museum is free). Metro Smolenskaya. www.pushkinmuseum.ru.

Pushkin Museum, 12/2 Prechistenka. Open 10am–6pm, Thursday noon–9pm; closed Monday and last Friday of month. (Every third Sunday of month museum is free.) Metro Kropotkinskaya. www.pushkinmuseum.ru.

Pushkin House Museum, 36 Staraya Basmanaya. Open 10am–6pm. Thursday noon–9pm; closed Mon/Tue and last Friday of month. (Every third Sunday of month museum is free.) Metro Krasniye Vorota. www.pushkinmuseum.ru.

Pushkin Museum of Fine Arts, 12 Volkhonka. Open 10am–7pm, Thursday 10am–9pm; closed Monday. Metro Kropotkinskaya. www.arts-museum.ru.

The **New Western Art Gallery** is next door at 10 Volkhanka, www.newpaintart.ru.

Richter Memorial Apartment, 2/6 Bol Bronnaya. www.sviatoslav-richter.ru. By appointment.

Roerich Museum, 3/5 Maly Znamensky Lane. Open 11am–7pm. Closed Monday. Metro Kropotkinskaya. www.icr.su. (Due to lack of funding, museum may be closed.)

Sakharov Human Rights Museum, 57/6 Zemlyanoi Val. Open 11am–7pm; closed Monday. (Entrance is free.) Metro Kurskaya. www.sakharov-center.ru.

Shalyapin Memorial House, 25 Novinsky Bul. Open 11am–7pm, Thursday noon–9pm, Sunday 11am–5pm; closed Mon/Tue and last Friday of month. Metro Barrikadnaya. www.shalyapin-museum.org.

Skryabin Memorial Museum, 11 Bolshoi Nikolopeskovsky Lane Open 11am–7pm, Thursday 11am–9pm; closed Monday and last Friday of month. (Every third Sunday of month museum is free). Metro Arbatskaya. www.anscriabin.ru.

St Basil's Cathedral, 2 Red Square. Open 11–6pm (winter until 5pm). Metro Okhotny Ryad. www.saintbasil.ru.

Stanislavsky Memorial Museum, 6 Leontevsky Lane. Open 11am–6pm, Thursday 11am–9pm; closed Mon/Tue. Metro Tverskaya. www.mxat.ru/museum.

Tchaikovsky Museum, 46/54 Kudrinkskaya Sq. Open 10am–7pm; closed Mon/Tue. Metro Barrikadnaya.

Tolstoy Country Estate Museum, 12 Pyatniktskayal. Open 10am–6pm, Thursday noon–8pm; closed Monday. Metro Novokuznetskaya. www.tolstoymuseum.ru.

Tolstoy Museum, 11 Prechistenka. Open 10am–6pm, Thursday noon–8pm; closed Monday. Metro Kropotkinskaya. www.tolstoymuseum.ru.

Tolstoy Museum, 21 Lva Tolstovo. Open 10am–6pm, Thursday noon–8pm; closed Monday. Metro Park Kultury. www.tolstoymuseum.ru.

Tropinin Museum, 10/1 Shchetininsky Lane. Open 12–7pm Sat/Sun 10am–5pm; closed Tue/Wed. Metro Polyanka/Tretyakovskaya.

Tretyakov Gallery, 10/12 Lavrushinsky Lane. 10am–6pm, Thur/Fri 10am–9pm; closed Monday. Metro Tretyakovskaya. (**Gallery** also at 10 Krymsky Val, Metro Park Kultury; open 10am–7:30pm; closed Monday.) www.tretyakovgallery.ru.

Tsvetaeva House Museum, 6 Borisoglebski. Open 12–6pm, Thursday noon–9pm; closed Monday and last Friday of month. Metro Arbatskaya. www.dommuseum.ru.

Turgenev Museum, 37 Ostozhenka. Open 10am–6pm, Thursday noon–9pm; closed Mon/Tue and last Friday of month. (Every third Sunday of month museum is free.) Metro Park Kultury.

Vasnetsov (Appolinary) Memorial Apartment, 6 Furmanny Lane. Open 11am–5pm; closed Sun/Mon. Metro Chistiye Prudy.

Vasnetsov (Victor) Memorial House, 12 Vasnetsov Lane. Open 10am–5pm; closed Mon/Tue and last Thursday of month. Metro Sukharevskaya.

Vysotsky Cultural Museum, 3 Nizh. Tagansky. Open 11am–5.30pm; closed Sun/Mon. Metro Taganskaya.

Yermolova Memorial House, 11 Tverskoi Bul. Open noon–7pm, Thursday 1pm–9pm; closed Mon/Tue and last Friday of month. Metro Tverskaya.

Zoological Museum of Moscow University, 6 Bolshaya Nikitskaya. Open 10am–5pm; closed Monday and last Tuesday of month. Metro Aleksandrovsky. zmmu.msu.ru.

Zoo, 1 Bolshaya Gruzinskaya. Renovated in 1996. Open 10am–8pm, in winter, 10am–5pm; closed Monday. Metro Barrikadnaya. www.moscowzoo.ru.

LIBRARIES

There are 15 major libraries in Moscow where one can browse through books in reading rooms, but not take books out.

Library of Foreign Literature, 1 Nikoloyamskaya. Monday–Friday 9am–7.45pm; Saturday/Sunday 9am–6pm. Metro Kitai-Gorod. www.libfl.ru.

Russian State Library (formerly Lenin Library), 3 Vozdvizhenka. Open 9am–9pm; closed Sunday. Metro Biblioteka Imeni Lenina. www.rsl.ru.

Russian Art Library, 8/1 Bolshaya Dmitrovka. Open 8am–7pm; closed Sunday. Metro Teatralnaya. www.liart.ru/en.

Russian Historical Library, 9 Starosadsky Per. Monday–Friday 9am–9pm; Saturday 10am–8pm; closed Sunday. Metro Kitai-Gorod. www.shpl.ru.

ENTERTAINMENT
THEATERS

There are nearly 100 theaters and concert halls in Moscow. Theater, concert and circus performances on weekdays begin between 6pm and 8pm with matinée performances on weekends, with an earlier evening show. Tickets can be bought directly from theater and concert hall box offices, or from kiosks called 'Teatralnaya Kassa', found on streets, in underpasses, or inside/near entrances to many metro stations. (Tickets can often be reserved through a travel/service bureau in your hotel.) Many of the larger theaters have their own websites where tickets can be purchased online. For information on theater repertoires look for the free addition of the Moscow Times, in English, which lists theater, concert, circus and cinematic events (www.themoscowtimes.com); also check out www.expat.ru. You can also find out event schedules and order tickets by calling (495) 258-0000 or go online at www.parter.ru.

Amadeus Musical Theater, 12 Pyatnitskaya (in Leo Tolstoy Museum). www.amadei.ru.

Bolshoi Opera and Ballet Theater, 1 Teatralnaya Sq. Metro Teatralnaya. www.bolshoi.ru.

Bulgakov House and Theater, 10 Bol. Sadovaya (thru arch, Apt 50). Metro Maykovskaya. www.dombulgakova.ru.

Chekhov Academic Art Theater, 3 Kamergersky Lane. Metro Teatralnaya. www.mxat.ru/english.

(Chekhov Intl. Theater Festival: www.chekhovfest.ru/en).

Children's Musical Theater of Natalya Sats, 5 Vernadsky Pr. Metro Universitet. www.teatr-sats.ru.

Dramatic Arts Theater, 20 Povarskaya. Metro Arbatskaya. www.sdart.ru.

Cirque du Soleil at Luzhniki, www.cirque-du-soleil.me.

Estrada Theater, 20/2 Bersenevskaya Emb. (Red October District). Metro Borovitskaya. www.teatr-estrada.ru.

Fomenko Studio Theater, 29 Tarasa Shevchenko Emb. Metro Kutzovskaya. www.fomenko.theatre.ru.

Gogol Drama Theater (Gogol Center), 8a Kazakova. Metro Kurskaya. www.gogolcenter.ru.

Golden Mask Arts Festival, www.goldenmask.ru.

Hermitage Theater, 3 Karetny Ryad, Hermitage Gardens. Metro Pushkinskaya. www.ermitazh.theatre.ru.

Jewish Events, www.jewish-museum.ru.

Lencom Theater, 6 Malaya Dmitrovka. Metro Tverskaya. www.lenkom.com.

Maly Theater, 1/6 Teatralnaya Sq. Metro Teatralnaya. www.maly.ru.

Maly Theater Branch, 69 Bolshaya Ordynka. Metro Dobryninskaya. www.maly.ru.

Mayakovsky Theater, 19 Bolshaya Nikitskaya. Metro Pushkinskaya. www.mayakovsky.ru.

Mayakovsky Theater Branch, 21 Pushkarev. Metro Sukharevskaya. www.maykovsky.ru.

Meyerhold Center, 23 Novoslobodskaya. Metro Mendeleyevskaya. www.meyerhold.ru.

Mosoviet Theater, 16 Bolshaya Sadovaya. Metro Mayakovskaya. www.mossovet.theater.ru.

New Ballet, 25/2 Basmannaya. Metro Kraniye Vorota. Contemporary dance. www.newballet.ru.

New EuropeanTheater (NET), 10/46 Strasnoi Bulvar. Metro Chekhovskaya. www.netfest.ru.

Novaya (New) Opera, 3 Karatny Ryad. Metro Mayakovskaya. www.novayaopera.ru.

Obraztsov Puppet Theater, 3 Sadovaya Samotechnaya. Metro Mayakovskaya. www.puppet.ru.

Operetta Theater, 6 Bolshaya Dmitrovka. Metro Okhotny Ryad. www.mosoperetta.ru.

Pushkin Drama Theater, 23 Tverskoi Bul. Metro Pushkinskaya. www.teatrpushkin.ru.

Rossiya Theater, 2 Pushkin Sq. Metro Pushskinskaya. www.stage-musical.ru.

Russian Army Theater, 2 Suvorov Sq. Metro Novoslobodskaya. www.teatrarmii.ru.

Satircon Theater, 8 Sheremetyevskaya. Metro Marina Roshcha. www.satirikon.ru.

Satire Theater, 2 Triumphfalnaya Sq. Metro Mayakovskaya. www.satire.ru.

Sovremennik (Contemporary) Theater, 19 Chistoprudny Bul. Metro Chistiye Prudy. www.sovremennik.ru.

Stanislavsky Drama and Arts Theater, 23 Tverskaya. Metro Tverskaya. www.stanislavskydrama.ru.

Stanislavsky & Nemirovich-Danchenko Musical Theater, 17 Bolshaya Dmitrovka. Metro Chekhovskaya. www.stanmus.com.

Stas Namin Theater, 9 Krymsky Val, Bldg 33 (in Gorky Park). Metro Okyabrskaya. www.stasnamintheatre.ru.

Taganka Drama and Comedy Theater, 76/21 Zemlyonoi Val. Metro Taganskaya. www.taganka.theatre.ru.

Theater on Malaya Bronnaya, 4 Malaya Bronnaya. Metro Tverskaya. www.mbronnaya.theater.ru.

Vakhtangov Theater, 26 Arbat. Metro Arbatskaya. www.vakhtangov.ru.

Vysotsky Center, 3 Nizhny Tagansky Tupik. Metro Taganskaya. www.visotsky.ru.

Winzavod Art Complex at 14th Syromyatnichesky Lane (Bldg 6). Metro Kurskaya. With theater, music and dance performances. www.platformaproject.ru.

Yermolova Drama Theater, 5 Tverskaya. Metro Okhotny Ryad. www.ermolova.ru.

CONCERT HALLS

Crocus City Hall (Crocus City in northwestern Moscow, metro Myakinino). www.circus-hall.com.

Helikon Opera on Arbat, 11/2 Novy Arbat. Metro Arbatskaya. www.helikon.ru.

House of Unions Concert Hall, 1 Bolshaya Dmitrovka. Metro Okhotny Ryad. www.domsojuzov.ru.

Galina Vishnevskaya Opera Center, 25 Ostozhenka. Metro Park Kultury. www.opera-centre.ru.

Gnesin Music Concert Hall, 1 Maly Rzhevsky Lane. Metro Arbatskaya. www.gnesin-academy.ru.

House of Composers, 8/10 Bryusov Lane. Metro Okhotny Rad. www.house-composers.ru.

Kremlin Palace, the Kremlin (entrance through Borovitsky Gate). Metro Aleksandrovsky Sad. (The box office is near the metro station in the underground passage.) www.kremlin-gkd.ru.

Moscow Philharmonia, 31 Tverskaya. Metro Mayakovskaya. www.meloman.ru.

MMDM Moscow International House of Music, 8/52 Kosmodamianskyaya Emb. Metro Pavletskaya. www.mmdm.ru. This modern glass building has three halls, including Sverdlov Hall, with Russia's largest organ. It is home to the National Philharmonic of Russia (founded in 1991). www.nfor.ru/en.

Novaya Opera, 3 Karetny Ryad. Metro Mayakovskaya. www.novayaopera.ru.

Philharmonic Chamber Hall, 4/31 Triumphfalnaya Sq. Metro Mayakovskaya. www.meloman.ru. (Moscow Concert Hall is nearby at number 1. www.moscow-hall.ru.)

Pushkin Concert Hall, 12/2 Prechistenka (in Pushkin Museum). Metro Kropotkinskaya. www.pushkinmuseum.ru.

Tchaikovsky Conservatory Complex, 13 Bol. Nikitskaya Ul. Metro Biblioteka imeni Lenina. The complex is composed of four concert halls (including the Bolshoi and Maly) and several lecture buildings. www.mosconsv.ru. Once every four years, the prestigious Tchaikovsky Festival is held here, where competitions take place for the top pianist, cellist, violinist and opera singer. www.tchaikovsky-competition.net.

CIRCUSES

Bolshoi New Circus, 7 Vernadsky Pr. Metro Universitet. www.bolshoicircus.ru.

Clown Theater of Teresa Durova, 6 Pavlovskaya. Metro Tulskaya. www.ugolokdurova.ru.

Durov Animal Theater, 4 Durov. Metro Prospekt Mira. www.ugolokdurova.ru.

Kuklachyov Cat Theater, 25 Kutuzovsky Pr. Metro Kievskaya. www.kuklachev.ru.

Nikulin's Old Circus, 13 Tsvetnoi Bulvar. Metro Tsvetnoi Bulvar. www.circusnikulin.ru.

Summer Tent Circus, Nyeskuchny Gardens. Metro Oktybrskaya.

CINEMAS

Moscow has more than 100 cinemas. Most show movies in Russian; some screen foreign films in original language with subtitles.

35MM, 47/24 Pokrovka. Metro Krasniye Vorota. www.kino35mm.ru/en.

Center of Documentary Drama, 2/7 Zubosky Bulvar. Metro Park Kultury. www.cdkino.ru.

Dome Theater, 18 Olympisky Pr (in front of Renaissance Hotel). Metro Prospekt Mira. Films shown in original language, usually English. www.domecinema.ru.

Dome Restaurant in the Red October complex (3/10 Bersenevsky Lane, Metro Kropotkinskaya) has a 60-seat Cinema Lounge where art and foreign flicks are screened in the evenings (free with order).

Five Stars on Novokuznetskaya, 8 Sredny Ovchinnikovsky Lane (in Arkadia Mall) Another theater is at 25 Bakhrushina. Metro Paveletskaya. www.5zvezd.ru.

GUM Theater in the GUM shopping arcade on Red Square. www.gum.ru/projects/kinozal.

Illuzion Cinema, 1/15 Kotelnicheskaya Emb. Metro Taganskaya (inside Seven Sisters Bldg). Great for Soviet film buffs, as it screens both popular and obscure Soviet-era films.

Moscow Film Festival (annually) www.moscowfilmfestival.ru.

Oktyabr (October), 24 Novy Arbat. Metro Arbatskaya. With multiple screens, the largest auditorium seats 1500; films in 3D and IMAX. (Karo Films own many multiplex cinemas throughout the city.) www.karofilmru.

Roland Cinema, 12 Chistoprudy Bulvar. Metro Chistiye Prudy. Two theaters that show arthouse-type films and also hosts film festivals.

NIGHTCLUBS AND MUSIC

Transitioning from relatively no entertainment possibilities at all during the Soviet era—today, Moscow's nightlife is legendary. The Russian capital's nightclubs and bars have an international reputation for having some of the wildest partying crowds, the most cutting edge bands and innovative DJ's, the most glitzy and glamorous décor, the toughest face control and, of course, the most beautiful women in the world.

There are now hundreds of places offering nightly entertainment from all-night dance clubs to other music venues offering everything from rock, disco and techno to jazz, folk and blues. From upscale and expensive to eclectic and quirky, the varied nightspots have something for everyone where you can grab a bite, have a drink, listen to music and dance the night away.

Be aware that many have cover charges along with expensive drinks. Be prepared to walk through a metal detector upon entering, and pass the *feis kontrol* (face control) scrutiny of big bodyguard doormen. All serve food and alcohol, and most now take credit cards. (Keep a keen eye on your belongings.) Many venues function as restaurants or cafés by day and turn into a club at night. During the week, they are usually open from noon to midnight, and on Thur/Fri/Sat nights until 5 or 6am.

(Some are closed on Monday.) Remember the metro closes by 1am and does not open until 5:30–6am, and taxi rides home at night can be expensive.

Arma17, 5/17 Nizhny Susalny. Metro Kurskaya. The industrial factory area behind the Kursky train station houses a number of clubbing hotspots, and this one is popular with guest DJ's, dancing, and parties that carry on well into the next morning. (See Discoteque) www.arma17.ru.

ArtefaQ, 32 Bol Dmitrovka. Metro Chekhovskaya. Open 24 hours. Set on four levels, the complex functions as a gallery, restaurant, bar, and club. Music and dancing (mostly Disco) is on the basement level. www.artefaq.ru.

Artist Nightclub, 15/44 Rochdelskaya. Metro Krasnopresnenskaya. Glittery and extravagant, the compound has five bars and a large LED display around the main dance floor (along with scantily-clad dancers on podiums), with a second floor restaurant and lounge. Live music bands and DJ.s. www.artistclubmoscow.ru.

B2 Club, 8/1 Bol. Sadovaya. Metro Mayakovskaya. As one of the city's largest live music clubs (with five floors and seven bars), it offers everything from rock and jazz to Latino and ska. Open daily noon–6am. www.b2club.ru.

BB King (Moscow House of Blues), 4/2 Sadovaya Samotechnaya. Head thru the arch and look for half a red Cadillac and then go down into the cellar for a Cajun dish and blues music that kicks off around 8pm; club open till midnight. www. bbkingclub.ru.

Bard Club (Gnezdo-gluharya), 20 Tsvetnoi Bulvar. Metro Tsvetnoi Bulvar. (Bolshoi Hall and New Hall). Features different Russian bard performers and has song nights. www.gnezdogluharya.ru.

Chinese Pilot Dzhau Da (Kitaisky Letchik Jao Da), 25 Lubyansky Pr. Trendy club that hosts bands from all around Russia and Europe. Concerts on Thursday begin at 10pm and Fri/Sat at 11pm. (Free concerts on Monday nights) Metro Kitai-Gorod. www.jao-da.ru.

Chinatown, next door to the Pilot at 25/12, this basement café-bar has all types of music from folk and jazz to hip hop and pop rock. Evening concerts begin at 9pm, with a second on weekends at 10:30pm. www.chinatown.ru.

Club Che, 10 Nikolskaya. Metro Lubyanka. Open 24 hours. This restaurant-club, decorated in the style of the Cuban revolution, has Cuban-Mexican food, lots of cocktail choices and Cuban cigars. Evenings bring in DJ's, dancing and live music, with salsa nights. www.clubche.ru.

Discoteque, 5/5 Nizhny Susalny Lane. Metro Kurskaya. This industrial area behind the Kursky train station houses a number of clubbing hotspots in the former factories. DJ's and dancing (and the ubiquitous girls dancing in cages) until the wee morning hours. (See Arma 17.)

Duma Club, 11 Mokhovaya. Metro Okhotny Ryad. Good food, music and dancing till 6am. www.clubduma.ru.

Forte Jazz Club, 18 Bol. Bronnaya. Metro Pushkinskaya. Open 2pm to midnight. One of the city's oldest jazz clubs, the expansive hall with a raised stage has 9pm evening concerts of mainly jazz and modern blues (and singing). Food is primarily European. www.forteclub.com.

Garage Club, 8 Brodnikov Lane. Metro Polyanka. Open 24 hours. Most popular on Wednesday and Sunday nights with dancing to Rhythm & Blues. It is also packed in the wee hours of Sat/Sun morning when clubbers show up for the famous after party. www.garageclub.ru.

Gogol, 11 Stoleshnikov Lane. Metro Chekhovskaya. Open 24 hours. An informal and affordable club with good nosh, drinks and evening music in three rooms as a Parisian café, a beer hall, and, in summer, the action is in the courtyard under a gigantic circus tent. The music varies from funk and experimental to rock and disco. Concerts Thur–Sat at 9pm or 10pm. www.gogolclubs.ru.

Icon Club, (formerly Rai Moscow), 9 Bolotnaya Emb. Red October District. With one of Moscow's largest club spaces, it has lots of dance space and an iconic décor without straight angles, Live music, DJ's and cutting-edge acts; open Fri/Sat from 10pm until 6:30am. Tough face control. www.iconclub.ru.

Igor Butman Jazz Club, Named one of the world's top 100 jazz clubs by US Downbeat Magazine, it features acoustic mainstream, jazz rock, funk, soul, ethno jazz and blues performed by the world's best jazz musicians. The Club has two locations: one in the Taganka Theater Building at 2 Verkhnaya Radishchevskaya (Steaks Restaurant), Metro Taganskaya; and, the second is at 36/11 Novoslobodskaya, Metro Mendeleevskaya (by the Art Café). Concerts usually begin at 8:30pm. Often legendary Russian saxophonist, Igor Butman, and his big band play at one of the venues on Monday nights. www.butmanclub.ru.

Imperia Lounge, 5/7 Mantulinskaya. Metro 1905 Goda. Owned by Russian Standard Vodka, the upscale lounge has multiple levels, along with go-go dancers on pedastals. Expensive and elite, it also has über face control to get in. Open Thur–Sat 11pm–5am. www.imperialounge.livejournal.com.

Krizis Zhanra, 16/16 Pokrovka, Metro Chistiye Prudy. Inexpensive, popular nightclub filled with both locals and expats. Sun–Thur concerts at 9pm and Fri/Sat at 11pm. www.krizis zhanra.ru.

Krysha Mira, Tarasa Shevchenko Emb. Metro Kievskaya. With its rooftop terrace, known as the 'Roof of the World,' this exclusive party haven and ultratight face control nightclub even has an unmarked entrance. (It is located about 500m past the Radisson Hotel by the metal staircase.) www.kryshamira.ru.

Masterskaya, 3/3 Teatralny Proezd, Metro Teatralnaya. This quirky place is composed of a club, café and theater; the crowd tends to arrive after the 10pm evening concert and dancing begins at around 1am. www.mstrsk.ru.

Posh Friends, 5 Pushkinskaya Sq, Metro Pushkinskaya. Popular with the young, hip and well-dressed crowd, one has to be quite posh to get by face control. Italian/Japanese menu. Open Mon–Sat 11pm–6am. www.poshfriends.ru.

Propaganda, 7 Bol. Zlatoustinsky Lane. Metro Kitai-Gorod. One of the city's longtime popular nightclubs (open in 1997), it is a café by day, and the warehouse opens up at night to music and visiting DJ's. Friendly and affordable, Sunday is usually Gay Night. It is open daily noon to 6am. www.propagandamoscow.com/en.

Rhythm Blues Café, 19/2 Starovagankovsky. Metro Aleksandrovsky Sad. A country and blues joint that looks like an American Roadside tavern inside with live bands and line dancing. Fri/Sat open till 6am. www.rhythm-blues-café.ru.

Rolling Stone, 3 Bolotnaya Emb. Metro Kropotkinskaya. Sun–Thur noon-midnight and Fri/Sat noon–6am. Located in the trendy Red October Factory District, the place is covered by pics of the namesake magazine, with a small dance floor and all kinds of live music. (Even though casual, face control often decides who enters.)

Simachyov, 12/2 Stoleshnikov Lane. Metro Chekhovskaya. Owned by famous fashion designer, Denis Simachyov, it functions as a boutique-café by day and a very hip bohemian nightclub by night (with private dining available in catholic confessionals). Dress, as there is face control to gain entrance. www.bar.denissimachev.com.

Soho Rooms, 12 Savvinskaya Emb. Metro Sportivnaya. Open 24 hours. One of the hottest, most expensive and exclusive (super face control) of Moscow's nightclubs. With nightly music, bands and singers, it even has a swimming pool. www.sohorooms.com.

Solyanka, 11 Solyanka. Metro Kitai-Gorod. Located in an 18th-century merchant's house, the place serves as a restaurant /bar by day (with delicious Russian/European food), and guest DJ's come in on Thur/Fri/Sat nights and start spinning around 11pm until sunrise. Dress for face control. www.s-11.ru.

LGBT VENUES

Useful websites are: www.gay.ru, www.gaytours.ru, www.lesbi.ru and www.gayrussia.eu.

12 Volts, 12/2 Tverskaya. Metro Mayakovskaya. Open 6pm–6am. Opened by the founders of Moscow's lesbian movement, both gays and lesbians gather in this comfortable social café club with drinks and music. (Buzz at the door for admission) www.12voltclub.ru.

Central Station. In 2014, Russia's largest gay nightclub was forced to close after a series of antigay attacks and a decision from the Moscow Arbitration Court to end the club's building lease.

Maki Café, 3 Glinishchevsky Lane. Metro Pushkinskaya. (Fri/Sat open to 5am). This bar-restaurant (with Maki rolls as the speciality) gets lively in the evenings, and is frequented by gay and lesbians.

Propaganda, 7 Bol. Zlatoustinsky Lane. Metro Kitai-Gorod. Functions as a restaurant by day and lively club at night with DJ music and dance floor, with Sunday gay party night. www.propagandamoscow.com.

Secret, 7 (Bldg 8) Nizhny Susalny Lane. Metro Kurskaya. This gay nightclub (in a former factory area behind Kursky Station) has two dance floors and live music or drag shows on weekends. Free admission for any male aged 18–22.

TRAVEL AGENCIES AND TOUR COMPANIES

Hundreds of travel companies have opened throughout the city. If you have a touring question, inquire at a hotel service desk; they can also direct you to a speciality agency.

American Express, 33/1 Usacheva. Tel. (495) 933-8400. Can help with credit cards/travellers' checks air tickets, hotels, transfers and visas. Metro Okhotny Ryad. www.americanexpress.com.

Express to Russia, travel services and tours about Russia. www.expresstorussia.com

Capital Tours, 4 Ilyinka, Ent 6 (Gostiny Dvor) Metro Okhotny Ryad. Tel. (495) 232-2442. Specializes in Moscow city (day and night), museum and Kremlin Armory tours. www.capitaltours.ru. (The Moscow Visitor's Information Center is also in Gostiny Dvor.)

Go To RUSSIA Travel, 3/4 Pyatnitskaya (3rd fl) Tel. (495) 225-5012 (In US: 888-263-0023). Provides extensive travel services, visas, hotels, apartments. www.gotorussia.com.

Intourist Travel, 15/5 5th Donskoy Proezd. Metro Leninsky Pr. Offers air tickets, packaged tours, hotel and transportation services. www.intourist.com.

Marlis Travel, offers a wide selection of tours all around Russia. www.marlis.ru.

Online Moscow Resource, www.moscow.info.

Patriarshy Dom Tours, 6 Vspolny Per. Tel. (495) 795-0927 (in the States, 650-678-7076) offers a variety of English-language tours on any subject with trips also outside the city. (With a visa and booking dept as well.) The Moscow Times and other magazines post their monthly schedules. http://russiatravel-pdtours.netfirms.com or www.toursinrussia.com.

BOAT EXCURSIONS

Capital Shipping Company, www.cck-ship.ru. Frequent tour boats depart along the Moscow River May to September from the port by Kievsky Train Station and run roundtrip to the Novospassky Bridge (by the monastery), with stops at Sparrow Hills (Moscow University), Gorky Park, Krymsky Bridge, Bolshoi Kammeny (Big Stone) Bridge opposite the Kremlin, and Ustinsky Bridge near Red Square. (Once you get off the boat, your ticket is finished). Alternatively, buy a more expensive full day ticket, which allows you to get on and off at any stop. CCK also offers longer boat excursions outside of Moscow.

Radisson River Cruises, www.radisson-cruise.ru. The Radisson Royal (the former Hotel Ukraine) operates river boats that leave from its dock in front of the hotel. Check the website for departure schedules. The boats are equipped with ice cutters, so cruises operate year-round.

Longer Boat Cruises from one to several weeks ply routes north to St Petersburg and Valaam/Kizhi in Lake Ladoga, and east to Golden Ring towns (as Uglich, Kostroma and Yaroslavl). For more information, check out: **Mosturflot** (www.mosturflot.ru), **Orthodox Cruise Company** (www.cruise.ru), **Rechturflot** (www.rtflot.ru) and **Vodohod** (www.bestrussiancruises.com).

BUS EXCURSIONS—LOCAL AND OUTSIDE MOSCOW

Central Bus Station, 75 Shchyolkovskoye Shosse. Buses to Vladimir, Ivanovo, Kostroma, Rybinsk, Suzdal, Tula, Yaroslavl, Nizny Novgorod and other towns. Metro Shchyolkovskoye.

Capital Tours operates bus sightseeing excursions that depart from in front of the Bolshoi with 13 stops about town. Called Hop on-Hop off, the ticket is good for 24 hours to ride on the red double-decker buses. (There are Night Tours as well). Office is in Gostiny Dvor at 4 Ilyinka (Ent 6/7). www.capitaltours.ru.

CAR RENTALS

Moscow has nearly 50 car rental agencies scattered around the city offering everything from compact cars to minibuses. Inquire if a rental car comes with or without a driver. Check your insurance coverage; most policies do not cover Russia. (Make sure rental coverage includes theft and break-ins.) You may need to present an International Driver's License. Officers of the Road Patrol Service, who stand out on the street, can put out their stripe stick anytime and wave you to pull over (one does not have to do anything wrong to be pulled over). An officer can issue on the spot fines; try to negotiate, pay only in rubles, and get a receipt. Since most Moscovites drive without insurance, and driving in Moscow can be a traffic nightmare, it is recommended not to rent a car unless excursions into the countryside are planned. Always inquire at the hotel service desk for rental recommendations. If you do not know the city, it really is easier, safer (and cheaper) to get around with public transportation.

Avis, www.avis.com.

Europcar, www.europcar.com or www.europcar.ru.

Hertz, www.hertz.com or www.hertz.ru.

Thrifty, www.thrifty.com or www.thrifty.ru.

HEALTH CLUBS AND SAUNAS (*BANYAS*)

Most high-end hotels have fitness clubs, often with saunas and pools. For non-guests, some offer a daily entrance fee to use the facilities. Scores of other health clubs and western-style fitness centers (as Gold's Gym and Planet Fitness) have opened throughout the city. Check at your hotel service desk for recommendations.

Saunas/*Banyas***: (see also Special Topic on page 438) Bring towels (or else pay to rent one) and flip-flops. Men and women have their own separate sauna areas, and often the location has more expensive private banyas to rent as well. Many have *veniki* or bunched birch leaves for sale. For a listing of banyas and saunas: www.par. ru. If you have time for only one, go to Sandunovskiye!

Sandunovskiye (Sanduny) Bani, 14 Neglinnaya (Bldgs 3–7). Metro Kuznetsky Most. www.sanduny.ru.

Bani na Presnye (Krasnopresnensky), 7 Stolyarny Per. Metro Ulitsa 1905 Goda. www.baninapresne.ru.

Expeditisya, 6 Pevchesky Lane. Metro Kitai-Gorod. (Private banya) www. expedicia.ru.

Lefortovskiye Bani, 9a Lefortovsky Val, Metro Aviamotornaya. www.banya-lefortovo.ru.

Pokrovskiye Bani, 12 Bagrationovsky Proezd (Fili), Metro Bagrationovskaya. www. pokrovskiebani.ru.

Rzhevskiye Bani, 3a Bannyi Proezd, Metro Prospekt Mira. www.rzhevskie-bani.ru.

Spa Palestra, 4a 2nd Pechannaya, Metro Sokol. www.palestra.ru.

SPORTS

Bicycling: Moscow is a dangerous city for bicycling, but riding in parks, along the river, and other off-road areas can be delightful. (Some good biking locations are: Gorky, Bitsevsky, and Sokolniki Parks, the Botanical and NeskuchnyGardens, Sparrow Hills Nature Preserve and Krylatskoye Hills, which was built for the 1980 Olympics and has the only track venue for bike racing.) Bicycles are not allowed on the metro (except for folding ones), and to ride the local eletrichka trains you must buy a special ticket (bikes are permitted on long-distance trains with weight limits).

Some of the larger parks offer bike rentals. **Oliver Bikes** rent out all types from collapsible road bikes to mountain and tandem. 2/3 Pyantskaya, Metro Novokusnetskaya. Open noon–10pm; Sat/Sun 10am–10pm. www.bikerentalmoscow.com. For weekend city rides and longer distance tours around Russia (from the Golden Ring to Siberia) the **Russian Cycle Touring Club** organizes these. www.rctc.ru.

Golf: **Moscow Country Club in Nahabino** has Russia's first pro-18 hole/par-72 course, designed by American Robert Trent Jones, II (see Vicinity section). Located 30 kilometers (18 miles) northwest of the city at 31km Volokolamskoye Hwy, the complex also has a driving range, pro shop, hotel, fitness center/spa and tennis club. www.moscowcountryclub.ru/en.

Hiking: The Hikers, Walkers and Nature Lovers Club offers organized hikes. www. hike.narod.ru.

Vorobyovy Gory or Sparrow Hills is the wooded area by Moscow University (Metro Vorobyovy Gory) now an ecological park. Following the south shore of the Moscow River brings you to a series of wooded hiking trails (and a sandy beach), which you can walk along from the bank to University Square. (An ecotrain also runs along the river bank.) As another alternative, a paved pathway begins in the Neskuchny Gardens and stretches for several kilometers along the river. At the park's eastern entrance, bikes are for rent (and skates in winter). www.vorobyovy-gory.ru (See also Walking Tours).

Horse Riding: Equestrian Sports Center at 33 Balaklavsky Pr, has show jumping and an indoor riding school. Metro Kaluzhskaya. For a list horse rental locations, see www.expat.ru (Horse Riding Clubs).

Horse Racing takes place at the Hippodrome at 22 Begovaya, usually on Saturday, Sunday and Wednesday. Metro Begovaya. Includes mainly harness and thoroughbred horse racing (small-stake betting), with flat racing, *kachalki-in* lightweight carriages and occasional troika events in winter.

Ice Skating: There are scores of both indoor and outdoor skating rinks in Moscow. For a location listing, www.expat.ru (Skating Rinks). A year-round indoor rink is on the top floor of the **Evropeisky Shopping Center** at 1 Kievsky Sq, Metro Kievskaya. In winter, the ponds of **Gorky Park** turn into the city's largest ice-skating rink and the grounds into a huge cross country ski area. Both skates and skis can be rented in the park. (Bring an ID for the rental.)

Moscow Marathon is held annually in the city. The course, which is flat, starts at Red Square in front of St. Basil's Cathedral, and follows the Moscow River, passing the Kremlin, Cathedral of Christ Our Saviour, Gorky Park and the Peter the Great Monument, and finishes close to Red Square. www.moscowmarthon.org.

Skiing: Parks Sokolniki, Bittsa and Luzhniki offer cross-country skiing rentals and trails. Cross-country is also popular in nearby Peredelkino. If you have your own gear, practically any park allows cross-country skiing when it snows.

Snow Dome Snej (Snow) An indoor facility, it has both ski and snow board runs (and rents out equipment and warm clothes.) Located in northwestern Moscow (area of Krasnogorsk) north of Crocus City. www.dome.snow24.com.

The **Krylatskoye Ski Center** offers low-altitude mountain (3 runs, 10 lifts), cross-country, skiing and ice skating. **Ski Park Volen** (1 Troitskaya, www.volen.ru) is an hour's drive north of the city along the Dmitrovskoye Hwy. It has seven ski lifts, over 13 snowboard and ski trails, ice skating, cafés, restaurants, and wooden cottages for rent. **Sorochani**, in Kurovo Village (www.sorochany.ru), has ten runs.

Swimming and Water Park: Akvapark Kva-Kva Water Park, Yaroslavskoye Hwy (in XL Shopping Center). Metro VDNkH then by bus N333, about 1km past the MKAD. Filled with water slides, a Tsunami water ride and wave pools. Great for kids, and adults can enjoy the warm hydromassage jets. www.kva-kva.ru.

Chaika Sports Complex, 1/3 Turchaninov Land. Metro Park Kultury. Has an outdoor 50-meter, eight-lane swimming pool heated year round, along with a gym. www.chayka-sport.ru.

Luzhniki Stadium, 24 Luzhetkskaya Emb. Metro Sportivnaya. Besides the giant stadium (built for the 1980 Olympics) the complex has two outdoor and two indoor swimming pools (heated year-round), a sauna, gym and tennis court (Luzhniki, which seats 80,000, is also home to teams in Russia's football (soccer) league as Spartak and Torpedo.) www.luzhniki.ru.

Walking Tours: Capital Tours also offers walking tours of many museums and sites, such as the Kremlin, Lubyanka and the Gulag Museum. www.capitaltours.ru.

Patriarshy Dom Tours offers a variety of English-language tours on any subject with trips also outside the city. The Moscow Times and other magazines post their monthly schedules. http://russiatravel-pdtours.netfirms.com.

Moscow Mania has organized over 50 walking tours about the city for history fanatics. (There is also a branch in St Petersburg.) www.mosmania.com.

BANYA БАНЯ

Nothing gives a better glimpse into the Russian character than a few hours spent in a Russian bathhouse or *banya*. This enjoyable sauna tradition has been a part of Russian culture for centuries. Traditionally each village had its own communal bathhouse where, at different times, males or females would stoke wood-burning stoves and spend hours sitting, sweating and scrubbing. The Greek historian Herodotus reported from Russia in the fifth century BC: 'They make a booth by fixing in the ground three sticks inclined toward one another, and stretching around them wooden felts, which they arrange so as to fit as close as possible; inside the booth a dish is placed upon the ground, into which they put a number of red hot stones; then they take some hemp seed and throw it upon the stones; immediately it smokes, and gives out such a vapor that no Grecian hot mist can exceed; they are immediately delighted and shout for joy, and this hot steam serves them instead of a water bath.' Later, many homes even had their own private *banyas* and during winter naked bodies could be seen rolling in the snow after a well-heated sweat. Today the *banya* ritual is still a much favored pastime; this invigorating washing process has proudly been passed down from generation to generation.

Banya complexes are located throughout Russian cities and towns. Some of the most popular in Moscow are the Sandunovskiye, established in 1896, and Bani na Presnye, and St Petersburg the Dyegtyarniye or Krugliye Bani. Here the bather can spend many a pleasurable hour in the company of fellow hedonists. No *banya* is complete without a bundle of dried birch branches with leaves, called *veniki*, usually sold outside the complex. *Berioza* (birch) has always been a popular symbol of Russia, which claims more birch than any other country in the world. Buy a switch of birch and enter to pay the *banya* fee; the cashier can then point you in the right direction—*muzhchina* (men) or *zhenshchina* (women). Once inside, an attendant is there to assist you.

Many older *banyas* are housed in splendid prerevolutionary buildings; marble staircases, mirrored walls and gilded rooms, are filled with steam and cold pools. The best *banyas* even offer massage, body scrubs, facials and a café. Bring along a towel, shampoo, head-cap and flip-flops; otherwise you can often rent them there. It is recommended to leave valuables behind, or give them to the attendant for safe-keeping if there is no place to lock them up.

There are three main parts of the *banya*: the sitting and changing room, the bathing area and the sauna itself. The bathing area is usually one immense room filled with large benches. Soak your *veniki* in one bucket filled with warm water (it prevents the leaves from falling off), while using another to rinse yourself. Then carry the wet branches into the hot *banya* (start out on the bottom level then slowly work your way up). The custom is to lightly swat the body with a bunch of birch leaves: this is believed to draw out toxins and circulate the blood. It is also traditional to whack each other, and since you will easily blend in like a native, you may find your *banya* buddy asking if you would like your own back gently swatted!

An old Russian folk-saying claims that 'the birch tree can give life, muffle groans, cure the sick and keep the body clean'. Cries of *oy oy, tak khorosho* (how wonderful) and *s lyokim parom* (have an easy steam) eminate from every corner. When someone, usually one of the *babushki* (grandmothers) or *dyedushki* (elderly men), get carried away with flinging water on the heated stones, moans of *khavatit* (enough) resound from the scorching upper balconies, when lobster-red bodies come racing out of the hot steamy interior. (Even though temperatures are lower than in Finnish or Turkish saunas, the humidity makes it feel hotter.) Back in the washroom, the bather rinses alternately in warm and cold water or plunges in the cold pool and then uses a loofah for a vigorous rubdown. Go in and out of the steam as often as you like. Afterwards, wrapped in a crisp sheet or towel, your refreshed body returns to the sitting room to relax and sip tea, cold juices, or even beer or vodka. With skin glowing and soul rejuvenated, it is time to take an invigorating walk about the city!

The Neva is clad in granite
Bridges stand poised over her waters
Her islands are covered with dark green gardens
And before the younger capital, ancient Moscow
Has paled, like a purple clad widow
Before a new Empress...

Alexander Pushkin

(above) The front façade of the Pavlovsk Palace (built 1782–86) is graced with a statue of Paul I, a copy of the statue at Gatchina, Paul's other summer residence.

(opposite) Russian folk singers perform in front of Catherine's Palace at Tsarskoye Selo.

Nicknamed the "Venice of the North, St Petersburg is intersected by three main canal systems, known as the Moika, Griboyedov and Fontanka.

(above) Peter the Great in England, painted by Sir Godfrey Kneller in 1698

(opposite top) St Petersburg in the early 1800s. A view of the Strelka and lighthouse with the Peter and Paul Fortress in the distance. The city was a busy port even then. In one summer month alone, contrary to the impression given by this painting, over 19,000 ships anchored here from all over the world.

Dancers of the Mariinsky
(Kirov) Theater.
(bottom right) Ballet slippers
of the famous ballerina Anna
Pavlova in the Vagonova Ballet
School Museum.

(right) Statue of Alexander Pushkin in St Petersburg's Arts Square.

(opposite page) The St Peter and Paul Cathedral inside the Peter and Paul Fortress. When it was constructed in 1732 the spire, topped with an angel holding a cross, was the highest structure in Russia. Peter the Great purposely made it taller than the Bell Tower in Moscow's Kremlin (see picture on page 227). Its gilded spire was scaled and camouflaged by mountain climbers during the Siege of Leningrad to protect it from German bombing raids.

(below) The Hermitage on the Neva River. On the right the golden dome of St Isaac's Cathedral stands behind the spire of the Admiralty.

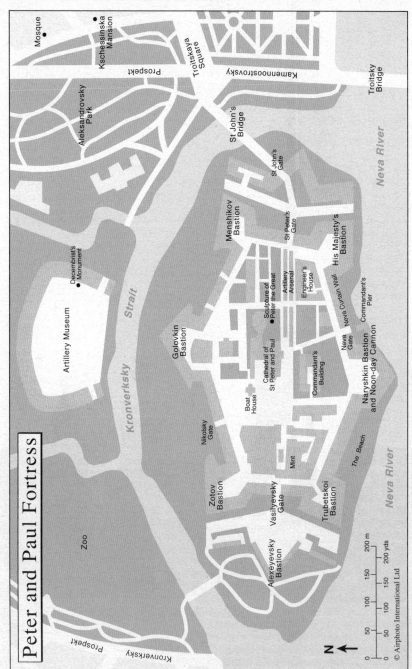

Peter and Paul Fortress

Mosque

Kschessinska Mansion

Prospekt

Troitskaya Square

Kamennoostrovsky

Troitsky Bridge

Neva River

St John's Bridge

Aleksandrovsky Park

St John's Gate

St Peter's Gate

Menshikov Bastion

His Majesty's Bastion

Decembrist's Monument

Artillery Arsenal

Engineer's House

Neva Curtain Wall

Commandant's Pier

Strait

Sculpture of Peter the Great

Golovkin Bastion

Artillery Museum

Cathedral of St Peter and Paul

Neva Gate

Commandant's Building

Naryshkin Bastion and Noon-day Cannon

Kronverksky

Boat House

The Beach

Neva River

Nikolsky Gate

Mint

Zotov Bastion

Vasilyevsky Gate

Trubetskoi Bastion

Zoo

Alexeyevsky Bastion

Kronverksky Prospekt

0   50   100   150   200 m
0   50   100   150   200 yds

N

© Airphoto International Ltd

(left) A St Petersburg couple celebrate their wedding day.

(below) Peter and Paul Fortress on Hare Island. The St Peter and Paul Cathedral is the burial place for over 30 czars and princes, including Nicholas II and his family.

St Petersburg

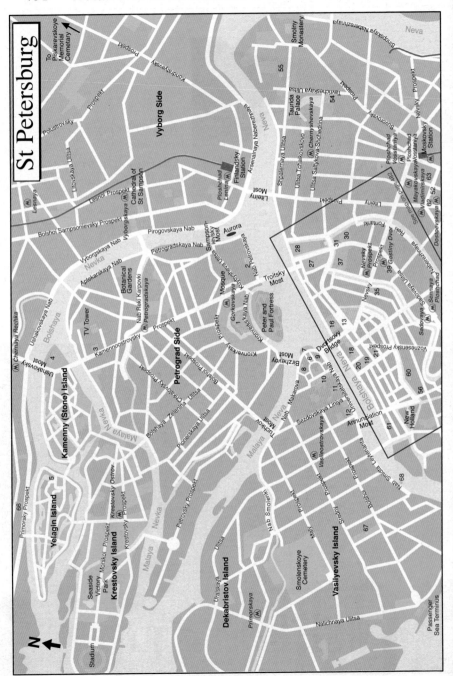

To Piskarevskoye Memorial Cemetery

Prospekt

Kondratyevsky Prospekt

Polustrovsky Prospekt

Litovskaya Ulitsa

Lesnaya

Vyborg Side

Lesnoi Prospekt

Vyborgskaya

Bolshoi Sampsonievsky Prospekt

Cathedral of St Sampson

Finlandsky Station

Ploshchad Lenina

Smolny Monastery

Arsenalnaya Naberezhnaya

55

Taurida Palace

Tavricheskaya Ulitsa

54

Shpalernaya Ulitsa

Ulitsa Tchaikovskovo

Ulitsa Chernyshevskaya

Ulitsa Saltykova-Shchedrina

Suvorovsky

Synopskaya Naberezhnaya

Neva

Nevsky Prospekt

Ploshchad Vosstaniya

Ploshchad Vosstaniya

Mayakovskaya Vosstaniya

Moskovsky Station

Vladimirskaya

62   52   63

Dostoevskaya

Pirogovskaya Nab

Petrogradskaya Nab

Aurora

Sampsonievsky Most

Nab Petrovskaya

Troitsky Most

Liteyny Most

Liteyny Prospekt

Prospekt

Reki Fontanki

Serpukhovskaya Ulitsa

Gostiny Dvor

Nevsky Prospekt

Sennaya Ploshchad

Sadovaya

Voznesensky Prospekt

28   27   30   31   37   35   39

Vyborgskaya Nab

Nevka

Aptekarskaya Nab

Botanical Gardens

Nab Reki Karpovki

Nab Petrogradskaya

Mosque

Gorkovskaya

Kronverkskaya Nab

Peter and Paul Fortress

Birzhevoy Most

Dvortsovy Bridge

16   13

18

19   20   21

60

56

New Holland

61

TV Tower

Kamennoostrovsky Prospekt

Petrograd Side

Bolshoi Prospekt

Bolshaya Zelenina Ulitsa

Pionerskaya Ulitsa

Tuchkov Most

Nab Makarova

Sezdovskaya Liniya

Universitetskaya Nab

Annunciation Most

3   4   5

Kamenny (Stone) Island

Ushakovsky Most

Chernaya Rechka

Ushakovskaya Nab

Bolshaya

Malaya Nevka

Yelagin Island

Primorsky Prospekt

66

Seaside Victory Park

Krestovsky Ostrov

Morskoi Prospekt

Krestovsky Prospekt

Krestovsky Island

Dekabristov Island

Uralskaya Ulitsa

Primorskaya

Nevka

Malaya

Petrovsky Prospekt

Nab Smolenki

Smolenskoye Cemetery

Vasilyevsky Island

67

68

Bolshoi Prospekt

Sredny Prospekt

Nab Leitenanta Shmidta

Nab Smidta

Nalichnaya Ulitsa

Passenger Sea Terminus

Stadium

N

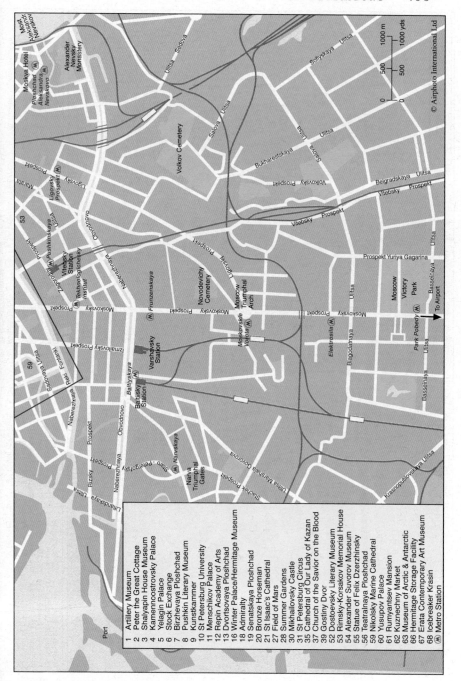

© Airphoto International Ltd

1000 m
500
0

1000 yds
500
0

1   Artillery Museum
2   Peter the Great Cottage
3   Shalyapin House Museum
4   Kamennoostrovsky Palace
5   Yelagin Palace
6   Stock Exchange
7   Birzhevaya Ploshchad
8   Pushkin Literary Museum
9   Kunstkammer
10 St Petersburg University
11 Menschikov Palace
12 Repin Academy of Arts
13 Dvortsovaya Ploshchad
16 Winter Palace/Hermitage Museum
18 Admiralty
19 Senatskaya Ploshchad
20 Bronze Horseman
21 St Isaac's Cathedral
27 Field of Mars
28 Summer Gardens
30 Mikhailovsky Castle
31 St Petersburg Circus
35 Cathedral of Our Lady of Kazan
37 Church of the Savior on the Blood
39 Gostiny Dvor
52 Dostoevsky Literary Museum
53 Rimsky-Korsakov Memorial House
54 Alexander Suvorov Museum
55 Statue of Felix Dzerzhinsky
56 Teatralnaya Ploshchad
59 Nikolsky Marine Cathedral
60 Yusupov Palace
61 Rumyantsev Mansion
62 Kuznechny Market
63 Museum of Arctic & Antarctic
66 Hermitage Storage Facility
67 Erata Contemporary Art Museum
68 Icebreaker Krasin
Ⓜ Metro Station

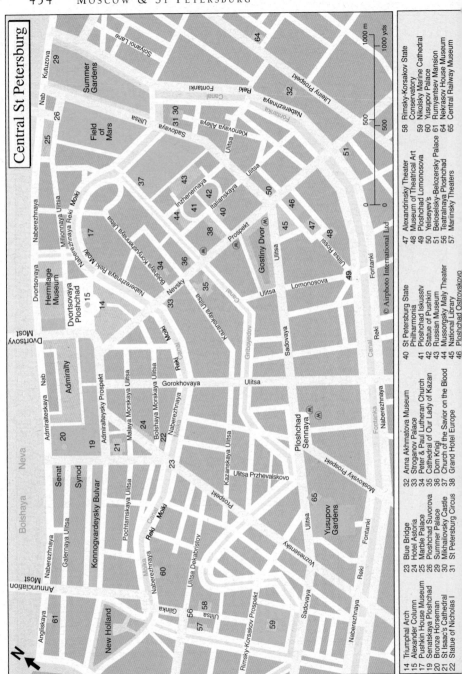

Central St Petersburg

14 Triumphal Arch
15 Alexander Column
17 Pushkin House Museum
19 Senatskaya Ploshchad
20 Bronze Horseman
21 St Isaac's Cathedral
22 Statue of Nicholas I

23 Blue Bridge
24 Hotel Astoria
25 Marble Palace
29 Ploshchad Suvorova
30 Summer Palace
31 St Petersburg Circus

32 Anna Akhmatova Museum
33 Stroganov Palace
34 Peter & Paul Lutheran Church
35 Cathedral of Our Lady of Kazan
36 Dom Knigi
37 Church of the Savior on the Blood
38 Grand Hotel Europe

40 St Petersburg State Philharmonia
41 Ploshchad Iskusstv
42 Statue of Pushkin
43 Russian Museum
44 Mussorgsky Maly Theater
45 National Library
46 Ploshchad Ostrovskovo

47 Alexandrinsky Theater
48 Museum of Theatrical Art
49 Ploshchad Lomonosova
50 Yeliseyev's
51 Beloselsky-Belozersky Palace
56 Teatralnaya Ploshchad
57 Mariinsky Theaters

58 Rimsky-Korsakov State Conservatory
59 Nikolsky Marine Cathedral
60 Yusupov Palace
61 Rumyantsev Mansion
64 Nekrasov House Museum
65 Central Railway Museum

© Airphoto International Ltd

e Winter Palace across Palace Square. In the center stands the Alexander Column commemorating the defeat of Napoleon in 1812.
f Building and the Guard's Headquarters curve around the far side of the square and are linked by the Triumphal Arch, which is
o Rossi's 16-ton sculpture of the Winged Glory.

The lavish baroque-style Winter Palace, with over 1,000 rooms, was commissioned by Elizabeth I in 1754; the blue-green walls are adorned with 176 sculpted figures.

(inset) Boat tours in St Petersburg include scenic excursions along the Neva River and its many canals.

(Opposite page) The Winter Palace houses the Hermitage Museum, exhibiting over 3 million items, dating from antiquity to the present.

(left) In 1914, the Benois family sold to the Hermitage Museum the famous Madonna and Child with Flowers, also known as the Benois Madonna, painted by Leonardo da Vinci in 1478.

(bottom) The Throne Room of Peter the Great was built to honor the czar in the early 1800s. The throne was crafted by a Huguenot silversmith and embroidered with a double-headed eagle. The czar's portrait with a woman (representing Minerva or the Spirit of Russia) was painted in 1730 for the Russian Ambassador to London.

Many lavish interiors, dating from the 18th to 20th centuries, are preserved within the Winter Palace.

Pushkin House Museum (see page 530). (top) Sketch of Alexander Pushkin. (bottom left) The writer's study and library of over 4,000 books. It is arranged exactly as it was when Pushkin died on the divan from a wound received in a duel. The clock is set to the moment of his death, 2.45pm, on January 29, 1837. (bottom right) The inkstand on Pushkin's desk is decorated with an Ethiopian figure which reminded him of his great-grandfather, Abram Hannibal, an African officer who became Peter the Great's chief military engineer in St Petersburg.

Inside the Hermitage Museum.
(opposite page) The Jordan Staircase (named after Jesus' baptism in the River Jordan) leads the visitor up marble steps from the Rastrelli Gallery, entrance to the museum's many halls including the Throne Room of Peter the Great (see picture on page 459).

(left) The ceiling of the Gallery is decorated with a painting of the gods of Mt Olympus.

(below) the Siberian green jasper Kolyvan Vase.
Visit www.hermitagemuseum.org.

(top) Alexander II invited Alberto Kavos to build a stunning center for opera and ballet; it was named the Mariinsky Theater after his wife, Maria Alexandrovna. The first season in the new building opened on October 2, 1860 with Glinka's A Life for the Tsar.

(bottom) A view of the Winter Palace, whose perimeter stretches over a kilometer along the Neva River Embankment.

St Petersburg

The Neva is clad in granite
Bridges stand poised over her waters
Her islands are covered with dark green gardens
And before the younger capital, ancient Moscow
Has paled, like a purple clad widow
Before a new Empress...

Alexander Pushkin

Illuminated by the opalescent White Nights of summer, when the sun hardly sets, then sunk into gloomy darkness in winter, St Petersburg's history is equally juxtaposed with great artistic achievement and violent political upheaval. This paradoxical place has long inspired a flood of poetry, arts and revolutions, and combines the personality of three unique cities into one. It was Petersburg for the czars, Petrograd for a nation at war, and Leningrad for the followers of the Bolshevik Revolution. A visitor today cannot help but get swept into the remarkable vortex of all three distinctly different atmospheres.

St Petersburg initially sprang from a collision of two very different cultures and adapted the tastes of both East and West to the far northern latitudes. Situated only 800 kilometers (500 miles) south of the Arctic Circle, the population grew up along the shores of the Neva River that winds around the 44 islands which comprise the city, and flows 74 kilometers (46 miles) from Lake Ladoga into the Gulf of Finland. The swift-flowing Neva, contrasted with the wide prospekts and unique architecture, all add to the city's mystery, character and charm.

Strolling along the enchanted embankments at any time of year, the first thing one notices is the incredible light that washes over the city. Joseph Brodsky, the Nobel prize-winning poet who was born in St Petersburg, wrote: 'It's the northern light, pale and diffused, one in which memory and eye operate with unusual sharpness. In this light... a walker's thoughts travel farther than his destination.'

It was Peter the Great who brought the majesty of the West to this isolated northern region. He called his new creation Sankt Pieterburkh, from the Dutch, and named it after Christ's first apostle, his patron saint. The city was one of the first in the world built according to preconceived plans, drawn up by the most famous Russian and European architects of the day. Only nine years after its inception in 1703, Peter the Great moved out of Moscow and proclaimed his beloved city the capital of the Russian Empire; it remained so for 206 years.

Over the next 150 years, sparked by the reigns of two great women—Peter's daughter, Elizabeth I, and then Catherine the Great—St Petersburg became the host to Russia's Golden Age and a Mecca to some of the world's greatest composers, writers, artists and dancers. As the catalyst for Russia's Renaissance, St Petersburg flowered in the music of Tchaikovsky, Glinka and Rimsky-Korsakov; the Ballets Russes of Diaghilev, Pavlova and Nijinsky; in the arts and crafts of Repin, Benois and Fabergé; and in the literature and poetry of Gogol, Dostoevsky and Akhmatova. St Petersburg's first two centuries were forged on beauty, innovation and progress.

But the city, born of a forceful will and determined vision, was also destined to become the cradle of turbulent revolutions. Around the time its name was Russianized to Petrograd during World War I, political and philosophical ideas flourished. By February 1917 the monarchy of Nicholas II had been toppled, and on October 24, 1917, Lenin gave the command for the start of the great October Revolution. The battleship *Aurora* fired a blank shot at the Hermitage—the signal for the beginning of what American writer John Reed termed 'the ten days that shook the world'. Red Army troops stormed the Winter Palace and the Bolsheviks seized control of the new Soviet State.

Practically overnight, Leninist and Communist ideals took the place of czars and the aristocracy. Czar Nicholas II and his family were executed in 1918 to thwart the hopes of a return to Romanov rule. Amidst all this turmoil, Lenin transferred the capital of the new Soviet Union back to Moscow. When Lenin died in 1924, ironically (he had hated the place) the city of Petrograd was renamed Leningrad in his honor.

But an even greater tragedy lurked in the shadows. Hitler invaded the USSR in 1941 and laid siege to the city for 900 days. In three years alone, more than half a million residents died from starvation or in the defense of their city. Then, during the subsequent years of Stalin's Great Terror, many of the city's finest were executed or sentenced to gulags and never heard from again. St Petersburg's monuments not only immortalize its crowning achievements, but also serve as testaments to thousands of persecuted souls.

Much has happened to St Petersburg over the past three centuries. She has lived through revolutions and repression, sieges and purges, isolation and humiliations. But through all of this, the city has retained its propensity for courage and change. The White Nights of her spirit have always shown through the darkness as on a midsummer's night. Subdued for many years by tragedy and war, the fairy-tale Sleeping Beauty has reawoken to find her glorious past, prolific poetry and dedicated subjects intact.

Today there is much to behold, and the city's heart is so unique that it has been named a World Heritage Site. One day of sightseeing brings you to the former palaces of Peter the Great, from his first modest cottage on the banks of the Neva River, to his stunning summer palace at Peterhof, modeled on Versailles. The fabulous Hermitage, created by Catherine the Great as her own personal museum, now contains one of the largest and most valuable art collections in the world. The center of Senate Square is marked by the celebrated statue of Peter the Great, known as the Bronze Horseman.

Another day of touring re-creates past splendors and revolutions as you stand in the Winter Palace or onboard the battleship *Aurora*. Nevsky Prospekt, the city's most popular thoroughfare, stretches five kilometers (three miles) from the golden-spired Admiralty to Alexander Nevsky Monastery, one of the largest Russian Orthodox centers in the country. A stroll along the Nevsky and adjoining side streets (many now being converted into pedestrian walkways, brimming with outdoor cafés in summer), or a boat trip through the numerous canals leads you past former palaces of aristocrats and on to the Mariinsky (Kirov) Ballet, where Balanchine and Baryshnikov once danced, or the Maly Theater to hear opera and music written by Stravinsky, Tchaikovsky and Shostakovich.

In 1991, as a grand gesture to honor its historic foundation, the country's second largest city of nearly 5 million people won the battle to change its name from Leningrad back to St Petersburg The new 'Pieter', as residents lovingly call their city, is rising forth to embrace its past and reclaim its heritage. In 1998, the remains of the executed family of Nicholas II were ceremoniously reburied in the Peter and Paul Cathedral. Even though Moscow is still the capital, St Petersburg residents resoundingly prefer their own city. At the Baby Palace, each newborn is honored with a ceremony and medal that reads, Born in St Petersburg. And Russia's current president, Vladimir Putin, who was born in St Petersburg, has one.

Putin's influence has raised the fortunes of the city as it continues to strive for a wider renaissance. For the 2003 tercentenary, the President earmarked $1.5 billion for refurbishments and celebrations, and everyone from world leaders to foreign tourists marveled at the beauty of the newly restored city. Few cities in the world can compare with St Petersburg—in its vast beauty, turbulent history and remarkable endurance of the human spirit. Now this extraordinary city pushes forward into the 21st century with renewed faith and optimistic vigor. As we embark on our timeless journey through this extraordinary place, let us recall the words of Alexander Pushkin, a long-time resident of the city:

> *Be beautiful, city of Peter*
> *Stay as unshakable as Russia*
> *And let no vain wrath*
> *Ever trouble the eternal dream of Peter.*

HISTORY

The delta at the mouth of the Neva River was settled long before the founding of St Petersburg. The Neva was an important trading route between Northern Europe and Asia. Finns, Swedes and Russians established settlements there at one time or another and frequently fought over the land. In the early 17th century, Russia's Time of Troubles, the nation's military power was so debilitated that Mikhail, the first of the Romanov czars, was forced to sign a treaty ceding the land to Sweden in 1617.

After Peter the Great returned from his tour of Holland, England and Germany, one of his first actions was to oust the Swedes from the Neva delta. (It had been more than 450 years since Alexander Nevsky had last defeated the Swedes). In the winter of 1702–3, Russian forces attacked and captured Swedish forts at Nyenshatz, a few miles upstream from the river's mouth, and Nöteborg on Lake Ladoga. Peter ordered that the keys to these forts be nailed to their gates. Two keys hanging from a sailing ship became the symbol representing the future of St Petersburg. On May 16, 1703, seven weeks after ousting the Swedes, Peter the Great lay the foundation stone of the Peter and Paul Fortress on an island near where the Neva divides into its two main branches. The primary role of the new settlement was as a military outpost, but right from the beginning Peter had greater designs.

While the construction of the fortress was under way, Peter lived in a rough log cabin nearby and from it planned his future capital. He decided that the hub of the new city was to be on the opposite bank of the Neva, at the present site of the Admiralty. Here he founded Russia's first great shipyard, where he built his navy. But Peter's project was hampered from the start by the occasional flooding of the Neva and by the lack of workers willing to move to the cold and isolated swamp. With typical ruthlessness, he ordered the conscription of 40,000 laborers to lay the foundations and dig the canals. It is estimated that approximately 100,000 people died from disease, exhaustion and floods during the first few years. 'The town is built on human bones,' the saying goes. The construction of the city began along the banks of the river and radiated inland along broad avenues from the shipyards. During this time, Peter adopted a city coat-of-arms that had crossed anchors topped with an imperial crown, inspired by the Vatican's crossed keys to paradise.

In 1712, three years after the Swedes were decisively defeated (the final end of the Great Northern War came in 1721 with the signing of the Nystad Treaty), Peter the Great decreed that Sankt Pieterburkh was now the capital of the Russian Empire. Unfortunately, the aristocracy and merchants did not share his enthusiasm. Peter did not have the patience to persuade them, so he simply commanded the 1,000 leading families and 500 of the most prominent merchants to build houses in the new capital. Aside from the Peter and Paul Fortress and Peter's cabin, the notable buildings of this era still standing are the Menschikov and Kikin palaces, the Alexander Nevsky Monastery and the Monplaisir Palace at Petrodvorets. The construction of St Petersburg was the first time—but certainly not the last—that the hand of the State intervened on a national scale in the lives of the Russian masses. (For more on Peter the Great, see Special Topic.)

By 1725, the year of Peter's death at age 52, St Petersburg had a population of 75,000 unwilling subjects. Over the next few years the future of the new capital was shaky due to the lack of Peter's strong hand. First his wife, Catherine I, ruled for two years, with Peter's friend, Alexander Menschikov, acting as *de facto czar*. When Catherine died, the aristocratic political faction managed to strip Menschikov of his power and sent him far away into Siberian exile. When the council, under the rule of 12-year-old Peter II (Peter's grandson), moved the imperial court back to Moscow, thousands of people thankfully left the half-built city. They stayed away until Peter II's early death, at age 14, from smallpox. In 1730, Peter's niece, Anna Ivanova, took the reins; and, two years later the Empress decreed that the capital would return to St Petersburg. Under Anna's ten year rule, the second great phase of the construction of St Petersburg began. She hired Bartolomeo Rastrelli, the son of an Italian sculptor hired by Peter the Great, to build her a Winter Palace (no longer standing), the first permanent imperial residence in the city. In 1740, she ordered the construction of a 24-meter-long (80-feet) and 10-meters-high (33-feet) ice palace complete with rooms and ice furniture on the frozen Neva. This was built for Prince Golitsyn who had been unfaithful to her and thus forced to marry an ugly Kalmyk tribeswoman from Central Asia in a mock ceremony. They were stripped naked and had to spend the night in the ice palace with only each other for warmth.

Anna died the same winter, and after the brief rule of another child czar, Ivan VI, the extravagant Empress Elizabeth, the second oldest-surviving daughter of Peter the Great, took the throne. During her 20-year reign, she went on to build many of the most important buildings in St Petersburg. At this time Rastrelli and other imported European architects had developed a style that later became known as Elizabethan rococo. Like a wedding cake, the basic structures disappeared underneath an ornate icing of pilasters, statuary and reliefs. The other recurrent theme was size. These buildings did not reach for the heavens like the churches of the Moscow Kremlin; they sprawled across acres of the flat, empty countryside of the new city. Huge architectural clusters like the Winter Palace, the Hermitage and the palaces at Peterhof and Pushkin, all painted an ethereal turquoise, were testament mostly to Elizabeth's power to do as she pleased. (As her father, she loved the pomp as much as the power. Elizabeth hosted elaborate masquerade balls, loved dancing and amassed over 15,000 dresses, changing her outfits seven times a day.) By the end of her rule, St Petersburg looked more like a stage set than a working city, with broad avenues built for parades and palaces like props for some lavish drama.

By the end of her reign in 1761—even though the imperial coffers were emptied, Elizabeth had succeeded in making her father's grandiose dream a reality.

After Elizabeth's death another weak czar, Peter III, took the throne and soon died under mysterious circumstances after forging an unpopular alliance with Prussia. The scepter was handed to his wife, Catherine II, an independently-minded German princess who ruled the empire for 34 years. (See Special Topic on Catherine the Great.) Under Catherine, later dubbed 'the Great', St Petersburg solidified its position as the artistic and political center of the empire, as intellectuals flocked to the now-thriving academies of arts and sciences. The latest political ideas from Western Europe were hotly debated among the aristocracy, and the streets and squares of the city were dotted with sculptures crafted by the finest European artists, including the enormous Bronze Horseman sculptural portrait of Peter the Great cast by the Frenchman Falconet. At the end of Catherine's reign in 1796, there was a profound sense of achievement in St Petersburg; in less than a century it had become one of the leading cities in the world with a population of 220,000. But there was also unease: the winds of change were blowing, and no one knew how to reconcile the new political ideas of St Petersburg with the profoundly conservative and deeply religious Russian countryside.

After her death, Catherine's son, the mentally unstable Paul I (1796–1801), built a fortress variously known as the Mikhailovsky or Engineer's Castle to protect himself from conspirators against the throne (see page 542). His paranoia proved justified, because in 1801, just 41 days after he moved in, his own courtiers strangled him to death in his very own bedroom. His successor was Alexander I, whose liberal reforms during the first half of his reign were wildly popular among the aristocracy and intelligentsia. After his victory over Napoleon in 1812 (and Russian troops even occupied Paris), monuments were built around the city, including the Alexander Column and Kazan Cathedral that celebrated an empire that now stretched half way across the globe. The latter half of Alexander's rule was less successful. In 1824, the city experienced its worst flood when 500 people were killed and hundreds of buildings destroyed. At the same time a number of revolutionary cells were formed within the aristocracy which plotted to overthrow the imperial system. When Alexander died in December 1825, these cells were violently opposed to the accession of his anointed successor, his younger brother Nicholas, who was known to be a conservative and sympathetic to the Prussians. When a group of aristocrats and guard officers, later known as Decembrists, took over Senate Square and demanded a constitutional government. Nicholas I ordered the army's cannons to fire on them, and the rebels fled in confusion. The main plotters were arrested and interned in the Peter and Paul Fortress (see page 507), where five of them were executed and 115 were sent to Siberia. Later, in 1849, this fortress was also the prison for the writer Fyodor Dostoevsky and the rest of the

Petrashevsky Circle of socialist revolutionaries. Under Nicholas' orders they were sentenced to death, led before a firing squad and then reprieved at the last minute and exiled to Siberia. Dostoevsky fashioned his book *Notes from the Underground* after this experience. In 1851, the first railway opened between St Petersburg and Moscow. Ten years later, in 1861, the next Czar Alexander II signed a decree to emancipate the serfs (at this time peasants made up 80% of Russia's population, half of which were serfs), allowing tens of thousands of freed families to flock into the capital to try and earn a living. By 1862 St Petersburg had a population of 532,000 and was the fourth largest city in Europe after Paris, London and Constantinople.

The period from Nicholas I through the Russian Revolution in 1917 was an era of more or less constant political repression of the aristocracy and intelligentsia. Paradoxically, in St Petersburg it was the time of a great flowering of creativity that gave us some of the masterpieces of world literature, music and ballet, with writers like Pushkin, Gogol and Dostoevsky; the Mighty Band of the composers Rimsky-Korsakov, Mussorgsky and Borodin; and the choreographers of the Mariinsky Ballet, whose dances are still performed today.

Political turmoil proceeded apace with the artistic ferment during the latter half of the 19th-century. St Petersburg was at the center, and a number of prominent revolutionary theorists, including the anarchist Mikhail Bakunin, and the writer Nikolai Chernyshevsky, spent time in the Peter and Paul Fortress. In March 1881, these activities finally bore fruit when a terrorist cell called the Peoples' Freedom Group succeeded in mortally wounding Czar Alexander II with a bomb on the banks of the Ekaterininsky Canal. This led to more decades of oppression under Alexander III and Nicholas II, which only served to heighten the political unrest. By this time the imperial system was not only unpopular among the St Petersburg elite but throughout Russian society. (See Special Topic on page 760, Genealogy of the Imperial Family.) In 1887, the brother of Lenin, Alexander Ulyanov, along with four others, attempted to assassinate Alexander III but did not succeed; they were all hung in the Kronstadt Fortress.

In 1905, Russia was given a portent of its future when a series of strikes by up to 100,000 soldiers and workers led to a huge demonstration in St Petersburg. A radical priest named Father Gapon led thousands of workers in a march to the Winter Palace to present a petition to Nicholas II (see page 494). As they entered Palace Square, soldiers opened fire and hundreds of unarmed protesters were killed or trampled. 'Bloody Sunday' shocked the nation and galvanized the revolutionary movement. Socialist intellectuals and workers formed mass parties for the first time and demanded a share of the power. Nicholas gave them a weak advisory body named the Duma, which was accepted by the moderates but not by the extreme left, and arrested as many revolutionary rabble-rousers as he could. Trotsky went to jail and Lenin escaped to Switzerland. (See Special Topic on page 598.)

When Russia went to war against Germany in 1914, St Petersburg's name was changed to Petrograd to avoid the Germanic implications of having a 'burg' at the end of its name. World War I was disastrous for the Russian Empire. The long and bloody war in the trenches sapped the economically and politically weak nation. Back in St Petersburg, the Czar and the Duma fought for power, while the charismatic priest Rasputin played mind games with the Czarina and her circle, and the people starved. On March 12, 1917, over a quarter of a million people in the capital rioted. They killed policemen, broke open the jails and set the courthouse on fire. The Czar ordered military troops to restore order, but soldiers stationed in the city refused to quell the rioters; instead they joined them. Three days later the czar abdicated, and Russia was ruled by the Provisional Government led by Alexander Kerensky. Thus ended three hundred years of Romanov rule and 500 years of czarist autocracy.

In April 1917, after a decade of exile and plotting, Vladimir Lenin arrived in Petrograd's Finland Station, and was met by a cheering mass of thousands. (His safe passage was arranged by German generals who hoped Lenin would distract Russia from its participation in the war.) From the top of an armored car in front of the station Lenin gave a speech rallying his Bolshevik Party and their allies, the Soviets of Workers and Soldiers, against Kerensky's government. Then followed months of agitation and attempted revolution which culminated in the events of the night of November 7, 1917.* The battleship *Aurora*, under the control of the Bolsheviks, fired several shells at the Winter Palace giving the signal for troops to storm the palace and other principal government buildings. Kerensky was later arrested in the Palace's White Dining Room behind the Malachite Hall. (He later escaped, lived in exile and died in New York in 1970 at the age 89.) The party of Lenin, Trotsky and Stalin was now in command of the Russian Empire. Soon after Lenin ordered the formation of the Extraordinary Commission for the Suppression of Counter revolution, the Cheka—later known as the KGB.

For the next three years civil war raged through the nation. The Soviets were attacked first by the Germans, then both by the White Russian army and the British Royal Navy. During that time Petrograd's population dropped from 2,500,000 to 720,000, due to extreme hardship. In March 1918, Lenin moved the Soviet Government to Moscow because Petrograd was vulnerable to German attack—and perhaps also because of his distaste for the artificial imperial city. (Pudovkin's 1927 silent film, *The End of St Petersburg*, was made to celebrate the Revolution's 10th

---

* In 45 BC Julius Caesar introduced the Julian calendar to the Western world. A new reformed calendar was introduced by Pope Gregory XIII in 1582 which calculated time more accurately. By the 20th-century the difference between the Julian and Gregorian calendars was 13 days. Russia continued to use the old Julian calendar until February 1, 1918. This is why the October Revolution came to be celebrated at the beginning of November.

Anniversary.) In 1922, the Soviet Union was officially established, merging Russia, Ukraine, Belarus and the Caucasus regions into one socialist state.

On July 17, 1918, probably under Lenin's orders, the former Czar Nicholas II, his family and four servants were secretly executed by a Bolshevik firing squad in the town of Yekaterinburg where they had been held in exile after Nicholas' abdication. Their unmarked graves were not discovered until 1991; the remains were reburied in 1998 in the Peter and Paul Cathedral (see page 509).

On Lenin's death in 1924, Petrograd was renamed Leningrad after a man who publicly despised the city and spent less than a year of his life there. Ominously, that same year, there was a great flood in his namesake city. During the next two decades Moscow became the center of cultural and political life, while Leningrad became identified as a center of shipbuilding and industry. Its tradition of political assassination nevertheless continued with the 1934 shooting of Leningrad Party leader Sergei Kirov at the Smolny Institute. Some say that Stalin was behind the shooting, and he certainly used it as the excuse to start the great purges, ushering in his long reign of terror.

Leningrad received its next great blow during World War II. For 900 days, from September 1941 to January 1944, the German army laid siege to the city and hundreds of thousands of inhabitants died, adding more bones to the foundations. By 1944 there were fewer than 600,000 people left, compared to a 1939 population of 3,100,000. The poet Mandalstam wrote, 'living in St Petersburg is like sleeping in a coffin.' (See pages 486–487/489.)

Adding further to the city's misery, Stalin instigated another purge in 1948–9, known as the Leningrad Affair, in which many of the city's artists and top Party members vanished forever or were sent to Siberia. In this purge it was apparent that the Moscow leadership remained suspicious of the Leningrad Party hierarchy because they retained some of the idealism of the original revolutionaries.

The years following the war were devoted to reconstruction of the city center and the development of huge satellite suburbs to the south. Thankfully, the government banned high-rises in the center, sustaining Catherine the Great's edict that no building should be higher than the Winter Palace.

Under Khrushchev and Brezhnev, Leningrad became even more of a second-rate provincial city. It was forced to concentrate on military matters and industrial accomplishments. In the stagnant atmosphere of these ensuing decades the city still nurtured a reactionary climate; this time it was between the suppressed artistic community and the brainwashed bureaucrats. It was no accident that the first major post-Stalinist trial of an artist (the Jewish writer Joseph Brodsky) took place in Leningrad. In 1964, Brodsky was sentenced to Siberian exile (and later expelled from the country); his crime—not having official permission to write poetry. Brodsky wrote about his beloved city: '...during the White Night, let your immovable earthly glory dawn on me, a fugitive.'

Members of the intellectual community were forced to reject professions not officially recognized. Thus to earn a living they had to take on such menial jobs as night-watchmen, janitors, furnace stokers and dock workers, while secretly pursuing their passions. Despite this ironclad curtain, forbidden works were secretly circulated in underground *samizdat* publications. The up-and-coming rock pioneers began *magnitizdat* where homemade music tapes were circulated like manuscripts. The poet Gorgovsky recalled the 1970s in Leningrad as 'dead, inert times, and fatal for art's breathing'.

The stifling censorship and cruel punishment drove many Leningrad artists to alcoholism, madness and even suicide. On top of all this, the unchecked industrial pollution of the city added further to the suffocation of the population. A popular joke was told during this time: A man is brought into the KGB and asked, "Is it true you are dissatisfied with Brezhnev?" "Of course not," the man replied. "If I'm dissatisfied with anyone, it is with Peter the Great. If only he had lost the Battle of Poltava, we would all be living in Sweden now."

PERIOD OF PERESTROIKA

With the advent of Gorbachev and his new policy of perestroika (restructuring), the harsh totalitarian regime that had ruled Leningrad for more than seven decades began to crack. In the 1980s the most popular and controversial TV program in the country, *600 Seconds*, was broadcast from Leningrad. Its brazen reporter Alexander Nevzorov exposed the corruption and misery of the old socialist system; he was hailed as the Russian 'Robin Hood'. The State also allowed long-banned and shelved works to officially appear—everything from film, prose and poetry to music, art and ballet. In the spring of 1987, almost half a century after their completion, Anna Akhmatova's poems *Requiem* and *Poem Without a Hero* were published. Other Leningrad authors such as Mandalstam, Zoshchenko and Nabokov were widely read for the first time. The two émigrés, composer Stravinsky and choreographer Balanchine, were allowed to return and visit the city of their birth, and their creations were played and staged in the Kirov Theater's repertoire.

In 1990, the economic law professor Anatoly Sobchak was elected Leningrad city council chairman. Later, as mayor, he brought about sweeping changes to crumbling Soviet dogma. During the August attempt to overthrow Gorbachev, Mayor Sobchak lead the city back into the political arena, and personally stopped putsch plotters from a planned military takeover of the city. Sobchak had allied himself with Captain Melnikov, the commander of the nearby Kronstadt naval base, and Melnikov had offered to protect Sobchak and the city council within the fortress. Instead of hiding, Sobchak rallied 250,000 residents into Palace Square (the site of past revolutions) in support of Yeltsin. When the coup failed, Sobchak became a national hero, second only to Yeltsin.

In the early years of glasnost (openness), a democratic movement pushed to change the city's name back to St Petersburg. On October 31, 1991 (the Soviet Union dissolved on Christmas Day, 1991), Leningrad was officially renamed Sankt Pieterburg. The Nobel prize-winning writer Joseph Brodsky was pleased: 'It is much better for them to live in a city that bears the name of a saint than that of a devil!'

St Petersburg Today

After the Baltic States broke away from the Soviet Union in May 1991, St Petersburg's presence as a major port increased sharply. The city was once again becoming the country's 'Window to the West.' But, hard-liners (calling themselves everything from pro-communists to imperialists and ultra-nationalists) continued to protest the difficult transitions. For example, in 1992, a coupon system for buying rationed food products was being used—forty percent of the city's budget went just to subsidizing meat. But, the city forged ahead with democratic reforms. St Petersburg was the first city in the new Russia to sell government-owned shops to private enterprises, open joint-ventures, and create a private banking sector. A stock and commodities market opened in the original 18th-century Stock Exchange. 'I believe the worst is over,' Mayor Sobchak announced a few years later from his Smolny Institute office. 'Privatization is moving along fast and we are slowly converting factories, which used to serve the defense industry, to making essential products for the city.' The mayor also returned many of the churches and religious buildings to the Orthodox Church, and innovative new theaters and artistic endeavors were opened throughout the city. St Petersburg began to re-evolve into the cultural and spiritual capital of her former years.

In 1996, the mayor, now called governor (governors are appointed by the Russian president rather than elected by the populace), was replaced by his deputy who, within the next several years, managed to balance the budget and garner a European bond backing—allowing for some major repairs of the city's wealth of architectural monuments. (Over 15,000 historic palaces, mansions, museums and theaters had deteriorated over time.) In March 1997, two centuries after the original patrols were created, the new *gorodovoy* ceremoniously marched down Nevsky Prospekt. These patrolmen, whose sole duty it is to make foreigners welcome, have extensive knowledge of the city and environs.

To usher in St Petersburg's 300th anniversary in 2003, the city selected an anthem, composed from a movement in the ballet, The Bronze Horseman, written in 1949 by composer Reinhold Glière. In 2001, the St Petersburg Union of

Composers chose the opening stanzas from Alexander Pushkin's famous poem, after which the ballet is named, and set them to Glière's music. However, they realized that in order to fit the meter of the music, Pushkin's famous words would have to be edited; but no one dared edit Pushkin, the national poet. So St Petersburg's governor staged a contest stating, "The lyrics have to be ceremonial, patriotic and fit well with the music." In all, 341 different texts were submitted from poets and teachers to pensioners and homemakers. The chosen winner was local poet, Oleg Chuprov, who worked for three months on ten versions. He said, "For me, an anthem is something that should unite people. It is like a confession of love." A special choir sang the city's praises during the 300th anniversary celebrations.

St Petersburg is today a proud showcase for the new Russia. The governorship of Valentina Matvienko (2003-2011) was marked not only by preservation initiatives but also new construction projects. In 2010, businessman Roman Abramovich acquired New Holland Island and is now turning it into a major cultural and commercial center. In 2013, after a decade in the making, the spectacular Mariinsky II opened its new stage, next to the original Mariinsky, on Theater Square. Not all the new innovations have gone without controversy. The Okhta project, the city's first planned skyscraper at 403-meters (1322-feet) tall (funded by Gazprom) was originally slated to be built near the Smolny Cathedral. But, after years of public outcry against the modern behemoth—whose towering presence many felt would destroy the historic heart of the city, the project was finally relocated (by the next governor) beyond the Kirovsky Islands on the Vyborg side and renamed the Lakhta Center. The completed building is cited to be the tallest structure in Europe.

This magnificent and soulful city seems to have always been trying to find a balance between order and chaos. But despite the difficulties, the city's inhabitants remain hopeful: Considering the conditions that were overcome to even build this city, the St Petersburg tradition will surely guide them.

After 300 years St Petersburg still exultantly stands at the forefront of determination and progress. Legend has it that as long as the statue of the Bronze Horseman remains in its place overlooking the Neva River, St Petersburg will never falter.

> *And high above him all undaunted*
> *Deaf to the storm's rebellious roars*
> *With hand outstretched, the Idol mounted*
> *On steed of bronze, majestic soars.*

Alexander Pushkin (see page 679)

THE OLD GUARD

*A*n old man of eighty-four attracted my attention in the Mikhailovsky gardens. He brandished a sabre-shaped walking-stick as he strode down the paths, his war medals dangled in ranks at his chest, and his features showed bellicose above a mist of white beard. He looked like God the Father peering over a cloud.

'I'm an Old Bolshevik,' he announced to me. 'One of the original Revolutionaries!'

A ghost from the twenties, he still exulted in the people's common ownership. He patted the tree trunks possessively as he marched by and frequently said 'This is my tree, and this is my tree.'

In 1907 he had become a revolutionary, and had been sent in chains to Siberia. But a fellow-prisoner, he said, had concealed a file in the lapel of his coat, and together they had cut through the manacles and fled back to Leningrad. Those were the days when Siberian exiles and prisoners—Trotsky, Stalin and Bakunin among them—escaped from Siberia with laughable ease and slipped over frontiers with the freedom of stray cats.

Then the old man had joined the Revolution and fought for the three years against the Whites. He settled into a military stride as he spoke of it, and thrust out his beard like a torpedo, while all the time his gaze flashed and fulminated over the gardens. 'Get off the grass, comrade!' he bellowed. A young mother, seated on the sward beside her pram, looked up in bewilderment. 'Get off our motherland's grass!'

He embodied the intrusive precepts of early Communism, whose zealots were encouraged to scrutinize, shrivel and denounce each other. He was the self-proclaimed guardian and persecutor of all about him, and he entered the 1980s with the anachronism of a mastodon. Farther on a girl was leaning in the fork of one of his precious trees. 'Keep away from there!' he roared. 'Can't you see you're stopping it to grow? Get off!' She gaped at him, said nothing, did not move. He marched on unperturbed. He even anathematized a mousing cat. 'What are you looking for, comrade? Leave nature alone!' He did not seem to mind or notice that nobody obeyed him.

We rested under a clump of acacias. 'When I was a boy,' he said, 'I saw these trees planted.' He pointed to the largest of them, which bifurcated into a gnarled arm. 'That tree was no taller than a little lamp-post then. The garden was private, of course, but as a boy I often squeezed in over the railings. The tsar and tsaritsa used to walk here in the summer.' His voice dwindled from an alsatian growl to purring reminiscence. 'Once, while I was hiding in the shrubs, I saw them myself... What were they like? It's hard to recall exactly. But she was a beautiful woman, I remember. She had her hand on his arm. And he seemed very large and handsome, and...' But he never finished. The lurking commissar in him erupted again. 'What are you doing, comrade?' Beneath us, a man was raking weeds out of an ornamental pond. 'How can you weed a lake?'

The gardener looked up stoically. 'I'm at work.'

Work. The magic syllable.

Immediately, as if some benedictory hand had passed its grace across the old man's brow, his expression changed to a look of benign redress. 'Fine,' he murmured, 'work.' For him the word had the potency of 'revolution' or 'collective.' The mousing cat, too, had been at work, I thought, but had been unable to voice this watchword.

Before we parted he said: 'I'll give you my address, not the real one. That's secret. You see,' he repeated, 'I'm one of the Old Bolsheviks.'

I wondered then if he were not deranged. He scribbled out his address on the back of a newspaper, in enormous handwriting. It was only as he was leaving me that I realized from his age that the history he had given me was nonsense. The tsars did not send lone boys of eleven to Siberia.

'How old did you say you were?' I asked. For he looked timeless.

'I know what you're thinking,' he answered. His eyes twinkled at me collusively. 'You Estonians, you're a clever lot. You're thinking that I can't have been sent to Siberia aged eleven. But actually I'm ninety-four...'— and he strode away through the trees.

Colin Thubron, Among the Russians, 1983

PETER THE GREAT (1672–1725)

Peter the Great, one of Russia's most enlightened and driven rulers, pulled his country out of her dark feudal past into a status equal with her European neighbors. Possessing an intense curiosity toward foreign lands, he opened Russia's window to the West and became the first ruler to journey extensively outside Russia. Standing at six feet seven inches, with a passionate will and temper to match his great size, Peter I, against all odds, also built a city that became one of the most magnificent capitals in all of Europe.

Peter's father, Czar Alexei, ruled the Empire from 1645 to 1676. Alexei's first wife had 13 children; but only two, Fyodor and Ivan, were destined to inherit the throne. Natalya Naryshkin became Alexei's second wife and gave birth to a son named Peter in 1672.

When Alexei died, his son, Fyodor III, succeeded to the throne and reigned from 1676 to 1682. During this time, his half-brother, Peter, along with ill-favored Natalya, were sent away from Moscow to live in the country. Instead of the usual staunch upbringing within the Kremlin walls, Peter had the freedom to roam the countryside and make friends with peasant children. When Fyodor died, a rivalry broke out between the two families as to which son would gain the throne. Peter won the first battle and was proclaimed czar at the age of ten. But soon Ivan's side of the family spread rumors to the Streltsy, or Musketeers (the military protectors of Moscow), that the Naryshkins were plotting to kill Ivan. The Streltsy demanded that Peter's half-brother be crowned, too. So, for a time, the throne of Moscovy was shared by the two boys, the feeble-minded Ivan V and the robust Peter I. In actuality, however, it was Sophia, Peter's older half-sister, who ruled as Regent for seven years with the help of her lover, Prince Golitsyn.

Peter spent most of this time back in the country, mainly engaged in studies that had a practical use. One fateful day, on his father's estate in Pereslavl-Zalessky, the young boy discovered a wrecked English boat that could sail against the wind. He had the boat repaired and learned how to sail it. In 1688, Peter built a flotilla on Lake Plescheyevo at Pereslavl-Zalessky to practice his ideas for a future navy. Infatuated now with sailing, he also immersed himself in the study of mathematics and navigation and tried to instill a maritime spirit into the whole of society. Naval training courses and marine sports clubs were offered to nobles, and jobs as seamen opened to the lower classes. Later, St Petersburg became one of the most important trading ports on the Baltic.

In addition, the young czar worked well with his hands and became an accomplished carpenter, blacksmith and printer; he even mended his own clothes. As a child, he loved to play soldiers, and drilled his companions in military maneuvers, eventually staging mock battles with weapons and in uniforms supplied by the Royal Arsenal. Peter was also fascinated with the techniques of torture. Later in his reign, fearing an assassination attempt, he would torture his first son, Alexei, to death.

Sophia was eventually removed from court affairs and sent off to live in Novodevichy Convent outside Moscow. When Ivan died, Peter I, at the age of 22, assumed the throne as the sole czar and took up his imperial duties with earnest. On the throne, his first real battle was against the Turks. His plan was to take the Sea of Azov at the mouth of the Don in order to gain access to the Black Sea. Peter built a fleet of ships, and for the first time in her history, Russia led a surprise attack from the water. The Turks were defeated in 1696 and Russia had her first southern outlet to the sea.

After this successful campaign, Peter set off on a long journey to the West. He traveled to England, France, and Germany, and worked as a shipbuilder in Holland. Back home, the Streltsy, with the help of Sophia, began to organize a secret revolt to overthrow the czar. Peter caught wind of their plans; upon his return, he captured and tortured almost 2,000 men and dissolved the corps. By this time, the now cultured ruler had lost interest in his first wife and sent her off to a convent in Sergiyev Posad, the equivalent of divorce.

Peter was greatly impressed by Western ways and, to him, change symbolized Russia's path to modernization. Knee-length coats became the new fashion. One of the new State laws prohibited the growing of beards. He also upended the established social order by forbidding arranged marriages and establishing a Table of Ranks, fourteen in all, which assigned social status on the basis of service to the country. In this way aristocratic inheritance was no longer the only way to elite status, as humble and hard-working men could be rewarded too. Since the church taught that man was created in God's image (ie with a beard), many believed Peter I to be the Antichrist. In addition, in the same year (1700), after centuries of celebrating the Russian New Year on September 1 (after crop harvests were completed), Peter I changed New Year's day to fall on January 1, to coincide with the West.

But Peter was as determined as ever to pull Russia out of her isolation. He tolerated new religions, allowing the practices of Catholics, Lutherans and Protestants, and even approving of the sacrilegious scientific stance taken by Galileo. He exercised State control over the Russian Orthodox Church by establishing the Holy Synod. This supremacy of the czar over the Russian Church lasted from 1721 until 1917. In 1721, Peter also declared himself Emperor of All Russia (see picture on page 445).

During the Great Northern Wars, while trying to chase the Swedes out of the Baltic, Peter organized the building of the first Russian fleet on the Gulf of Finland. After conquering the Swedes in 1709, the Russian navy returned to the city where thousands of citizens lined the Neva River embankments to cheer the victorious ships. (To this day, St Petersburg celebrates Navy Day, the last Sunday in July, when the naval fleet is paraded down the Neva.) Engravings of the city filled with ships decorated the proud czar's palaces. It was during this time that Peter met and fell in love with a good-natured peasant girl named Catherine, whom he later married; Empress Catherine ruled for two years after his death.

In 1703, Peter began the fanatic building of a new city in the north at a point where the Neva River drained into Lake Ladoga. The city was constructed on a myriad of islands, canals and swamps. The conditions were brutal and nearly 100,000 perished the first year alone. But within a decade, St Petersburg was a city of 35,000 stone buildings and the capital of the Russian Empire. Peter commissioned many well-known foreign architects: the Italian Rastrelli, the German Schlüter, the Swiss Trezzini and the Frenchman Leblond, who created Peter's Summer Palace of Petrodvorets. Montferrand later designed St Isaac's Cathedral, which took over 100 kilos of gold and 40 years to build. Peter brought the majesty of the West to his own doorstep. It was no small wonder that St Petersburg was nicknamed the Venice of the North.

Peter died looking out from his window to the West. Today in St Petersburg stands a monument to the city's founder, a statue of Peter the Great as the Bronze Horseman. The statue, made by the French sculptor, Falconet, shows Peter rearing up on a horse that symbolizes Russia, while trampling a serpent that opposes his reforms. Pushkin wrote that Peter 'with iron bridle reared up Russia to her fate'. By a great and forceful will, Peter the Great had successfully led Russia out of her darkness into the light of a Golden Age.

CULTURE

A political and social history tells only half the story of St Petersburg. Of equal consequence are the literary and artistic creations set in St Petersburg, because in them writers and artists have created a parallel city that lives just as much in the minds of the inhabitants. Since the reign of Elizabeth, the realms of fiction, poetry, symphony, opera and ballet have all collaborated to produce an intellectual St Petersburg that is one of the great artistic creations of humankind.

LITERATURE

In the earliest years of St Petersburg, Peter the Great emphasized the practical sciences, particularly engineering, and his image of the city as a glorified barracks left little room for the arts. St Petersburg's first great contributor to Russian culture, Mikhail Lomonosov, arrived in the city in 1736 and went on to become the director of the Academy of Sciences.

Lomonosov was a kind of Russian Benjamin Franklin—a chemist, physicist, geologist, educator, historian and poet. He had also studied in the West and was a friend of the French philosopher Voltaire. Lomonosov devoted his life to bringing the ideas of the European Enlightenment to Russia and at the same time tried to advance Russia's cultural thought in distinctly Russian ways. Up to this time, a complicated and archaic Church Slavonic had remained the liturgical and literary language of Russia for over seven centuries, until Peter the Great tried to simplify the Church Cyrillic into the 'civil alphabet' (*grazhdansky* shrift) a written form to be used in secular books. One of Lomonsov's crowning achievements in the cultural sphere was his new codified version of Russian grammar, which encouraged the use of language of the common people in Russian literature.

If Lomonosov was the genius of the 18th century, then Alexander Pushkin was the soul of the 19th-century. Pushkin, known as the Father of Russian Romanticism, was born into an aristocratic family; his mother was the granddaughter of Peter the Great's Abyssinian general, Hannibal, and the poet was proud of his nobility and African blood. In 1811, Pushkin was sent to the school at Tsarskoye Selo (also called Pushkin, see page 646) where he began to write light romantic poetry. In his 20s he led a life of aristocratic dissoluteness in the salons and bordellos of the imperial capital. Many of his friends were politically active young officers associated with the Decembrist group, which Pushkin was never asked to join because they considered him too frivolous for their revolutionary mission. Nevertheless, he wrote some mildly seditious poems; one of them, *Ruslan and Ludmilla*, caused such a stir with the younger generation that it was censored by Alexander I, who also exiled the poet to the Caucasus in 1820. (See page 668.)

During his exile from St Petersburg he wrote some of his most famous works, including the epic *Boris Godunov*, the story of the pretender to the Russian throne at the start of the Time of Troubles in the early 17th century. At the end of his exile Pushkin began his masterpiece *Evgeny Onegin*, a novel in verse, partly set in the imperial capital that ridicules aristocratic society while telling the story of two star-crossed lovers, Onegin and Tatyana. In 1830, he began to publish the *Literary Gazette*, a newpaper about literature where he contributed his poetry and excerpts from his novels, such as *The Negro of Peter the Great*. His famous novel *Queen of Spades* came out in 1833; the gambler Ghermann (Herman) symbolized the secret craving of the people to take a hand in the gamble of winning freedom during an opportunistic age. That same year Pushkin completed his last narrative poem *The Bronze Horseman*, revered as one of the greatest works about St Petersburg (see page 679). In it a young government clerk watches a huge storm cause a flood in St Petersburg that destroys most of the city and kills thousands, including his fiancée. Driven mad by grief, he comes upon Falconet's statue of Peter the Great, the Bronze Horseman, and he associates Peter's terrible imperial power with the destructive force of the flood. The mad clerk shakes his fist at the statue, and the horseman comes to life in a rage and chases him out of the square with a great clattering of bronze hoofs. In 1836, Pushkin was mortally wounded in a pistol duel over his wife's honor and died on January 29 1837 (old-style calendar) at the age of 37. Immediately upon his death he was lionized as the greatest Russian writer and that acclaim continues to this day. He was buried in Pskov near the family's Mikhailovskoye Estate in the Svyatogorsky Monastery. In 2014, Russia celebrated the 215th anniversary of their beloved poet's birth. Pushkin in his own words had predicted:

> News of me then will cross the whole of Russia
> And every tribe there will have heard my name...
> And they will all love me, because my songs.
> Evoked some kindness in a cruel age.

Pushkin's mantle was inherited by Nikolai Gogol, a Ukrainian-born writer. Upon Pushkin's death, Gogol declared, 'In him, as in a dictionary, is contained all the riches, the strength and flexibility of our tongue. Pushkin is a rare and perhaps unique phenomenon of the Russian spirit... I did not write a single line without imagining him standing before me.' In his play *The Inspector General*, Gogol satirized the vast bureaucratic state that had taken over the Russian Empire. *The Nose* is a satirical short story that tells of a St. Petersburg official whose nose leaves his face and develops a life of its own. Gogol's famous short story *The Overcoat* is more enigmatic. A petty government clerk in St Petersburg invests all his savings in a new overcoat, but as he is returning home late at night he loses it to a band of robbers. After he discovers that none of his superiors will help him find his coat he dies of grief, only to reappear on the streets of St Petersburg as an avenging ghost.

(The four stories, *Nevsky Prospekt*, *Diary of a Madman*, *The Nose* and *The Overcoast*, all set in St Petersburg, have become known collectively as the Petersburg Tales.) Gogol followed *The Overcoat* with *Dead Souls* (see Excerpt on page 240), which was to be the first volume of a projected trilogy envisioned as a sort of Russian divine comedy about sin, atonement and salvation. As Gogol wrote the second volume he began to go mad, thinking that the flames of hell were licking at his heels; on the evening of February 24, 1852, he burned the manuscript. Soon thereafter, the writer took to his bed, refused all food and died nine days later at the age of 42. Nikolai Gogol was regarded as the greatest satirist of the regime of Nicholas I; thus, the government allowed no obituary or public tribute to be printed.

'Just imagine: the censorship here already forbids all mention of his [Gogol's] name!' wrote Ivan Turgenev, one of Russia's finest prose writers. In protest, he wrote the eulogy, *In Memory of Gogol*, in which he also symbolized the plight of the oppressed Russian peasant and his opposition to serfdom. After it was circulated in 1852, Czar Nicholas I exiled Turgenev from St Petersburg to his country estate.

Born in the Ukraine in 1818 to a rich aristocratic family, Turgenev graduated from Moscow University and later St Petersburg University's Philosophy Department. By the time of his graduation, he had already authored numerous plays, poems and novels (including *A Month in the Country*, *The Boarder*, *Mumu* and *First Love*), but it was his collection of short stories, *Notes of a Hunter* (*Zapiski Okhotnika*), which brought him national acclaim. A great critic of the socio-political and revolutionary climate of his time (serfs were finally emancipated in 1861), his other popular writings include, *Diary of a Superfluous Man* (1850), *Rudin* (1856), *Nakanune* (On the Eve, 1860), *Dym* (Smoke, 1867), and his last novel, *Virgin Soil* (1877).

With over 100 works, Turgenev is probably best remembered for his novel, *Father and Sons* (1862), which incorporated his three favorite themes: the tumultuous political protests and changes within Russia; the blind, impersonal force of nature; and the overriding importance of love in human relations. Before his death in 1883, Turgenev wrote of the deep love for his country, 'Russia can go without each of us, but none of us can go without her.' He is buried in the Volkovskoye cemetery in St Petersburg.

The next great St Petersburg writer was Fyodor Dostoevsky, who although anguished and epileptic managed to live a full lifespan to age 59. (He wrote, 'we all came out of Gogol's Overcoat.') Born in Moscow in 1821, Dostoevsky later moved to St Petersburg and entered the Military Engineering Academy in 1838. Upon his graduation, he served in the civil service, but gave it up to pursue a writing career. By age 25 Dostoevsky had published his first two books, *The Double* and *Poor Folk*, in which he explored social issues of the day. In 1848, he penned the short story *White Nights* about a lonely nameless narrator who falls in love with a woman who eventually leaves him to return to her former lover. (From 1957 to 2008 nine international film directors adapted the story for cinema!) During this time, Dostoevsky fell in with a group of young liberal thinkers, known as the Petrashevsky Circle who met to discuss current political issues as the liberation of the serfs. They were arrested by Czarist police in 1849, and sentenced to death by Nicholas I. After spending eight months in the harsh prison of Peter and Paul Fortress, the men were led out to the gallows for execution when, at the last minute, a messenger came riding into the square with a pardon from the Czar, who had commuted their sentences to hard labor. Dostoevsky was exiled to Omsk in Siberia for four years. When he returned he wrote *Memories from the House of the Dead* about his Siberian experiences, and the acclaim at its publication in 1860 launched his career as a writer. (In *The Idiot*, the character of Prince Myaskin tells a story about a mock execution that resembled Dostoevsky's own). Most of Dostoevsky's novels were written in serial form for magazines so he could stay one step ahead of his many creditors. He took his subject matter from popular melodramas and sensational newspaper stories and wrote about them with the methods of psychological realism, exploring the depths of the human subconscious, a form that he pioneered. His greatest novel, *Crime and Punishment*, tells the story of Raskolnikov, an impoverished former student who murders an old woman—a pawnbroker, and feels such guilt that by the time he is finally brought to justice he welcomes it. Dostoyevsky spent nearly two years writing *The Brothers Karamazov*, published as a serial in *The Russian Messenger* and completed in November 1880. It is a philosophical novel that enters deeply into the ethical debates of God, free will, and morality. The writer had intended it to be the first part in an epic story titled *The Life of a Great Sinner*, but he died less than four months after its publication. (See Literary Excerpt, page 578.)

Late in life Dostoevsky became a devout believer in Orthodox Christianity. Luckily for world literature he never lost his commitment to artistic realism, so his novels show the passionate struggle of trying to reach, but never attain, an ideal goal. When Dostoevsky died in 1881, thousands of Russians, ordinary citizens and fellow writers alike, accompanied his coffin to the Alexander Nevsky Monastery for a hero's burial.

Anton Chekhov (1860–1904), famous for such plays as *The Cherry Orchard*, *Three Sisters* and *The Seagull*, had his first stories published in St Petersburg magazines. As a realist and the first truly modern playwright, he expressed human drama in plain and simple words. He said, "Everything on stage should be just as complex and, at the same time, as simple as in life." He also loved contributing to the city's monarchist daily newspaper *Novoye Vremya* (*New Times*), which even the czar read. From 1885 to 1888, Chekhov wrote hundreds of stories for the St Petersburg weekly magazine *Fragments*; and, in total, wrote more than 400 short stories and novellas. He died of tuberculosis at the age of 44.

In 1906, the twenty-six-year-old writer and poet Alexander Blok was published in the St Petersburg weekly periodical *Niva*. He soon ignited the new Symbolist movement that heralded Russia's Silver Age of Literature which included other writers and poets, such as Andrei Bely, Vladimir Solovyov, and Sergei Yesenin. After many years of classical and realist prose, readers regained an interest in poetry, not popular since the era of Pushkin. Many of the symbolists looked upon the Revolution as an event that would purge Russia of its sins and bring on a new era of wholesome equality. Poets readily participated in political and spiritual themes that thrived in the dissident and decadent atmosphere of the times.

Blok's poems were also filled with erotic and romantic motifs, and the handsome blonde poet soon had a massive cult following among the female population. (His first book of poetry was *Verses on the Beautiful Lady* in 1904.) But soon frustrated with the new Soviet regime, Blok wrote the narrative epic poem *The Twelve* in 1918, about an army patrol who transform into the twelve apostles while walking through ruined Petrograd after the Revolution; led by Christ, they hope for redemption. A year later, Blok was arrested by the Cheka police for participating in anti-Soviet conspiracies. He was eventually released, but as he later wrote to a friend: 'I'm suffocating... and the old music is gone.' One of the last poems Blok penned was: 'Pushkin! Having you to guide us. We sing secret freedom's song! With your help we'll bear this onus. Help the silent struggling throng!' Thereafter broken, Blok never again picked up his pen. When he died in Leningrad on August 7 1921, at the age of 40, his friends knew that the lack of creative freedom had stifled his spirit. The obituary in Pravda for one of the greatest poets of the 20th century was composed of one sentence: 'Last night the poet Alexander Blok passed away.' *The Artist* ends with:

> The wings have been clipped and the song sung—so often
> Does it please you to stand by the sill in the sun?
> The song gives you pleasure? But, I, in exhaustion,
> Wait, bored as before, for a new one to come.

Two weeks after Blok's funeral Nikolai Gumilyov, the ex-husband of the poet Anna Akhmatova, was arrested on false charges by Bolshevik police for participating in anti-Soviet propaganda. Before his arrest Gumilyov had written a poem called *The Streetcar Gone Astray*, about the outcome of the Revolution. He was executed by firing squad without a trial. Prior to the Revolution he had founded a new poetry movement in St Petersburg known as Acmeism. Their idea was to reject the ethereal aspects of symbolism and write about the direct and tangible 'salty skin of the earth'.

The cofounder of the Acmeist movement, Osip Mandalstam, possessed a prophetic understanding of the country's suffering and fate as expressed in his three collections of poetry: Stone, Tristia and Poems. Mandalstam also did not escape persecution under Stalin, and was eventually sentenced to five years hard labor for counterrevolutionary activities. He died in 1938, at the age of 48, from heart failure in a freezing transit camp in Vladivostok, Siberia; he wrote, "only in Russia is poetry respected—it gets people killed." His widow Nadezhda Mandalstam wrote an incredibly moving memoir about her life with Osip. It was published in two large volumes entitled *Hope Against Hope and Hope Abandoned*. (*Nadezhda in Russian means 'hope.'*)

With these quintessential St Petersburg poets dead, the new regime severely underscored the fact that the cultural elite would be under their control. Not able to live with his own disillusionment, the futurist poet Vladimir Mayakovsky shot himself in 1930 while playing Russian roulette at the age of 36. His suicide stunned an already desolate nation. It was Anna Akhmatova who took up the poetic reins during these times of terror. (See Special Topic on page 675.)

Her contemporary, Vladimir Nabokov, made his debut as a poet in St Petersburg, though he emigrated to Europe in 1919 and then in 1940 to America. Born in the city in 1899, Nabokov frequently used St Petersburg as a theme for his stories. Some of his classic works include *Pale Fire, Pnin, Laughter in the Dark* and *Lolita*—later made into a film by Stanley Kubrick. Nabokov's brilliant autobiography *Speak, Memory* was one of the first contemporary books to introduce the city of St Petersburg to an international audience. He also wrote a splendid little biography of Nikolai Gogol which begins with the writer's death and ends with his birth.

In 1903, Ivan Bunin won the Pushkin Prize for Literature, and in 1909, was elected to the Academy of Sciences in St Petersburg. Like Turgenev and Chekhov, Bunin portrayed the reality of Russian life while encompassing the themes of universal human passions and struggles. Some of his works include, *The Village* (1910), *Dry Valley* (1911), *The Brothers* (1914) and *Nooselike Ears* (1916). In the wake of the Russian revolution, Ivan Bunin (then aged 48) and his wife fled to the Black Sea port of Odessa. Living here during the years of 1918 and 1919 (before they emigrated to France), Bunin kept a diary of his observations on revolutionary events entitled *Cursed Days*, in which he reflected, 'I will never accept that Russia has been destroyed... Socialism contradicts and is completely unsuited to the human soul.' He predicted, only wrong in his timing, that 'in twenty five years, the passion for individualism would rise from the ashes of communism.' In 1933, Bunin received the Nobel Prize for Literature, the first Russian writer to ever be awarded this honor. Boris Pasternak (1890–1960) would later receive the Nobel Prize for *Dr Zhivago* in 1958.

With Akhmatova's death in 1966, the one heroic figure that had connected the three eras of St Petersburg, Petrograd and Leningrad was gone. Joseph Brodsky, born on Vasilyevsky Island in 1940, was considered the heir apparent to both Nabokov and Akhmatova. And, in the late 1950's, during the Khrushchev thaw, Brodsky and other young poets, known as Akhmatova's Orphans, gathered in her apartment to discuss and read their works. But, in 1964, the writer, accused of social parasitism (being unemployed) was sentenced to five years hard labor in the Arctic Circle for writing poetry without official permission. Interrogated at the trial about where his poetry came from, he replied: 'I thought that it came from God.' After being imprisoned three times and twice thrown into a madhouse for his writings, Brodsky was finally expelled by Brezhnev from the Soviet Union in 1972. He wrote:

> I let the burnished gaze of the warden into my dreams.
> Gnawed the bread of exile, leaving no crusts.
> I allowed my chords to voice every sound, but for howls:
> I switched to a whisper. Now I am forty.
>
> May, 24, 1980.

The old regime tried to erase his existence from history, but Brodsky received international acclaim when he won the Nobel Prize for Literature in 1987. He became an American citizen in 1980 and died in New York in 1995. In Brodsky, Leningraders felt that the Nobel Prize also honored the other literary geniuses who were never recognized by their own country.

In 1964, shocked by Brodsky's trial, the writer Andrei Bitov began work on his novel *Pushkin House*, a requiem for the disillusioned St Petersburg intelligentsia. The novel's hero works at Leningrad's Pushkin House, the research academy of Russian literature. Bitov uses this theme to interweave writings by many of the city's past respected authors—from Pushkin to Akhmatova. It was published in 1978 by an American publishing house, but was not allowed past Soviet censors until 1987, when it immediately became a sensation during Gorbachev's glasnost era.

Another work that had laid in a desk drawer for 20 years, and also finally was published in 1987, was *Children of the Arbat* by Anatoly Rybakov, one of the milestones of perestroika. The novel was fairly autobiographical—in 1933 Rybakov was arrested and sentenced to three years in exile for obscure counter-revolutionary activities. He eventually joined the army during WWII and participated in the storming of Berlin. The book was the first literary description of Stalin's regime and the era of Soviet stagnation. It was ardently read and passed from hand-to-hand in underground xeroxed *samizdat* fashion. In 1999, Rybakov died in his sleep, at the age of 87.

By 1990 many long-banned works by authors such as Nabokov, Pasternak, Akhmatova and even Solzhenitsyn were published and distributed among a new generation of Russian readers. Many foreign authors were also translated into Russian for the first time. But ironically, with the demise of socialism, the Writers' Union and most State-subsidized publishing also collapsed. Post-perestroika Russia appeared just as devastated as its corrupt Communist shadow; this time however, instead of for political reasons, contemporary writers were stifled out of economic needs.

A CULTURAL EXTRAVAGANZA

*I*n the season of 1903–4 Petersburg witnessed concerts in the grand manner. I am speaking of the strange, never-to-be surpassed madness of the concerts of Hoffmann and Kubelik in the Nobility Hall during Lent. I can recall no other musical experiences, not even the premiere of Scriabin's Prometheus, that might be compared with these Lenten orgies in the white-columned hall. The concerts would reach a kind of rage, a fury. This was no musical dilettantism: there was something threatening and even dangerous that rose up out of enormous depths, a kind of craving for movement; a mute prehistorical malaise was exuded by the peculiar, the almost flagellant zeal of the halberdiers in Mikhaylovsky Square, and it whetted the Petersburg of that day like a knife. In the dim light of the gas lamps the many entrances of the Nobility Hall were beset by a veritable siege. Gendarmes on prancing horses, lending to the atmosphere of the square the mood of a civil disturbance, made clicking noises with their tongues and shouted as they closed ranks to guard the main entry. The sprung carriages with dim lanterns slipped into the glistening circle and arranged themselves in an impressive black gypsy camp. The cabbies dared not deliver their fares right to the door; one paid them while approaching, and then they made off rapidly to escape the wrath of the police. Through the triple chains the Petersburger made his way like a feverish little trout to the marble ice-hole of the vestibule, whence he disappeared into the luminous frosty building, draped with silk and velvet.

The orchestra seats and the places behind them were filled in the customary order, but the spacious balconies to which the side entrances gave access were filled in bunches, like baskets, with clusters of humanity. The Nobility Hall inside is wide, stocky, and almost square. The stage itself takes up nearly half the area. The gallery swelters in a July heat. The air is filled with a ceaseless humming like that of cicadas over the steppe.

Osip Mandelstam, The Noise of Time, 1922

In the early 1990s, the International Booker Prize Committee instituted a special Smirnov-Booker Russian novel prize to annually recognize the new generation of Russian writers. In 1999, Mikhail Butov (a former TV antenna repairman) won the $12,500 prize for his novel *Svoboda (Freedom)*. The novel tells the story of the country's first liberated generation (born in the 1960s) who grew up in the final era of Soviet stagnation and passed into adulthood during the reform years of the late 1980s. Butov's protagonist wants out of the old way of life, but does not yet know how to fit into the new climate the tumultuous changes have created. 'Unfortunately,' Butov explained, 'winners of the Russian Booker don't automatically see their books printed in huge print runs... *Svoboda* was first printed in 2,500 copies. It was only in the Soviet past that books were printed in the millions!'

The Russian Booker Prize, the country's premier literary award, is handed out each year to the best work of fiction written in the Russian language A jury chooses a short list of the six best novels from a long list of nominees, and the winner receives a monetary award of about $20,000. In 2011, a 'Novel of the Decade' was chosen—Alexander Chudakov won posthumously for *A Gloom Is Cast Upon the Ancient Steps*, which takes place in a fictional town in Kazakhstan and describes life under Stalinist Russia. The National Bestseller is the annual Literary Prize awarded to a St Petersburg author for the best novel written in Russian. In 2014, the winner was 31-year-old St Petersburg poet, Kseniya Buksha for *Freedom Factory*, her novel about a defense industrial factory; the award came with a prize of R250,000 (www.rus-lit.org).

In 2006, the first winner of a new Russian literary prize, called the Big Book (*Bolshaya Kniga*), was Dmitry Bykov for his biography on Boris Pasternak (author of *Dr Zhivago*). Sponsored by the Russian government and backed by Russian oligarchs, the prize came with winnings of three million rubles ($100,000). In 2012, London's Pushkin House began the annual Russian Book Prize to reward non-fiction writing on Russia. For a list of books, authors and current prize winners: www.pushkinhouse.org.

With the advent of a new century, Russian literature has slowly begun to recover with a revitalized exuberance and freshness of vision. Realist writers Tatyana Tolstaya and Alexandra Marinina create moving portraits of everyday lives in Russia. Aside from the classics and innovative contemporary novels (such as Victor Pelevin's *Buddha's Little Finger*, *Omon Ra*, and *Generation P* (Babylon)), even pulp fiction, romance (nicknamed 'love-burgers' for the way they are mass produced—like fast-food) action thrillers and detective novels (the latter claims a whopping 38 percent of the Russian fiction market, science fiction and mysticism, a 26 percent share) have become more popular than ever. Among Russia's best-selling authors is Grigory Chkhartashvili, whose pen name, Boris Akunin, is a play on words for the

19th-century Russian anarchist Mikhail Bakunin. Akunin's first detective novel, *The Winter Queen*, is set in both Moscow and St Petersburg. The central charismatic character, Erast Petrovich Fandorin, begins his adventures in 1876, the day of Bakunin's death. Many of Akunin's novels have now been translated into English, and several have been made into feature films.

Translated foreign works by leading authors, such as Tom Clancy and Barbara Cartland (nicknamed 'Baba Katya'), and works on new technologies (such as the 'for Dummies' series—*dlya Chainikov*) are also widely read. As one noted Russian writer observed, 'Dissidence via literature has evaporated. Back then our most widely read literature, the *samizdat* 'underground' books served a different function. Today literature has simply become a pastime.'

BALLET

The first *balli*, or *balletti*, originated in Italy during the Renaissance, when dance became an important social function in court life. Men would entertain at court festivities in routines combining music, dancing, singing and acting; women, on the other hand, were forbidden to dance openly in public. By the late 15th century, it was the vogue for court entertainment to be combined with banquets—each course was accompanied by a new scene in the story. Menus still list the entrées as they did five centuries ago. The French soon copied the Italians by staging their own *ballets de cour*. Their courts brought in Italian dancing masters, and many outstanding French painters and poets collaborated in the elaborate displays. These staged spectacles were set up to glorify the power and the wealth of the monarchy.

King Louis XIV of France was an avid dancer himself and took the part of the sun in the *Ballet de la Nuit*. Later in life, when Louis could no longer dance, he established the first *Académie Royale de Musique* (now the Paris Opera) where a dancing school was added that set the foundation of classical ballet.

As the Italians invented the idea of the *balli* as a combination of all the arts, the French developed this new vision of dance into a professional school, the *danse d'école*. A style of classical dancing was born with its own vocabulary of individual steps, the five positions of the feet (fashioned from court ballroom dance moves) and synchronized group movements. French terminology is still used today.

This form of ballet-dance was first staged in Moscow in 1672 by a German ensemble for Czar Alexei I. The theatrical performance, lasting ten hours, was based on the Bible's Book of Esther. Alexei's daughter, Sophia (the future regent), was very fond of dancing herself and composed comedy ballets, such as *Russalki* (the Mermaids). Sophia's half-brother, Peter the Great, encouraged Western dance and later, as czar, brought in many French, English and Polish companies for lavish productions in his new city of Sankt Pieterburkh. Later the St Petersburg Imperial Ballet was founded in 1738.

During the reigns of Elizabeth (1741–61) and Catherine the Great (1762–96), many French and Italian masters took up residence in St Petersburg and Moscow. By the turn of the century St Petersburg was approaching the peak of its cosmopolitan fame. It had four separate opera houses with permanent companies, all fully supported by the czarinas and czars. While ballet grew in popularity and artistic importance in Russia, it declined throughout the rest of Europe.

One of the most influential characters of the early Russian ballet scene was the Frenchman Charles Didelot, who arrived in Russia in 1801. He taught at the St Petersburg Imperial Ballet School for more than 25 years and wove French classical and Russian folk themes through the new romantic style of the times. He was the first to translate Pushkin's poems, *The Prisoner of the Caucasus* and *Ruslan and Ludmilla*, into the physical world of ballet. Under his direction, the ballet was made into a grand spectacle, incorporating the entire *corps de ballet*, costumes, scenery, and even special effects—dancers were fitted with wings and live pigeons flew across the stage.

Another of St Petersburg's well-known dancers was the Frenchman Marius Petipa (1819–1910), who came to Russia in 1847. Petipa was the master of the grand spectacle and produced an original ballet for the opening of each new season. During his 56-year career on the Russian stage, Petipa choreographed over 60 ballets for the Imperial Ballet, highlighting solos within each performance. In the early 1890s this grand master worked almost exclusively with Tchaikovsky, choreographing *Sleeping Beauty*, *The Nutcracker*, and *Swan Lake*. It was Petipa who brought the Imperial Ballet to the pinnacle of the ballet world.

All the St Petersburg ballets premièred at the Mariinsky Theater. Built by Albert Kavos in 1860, it was named after Maria, wife of Czar Alexander II. (In 1935, it was renamed the Kirov, after the prominent Communist leader under Stalin; but in 1992, the original name was restored.) The Mariinsky remains one of the most respected names in the ballet world. It is situated in St Petersburg on Ploshchad Teatralnaya (Theater Square; see page 586). This section of land was once the location for St Petersburg carnivals and fairs. (In the 18th-century, it was known as Ploshchad Karusel, Merry-Go-Round Square.) This gorgeous 1,700 seater, five-tiered theater is decorated with blue velvet, gilded stucco, ceiling paintings and chandeliers.

By the end of the 19th-century the Mariinsky Theater had almost 200 permanently employed dancers, graded in rank. Each graduate of the Imperial Ballet School was placed into the *corps de ballet*; only a few rose to coryphée, *sujet*, prima ballerina and lastly *prima absoluta* (or, for a man, soloist to the czar). They were employed by the czar for 20 years and retired with full pensions. Ballet dancers were often invited to court banquets, and favorites received many luxurious presents from admirers and the royal family themselves. Nicholas II bestowed large gifts of diamonds and emeralds upon his jewel *danseuse* Kchessinskaya, which she often wore during performances. (See page 56.)

As the spirit of revolution hung in the air, the Imperial Ballet's conventional classical style plunged into decline. It was the St Petersburg artistic entrepreneur Sergei Diaghilev (1872–1929), who revived the stagnating Imperial Ballet with the individual and innovative style of the Ballets Russes. Diaghilev brought Russia's best dancers, choreographers, musicians and artists together to create some of the most stunning spectacles that the world had ever known. His dancers were Pavlova, Karsavina and Nijinsky; his choreographers Fokine, Massine, Nijinskaya (Nijinsky's sister) and later Balanchine; musicians Tchaikovsky, Chopin, Stravinsky and Rimsky-Korsakov; and artists Benois, Bakst, Goncharova and even Picasso. During the first season abroad in Paris in 1909, the repertoire of the Ballets Russes consisted of Borodin's *Polovtsian Dances* from *Prince Igor*, Chopin's *Les Sylphides* and *The Banquet*, with music by Tchaikovsky, Mussorgsky and Rimsky-Korsakov. The programs were designed by the French writer Jean Cocteau and posters painted by Moscow artist Valentin Serov. Even Erik Satie joined the group of musicians. In the center of all this furor were two of the most magnificent dancers of the 20th-century, Anna Pavlova and Vaslav Nijinsky.

Born the illegitimate daughter of a poor laundress, Pavlova did not seem destined for the stage. But in 1891, at the age of ten, this petite dark-eyed beauty was accepted into the St Petersburg Imperial Ballet School. When she graduated in 1899, the stunning performer leaped right into solo roles in the Mariinsky Theater. Anna then left to dance with the Ballets Russes; after her first performance in Paris, a French critic exuberantly claimed: 'She is to dance what Racine is to poetry, Poussin to painting, Gluck to music.' Pavlova was known for her dynamic short solos, filled with an endless cascade of jumps and pirouettes as in *The Dying Swan* and *The Dragonfly*.

Nijinsky was heralded as the greatest male dancer of his day—dancing was in his blood. For generations his family worked as dancers, acrobats, and circus performers. Vaslav was born in Kiev in 1888, where his Polish parents were performing. When he was 11, his mother enrolled him in the St Petersburg Imperial Ballet School, where he studied for eight years. His graduation performance so impressed the *prima absoluta* ballerina Matilda Kchessinskaya that he immediately began his career at the Mariinsky Theater as a principal soloist.

His full genius emerged at the Ballets Russes' 1909 Paris debut. One spectator felt that 'his was the victory of breath over weight, the possession of body by the soul.' In 1911, Nijinsky was fired from the Imperial Ballet for not wearing the required little pair of trunks over his tights when he danced *Giselle*; this did not go down well with the dowager empress, who witnessed with crimson face the entire performance. His range in roles was astonishing. Everywhere he went, Nijinsky captured the hearts and adoration of the critics and audiences. One American

THE PETITION OF JANUARY 9, 1905

A Most Humble and Loyal Address of the Workers of St Petersburg Intended for Presentation to HIS MAJESTY on Sunday at two o'clock on the Winter Palace Square.

SIRE:
We, the workers and inhabitants of St Petersburg, of various estates, our wives, our children, and our aged, helpless parents, come to Thee, O SIRE, to seek justice and protection. We are impoverished; we are oppressed, overburdened with excessive toil, contemptuously treated. We are not even recognized as human beings, but are treated like slaves who must suffer their bitter fate in silence and without complaint. And we have suffered, but even so we are being further pushed into the slough of poverty, arbitrariness, and ignorance. We are suffocating in despotism and lawlessness. O SIRE, we have reached that frightful moment when death is better than the prolongation of our unbearable sufferings.

Hence, we stopped work and told employers that we will not resume work until our demands are fulfilled. We did not ask much; we sought only that without which there is no life for us but hard labor and eternal suffering. Our first request was that our employers agree to discuss our needs with us. But even this we were refused. We were prohibited even from speaking of our needs, since no such right is given us by law. The following requests were also deemed to be outside of the law: the reduction of the work day to eight hours; our manual participation in determining the rates for our work and in the settlement of grievances that might arise between us and the lower managerial staff; to raise the minimum daily wages for unskilled workers, and for women as well, to one ruble; to abolish overtime work; to give our sick better medical attention without insults; and to arrange our workshops so that we might work there without encountering death from murderous drafts, rain, and snow.

According to our employers and managers, our demands turned out to be illegal, our every request a crime, and our desire to improve our conditions an insolence, insulting to them. O SIRE, there are more than 300,000 of us but we are human beings in appearance only, for we, with the rest of the Russian people, do not possess a single human right, not even the right to speak, think, gather, discuss our needs, and take steps to improve our conditions. We are enslaved, enslaved under the patronage and with the aid of Thy officials. Anyone of us who dares to raise his voice in defense of the working class and the people is thrown into jail or exiled. Kindheartedness is punished as a crime. To feel sorry for a worker as a downtrodden, maltreated human being bereft of his rights is to commit a heinous crime! The workers and the peasants are delivered into the hands of the bureaucratic administration, comprised of embezzlers of public funds and robbers, who not only care nothing for the needs of the people, but flagrantly abuse them. The bureaucratic administration brought the country to the brink of ruin, involved her in a humiliating war, and is leading Russia closer and closer to disaster. We, the workers and people, have no voice whatsoever in the spending of huge sums collected from us in taxes. We do not even know how the money, collected from the impoverished people, is spent. The people are deprived of the opportunity to express their wishes and demands, to participate in the establishment of taxes and public spending. The workers are deprived of the opportunity to organize their unions in order to defend their interests.

O SIRE, is this in accordance with God's laws, by the grace of which Thou reignest? Is it possible to live under such laws? Would it not be preferable for all of us, the toiling people of Russia, to die? Let the capitalists—exploiters of the working class and officials, the embezzlers and plunderers of the Russian people, live and enjoy their lives.

Translated by Walter Sablinsky

critic noted, 'few of us can view the art of Nijinsky without emotion... he completely erased the memory of all male dancers that I had previously seen.'

Nijinsky danced with Pavlova in *Cleopatra* and as the ethereal spirit in *Le Spectre de la Rose*. Jean Cocteau, who saw his first performance in Paris, exclaimed that Nijinsky's jumps 'were so poignant, so contrary to all the laws of flight and balance, following so high and curved a trajectory, that I shall never again smell a rose without this unerasable phantom appearing before me.' Fokine choreographed up a storm of innovative and dynamic ballets and stressed strong male dancing; Nijinsky danced in almost all his creations, including *Le Pavillion d'Armide*, *Sheherazade*, *The Firebird*, *Narcisse*, *Daphnis and Chloe*, and *Le Dieu Bleu* (The Blue Clown). In his diary, Nijinsky wrote 'I am beginning to understand God. Art, love, nature are only an infinitesimal part of God's spirit. I wanted to recapture it and give it to the public... If they felt it, then I am reflecting Him. The world, in turn, would regard him as *Le Dieu de la Danse*.

His first choreographic work, *L'Après-Midi d'un Faune*, was performed in 1912. Even though only eight minutes long, it managed to cause a scandal that rocked even Paris. With his natural faun-like eyes, waxed pointed ears and horns, and dressed only in tights with a curly golden wig, Nijinsky danced around seven lively nymphs. At the end of the ballet, each nymph fled as she dropped her veil. During this flight of passage, he caught up with each nymph and swept down under her in one convulsive, erotic movement. The audience gasped audibly.

Nijinsky's *Le Sacre du Printemps*, performed a year later on May 29, 1913, stopped just short of causing a riot in Paris; even the composer, Igor Stravinsky, had to flee the theater. The story of the ballet weaves around the ritual of the pagan rites of spring. The dancers' movements were not traditional gentle swayings and graceful turns, but asymmetrical rhythms and gestures, twists and jerks. By the time the first act was completed, many spectators were already hissing and screaming; the music was barely audible over the cries of emotional insults.

Nijinsky gave his last dance in Switzerland in 1919, at the age of 31, ten years after his first performance. By then he had already embarked on his voyage into madness; his memory became a blank. Prophesying in his diary, he had written, 'people will leave me alone, calling me a mad clown.' Nijinsky lived out the rest of his days in an asylum; his body died in 1950.

On the night of March 15, 1917, the day Nicholas II abdicated the throne to the Provisional Government, *Sleeping Beauty* was performed at the Mariinsky Theater in Petrograd. This parable, about a kingdom plunged into a century-long sleep on the whim of an evil witch, prophetically foretold the fate of an entire nation. (After the revolution the Mariinsky was renamed the Kirov Theater, after Leningrad Party Boss Sergei Kirov, who was later assassinated in 1934.)

During the Soviet era, one of the most famous ballerinas was Galina Ulanova (1910–1998), whose father was the director of the Imperial Mariinsky and mother a dancer and teacher at the Imperial school. In 1944, on Stalin's personal order, she left the Kirov Ballet for Moscow's Bolshoi to become the Prima Ballerina, where she danced all the greatest roles in classical ballet.

"Galina was an angel, and danced like one," stated another extraordinary dancer of the time, Maya Plisetskaya, who rose to fame in 1945 when she premiered in Prokofiev's ballet, *Cinderella*. Rodion Schedrin, her husband, composed a special ballet for her based on Bizet's opera *Carmen*. But it was her portrayal of the dying swan in Tchaikovsky's *Swan Lake* that became her signature role. Each year in St Petersburgh there is an annual ballet contest bearing her name, 'Maya.'

As Ulanova and Plisetskaya, the troika of today's reigning ballerinas, Lopatkina, Vishneva and Zakharova are also products of the famed Vagonova Ballet School on Rossi Street. Dating back over two centuries to the Imperial Ballet academy, the famous St Petersburg academy was renamed after Agrippina Vagonova who taught here between 1921 and 1951, and exemplified the Russian dance style in her book, *Basic Principles of Classical Ballet*. Each year over 2,000 hopefuls apply for the eight-year study program, and only about 100 are chosen. The Vagonova remains one of the world's premiere ballet institutions; and over former years, it has produced numerous other ballet icons, such as Karsavina, Semenova, Kolpakova, Makarova, Nureyev, Balanchivadze (Balanchine) and Baryshnikov.

From the 1930's to the 1960's, the Ballets Russes (which eventually dissolved into two different troupes, the Original Ballet Russes, and the Ballet Russes of Monte Carlo), continued to revolutionize ballet with groundbreaking productions around the world. In 2005, American filmmakers, Dayna Goldfine and Dan Geller, created a fabulous documentary, entitled *Ballet-Russes*, for which they interviewed the surviving dancers during their first-ever reunion in 2000. These included: Dame Alicia Markova who, until her death in 2004, continued to coach dancers in London; George Zoritch (1917–2009); Frederic Franklin (1914–2013), who traveled the world in his nineties to teach Ballet-Russes choreographies; and the famed teenage "Baby Ballerinas" Irina Baranova, Tamara Toumanova (1919–1996) and Tatiana Riabouchinska (1917–2000). The film creatively intertwines the interviews with fascinating archival footage and old photographs of the talented dancers, and brilliantly celebrates the remarkable legacy of the Russian dance world and the Ballets Russes.

MUSIC

The development of Russian music in St Petersburg followed the same patterns as literature, only later. In the 1830s and 40s Mikhail Glinka, a close friend of Pushkin, composed many symphonies and two operas based on Russian folk songs from his childhood. Glinka put these folk themes together with many of Pushkin's poems and produced some of the first distinctly Russian musical works. One of his most famous pieces is *Ruslan and Ludmilla,* an opera based on Pushkin's mock-romantic epic about the court of Kievan Russia.

Glinka's 1836 patriotic opera *Ivan Susanin* (later renamed, over his objection, *A Life for the Czar*) is about a peasant who saved the first Romanov czar from a Polish invasion. Composed at a dinner in honor of Glinka after its premiere, Pushkin wrote, 'By this innovation giver. Everyone will be amazed; Moscow to the Neva River. Our Orpheus will be praised.' (Glinka's *Patriotic Song* was the tune for the Russian national anthem from 1991 to 2000.) Another of his popular works, *Farewell to Petersburg,* is composed of a kaleidoscope of sounds that mixes Spanish boleros, Jewish songs and Italian barcaroles. *Travel Song* depicts images in sound of the first Russian railway, built between St Petersburg and the czar's palace in Tsarskoye Selo. Russians consider Glinka to be the father of their national music.

By the mid-19th-century St Petersburg had become a major musical center and Berlioz, Verdi, Strauss and Wagner conducted their works there. In response to this invasion of Western talent, particularly Wagner, whom they believed had imperial aspirations, a group of Russian composers banded together to create a musical style that was uniquely Russian (using unique tonal and harmonic devices). Known as the 'Mighty 'Handful' (*Moguchaya Kuchka*), the five composers were Cesar Cui, Mily Balakirev, Nikolai Rimsky-Korsakov, Alexander Borodin and Modest Mussorgsky. The Band followed Glinka's example and composed music based on folk songs and themes from Russian literature. Borodin's most famous work was the opera *Prince Igor,* which was based on an old Russian heroic song and included the famous Eastern dance number *The Polovtsian Dances.* Rimsky-Korsakov also wrote a number of operas based on mythic-historical themes from early Russian history and folklore. Mussorgsky, an epileptic like Dostoevsky, was the most artistically ambitious of the Band. He began by writing works based on Gogol's stories, which he considered were the closest to the Russian soul. Another piece tried to reproduce musically the babble in the marketplace at Nizhny Novgorod. Mussorgsky's two greatest works are the opera *Boris Godunov,* based on Pushkin's poem, and *Pictures from an Exhibition,* inspired by the drawings of his friend Viktor Hartman. *Khovanshchina,* the first part of an unfinished trilogy, is a kind of tone poem rendition of Russian-style chaos and social anarchy set at the end of the Time of Troubles just before Peter took the throne. While Mussorgsky was finishing this piece he went mad, and died a few weeks after Dostoevsky in 1881. He was buried near the writer in the Alexander Nevsky Monastery (see page 576).

As the Mighty Handful was striving to lead Russia back to her roots, another faction, led by Anton Rubenstein, preferred the influence of European-oriented music. Rubenstein, a piano prodigy, organized state sponsorship for musical training; the St Petersburg Conservatory became the first of its kind in Russia. The talented performer and composer charmed audiences with his piano pieces that included *Kamenny Island* and *Soirées à St Petersburg*.

In 1862, Peter Tchaikovsky, then aged 22, was accepted as part of the first group of students into the St Petersburg Conservatory, having earlier received a degree in law. During his time, St Petersburg was a melting pot of sounds—everything from French waltzes and Italian arias to military marches and Gypsy songs. Their effect can be recognized in his first three symphonies, and in the *Slavonic March* and *1812 Overture*. In his popular opera *Queen of Spades*, based on Pushkin's novella, Tchaikovsky rekindled a patriotic theme. The talented musician also composed for the Mariinsky Ballet; some of his most evocative works include *The Nutcracker*, *Sleeping Beauty* and *Swan Lake*.

Alexander III was enraptured with the composer's genius and in 1888 granted him a lifetime annual pension of 3,000 rubles. In 1891, Tchaikovsky was even invited to conduct at the grand opening of New York's Carnegie Hall. Tchaikovsky's most popular symphony is considered to be the Sixth (*Pathétique*), written shortly before his death. Peter Tchaikovsky became one of the world's most popular composers.

Sergei Prokofiev (1891–1953) studied piano, and composition at the St Petersburg Conservatory under Rimsky-Korsakov. He wrote numerous sonatas, concertos and symphonies, composed for the ballets *Romeo and Juliet* and *Cinderella*, and collaborated with the filmmaker Sergei Eistenstein on his screen epics *Alexander Nevsky* and *Ivan the Terrible*. In Prokofiev's well-known *Album for Children*, he created the classic 'Peter and the Wolf.'

The Bolshevik Revolution would put a serious damper on experimentation in Russian music. Many composers such as Stravinsky, Rachmaninov and Prokofiev later fled Russia for the West. Prokofiev eventually returned to Russia in the mid 1930's, where he remained until his death. Ironically he died on March 5, 1953, the same day as Stalin; he is buried in Moscow's Novodevichy Cemetery. Igor Stravinsky, who had composed the music for some of the finest Mariinsky ballets, eventually settled in America where he helped score Walt Disney's animated film Fantasia in 1940. Abroad, Stravinsky also began a close collaboration with Diaghilev and the Ballet Russes, where *The Firebird*, *Petrouchka* and *Le Sacre du Printemps* (*The Rite of Spring*) became phenomenal successes. In 1937, the New York Metropolitan opera staged *Apollon*

Musagéte and Le Baiser de la Fée—the composer's special tribute to Tchaikovsky. Stravinsky said, "I know that the twelve notes in each octave and the varieties of rhythm offer me opportunities that all of human genius will never exhaust."

Leningrad's greatest musical resident after the Revolution was Dmitri Shostakovich, born in the city on September 25 1906. (The 100th Anniversary of his birth was celebrated in 2006.) He studied at the St Petersburg Conservatory, both as a composer and pianist. His graduation thesis was the First Symphony, which was played at the Leningrad Philharmonic in 1926, when the composer was just 19 years old. His Second Symphony was named *Dedication to the October Revolution*, and his Third honored May Day, the official holiday of the proletariat. Boxed in by the demands of socialist realism, Shostakovich soon found an outlet by experimenting with constructionist principles and the avant-garde.

In 1930, tiring of this nonsensical propaganda, Shostakovich followed with an experimental opera entitled *The Nose*, based on Gogol's unsettling 1836 novel about a St Petersburg aristocrat. Even though Shostakovich called it 'a satire on the era of Nicholas I', the innate message of the story was not lost on Soviet censors. It was removed from the repertoire and not restaged again for more than 40 years. Following this Shostakovich feared for his life living under Stalin, and he kept a toothbrush and towel permanently packed in a bag, expecting an arrest to come at any moment. He later credited his survival to his movie scores, used for propaganda purposes by the Soviet Union (he frequently composed scores for Eisenstein's films, see Special Topic on page 220).

On the eve of the purges in 1937, Shostakovich wrote his tragic Fourth Symphony, which was withdrawn from its premiere and not heard in public again until 1961. During the midst of the purges he premiered his Fifth Symphony in Leningrad; with its slow requiem-like movements, it clearly represented the tragedies of the times.

Saved by the patriotic events of World War II, Shostakovich fervently began to compose his famous Seventh Symphony, dedicated to the fate of Leningrad. It was broadcast throughout the country on March 5, 1942 during the German blockade. Ironically, on April 11, Shostakovich was bestowed with the country's highest cultural award, the Stalin Prize. (The composer later declared that the symphony was written as a protest against both Hitler and Stalin.) The score was flown on a bomber to the United States and leading conductors vied for the honor of its American premiere—Toscanini won. His Eighth Symphony was strongly denounced by the authorities. It was only in 1949 that Shostakovich produced Stalin's desired masterpiece, *Song of the Forests*. Shostakovich was eventually internationally honored with the Sibelius Prize and, in 1958, with an honorary doctorate from Oxford University.

All told, Shostakovich wrote fifteen symphonies and works in every major genre, including concertos, sonatas, quartets, and the operatic masterpiece, *Lady Macbeth of the Mtsensk District*. Today he is the namesake for the acclaimed Shostakovich Philharmonia on Arts Square in St Petersburg.

Today both Russians and foreign visitors alike enjoy performances by these and other contemporary composers in the theaters and philharmonic halls of Moscow and St Petersburg. UNESCO named 1989 as the year of the composer Modest Mussorgsky. In the spring of 1990, the renowned cellist and conductor Mstislav Rostropovich and his opera singer wife, Galina Vishnevskaya, were allowed to return to Russia after 16 years of exile. In 2007, Rostropovich was honored by President Putin in the Kremlin for his 80th Birthday shortly before he passed away.

During the reform years of the 1980s, Leningrad's most popular musician was Boris Grebenshchikov, considered the country's equivalent of Bob Dylan. He founded his band, Akvarium (Aquarium) in 1972, but they toiled for many years in the 'unofficial' underground (the government did not recognize rock n' roll—in an early popular song, Grebenshchikov sang, 'I'm tired of being the ambassador of rock n' roll/In a country that can't feel the beat'). In 1980, after the band performed at a national music festival, Grebenshchikov was labeled an anti-Soviet agitator, fired from his job as a computer programmer, and forced to work as a janitor.

But eventually, during glasnost, the singer/songwriter had his band's illicit homemade recordings officially released, which immediately sold millions of copies. (This also meant that the government made a hefty profit. The irony was not lost on Grebenshchikov. A song on the *Equinox* album: 'We were silent like dogs/As they sold off all they could sell/Including our children...')

By 1989, when the walls between East and West were crumbling, the Russian rock superstar had an American record contract, a US Tour, a documentary film, videos for MTV, and interviews with *Rolling Stone* magazine. Today, he performs around the world, and is still going strong (see www.planetaquarium.com for tour schedules). Grebenshchikov continues to sing the final lines from his now famous song, *Railroad Water*: 'I wrote these songs at December's end/Naked, in the snow, by the light of the moon/But if you can hear me/Maybe it wasn't in vain.' He speaks for all his country's artists who were suppressed during the Soviet regime. One of Aquarium's classic albums is *Peski Peterburga*.

Another popular album was *Chorny Pyos Peterburg* by rock band DDT, led by Yuri Shevchuk. One of the most famous early Russian rockers who became an idol to millions was Kino's lead singer/songwriter Viktor Tsoy, born in Leningrad in 1962; his father was a Soviet-Korean engineer. (Tsoy's first band was called Ward No. 6 after Chekhov's famous story.) By 1988, the album *Blood Type (Gruppa Krovi)* created Kinomania across the USSR. The next album *A Star Named the Sun* culminated in a famous concert at Moscow's Luzhniki Stadium in 1989. The following year Tsoy died tragically in a car accident at the age of 28. Tsoy retains cult status today: Tsoy's Wall remains in Moscow's Arbat, and each year on August 15, the anniversary of his death, fans still gather to play and sing his tunes by his grave in St Peterburg's Bogoslovskoye Cemetery.

In 1987, Igor Matvienko created another popular St Petersburg group, Lyube, devoted to working class Russians. Their first album, *Atas* ("Be Alert!" in Russian slang) came out in 1991; and their subsequent album, *Who Said We Were Living Poorly?* was marked by nostalgia for socialism's lost way of life. The 1996 album *Battalion Commander* was dedicated to those who fought in Chechnya; and, in 2000, *Polustanochki* (a small station on a railway where a train does not even stop) was for all those persecuted Russians who had been forgotten along the way. The meaning of their next record, *Davai Za* (Here's to) was a hymn to Russia's past and its people who managed to survive the horrors and dangers of the 20th-century. Today, new Russian music ensembles abound, from rock group, Uma Thurman (a band from Nizhny Novgorod whose favorite actress is!), and punk group Leningrad (with lead singer Sergei Shnurov) to the popular world-touring 'Bering Strait,' that blends country, rock and bluegrass sounds. The all female punk rock group, Pussy Riot, garnered international fame after their arrest for trying to perform in Moscow's Cathedral of Our Savior in 2012. (A documentary on this story, *Pussy Riot: A Punk Prayer* is available on Netflix.)

Many famed western groups have now come to perform in Russia. In 2003, former Beatle Paul McCartney played in a packed Red Square in Moscow. The songs included classics 'Let It Be' and 'Back in the USSR'. President Vladimir Putin, who was also in the audience, confessed that he had been an avid Beatle's fan during his childhood; Sir Paul then performed one year later in St Petersburg's Palace Square; he also received an honorary doctorate from the St Petersburg Conservatoire. Today, St Petersburg remains the center for *Russky Rok* and a magnet for musicians and music lovers alike where clubs abound offering every type of music.

ART

During Russia's Golden Age in the 19th-century, the arts strove to portray the realistic aspects of Russian life. Russian art grew beyond the depiction of spiritual realms, as symbolized by frescoes and icons, to encompass the whole contemporary world of the common man with his hopes, sufferings and desire for change. In 1827, Karl Bryullov's masterpiece *The Last Days of Pompeii* was exhibited in St Petersburg. The public compared the Italian romantic upheaval to St Petersburg's tendency to natural disaster. Another meaning—of citizens forced to flee their burning city—symbolized the Decembrist uprising that had taken place only two years before.

The painter Ilya Repin greatly influenced the artistic developments of the late 19th-century. Repin's arrival at the St Petersburg Academy of Arts in 1863 coincided with one of the most significant events of the city's artistic life: a group of 14 art students led by Ivan Kramskoi rebelled against the strict conservative academic standards and were soon forced to resign. In 1870, this group formed their own artistic movement known as the *Peredvizhniki*, or Wanderers. They formed the Association of Travelling Art Exhibits to give all areas in Russia the chance to follow the achievements of Russian Art, which they perceived should depict the real and arduous lives of the people and be a catalyst for social change. Over 25 Russian artists participated, including Ghe, Levitan, Maximov, Perov, Petrov-Vodkin, Polenov, Savrasov, Serov, Surikov, and Apollinary and Viktor Vasnetsov. In his last year at the academy, Repin painted *The Barge Haulers on the Volga*, symbolizing the heavy burdens borne by the Russian people (see page 326); He also painted historical portraits as *Cossacks Writing a Letter to the Turkish Sultan*. After graduation he joined the *Peredvizhniki* and, in 1887, while living in Moscow, Repin frequented the art salons of Pavel Tretyakov and Savva Mamontov.

When Repin witnessed the public execution of five people who had taken part in the assassination of Alexander II, it had a great impact on his artistic life. Soon after, he moved back to St Petersburg and explored revolutionary ideas. Like his literary contemporaries, Repin strove to capture the moral and philosophical issues of the time. His paintings *Arrest of a Propagandist*, *They Did Not Expect Him* (concerning the unexpected return of a political exile to his home) and *Ivan the Terrible and his Son—16 November 1581* (the date Ivan IV killed his son in a fit of rage; see picture on page 326) can now be seen along with many of his other works in Moscow's Tretyakov Gallery.

In 1899, Repin bought an estate (now a museum, see page 643) outside St Petersburg that he named the Penates, after the Roman gods who protected home and family, and continued to live and paint there until his death in 1930, aged 86. St Petersburg's Repin Institute of Painting, Sculpture and Architecture is one of the largest art schools in the world.

In 1898, Diaghilev, Bakst and Benois created Russia's first art magazine Mir Iskusstva (World of Art), which caused an immediate sensation throughout St Petersburg. The innovative journal introduced art concepts from around the world: Postimpressionism, pointillism, cubism, art nouveau, and finally Malevich's abstract supremetism. These artists now wanted to free Russia from the old artistic standards established by such groups as the Wanderers. By the turn of the century, Russia was an innovative hub of the *avant garde*, considered by many as the Silver Age of Russian art. It was the time of Chagall, Kandinsky, Malevich, Rodchenko, Roerich and Vrubel During this time the husband-wife team of Mikhail Larionov and

Natalya Goncharova were the center of the group known as the Knave of Diamonds that developed neo-primitivism, and worked closely with the Ballet Russes to create costumes and set designs. By 1910, the avant-garde maximalists and futurists were at the center of design and art. (See pages 60–61.)

In 1903, Boris Kustodiev graduated from the St Petersburg Academy of the Arts with a gold medal for his colorful painting "Village Bazaar". His other realistic paintings (based on scenes from ordinary Russian life) include "A Merchant's Wife at Tea" (1918), "The Blue House" (1920), "A Sailor and His Mistress" (1920), and "Portrait of Fyodor Shalyapin" (1922). (He eventually became so famous that the Uffizi Gallery in Italy ordered a self-portrait.) Kustodiev's paintings and drawings contain nearly all the remarkable Petersburg people of the 1917 era. The 'World of Art' members would frequently gather at his apartment for concerts, literary readings and art exhibitions. Alexander Benois wrote of his works: "It seems to me that the real Kustodiev is the Russian fair, multicolored, with large print fabrics, barbarous battles between colors, the Russian land and the Russian village, with its harmonics, gingerbread, boldly dressed girls and jaunty young fellows." Today, some of his paintings are mounted in St Petersburg's Russian Museum, and Moscow's Tretyakov Gallery exhibits the famous 'Moscow Traktir.' (See page 62.)

The avant-garde painter Kazimir Malevich was renowned in St Petersburg for his theatrical costumes and scenery, along with his innovative paintings that included *Victory Over the Sun*. His *Black Square* paintings, which Malevich said represented the universality of existence and the ultimate zero form, became the icon of Russian abstract art. The painter believed that this pure simple style of color and shape would act as a catalyst to the unconscious and open a way to spiritual transcendence. Examples of this period are on exhibit at the Hermitage Museum.

The renaissance in Russian art was brought to an end by the stifling effects of Socialist Realism, where art not only had to have a social purpose (such as posters and banners), but one sanctioned by the State. After the death of Stalin, the government permitted a Conceptualist group to form; and, in 1962, artists were allowed to set up an exhibit in Moscow that attracted thousands. But when Krushchev attended and labeled it 'dog shit,' it was shut down and the movement again forced to hunker underground. The Erarta Museum and Galleries of Contemporary Art on St Petersburg's Vasilevysky Island has a large and fascinating display of Soviet underground art from this period.

During the period of Perestroika, artists once again had the freedom to exhibit their works. (In 1988 Sotheby's held the first auction of Russian art, with one painting selling for over $400,000.) In the late 1980's a number of artists and musicians moved into an abandoned building near Vosstaniya (Uprising) Square in

Leningrad and created an artistic collective known as Pushkinskaya 10. Today the center, known as the Free Culture Society, consists of museums, galleries and artist studios (the entrance is at 53 Ligovksky Pr). In 1998, the Center opened the Museum of Non Conformist Art with a 20th/21st-century collection of 'Unofficial Art.' Four years later, Timur Novikov founded the Neo-Academic Movement along with the New Academy of Fine Arts. Today, this legendary locale also showcases contemporary paintings, photographs, sculptures, visual arts and music and has grown into an artistic and cultural institution.

In 2007, after the death of her husband, acclaimed cellist Mstislav Rostropovich, Galina Vishnevskaya put up for sale their unique art collection of 450 items, which included antique furniture, porcelain and works by artists such as Roerich and Repin. Russian billionaire, Alisher Usmanov, purchased all for $72 million and donated it to Russia. The collection is now on display in the Konstantin Palace outside of St Petersburg. Three years earlier, another Russian billionaire, Viktor Vekselberg, had paid $90 million for the Forbes Fabergé collection and also gifted it to Russia.

In 2008, the St Petersburg Konstantinovsky Charitable Fund (controlled by the office of the President) purchased the unique Lobanov-Rostovsky Russian Theater Art Collection, comprised of over 800 pieces of Russian stage and costume design devoted to the period between 1890 and 1930. Many of the works were made especially for Diaghilev's Ballets Russes and include costumes, drawings, paintings, posters and water colors. Plans are to build a special venue near the Konstantinovsky Palace to exhibit the collection. (Earlier, in 1987, Prince Nikita Lobanov-Rostovsky, born in 1935 to Russian émigré parents, donated 80 other works of art to Pushkin's Museum of Personal Collections in Moscow.)

The outstanding documentary film, *The Desert of Forbidden Art* (available on Netflix or at www.desertofforbiddenart.com) traces the incredible story of defiant visionary Igor Savitsky (1915–1984), an artist and museum curator, who over his lifetime cunningly acquired more than 80,000 avant-garde works of art, banned during Soviet times, and hid the illegal collection from the KGB in western Uzbekistan's Nukus Museum, now renamed the Savitsky Art Museum.

Today, in Russia, the art scene is once again booming and scores of museums, exhibition halls and galleries, displaying and selling the works of contemporary artists, grace the streets of Moscow and St Petersburg.

GETTING AROUND

ORIENTATION

St Petersburg is 660 kilometers (410 miles) north of Moscow on the same latitude as Helsinki and Anchorage, and lies at the mouth of the Neva River as it flows into the Gulf of Finland. The city is divided into several districts and islands, and taking a few moments with a map to familiarize yourself with these areas will make a visit to St Petersburg easier and more enjoyable.

The eastern bank of the Neva is known as the Vyborg Side (see Finland Station on page 580). At the eastern tip of Vasilyevsky Island the river splits into two main branches: the Bolshaya (Big) and Malaya (Small) Neva. Here the northern bank is known as Petrogradskaya or the Petrograd Side (see Across the Kronverk Strait on page 511), and includes the islands of Zayachy, Petrogradsky, Petrovsky, Kronversky and Aptekarsky. To the northwest are the Kirov Islands (see page 515) comprised of the Krestovsky Yelagin and Kammeny (Stone) Islands. Many of the city's sights are to be found on the south bank of the Neva, known as the mainland or heart of the city.

St Petersburg was originally spread over 101 islands. Today, because of redevelopment, there are 44 islands that make up one-sixth of the area of the city. These are connected by 620 bridges, which span 100 waterways and canals. St Petersburg is a cultural treasure house with over 200 museums and galleries, 50 theaters and concert halls and hundreds of well-preserved palaces and monuments.

Consider purchasing a 2-, 3- or 5-day electronic Petersburg City Card, which offers visits to 40 museums along with discounted transportation and other tours. www.petersburgcard.com/eng.

ARRIVAL

See Getting There and Getting Around sections (pages 71/78) for details of international arrivals. Passengers arriving at the new Pulkovo Airport (opened December 2013), located 20 kms/12 miles south of the city, can choose between a taxi or an express or local bus into town. The taxi booking stand is in the Arrivals area. You'll be given a receipt with the set price to your destination. If on a budget, the airport's Bus 39 runs to Moskovskaya Metro station from 5:30am–1:30am, or Minivan Taxi K39 from 7am to 11:30pm; pick ups are every 15 minutes for the half-hour run to/from the airport. For questions, inquire at Information Stands within the airport. The new airport, with its glass skylights and geometric panels, took three years to construct and unites the international and national terminals. Domestic passengers will continue to depart from Pulkovo I once renovations are completed. www.pulkovoairport.ru/en.

Those arriving in St Petersburg by train or bus will find the main stations located around the city center, each with its own Metro station. You can either jump on the Metro (if you have little luggage) or take a taxi from here to your destination. (See By Train, pages 71/79.)

For more on Metro travel, see page 134. (There are five metro lines and the deepest station is Admiralteyskaya at 86 meters/282 feet below ground.) The best line for a metro tour is the M1 Red Line with a journey from Ploshchad Vosstaniya (Uprising Square) south to Avtovo. (You can get on and off as many times as you like with one ticket while riding underground.) Pl Vosstaniya has Stalin and Lenin (on a tank and with the Kronstadt soldiers); Tekhnologischesky Institut has reliefs of famous scientists and their achievements; Baltiiskaya carries a naval theme with a mosaic depicting the Aurora Battleship of the 1917 revolution at the end of the platform; Narvskaya is chocked full of carvings of artists, teachers and engineers along with a sculptured relief of Lenin and a triumphant proletariat rejoicing over the escalators; Kirovsky Zavod is named after an engineering plant with decorations of industrial oil wells; and the Avtovo station's marble and glass columns hold up the roof while a bright red and gold mosaic gleams at the end of the platform.

SIGHTS
PETER AND PAUL FORTRESS

The origins of the city can be traced back to the Peter and Paul Fortress, known as Petropavlovskaya Krepost in Russian. Peter the Great was attracted to Zayachy Ostrov (Hare Island), situated between the Neva and the Kronverk Strait, because of its small size and strategic position in the area. On May 16, 1703, Peter himself laid the first foundation stone of the fortress, named after the apostles Peter and Paul. (Their Orthodox feast day is celebrated on July 12.) The fortress was designed to protect the city from invading Swedes, and was built as an elongated hexagon with six bastions that traced the contours of the island. Over 20,000 workers were commissioned and within only six months the earthen ramparts were set in place. Work continued on the fortress, replacing the wooden buildings with brick and stone until its completion in 1725. The new walls were over 12 meters (39 feet) thick and 300 guns were installed. Soon after its completion the fortress lost its military significance and over the next 200 years it served instead mainly as a political prison. In 1922, the fortress was opened as a museum complex. The grounds are open 6am to 9pm. The Peter and Paul Cathedral is open 10am–7pm and Sunday 11am–7pm (services are held on Sat/Sun); the Trubetskoi Bastion Prison is open from 10am–7pm and on Tuesday until 6pm. Permanent displays and exhibition halls are open 11am–7pm and Tuesday until 6pm. The last admission is one hour before closing time. The complex is closed on Wednesdays. The Bell-tower in the cathedral is open from May 1 to Sept 15 by guided tour only. Metro Gorkovskaya. www.spbmuseum.ru.

Three ticket combinations are offered, which include a separate entrance fee for each display or one ticket good for two permanent displays; the ticket for four displays (Cathedral, Prison, two museums) is valid for two days. (Discounted tickets are offered to students and seniors.) Audio guides in English are available.

The visitor's entrance to the fortress is at **St John's Gate**, on the east side of the island not far from Kamennoostrovsky (formerly Kirov) Prospekt. While crossing **St John's (Ioannovsky) Bridge**, the city's oldest, note the bronze hare installed atop one of the pylons. Legend has it that, in 1703, while Peter the Great was investigating the area, he got some water in his boot; so he took it off and set it on the grass to dry. Later, as the story goes, when Peter went to put his boot back on, he discovered a hare inside it. Peter reportedly laughed and named the area 'Hare's Island.'

At the end of the bridge is **St Peter's Gate** (1718), the main entrance and oldest unchanged structure of the fort. Hanging over the archway is a double-headed eagle, the emblem of the Russian Empire, along with bas-reliefs of the apostle Peter. The carver Konrad Osner gave the apostle the features of the czar. North of the entrance is the **Museum of Space Exploration and Rocket Technology** and the **History of Peter and Paul Fortress Museum**. South of the gate is **His Majesty's Bastion**, used as a dungeon for Peter's prisoners.

Ironically, the first prisoner was Peter's son, Alexei, who was suspected of plotting against the czar. Peter supervised his son's torture and Alexei died here in 1718. (Peter had Alexei buried beneath the staircase of the cathedral, so he would always be 'trampled upon'.) An outer fortification built to cover an entrance into the western end of the fort is known as the **Alexeyevsky Ravelin**, after Peter's son. The history of the fortress is also closely connected with revolutionary movements. Catherine the Great locked up Alexander Radishchev, who criticized the autocracy and feudal system in his book *Voyages from St Petersburg to Moscow*. In 1825, the Decembrists were imprisoned here; five were executed on July 13, 1826, and hundreds of others were sentenced to hard labor in Siberia. In 1849, members of the Petrashevsky political movement, including Dostoevsky, were held in the nearby **Trubetskoi Bastion** after being sentenced to death. On December 22, 1849, after spending eight months in the Fortress, they were led out to a square and dressed in white canvas robes and hoods. The firing squad aimed their rifles at the men. 'I was in the second row, and had less than a minute to live,' Dostoevsky recalled in horror. But instead of hearing gunshots, a drum roll sounded. Nicholas I had decided to commute the death sentences to exile in Siberia. Dostoevsky was sent to Omsk Prison, where he spent four years shackled day and night; he would not write again for over ten years. Nikolai Chernyshevsky wrote his influential novel *What Is To Be Done?* while imprisoned in the Fortress for two years in 1862. In the 1880s many members of the Narodnaya Volya (Peoples' Freedom Group) were placed in the bastion's solitary-confinement cells—or executed for the assassination of Alexander II. In 1887, five prisoners were executed for the attempt on the life of Alexander III, including Lenin's brother, Alexander Ulyanov. The writer Maxim Gorky was once incarcerated for writing revolutionary leaflets. The cells have been reconstructed to their former 19th-century appearance, and biographies of many of the former inmates are posted on the doors.

During the October 1917 Revolution, when the fortress' last stronghold was captured by the Bolsheviks and the political prisoners set free, a red lantern was hung in the southern **Naryshkin Bastion** signaling the battleship *Aurora* to fire the first shot of the Revolution. Today, every day at noon a blank cannon shot is fired from the Naryshkin Bastion (be prepared!). It has been sounded every day (except during the Siege of Leningrad) since a similar salute in 1721 proclaimed the end to the Great Northern War. Locals also call it the Admiral's Hour; according to tradition the cannon was fired daily after an admiral drank his glass of noon-day vodka. The shot also let the townspeople know the time.

A straight path from St John's gate leads to **St Peter and Paul Cathedral**, built between 1712 and 1732 in Dutch style by Swiss architect Domenico Trezzini (1670–1734). Peter the Great laid the cornerstone. The cathedral, with its long slender golden spire topped with an angel holding a cross, is the focal point of the square. The belfry, towering to 122.5 meters (402 feet), used to be the highest structure in the entire country; Peter purposely had the spire built higher than the Ivan the Great Bell Tower in Moscow's Kremlin. (During the Siege, mountain climbers courageously scaled the spire in order to camouflage and protect it from German bombing raids.)

The interior gilded wooden iconostasis was carved between 1722 and 1726, and holds 43 icons. The cathedral is the burial place for over 30 czars and princes, including every czar from Peter I to Nicholas II. (There are no tombs for Ivan VI or Peter II, both of whom were murdered.) Peter the Great himself chose his resting place to the right of the altar. The sarcophagi of Alexander II and his wife took 17 years to carve from Altai jasper and Ural red quartz. In 1994, Queen Elizabeth II paid a visit here to her Romanov ancestors' tombs. This was the first visit by a British monarch to Peter and Paul Fortress in over 75 years.

The last czar, Nicholas II, along with his murdered family and friends were finally given an official burial in the cathedral on July 17, 1998 (80 years to the day after they were shot by a 12-man Bolshevik firing squad while under house arrest in Yekaterinburg, 1450 kilometers/900 miles east of Moscow). They were buried in the

Chapel of St Catherine the Martyr in the cathedral's southwest side. Positive DNA identifications had been made on the nine skeletons exhumed in 1991 (but discovered in 1979) from unmarked graves in the Ural Mountains, near Yekaterinburg. (For some of the verification, researchers used DNA from Britain's Prince Philip whose grandmother and the Czarina were sisters.) Results concluded that the bodies belonged to Nicholas II, his wife, three (of their five) children, the doctor and three servants. (In a breach of tradition, the servants were also allowed burial in the lower vault.) The Czar and his family were canonized as passion bearers by the Russian Orthodox Church in 2000.

In 2007, archeologists discovered a second grave located about 70 meters (230 feet) from the first, which contained 44 broken and burned bone fragments. After extensive mitochondrial DNA testing, a 2009 analysis concluded that the bones were from a young female and male from the Romanov family believed to be the missing daughter Maria and hemophiliac son, Alexei. A burial decision is still being formalized by the Orthodox Church.

In 1999, the remains of Czarina Maria Fyodorovna, the Danish-born princess who was the mother of Nicholas II, were also allowed burial next to her husband, Alexander III, who had died in 1894. Maria Fyodorovna married Alexander III in 1866, and the couple had six children. After the Bolshevik Revolution, she fled Russia to Denmark. She died in 1928 with no knowledge about the fate of her family.

Outside the cathedral entrance is a small pavilion with a statue of the Goddess of Navigation. The **Boat House** was erected in 1761 to house a small boat that was built by Peter the Great. (Today, this Grandfather of the Russian Fleet is on display at the Central Naval Museum.) An information center and ticket office is inside the Boat House, open daily 10am–6:30pm. Directly in front of the cathedral is the yellow and white building of the **Mint** (1800–1806). In 1724, Peter the Great transferred the Royal Mint from Moscow to St Petersburg. The first lever press in the world was used here in 1811. The Mint still produces special coins, medals and badges. Beyond the Mint are the Alexeyevsky, Zotov and Trubetskoi Bastions.

As you leave the Cathedral look for the **Statue of Peter the Great**, a large figure of the czar (with strangely proportioned head and hands) seated in an armchair. Unveiled on June 7, 1991, it was sculpted and donated by St Petersburg artist Mikhail Chemiakin, just before the city regained its historical name. The statue is an interpretation of Peter I's wax effigy (now in the Hermitage collection) made by sculptor Carlo Rastrelli (father of architect, Francesco Rastrelli) in 1725, right after the czar's death. The head is an actual cast from the life mask of Peter the Great (also in the Hermitage) made by Rastrelli in 1719. Rub Peter's right forefinger, meant to bring good luck!

The next structure is the stone **Commandant's Building**, built as the commander's headquarters and the interrogation center for prisoners. It now houses the **Museum of History of St Petersburg and Petrograd from 1703 to 1918**. Next door, the old Engineer's House shows temporary exhibitions. Behind these stands the **Neva Gate**, once known as the Gate of Death, because prisoners were led through it to the execution site. Now it leads to the beach area (with a spectacular view of the city) that is quite crowded in summer with sunbathers. The Walrus Club gathers here in winter to swim between the ice floes of the Neva. Anyone is welcome to join in!

As you pass through the gate notice the plaques that record the city's many floods. In the disastrous flood of 1824, the entire Vasilyevsky Island across to both the Petrograd Side and the mainland were underwater. Nikolai Gogol wrote, 'Now the belfry spire is alone visible from the sea.'

The **Neva Curtain Wall** (included on a complete display ticket) contains exhibits on the history of the fortress, including a short film. For an extra fee, a visitor can climb up and walk along the fortress wall with great views of the Hermitage and Winter Palace on the other side of the Neva River.

ACROSS THE KRONVERK STRAIT

Exiting the fortress by way of St John's Bridge brings you to **Troitskaya Ploshchad** (Trinity Square, formerly Revolution Square) where many of the first buildings of the city once stood. These included the Senate, Custom House and Troitsky Cathedral, where Peter was crowned emperor in 1721. Today the square is a large garden.

Crossing the Neva is the **Troitsky Most** (formerly Kirov Bridge) with a splendid view of the fortress. This is the city's longest bridge, built between 1897 and 1903 from French designs, to commemorate the silver wedding anniversary of Alexander III. The small path to the northwest of St John's Bridge circles around the Kronverk Strait; it leads to a small obelisk, a monument to the Decembrist revolutionaries, erected on the spot where Nicholas I executed the five leaders of the 1825 uprising. A witness described the execution: 'The hangmen made them stand on a bench and put white canvas hoods over their heads. Then the bench was knocked from under their feet. Three men whose ropes had broken fell on the rough boards of the scaffold bruising themselves. One broke his leg. According to custom, in such circumstances the execution had to be canceled. But in an hour, new ropes were brought and the execution carried through.'

Past the obelisk is a large building that was once the artillery arsenal. Today it is the **Kronverk Artillery, Engineers and Signals Museum**, established by Peter the Great to display the history of Russian weaponry. Today it houses more than 50,000 exhibits of artillery, firearms, engineering equipment and military paintings; there is also an outdoor display of tanks. The centerpiece is Lenin's armored car that he returned from Switzerland to Russia in, arriving at Finland Station in April, 1917. Open 11am–6pm; closed Mondays, Tuesdays and last Thursday of the month. www. artillery-museum.ru.

Behind the museum is **Kronversky Island**, and Kronversky Prospekt does a half-circle loop all around the northern side of the Strait. (The writer Maxim Gorky lived at number 23 from 1914 to 1921.) Inside the **Alexandrovsky Park**, at number 1, is the **St Petersburg Zoo** and gardens, with over 1,000 animals (10am–8pm in summer, and 10am–6pm in winter; www.spbzoo.ru.) To the east, at 4 **Aleksandrovsky Park**, is the **Planetarium**, open 10:30–8pm; closed Mondays. www.planetary-spb.ru. Nearby is the **Baltic Dom Theater** which hosts an annual festival from Baltic countries, along with Russian plays and other experimental theater. At 7 Kronverksky Prospekt, with it azure dome and stunning minarets, is the city's working **Mosque** (1910–1914), modeled on Samarkand's magnificent Gur Emir Mausoleum where Tamerlane is buried.

Petrogradsky Island is north of Kronversky Island and the Fortress, and thus this area is known as the Petrograd side (so named when the city was known as Petrograd during WW II.) Up to the revolution this district was a fashionable area in which to live and many Style-Moderne mansions and other architectural gems still grace this neighborhood. Take the Gorkovskaya Metro one stop north to Petrogradskaya. A five-minute stroll west along the southern embankment of the Karpovka River to number 32 brings you to the **Toy Museum** that exhibits all types of toys (both hand- and factory-made) from all over the country. Open 11am–6pm; closed Mondays. In the area, at number 3 Lenina, is the **Yelizarov Museum** (3rd fl, Apt. 24), where Lenin and his wife lived before the revolution from April to July, 1917. (Lenin's eldest sister, Anna, was married to Mark Yelizarov.) Personal items and memorabilia remain, such as Lenin's telephone that still bears the home number. In 1913 the building was constructed in the style of Art Moderne to appear as a large ocean liner. Open 11am–4pm; closed Sundays and Wednesdays. (Press 24 on the intercom for entry.)

Heading east on Levashovsky Prospekt, make a left on Kamennoostrovsky Prospekt to number 2 Ul Professora Popova (one block north across the river). The grey-painted 19th-century wooden cottage is the **Avant-Garde Museum**, once the home of avant-garde and Cubo-Futurist artist Mikhail Matyushin (1861–1934) who developed his own concept of the fourth dimension, connecting musical and visual arts. Open 11am–6pm, Tuesday till 5pm; closed Wednesdays. www.spbmuseum.ru.

A few minutes walk further east, to number 10, brings you to special gardens, where medicinal plants and herbs were grown for the city's apothecaries. This is how the island got its nickname of Aptekarsky (Apothecary). The **Botanical Gardens** are now located here along with the **Botanical Greenhouse**, filled with over 80,000 plants. (The entrance is by the river at Aptekarsky Prospekt.) The grounds are open 10am–6pm, Greenhouse from 11am–4pm (May–Sept); closed Fridays. On the northeast end of the island looms the 50,000-watt **TV Tower**; standing at 321 meters (1,053 feet), it is open for tours offering great views of the city; a café is on the second deck.

A few blocks west of the TV Tower, at 2-B Graftio Ulitsa, is the **Shalyapin House Museum** with exhibits on the life of the famous Russian opera singer who lived here from 1914 to 1922 (and then he fled Russia). Open 11am–7pm, Wed 1pm–9pm; closed Mondays, Tuesdays and the last Friday of the month. It also has occasional chamber music performances. www.theatremuseum.ru.

Heading south on Kamennoostrovsky Prospekt brings you to Leo Tolstoy Square (near Petrogradskaya metro). At number 35 is the **House With Towers** whose architecture is a striking mix of both neoclassical and neo-gothic styles. Its two hexagonal towers are based on the gatehouse of Maxstoke Castle in Wartwickshire, England. Built as an apartment building in 1910–1915 by factory-director Konstantin Rosenshtein, it was designed in the highest standards of the time by architect Andrei Belogrud; the apartments contained everything from sunken bathtubs and gas stoves to indoor heated closets for drying laundry; a car garage was in the courtyard.

Sergei Kirov (1886–1934), regional head of the Leningrad Party before he was murdered, lived for ten years at 26–28 Kamennoostrovsky Prospekt. The **Kirov Museum** on the fourth floor (ticket office on 5th floor) shows how the Bolshevik elite lived, and displays Kirov's possessions along with many great examples from Soviet 1920s technology, including a hotline to the Kremlin and the first Soviet typewriter. One of the rooms has been reconstructed to Kirov's office at the Smolny complete with a display of bloodstained clothes he was killed in. Open 11am–6pm, Tuesday till 5:30pm; closed Wednesdays, www.kirovmuseum.ru. Continuing south on the prospekt, notice the castle-like architecture scattered around Avstriiskaya Square.

South of the Mosque, at 2–4 Kuibysheva, is the art-nouveau style **Kshesinskaya Mansion** (built between 1902 and 1906 by architect Alexander Gogen) which formerly belonged to Matilda Kshesinskaya, a famous Russian ballerina and mistress of Nicolas II before he married in 1894. After the revolution, the prima ballerina fled the country and, later in 1921, she married Grand Duke Andrei Vladimirovich, cousin of Nicholas II, in Cannes, France. In 1936, at age 64, she gave a farewell performance at London's Covent Garden, where she received 18 curtain calls. In 1960 she published her memoirs, *Dancing in Petersburg: The Memoirs of Mathilde Kschessinska*, still in print today. (She died in Paris in 1971, age 99.) Today the restored mansion houses the **Museum of Political History** with exhibits on Russian political parties from 1905 to the 1990's, along with a few displays on Kshesinskaya. The building briefly served as Bolshevik headquarters when Lenin gave inspirational speeches from the balcony. Frequent concerts are held here in the chamber music hall. Open 9am–6pm, Wed 10am–8pm; closed Thursdays and last Monday of month. (Another branch of the Political Museum is at 2 Gorokhovaya, metro Admiralteyskaya.) www.polithistory.ru. (See page 56.)

The **Lidval Building** (1–3 Kamennoostrovsky Prospekt), an apartment block built in 1902, is named after the city's favorite architect of the Style-Moderne, Fyodor Lidval; look closely and you will see a menagerie of figures that jump out of the stone: fish, owls, spiders and webs.

Head east on Petrovsky Embankment along the Neva River and you'll pass the two-ton granite figures of Shih-Tze, brought from Manchuria in 1907, poised on the steps by the Neva. In China these sculptures guarded the entrances to palaces. Behind them, at number 6, is the **Cottage of Peter the Great**, one of the oldest surviving buildings of the city. It was constructed in a mere three days in May 1703 out of pine logs painted to look like bricks. One room was a study and reception area and the other was used as a dining room and bedroom. The largest door was 1.75 meters (five feet, nine inches) high—Peter stood at 2 meters (six feet seven)! From here Peter directed the building of his fortress, in view across the river. (Once his summer palace was completed, Peter stopped living here altogether.) In 1784, Catherine the Great encased the tiny house in stone to protect it. The cottage is now a museum, displaying his furniture, household utensils, a cast of his hand and a small boat with which Peter is supposed to have saved a group of fishermen on Lake Ladoga in 1690. A bronze bust of Peter can be found in the garden. Open 10am–6pm, Thursday 1pm–9pm; closed Tuesdays.

The beautiful blue building of the **Nakhimov Naval School**, at number 4, is a short walk farther east, where young boys learn to carry on the traditions of the Russian fleet. The **Battleship Aurora** was anchored in front of it on the Bolshaya Nevka River. The cruiser originally fought during the Russo-Japanese War (1904–05). In October 1917, the sailors mutinied and joined in the Bolshevik Revolution. On the evening of October 24, following the orders of Lenin and the Military Revolutionary Committee, the Aurora sailed up the Neva and at 9.45pm fired a blank shot to signal the storming of the Winter Palace. (It was sunk by the Germans during WW II, but later raised and repaired.) In 1948, it was moored by the Naval School and later opened as a museum in 1956. Displays include many revolutionary photographs, documents, the gun that fired the legendary blank shot, and the radio room where Lenin announced the overthrow of the Provisional Government to the citizens of Russia. Currently the Aurora is under restoration in Kronstadt. www. aurora.org.ru.

KIROV ISLANDS

The northernmost islands are collectively called the Kirov Islands, the largest of which are known as Krestovsky, Yelagin and Kamenny (Stone). They lie between the Malaya, Srednaya and Bolshaya (Small, Middle and Large) Nevka, tributaries of the Neva. These wooded islands, filled with canals, lakes and ponds are a lovely place to have a stroll any time of year.

Stone Island Bridge leads from the end of Kamennoostrovsky Prospekt on the Petrograd Side (about a 15-minute walk north of Petrogradskaya Metro station) to **Stone Island**, a popular summer resort area in the days of Peter the Great who is said to have planted an oak tree by the southern Krestovka Embankment (and the Maly Krestovsky Bridge) in 1718. Even though the large oak died, it was replaced by a new one, and is still known as **Peter's Tree**. In 1765, Catherine the Great bought the lands for her son, and the following year erected the classically designed **Kamennoostrovsky (Stone Island) Palace** on the eastern tip of the island; it is closed to visitors, though one can visit the restored **Gothic Church of St John the Baptist** (1776) in the grounds. Another way to the island is from Chornaya Rechka metro on the Vyborg side; walk south across the bridge over the Bolshaya Nevka to the island.

Today the 107-hectare (265-acre) island is filled with holiday centers and beautiful old dachas—some of the finest wooden buildings in Russia originally constructed by wealthy aristocratic families at the turn of the century. (Many have guarded gates and are now owned by 'New Russian' businessmen.) A wonderful example on the northwest shore is the lavish mansion of Senator Polovtsev who barely escaped when the Bolsheviks took possession of it. Another is the Dolgoruky Mansion, which stands on the southern embankment near Kamennoostrovsky Prospekt. The building, at 13 Bolshaya Alleya, is a fairy-tale castle built in art nouveau style. On the other side of the island is the wooden **Kamenny Island Theater**, a classical giant with an eight-column portico, erected in just 40 days in the early 1820s.

Another interesting site is the equine cemetery for the steeds of Mad Czar Paul I. A large park fills the southwest corner, and the western footbridge leads to Yelagin Island.

Yelagin Island is connected by three bridges—from Kamenny Island to the east, Krestovsky Island to the south and Primorsky Prospekt to the north. (Boat rentals are available by the Yelagin Bridge that crosses the Bolshaya Nevka to Primorsky.) It was once owned in the late 18th century by wealthy aristocrat Ivan Yelagin; after his death it became the summer destination of the czars. In 1817, Alexander I bought the island for the summer residence of his mother Maria Fedorovna; he then had Carlo Rossi build the elegant **Yelagin Palace** (1818–1824) near the northeastern shore, Rossi's first commission in the city. Today, along with beautifully restored furnishings, it houses an exhibit of decorative and applied arts. In the Orangery and garden is the Glass Museum that has a collection of over 8,000 items that display the history and traditions of Russian glass artistry. Open 10am–6pm; closed Mondays and last Tuesday of month. Besides the main palace, there are also three outdoor pavilions, the kitchen and stable buildings. Rossi went on to plan and landscape the entire island, adding parks, ponds and shady tree-lined pathways. Today the **Kirov Park** takes up most of the western half of the island; carnivals are held here, especially during the White Nights in June. In winter this car-free island becomes a wonderland of cross-country skiing, ice skating and sledding (skis and skates are available for hire). In warmer months, rent roller blades to glide along the many wooded paths. It has also been a long tradition to watch the sunset over the Gulf of Finland from the western tip of the island. Admission to the park is free Monday to Friday, with a small entrance fee on Sat/Sun and holidays. The closest metro station is Staraya Derevnya, north of the island. www.elaginpark.org.

Just across the northern bridge, at 91 Primorsky Prospekt, is the **Buddhist Datsun** or Temple. It was built between 1909 and 1915 by Pyotr Badmaev, Buddhist physician to Nicholas II, combining Tibetan and art-nouveau styles. The monastery's abbot was Lama Aguan Dordjiev, a legendary Buddhist teacher and scholar from Buryatia. Donations were given by the Dalai Lama and Nikolai Roerich, a leading artist and figure of the spiritual and occult. Having been shut down after the Revolution, the buildings were returned to the Buddhist community in 1990. (The 14th Dalai Lama, Tenzin Gyatso, visited the city and temple in 1987.) In 2003, the kingdom of Thailand restored the large golden Buddha that was damaged during the revolution. Today, the temple and monastery are run by monks from the Buryatia Republic, Russia's largest Buddhist area, situated along Lake Baikal in southeastern Siberia. Open daily 9am–7pm with services at 10am and 3pm. Metro Staraya Derevnya.

About a 10-minute walk east of the metro station is the Staraya Derevnya **Hermitage Restoration and Storage Center** at 37 Zausadebnaya, a large golden-glass state-of-the-art complex that acts as a depository and restoration center for the museum. Guided tours are at 11am, 1pm, 1:30pm, 3:30pm; closed Mondays and Tuesdays. The group is led through only a handful of its many rooms, but includes paintings, carriages and furniture; some of the highlights are the Turkish Ceremonial Tent presented to Catherine the Great by a Sultan in 1793, and the large mythical Garuda bird, carved from wood and gifted to the city by Indonesia for its 300th anniversary. www.hermitagemuseum.org.

Krestovsky is the largest island in the group and once belonged to the wealthy Beloselsky-Belozersky family (their mansion is at 41 Nevsky Prospekt) who acquired the island from Count Razumovsky in 1803. On the grounds of the estate, on July 5, 1908, a duel was fought between Counts Nicholas Yusupov and Arvid Manteuffel after Yusupov caused a great scandal by having an open affair with the other's wife. Yusupov was mortally wounded after the second round of shots. Years later on January 1, 1917, the corpse of Grigory Rasputin was found in the ice of the Malaya Nevka, near Bolshoi Petrovsky Bridge. Rasputin was killed by Felix Yusupov, Nicholas' younger brother. On the western side of the island the **New Zenit Stadium** (built on the site of the former Kirov Stadium) hosts the home soccer matches of Football Club Zenith. (The Dynamo and Spartak Stadiums are on the southern end of the island; Petrovsky Stadium is on Petrovsky Island near metro Sportivnaya.) One of the main attractions of the island is **Seaside Victory Park** (Primorsky Park Pobedy), built after the war in 1945. Leningrad poet Anna Akhmatova wrote: 'Early in the morning, the people of Leningrad went out. In huge crowds to the seashore, and each of them planted a tree up on that strip of land, marshy, deserted. In memory of that Great Victory Day.' Within two weeks, 45,000 oaks, birch, maples and other trees, and 50,000 shrubs were planted over 450 acres. At the center of the island (next to the Krestovsky Ostrov metro station) is **Divo Ostrov**, a small Disney-style amusement park with many rides from Ferris wheels to roller coasters; one can also rent bikes and rollerblades. Open noon–8pm (from 11am on Sat/Sun) June–August, and Sat–Sun only 11am–8pm Sept–May. www.divo-ostrov.ru.

THE STRELKA OF VASILYEVSKY ISLAND

Vasilyevsky is the largest island in the Neva Delta, encompassing over 4,000 acres. At the island's eastern tip, known as the Strelka (arrow or spit of land), the Neva is at its widest and branches into the Bolshaya (Big) and Malaya (Small) Neva. The Dvortsovy Most (Palace Bridge) spans the Bolshaya Neva to the west bank and the Birzhevoy Most (Commerce Bridge) crosses the Malaya Neva to the Petrograd Side. From the Strelka one looks out upon a spectacular panorama of Peter and Paul Fortress, the Winter Palace, Admiralty and St Isaac's Cathedral. In summer a fountain shoots water out from the middle of the Neva. The closest metro stop to all the main sights is Vasileostrovskaya.

At first Peter chose to build his city, modeled after Venice, on Vasilyevsky Island. But when the Neva froze over in winter, the island was cut off from the rest of Russia. By the mid-18th century it was decided instead to develop the administrative and cultural centers on the south bank of the Neva. However, many of the original canals are still present on the island, whose streets are laid out as numbered lines (where canals were planned) and crossed by three major avenues.

After the completion of the Peter and Paul Fortress, vessels docked along the Strelka. The first wooden Exchange Building was built near the fortress for foreign merchants only. According to tradition Russian traders made their deals at local fairs; but, by the end of the 18th century, they were also allowed to participate in stock exchange deals. Between 1805 and 1816 the present **Stock Exchange** was erected according to the designs of Thomas de Thomon. Thousands of piles were driven into the riverbed to serve as the foundation for a granite embankment with steps leading to the Neva, flanked on each side by two large stone globes. The Exchange has 44 white Doric columns, and the sea-god Neptune in a chariot harnessed to sea horses stands over the main entrance. This building still serves as the city's stock exchange. (In 2013, the **Central Naval Museum** was relocated to 69 Bolshaya Morskaya by the Kryukov Canal on the mainland.)

Birzhevaya Ploshchad (Commerce Square) lies in front of the Exchange. The dark red **Rostral Columns**, 32 meters (105 feet) high, stand on either side. These were also designed by de Thomon and constructed from 1805 to 1810. The Romans erected columns adorned with the prows of enemy ships, or rostrals, after naval victories. These rostral columns are decorated with figures symbolizing the victories of the Russian fleet. Around the base of the columns are four allegorical figures, representing the Neva, Volga, Dnieper and Volkhov rivers. The columns also acted as a lighthouse; at dusk hemp oil was lit in the bronze bowls at the top. Nowadays gas torches are used, but only during festivals. This area is one of the most beautiful spots in all St Petersburg, offering a large panoramic view of the city. Imagine the days when the whole area was filled with ships and sailboats. The Frenchman Alexandre Dumas was obviously captivated with the area on his first visit over a century ago: 'I really don't know whether there is any view in the whole world which can be compared with the panorama which unfolded before my eyes.'

Two gray-green warehouses, built between 1826 and 1832, stand on either side of the Exchange. The southern building is the **Zoological Museum** with a collection of well over 40,000 animal species, including a 44,000-year-old preserved woolly mammoth, nicknamed Dima, discovered in the Siberian permafrost in 1902. The upper floor contains an immense collection of insects, including a live insect zoo. Open 11am–6pm; closed Tuesdays. www.zin.ru.

The eight-columned **Customs House** (1829–32) at 4 Makarov Embankment (Naberezhnaya Makarova) is topped with mounted copper statues of Mercury (Commerce), Neptune (Navigation) and Ceres (Fertility). The cupola was used as an observation point to signal arriving trade ships. It is now the Russian Literature Institute or the **Pushkin House**. In 1905, the museum purchased Pushkin's library. Other rooms contain exhibits devoted to famous Russian writers from the 18th and 19th centuries. (The Pushkin House Museum is at 12 Moika Embankment.) Open 11am–4pm; closed Sat/Sun. www.pushkinskijdom.ru.

The baroque-style green and white **Kunstkammer** (1718–34), nicknamed the Palace of Curiosities, is located at the beginning of University Embankment

(Universitetskaya Naberezhnaya) at number 3, and extends west along the Bolshaya Neva. Nearly every building in this district is a monument of 18th-century architecture. Kunstkammer, stemming from the German words kunst (art) and *kammer* (chamber), was the first Russian museum open to the public. Legend has it that Peter the Great, while walking along the embankment, noticed two pine trees entwined around each other's trunks. The czar decided to cut down the trees and build a museum on the spot to house 'rarities, curiosities and monsters'. (The tree was also in the museum.) In order to attract visitors, admission was free and a glass of vodka was offered at the entrance. (The Czar wanted to create a scientific museum to dispel superstitions about disease and illness.) Today the Kunstkammer is made up of the **Museum of Anthropology and Ethnography** which continues to exhibit a rather gruesome collection with labels such as 'double-faced monster' and 'two-headed mutant.' Other exhibitions feature native peoples from around the world.

The Kunstkammer became known as the 'cradle of Russian science' and was the seat of the Academy of Sciences, founded by Peter I in 1724. The famous scientist and writer Mikhail Lomonosov worked here from 1741 to 1765. The third floor houses the **Lomonosov Museum** with a re-creation of his laboratory. The Museums are open 11am–6pm; closed Mondays and last Tuesday of month. www.kunstkamera.ru.

The first Russian astronomical **Observatory** was installed in the museum's tower. The large **Gottorp Globe** had a model of the heavens in its interior where a mechanism was regulated to create the motion of the night sky, a forerunner of the planetarium. It is three meters (ten feet) in diameter—large enough for 12 people to fit inside. (Entrance to the Observatory is only by guided tour.) When the Kunstkammer eventually became too small, a new building was constructed next to it for the Academy of Sciences. Completed in 1788, it was designed by Giacomo Quarenghi. A statue of Mikhail Lomonosov stands outside the Academy.

Peter I commissioned the architect Domenico Trezzini to design the 400-meter (1312-foot) long **Twelve Collegiums** (1722–42) next to the Kunstkammer (along Mendeleyevskaya Liniya) for his Senate and colleges, which replaced more than 40 governmental departments. After governmental orders were announced, they were posted outside the colleges for the public to read. By the beginning of the 19th-century the colleges had been replaced by ministries.

St Petersburg University, founded in 1819, moved into the buildings of the Twelve Collegiums in 1838, where it continues to operate today. Many prominent writers and scholars studied here. Lenin passed his bar exams and received a degree in law. A few of of the teachers were renowned physiologist Ivan Pavlov, and Alexander Popov who was one of the first to communicate messages by radio waves. On March 24, 1896, Popov demonstrated transmission of radio waves here between different campus buildings. Dmitri Ivanovich Mendeleyev (1834–1907), a prolific inventor and chemist, lived at 7/9 Mendeleyevskaya Liniya while he was a professor at the University. Mendeleyev is best known for his work on arranging the then 63 known elements into a Periodic Table based on atomic mass, which he published in Principles of Chemistry in 1869. He even predicted the existence and properties of new elements, and went on to study the origin and nature of petroleum. (A famous portrait of Mendeleyev was painted by Ivan Kramskoi in 1878.) In 1893 Mendeleyev became director of the Bureau of Weights and Measures; and, a year later, Alexander III commissioned him to create a standard for vodka; the chemist figured the optimal alcohol content to be 38%. Because, at the time, taxes on vodka were based on strength, it was rounded off to 40% to make it easier on officials to compute amounts. The apartment, where he lived from 1866–1890, is now the **Mendeleyev Museum**, open 11am–4pm; closed Fri/Sat/Sun. (Entrance is by pre-booked guided tour.) The red and white buildings are now part of St Petersburg University, which has more than 20,000 students.

Not far from the university at 15 University Embankment is the yellow baroque-style **Menschikov Palace**. Prince Alexander Menschikov was the first governor of St Petersburg and did much for its development. Peter the Great presented his close friend with the whole of Vasilyevsky Island in 1707 (but later took it back). The palace, built between 1710 and 1714, was the first stone residential structure on the island. Also known as the Ambassadorial Palace, it was the most luxurious building in all of St Petersburg. After the death of Peter the Great in 1725, Menschikov virtually ruled the country until he lost a power struggle (after the death of Catherine I) and was exiled to Siberia in 1727, where he died two years later. The First Cadet Corps took over the palace as their Military College in 1831. Today the beautifully restored palace, one of the few private houses preserved from the first quarter of the 18th century, is part of the Hermitage Museum with collections of 18th-century Russian culture in over 20 rooms, including the magnificent Grand Hall where banquets and balls were held. (Look for the English fact sheet displayed in each room; an audio guide is also available.) Chamber music concerts are frequently held in the evenings. Open 10.30am–6pm, Sunday till 5pm; closed Mondays. (Free admission first Thursday of month.) The Hermitage Two-Day Combined Ticket can be used for entrance.

Peter the Great had the idea to create a Russian artistic school; and a year before his death an engraving school was opened in the Academy of Sciences. But it was not until 1757 that Count Ivan Shuvalov created the Academy of Fine Arts. The Academy (1765–1788) was the city's first structure built with classical designs. Over the entrance is a bronze inscription: 'To Free Arts. The year—1765.' Many of Russia's most prominent artists and architects graduated from here. Today it is the largest art school in the world, and known as the **Repin Institute of Painting, Sculpture and**

Architecture (named after the renowned Russian painter). Part of it houses the **Academy of Arts Museum** that depicts the educational history of Russian art and architecture along with artwork displays by faculty and academy students. The third floor has models used for the Alexander Nevsky Monastery, the Smolny and St Issac's Cathedral. Open 11am–7pm; closed Mondays and Tuesdays. (Ticket office on 2nd floor) www.nimrah.ru.

When the Academy was built, the city's seaport was still situated here along the Neva. The river was only navigable 200 days a year (the rest of the time it was frozen). In one month alone, in May 1815, this port area received 19,327 ships— among them, 182 English, seven American, 36 Scandinavian and 69 German. In 1885, the port was transferred to Kronstadt, and later moved to Gutuevsky Island (southwest of the city) where it remains today.

In front of the Academy two pink-granite **Egyptian Sphinxes**, over 3,500 years old, flank the staircase leading down to the water; they were brought to the city in 1832, and each weighs 23 tons. They were discovered in the early 1800s during an excavation of ancient Thebes and personify the Pharaoh Amenkhotep III, who once ruled Egypt.

The **Annunciation** (Blagoveshchensky) **Bridge**, named after a neighboring Cathedral, crosses the Bolshaya Neva from University Embankment. Constructed between 1843 and 50, it was the first permanent bridge across the Neva. Later the bridge was renamed Nikolayevsky after Nicholas I; in the middle of the bridge was a chapel with the mosaic image of St Nicholas, the patron saint of navigators. (It recently reverted back to its original name.) Today it is also the last bridge before the river flows into the Gulf of Finland. During the White Nights, it is quite lovely to watch the numerous bridges of the city open and close in the early morning. (In summer the Blagoveshchensky is up from 1:25am–2:45am and 3:10am–5am; Dvortsovy (Palace) from 1:25am to 4:50am and Tuchkov from 2am–2:55am and 3:35am–4:55am.)

The main pedestrian and commercial streets of the Island are the 6-ya and 7-ya Liniya. Full of restaurants and shops, enjoy a leisurely stop at a summer sidewalk café. At 29 6-ya Liniya is the (New) **Novy Museum**, established by art collector Aslan Chekhoev to exhibit his collection of Soviet and contemporary Russian art. Open noon–7pm; closed Mon/Tues/Wed. www.novymuseum.ru. Nearby, at 74 Sredny (Middle) Prospekt, is the **Geological Museum** which contains thousands of prehistoric fossils, rocks and dazzling gems from all over Russia. The centerpiece is a huge map of the Soviet Union made up of thousands of semi-precious stones; it won the Grand Prix prize at the 1937 Paris World Exposition. Open 10am–4pm; closed Sat/Sun. To get in, call on the in house phone, and someone will escort you to the museum's upper floors.

Along the Lieutenant Schmidt Embankment (a continuation west of University Embankment) at 14/15-ya Liniya stands the Byzantine **Assumption Cathedral**, built in 1895 by architect Vasily Kosyakov on the site of the former monastery. During the Soviet era the church was used as an indoor ice-skating rink, and today is under restoration.

The legendary **Icebreaker Krasin**, built in Great Britain in 1917, is anchored at number 22L along this embankment, and can be visited by guided tour that starts every hour from 11am–5pm; the engine room can be visited on Saturday and Sunday at 1pm and 3pm; closed Mondays, Tuesdays and last Wednesday of month. At the time, the Krasin was the world's most powerful icebreaker, which took part in many Arctic missions. In 1928, it rescued an Italian expedition led by Umberto Nobile, whose airship, Italia, had crashed on the ice while returning from the North Pole. The Krasin was decommissioned in 1971. www.krassin.ru/en.

After the icebreaker, visit the Narodovolets **Peoples' Will D2 Submarine** at 10 Shkipersky Protok. It was one of the first diesel-fueled submarines built in the Soviet Union, and operated from 1931 to 1956. Guided tours leave on the hour and take the visitor through the sub where you can imagine how the crew of over 50 worked and lived. Open 11am–5pm; closed Mondays and Tuesdays. Located just west of Nalichnaya St and north of Sredny Prospekt; closest metro Primorskaya.

At 2 29-ya Liniya (just north of Bolshoi Prospekt) is the **Erarta Museum and Galleries of Contemporary Art**. Opened in 2010 in a restored Stalinist-era building, this splendid space is spread over five floors where the left side displays the permanent collection of over 2000 works of Russian art from the 1950's to the present day, with special focus on Soviet underground art. The right side houses temporary exhibits with many of the pieces for sale. The building also has a restaurant, café and store. Open 10am–10pm; closed Tuesdays. (To get here take Bus 6 or Tram 6 west from Vasileostovskaya Metro.) www.erarta.com (check out the online store).

The **Park Inn by Radisson Pribaltiiskaya Hotel** is at the western end of the island, not far from Primorskaya (Maritime) Metro station. Located in the hotel is the popular **Waterville Aquapark** with loads of waterslides, waterfalls and wave pools. From a 25-meter lap pool to shallower waters for kids, the complex also contains a Finnish sauna, Russian *banya* and Turkish *hammam*. www.waterville.ru. After a rejuvenating steam, go outside to watch a spectacular sunset over the Gulf of Finland from the embankment behind the hotel. A few minutes walk down the road from the hotel is the International Seaman's Club, near the Morskoi Vokzal (Marine Terminal), where most cruise ships dock. Marine Glory Square is in front with permanent glass pavilions that house international exhibitions. The Dekabristov (Decembrist) Island lies farther to the north.

For the next 320 kilometers (200 miles), the Gulf of Finland off Vasilyevsky Island is known as Cyclone Road. Cyclones traveling west to east create what is known as the long wave. It originates in the Gulf during severe storms and then rolls toward St Petersburg. Propelled by high winds, it enters between the narrow banks of the Neva with great speed. The city has experienced over 300 floods in its 300-year history. A 29-kilometer (18-mile) barrier has been built across a section of the Gulf to control the flooding. Much controversy surrounds the barrier, since many scientists believe that it is changing the ecological balance of the area.

PALACE SQUARE (DVORTSOVAYA PLOSHCHAD)

Palace Square was the heart of Russia for over two centuries and is one of the most striking architectural ensembles in the world. The Italian architect, Carlo Rossi, was commissioned to design the square in 1819. The government bought up all the residential houses and reconstructed the area into the Ministries of Foreign Affairs and Finance, and the General Staff Headquarters of the Russian Army. These two large yellow buildings curve 580 meters (1902 feet) around the southern end of the Square and are linked by the **Triumphal Arch** (actually two arches), whose themes of soldiers and armor commemorate the victories of the War of 1812. It is crowned by the 16-ton Winged Glory in a chariot led by six horses, which everyone believed would collapse the arch. On opening day Rossi declared: 'If it should fall, I will fall with it.' He triumphantly climbed to the top of the arch as the scaffolding was removed.

The Square was not only the parade ground for the czar's Winter Palace, but a symbol of the revolutionary struggle as well, and was in fact the site of three revolutions: the Decembrists first held an uprising near here in 1825. On Sunday January 9, 1905, over 100,000 people marched to Palace Square to protest intolerable working conditions. The demonstration began peacefully as the families carried icons and pictures of the czar. But Nicholas II's troops opened fire on the crowd and thousands were killed in the event known as Bloody Sunday. After the massacre, massive strikes ensued. In October of the same year, the St Petersburg Soviet of Workers' Deputies was formed. Twelve years later, in February 1917, the Kerensky Government overthrew the autocracy. At 1.50am on October 26, 1917, the Bolshevik Red Guards stormed through Palace Square to capture the Winter Palace from the Provisional Government. John Reed, the famous American journalist, wrote of the Revolution that on that night 'on Palace Square I watched the birth of a new world.' (see Literary Excerpt).

In 1920, the anniversary of the Revolution was celebrated by thousands of people rushing through the square to dramatically reconstruct the storming of the Winter Palace. (Eisenstein's famous film *October* immortalized this embellished image.) In actuality, only one blank shot was fired by the *Aurora* Battleship, and one soldier killed—the Provisional Government surrendered virtually without a fight. For decades thereafter, parades and celebrations were held on May Day and Revolution Day. Today, Palace Square remains the heart of the city.

As you enter Palace Square from Bolshaya Morskaya Ulitsa, an unforgettable panorama unfolds. The **Alexander Column** stands in the middle of the square, symbolizing the defeat of Napoleon in 1812. Nicholas I had it erected in memory of Alexander I. The 700-ton piece of granite took three years to be extracted from the Karelian Isthmus and brought down by barges to the city. Architect Auguste Montferrand supervised the polishing in 1830, and by 1834 the 14.5 meter (48-foot) high column was erected by 2,500 men using an elaborate system of pulleys. The figure of the angel (whose face resembles Alexander I) holding a cross was carved by sculptor Boris Orlovsky. The Guard's Headquarters was built by Karl Bryullov (1837–43) and now serves as an administrative building. The **General Staff Museum**, reopened in 2013 after extensive renovation, is on the eastern side of the Arch; the entrance is underneath the clock. It hosts displays of temporary exhibitions from the Hermitage Collection, and other paintings, graphics and applied arts from Russia and Western Europe. Open 10:30am–6pm, Sunday till 5pm; closed Mondays.

The main architectural wonder of the Square is the **Winter Palace**, standing along the bank of the Neva. This masterpiece, designed by Francesco Bartolomeo Rastrelli, was commissioned by Elizabeth I, daughter of Peter the Great, who was fond of the baroque and desired a lavish palace decorated with columns, stucco and sculptures. It was built between 1754 and 1764, as Rastrelli remarked, 'solely for the glory of all Russia'. At this time, the Winter Palace cost two and a half million rubles, equal to the value of 45 tons of silver. The Palace remained the Imperial official residence until the February 1917 Revolution. The magnificent complex extends over eight hectares (20 acres) and the total perimeter measures two kilometers (over a mile). There are 1,057 rooms (not one identical), 1,945 windows, 1,886 doors and 117 staircases. The royal family's staff consisted of over 1,000 servants. At 200 meters (656 feet) long and 22 meters (72 feet) high, it was the largest building in St Petersburg. After the 1837 fire destroyed a major portion of the Palace, architects Bryullov and Stasov restored the interior along the lines of Russian classicism, but preserved Rastrelli's light and graceful baroque exterior. The blue-green walls are adorned with 176 sculpted figures. The interior was finished with marble, malachite, jasper, semiprecious stones, polished woods, gilded moldings and crystal chandeliers. In 1844, Nicholas I passed a decree (in force until 1905) stating that all buildings in the city (except churches) had to be at least two meters (6.5 feet) lower than the Winter Palace. During World War II the Winter Palace was marked on German maps as Bombing Objective number 9. Today the Winter Palace houses the

Hermitage Museum—the largest museum in the country, which contains one of the largest and most valuable collections of art in the world, dating from antiquity to the present. Its buildings are home to over 16,000 paintings, 600,000 drawings and prints, 12,000 sculptures, 250,000 works of applied art, 700,000 archeological exhibits and 1 million coins and medals—over 3 million items in all. For the museum's 250th anniversary in 2014, it opened its own Fabergé collection in the newly renovated eastern wing.

Peter the Great began the city's first art collection after visiting Europe. In 1719, he purchased Rembrandt's *David's Farewell to Jonathan*, a statue of Aphrodite (*Venus of Taurida*), and started a museum of Russian antiquities (now on display in the Hermitage's Siberian collection).

In 1764, Catherine the Great created the Hermitage (*Ermitazh*—a French word meaning secluded spot) in the Winter Palace for a place to display 225 Dutch and Flemish paintings she had purchased in Berlin. Her ambassadors, who included Prince Dmitry Golitsyn and Denis Diderot, were often sent to European countries in search of art. In 1766, Golitsyn secured the purchase of Rembrandt's *Return of the Prodigal Son* from a private collector, regarded by many as one of the greatest works of art in the Hermitage. In 1769, Catherine II purchased the entire collection of Count von Brühl of Dresden, which included over 600 paintings and 1,000 drawings. The Hermitage held almost 4,000 paintings at the time of her death. Subsequent czars continued to expand the collection: Alexander I bought the entire picture gallery of Josephine, wife of Napoleon, and Nicholas I even purchased pictures from Napoleon's stepdaughter. Until 1852, the Hermitage was open only to members of the royal family and aristocratic friends. Catherine the Great wrote in a letter to one of her close friends that 'all this is admired by mice and myself'. A small list of rules, written by Catherine, hung by the Hermitage's entrance (see page 532). In 1852, Nicholas I opened the Hermitage on certain days as a public museum (but still closed to common people), and put it under the administrative direction of curators. After the 1917 Revolution, the Hermitage was opened full-time to the public.

The Hermitage occupies several other buildings in addition to the Winter Palace. The **Small Hermitage**, constructed by Vallin de la Mothe between 1764 and 1767, housed Catherine's original collection. Stackenschneider's Pavilion Hall is decked with white marble columns, 28 chandeliers, the four Fountains of Tears and the Peacock Clock. The royal family would stroll in the Hanging Gardens in summer, along with pheasants and peacocks. In winter, snow mounds were built for sledding. The **Large (Old) Hermitage** was built right next to it to provide space for Catherine's growing collection. The **Hermitage Theater**, Catherine's private theater, is linked to the Old Hermitage by a small bridge that crosses the Winter Ditch canal. The theater was built by Giacomo Quarenghi in 1783–1785, designed by Leo von Klenze, and modeled after the amphitheaters of Pompeii. Today concerts and ballets are staged in this intimate space. The **New Hermitage** (1839–52), located behind the Old Hermitage, houses additional works of art. Its main entrance off Millionnaya Ulitsa is composed of the ten large and powerful **Statues of Atlas**. They were designed by sculptor Terebenyev who personally participated in the carvings of these huge blocks of polished gray marble. The first figure took a year and a half to complete. Three more years were spent cutting the other nine. The figures of Atlas became the official emblem of the Hermitage.

The Hermitage collection spans a millennium of art and culture. Mikhail Piotrovsky, the museum's director stated, 'The Hermitage is a symbol of not only Russian but human civilization.' It is said that if a visitor spent only about half a minute at each piece, it still would take nine years to view them all! Plan to spend at least half a day here and this will only cover the initial highlights of the museum's collection.

The easiest way into the Hermitage is to purchase a ticket through the website: www.hermitagemuseum.org. (Make sure to print out the voucher.) A one-day ticket allows for a visit to the Winter Palace/Hermitage and its five interconnected buildings. A two-day Combined Entrance ticket also grants entry to four other Hermitage sites ((Winter Palace of Peter I, Menshikov Palace, Museum of Imperial Porcelain and the Hermitage Preservation and Storage Center, valid over two consecutive days.) Any ticket voucher is valid for 6 months so you can enter at anytime. You must present the Voucher and an ID at the entrance. By having a pre-purchased Voucher, a visitor does not have to stand in often long ticket lines. Go directly inside the Museum to the Cashier or Information Desk, and a guide will direct you to the proper counter where you redeem the voucher to receive an entrance ticket. (Free maps of the museum are available in different languages.) During summer months, the group and voucher entrance to the museum is located in front of the Winter Palace off the Palace (Dvortsovaya) River Embankment. The regular ticket lines are on the other side, off Palace Square. (In winter, this southern side often acts as the main entrance for everyone.) Inside the courtyard, signs are posted with times of daily English tours, and when group tours are available for the **Treasure Gallery: Gold and Diamond Rooms** (for an additional cost).

A visitor must check all coats, large bags, backpacks, umbrellas, etc. (smaller handbags are permitted) at the cloakrooms before going through the ticket turnstile and X-Ray control. Audio guides are for rent in the Jordan Gallery by the Jordan Staircase. To the rite of the entrance, down the hall, is the Interactive Center (with computer presentations of the museum's history and exhibits), a Wifi internet café, and numerous shops. Credit cards are accepted. www.hermitageshop.org.

The museum complex is open 10:30am–6pm, Wednesday 10:30pm–9pm; closed Mondays. The first Thursday of each month, entrance to the museum is free. Closest metro stop is Admiraleyskaya.

Upon entering, pass through the **Rastrelli Gallery** and up the white marble steps of the lavish **Jordan Staircase** (named after Christ's baptism in the River Jordan) to the first floor. Both clergy and court descended the staircase each year on January 6 to celebrate the 'Blessing of the Waters.' The procession then continued outside to the Neva River where a hole was cut through the ice, and water blessed and bottled for later use in baptisms in the city's churches.

On the first floor are the State Rooms of the Winter Palace. The top of the Staircase opens onto **Field Marshals' Hall** (Room 193), and the **Throne Room of Peter the Great** (Room 194). The **Armorial Hall** leads to the magnificent **1812 Gallery** (Room 197), designed to commemorate the Napoleonic Wars. Portraits of over 300 generals who fought against Napoleon cover the walls from floor to ceiling. The Italian architect, Carlo Rossi, modeled the gallery after the Waterloo Chamber at Windsor Castle. In front of the gallery is the great **Hall of St George** (Room 198) where the imperial throne once stood, and czars held elaborate receptions. The ceiling is a mirrored pattern of the inlaid floors, and a bas-relief of St George, protector of Russia, hangs in the room. The white and gold ceremonial **Pavilion Hall** (Room 204) with 28 chandeliers overlooks the Neva River and Catherine the Great's Hanging Gardens. The floor mosaic is copied from a Roman Bath. The centerpiece is the magnificent **Peacock Clock**, created by James Fox in 1772. Look closely at one of the toadstools where a revolving dial tells the time. On the hour, the peacock would spread its colorful wings, and all the animals come to life. The ornate **Palace Church** (Room 271) was the Romanov's private chapel and here Nicholas II married Alexandra Fyodorovna in 1894.

On the western side of the palace were the Imperial private apartments: Alexander II's are Rooms 289 & 304–308, and Nicholas II and his family, Rooms 175–189. Walking along the Corridor leads to the **Rotunda** and the **Moorish Dining Hall** (Rooms 155–156), which open onto the resplendent **Malachite Hall** (Room 189), designed by Bryullov as the Royal Drawing Room. Everything in this space, from pillars to vases, is carved from bright green malachite extracted from the Ural Mountains. When the Bolsheviks raided the Winter Palace in October 1917, it was in the next **White Dining Room** (Room 188) where Kerensky's Provisional Government members were captured. The clock on the mantelpiece is set to the time of their arrest at 2.10am. Circling back towards the Jordan Staircase, you will pass through **Nicholas Hall** (Room 191), once used to stage balls of up to 5,000 people. The portrait of Nicholas I gave the ballroom its name.

Due to the museum's layout, a visitor must first go up to the first floor and descend to the ground floor via a staircase on the other side of the main entrance. Exhibits on the ground floor encompass ancient Egyptian, Eurasian, Central Asian, Far Eastern and Russian art and culture. One of the most famous of the items that Nicholas I had placed in the New Hermitage was the **Kolyvan Vase**; standing 2.57-meter (8.4-feet) high its elliptical bowl is five yards long and three yards wide. The vast piece of jasper from which it was cut was unearthed in the Siberian Altai Mountains in 1819; the rough cut was not completed until 1831. The stone was then moved over the mountains to the town of Kolyvan, were it took another 12 years to cut and polish the 19-ton giant urn at a cost of over 30,000 silver rubles. Then, in 1843, it took over 150 horses to haul the vase across the wintry ice to the docks of Barnaul where it was put on a ship bound for St Petersburg. Eventually, it was moved to the New Hermitage where the walls were literally built around it. The vase still stands on the ground floor in the Hall of the Big Vase surrounded by Greek and Roman antiquities.

Over a quarter million pieces of ancient and oriental art and culture from Egypt (Room 100), Babylon, Byzantium, China, India, and the East occupy both the ground and second floors. (In the 1920s, academician Josif Orbelli wrote to Stalin advocating that no eastern art from the Oriental Department be sold abroad. Stalin agreed. Thus, in future years, the museum staff began to assign all treasures of uncertain origin to the Oriental Department to cunningly prevent their sale out of the country.)

Over 650,000 items in the collection of Western European, Byzantine and Central Asian art are also found on the first and second floors. Room sections include British (298–301), Dutch (249–254), Flemish (245–247), French (272–297), German (263–268), Italian (207–238), Spanish (239–240) and Russian culture and art (151–161), with famous paintings by Botticelli, Caravaggio, Da Vinci, El Greco Raphael, Rembrandt and Rubens. In addition there are numerous displays of china, furniture, handicrafts, jewelry, porcelain, rare coins, silver, sculpture and tapestries.

The top second floor showcases Impressionist and Post-Impressionist artists that include works by Cézanne, Degas, Gauguin, Matisse, Monet, Picasso, Renoir, Toulouse-Lautrec and Van Gogh. Room 334 is devoted to Russian Avant-Garde with paintings by Kandinsky and Malevich. Rooms 321–331 represent the Barbizon School and Romanticism; and Rooms 351–400 hold a vast collection of Oriental and Middle Eastern Culture and Art. The museum has room to display only 20 percent of its incredible treasures.

In 1995, the Hermitage opened a highly controversial exhibition entitled *Hidden Treasures Revealed* (Rooms 143–146), composed entirely of art confiscated by the Red Army from private German collections when it swept across Eastern Europe into Berlin at the end of World War II. The paintings, estimated to be worth several million dollars, are by Impressionist and Post-Impressionist artists. The centerpiece is Degas' 1875 painting *Place de la Concorde*, believed destroyed during the war. Stored secretly for over half a century in a small room on the museum's second floor, the unveiled collection includes many other paintings by Cézanne, Gauguin, Matisse, Monet, Renoir and Picasso. In all, during the war, the two countries pilfered from one another an estimated five million artworks. The dispute over who is the rightful owner of these paintings continues through today.

A fabulous film to rent is Alexander Sokurov's *Russian Ark*, which takes the viewer (this was the first feature film ever shot in one continuous take) through 33 rooms of the Winter Palace and 300 years of Russian history. One of the film's characters is the Marquis de Custine (1790–1857), who wrote extensively about his travels in Russia (see page 532).

If you can't get enough of the Hermitage, visit its **Restoration and Storage Center** (included in the Two-Day Combined Ticket) at 37 Zausadebnaya on the Vyborg side (metro Staraya Derevnya). As the largest preservation complex of its kind in the world, exhibits include art, furniture and carriages. Group tours are offered at 11am, 1pm, 1:30pm, 3:30pm; closed Mon/Tues.

Leaving the Hermitage walk out to the Neva River and east along the embankment to **Peter the Great's Winter Palace** (at number 32), where he lived from 1720 until his death in 1725. It was long thought that Peter's main residence had been destroyed in 1785 in order to make way for the Hermitage Theater. But research in the 1970's and 1980's revealed that the architect Quarenghi had retained much of the palace's structure, and that a significant portion of the former courtyard was located beneath the theater's stage, along with other suites of private rooms used by Peter and his wife, Catherine, that faced the Winter Canal. After extensive renovation, rooms were opened to the public in 1992. These include Peter the Great's study, dining area and turnery (lathe workshop) where personal articles of the Emperor decorate the rooms. Other items on display are a replica of Peter I sitting on his throne, a gilded carriage and Rastrelli's wax effigy portrait of the Czar. Open 10:30am–6pm, Sunday till 5pm; closed Mondays. (The Hermitage Two-Day Combined Ticket is good for entrance.) (See pages 548–549.)

Walking behind the Hermitage Theater towards Millionnaya St. and through the Choristers' Passage takes you across the **Pevchesky Most (Singers' Bridge)**, also known as the Yellow Bridge. (The four small bridges that cross the Moika west up to St Issac's Cathedral are color coded and known as the Yellow, Green Red and

Blue.) The Yellow leads to the former Imperial Court Choir Capella (founded in Moscow in 1473) at number 20, now the **Glinka Capella House** that hosts performances of organ and choral music. www.glinka-capella.ru.

At 12 Moika Embankment is the **Pushkin House Museum** where the poet, considered the fountainhead of Russian literature, lived from October 1836 until his death on January 29, 1837. Alexander Pushkin died from a wound (he was shot in the stomach) following a duel with a French soldier of fortune named George D'Anthès, who had been publicly flirting with Pushkin's beautiful wife Natalya. A statue of Pushkin stands in the courtyard. The rooms have all been preserved and contain the poet's personal belongings and manuscripts. The study is arranged exactly as it was when Pushkin died on the divan two days after the duel, at age 37. The clock is even set to time of death at 2.45. The next room displays the clothes worn during the duel and his death mask. The museum is open 10.30am–6pm, Monday noon–8pm; closed Tuesdays and last Friday of month. Metro Nevsky Prospekt. www.museumpushkin.ru. (See pages 205 and 667.)

On January 27, Alexander Pushkin met up with his attendant at a shop at 18 Nevsky Prospekt (today it is the Literatornoye Café) and they continued on by sleigh to the Chornaya Rechka (Black River) area on the Vyborg Side of the city to fight the duel with D'Anthès, who ironically was married to Natalya's sister. Today a marble monument marks the spot of the famous duel (not far from Chornaya Rechka metro stop). In Pushkin's famous epic poem, *Yevgeny Onegin*, the St Petersburg protagonist rejects the love of Tatyana while trying to seduce her sister, Olga, who is engaged to his best friend, Lensky. In the end, in this tale of unrequited love, Lensky also challenges Onegin to a duel where one is killed.

THE AREA OF SENATE SQUARE (SENATSKAYA PLOSHCHAD)

Walking west of the Winter Palace along the Neva, you come to another chief architectural monument of the city, the **Admiralty**, recognizable by its tall golden spire topped by a golden frigate, the symbol of St Petersburg after Peter the Great. The best views of the building are from its southern end. A beautiful fountain stands in the middle of the **Admiralty Gardens** surrounded by busts of Glinka, Gogol and Lermontov. In 1704, Peter the Great ordered a second small outpost constructed on the left bank of the Neva, opposite the main town. This shipyard was later referred to as the Admiralty. Over 10,000 peasants and engineers were employed to work on the Russian naval fleet. By the end of the 18th century the Navy had its headquarters here, and remained until 1917. Whenever the Neva waters rose during a severe storm, a lantern was lit in the spire to warn of coming floods. In 1738, the architect

Ivan Korobov replaced the wooden tower with a golden spire, topped by the weather-vane *korablik*—the little ship. From 1806 to 1823, the structure was again redesigned, this time in Russian Empire style by Adrian Zakharov, an architectural professor at the St Petersburg Academy. The height of the spire was increased to 72.5 meters (238 feet) and decorated with rows of white columns, 56 mythological figures and 350 ornamentations based on the glory of the Russian fleet. The scene over the main-entrance archway depicts Neptune handing over his trident to Peter the Great, a symbol of Peter's mastery of the sea. In 1860, many of the statues were taken down when the Orthodox Church demanded the 'pagan' statues removed. Today the Admiralty houses the Higher Military Naval College. (It is closed to visitors.)

Across the street from the Admiralty is the building of the former city police administration that was once known as the All Russia Extraordinary Commission for Combating Counter-revolution, Sabotage and Speculation—the Cheka. Today, here at 2 Gorokhovaya, the building houses the **Museum of the History of Political Police** that traces the history of the secret police from czarist times through the Cheka up to the KGB. One room recreates the office of Felix Dzerzhinsky, the first chairman of the Cheka. His best-remembered words were that a member of the Cheka 'must have clean hands, a warm heart and a cold head'. Open 10am–6pm; closed Sat/Sun. Metro Admiralteyskaya. (Another branch of the museum is at 2/4 Kuibysheva, Petrograd side. Metro Gorkovskaya.) www.polithistory.ru.

Beside the Admiralty is the infamous **Senate Square**, formerly known as Decembrists' and Peter's Square. In 1925, to mark the 100-year anniversary of the Decembrist uprising, the area was renamed Decembrists' Square. (In 2008, its name reverted to Senate.) After the Russian victory in the Patriotic War of 1812 and the introduction of principles from the French Enlightenment, both the nobility and peasants wanted an end to the monarchy and serfdom. An opportune moment for insurrection came on November 19, 1825, when Czar Alexander I unexpectedly died. A secret revolutionary society, consisting mainly of noblemen, gathered over 3,000 soldiers and sailors who refused to swear allegiance to the new czar, Nicholas I. The members compiled the Manifesto to the Russian People, which they hoped the Senate would approve. (They did not know that the Senate had already proclaimed their loyalty to Nicholas.) They decided to lead an uprising of the people in Senate Square on December 14, 1825, and from here to capture the Winter Palace and Peter and Paul Fortress. But Nicholas I discovered the plan and surrounded the square with armed guards. The Decembrists marched to an empty Senate, and moreover, Prince Trubetskoi, who was elected to lead the insurrection, never showed up! Tens of thousands of people joined the march and prevented the guards from advancing on the main parties. But Nicholas I then ordered his guards to open

CODE OF THE EMPRESS CATHERINE

*A*t the entrance of one hall, I found behind a green curtain the social rules of the Hermitage, for the use of those intimate friends admitted by the Czarina into the asylum of Imperial Liberty.

I will transcribe, verbatim, this charter, granted to social intimacy by the caprice of the sovereign of the once enchanted place: it was copied for me in my presence:-

RULES TO BE OBSERVED ON ENTERING

ARTICLE I
*On entering, the title and rank must be put off,
as well as the hat and sword.*

ARTICLE II
*Pretensions founded on the prerogatives of birth, pride,
or other sentiments of a like nature must also be left at the door.*

ARTICLE III
Be merry; nevertheless, break nothing and spoil nothing.

ARTICLE IV
Sit, stand, walk, do whatever you please, without caring for anyone.

ARTICLE V
*Speak with moderation, and not too often,
in order to avoid being troublesome to others.*

ARTICLE VI
Argue without anger and without warmth.

ARTICLE VII
*Banish sighs and yawns, that you may not communicate ennui,
or be a nuisance to anyone.*

ARTICLE VIII
*Innocent games, proposed by any members of the society,
must be accepted by the others*

ARTICLE IX
*Eat slowly and with appetite; drink with moderation,
that each may walk steadily as he goes out.*

ARTICLE X
*Leave all quarrels at the door; what enters at one ear must go out the
other before passing the threshold of the Hermitage.*

*If any member violates the above rules, for each fault witnessed by two
persons, he must drink a glass of fresh water (ladies not excepted);
furthermore, he must read aloud a page of the* Telemachiad *(a poem by
Trediakofsky). Whoever fails during one evening in three of these articles,
must learn by heart six lines of the* Telemachiad. *He who fails in the tenth
article must never more re-enter the Hermitage.*

Marquis Astolphe Louis Leonard de Custine, Russia, 1854–5

fire on the crowds. Hundreds were killed and mass arrests followed. Over 100 people were sentenced to serve 30 years in penal servitude. Five leaders of the rebellion were hanged in Peter and Paul Fortress. Others received such ludicrous sentences as having to run a gauntlet of a thousand soldiers 12 times, amounting to 12,000 blows by rod; if they survived, they would be set free! Even though the 1825 uprising was unsuccessful, 'the roar of cannon on Senate Square awakened a whole generation', observed the revolutionary writer Alexander Herzen.

In 1768, Catherine the Great wanted to commission a magnificent monument to her predecessor, Peter the Great. She considered herself Peter's political heir; he had begun to open Russia to the modern world, and Catherine had brought Europe into her country's domain. It was her close friend in France, Denis Diderot, who invited Etienne Falconet (who had written an article for Diderot's *Encyclopédie*) to Russia. The French sculptor said he was prepared to devote eight years of his life to it. In fact, Falconet toiled for 12 years to create, in his words, 'an alive, vibrant and passionate spirit.' He successfully designed the symbolic rider (Peter is depicted three times life size) on a rearing horse, crushing a serpent underfoot. Marie Collot, Falconet's pupil and future wife, sculpted the head (based on a bronze bust of Peter fashioned during his lifetime by Carlo Rastrelli), and the Russian sculptor, Fyodor Gordeyev, the snake.

In addition, Falconet wanted to place his monument atop natural stone. And it was Catherine the Great who went to great lengths to transfer an enormous granite stone, shaped like a wave about to break, over ten kilometers (six miles) to the city. It had been split by lightning and was known as Thunder Rock. Peter the Great was said to have often climbed this very rock to view his emerging city. Weighing 1,600 tons, it was eight meters (26 feet) high, 13.5 meters (44 feet) long and ten meters (33 feet) wide. Catherine offered 7,000 rubles as a reward to the person who invented a way to quickly transport it to the city. A Russian blacksmith came up with a plan. First, an entire road was cut through the forest to the gulf. With the help of levers, the boulder was lifted atop a log platform. Then two large, parallel grooves were carved out along the path (rather like a railroad track). Thirty copper balls, acting like ball bearings, were placed along the grooves. Over 100 horses took five months to pull the 'moving mountain' nine kilometers to the sea. The boulder was then placed upon a raft and towed to Senate Square.

After three attempts to cast the huge statue, Falconet finally succeeded in 1782. It was in this year that the masterpiece was unveiled, the 100th anniversary of Peter's ascension to the throne. In a play of words, Catherine had inscribed: *Petro Primo Catharina Secunda*—'To Peter I from Catherine II, 1782.' This monument became known as the **Bronze Horseman**, after the popular poem by Pushkin. (See page 679.) Today the statue is looked on as the symbol of St Petersburg, a sign of its splendor and endurance. It has remained a constant through nearly three tumultuous centuries. Legend has it that as long as the Bronze Horseman remains, St Petersburg will never perish.

The first governing Senate was established by Peter the Great in 1711 and ruled the country while the czar was away. Peter put the Church and ecclesiastical members under State control in 1721 by founding the Holy Synod. Carlo Rossi supervised the construction of the yellow-white **Senate, Synod and Supreme Court buildings** between 1829 and 1836, which are joined by an arch, symbolizing Faith and Law. Today they house the Central State Historical Archives and the Yeltsin Presidential Library. Take a stroll down the small Galernaya Ulitsa that lies beyond the arch; this was the area of the galley shipyards. The two Ionic columns standing at the start of the next boulevard bear the Goddesses of Glory. These monuments commemorate the valor of Russia's Horse Guards during the war against Napoleon. The building that looks like an ancient Parthenon temple is the Royal Horse Guard **Manège**, built between 1804 and 1807 from designs by Quarenghi, where the czar's elite equestrian troops were trained. It enjoyed later incarnations as a concert hall and trade show center. Today it houses rotating art exhibtions; in December an annual retrospective is held with paintings and sculptures by local artists. In front of the portico are marble statues of the mythological heroes Castor and Pollux. www.manege.spb.ru.

ST ISAAC'S SQUARE (ISAAKIYEVSKAYA PLOSHCHAD)

The whole southern end of Senate Square is framed by the grand silhouette of **St Isaac's Cathedral**. In 1710, the first wooden church of St Isaac was built by Peter I, who was born on the feast day that celebrated the sainthood of Isaac of Dalmatia; it was replaced in 1729 by one of stone. At that time the church was situated nearer to the banks of the Neva and it eventually began to crack and sink. Thus, in 1768, it was decided to build another church farther away from the riverbank. But, on its completion in 1802, the church was not deemed grand enough for the growing magnificence of the capital. After the War of 1812, Czar Alexander I announced a competition for the best design of a new St Isaac's. The young architect Auguste Montferrand presented an elaborate album filled with 24 different variations, from Chinese to Gothic, for the czar to choose one. Montferrand was selected for the monumental task in 1818, and the czar also assigned the architects Stasov, Rossi and the Mikhailov brothers to help with the engineering.

The cathedral took 40 years to build. In the first year alone, 11,000 serfs drove 25,000 wooden planks into the soft soil to set a foundation. Each of the 112 polished granite columns, weighing 130 tons, had to be raised by a system of pulleys. The system was so efficient that the monolithic columns were each installed in a mere 45 minutes. The domed cathedral has a total height of 101.5 meters (333 feet). An observation deck along the upper colonnade (262 steps to climb) provides a magnificent view of the city. The State spared no expense—the cathedral cost ten times more than the Winter Palace. Nearly 100 kilograms of gold leaf was used to gild the dome, which in good weather is visible 40 kilometers (25 miles) away. The interior is faced with 14 different kinds of marble, 43 other types of stone and mineral and 16,000 kg of malachite.   Inside the western portico is a bust of Montferrand, holding a model of the cathedral, made from each type of marble. (Montferrand died one month after the completion of the cathedral. He had asked to be buried within its walls, but Czar Alexander II refused. Instead, the architect was buried in Paris.) The 4000-sq-meter (43,000-sq-feet) interior can hold 14,000 people and is filled with over 400 sculptures, paintings and mosaics by the best Russian and European masters of the 19th-century. Twenty two artists decorated the iconostasis, ceilings and walls. The altar's huge stained-glass window is surrounded by frescoes by Karl Bryullov, who also painted the frescoes in the ceiling of the main dome. A St Petersburg newspaper wrote that the cathedral was 'a pantheon of Russian art, as artists have left monuments to their genius in it'. On May 29, 1858, St Isaac's was inaugurated with much pomp and celebration as the main cathedral of St Petersburg. In 1931, it was opened by the government as a museum. (Services are sometimes held during special religious holidays.) Open 10:30am–6pm, evening admission 6pm–10:30pm from May 1–Sept 30. The upper Colonnade walkway is open 10:30am–6pm, from May 1–Oct 31 6pm–10:30pm, and during the White Nights (Jun 1–August 20) 6pm–4:30am; closed Wednesdays. Metro Admiralteyskaya. www.cathedral.ru.

St Isaac's Square, in front of the cathedral, was originally a marketplace in the 1830s. At its center stands the bronze Statue of Nicholas I constructed by Montferrand and Klodt between 1856 and 1859. The czar, who loved horses and military exploits (nicknamed Nicholas the Stick), is portrayed in a cavalry uniform wearing a helmet with an eagle. His horse rests only on two points. The bas-reliefs around the pedestal depict the events of Nicholas' turbulent rule. One of them shows Nicholas I addressing his staff after the Decembrist uprising. The four figures at each corner represent Faith, Wisdom, Justice and Might, and depict the faces of Nicholas' wife and three daughters, who commissioned the statue.

The two buildings on each side of the monument were built between 1844 and 1853 and now house the Academy of Agricultural Sciences. Behind the monument is the Blue Bridge (1818), which is painted accordingly. It is the widest bridge in the city (at 97.3 meters/320 feet); even though it appears to be a continuation of the square, it is actually it spans over the Moika (this river is 5 km long and crossed by 15 bridges). There was a slave market here before the abolition of serfdom in 1861.

Many of St Petersburg's bridges were named after the color they were painted; up river are the Red, Green and Yellow bridges. On one side of the bridge is an obelisk crowned by a trident, known as the Neptune Scale. Five bronze bands indicate the level of the water during the city's worst floods. The Leningrad poet Vera Inber wrote of this place:

> Here in the city, on Rastrelli's marble
> Or on plain brick, we see from time to time
> A mark: 'The water-level reached this line'
> And we can only look at it and marvel.

Beyond the bridge stands the former Mariinsky Palace. It was built between 1839 and 1844 for Maria, the daughter of Nicholas I. In 1894, it was turned into the State Council of the Russian Empire. In 1901, the artist Repin painted the centennial gala, entitled *The Solemn Meeting of the State Council* which can be viewed today at the Russian Museum. In 1917, the Palace was the residence of the Provisional Government. It now houses the St Petersburg City Assembly (the city parliament).

The seven-story **Hotel Astoria**, on the northeast side of the square, was built in 1912 by architect Fyodor Lidval in a Russian interpretation of art nouveau called northern moderne. It became the grandest hotel in the city. During the early 1900s, St Petersburg was alive with the innovative creations of the Ballet Russes by Diaghilev and Stravinsky. In turn, Lidval designed the hotel with rounded corners, swirling mirrors and artistic plasterwork. During the 1917 revolution, demonstrators stormed the hotel, but it remained open. The hotel became a field hospital during WW II. And, during the 900-day Siege of Leningrad, Hitler even planned to hold his victory party here; he sent out engraved invitations for a banquet to be held at the Astoria on November 7 1942, as soon as he had captured the city. Of course, this never took place. The hotel has been completely renovated, and today stands as a proud symbol of the new spirit of St Petersburg. The other side of the building is now the Angleterre Hotel.

In front of the Astoria is the Lobanov-Rostovsky Mansion. Montferrand built this for the Russian diplomat between 1817 and 1820. Pushkin mentioned the marble lions in front of the house in the *Bronze Horseman*, when the hero climbed one of them to escape the flood. The mansion is referred to as the **House with Lions**.

On the southwest side of the square is the former Intourist Building, originally built in 1910 to accommodate the German Embassy. It was designed by German architect Berens, who became one of the founders of the new *Jugendstil* style. Behind this building, at 47 Bolshaya Morskaya is the **Nabokov House Museum**. The famous prolific writer was born in this lovely 19th-century apartment over a century ago in April 1899. This house and St Petersburg are lovingly described in his autobiography, *Speak Memory*. Other works include *Pale Fire, Laughter in the Dark* and *Lolita*—the immensely controversial novel written in 1955 (and later made into a classic movie by Stanley Kubrick). On view in the museum are photographs, books and original *samizdat*—secretly circulated hand-copied Nabokov works officially banned for print in Soviet times, along with a part of his extensive butterfly collection. His family, liberal aristocrats, fled to England via Greece in 1919, and Nabokov later resided in Germany, France, the US and Switzerland, where he died in 1977. The museum also hosts annual April readings from Nabokov's works. Open 11am–6pm, Sat/Sun noon–5pm, closed Mondays. Metro Admiralteyskaya. www.nabokovmuseum.org. The family estate at Rozhdestveno, outside St Petersburg, can also be visited. (See Vicinity of St Petesburg, page 659.) Down the street, at number 37, is the **Rosphoto Photography Center** that showcases photography and mixed media presentations from all around Russia. Open 11am–7pm, Thursday till 9pm. www.rosphoto.org.

A few blocks west, at 4 Pochtamtskaya (Postal) Street, is the **Popov Central Museum of Communications** housed within the former 18th-century mansion of Prince Bezborodko, Chancellor of the Russian Empire. On May 7, Russia celebrates Radio Day. On this day, in 1895, Alexander Popov demonstrated his invention of the radio receiver at St Petersburg University with a range of 600 meters. Two years later, the range had increased to five kilometers, and by 1901, to 150. In 1900, Popov won a gold medal at the Paris World's Fair. (In 1897, it was the Italian Guillermo Marconi who received the first radio receiver patent.) The museum contains a history of all manner of communications from the Pony Express and an antique telephone switchboard to the large communications satellite Luch-15, with lots of multimedia and interactive explanations. Open 10:30am–6pm; closed Sundays, Mondays and last Thursday of month. Metro Nevsky Prospekt. www.rustelecom-museum.ru.

At 9 Pochtamtskaya is the General Post Office (1782–89), with the Clock of the World mounted on its archway. **The Museum of the History of Religion**, at number 14, exhibits work on world religions, including Buddhism, Christianity, Judaism, Islam and Russian Orthodoxy that includes art, texts and other ritual items. Open 10am–6pm, Tuesday 1pm–9pm; closed Wednesdays. www.gmir.ru.

A few blocks north, at 4 Konnogvardeysky Bulvar is the private **Russian Vodka Museum**, which traces the history of vodka from its origin to the international vodka industry of today, along with Russian dining and drinking traditions. For an added charge, a visitor can also have a *tasting tour* with *zakuski* appetizers—or if you have a meal in the Imperial-style restaurant (Russian Vodka Room No 1 with a huge vodka list), you can then visit the museum, with a tasting included, for a small fee. Open noon–10pm. www.vodkamuseum.su.

Dostoevsky lived nearby at 23 Malaya Morskaya before his imprisonment, in 1849, in the Peter and Paul Fortress for his participation in a radical intellectual group. Here he wrote *Netochka Nezvanova* and *The White Nights*. Dostoevsky's main museum is located at 5/2 Kuznechny Pereulok, near Vladimirskaya Metro (closed Mondays).

FIELD OF MARS (POLYE MARSOVO)

A short walk east from the Hermitage, to number 5 Millionnaya, brings you to the **Marble Palace**, a masterpiece of neoclassicism. In 1768, Catherine the Great commissioned Antonio Rinaldi to build a palace for her favorite, Count Grigory Orlov. (He had helped Catherine ascend to the throne in 1762.) In turn, Orlov's response was to present the Empress with one of the world's largest cut diamonds, weighing 189.6 carats. (The 'Orlov' diamond was later mounted in the royal scepter.) Upon his retirement in 1783, Catherine wrote in a letter to him: "I shall never forget how much I owe to your family, nor the qualities with which you are endowed and how useful they can be to our Motherland." This was the only building in St Petersburg faced both inside and outside with colored marble, 32 different kinds. Marble came from Karelia in the Baltic region, and the islands of Lake Ladoga; further expeditions were carried out all the way to the Urals. Over 100 stonemasons worked daily for years to polish and fit the granite and marble pieces throughout the palace.

Since Orlov died before the palace's completion in 1785, Catherine the Great gifted it first to a Polish King and then to her grandson, Grand Prince Konstantin Pavlovich. In 1832, Nicolas I gave the palace to his second son, Konstantin Nikolayevich; and one of last owners of the palace was the brother of Alexander II. From 1844–51, the architect Alexander Bryullov was commissioned to redo parts of the interiors. The palace was closed after the 1917 revolution when many of the rooms acted as offices for various Socialist organizations.

Upon entering the palace, the **Grand Marble Staircase** contains bas-relief and allegorical sculptures, one a portrait of the architect Rinaldi himself. One of the palace's highlights is the **Marble Hall**, whose ceiling depicts 'The Wedding of Cupid and Psyche,' painted in 1775. In 1937, the Marble Palace opened as the Leningrad branch of the Central Lenin Museum, with over 10,000 exhibits in 34 rooms relating to Lenin's life and work. After the 1991 failed coup, the Lenin Museum was removed from the Marble Palace which now, as a branch of the Russian Museum, displays 18th/19th century European art (entitled Foreign Artists in Russia), a 20th-century Modern Art Collection from the Ludwig Museum in Cologne, Germany, other works of Pop Art, as well as rotating temporary art exhibitions. The outdoor **Clock Tower** was restored in 1999, when three large bells were hung and connected by ropes to the clock's mechanism. Today, their chimes ring out every 15 minutes across the Neva and Summer Gardens. During the 1990's, Lenin's armored car was removed from the courtyard and replaced by the equestrian **Statue of Alexander III**. The palace is open 10am–6pm, Monday till 5pm; closed Tuesdays. Closest metro is Nevsky Prospekt. (A combined entrance ticket can be bought for the Marble and Stroganov Palaces, Mikhailovsky Castle and Russian Museum, good for 3 days.) www.rusmuseum.ru.

Right in front of the Troitsky Bridge is **Suvorov Square** (Ploshchad Suvorova), with the **Statue of Alexander Suvorov**, the Russian generalissimo depicted as Mars, the God of War. The square opens on to one of the most beautiful places in St Petersburg, the **Field of Mars**. Around 1710, Peter the Great drained the marshy field and held parades after military victories. The festivities ended in fireworks (known as amusement lights), so the square was called Poteshnoye Polye (Amusement Field). By the end of the 18th century the area was used as a routine drill field, which destroyed the grass; for a while the field was nicknamed the St Petersburg Sahara. When in 1801 the monument to Field Marshal Suvorov was placed here, the area became known as Marsovo Polye (Field of Mars). It was moved to its present location, Suvorov Square, in 1818. The 12-hectare (30-acre) field is bordered on the west by the **Barracks of the Pavlovsky Regiment**. Because of their heroic deeds this regiment was rewarded with a magnificent barracks, built between 1817 and 1820. The Pavlovsky Grenadier Regiment was the first among the czar's armies to take the side of the people during the February 1917 Revolution. It is now the St Petersburg Energy Commission. The southern side is bordered by the Moika River and Griboyedov Canal, and the eastern side by the Swan Canal (Lebyazhya Kanavka).

The **Memorial to the Fighters of the Revolution** stands in the center of the field. On March 23, 1917, 180 heroes of the February uprising were buried here in mass graves. The next day the first granite stone was laid in the monument foundation, which was unveiled in 1920. On each of the eight stone blocks are words by the writer Anatoly Lunacharsky. One reads: 'Not victims, but heroes, lie beneath these stones. Not grief, but envy, is aroused by your fate in the hearts of all your grateful descendants.' During the 40th anniversary of the Revolution in 1957, the eternal flame was lit in memory of those killed.

The eastern side of the field opens up on the lovely Letny Sad or **Summer Garden** with over 250 sculptures made by 17th and 18th century Italian masters. The main entrance to the garden is from the Kutuzova Embankment. A beautiful black and golden grille (1770–84 by Yuri Felten) fences it. The open railing, decorated with 36 granite columns and pinkish urns, is one of the finest examples of wrought-iron work in the world. The Summer Garden, the city's oldest, was designed by Jean-Baptiste Leblond in Franco-Dutch style in 1704. Peter the Great desired to create a garden more exquisite than Versailles. On 25 acres of land he planted trees and had hothouses, aviaries, grottos and sculptures placed within. Some copies of the original statues are *Peace and Abundance*, the busts of John Sobiesky (a Polish king), Christina (a Swedish queen), the Roman empress Agrippina, and Cupid and Psyche. The Swan Canal dug on the western side was filled with swans and had a tiny boat for Peter's favorite dwarf jester. The garden also had many fountains depicting characters from Aesop's *Fables*.

The water for the fountains was drained from a river on its east side; the river was named **Fontanka**, from the Russian *fontan* (fountain). Pipes made from hollowed logs ran from the Fontanka to a city pool, from which a 1.6-kilometers (one-mile) pipeline brought water to the gardens. The Fontanka formed the southern border of the city in the mid-18th century. At this time the first stone bridge was built where the Fontanka flows into the Neva. It is still known as **Prachechny Most** (Laundry Bridge) because it was located near the Royal Laundry. The gardens received their name from the many festivals that Peter the Great loved to hold in summer; the area became the center of social life in St Petersburg.

Many of the fountains, pavilions and statues were destroyed during the 1777 and 1824 floods. The Summer Garden was open only to nobility until, in the mid-19th-century, Nicholas I issued a decree stating that it would be 'open for promenading to all military men and decently dressed people. Ordinary people, such as *muzhiks* (peasants) shall not be allowed to walk through the garden.' After the Revolution the garden was opened fully to the public. In 2012, the gardens were reopened after an extensive two-year restoration. The Summer Gardens are open May 1 to September 30 10am–10pm; closed Tuesdays and earlier in winter months.

After the garden was designed, Peter had his Letny Dvorets or **Summer Palace** built at the northeastern end by the Neva. Following its completion in 1712 by Domenico Trezzini, Peter moved from his cottage into the palace. The modest stone building was decorated with 29 terracotta figures and a weather vane of St George slaying the dragon. There are 14 rooms, seven on each floor. Peter lived on the ground floor, and his wife Catherine on the second. The czar received visitors in the reception room, and the empress enjoyed baking Peter's favorite pies in the kitchen. Nearby stood one of Peter's favorite statues, the *Venus of Taurida* (now in the Hermitage); the czar purchased it from the Pope. The House is open 10am–6pm; closed Tuesdays and first Monday of month. Closest Metro Nevsky Prospekt/ Chernyshevskaya. (The Palace is often closed for renovation.)

Behind the Summer Palace is an interesting bronze **Monument to Ivan Krylov** (1854) by the sculptor Peter Klodt, dedicated to the popular Russian fabulist. There is also a playground for children with subjects from Krylov's fables. Nearer to the fountain are the Chainy Domik or **Tea House**, built in 1827 by Ludwig Charlemagne, and the **Coffee House** built by Carlo Rossi in 1826 (it is also known as Rossi's Pavilion). Recitals are now held here. The outside sculpture of *Peace and Abundance* symbolizes the peace treaty made with Sweden in 1721. It was a gift to Nicholas I from the Swedish king, Karl Johann.

MIKHAILOVSKY (ENGINEER'S) CASTLE

Crossing the Moika Canal and continuing along the banks of the Fontanka to 2 Sadovaya, leads to the **Mikhailovsky Castle**, built between 1797 and 1800 by the Italian architect Vincenzo Brenna for Czar Paul I (1754–1801). Paul did not like his mother Catherine the Great's residence (she died in 1796) in the Winter Palace, and fearing attempts on his life, he ordered the Medieval-like complex constructed as an impregnable fortress. The Mikhailovsky Castle (the archangel Michael was Paul's patron saint) was bordered in the north by the Moika Canal and the east by the Fontanka. Two artificial canals, the Resurrection and Church, were dug on the other sides creating a small island (they have since been filled in). Drawbridges, protected by cannons, were raised at 9pm when the czar went to bed. In spite of all this, 40 days after he moved in, Paul was strangled in his sleep in his own bedroom by one of his guards on March 12, 1801. (In all, Paul was heir to the throne for 40 years, and was czar for exactly four years, four months and four days.)

In February 1819, after a military engineering school was opened in the building, it became known as Engineer's Castle. Dostoevsky went to school here as a cadet from 1838 to 1843. In front of the castle's main entrance is a **Statue of Peter the Great**, created by Carlo Rastrelli while Peter was still alive. It was supposed to be erected near the Twelve Collegiums on Vasilyevsky Island. However, it was not completed until 1746, during the reign of Elizabeth I. And since the empress did not particularly like the statue it ended up in storage. In 1800, the monument was placed in its current location. Paul I ordered the inscription placed upon its base: 'To Great-Grandfather—From Great-Grandson. The Year 1800.' On the sides of the pedestal are bronze reliefs depicting major victories of Peter the Great. Today the Mikhailovsky Castle is part of the Russian Museum complex; the ground floor contains temporary exhibits and upper floors house a Portrait Gallery and works painted by 18th- and 19th-century foreign artists while living in Russia. Several lavishly-restored state rooms, including the Czarina's throne room, can also be viewed. Open 10am–6pm; closed Tuesdays. Metro Gostiny Dvor (A combined entrance ticket can be bought for the Mikhailovsky Castle, Marble and Stroganov Palaces and Russian Museum, good for 3 days.) Not to be confused with the castle, the Mikhailovsky Palace is the Russian Museum. www.rusmuseum.ru.

CATHERINE THE GREAT (1729–1796)

Peter the Great propelled Russia into the 18th-century; Catherine II completed it by decorating his creation in European pomp and principle. Born Sophie Frederika Augusta in 1729 to the German prince of Anhalt-Zerbst, she was chosen as the future bride, at the age of 14, to Peter III, the half-wit grandson of Peter the Great. When Peter III ascended the throne in 1762, he threatened to get rid of Catherine by imprisoning her in a nunnery (and marrying his pockmarked mistress). This only fueled Catherine's ambitions; she said, 'either I die or I begin to rule'. That same year a secret coup, headed by her lover Grigory Orlov and his brothers, overthrew the unpopular Peter. When he was killed by drunken guards a week later, Catherine became the first foreigner ever to sit upon the Russian throne; she would rule for 34 years. Catherine was clever and adventurous and had fallen deeply in love with her new homeland (instead of with her husband). She immersed herself in the problems of politics and agriculture and worked toward basing the government on philosophic principles rather than on religious doctrines or hereditary rights. Because of her European roots, Catherine held a fascination for France and avidly worked to link French culture with that of her adopted nation. She read Voltaire, Montesquieu and Rousseau and sent emissaries to study in foreign lands; she also began the education of noblewomen. The Russian aristocracy soon incorporated French culture into their daily lives, giving the noblemen a common identity. The French language also set them apart from the Russian peasantry. In 1780, she further initiated the Declaration of Armed Neutrality, helping the American colonies in their struggle for independence.

Catherine described her reign as the 'thornless rose that never stings'. Along with autocratic power, she ruled with virtue, justice and reason. By the publication of books and newspapers, and instruction by Western-trained tutors, education spread throughout the provinces, where before much of the learning originated from the Church. This allowed Russian culture to cut loose from its religious roots. Paper money was introduced, along with vaccinations; the day of Catherine's smallpox vaccination became a national feast day.

Scientific expeditions were sent to Far Eastern lands and hundreds of new cities were built in Russia's newly conquered territories. Along the coast of the Black Sea, the cities of Odessa, Azov and Sevastopol were constructed on the sites of old Greek settlements. With the formation of the Academy of Sciences, Russia now contributed to the Renaissance Age and would never again stand in the shadows. One of the most important figures of the time, Mikhail Lomonosov, scientist, poet and historian, later helped to establish Moscow University.

Catherine spared no expense to redecorate St Petersburg in the classical designs of the time. Wanting a home for the art that she began collecting from abroad, Catherine built the Hermitage. It was connected to her private apartments and also served as a conference chamber and theater. Besides the exquisite treasures kept within, the Hermitage itself was constructed of jasper, malachite, marble and gold. The Empress' extravagant reputation filtered into her love life as well. She had 21 known favorites, and loved being exceedingly generous to them—during her rule she spent nearly 100 million rubles on them. (Russia's annual budget, at the time, was 40 million rubles.) Among Catherine's ladies-in-waiting was a *probolshchitsa*, whose sole task was to test the virility of the Czarina's potential admirers. Platon Zubov, at age 22, was the Empress' lover when she was well into her sixties.

Unfortunately it became increasingly difficult for Catherine to maintain her autocratic rule while at the same time implement large-scale reform. Her sweeping plans for change planted the seeds for much more of a blossoming than she bargained for. The education of the aristocracy created a greater schism between them and the working class and her reforms further worsened the conditions of the peasantry. As the city took the center of culture away from the Church, more and more Old Believers were left disillusioned with her rule. Catherine tore down monasteries and torched the old symbols of Muscovy. In an Age of Reason, she had a deep suspicion of anything mystical.

Huge sums of money were also spent on constructing elaborate palaces for her favorite relations and advisors. One of these was Prince Grigory Potemkin, her foreign minister, commander-in-chief and greatest love for almost two decades. It was he who organized a trip for Catherine down the Dnieper River to view the newly accessed Crimean territories. The prince had painted façades constructed along the route to camouflage the degree of poverty of the peasants. These 'Potemkin villages' were also to give the appearance of real towns in the otherwise uninhabited areas. Finally in 1773, Pugachev, a Don cossack, led a rebellion of impoverished cossacks, peasants and Old Believers against the throne and serfdom. Pugachev was captured and sentenced to decapitation, but ended up exiled in Siberia.

It was not only the peasantry and the Church that felt alienated. The aristocracy too grew dissatisfied with the new European truths and philosophies. Those who yearned for more considered themselves a new class, the intelligentsia. Searching for their own identity amidst a surge of French principles, the intelligentsia proceeded not only to understand Voltaire's logic but to incorporate its heart and spirit as well.

By grasping the ideals of a foreign Enlightenment, Catherine II unknowingly gave birth to Russia's own. The catalyst of change, along with teaching people to think for themselves, brought despotism into deeper disfavor and paved the road to revolution. After the fall of the Bastille, Catherine turned her back on France. In a panic, she tried to dispose of all that she had helped create. Censorship was imposed throughout Russia, and Catherine attempted to slam shut the window to the West less than a century after Peter had opened it. But from this period of discontent and new search for meaning, Russia would give birth to some of the greatest writers and thinkers of all time. The West would be captivated by the works of Pushkin, Dostoevsky and Tolstoy, and Lenin would later lead Russia out of five centuries of autocratic rule. Peter the Great had built the wheels and Catherine set them in motion; there was to be no turning back.

In the year 2000, 25 percent of Russians polled named Catherine the Great as "the

cleverest Russian woman of all time". The Pulitzer Prize-winning author of *Peter the Great, Nicholas and Alexandra* and *The Romanovs*, Robert K Massie, has written another masterpiece of narrative biography with his book *Catherine the Great: Portrait of a Woman* which presents the extraordinary story of this obscure German princess who became one of the most remarkable, powerful, and captivating women in history.

The young German Princess Catherine II arrived in St Petersburg to marry Peter III. She went on to become the first foreign woman to rule Russia, and later received the title of Catherine the Great for her many accomplishments during her 34-year reign.

In 1768, Catherine the Great commissioned the French sculptor, Etienne Falconet, to create a magnificent monument to Peter the Great, who is depicted on a rearing horse, crushing a serpent underfoot. The enormous granite base, shaped like a wave about to break, was transferred over

10 kilometers to the city. The masterpiece was unveiled during the 100th anniversary of Peter's ascension to the throne. The inscription reads, 'To Peter I from Catherine II, 1782.'

Peter I on His Deathbed, *painted in 1725 by Tannauer Johann-Gottfried.*

Peter the Great's Winter Palace (at 32 Palace Embankment), where the Czar lived from 1720 until his death in 1725. The interior rooms include his study, dining room and a gilded carriage.

(right) During the cold winter months members of the Walrus Club chop through the ice to swim in the freezing waters. They believe that this activity promotes health and a hardy disposition.

(below) In 1715, Mikhail Anichkov built the first bridge over the Fontanka Canal, and Peter Klodt's famous horse-tamer sculptures were later installed in 1851. Behind Anichkov Bridge, on Nevsky Prospekt, stands the Beloselsky-Belozersky Palace designed in 1847 by court architect, Andrei Stakenschneider, in the baroque-style of the Winter Palace.

(opposite) Bank Bridge spans the Griboyedov Canal near Nevsky Prospekt. This lovely footbridge is adorned with lion-griffins; in ancient Greece griffins were said to stand guard over gold. At the time this bridge was built, around 1800, it led to the National Bank.

Modeled on St Basil's Cathedral in Moscow, the elaborately-decorated Savior Church on Spilled Blood was erected near the Griboyedov Canal off Nevsky Prospekt on the spot where Alexander II was assassinated by a revolutionary group in 1881.

(above) St Petersburg is filled with a wealth and variety of splendid architecture, dating from the 18th and 19th centuries.

(below) *The famous Rossi Street was designed by Carlo Rossi to follow the canons of classical antiquity—its height and width are identical at 22 meters (72 feet), and its length at 220 meters (720 feet) is exactly ten times the width. Between 1828 and 1834, Rossi also designed the street's five Neo-classical buildings; at the end stands the Russian Museum, established in 1895 by Nicholas II.*

(left) *The famous Vaganova Ballet Academy on Ulitsa Rossi. Portraits of former students, such as Natalia Makarova, Mikhail Baryshnikov and Rudolph Nureyev, grace the wall.*

Tikhvinskoye Cemetery in Alexander Nevsky Monastery contains the graves of many notable Russians, including composers Alexander Borodin (1834–1887), Mikhail Glinka (1804–1857), Modest Mussorgsky (1839–1881) and writer Fyodor Dostoevsky (1821–1881).

The beautiful ensemble of St Nicholas Marine Cathedral (1753–1762) was built in honor of St Nicholas, protector of seamen; it combines old Russian traditions of a gilded five-domed church with baroque decorations.

The funeral of St Petersburg's famous poet Anna Akhmatova was held at St Nicholas Marine Cathedral in 1966. The cathedral's four-tiered baroque bell tower stands beside the Kryukov Canal.

(above) The lavish Yusupov Palace, situated along the Moika Canal near the Mariinsky Theater, was the home of the wealthy Prince Felix Yusupov, best known for participating in the murder of Rasputin in 1916. Today, his palace is a museum that contains the family's personal opulent theater (shown here), and other rooms, including the drawing room where Rasputin was killed.

(left) Today, concerts and theater performances are held in the palace. www.yusupov-palace.ru.

On the other side of Mikhailovsky Castle, at 3 Fontanka Embankment (Naberezhnaya Reki Fontanki), is the **Bolshoi St Petersburg Circus**, which celebrated its 135th anniversary in 2012. The circular building of the circus was constructed in 1877 by Kenel, (and was known as the Circus Ciniselli), making it one of the oldest permanent circus buildings in the world. During the intense revolutionary years, some of Russia's finest artists, such as Chekhov, Gorky, Eisenstein and Stanislavsky, focused their attention on the circus, so much so that the Soviet Government decided not to abolish it. (See Special Topic on the Russian Circus) www.circus.spb.ru/en. Inside there is also the **Museum of Circus History and Variety Art** (established in 1928 as the world's first circus museum), with over 100,000 circus-related items (group excursions are on Tues/Wed/Fri). www.circus.spb.ru/en/museum. The building is slated to be closed for a massive restoration process through the end of 2015.

Crossing the Fontanka Canal to 15 Solyanoi Lane is the **Stieglitz Museum of Applied Arts**, In 1878, Baron Alexander von Stieglitz (1814–1884) founded the School of Technical Drawing & Design and began accumulating a vast array of European and Oriental decorative arts and crafts, including furniture, glassware, metalworks, porcelain, tapestries and tiled stoves. To accommodate this vast collection, his son had a building constructed, in Neo-Renaissance style by architect Maximilian Messmacher (between 1885–1896), where each hall is decorated in a different style, including Baroque, Flemish, Italian and Renaissance; the opulent Terem Room resembles the Moscow Kremlin's Terem Palace. Today, this gem of a museum contains over 30,000 items, and the Applied Arts Academy is next door. Enter through the Academy Building (at number 13), go up the grand staircase, turn right at the top, walk along the corridor and then down the first narrow staircase on your left to the next floor. The museum's entrance and ticket counter is on the lower landing of the staircase. Open 11am–5pm; closed Sundays, Mondays and last Friday of month (and Academy holidays in August). Metro Chernyshevskaya. www.stieglitzmuseum.ru.

Nearby, at 9 Solyanoi, is the **Museum of the Defense and Siege of Leningrad** with exhibits concerning the 900-day blockade of the city from September 8 1941 to January 17, 1944. Open 10am–5pm, Wednesday 12:30pm–9pm; closed Tuesdays and last Thursday of month. Nearest Metro is Chernyshevskaya. www.blokadamus.ru.

Not far from the museum, on Transfiguration Square, stands the gilded Neoclassical **Cathedral of the Transfiguration of Our Savior**, first built in 1743 on the site where the Preobrazhensky Guards (the Czar's bodyguards) had their headquarters. The church was later restored by architect Vasily Stasov (from 1827–1829) to celebrate Russia's victory over the Turks. Metro Chernyshevskaya.

At number 36 Liteiny Prospekt is the **Nekrasov Apartment Museum** which displays the works and personal items of writer Nikolai Nekrasov (1821–77) who was a popular poet and editor of the literary magazine *Sovremennik* (Contemporary). Open 10:30am–6pm; closed Mondays, Tuesdays and last Friday of month. Metro Chernyshevskaya. www.museumpushkin.ru.

Back along the eastern Fontanka Canal Embankment, at number 34, is the **Sheremetyev Palace**, once the center of the city's largest aristocratic estate given to Field Marshal Boris Sheremetyev (1652–1719) by Peter the Great in 1712. The Palace was later built in the 1740's by his son, Pyotr Borisovich, with the elegant baroque exterior façades painted in yellow and white. The magnificent wrought-iron fence is decorated with the family's gilded coat-of-arms. The palace is also known as 'the Fountain House' for the opulent arrangement of fountains that once decorated its gardens. The theatrical passion of Nikolai Petrovich Sheremetyev (1751–1809) created one of the finest theatres in 18th century Russia; and, in 1801, he married one of the stars of his serf opera, the soprano Praskovia Zhemchugova, in what became one of the most celebrated (and controversial) romances of the day. (See Kuskovo Estate in Vicinity of Moscow). The Sheremetyev's famous serf theater troupe and orchestra frequently performed in the palace.

Today one wing of the palace is the **Museum of Musical Instruments** with one of the world's largest collections. On the first floor is an elegant display of the evolution of harp design, and other Arctic tribal instruments, such as the glass harmonica. On the second is Tchaikovsky's piano, along with harpsichords, spinets, and early mechanical pianos. Open 11am–7pm; closed Tuesdays and last Wednesday of month. Closest Metro Vladimirskaya. www.theatremuseum.ru.

The southern wing of the palace houses the **Anna Akhmatova Memorial Museum**, in the third floor apartment where the celebrated 20th century poet (see Special Topic) lived from 1924 to 1941 and 1944 to 1954. (The entrance is from 53 Liteiny Prospekt through the arch into the gardens.) Akhmatova first lived here with her second husband, Vladimir Shileiko, and then later moved back with her third common-law husband, Nikolai Punin, an art historian. (By this time her first husband, Nikolai Gumilyov, had been arrested and shot, and her son imprisoned. Punin was later twice arrested, and died in a Siberian labor camp in 1953). The modest spare rooms contain the original furniture, with other exhibits of photographs, publications and films. In the cramped kitchen, a recording, read in Akhmatova's own voice, plays her famous poem 'Requiem.' The motto on the Sheremetyev's coat-of-arms, *Deus Conservat Omnia* (God Preserves All) became the symbol for one of Akhmatova's most masterful works, "Poem Without a Hero", written during the Seige of Leningrad—'He will visit me at the Fountain Palace... But death he shall bring.' Other sections are dedicated to her son, historian and geographer Lev Gumiliev (1912–1992), and the poet Joseph Brodsky (1940–1996). Downstairs is a bookshop and video room where documentaries on Akhamatova and her contemporaries can be viewed. The museum often hosts literary and musical evenings. Open 10.30am–6.30pm, Wednesdays 1pm–9pm, closed Mondays. Audio guides available. www.akhmatova.spb.ru. (The Lev Gumilev Memorial Apartment Museum is at 1/15 Kolomenskaya, open 10:30am–5:30pm; closed Sun/Mon. Metro Dostoevskaya.)

Akhmatova wrote of St Petersburg:

> But not for anything would we exchange this splendid
> Granite city of fame and calamity,
> The wide rivers of glistening ice,
> The sunless, gloomy gardens,
> And, barely audible, the Muse's voice.

NEVSKY PROSPEKT

In the words of Nikolai Gogol: 'There is nothing finer than the Nevsky Prospekt.... In what does it not shine, this street that is the beauty of the capital.' Nevsky Prospekt, which locals refer to as Nevsky (it derives from the Neva River), is the main thoroughfare of the city and the center of business and commercial life. A stroll down part of it during any time of day is a must, for no other street like it exists anywhere in the world. It is a busy, bustling area, filled with department stores, shops, cinemas, restaurants, museums, art studios, cathedrals, mansions, theaters, libraries and cafés. The Nevsky is made even more interesting and beautiful by the stunning architectural ensembles that line the 4.8-kilometer (three-mile) long route that stretches from the Admiralty to Alexander Nevsky Monastery. It also brims with history; you can find the spot where Pushkin lived, where Dostoevsky gave readings of his works, and where Rimsky-Korsakov and Tchaikovsky premiered their music.

Shortly after the Admiralty was completed, a track was cut through the thick forest, linking it with the road to Novgorod and Moscow. This main stretch of the city was known as the Great Perspective Road. The road took on the name of Neva Perspectiva in 1738, when it was linked to another small road that ran to Alexander Nevsky Monastery. In 1783, the route was renamed Nevsky Prospekt. Peter the Great had elegant stone houses built along the Nevsky and ordered food sold in the streets by vendors dressed in white aprons. The first buildings went up between the Admiralty and Fontanka Canal. The area, nicknamed St Petersburg City, was a fashionable place to live, and it became the center for banks, stores and insurance offices. The architects desired to create a strong and imposing central district and constructed the buildings out of granite and stone brought in from Sweden.

Beginning at the Admiralty, where the street is at its narrowest—25 meters (82 feet), walk along to 9 Nevsky. On the corner you will find Vavelberg's House, which was originally a bank. The large stone house was built in 1912 by the architect Peretyatkovich to resemble the Doge's Palace in Venice and Medici in Florence. Here the Nevsky is intersected by Malaya Morskaya Ulitsa (formerly Gogol Street), where the writer Nikolai Gogol lived at number 17 from 1833 to 1836 and wrote *Taras Bulba*, *The Inspector General* and the first chapters of Dead Souls. At 10 Malaya Morskaya is the Queen of Spades residence, the house of the old countess on whom Pushkin based his story of the same name. Tchaikovsky lived at 13 Malaya Morskaya for many years up until his death in 1893 (see Klin, in Vicinity of Moscow).

The next intersection on the Nevsky is Bolshaya Morskaya Ulitsa (formerly Herzen Street). The writer Alexander Herzen lived at number 25 for a year in 1840. Fabergé had its main studios at number 24 (see Special Topic). The architect Carlo Rossi laid out the street along the Pulkovo Meridian (which was the meridian on old Russian maps) so that at noon the buildings cast no shadows on the street.

The oldest buildings are at 8 and 10 Nevsky. Built between 1760 and 1780, they are now exhibition and gallery halls for work by St Petersburg artists. The house at number 14 (built in 1939) is a school. A pale blue rectangular plaque on its wall still reads: 'Citizens! In the event of artillery fire, this side of the street is the most dangerous!' The house with columns at number 15 was built in 1768 as a stage site for one of Russia's first professional theaters. Later a small studio was connected to the theater where Falconet modeled the Bronze Horseman. Years later, the space became Talon's, the famous Restaurant of French Chef, Pierre Talon. Alexander Pushkin wrote of Talon's in his 1825 verse novel *Evgeny Onegin*: 'He mounts the sledge…he's flown to Talon's…the cork goes flying up, wine of the Comet fills the cup.' The 1811 vintage champagne, Comet Wine, was named after the year when the Great Comet appeared throughout Europe.

The building at number 18 was known as Kotomin's House (1812–16), after the original owner. Pushkin, who lived nearby at 12 Moika Embankment, often frequented the confectioner's shop, Wolf and Beranger, that was on the ground floor. It was here on January 27, 1837, that Pushkin met up with his attendant on the way to his fatal duel with George D'Anthés. The second floor is now the **Literaturnoye Café**, a popular spot to eat that offers piano and violin music. (A wax figure of Pushkin sits in a chair on the ground floor.) Outside the café, you can have your portrait drawn by one of the numerous artists.

The section on the north side of the Nevsky beyond the Moika Canal was once reserved for churches of non-Orthodox faiths. The Dutch church at number 20 was built between 1834 and 1836 by Paul Jacquot. The central part functioned as a church and the wings housed the Dutch Mission. At 22–24 Nevsky is the

Romanesque-style **Peter and Paul Lutheran Church** (1833–38). In the yard behind the church was the Peterschule, one of the oldest schools in the city, established in 1710; the musician Modest Mussorgsky graduated from here in the mid 1800's. From 1963 to 1992 the church served as a swimming pool; today it houses the German Lutheran community of Saints Peter and Anna, the office of the Archbishop, the Society of Russian-German relations and a small exhibit of art work on the second floor.

Across the street, at number 17, is the salmon-pink Baroque style **Stroganov Palace**, built by Rastrelli in 1754 after the two-story house of Baron Sergei Stroganov burnt down. The Baron was the son of Grigory Stroganov, a wealthy industrialist, mine owner and patron of the arts. The Stroganov family owned and developed vast amounts of land in Siberia (yes, one member of the family invented the well-known beef dish), and their coat-of-arms, depicting two sables and a bear, lies over the gateway arch. Seven generations of Stroganovs lived in the palace from the mid 18th century right up until 1918. Alexander Sergeyevich Stroganov (1733–1811) was the president of the Academy of Fine Arts and Director of the Imperial Library. In the 1790s he hired architects to remodel the interior decor in Neoclassical style. Today, the restored Palace includes period furniture and sculptures, the Arabesque Dining Room, Rastrelli Hall, remarkably ornate Mineral Study (which housed the Count's library and collection of precious stones and minerals), and the Picture Gallery, home to his impressive art collection, including works by Rembrandt and Poussin. The Art Salon Shop is on the first floor. The Palace is open daily 10am–5pm; closed Tuesdays. (A combined ticket for the Stroganov and Marble Palaces, Mikhailovsky Castle and Russian Museum can be purchased, good for three days.) www. rusmuseum.ru. The nearest Metro is Nevsky Prospekt.

Next along the Nevsky stands the majestic, semicircular colonnade of the **Cathedral of Our Lady of Kazan**. The Kazansky Sobor was named after the famous icon of Our Lady of Kazan that used to be here; it is now on view at the Russian Museum. The architect Andrei Voronikhin, a former serf, faced two challenges in 1801. First, Paul I wished the cathedral modeled after St Peter's in Rome, and second, the Orthodox Church required the altar face eastwards (which would have had one side of the cathedral facing the Nevsky). Voronikhin devised 96 Corinthian columns to fan out 111 meters (364 feet) along the prospekt. The bronze Doors of Paradise, replicas of the 15th-century Baptistery doors in Florence, opened on the Nevsky side. The structure took ten years to build and at that time was the third largest cathedral in the world. The Dome stands at 80 meters (262 feet) high. The brick walls are faced with statues and biblical reliefs made from Pudostsky stone, named after the village where it was quarried. The stone was so soft when dug out that it was cut with a saw. It later hardened like rock when exposed to air. Inside, there are 56 pink granite columns and polished marble and red-stone mosaic floors. In niches around the columns are statues of Alexander Nevsky, Prince Vladimir, St John the Baptist and the Apostle Andrew. The interior was also decorated by the outstanding painters Bryullov, Borovikovsky and Kiprensky. On June 13, 1813, Field Marshal Mikhail Kutuzov was buried in the northern chapel. The general stopped to pray at the spot where he is now buried before going off to the War of 1812. Many trophies from this war, like banners and keys to captured fortresses, hang around his crypt. In 1837, the two statues of Kutuzov and Barclay de Tolly were put up in the front garden The cathedral is open 9am–10pm; services are usually held at 10am and 6pm. www.kazansky-spb.ru.

To the right of the main entrance is a small square surrounded by a beautiful wrought-iron grille called Voronikhin's Railing. In 1876, the first workers' demonstration took place in front, with speeches by the Marxist, Georgi Plekhanov. A square and fountain were later added to prevent further demonstrations. But the area remains to this day a popular spot for summer picnics, as well as for political and religious demonstrations.

Walking behind the cathedral and south along the **Griboyedov Canal** leads to the lovely footbridge of **Bankovski Most** (Bank Bridge), adorned with winged lion-griffins (see picture on pages 553). At the time it was built in 1800, the bridge led to the National Bank; according to Greek mythology, griffins stood guard over gold. On the other side of Nevsky, also on the canal, is **Dom Knigi** (House of Books). This polished granite building topped by its distinguishing glass sphere and globe, was originally built in art-nouveau style between 1902 and 1907 by the architect Suzor for the American Singer (Sewing Machine) Company. The first two floors now make up one of the largest bookstores in the country. Posters, calendars and postcards are sold on the first floor, and the Café Singer, on the second, offers superb views of the Nevsky and Kazan Cathedral. www.spbdk.ru.

The Kazansky Bridge crosses the canal and was built by Ilarion Kutuzov, the father of the military leader. A few minutes' walk along the canal to the north stands the eye-popping **Cathedral of the Savior on Spilled Blood** (Spasa Na Krovi) with its phantasmagoria of colored mosaics and onion domes, built between 1883–1907. It was modeled on St Basil's in Moscow and erected on the spot where Czar Alexander II was assassinated by a member of Peoples' Will, a group of revolutionaries pushing for more liberal reforms. On March 1, 1881, the Czar was returning from a military parade to the Winter Palace in a special armored coach built in Paris. (There had been six previous attempts on his life.) When it reached the embankment of the Griboyedov Canal, a terrorist jumped out and tossed a bomb beneath the hooves of the galloping horses. The emperor leapt out of the burning carriage unharmed. But another man then threw a second bomb. This time the

Emperor was mortally wounded, both legs torn off. (Alexander II had emancipated the serfs in 1861; and, ironically, he was on his way to sign a draft for further constitutional reforms that very day.) His successor, Alexander III, ordered architect Alfred Parland to build the altar where the former czar's blood fell on the cobblestones. After many years of restoration (the church took 24 years to build and 27 to restore), the cathedral reopened to visitors in 1997. The walls inside are decorated with 7000 sq meters (75,000 sq feet) of mosaics designed in the style of both Byzantine and modern icon painting. A jasper canopy, in the western apse, marks the spot where the czar was murdered. The height from floor to cupola is 81 meters (265 feet), corresponding to the assassination year. Surrounding the exterior 20 granite plaques record the accomplishments of Alexander II's reign, and the 144 mosaic coat-of-arms represent regions and towns of Russia during his time. The cathedral and museum are open 10:30am–6pm, evening admission 6pm–10:30pm from May 1–Sept 30; closed Wednesdays. The ticket counter is located at the other side of the church. eng.cathedral.ru. Behind the Church, towards the Moika Canal, is a large and lively daily **Souvenir Market** full of interesting items, as handicrafts, Matryushka dolls and Soviet paraphernalia for sale. The narrow **Bridge of Kisses** (Most Polseluyev) crosses the Moika Canal.

The Philharmonic Society, where Wagner, Liszt and Strauss performed was at 30 Nevsky Prospekt. Today the building is known as the *Maly Zal* or **Small Hall**, part of the Shostakovich Philharmonia. (www.philharmonia.spb.ru). The **Catholic Church of St Catherine**, built between 1763 and 1788 in baroque-classical design by Vallin de la Mothe, is at 32–34 Nevsky. It is the oldest Catholic Church in St Petersburg. Stanislas Ponyalovsky, the last king of Poland and one of the many lovers of Catherine the Great, is buried inside. Religious services are also held here. In front of the church is a vibrant art market, filled with paintings and portrait artists. The **Armenian Church of St Catherine**, at 40–42 Nevsky, was built between 1794–1798 by Yuri Felten (born Georg Veldten in Russia to a family of German immigrants). Felten (1730–1801) was a court architect of Catherine the Great. During the Soviet Union it was used as a warehouse, and returned to followers for worship in 1992. So many churches were opened on Nevsky Prospekt in the 18th century that it was nicknamed the Street of Tolerance.

The corner building at 31–33 was known as Silver Row. Built between 1784 and 1787 by Quarenghi, it was used as an open shopping arcade, where silver merchants would set up their display booths. In 1799, the structure was made into the Town Hall or **City Duma**, and in 1802, a European Rathaus tower was installed. This served as a fire watchtower (various colored balls raised indicated where in the capital a fire had broken out), and part of a 'mirror telegraph' that linked the residences of the czar in the city to Tsarskoye Selo. A beam of light was flashed along other aligned towers to announce the ruler's arrival or departure. The small building (off Dumskaya St) that stands between the City Duma and Gostiny Dvor holds the **Central City Theater Booking Office**, where tickets for drama, music and ballet are sold. Along the front of Gostiny Dvor are kiosks selling tickets for various types of excursions throughout the city.

At number 35 Nevsky is the **Bolshoi Gostiny Dvor** (Big Guest or Merchant Yard) department store. Visiting merchants used to reside in *gostiniye dvori* guest houses, which also served as their places of business. From 1761 to 1785 the architect Vallin de la Mothe built a long series of open two-tiered arcades, where merchants had their booths. It was not only a commercial center; representatives of all the estates of the capital were also found here. The Duke of Wellington, invited to Russia by Alexander I, loved to stroll past the many galleries, which stretched more than 230 meters (750 feet) along the Nevsky (the building's perimeter is more than 1 km long). Pushkin and Dostoevsky shopped here as well and mentioned the *Gostiny Dvor* in their works. In 1917, the Bolsheviks threw out the merchants and transformed the space into a State-run store. But some traders, not believing the Revolution would actually last, stashed 128 kilograms of gold inside the walls of the store, found by workers in 1965. Today the newly renovated two-story building is the largest department store in the city and a popular place for shopping (open daily 10am–10pm).www.bgd.ru. Behind Gostiny Dvor, at 26 Sadovaya, is the ornate Baroque-style **Vorontsov Palace**, built between 1749 and 1757 by Rastrelli for diplomat Count Mikhail Vorontsov. After decorating the interior and amassing a huge debt, Vorontsov had to sell his palace to the Imperial Estates. Paul I later passed it on to the Knights of Malta (Napoleon took the island in 1798); and 12 years later it was turned into an elite military college. Today it functions as a branch of the Suvorov Military College. In the courtyard look for the circular green and gold sign 'Military Shop', where everything from uniforms and boots to sailor shirts and caps are for sale.

Opposite Gostiny Dvor, at 48 Nevsky, is the three-story **Passazh** arcade, opened in 1848, with a beautiful glass roof, another shopper's delight. The Passazh became the first area in the city where trade, amusements and shops flourished in one place. In 1860 a special literature evening was held here, featuring famous authors that included Goncharov, Nekrasov, Ostrovsky, Turgenev and Dostoevsky. Open 10am–9pm, Sunday 11am–9pm. www.passage.spb.ru/en.

The art-nouveau **Grand Hotel Europe** is on the corner of Nevsky and Mikhailovskaya Ulitsa. Built in the 1870s, it was completely renovated between 1989 and 1991 by a Russian-Swedish joint venture. It has many antiques including one of Catherine the Great's carriages (available for guests). The hotel has a number of elegant restaurants, bars, and cafés. Across from the hotel, at 2 Mikhailovskaya, is the **Shostakovich St Petersburg Academic Philharmonic**, built in 1834–1839 by French architect Paul Jacquot for the Assembly of Nobility. (Carlo Rossi designed the exterior façades.) The Tricolor Hall (now the *Bolshoi Zal* or **Grand Hall**) was used by the Nobility Club to host charitable events. At the turn of the century, American dancer, Isadora Duncan, made her Russian debut on its stage. Founded in 1882, as the Imperial Music Choir, the St Petersburg Philharmonic is the oldest symphony orchestra in Russia. The works of many Russian composers, such as Glinka, Rachmaninov, Rimsky-Korsakov and Tchaikovsky were first heard at the Philharmonic. Wagner was the official conductor during the 1863 season. Dmitri Shostakovich premiered his First Symphony here in 1926; and he later lived in Leningrad during the 900-day siege. In July 1941, Shostakovich began to write his Seventh Symphony, while a member of an air-defense unit. Hitler boasted that Leningrad would fall by August 9, 1942. On this day, the Seventh (or Leningrad) Symphony, conducted by Karl Eliasberg, was played in the Philharmonic and broadcast throughout the world. 'I dedicate my Seventh Symphony to our struggle with fascism, to our forthcoming victory over the enemy, and to my native city, Leningrad.' After the fall of the Soviet Union, the Philharmonic was named after Shostakovich in his honor. The Maly Zal or **Small Hall** is at 30 Nevsky Propspekt. www.philharmonia.spb.ru.

The square in front of the Philharmonic is called **Arts Square** or Ploshchad Iskusstva. In the mid-18th century Carlo Rossi designed the square and the areas in between the Griboyedov and Moika Canals and Sadovaya Ulitsa. The center of the square is dominated by the **Statue of Alexander Pushkin**, sculpted by Mikhail Anikushin in 1957 to mark the 120th anniversary of the poet's death. The square is surrounded by the Mikhailovsky Theater and the Russian Museum. Along Italyanskaya, not far from the Philharmonic, at no 13, is the **Theater of Musical Comedy**, the only theater in the city that stayed open during the siege. Next to it, at number 19, is the **Komissarzhevskaya Drama Theater**, named after Russian actress Vera Komissarzhevskaya who acted in many of Vsevolod Meyerhold's stage productions. At the turn of the century, she formed her own acting troupe where they performed in the nearby Passazh concert hall. The actress was artistic director of the theater from 1904 to 1906, when the company staged plays (including by Chekhov and Gorky) around the political mood of the times.

Behind the square on Inzhenernaya Ulitsa (Engineer's Street) stands the majestic eight-columned building of the **Russian Museum**, second largest art museum in the city that focuses solely on Russian art from ancient church icons to contemporary painting. Upon the birth of his youngest son Grand Duke Mikhail Pavlovich in 1798, Paul I set aside funds for the building of a palace. Construction did not begin for another 21 years, by which time his elder brother, Alexander I, was on the throne. Alexander chose Carlo Rossi, the Italian-Russian master of Neoclassicism, to design the palace. He was granted a huge plot of land and, between 1819–1827, Rossi created a meticulously planned ensemble of parklands and architecture with two different facades, one facing the Field of Mars across the Moika River, and the other towards Nevsky Prospekt. The Palace was the home of the Grand Duke and his wife, and then to their children and grandchildren until Nicholas II decided to buy the building and convert it into a public museum in honor of his father Alexander III, who had amassed his own art collection (he died in 1894). Between 1895 and 1897 architect Vasily Svinin transformed the palace interiors into gallery halls; and the museum opened in March 1898. As the collection expanded, the **Benois Wing** on the Griboyedov Canal (originally the Exhibition Pavilion of the Academy of Arts) was added between 1914 and 1919, and today houses the modern art collection. A splendid wrought-iron fence (embossed with the double-headed eagle) separates the palace from the square. The courtyard allowed carriages to drive up to the front portico, where a granite staircase lined with two bronze lions still leads to the front door.

As you enter the Museum, pick up a map before ascending the main staircase. The nearly 1,000-year history of Russian art is represented by over 300,000 items in over 100 halls, the most complete gathering of Russian art anywhere in the world. The rooms display the artwork in chronological order; and the vast collection includes religious icons, folk art, graphic, decorative & applied art, drawings & water colors, sculptures, coins & medals, Classicist, Landscape & Impressionist artists, and a large exhibition of avant-garde, Soviet and modern art. The grand **Hall of White Columns** was so admired by the czar that he ordered a wooden model made for King George IV of England. The government has signed over the Stroganov and Marble Palaces, and Mikhailovsky Castle to the Russian Museum which has doubled its display space. Open 10am–6pm, Thursday 1pm–9pm; closed Tuesdays. A combined ticket for the Russian Museum, Mikhailovsky Castle, and the Stroganov & Marble Palaces can be purchased, good for three days. www.rusmuseum.ru. In 2002, the nearly 9 hectares (20 acres) of the **Mikhailovsky Gardens** reopened to the original 19th-century design; open 10am–10pm May–Sept, till 8pm in winter; closed April.

To the right of the museum, at 4/1, is the **Museum of Ethnography**, in the large classical building, with displays of traditional customs and crafts of more than 150 of Russia's ethnic populations. The centerpiece is the grand Marble Hall Gallery surrounded by pink Karelian columns. Open 10am–6pm, Tuesday till 9pm; closed Mondays and last Friday of month. www.ethnomuseum.ru.

In Arts Square, the statue of Pushkin gestures to the building known as the **Mikhailovsky Theater**. Built in 1833 by Bryullov, this elaborate multi-tiered theater originally housed a permanent French troupe; today it is home to the State Academic Opera & Ballet Company, and is the second most popular theater in the city; it is usually easier and cheaper to get tickets for performances here than at the Mariinsky. www.mikhailovsky.ru.

The building next door, at number 5, was the site of the **Stray Dog Café**, a favorite cellar hangout for the artistic elite of St Petersburg where they gathered around midnight and did not leave until dawn. Opened on New Year's Eve 1912, the club was the country's greatest bohemian meeting spot until it was closed down in the spring of 1915. After the Revolution and Stalinist terrors, Russia would never again know such a free and vibrant artistic period. The ballerina Tamara Karsavina danced works by Michel Fokine; Mayakovsky, Blok and Mandalstam read their poetry; and Anna Akhmatova and her husband Nikolai Gumilyov formed a new movement of poetry known as Acmeism. Later, after Stalin took control of the country, many of these artists, writers and musicians died in Siberian gulags or ended their lives abroad. Today, the underground café is still known as the Stray Dog (*Podval Brodyachey Sobaki*) with music and literary performances in the evening. Open 11:30am–11:30pm. www.vsobaka.ru.

The **Brodsky House Museum** at 3 Arts Square exhibits items on the life of artist Isaak Izrailaevich Brodsky, who lived here from 1924 until his death in 1939. A student of Ilya Repin, Brodsky was instrumental in creating the new art movement of socialist realism. He also collected works by many other 19th-century artists, many of which are exhibited here. The museum is open noon–7pm; closed Mondays and Tuesdays. www.nimrah.ru/musbrod.

Continuing down the Nevsky, the **Russian National Library** stands on the corner of Nevsky and Sadovaya. Built in 1801 by Yegor Sokolov, it opened in 1814 as the Imperial Public Library. In 1832, Carlo Rossi built further additions. The statue of Minerva, Goddess of Wisdom, stands atop the building. It is one of the largest libraries in the world with over 25 million books. A reading room is inside, but no books can be taken out.

The library faces **Ostrovsky Square** (formerly Alexandrinkskaya) named after the celebrated playwright Alexander Ostrovsky (1823–1886). A **Statue of Catherine the Great** (1873) graces the center. Catherine, dressed in a long flowing robe, stands on a high rounded pedestal that portrays the prominent personalities of the time: Potemkin, Suvorov, Rumyantsev and Derzhavin, to name a few. To the left are two classical pavilions, designed by Rossi, in the Garden of Rest.

Behind the square is the **Alexandrinsky Theater** (formerly the Pushkin State Drama Theater), a veritable temple to the arts. Flanked by Corinthian columns, the niches are adorned with the Muses of Dance, Tragedy, History and Music. The chariot of Apollo, patron of the arts, stands atop the front façade. The Neoclassical yellow building, erected by Rossi in 1828, was named after Alexandra, the wife of Nicholas I, and housed Russia's first permanent theater group. This is where, in 1896, Anton Chekhov premiered *The Seagull*, not initially well received by critics or the public. Today, as the oldest drama theater in Russia, it has a varied repertoire of classical and modern plays. www.alexandrinsky.ru. Behind the theater, at number 6, is the **Museum of Theatrical Art and Music**, exhibiting the history of Russian drama and musical theater. Open 11am–6pm, Wednesdays 1pm–7pm; closed Tuesdays and last Friday of month. www.theatremuseum.ru.

The famous **Ulitsa Rossi** (named after architect Carlo Rossi) stretches from Ostrovsky to Lomonosov Squares. The street was designed by Rossi to follow the canons of classical antiquity—its height and width are identical at 22 meters (72 feet), and its length at 220 meters (720 feet) is exactly ten times the width. Between 1828 and 1834, Rossi also designed five Neoclassical buildings on the street. In 1738, twelve boys and twelve girls (children of court servants) were the city's first ballet students, attending a school started by Empress Anna, the same year that she founded the St Petersburg Imperial Ballet. Today, at number 2, the yellow-and-white two-story complex houses the world-renowned **Vagonova Ballet Academy**. The school bears the name of Agrippina Vagonova, who taught here between 1921 and 1951; her 1934 'Fundamentals of Classical Ballet' became known as the Vaganova Method. Some famous pupils of the Imperial Ballet and Vagonova have been Pavlova, Ulanova, Petipa, Nijinsky, Fokine, Balanchine and Nureyev. Of the 500 10-year-olds who are invited to audition each year, only 60 are admitted to the boarding school's eight-year program. The graduates hope to go on to a professional ballet company such as the Mariinsky. A museum inside the school on the first floor contains historical displays, such as Pavlova's ballet shoes and Nijinsky's costumes. Posters and pictures trace the history of ballet from Diaghilev to Baryshnikov who, along with Natalia Makarova, attended the Vagonova School. (The museum is closed to the general public—but if you express an interest in ballet, you may get in.) See Ballet on page 491.

Back on Nevsky Prospekt in the corner building across the street is the impressive **Yeliseyev's Emporium**, once the most luxurious food store in St Petersburg. The well-known Russian merchant Yeliseyev had this imposing art-nouveau structure built in 1902. Today the store is once again stocked with a wide assortment of goods and it is well worth seeing the interior, which includes a small café (see Special Topic). Open 10am–10pm. The **Demmeni Marionette Theater**, opened in 1918, is at 52 Nevsky (www.demmeni.ru), and the **Akimov Comedy Theater**, founded in 1929, is at number 56. The **Avrora Movie Theater**, at number 60, opened in 1913 as the Piccadilly Picture House, and was renamed the Aurora (after the famous Battleship) in 1932. Here a young Dmitri Shostakovich played piano to accompany silent movies. Go through the courtyard inside to the cinema where tickets can be bought. www.avrora.spb.ru.

The area around the Fontanka Canal (the old southern border of the city) was first developed by an engineering team headed by Mikhail Anichkov. He built the first bridge across the Fontanka here in 1715 and it is still named after him. In 1841, a stone bridge with four towers replaced the wooden structure. Peter Klodt cast the tamed-horse sculptures a century ago and today they give the bridge its distinguishing mark. During World War II the sculptures were buried by the Palace of Young Pioneers across the street. The **Anichkov Most** (Bridge) is a popular hangout, and boats leave frequently from the Fontanka Quay for a city tour of the canals and waterways. AngloTourismo provides tours in English, and from May 5 to September 30 covered boats depart every 1.5 hours from 11am to 6:30pm, and until 12:20am during the White Nights summer months. www.anglotourismo.com.

A few blocks down the Fontanka, at 21 (on the corner of Italyanskaya), is the city's first **Fabergé Museum** housed in the 18th-century Neoclassical **Shuvalov Palace**, formerly owned by the Vorontsov and Naryshkin families (Countess Maria Naryshkina was lady-in-waiting to Catherine the Great, and later Sofiya Naryshkina married Count Pyotr Shuvalov.) In 1965, it was turned into the House of Peace and Friendship and later Soviet offices. In 2006, the Links of Time Foundation, owned by Russian Entrepreneur Viktor Vekselberg, restored the palace (over seven years), which features a marble staircase, large ballroom, the Blue Drawing Room, and 12 galleries with an area of 4700 sq meters (50,000 sq. feet) of exhibition space. In 2004, Vekselberg acquired over 200 Fabergé objects, owned by the Forbes Foundation in New York, for over $100 million, which include silver, jewelry and fifteen Fabergé eggs. Vekselberg has gone on to assemble the largest collection of Fabergé in the world, now with over 1500 pieces. Other items in the museum collection feature paintings, enamel work, porcelain and textiles. Entrance to the museum is by pre-arranged tour. www.fsv.ru/en.

On the other side of Nevsky Prospekt, (on the Fontanka's west side) stands the ornate **Anichkov Palace**. Empress Elizabeth (Peter's daughter) commissioned the architects Dmitriyev and Zemtsov to build a palace on the spot where she stayed on the eve of her coronation in 1741. Upon its completion in 1751, Elizabeth gave the Anichkov Palace to her favorite, Count Alexei Razumovsky. Later, Catherine the Great gave it to her own favorite, Count Grigory Potemkin, who frequently held elaborate balls here. After that, in 1794, it became part of His Majesty's Cabinet and

Nicholas II frequently stayed here. In 1936 the palace was turned into a Young Pioneer's Club headquarters. Today, it is known as the Palace of Creative Youth with after school clubs for children. Several times a month there are group tours of the Palace and its Museum of History. Check at the ticket booth in front of the palace on Nevsky. At number 65 (on the Fontanka) is the **Bolshoi Drama Theater**, one of the city's grandest theaters whose repertoire features Russian drama. www.bdt.spb.ru.

The grand **Beloselsky-Belozersky Palace**, at 41 Nevsky, was commissioned in 1847 by Princess Elena Beloselskaya-Belozerskaya who petitioned Nicholas I to use his court architect, Andrei Stakenschneider to design it in the baroque style of the Winter Palace with grand rococo façades; and as can be imagined, many a lavish party was thrown here. In 1884, the building was sold to Grand Duke Sergei Alexandrovich, the brother of Alexander III. (The Grand Duke was later killed by a bomb in the Moscow Kremlin.) Today, the Palace is home to a Cultural Center with regular concerts of chamber music. Several times a month group tours of the palace are given by appointment only; reservations can be booked through the website: www.beloselskiy-palace.ru.

Following the Nevsky a bit farther up you come to Ulitsa Marata by Metro Mayakovskaya. At number 24 Marata is the **Museum of the Arctic and Antarctic** (in the Church of St Nicholas) that traces the history of Russian and Soviet polar explorations. Open 10am–6pm, Sunday till 5pm; closed Mondays, and last Friday of month. www.polarmuseum.ru.

A few blocks south, Marata intersects with Kuznechny Lane, and at 5/2 is the **Dostoevsky Literary Museum**, where the famous author lived from 1878 until his death. The study where he wrote *The Brothers Karamazov* has been preserved, along with other rooms, devoted to his writings. Of particular interest is Dostoevsky's map of St Petersburg with marked locations used in his novels. In *The Adolescent*, Dostoevsky wrote of his own vision of St Petersburg and the Bronze Horseman: 'A hundred times amid the fog I had a strange but persistent dream: "What if, when this fog scatters and flies upward, the whole rotten, slimy city goes with it, rises with the fog and vanishes like smoke, leaving behind the old Finnish swamp, and in the middle of it, I suppose, for beauty's sake, the bronze horseman on the panting, whipped horse?"' Dostoevsky lived in this house with his devoted wife Anna Grigoryevna and children. (Anna recopied his daily writings, usually composed the night before, and edited all of his books). On the evening of February 7, 1881, while writing in his spare and orderly study, the author dropped his pen, and it rolled under a heavy bookcase. When Dostovesky tried to move it, his fragile lungs began to hemorrhage (he had emphysema), and he died two days later, aged 59. (Dostoevsky also lived nearby at 11 Vladimirsky Prospekt, his first residence after leaving the military academy in the Mikhailovsky Castle; in this single-room apartment on the second floor, he created his first novel, *Poor Folk*.) The museum is open 11am–6pm, Wednesday 1pm–8pm; closed Mondays. Metro Vladimirskaya. www.md.spb.ru

At number 3 is the **Kuznechny Market** (a lively blue-collar market in Dostoevsky's time), still one of the most colorful in the city; it has a wide variety of produce and household goods at bargain prices. Kuznechny Lane ends at the five-domed **Vladimirskaya Cathedral**, designed by Trezzini in the 1760's and built in the Neoclassical and baroque styles. It is said that Dostoevsky frequently attended church services here. For over 60 years, the Soviets operated a factory in the complex, but the cathedral has since been returned to the church. Inside, take a look at the baroque-style iconostasis, originally inside the Anichkov Palace, and installed here in 1808. Open 8am with a 6pm service.

Walking south Vladimirsky turns into, Zagorodny Prospekt, and at number 28, is the **Rimsky-Korsakov Museum**, home of the great 19th-century Russian composer (1844–1908), who lived here for the last fifteen years of his life. Here is where he composed 11 of his 15 operas, including *Fairy Tale of the Czar Sultan*, *The Czar's Bride* and *The Golden Rooster*. All four rooms, including the study and dining hall, have been restored to their original appearance where a Becker grand piano stands in the living room. The composer enjoyed hosting musical soirées that became known as Korsakov's Wednesdays; the tradition continues today with Wednesday evening concerts. Three times a year, including on the composer's Birthday, March 18th, concerts are held in the living room. Open 11am–7pm, Wednesday 1pm–9pm; closed Mondays and last Friday of month. Metro Vladimirskaya. www.theatremuseum.ru. At number 27, is the **Jazz Philharmonic Hall**, founded by jazz violinist and composer David Goloshchokin, where bands play jazz and Dixieland in the Bolshoi and smaller Ellington Halls. www.jazz-hall.spb.ru.

From the museum, heading east to the other side of Razyezzhaya Ulitsa towards Ligovsky Metro brings you to **Loft Project Etagi** at 74 Ligovsky Prospekt. The former Smolninsky Bread Factory has been transformed into one of the city's most exciting contemporary art complexes with three galleries, two large exhibition spaces, shops and the Café Green Room on the third floor. Open noon–10pm. www. loftprojectetagi.ru. Continuing north to number 73, you will discover the **Bread Museum** that displays the role of bread in the city's history that includes examples of daily bread rations during the Siege of Leningrad, along with a 19th-century model bakery. Open 10am–4pm; closed Sat/Sun. www.colobki.ru.

At 53 Ligovsky Prospekt is another great art locale, **Pushkinskaya 10**, one of the main artistic and music scenes of St Petersburg. In 1988 a group of artist-squatters took over this abandoned apartment block, where they set up studios; today the complex has blossomed into numerous contemporary and alternative art galleries, such as the 4th floor **Museum of Non-Conformist Art** and the **New Academy of Fine Arts Museum**, with more exhibition and studio space on other floors. On the ground floor is the funky **Temple of Love, Peace & Music** where collector Kolya Vasin displays his large collection of John Lennon Beatle paraphernalia (Friday 6pm–8pm). In addition, in the courtyard, the music clubs **Experimental Sound Gallery, Fabrique Novelle** and **Fish Fabrique** (www.fishfabrique.spb.ru) host concerts that range from rock to experimental and electronic music. For exhibit information, see www.p-10.ru. Another popular contemporary art venue is the **Rizzordi Art Foundation** (49 Kurlyandskaya, Metro Baltiyskaya), located in a renovated 4000 square-meter brewery; it showcases local contemporary artists along with other educational programs. www.rizzordi.org.

Back on Nevsky Prospekt, **Vosstaniya Square** (Uprising/Insurrection) so named when troops of the czar refused to shoot a group of unarmed demonstrators during the February 1917 uprising. (It was formerly known as **Znamenskaya Square** after the Church of the Sign that had stood nearby.) One of the interesting buildings on the Square is **Moskovsky Vokzal** (Moscow Railway Station), built by the architect Konstantin Thon in 1847. The St Petersburg–Moscow railway line opened on November 1, 1851.The word *vokzal* (derived from the English Vauxhall Station) is used for a station and now St Petersburg has five major *vokzals* in the city: Moskovsky, Finlandsky, Ladozhsky, Baltiisky and Vitebsky. The latter was also known as Tsarskoye Selo, the station connecting Russia's first railroad line to the czar's summer residence. The Ploshchad Vosstaniya Metro station is near the Square.

By 140 Nevsky and 1 Dyegtyarnaya St are the popular **Dyegtyarniye Bani**, where visitors can experience a Russian banya. (See Special Topic.) www.d1a.ru. Nearby, at 12 Poltavskaya, is the **Police History Museum** which chronicles the history of the Ministry of Internal Affairs from the reign of terror that began in the 1920's up to the Mafia and other criminality of today. (By appointment only.)

The **Hotel Moskva** stands at the end of Nevsky Prospekt at 2 Alexander Nevsky Square (Ploshchad Aleksandra Nevskovo) with a metro station of the same name. Across the street is the **Alexander Nevsky Monastery**, a large complex of church and religious buildings. This is the oldest monastery in St Petersburg. Peter the Great founded the monastery in 1710 and dedicated it to the Holy Trinity and military leader Alexander Nevsky (1221–1263), Prince of Novgorod, who won a major victory near this spot on the Neva against the Swedes in 1240. In 1724, Peter I had one of his favorite architects, Domenico Trezzini, build the first church. Upon its completion, the remains of Alexander Nevsky were transferred from the Golden Ring town of Vladimir to this church. In 1746, the Empress Elizabeth commissioned a rococo-style sarcophagus and donated over one-and-a-half tons of silver to create the largest silver monument in the world. Designed by court portrait painter Georg Christoph Groot, it is five meters (16 feet) long, topped on both sides by angels holding inscribed shields. During the Stalin years, the government wanted to melt it down to earn badly needed hard currency. Fortunately, protests by members of the art community saved it. (But sadly, the solid silver iconostasis in the Kazan Cathedral was melted down. Ironically, the relics of Prince Nevsky were moved and exhibited in the cathedral's Museum of Atheism, but were returned to this location in 1989.) Later, Catherine the Great commissioned Ivan Starov to build a new church (1776–1790), known as the **Holy Trinity Cathedral** or Troitsky Sobor. Inside, to the right of the iconostasis, stands the Chapel of Alexander Nevsky, where the relics of the saint are buried. (This silver casket is a smaller variation of the original.) In 1797, Paul I bestowed the title of *Lavra* on the monastery, the highest title in Orthodox hierarchy; there were only four of this distinction in all of Russia. (Another *lavra* is the Trinity-Sergius Monastery in the Golden Ring town of Sergiyev Posad.) Every year on September 12, Alexander Nevsky Day, huge processions take place at the cathedral. The grounds are open 6am–8pm, and each day around sunset a monk climbs the tower and rings the bells by hand. www.lavra.spb.ru.

Opposite the cathedral is the **Metropolitan's House** (1775–1778), today the official residence of the city's leader of the Russian Orthodox community. The 20th-century **Nikolsky Cemetery** is behind the cathedral (with the Church of St Nicholas) that includes the graves of historian, Lev Gumilev, former mayor Anatoly Sobchak and Duma deputy and human rights activist Galina Starovoitova, who was murdered outside her apartment building in 1998. Near the canal is the **Orthodox Academy**, a Theological Seminary, which trains hundreds of students for the clergy.

The **Annunciation Church** (Blagoveshchensky Sobor), the oldest church in the complex, now houses the **Museum of Urban Sculpture** (the museum includes all the cemeteries), containing tombs of royals and czarist generals. Open 11am–5pm, closed Mondays and Thursdays. In 1716, Peter the Great buried his sister Natalie in the 18th century **Lazarevskoye Cemetery** (to the left of the main entrance), St Petersburg's oldest cemetery with over 1,000 headstones. Other graves include those of Lomonosov, and architects Quarenghi, Starov, Voronikhin and Rossi. (The Church of St Lazarus is closed to visitors.) To the right of the main entrance is the **Tikhvinskoye Cemetery** known as the Necropolis of Artists. Here are the carved gravestones of many of Russia's greatest figures such as Tchaikovsky, Borodin, Glinka, Rimsky-Korsakov, Mussorgsky, and Dostoevsky. Both are open from 9:30am to 6pm. Tickets can be bought at the entrance to the cemeteries. www.gmgs.ru. The Alexander Nevsky Bridge (Most Aleksandra Nevskovo), the city's largest bridge, crosses the Neva from the Monastery.

HOLIDAY SEASON

*F*orgive the triviality of the expression, but I am in no mood for fine language... for everything that had been in Petersburg had gone or was going away for the holidays; for every respectable gentleman of dignified appearance who took a cab was at once transformed, in my eyes, into a respectable head of a household who after his daily duties were over, was making his way to the bosom of his family, to the summer villa; for all the passersby had now quite a peculiar air which seemed to say to every one they met: 'We are only here for the moment, gentlemen, and in another two hours we shall be going off to the summer villa.' If a window opened after delicate fingers, white as snow, had tapped upon the pane, and the head of a pretty girl was thrust out, calling to a street-seller with pots of flowers—at once on the spot I fancied that those flowers were being bought not simply in order to enjoy the flowers and the spring in stuffy town lodgings, but because they would all be very soon moving into the country and could take the flowers with them. What is more, I made such progress in my new peculiar sort of investigation that I could distinguish correctly from the mere air of each in what summer villa he was living. The inhabitants of Kamenny and Aptekarsky Islands or of the Peterhof Road were marked by the studied elegance of their manner, their fashionable summer suits, and the fine carriages in which they drove to town. Visitors to Pargolovo and places further away impressed one at first sight by their reasonable and dignified air; the tripper to Krestovsky Island could be recognized by his look of irrepressible gaiety. If I chanced to meet a long procession of wagoners walking lazily with the reins in their hands beside wagons loaded with regular mountains of furniture, tables, chairs, ottomans and sofas and domestic utensils of all sorts, frequently with a decrepit cook sitting on the top of it all, guarding her master's property as though it were the apple of her eye; or if I saw boats heavily loaded with household goods crawling along the Neva or Fontanka to the Black River or the Islands—the wagons and the boats were multiplied tenfold, a hundredfold, in my eyes. I fancied that everything was astir and moving, everything was going in regular *caravans to the summer villas. It seemed as though Petersburg threatened to become a wilderness, so that at last I felt ashamed, mortified and sad that I had nowhere to go for the holidays and no reason to go away. I was ready to go away with every wagon, to drive off with every gentleman of respectable appearance who took a cab; but no one—absolutely no one—invited me; it seemed they had forgotten me, as though really I were a stranger to them!*

I took long walks, succeeding, as I usually did, in quite forgetting where I was, when I suddenly found myself at the city gates. Instantly I felt lighthearted, and I passed the barrier and walked between cultivated fields and meadows, unconscious of fatigue, and feeling only all over as though a burden were falling off my soul. All the passersby gave me such friendly looks that they seemed almost greeting me, they all seemed so pleased at something. They were all smoking cigars, every one of them. And I felt pleased as I never had before. It was as though I had suddenly found myself in Italy—so strong was the effect of nature upon a half-sick townsman like me, almost stifling between city walls.

There is something inexpressibly touching in nature round Petersburg, when at the approach of spring she puts forth all her might, all the powers bestowed on her by Heaven, when she breaks into leaf, decks herself out and spangles herself with flowers ...

Fyodor Dostoevsky, White Nights, *1918*

FINLAND STATION (FINLANDSKY VOKZAL)

The Finland Railway Station is located on the right bank of the Neva (the Vyborg Side), a little east of where the cruiser *Aurora* had been docked. It is a short walk from the Petrograd Side across the **Sampsonievsky Most** (Sampson Bridge), over the Bolshaya Nevka, to Finland Station. The station dates back to 1870, and was rebuilt in the 1970's. It was from here that Lenin secretly left for Finland in August 1917, after the Provisional Government forced him into hiding. A few months later he returned on the same locomotive, disguised as a railway fireman, to direct the October uprising. This locomotive, engine number 293, is on display behind a glass pavilion in the back of the station by the platform area. A brass plate on the locomotive bears the inscription: 'The Government of Finland presented this locomotive to the Government of the USSR in commemoration of journeys over Finnish territory made by Lenin in troubled times. June 13, 1957.'

A towering **Monument to Lenin** stands in Lenin Square (Ploshchad Lenina) opposite the station. After the February 1917 Revolution overthrew the czarist monarchy, Lenin returned to Petrograd from his place of exile in Switzerland on April 3, 1917. (He arrived aboard a sealed train provided by Russia's WWI enemy, the Germans, who hoped Lenin would undermine the government and take Russia out of the war.) Upon arrival, Lenin gave a stirring speech to the masses from the turret of his armored car. Originally the Lenin monument was erected on the spot where he gave the speech. But during construction of the square the statue, portraying Lenin standing on the car's turret addressing the crowd with an outstretched hand, was moved closer to the Neva embankment, where it stands today; it was unveiled on November 7, 1926. Ploshchad Lenina Metro station is also at the Finland Station.

Farther north, near Vyborgskaya Metro station, at 41 Bolshoi Sampsonievsky Prospekt, stands the **Cathedral of St Sampson—Host of Wanderers**. Peter the Great defeated the Swedes in the Battle of Poltava (1709) on the feast day of St Sampson, and a wooden church was built to commemorate the victory. Later, between 1728 and 1733, this five-domed light-blue baroque church replaced it. (It is rumored that Catherine the Great secretly married her long-time lover Grigory Potemkin here in 1774.) A lovely gilded iconostasis crowns the altar, with an enormous silver chandelier above it. On either side of the nave are two large panels forming the Calendar of Saints, each representing six months where each day is marked by an icon of the appropriate saint's feast day. Many of the city's preeminent architects such as Rastrelli, Leblond and Trezzini are buried in the neighboring cemetery. Open 10:30am–6pm; closed Wednesdays.

In Vyborg's northeast region lies **Piskarevskoye Memorial Cemetery**. Here are the common graves of over half a million Leningraders who died during the 900-day siege, marked only by somber mounds of dirt and their year of burial (see pages 582 and 602). The central path of the cemetery leads to the **Statue of the Mother Country**, holding a wreath of oak leaves, the symbol of eternal glory. Two museum pavilions are on either side of the entrance, where one realizes the horrors that faced the citizens of this city. The cemetery register is open at a page with the entries: 'February, 1942: 18th—3,241 bodies; 19th—5,569; 20th—10,043.' Another display shows a picture of 11-year-old Tanya Savicheva and pages from her diary: 'Granny died 25 January, 1942 at 3pm. Lyoka died 17 March at 5am. Uncle Vasya died 13 April at 2am. Uncle Lyosha 10 May at 4pm. Mama died 13 May at 7.30am. The Savichevs are dead. Everyone is dead. Only Tanya remains.' Sadly, Tanya later died after she was evacuated from the city. A memorial day to the Siege of Leningrad is held here every year on September 8 (the day the Blockade began) and May 9 (Victory Day). The cemetery is located at 74 Nepokorennikh Prospekt, and the grounds and museum are open daily 10am–6pm (in summer the cemetery is open until 9pm). The nearest Metro station is Ploshchad Muzhestva, and then by bus 123 or 138. www.pmemorial.ru.

Crossing the Neva in front of Finland Station and then over the **Liteiny Most** bridge, with its beautiful railings, decorated with mermaids and anchors, leads to 4 Liteiny Prospekt and the granite Constructionist-style Interior Ministry Building, known today as **Bolshoi Dom**. In 1932, it was built on the site of a czarist court where revolutionaries (including Lenin's brother) were tried for their unsuccessful attempt to assassinate Alexander III. During the Soviet era, the complex was the secret police center of Stalin's purges and later KGB headquarters; Vladimir Putin even worked here. In 2010, the 'Big House' made headlines when subversive art collective *Voina* (War) drew a 63-meter (206-foot) long phallus on the surface of the nearby Liteiny Bridge, which when raised in the evening, erected the painting and made quite a gesture of defiance to the Federal Security Bureau.

Further east along Robespierre Embankment (architect of an earlier reign of terror elsewhere) stands the three-meter high bronze **Monument to Anna Akhmatova**. (See Special Topic on page 675), dedicated in 2006 to mark the 40th anniversary of the beloved poet's death. It stands directly across from the former notorious Kresty (Crosses) Prison, built in 1892, where up to 17 prisoners would be stuffed into a 3 square-meter cell. Akhmatova's son, Lev Gumilev, was imprisoned here, and she spent countless days in line to hear word of his fate. The inscription on the monument comes from her epic poem, *Requiem*: "...And if someday in this country; they decide to erect a monument to me, I agree to this honor; but only on the condition that it stand; not by the sea, where I was born...But here, where I stood for 300 hours; and where they never unbarred the door for me...."

STATE OF SIEGE

What an incredible thing is this feeling of hunger. One can get used to it as to a chronic headache. For two successive days I have been waiting with blind resignation for one glutinous piece of bread, without experiencing acute hunger. That means the disease (ie hunger) has gone over from the acute stage to the chronic.

It's dark. I couldn't stop myself getting out that precious candle-end, hidden away in case of dire emergency. The darkness is terribly oppressive. Mila's dozing on the sofa. She is smiling in her sleep, she must be dreaming of a sandwich with smoked sausage or of thick barley soup. Every night she has appetizing dreams, which is why waking up is particularly tormenting for her.

The entire flat is appallingly cold, everywhere is frozen, stepping out into the corridor involves putting on one's coat, galoshes and hat. The bleakness of desolation everywhere. The water supply is non-existent, we have to fetch water from more than three kilometres away. The sewage system is a thing of the distant past—the yard is full of muck. This is like some other city, not Leningrad, always so proud of its European, dandyish appearance. To see it now is like meeting a man you have become accustomed to seeing dressed in a magnificent, thick woollen overcoat, sporting clean gloves, a fresh collar, and good American boots. And here you suddenly meet that same man completely transformed—clothed in tatters, filthy, unshaven, with foul-smelling breath and a dirty neck, with rags on his feet instead of boots.

Yesterday's Leningradskaya Pravda published an article by the chairman of the Leningrad Soviet, comrade Popov, entitled 'On the Leningrad Food Situation'. After calling on all citizens to summon their courage and patience, comrade Popov goes on to speak of the very real problems of theft and abuse in Leningrad's food distribution network.

My candle-end has almost burnt down. Soon darkness will descend upon me—until morning...

17th January. Old age. Old age is the fatigue of the well-worn components that are involved in the working of a human body, an exhaustion of man's inner resources. Your blood no longer keeps you warm, your legs refuse to obey you, *your back grows stiff, your brain grows feeble, your memory fades. The pace of old age is as unhurried as the slow combustion of the almost burnt-out logs in a stove: the flames die away, lose their colour, one log disintegrates into burning embers, then another—and now the last flickering blue flames are fading—it will soon be time to shut off the flue.*

We are, all of us, old people now. Regardless of age. The pace of old age now governs our bodies and our feelings.... Yesterday at the market I saw a little girl of about nine, wearing enormous felt boots which were full of holes. She was bartering a chunk of dubious-looking brawn—probably made from dog meat—for 100 grammes of bread. Her eyes, hardly visible beneath a pair of heavy lids, looked terribly tired, her back was bent, her gait slow and shuffling, her face puckered and the corners of her mouth turned down. It was the face of an old woman. Can this ever be forgotten or forgiven?

23rd January, 11a.m. Slowly, laboriously, like emaciated people toiling up a hill, the days drag by. Monotonous, unhealthy, withdrawn days in a now silent city. Leningrad's nerve centres, which have until recently kept the life of the city going, fed it vital impulses—the power-stations—have ceased to function. And all the nerve fibres extending over the city lie dormant, inactive. There is no light, no trams or trolley-buses are running, the factories, cinemas, theatres have all stopped working. It is pitch black in the empty shops, chemists', canteens—their windows having been boarded up since autumn (as protection from shell fragments). Only the feeble, consumptive flame of a wick-lamp flickers on every counter.... Thickly coated in snow, the tram, trolley-bus and radio cables hang listlessly above the streets. They stretch overhead like an endless white net, and there is nothing to make them shed their thick snow cover.

The great city's nervous system has ceased its function. But we know that this is not death, but only a lethargic sleep. The time will come when the sleeping giant will stir, and then rouse himself...

Alexander Dymov, Winter of 1942, *translated by Hilda Perham*

On the southeast corner of Potyomkinskaya and Shpalernaya is the **Indoor Flower Market**, with an impressive Butterfly House. Throw a coin in the wishing well! Open 11am–8pm, Monday 2pm–8pm. At number 56 is the **World of Water Museum**, with interesting exhibits on the history of the city's waterways and water system; the building also houses St Petersburg's water treatment company, Vodokanal. Open 10am–6pm; closed Monday and Tuesday.

Across the street, at number 47, stands the magnificent **Tauride Palace**. This Neoclassical mansion was built by Ivan Starov between 1783 and 1789 for Prince Grigory Potemkin-Tavrichesky as a gift from Catherine the Great for his successful capture of the Izmail Fortress from Turkey. Potemkin was commander-in-chief of the Russian Army in the Crimea during the Turkish Wars. For his victories, Potemkin was given the title of Prince of Tauris (the ancient Greek name for Crimea). On May 11, 1791, Potemkin hosted one of the most extravagant parties of Catherine's reign (partly as a thank you for the palace, and also as an attempt to woo back the Empress' attention from her new lover Platon Zubov). The palace halls were illuminated by 140,000 torches and 20,000 wax candles, and as the Empress entered the palace 300 musicians and singers broke into song, "Triumph's thunder, loudly rumble…" written by popular poet Gavrila Derzhavin. After the deaths of Potemkin (within 5 months of the party) and Catherine II (five years later), the new czar Paul I (who immensely disliked his mother and her favorites) converted the palace into equestrian barracks and stables. It was later renovated and became the seat of the State Duma in 1906. On February 27, 1917, the left wing of the palace held the first session of the Petrograd Soviet of Workers. Today the mansion is known as the Tauride or Tavrichesky Palace, and houses the Parliamentary Assembly of the CIS Member States; it is closed to the public. But a visitor can stroll through the lovely **Tauride Gardens**, once considered St Petersburg's finest in the 18th century when intricate pavilions, small bridges and carved statues dotted the landscape, and Venetian gondolas and boats sailed on the enormous pond. Today the gardens are also known as City Childrens' Park. Just east of the gardens stands one of the last remaining statues of **Felix Dzerzhinsky**, founder of the infamous Cheka that later became the KGB. On the south side of the gardens, at 43 Kirochnaya, is the **Alexander Suvorov Museum**, the great 18th-century Russian military leader under Catherine the Great and Paul I. Open 10am–6pm, Wednesday 1pm–9pm; closed Mondays. www.suvorovmuseum.ru.

Across the street from the front of the palace, at 9 Stavropolskaya, is **Kikin Hall**. Built in 1714, it is one of the city's oldest residential buildings and surviving examples of Petrine Baroque. It belonged to Boyar, Alexander Kikin, the Admiralty Councilor to Peter the Great. When he was accused of a plot, along with Peter's son Alexei, to assassinate the Czar in 1718, Kikin was put to death. Peter I then turned the palace into Russia's first natural science museum. The collections were later moved to the Kunstkammer on Vasilyevsky Island. Today the two-story palace is the St Petersburg Musical Lycée. The closest Metro station is Chernyshevskaya.

THE SMOLNY

Several years after the founding of Peter and Paul Fortress, the tar yards, *smolyanoi dvori*, were set up at the Neva's last bend before the gulf to process tar for the shipyards. Later, in 1748, Elizabeth I established the monastery and convent in this area; she had intended to take the veil at the end of her rule. The baroque (combined with Russian traditional), five-domed, turquoise and white Smolny complex (at 3/1 Rastrelli Square) is truly one of Francesco Bartolomeo Rastrelli's greatest works. After Elizabeth died (in 1761), the complex was still not fully completed. (The Empress lavishly spent State funds—she had over 15,000 gowns, and at her death only six rubles remained in the Treasury.) Vasily Stasov later completed the structure, adhering to Rastrelli's original design. When the new classicism vogue in architecture replaced baroque, Rastrelli fell into disfavor under Catherine II, who called baroque 'old fashioned whipped cream'. Today the Smolny Cathedral is used as a musical concert hall and exhibition space. (It is no longer a working church.) A visitor can buy a ticket to climb the 277 steps to one or both of the 63-meter (206-foot) bell towers for spectacular city views. Open 10am–7pm; closed Wednesdays. eng.cathedral.ru.

In 1764, Catherine the Great established the Institute for Young Noble Ladies next to the **Smolny Convent**, Russia's first school for daughters of nobility; they were educated here from the age of six to 18 and prepared for a life in high society.; afterwards many of the women became maids-of-honor in the court. A series of portraits of the first graduates can be found in the Russian Museum. Between 1806 and 1808, the architect Giacomo Quarenghi erected additional buildings, together known as the **Smolny Institute**, which also came to educate girls of lower estates. Today the Church of the Resurrection and the former convent is a small museum, and additional parts of the complex serve as concert halls.

In August 1917, the girls were dismissed and the institute closed. The building became the headquarters for the Petrograd Bolshevik Party and the Military Revolutionary Committee. On October 25, 1917, Lenin arrived at the Smolny and gave the command for the storming of the Winter Palace. On October 26, the Second All-Russia Congress of Soviets gathered in the Smolny's Assembly Hall to elect Lenin as the leader of the world's first Socialist Government of Workers and Peasants, and to adopt Lenin's Decrees on Peace and Land. John Reed wrote in his book *Ten Days That Shook the World* that Lenin was 'unimpressive, to be the idol for a mob, loved and revered as perhaps few leaders in history have been. A leader purely by virtue of intellect; colorless, humorless, uncompromising and detached, without picturesque idiosyncrasies—but with the power of explaining profound ideas in simple terms...he combined shrewdness with the greatest intellectual audacity.' (See page 144 for a further extract.) Lenin lived at the Smolny for 124 days before transferring the capital to Moscow. In 1925, two porticoes were built at the main entrance with the inscriptions: 'The first Soviet of the Proletarian Dictatorship and Workers of the World, Unite!' A bronze monument of Lenin was set up on the tenth anniversary of the Revolution. And it was here, on December 1 1934, that Leningrad Communist Party head, Sergei Kirov, was assassinated on probable orders of Stalin, which led to other purges that became known as the Great Terror. Today some of the rooms where Lenin lived are part of the Lenin Museum. The rest of the buildings house St Petersburg's governor offices. (Putin worked here for six years in the 1990's.) Open 10am–6pm; entrance by appointment only. The nearest Metro is Chernyshevskaya.

In 2006, one of the country's largest companies, Gazprom, began its fight to erect Gazprom City and the city's first skyscraper at 403-meters (1322 feet) directly across from the Smolny Cathedral. The ultra-modern complex's design was with five twisted sides, evoking images of a gas-fueled flame, a strand of DNA and a lady's high-heeled shoe! But, after years of public outcry against the modern behemoth—claiming the towering presence would destroy the city's historic heart, the project was finally relocated beyond the Kirovsky Islands on the Vyborg side and renamed the Lakhta Center. The completed building is cited to be the tallest structure in Europe.

THEATER SQUARE (TEATRALNAYA PLOSHCHAD)

The southwest part of the city is known as the Kolomna District, named after the largest of seven islands that make up the area. Along Glinka and Dekabristov Streets lies **Theater Square** or Teatralnaya Ploshchad. This section of land was once the location for St Petersburg carnivals and fairs. In the 18th century it was known as Ploshchad Karusel (Merry-Go-Round Square). When the Bolshoi Stone Theater opened in 1783, on the site of today's Rimsky-Korsakov Conservatory, the square became known as Teatralnaya. Later, Nicholas I ordered the construction of an Imperial Circus (modeled on the Circus Olympique in Paris), which opened in 1849 opposite the Bolshoi Theater. When the Circus caught fire and burned down in 1859, Alexander II invited Alberto Kavos to build a stunning theater for opera and ballet on the site. The following year, the **Mariinsky Theater** opened, named after Empress Maria Alexandrovna. (It was renamed the Kirov Theater from 1935 to 1992, after a prominent Communist leader.) The five-tiered theater seats 1800 and is decorated with blue velvet chairs, gilded stucco, ceiling paintings and chandeliers. The golden eagles and royal insignia, removed after the revolution, have been reinstated on the Royal and Grand Ducal boxes.

In the 19th-century St Petersburg was the musical capital of Russia. At the Mariinsky Theater performances were staged by Russia's most famous composers, choreographers and singers. Under Petipa, Ivanov and Fokine, Russian ballet took on worldwide recognition (see page 491). The Fyodor Shalyapin Memorial Room, named after the great opera singer, is open during performances. (The Shalyapin House Museum is located at 26 Graftio Ulitsa on the northern Petrograd Side.) In 2000, the US Library of Congress announced a program to help the theater preserve its unique collection of musical scores collected by the theater since czarist times. The Mariinsky continues to stage some of the world's finest ballets and operas, and tours many countries throughout the world.

In 2013, after nearly a decade in the making, the new **Mariinsky II**, designed by Canadian architects Diamond & Schmitt, opened by the original Mariinsky, on the corner of Dekabristov and the Kryukov Canal. The seven-story limestone building (also with three underground levels) includes the main 2000-seat hall, rehearsal stages for ballet and opera companies, staff offices and a rooftop amphitheater, venue for the summer *Stars of the White Nights festival*. The **Concert Hall**, opened in 2006, is next door at 37 Dekabristov. (It was built on the spot where a 2003 fire destroyed most of the costumes and sets being stored in the Warehouses here.) One can check performance listings, and buy tickets at www.mariinsky.ru. Mariinsky box offices are open 11am–7pm, and theater kiosks throughout the city also sell tickets.

Opposite the Mariinsky stands the **Rimsky-Korsakov State Conservatory**, Russia's first advanced school of music. The first wooden building on this site was used as a theater, and in 1783 was replaced by the Bolshoi Kammeny (Stone) Theater. In 1803, the drama troupe moved to the Aleksandrinsky Theater, but the opera and ballet remained at the Bolshoi. In 1836, the theater staged the first performance of Glinka's opera *A Life for the Tsar*, and in 1842 premiered Glinka's second opera, *Ruslan and Lyudmila*. Eventually, the theater fell into such a state of disrepair that it had to close its doors, and the ballet and opera companies were transferred to the Mariinsky. In 1889, extensive restoration work began on the building; and in 1896 its doors this time opened as the Music Conservatory, originally founded in 1862 by pianist and composer Anton Rubinstein. (In 1871, Rimsky-Korsakov became part of the faculty, and the Conservatory was named after him in 1944.) Some of the graduates include Tchaikovsky, Prokofiev and Shostakovich. The *Bolshoi Zal* (Big Hall) and *Maly Zal* (Small Hall) often host concerts (many free of charge) by students and alumni. On either side of the conservatory stand the monuments to Mikhail Glinka, and Rimsky-Korsakov (whose museum is not far from the Vladimirskaya Metro station, at 28 Zagorodny Prospekt.) www.conservatory.ru.

Walking a few blocks west to 2 Lermontovsky Prospekt brings you to the **Grand Choral Synagogue**, designed by Vasily Stasov with a 47-meter (154-foot) high cupola and wedding chapel that opened in 1893 to serve the city's growing Jewish community. The complex also contains the Small Synagogue, a Jewish restaurant and Kosher shop with Jewish food, books, art and music; in Summer the synagogue also hosts musical performances. Open 8am–8pm, services 10am Saturday. Through the website, a visitor can organize an English language tour of the facility, and a longer excursion of 'Jewish-St Petersburg.' www.jewishpetersburg.ru.

At the west end of Ulitsa Dekabristov at number 57 by the Pryazhka Canal, is the **Alexander Blok Museum**, home of the great Symbolist poet during the last eight years of his life from 1912 to 1920. Blok lived on the 3rd floor with his wife Lyubov (daughter of scientist Dmitri Mendelyeev), and his mother resided on the 2nd. Blok expressed his disillusion with the Revolution in his 1918 poem *The Twelve* which describes the march of 12 Bolshevik soldiers through the streets of Petrograd during a raging blizzard. The rooms display original copies of his works, items connected with the poet and his literary circle, his death mask and a drawing of Blok on his deathbed. Chamber concerts are occasionally held here. Open 11am–6pm, till 5pm on Tuesday; closed Wednesdays. www.spbmuseum.ru.

From the museum head north to the Moika Canal, and at number 211 is the Mansion of Grand Duke Alexei, son of Alexander II. Note the Duke's monogram on the wrought-iron fence. Built in 1882–1885 by Maximilian Messmacher, each façade reflects a different architectural style of the times. Today the mansion houses the **St Petersburg House of Music** where musical concerts are held. Appointment only tours are usually given on Tuesday and Thursday at 4pm; check the website: www.spdm.ru.

A short walk south down Glinka leads to the blue–stucco and golden-domed **St Nicholas Marine Cathedral**, built between 1753 and 1762 by Chevakinsky in honor of St Nicholas, the protector of seamen. Naval officers once lived in the area, thus the full name of Nikolsky Morskoi (Marine) Sobor. Standing at the intersection of the Griboyedov and Kryukov canals, the ice blue and white church combines the old Russian five-dome tradition with the baroque. A lovely carved wooden iconostasis is inside and a four-tiered bell tower stands by itself in the gardens. The interior is filled with golden candlelight and smell of incense, as worshippers kiss ancient icons and softly voice Orthodox prayers. (A small shop sells icons and other religious items.) Thousands came here to attend the funeral of the famous poet Anna Akhmatova on March 10, 1966. (She is buried in the village of Komarovo northwest of the city, near Repino; see pages 643 and 675.) Open 9am–7pm. From the Staro-Nikolsky Bridge, you can look north onto seven bridges that cross the canals towards the Neva River.

South across the Fontanka Canal, at 7 Izmailovsky Prospekt, is the **Trinity Cathedral** with its stunning blue cupolas emblazoned with golden stars. Built in 1828, it was the church for the Izmailovsky Guards, who lived next door. Here, Dostoevsky married his second wife, Anna Snitkina, in 1867. In honor of the Russian victory over the Turks, the memorial Column of Glory was assembled from 128 Turkish cannons in 1878. (This is a replica of the original that was destroyed by Stalin.) Daily service at 10am, and 5pm on weekends. Metro Tekhnologichesky Institut.

From the Nikolsky Gardens, at the opposite end of Glinka, at 94 Moika Embankment (Naberezhnaya Reki Moiki), is the **Yusupov Palace** that dates back to 1770. The Yusupov family, one of the richest in Russia, purchased the palace in the 1830's, and owned over 40 estates throughout the country. The last owner of the palace (he was born here in 1887) was the flamboyant Prince Felix Yusupov, quite the eccentric dandy who often attended society balls cross-dressing as a woman. The palace interiors are sumptuously preserved, filled with 19th-century chandeliers, furniture, frescoes, paintings and tapestries. After the Revolution, when the family was forced to flee the country, the immense Yusupov art collection was placed in the Hermitage. Rooms include the tiled Moorish Drawing Room and Turkish Study on the ground floor. On the second are the ballroom, banquet hall and ornate rococo-style 180-seat private theater, which hosted recognized artists of the day, including Pavlova, Glinka and Shalyapin. (Concerts are still held here today.)

Yusupov was most famously responsible for the assassination of Grigory Rasputin (the starets who exerted much influence in the court of Nicholas II) in December 1916. Rasputin was first lured to the palace by an opportunity to socialize with the Count's wife Irina Alexandrovna (the czar's niece). While music played upstairs (Yankee Doodle Dandy) to give the impression the couple were entertaining (his wife was not at home), Rasputin was asked to wait in a downstairs drawing room where he was given cakes laced with cyanide. Nothing happened—the sugar in the cakes is thought to have neutralized the poison. In desperation Yusupov finally went down and shot the monk, and then hurried upstairs to tell his four other accomplices (one of them Grand Duke Dmitri). During this time, Rasputin revived and managed to drag himself out into the courtyard, where the conspirators then ran after him and shot the mad monk three times more. Finally, they tied up Rasputin's body, rolled it in a carpet, and threw it through a hole in the ice of the river. Three days later, the body was found floating under the ice downstream. An autopsy showed that Rasputin had water in his lungs and rope burns on his wrists, proving he had still been alive after all the attempts to kill him. After Yusupov fled Russia and settled in France, he wrote *Lost Splendor: The Amazing Memoirs of the Man Who Killed Rasputin* in 1952, and it is still in print today. Yusupov died in 1967 and is buried in Paris' Sainte-Geneviève-des-Bois Russian Cemetery.

The palace also houses the **Rasputin Museum** and you can actually stand in the small basement room where Rasputin was poisoned; mannequins in period dress are posed in re-enactment. Rasputin's daughter, Maria Grigorievna Rasputina, emigrated to the United States in 1937; she died in Los Angeles in 1977, having just published her own book, *Rasputin: The Man Behind the Myth*. The Palace is open from 11am to 5pm; purchase an English audio guide for a tour of the rooms. A separate ticket for the Rasputin Museum is necessary; excursions are at 1:45pm in Russian (closed Sundays). www.yusupov-palace.ru.

Crossing the Moika Canal, walk north up Ulitsa Truda to Truda Square and the **Central Naval Museum**, the largest of its kind in the world. (The entrance is from the Kryukov Canal.) In 2013, the museum moved from the Stock Exchange on Vasilevsky Island to this large renovated space in the Kryukov barracks that eventually will contain 19 exhibition halls, restoration workshops, scientific and technical libraries, and a café and conference center. Peter the Great originally opened the museum in the Admiralty in 1709 to store models and blueprints of Russian ships. His collection of models numbered over 1,500, and today the museum contains half a million items on the history of the Russian fleet; included is the *Botik*, Peter's first boat. The exhibits include 18th–19th century naval guns, artillery systems & instruments, ship models, nautical maps and Russian battle paintings. The city celebrates Navy Day on July 28th, when ships from the Russian fleet parade along the Neva River. Open 11am–6pm; closed Mondays and Tuesdays. www.navalmuseum.ru.

On the other side of the Kryukov Canal you will see a number of brick buildings over on a small triangular island. These were the storehouses for ship timber during the time of Peter the Great when shipbuilding also took place here. Manmade canals created this small island known as **New Holland** or Novaya Gollandiya, The New Admiralty Canal, dug in 1717, once connected the island with the Admiralty. Konnogvardeysky (formerly Trade Union) Boulevard was partly laid along the route of the canal. Jean-Baptiste Vallin designed the impressive red-brick and granite arch. Up until 2004 it was owned by the Baltic Fleet and closed to visitors. In 2010, businessman and entrepreneur, Roman Abramovich, acquired New Holland Island and is now turning it into an art, cultural and commercial center. www.newhollandsp.com.

Walk a few blocks north to the Neva River, and at 44 English Embankment (Angliskaya Naberezhnaya) is the Neoclassical-style **Rumyantsev Palace**, named after prominent statesman, Count Nikolai Petrovich Rumyantsev (1754–1826) who founded the museum which contained the vast collection of historical and cultural artifacts he had gathered over many years of diplomatic service in different European countries. On his death, the collection was moved to Moscow, and formed the basis of the Russian National Library. Today the museum has over 4000 exhibits on 20th-century St Petersburg's history, but also includes information in several opulent staterooms on the mansion and its owners. Open 11am–6pm Tuesday till 5pm; closed Wednesdays. www.spbmuseum.ru.

THE SENNAYA DISTRICT AND MOSCOW AVENUE (MOSKOVSKY PROSPEKT).

Moskovsky Prospekt runs for nearly 16 kilometers (10 miles) in a straight line from **Sennaya Square** (and Sennaya Ploshchad Metro station) to the airport. The avenue follows the line known as the Pulkovo Meridian (zero on old Russian maps) that led to the Pulkovo Astronomical Observatory. The square was known even in czarist times as Sennaya Ploshchad or Haymarket, the underbelly of St Petersburg, filled with beggars, drunks and pickpockets. (Particularly after the emancipation of the serfs in 1861, thousands of peasants and poor workers flooded the city, which offered little housing. Tenement-like slums swelled up in this district, where often ten people to a room slept in shifts. Taverns and brothels lined the streets.) In 2003, for the city's tercentennial celebrations, money was spent on giving the district a major facelift, but alleyways around the square still evoke some of the past shabbiness. The Sennoi Market is at 4 Moskovsky Prospekt (Peasants would come to the Haymarket to sell hay and produce from the countryside.)

The area was the scene for many of Dostoevsky's novels—including *The Idiot* and *Crime and Punishment*. Today, it is still easy to imagine how the place fueled Dostoevsky's creative imagination. In Dostoevsky's time Stolyarny Alley was filled with drunkards and prostitutes, and brazen crowds bustled through the night in this Haymarket district. At 5 Stolyarny is the **Rodion Raskolnikov House**, where Dostoevsky's character from *Crime and Punishment* lived. (On the fifth floor is Russian graffiti that reads, 'Don't Kill, Rodya!') Dostoevsky described this house and yard in detail—Rodion stole the murder ax from the basement, and it was 730 paces between the murderer's house and his victim's. Even the stone under which Raskolnikov hid the stolen goods was real. Raskolnikov later knelt on Sennaya Square repenting his crime. A sculpture of Dostoevsky stands by the house (which is closed to the public).

Walking south, Stolyarny intersects with Kaznachevskaya Ulitsa (at this time, the street was known as Malaya Meschanskaya or Petit Bourgeois). Dostoevsky lived at number 1 from 1861 to 1863, and at number 9 for a month in 1864. He then moved to number 7 until 1867, where he wrote *The Gambler* and finished his famous novel *Crime and Punishment*. (The author lived at more than 20 residences in his 28 years in St Petersburg, mostly in the Haymarket and Vladimirsky areas.) Imagine Dostoevsky as Raskolnikov, leaving his house and walking south toward the Griboyedov Canal. Crossing the Kokushkin Bridge, he turns right onto Sadovaya Ulitsa and continues past the **Yusupov Gardens**. He then turns right into Rimsky-Korsakov Prospekt, walking several blocks until arriving at Srednaya Podyacheskaya. The entrance to the old-lady **Moneylender's House** (approximately 730 paces from Dostoevsky's doorstep) is at 104 Griboyedov Embankment. Head through the tunnel to block 5 (apartments 22–81). Look for the brass balls placed at the corners of the banisters by the residents; they lead to the pawnbroker's apartment, number 74, just after the third floor. The saintly prostitute Sonya Marmeladova lived further down the Canal at either 63 or 73. (Dostoevsky's Literary Museum is located at 5/2 Kuznechny Pereulok, close to Vladimirskaya Metro station; see page 574.)

Walking a few blocks west along Sadovaya Ulitsa brings you to the **Central Railway Museum**, at number 50, with more than 6,000 exhibits on Russian railway and bridge history. One of the oldest engines dates back to 1897—a 47-ton steam engine that could travel at 32 kilometers (19 miles) an hour. Another display showcases a 1903 Trans-Siberian compartment, decked out with a bathtub and piano salon, and a model ship that carried train cars across the frozen Lake Baikal in winter. Another engine carries the initials FD, those of Felix Dzerzhinsky, who became the first Soviet head of the railroads and secret police. In 1918, the S-68 steam engine transported the first Soviet government from St Petersburg to Moscow. Other items include the world's first diesel locomotive, designed in 1924, and the very last passenger steam engine built in 1956. Open 11am–5pm; closed Fridays and Saturdays. Metro Sadovaya. www.museum.ru/museum/railway   (For serious train buffs, other locations are the **Museum of Railway Technology**, at 118 Obvodnov Canal, metro Baltiiskaya, behind the Warsaw station. It has scores of 19th-century engines and carriage cars; open 11am–5pm; closed Mondays. Another is outside town at Provozny Muzei, a few stops from Vitebsky Station, which houses another collection of old locomotives and train cars.)

Back on Moskovsky Prospekt, continue south past the Obvodnovo Canal and Novodevichy Cemetery to the **Moscow Triumphal Arch**. It was built between 1834 and 1838 by Vasily Stasov to commemorate the Russian victories during the Russo-Turkish War (1828–1829), and was the largest cast-iron structure in the world in the mid-19th-century. Modeled on the Brandenburg Gate in Berlin, the arch was decorated with figures representing Winged Victory, Glory and Plenty. It once marked the end of the city where a road toll was collected. In 1936, Stalin had it taken down; but the Arch was put back up during the Siege of Leningrad when it was hoped that it would serve as a barricade. Metro Moskovskiye Vorota (Gates).

South of the Arch is the 70-hectare (170-acre) **Moscow Victory Park**, through which runs the Alley of Heroes. The park was laid out by tens of thousands of Leningraders after World War II; metro Park Pobedy (Victory).

Continuing south down Moskovsky Prospekt brings you to the stone Gothic-style **Chesme Palace**, at 15 Gastello, a triangular building with three corner towers. Catherine the Great commissioned Yuri Felten to build the palace in 1774. It was named after the Russian victory in 1770 over the Turkish fleet in Chesme Bay. It later became a rest stop for the empress between the city and Tsarskoye Selo. It was here too that Rasputin's body lay in state after his murder in 1916. The famous Chesme (Green-Frog) Dinner Service was commissioned by Catherine the Great from Wedgewood pottery in England; it is now on display in the Hermitage. Today the palace is part of the Institute of Aviation Technology, and closed to the public. The nearby **Chesme Church**, at 12 Lensoveta, built between 1777 and 1780, appears as a Gothic red and white fairy-tale concoction with fancy Russian-style *kokoshniki* (named after a Russian woman's head-dress) decorating the archways that outline the five-domed roof. It is also known as the Church of Nativity of John the Baptist. The graveyard is a burial site for those who died at war. Open 9am–7pm with regular daily services. Metro Moskovskaya.

The **Monument to the Heroic Defenders of Leningrad** (unveiled 30 years after the Siege on May 9, 1975) is the focal point of **Victory Square**. The heroic sculpted figures, called *The Victors*, look out on where the front once ran. (Notice how close the Germans came to capturing the city.) Pink granite steps lead to a 48-meter (157-foot) high Obelisk (dated 1941–45) that stands inside a circle symbolizing the breaking of the blockade ring. (On January 17, 1944, Leningrad was declared liberated from the Nazi blockade, which had lasted 882 days from when the final rail line into the city was cut on September 8, 1941.) An eternal flame burns at the base. In the underground **Memory Hall** is an exhibition space, lit by 900 bronze lamps, devoted to the Siege. The sound of a metronome was the only thing heard on the radio to indicate that the city had not fallen to the Germans. In the center hangs an electrified map that shows the various front and defensive lines during the war. Open 10am–6pm, Tuesday till 5pm; closed Wednesdays and last Tuesday of month. Metro Moskovskaya.

> *And on this starless January night,*
> *Amazed at its fantastic fate,*
> *Returned from the bottomles depths of death,*
> *Leningrad salutes itself.*
>
>   Anna Akhmatova

The **Green Belt of Glory** is a memorial complex that stretches 230 kilometers (143 miles) along the front line of 1941–44. Around **Moscow Square** (Moskovskaya Ploshchad) Stalin tried to transplant the heart of the old city to beat anew in these concrete suburbs, filled with gloomy apartment blocks. At 212 Moskovsky Prospekt is the **House of Soviets**, built in 1936 to house the central administration of the city. A great example of Stalinist design, the façade is filled with bas relief and symbolic friezes; today the building contains offices of the Regional Administration.

Moskovsky Prospekt was built in the early 18th-century to connect the royal residences in St Petersburg to Tsarskoye Selo. Later the road was continued all the way to Moscow. Today, on the way to Tsarskoye Selo, the prospekt passes the famed **Pulkovo Astronomical Observatory**, which once served as part of a 'mirror telegraph' that linked the residences of the czar. After crossing the Kuzminka River, you come to the **Egyptian Entrance Gates** of the city. The gates were built in 1830 and designed by the British architect Adam Menelaws, who incorporated motifs from the Egyptian temples at Karnak. A **Statue of Alexander Pushkin** stands to the left of the gates marking the beginning of the town of Tsarskoye Selo (see page 646).

To the northwest, not far from the Baltic (Baltiisky) Railway Station at Narvskaya Metro station is the **Narva Triumphal Arch** which celebrates the successful outcome of the War of 1812. In 1814, the first gates were erected at the Narva outpost to meet the Russian Guards returning from France. Two decades later, the present gates were designed by Vasily Stasov and built of bricks covered with copper sheets. The Chariot of the Goddess of Victory crowns the arch; the palm and laurel branches symbolize peace and glory. Four Russian armored warriors decorate the bottom; gold letters describe the regiments and places of battle. Words inscribed on the arch in both Latin and Russian read: 'To the Victorious Russian Emperor Guard. Grateful Motherland. On 17 August, 1834.'

> *A different time is drawing near...*
> *But the holy city of Peter*
> *Will be our unintended monument.*
>
> Anna Akhmatova

YELISEYEV'S

This store, whose nickname was the Temple of Gluttons, has a long and fascinating history. In Moscow the building was originally the personal mansion of Catherine the Great's State Secretary, Prince Kozitsky, whose wife was the heiress of a Siberian goldmine. The mansion was the largest and grandest in the city.

In the 1820s, their granddaughter Princess Volkonskaya turned the drawing room into one of Russia's most prestigious salons. All the great literary figures gathered here, including Pushkin, who presented his latest poems. But in 1829, when the princess left for Italy, the mansion fell into other hands.

By the mid-1850s, the dreaded Princess Beloselskaya-Belozerskaya, a relative of Volkanskaya, was living in the mansion; she was a total recluse and only left it to attend church on Sundays. (The family's St Petersburg mansion is at 41 Nevsky Prospekt.) She was not popular at home since she had her servants beaten every Saturday (it was a common practice in that era to single out a few for reprimand). Not surprisingly, some of these servants ran away, and eventually banded together in the house across the street. Many Muscovites believed the dark house to be haunted, claiming to see devils and ghosts, and would not even walk by, especially at night. The bandit-servants decided to lend credence to this belief. One night they dressed up like ghosts and spooked the old princess right out of her house. Some time afterwards, an animal trainer took up residence in the mansion with his black panther.

A number of years later, Grigory Grigoryevich Yeliseyev bought the vacant building. Grigory's grandfather Pyotr had won his freedom in 1813, when his master rewarded him for discovering how to produce strawberries in winter. Pyotr went off to open a wine store in St Petersburg where he soon became a member of the merchant class. His sons in turn founded the Yeliseyev Brothers Trading House, which specialized in foreign wines and other goods from tea and spices to rum and tobacco. The firm established links with the largest trading houses across Europe from Britain to Spain, and to ship the many foreign wares, several Dutch steamships were purchased.

The Yeliseyev business reached its heyday with the third generation. It was Grigory who opened the popular chain of food emporiums from St Petersburg to Kiev. The firm also built spacious warehouses, butcheries, fish canneries and chocolate factories. The shops were filled with mouth-watering delicacies, such as Belgian Oostende oysters, smoked sturgeon, stuffed turkeys, beluga caviar, exotic fruits and Swiss and French cheeses. Its wine cellars were scattered around the world; at one point the Yeliseyevs purchased entire grape harvests in some French provinces. For promoting Russia's national trade industry, Grigory Yeliseyev was ennobled. He was also honored with France's highest award, the Legion of Honor.

Throngs of people turned out for the Moscow Yeliseyev's grand opening in 1899. There was one unexpected hitch—the liquor department turned out to be less than 50 yards from the neighboring church, which contravened the sacred law. So builders had to do a quick restructuring and move it one yard further away. The popular writer Vladimir Gilyarovsky, who lived in the area, wrote in *Moscow and Muscovites*: 'Passers-by stared at the mountains of imported fruits

A trolleybus on Nevsky Prospekt near Ostrovsky Square passes Yeliseyev's
Food Emporium, 115th anniversary in 2014.

which looked like cannon balls, a pyramid of coconuts each the size of a child's head, bunches of tropical bananas so large you could not get your arms around them and unknown inhabitants of the ocean depths. Overhead, electric stars on tips of wine bottles flashed in enormous mirrors, the tops of which were lost somewhere up in the heights....' The store was a huge success. The Yeliseyevs even dreamed of cornering the American market and opened a chain of shops in the United States.

In his fifties, Grigory fell in love with the wife of a prominent St Petersburg jeweler. The millionaire's children and grandchildren opposed a divorce and his broken-hearted wife succeeded with suicide on her third attempt. When World War I broke out, Grigory married his lover and fled to France where he died in Paris in 1942. After this scandal, Yeliseyev's sons renounced their heritage, which included the store. This was probably just as well since the family would have lost everything anyway during the Bolshevik Revolution which broke out soon after.

The saga does not end there. Under Brezhnev, the director of Gastronom #1 (as the store was now called) was Yuri Konstantinovich Sokolov. As a friend of Brezhnev's daughter Galya, Sokolov was quite well-connected. At the store, Sokolov made up quotas and took many choice picks for himself; he also wrote a lot of food off as spoiled or sold it even more profitably on the black market. Of course, Sokolov became popular and wealthy, and was known for throwing great parties. But when Brezhnev died in 1982 and Andropov took over, the glorious days of corruption and stagnation were numbered. The head of Moscow Trade received a 15-year prison sentence, the director of another Gastronom six years, and Sokolov found himself sentenced to death—he was executed by firing squad in 1984. The police found gold, jewelry and huge bundles of rotting rubles buried in his backyard.

Today the new owners of the shops have renamed them Yeliseyev's, hoping to capitalize on their intriguing past. In the Moscow shop, a bust of Grigory Yeliseyev stands in the entrance hall, put up in 1989 to celebrate the store's 90th anniversary—the store marked its centennial jubilee with further celebrations in 1999. The Moscow store is located at 14 Tverskaya, and in St Petersburg the lavish art-nouveau building is at 58 Nevsky Prospekt.

LENIN AND THE RUSSIAN REVOLUTION

Lenin, founder of the first Soviet State, was born Vladimir Ilyich Ulyanov, on April 22, 1870. Vladimir, along with his five brothers and sisters, had a strict but pleasant childhood in the small town of Simbirsk (now Ulyanovsk) on the Volga River. On March 1, 1887, when Vladimir was 17, a group of students attempted to assassinate Czar Alexander III in St Petersburg. Vladimir's older brother, Alexander, was one of five students arrested. They were imprisoned in Peter and Paul Fortress in St Petersburg, and on May 8 were hung in the Fortress of Schlüsselburg (Kronstadt).

As a marked family of a revolutionary, the Ulyanovs left Simbirsk for Kazan, where Vladimir attended Kazan University. In December 1887, after the local papers reported the news of student riots in Moscow, 99 Kazan students protested against the strict rules of their university. Ulyanov, one of them, was immediately expelled, exiled to the town of Kokushkino and kept under police surveillance. Here Vladimir began to study the works of Karl Marx (*Das Kapital*, and the *Communist Manifesto*) and Chernyshevsky (*What Is To Be Done?*). Thereupon, he decided to devote his life to the revolutionary struggle. Lenin wrote that 'my way in life was marked out for me by my brother'.

Since he was refused permission to enter another university, the young Ulyanov covered the four-year law course independently, in a little over a year. He then journeyed to St Petersburg and passed the bar exam with honors. With his law degree, Ulyanov moved to the Asian town of Samara, where he defended the local peasants and secretly taught Marxist philosophy.

In 1893, he left again for St Petersburg, where he formed the revolutionary organization, the League of Struggle for the Emancipation of the Working Class. At 24, in 1894, Vladimir Ulyanov published his first book, *What Are the Friends of the People?* During a secret meeting of the League of Struggle, Ulyanov decided to publish an underground newspaper called the *Workers' Cause*. That same day he was arrested by the police, along with hundreds of other people from the League. Ulyanov was exiled to Siberia, as was Nadezhda Konstantinovna Krupskaya. They were married in the small village of Shushenskoye on July 22, 1898.

While in exile, the League planned the first party newspaper, called *Iskra* (*Spark*), inspired by words from a Decembrist poem, 'A spark will kindle a flame'. After the Ulyanovs' release, they settled in the town of Pskov outside St Petersburg (see page 665). Since it was illegal to disseminate any print media criticizing the government, they eventually moved abroad. The first issues of *Iskra* were published in Leipzig, Germany. During these years abroad, Ulyanov wrote books on politics, economics and the revolutionary struggle. In December 1901, Vladimir Ulyanov began signing his writings with the name of Lenin.

In 1903, the Russian Party Congress secretly gathered in London. During this meeting, the Social Democratic Workers Party split into two factions: the Bolsheviks (Majority) and the Mensheviks (Minority). After the session, Lenin led the Bolsheviks to the grave of Karl Marx and said, 'Let us pledge to be faithful to his teachings. We shall never give up the struggle. Forward, comrades, only forward.'

By 1905, widespread unrest was sweeping across Russia. A popular May Day song was often sung: 'Be it the merry month of May. Grief be banished from our way. Freedom songs our joy convey. We shall go on strike today.' Workers at the Putilov factory in St Petersburg began a strike that triggered work stoppages at over 350 factories throughout the city. On Sunday, January 9, 1905, thousands of workers lined the streets of St Petersburg. In a peaceful protest, the crowd carried icons and portraits of the czar. The procession walked toward the Winter Palace and congregated in Decembrists' Square (now known as Senate Square; see page 530). The palace guards opened fire. More than 1,000 demonstrators were massacred in what is known today as Bloody Sunday. Not long afterward, sailors manning the *Potemkin*, largest battleship in the Russian Navy, also protested against their miserable working conditions. In a mutiny headed by Afanasy Matyushenko, the sailors raised their own revolutionary red flag on June 14, 1905.

The Geneva newspapers carried the news of Bloody Sunday and Lenin decided to return to St Petersburg. He wrote in his newspaper *Vperyod* (*Forward*): 'The uprising has begun force against force. The Civil War is blazing up. Long live the Revolution. Long live the Proletariat.' But it was still too dangerous for Lenin to remain in Russia. Two years later he left again for the West, and over the next ten years, lived in Finland, Sweden, France and Switzerland.

Accounts of a new Russian Revolution were published throughout the West in February, 1917. Lenin immediately took a train to Finland and on April 3 proceeded in an armored car to Petrograd (the city had been renamed in 1914). Today the train's engine is displayed at St Petersburg's Finland Station, where Lenin first arrived (see page 580).

In Petrograd, Lenin lived on the banks of the Moika River and started up the newspaper *Pravda* (*Truth*), which was outlawed by the new Kerensky Provisional Government. Lenin was later forced into hiding outside the city on Lake Razliv (see page 642). The hut and area where he hid out has been made into a museum. With his beard shaved off and wearing a wig, Lenin was known as Konstantin Ivanov.

On the grounds of the Smolny Cathedral (see page 585), a finishing school served as headquarters for the Petrograd Workers Soviet, which organized the Red Guards. During the summer of 1917, more than 20,000 workers in Petrograd were armed and readied for a Bolshevik uprising. Lenin gave the command for attack from the Smolny on October 24, 1917. To signal the beginning of the Great October Socialist Revolution, the battleship *Aurora* fired a blank shot near the Hermitage. The Red Guards stormed the Winter Palace and almost immediately defeated the White Guards of the Provisional Government; the Moscow Kremlin was taken two days later.

Vladimir Ilyich Lenin, father of the 1917 October Socialist Revolution and leader of the Bolshevik Party. This statue used to stand on one of the highest spots in the Kremlin gardens in Moscow, known as Kremlin Hill, but was removed in 1997.

On October 25, the Second Congress of Soviets opened in the Smolny and Lenin was elected chairman of the first Soviet State; Trotsky was his Foreign Minister. Sverdlov, Stalin, Bobnov and Dzerzhinsky (later to head the Cheka, which authorized police to 'arrest and shoot immediately all members of counterrevolutionary organizations') were elected to the Revolutionary Military Committee. Lenin introduced a Decree on Land, proclaiming that all lands become State property. At the end of the Congress, all members stood and sang the Internationale, the proletarian anthem: 'Arise ye prisoners of starvation. Arise ye wretched of the earth. For Justice thunders condemnation. A better world's in birth.' On March 11, 1918, Lenin moved the capital from Petrograd to Moscow. He lived in a room at the National Hotel across from Red Square. The Bolsheviks, known as the Communist Party, had their offices in the Kremlin.

During the last years of Lenin's life, the country was wracked by war and widespread famine. He implemented the NEP (New Economic Policy) that allowed foreign trade and investment, but he did not live long enough to bear witness to its effects. Lenin died at the age of 54 on January 21, 1924. The cause of death was listed as cerebral sclerosis, triggered, as stated in the official medical report, by 'excessive intellectual activity'. (It's suspected he really died of syphilis.) In three days a wooden structure to house his body was built on Red Square. Later, it was replaced by a mausoleum of red granite and marble. For decades, thousands lined up daily to view his embalmed body and witness the changing of the guards. A "Commission for the Immortalization of Lenin's Memory" was founded; and the Commission even approved selected Lenin designs and statues to be cloned throughout Russian towns and villages. Alexander Sokurov's 2001 film *Telets* (Taurus) is a neo-realistic story that attaches human features to the Communist idol; Lenin is shown simply as a miserable, sick, and dying old man.

Soon after his death, Petrograd's name was changed to Leningrad in his honor; it bore this epithet until 1991, when the city's name reverted back to St Petersburg (in Soviet times the city had 103 monuments to Lenin). Today, even though the Red Square mausoleum is still opened to visitors, the changing of the guards has stopped. The current government is reviewing proposals to close the mausoleum and give Lenin's body a burial elsewhere, either on Kremlin grounds or, ironically, back in St Petersburg.

THE SIEGE OF LENINGRAD

It's now the fifth month since the enemy has tried to kill our will to live, break our spirit and destroy our faith in victory.... But we know that victory will come. We will achieve it and Leningrad will once again be warm and light and even gay.

Olga Bergholts, Leningrad Poet

For 900 days between 1941 and 1944, Leningrad was cut off from the rest of the Soviet Union and the world by German forces. During this harsh period of World War II, the whole city was linked to the outside world only by air drops and one dangerous ice road, The Road of Life (opened only in winter), that was laid across the frozen waters of Lake Ladoga.

The invading Nazis were determined to completely destroy Leningrad, and Hitler's goal was to starve and bombard the city until it surrendered. The directive issued to German command on September 29, 1941 stated: 'The Führer has ordered the city of St Petersburg to be wiped off the face of the earth.... It is proposed to establish a tight blockade of the city and, by shelling it with artillery of all calibers and incessant bombing, level it to the ground.' Hitler was so certain of immediate victory that he even printed up invitations to a celebration party to be held in the center of the city at the Hotel Astoria.

But the Germans did not plan on the strong resistance and incredible resilience of the Leningrad people. For almost three years, the Nazis tried to penetrate the city. All totaled, over 100,000 high-explosive bombs and 150,000 shells were dropped on the city. The suffering was immense: almost one million people starved to death. At one point, only 125 grams (four ounces) of bread were allocated to each inhabitant per day. The winters were severe with no heat or electricity. There are many stories, for example, of mothers collecting the crumbs off streets or scraping the paste off wallpaper and boiling it to feed their hungry children. Tanya Savicheva, an 11-year-old girl who lived on Vasilyevsky Island, kept a diary that chronicled the deaths of her entire family. It ended with the words: 'The Savichevs died. They all died. I remained alone.' Tanya was later evacuated from Leningrad, but died on July 1, 1944 (see Piskarevskoye Memorial Cemetery, page 581).

Damage to the city was extensive. More than half of the 18th- and 19th-century buildings classified as historical monuments were destroyed; over 30 bombs struck the Hermitage alone. Within one month of the German invasion in June 1941, over one million works of art were packed up by the Hermitage staff and sent by train to Sverdlovsk in the Urals for safekeeping. Other works of art and architecture that could not be evacuated were buried or secretly stored elsewhere within the city. Over 2,000 staff members and art scholars lived in 12 underground air-raid shelters beneath the Hermitage in order to protect the museum and its treasures. Boris Piotrovsky, the Hermitage's former director, lived in one of these shelters and headed the fire brigade. He noted that 'in the life of besieged Leningrad a notable peculiarity manifested itself—an uncommon spiritual strength and power of endurance... to battle and save the art treasures created over the

The Tomb of the Unknown Soldier outside the Kremlin walls in Moscow.
An eternal flame honors the memory of the 20 million Russians who died during World
War II. It was moved to this site from the Field of Mars in St Petersburg in 1967.

millennia by the genius of humanity.' Architect Alexander Nikolsky, who also lived in an air-raid shelter, sketched the city during the entire blockade. His pencil and charcoal drawings can be seen today in the Hermitage Department of Prints and Drawings.

The city's outskirts were the worst hit. The palaces of Peter the Great, Catherine II, and Elizabeth I were almost completely demolished. Peter's Palace of Petrodvorets was put to use as a Nazi stable. The Germans sawed up the famous Sampson Fountain for wood and took rugs and tapestries into the trenches.

The Soviet author, Vera Inber, was in Leningrad during the Siege. She wrote the narrative poem *Pulkovo Meridian* about the Pulkovo Astronomical Observatory outside Leningrad, where many scientists were killed when it was struck by an enemy bomb.

Dmitri Shostakovich's Seventh Symphony was composed in Leningrad during the siege and broadcast from the city around the world on August 9, 1942. Shostakovich was a member of the fire-defense unit housed in the Leningrad Conservatory. During bomb attacks, Shostakovich would hurriedly write the Russian letters BT, which stood for air raid, on his score before running to his post on the roof of the conservatory.

On January 27, 1944, Leningraders heard the salute of 324 guns to celebrate the complete victory over German troops. Even though most of the buildings, museums, and palaces have now been restored, the citizens of St Petersburg will never forget the siege, during which every fourth person in the city was killed. May 9, a city holiday, is celebrated as Liberation Day. Schoolchildren take turns standing guard at cemeteries.

Over half a million of the people who died between 1941 and 1943 are buried in mass graves at Piskarevskoye Cemetery outside St Petersburg. Inside the pavilion is a museum dedicated to the Siege of Leningrad. Outside, the Statue of the Motherland stands over an eternal flame. At the base of the monument are inscribed words by Olga Berggolts. The end of the inscription reads: 'Let no one forget. Let nothing be forgotten.'

In front of the Peterhof Palace the five-ton Sampson Fountain wrestles open the jaws of a lion from which a jet of water shoots over 20 meters (65 feet) into the air.

The great Cascade Fountain stands in front of Peterhof, Peter the Great's Summer Palace. Its 66 fountains, 17 waterfalls and 142 water jets all flow without the aid of a single pump.

(top) Russian folk singer wears a traditional peasant costume—sarafan jumper, embroidered blouse and tall kokoshniki headdress. (bottom) The Rocket hydrofoil takes tourists on trips along the Neva River and out to Peterhof Palace on the Gulf of Finland.

Peter the Great's Palace, Peterhof, was designed to resemble the French palace of Versailles. The rooms have magnificent parquet floors, painted ceilings and even Chippendale furniture.

(above) The centerpiece of Kronstadt is the Seaman's Cathedral, built in Neo-Byzantine style, which honors all those who perished at sea, and killed during the famous 1921 Kronstadt rebellion against the Bolsheviks.

(left) A 19th-century ball is held annually at Catherine's Palace. Dressed in turn-of-the-century aristocratic costume, city folk gather to celebrate their historical roots.

(opposite) During the reign of Elizabeth I over 100 kg of gold was used to decorate the summer palace exteriors and onion domes of the church.

In the town of Tsarskoye Selo, Catherine's Palace was built to honor Catherine I, wife of Peter the Great. After their daughter, Elizabeth I, inherited the estate in 1741, she transformed the palace into a grandiose baroque-style summer residence on a scale to rival Versailles.

(top) The entrance gate to Catherine's Palace (Yekaterinsky Dvorets) is decorated with the Russian czarist crest of the double-headed eagle, adopted by Ivan the Great in the 15th-century.

(bottom) The 18th-century Catherine's Palace in Tsarskoye Selo, designed by Rastrelli, is over 300 meters (980 feet) long. At the time it was the longest palace in the world. Two types of gardens make up Catherine Park, the naturalistic and formal. In front of the palace, beds of symmetrical red and black arabesque shapes gradually lead into a wilder area of wooded paths and fish-filled ponds.

The Yantarnaya Komnata *or Amber Room in Catherine's Palace remained intact for nearly two centuries until WWII, when the Germans dismantled and shipped the panels out of the country, never to be found again. More than 500,000 pieces of amber were used to reconstruct a near replica of the famous Amber Room, which opened to the public in 2003 for St Petersburg's 300th anniversary.*

Inside Catherine's Palace, the Great Hall of Light measures nearly 1,000 square meters. With gilded stucco decorating the walls, the entire ceiling is covered by an immense fresco entitled 'The Triumph of Russia.'

A replica of one of Empress Elizabeth I's many resplendent ball gowns.

The luxurious White Dining Room in Catherine's Palace with a traditional blue-and-white tiled stove in the corner.

The Green Dining Room was designed by Charles Cameron, a Scottish architect, for Paul I and his wife. The room's pistachio-colored walls are lined with stucco figures by Russian sculptor, Ivan Martos.

In the Great Hall, a couple dance in period costumes by the large arched and mirrored windows.

(above, left & top right) The Alexander Palace at Tsarskoye Selo was built by Catherine the Great for her grandson, the future Alexander I, and presented to him for his marriage. The last Czar, Nicholas II, preferred it as his primary residence. The family would often take tea with Rasputin in the Maple Drawing Room with the polar bear rug. After Nicholas II abdicated in March 1917, the family lived here under house arrest for six months.

(right) The estate at Strelna was first created by Peter the Great in 1706, and completed by Paul I in 1797 for his second son. Today, after being fully restored, the complex is known as the Palace of Congresses, used to host government functions. Over 50 rooms are open to the public, including permanent art collections. A Monument to Peter the Great stands in front.

The Palace of Paul I, Pavlovsk, is filled with statues, tapestries and hand-painted ceramics. (top left) The Empress' Bedroom was modeled after a state bedroom in Versailles. The bed was crafted in Paris by the Jacob studio. The floor is inlaid with arabesque designs that mirror the painted ceiling. (bottom right) The royal family's private chapel.

(top) The royal bedchamber of Paul I and his wife Maria Fyodorovna contains an elegant four-poster bed by Henri Jacob, and the famous Sèvres toilet service, gifted to them by Marie Antoinette, during their visit to Paris in 1782.

(bottom) Paul I (son of Catherine the Great) had the Gatchina Palace redesigned to look like a medieval castle. Later, Alexander III, after an assassination attempt, made the fortified estate into his permanent residence. Today, the complex is open as a museum.

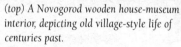

(top) A Novogorod wooden house-museum interior, depicting old village-style life of centuries past.

(middle) Situated outside of Novgorod is the Open Air Museum of Wooden Architecture, filled with log buildings and old izba cottages, dating back to the 16th-century.

(right) Anna Akhmatova (1889–1966) was one of St Petersburg's legendary poets. This portrait of her was painted by Natan Altman in 1914. Earlier, during a trip to Paris in 1910, she befriended the artist Amedeo Modigliani who, enamored with her beauty, frequently sketched her portrait. She is buried in the village of Komarovo, near Repino (see page 675, special topic).

VICINITY OF ST PETERSBURG

If you have time, it is well worth planning on making a few excursions outside of St Petersburg. Day trips to Peter the Great's Summer Palace on the Gulf of Finland, or to the towns of Tsarskoye Selo and Pavlovsk are highly recommended. Here are 15 areas from which to choose.

A two, three or five day electronic Petersburg City Smart Card offers visits to more than 40 museums around St Petersburg and its environs, along with discounted transportation and other tours. www.petersburgcard.com.

PETERHOF (Петергоф) OR PETRODVORETS (Петродворец)

Peterhof is located 30 kilometers (20 miles) west of the city, on the shores of the Gulf of Finland. Peter the Great named his imperial residence Peterhof; but during World War II its name was dutifully Russianized to Petrodvorets (Peter's Palace). Even though the name reverted back to Peterhof in 1992, many still refer to the area as Petrodvorets.

While Peter the Great was supervising the building of the Kronstadt fortress, he stayed in a small lodge on the southern shore of the Gulf of Finland. After Russia defeated the Swedes in the Battle of Poltava in 1709, Peter decided to build his summer residence, Peterhof, so that it not only commemorated the victory over Sweden (and of gaining access to the Baltic), but also the might of the Russian Empire. The design of Peterhof was greatly influenced by Louix XIV's Palace of Versailles in France.

Unfortunately, one ticket does not grant entry to all Peterhof sights. A visitor must first buy a ticket to enter the grounds, and then pay an entry fee for each additional museum—there are more than 15 in all. (A foreigner is charged more than a Russian; and a photo/video permit is an extra fee.) If arriving by hydrofoil, buy a park entrance ticket by the pier; one can also buy a map of the park at kiosk entrances. For more information, see the website: www.peterhofmuseum.ru. Online you can buy a ticket to the Lower Park (but need to print it out to gain entrance) and decide what museums you would like to visit. With a Petersburg Smart Card, visitors get free admission to the Lower Park. (From mid-October through end of April the City Card also grants free admission to the Grand and Cottage Palaces.) You can also buy a Card at special kiosks marked with a Petersburg Card Logo.

The Palace Grounds are open daily 9am–8pm (Saturday till 9pm), and most exhibits from 10.30am–6pm. (Ticket offices usually close an hour earlier.) Museums are closed on different days (see each individual listing below), but all are open Thursday through Sunday. The Grand Palace is closed Mondays and the last Tuesday of each month. For foreign groups and individuals the Grand Palace is open 10:30am–noon and 2:30pm–4:15pm, so make sure and come here first—for it gets quite crowded in summer months. (Tickets are sold near the lobby, and any photography/video is forbidden.) Fountains operate from 10am–6pm (till 8:50pm on Saturday and 7pm on Sunday); launch of the Great Cascade is daily at 11am. (The fountains and some of the smaller palaces are closed between October 15 and April 30.) In summer, it is advised to cover up or bring along mosquito repellent, as the palace grounds and fountains tend to attract swarms of them.

GETTING THERE

The most enjoyable and convenient way to Peterhof is by hydrofoil. From May to September (daily every 20 minutes from 9:30am; the last leaves Peterhof at 7pm), the *Rocket* or *Meteor* jets across the Gulf of Finland to the Peterhof Marine Canal in less than 30 minutes. Catch the hydrofoil at the pier right in front of the Hermitage Museum (and buy a round-trip to avoid long ticket lines on the return).

You can also travel on a commuter train from Baltic (Baltiisky) Railway Station (Metro Baltiiskaya) to Novy Peterhof (not Stary Peterhof); they depart every half hour or so, and the trip takes 40 minutes. From the station it is then about a 20-minute walk north to the palace grounds.

To build Peterhof, Peter the Great summoned architects from around the world: Rastrelli, Leblond, Michetti, Braunstein and the Russian, Mikhail Zemtsov. Over 4,000 peasants and soldiers were brought in to dig the canals, gardens and parks in the marshy area. Soil, building materials and tens of thousands of trees were brought in by barge. Peter helped to draft the layout of all the gardens and fountains—built by Vasily Tuvolkov, Russia's first hydraulics engineer. Over 20 kilometers (12 miles) of canals were constructed in such a way that 30,000 liters (7,925 gallons) of water flowed under its own pressure to 144 fountains—quite a marvel for its time.

Leading up from the hydrofoil pier is Water Avenue, crisscrossed by bridges and water sprays as it leads up to the famous **Cascade Fountain**. Crowning the front of the palace, it has 17 waterfalls, 142 water jets, 66 fountains (including the two cup fountains on either side), 29 bas-reliefs and 39 gilded statues, all of which have allegorical significance. The Russians won the Battle of Poltava on June 27, 1709— St Sampson's Day. The five-ton **Sampson** wrestles open the jaws of a lion (a symbol for conquering Sweden for a lion was featured on the country's coat of arms) with his bare hands. From the lion's gaping jaws a jet of water shoots over 21 meters (70 feet) into the air, first unveiled by Rastrelli in 1735 to commemorate the 25th Anniversary of Russia's victory over Sweden. The eight dolphins around the feet of Sampson represent the peace of the sea. Around the rock pedestal stand the heads

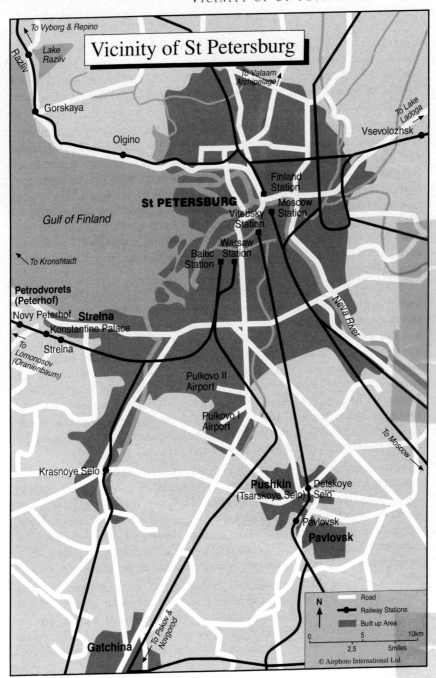

Vicinity of St Petersburg

To Vyborg & Repino

Lake Razliv

Razliv

Gorskaya

Olgino

To Valaam Archipelago

St PETERSBURG

Finland Station

Moscow Station

Vitebsky Station

To Lake Ladoga

Vsevolozhsk

Gulf of Finland

Warsaw Station

Baltic Station

To Kronshtadt

Neva River

Petrodvorets (Peterhof)

Novy Peterhof   **Strelna**

Konstantine Palace

To Lomonosov (Oranienbaum)

Strelna

Pulkovo II Airport

Pulkovo I Airport

To Moscow

Krasnoye Selo

Pushkin (Tsarskoye Selo)

Detskoye Selo

Pavlovsk

Pavlovsk

N

Road
Railway Stations
Built up Area

0   5   10km

2.5   5miles

To Pskov & Novgorod

Gatchina

© Airphoto International Ltd

of four lions (the four points of the compass) that symbolize the universal glory of Russia's might. (Water from the Cascade Fountain launches daily at 11am.) Each May, the official opening of the fountains at Peterhof is an all-day festival, with classical music and fireworks blasting, as each section of the park's fountains is turned on one by one.

On the upper grotto, the Tritons, gods of the sea, blow trumpet fountains heralding the victory. And on the central terrace flows the Basket fountain, signifying wealth and abundance. Around the lower terrace stands the mythological hero Perseus, representing the mighty Peter the Great himself, who had conquered the Medusa-like enemy. At the reservoir that surrounds the Great Cascade, look for the **Favoritny Fountain**, slightly hidden by the western colonnade. Four brightly painted ducks chase the dog, named Favoritka. If you listen closely you can hear the quacking of the ducks and the dog barking. The **Grottoes of the Grand Cascade** are open daily 11am–6pm; the **Museum of Fountain Matters** from 10:30am–6pm; closed Mondays.

Fountains also grace the back of the palace. The first, in the Upper Park, is known as the **Mezheumny**. A dragon with spread wings stands in the center pool surrounded by four dolphins. Since this fountain has often changed its appearance, its name actually means 'vague.' The center fountain is that of **Neptune** (set up in 1799), who holds a trident, signifying his dominion over the seas. Four water-breathing sea monsters stand along his pedestal and other riders on winged sea horses direct eight dolphins that swim along the walls of the fountain. These fountains were brought to Russia from Nuremberg, Germany. The next fountain in the Upper Park is that of the **Oak Fountain**. Originally appearing as an Oak Tree, it now contains a marble statue of Cupid. Right by the walls of the Palace are the **Square Ponds**, flanked by statues of Apollo and Venus.

The upper and lower parks and gardens cover over 120 hectares (300 acres), stretching around the palace to the Gulf of Finland. When warm, it is wonderful to have a picnic (bring one with) on the grounds or beach, stroll in the gardens, and spend the entire day here. In June during the White Nights, a variety of festivals and musical concerts are held on the palace grounds. (During the time of the czars, the city's inhabitants were invited here for one day a year to celebrate the festival of the summer solstice. Fireworks were set off from pontoons along the lake.)

After a stroll around the grounds, it is time to visit its centerpiece, the **Grand Palace**. To enter it is mandatory to join a group tour, which are held in different languages. If you cannot find one in English, join any tour and once inside, you can slip off on your own (do not let the feisty guards at the door deter you). Tickets are sold in the lobby where you pick up your *ta'pochki* (slippers) to put over your shoes. The Grand Palace is open 10.30am–6pm, closed on Mondays and the last Tuesday

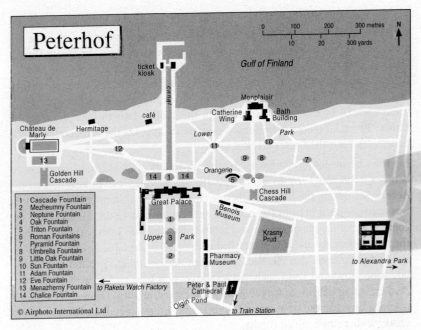

Peterhof

- Gulf of Finland
- ticket kiosk
- canal
- café
- Monplaisir
- Catherine Wing
- Bath Building
- Château de Marly
- Hermitage
- Lower Park
- Golden Hill Cascade
- Orangerie
- Chess Hill Cascade
- Great Palace
- Benois Museum
- Krasny Prud
- Upper Park
- Pharmacy Museum
- to Raketa Watch Factory
- Peter & Paul Cathedral
- to Alexandra Park
- Olgin Pond
- to Train Station

1 Cascade Fountain
2 Mezheumny Fountain
3 Neptune Fountain
4 Oak Fountain
5 Triton Fountain
6 Roman Fountains
7 Pyramid Fountain
8 Umbrella Fountain
9 Little Oak Fountain
10 Sun Fountain
11 Adam Fountain
12 Eve Fountain
13 Menazherny Fountain
14 Chalice Fountain

© Airphoto International Ltd

of the month. For foreign groups and individuals, tours are conducted between 10:30am–noon and 2:30pm–4:15pm.

The **Grand Palace** was built between 1714 and 1724, designed by Friedrich, Michetti and Leblond in classical and baroque styles. It stands on a hill in the center of the Peterhof complex and overlooks the parks and gardens. Later, architect Francesco Rastrelli (son of sculptor Carlo Rastrelli) made changes and added larger wings (1747–54) for Empress Elizabeth. After Peter's death, the palace passed on to subsequent czars and was declared a museum after the revolution.

The palace is three stories high with over 30 rooms that contain the numerous galleries. The central exhibition rooms lead to **Peter the Great's Oak Study** and on to the **Royal Bedchamber**. The rooms have magnificent parquet floors, gilded ceilings and crystal chandeliers, and are filled with exquisite *objets d'art* from around the world. (Most of these pieces are original, as they were removed from the palace before the German occupation.) The Cavalier or **Crimson Room** has furniture by Chippendale. The walls of the **Oak Study** are adorned with portraits of Empress Elizabeth, Catherine the Great and Alexander I. From the Dressing Rooms and Lounge, you enter the **Partridge Chamber,** so named for the silk ornamental partridges that covered the walls. It is decorated with 18th-century French silk-upholstered furniture, porcelain and clocks.

The **Portrait Gallery**, in the central hall of the palace, is filled with portraits by such painters as Pietro Rotari (the whole collection was acquired by Catherine the Great) and serves as an interesting catalog of period costumes. The **White Dining Hall**, once used for State dinners, is decorated in classical style with white molded figures on the walls and a crystal and amethyst chandelier. The table is ceremoniously laid out for 30 people with 196 pieces of cream-colored English porcelain, commissioned by Catherine the Great. In the 1750s, Rastrelli built the adjacent **Throne Room** for official receptions. A portrait of Catherine the Great on horseback hangs over Peter the Great's first throne.

The **Chesme Room** commemorates the war victory of Russia over Turkey, fought between 1768 and 1774. In 1770, Russia finally defeated the Turkish fleet in the Aegean Sea during the battle of Chesme Bay. The German artist Philippe Hackert was commissioned to paint the victory scenes for the hall. Count Alexei Orlov (the commander of the famous battle and brother of Catherine's lover, Grigori) checked the artist's sketches and was dissatisfied with one that depicted an exploding ship. Hackert mentioned that he had never seen such a thing. So Orlov ordered a 60-cannon Russian frigate, anchored off the coast of Italy, packed with gunpowder. Hackert had to journey to Italy to witness the exploding ship. The rest of the palace is joined by numerous galleries and studies, and at the east end is a Rastrelli rococo chapel with a single gilded cupola.

Hitler invaded Russia on June 22, 1941. When the Nazis reached Peterhof on September 23, many of the art pieces and statues had still not been evacuated. The German army spent 900 days here and virtually destroyed the complex. Monplaisir was an artillery site, used to shell Leningrad. The Germans cut down 15,000 trees for firewood, used tapestries in the trenches, plundered over 34,000 works of art and made off with priceless objects, including the Sampson statue, which was never recovered. After the war massive restoration work began, and on June 17, 1946, the fountains flowed once again. The Sampson statue was restored, according to surviving pre-war photos, and was returned to its former site the following year. The head of the Hermitage, Joseph Orbelli, who lived in the museum during the siege, remarked: 'Even during our worst suffering, we knew that the day would come when once again the beautiful fountains of Petrodvorets would begin to spray and the statues of the park flash their golden gleam in the sunlight.' There are black-and-white photographs on display in the Exhibition Room that show the extensive damage to the palace. Every year, at the end of August, the Sampson Holiday is marked on the day when the statue was returned to Peterhof.

Leningrad poet Olga Bergholts visited Peterhof after the siege and wrote:

> *Again from the black dust, from the place*
> *of death and ashes, will arise the garden as before.*
> *So it will be. I firmly believe in miracles.*
> *You gave me that belief, my Leningrad.*

Exiting the palace, walk right (east) down the main walkway to 8 Dvortzovaya Square and the **Benois Museum**, designed by Nikolai Benois. This building includes works by the architect Benois (1813–90) and other generations of the Benois family. Nikolai became the godson of Empress Maria Fyodorovna, and was educated at her expense (his father was Paul I's French chef). His son, Alexander, became a famous stage designer and artist who worked with Serge Diaghilev in the Mariinsky (his maternal grandfather Albert Kavos built this theater) and on the World of Art magazine, *Mir Iskusstva*. In 1914, the Benois family sold to the Hermitage Museum the famous Benois *Madonna*, painted by Leonardo da Vinci; it had been in the family for four generations, and is said to have been originally purchased in Astrakhan. (The British actor, Peter Ustinov, was related to the Benois family.) The museum is open 12:30pm–5pm, closed Mondays.

The **Apothecary Museum and Herbarium** was once the center for growing medicinal herbs for the royal family. Today, it still serves as a functioning pharmacy and a staff member can prepare herbal teas and tonics. The five-domed **Peter and Paul Cathedral**, at number 32 St Petersburg Prospekt, was built in the 1890s, and is slowly being restored (it was used as a Soviet-era movie cinema).

Strolling back down towards the Gulf, head west to the two-story **Château de Marly**, built between 1719 and 1723 by German architect Johann Friedrich Braunstein in the style of Louis XIV. (Peter I had visited the hunting-lodge palace of the French Kings in Marly-le-Roi.) The balconies' wrought-iron railings are emblazoned with the monogram of Peter the Great. This palace is open 10:30am–6pm, closed Mondays. In front of it flows the **Golden Hill Cascade**, commissioned in 1721 by Peter the Great and built by Italian architect Niccolo Michetti. All the mythological gods and goddesses that adorn the walls glorify the bounty of Russia's achievements. The front fountain, with its two huge jets, is known as the **Menazherny**, from the French *ménager*, to economize.

Heading east down the path leads to the two-story baroque-style structure known as the **Hermitage Pavilion**, built in 1725 by Braunstein from the designs of Peter the Great. The retreat was surrounded by a moat and had a drawbridge that could be raised to further isolate the guests. The first floor consisted of one room with a large dining table that could be lifted from or lowered to servants on the ground floor below. The guests placed their written food orders on the table, rang a bell, and then it would be lowered and lifted with their requests. In 1797, when Paul I got stuck in the lift ascending to the first floor, he ordered an oak staircase built but it has since been replaced. Today, the building houses over 100 paintings by 18th-century European artists. It is open daily 10:30am–6pm, closed Tuesdays. The **Lifting Table** operates Saturday and Sunday at 1pm, 2pm, and 3pm. The **Lion Cascade Fountain** stands near the front of the Hermitage.

Crossing the canal, continue east to **Monplaisir**, built between 1710 and 1723. While the Grand Palace was under construction, Peter lived in this seven-room Dutch-style villa that he called Monplasisir (My Pleasure), situated beside the waters of the Gulf of Finland. Even after the larger palace was completed, Peter preferred to stay in this smaller and cozier brick abode while he visited Peterhof.

At the entrance, in the garden, stands the Wheatsheaf fountain and the four gilded statues of Psyche, Apollo, Faun and Bacchus—all basically designed (including Monplaisir) by Peter himself. Rooms include the Lacquered Study, the Ceremonial Hall, Peter the Great's Naval Study, his Bedroom (the patch-work quilt on the bed, and the Chinese-dressing gown and nightcap are said to have belonged to the czar) and the Dutch-tiled kitchen. The complex is open daily 10.30am–6pm (May 24 to October 13); closed the first Monday of each month. (The ticket kassa is along the western side of the palace.)

In 1762, when Catherine the Great's husband, Peter III, threatened divorce (his mistress was the pock-marked Elizaveta Vorontsova), the empress came to live in a building adjoining Monplasir. (In the 1740's, Elizabeth I had the original Tea House demolished and rebuilt by Francesco Rastrelli to stage large balls and receptions.) On July 28 1762, the day of their planned coup, Catherine's lover, Count Grigori Orlov, picked her up here from Peterhof. Soon after, Czar Peter was mysteriously strangled in his sleep (probably instigated by the Orlov brothers). The whole army came out to pledge its allegiance to Catherine when she returned to the Winter Palace. Today, it is known as **Catherine's Wing** with exhibits of historical items in its large rooms that include the Yellow Hall, and bedroom and study of Alexander I. This building is open 10.30am–6pm, and closed the last Thursday of each month. The **Bath Wing** stands at the opposite eastern end of Monplaisir, built in 1865 for the wife of Alexander II (open 10:30am–6pm; closed Wednesdays). The adjacent **Assembly Hall**, designed by Zemtsov in 1726, has exhibits of 18th-century Russian tapestries.

Exiting Catherine's Wing, walk along the southwest path to the **Adam Fountain**. This statue was brought to Russia from Venice by Peter the Great in 1718. On the other side of the Marine Canal stands the **Eve Fountain**, also fashioned from marble by the Venetian sculptor, Giovanni Bonazza.

Heading east from the Adam Fountain, you will pass the **Monument to Peter the Great**, crafted by a Russian sculptor in 1884. The next pond contains the **Sun Fountain** with 16 golden dolphins. The interior golden disks slowly rotate with 72 jets of water, creating the effect of golden rays streaming from the sun. The **Pyramid Fountain** is down the southeast path. Peter the Great designed this water pyramid, consisting of seven tiers and 505 jets. The center of the area consists of many trick fountains. A circular seat is positioned under the **Little Umbrella Fountain**. If you are tempted to have a short rest on the bench under the umbrella, be ready to scramble—as 164 jets spray out water as soon as anyone sits down! As you scamper away, you will approach the **Little Oak Fountain**, which has dozens of hidden jets (as do the artificial tulips) that spray as any weight approaches the oak tree. When you run off to the nearby bench to catch your breath, you will now get drenched by 41 more jets! And beware, too, of the **Three Fir Trees**!

Walking south towards the palace brings you to two **Roman Fountains**, built by Karl Blank and Ivan Davydov in 1739. They were modeled after those at the Cathedral of St Peter in Rome. In front of these, **Chess Hill**, with a checkerboard design, contains some of the best waterfalls, cascading over bronze dragons, and flanked by marble figures of mythological heroes. The **Triton Fountain** (Neptune's son) presides over the semi-circular **Orangerie**, once used as a greenhouse; it is now the Grand Orangerie restaurant.

One can grab a bite to eat at numerous cafés on the grounds. Besides the Grand Orangerie, off the main Marine Pier, located down the western path, is the **Shtandart Restaurant**, an upscale eatery that overlooks the Gulf of Finland. www.restaurantshtandart.spb.ru. Inside the Grand Palace is the the Kafe Dvortsovoye, and the Monplasir Café is situated next to Peter's retreat.

After a brief respite continue east along any of the main paths to **Alexandra Park**, developed by Nicholas I and his wife, after whom the park is named; the park is open daily 9am–10pm. Near the park entrance stands the Gothic-style **Court Chapel** (with 43 saints along the outer walls), built in 1831 as the Czar's private chapel. The **Cottage Palace** was designed in 1829 by Adam Menelaws to resemble an aristocratic Englishman's cottage. During WWII, the museum staff saved 1,981 of the 2,500 pieces in the cottage and these are on exhibit today. Some of the rooms to be visited are the Studies of Empress Alexandra Fyodorovna and Nicholas I, the Library, Dining Hall, Reception Halls, and the classroom of their son, the future Alexander II (full of interesting daguerreotypes). The last building in this area is the **Farm Palace**, originally used as a storage house, but later converted into a summer palace by Alexander II. All are open 10:30am–6pm; closed Mondays. Nearby is the building of the **Imperial Telegraph Station**, constructed in 1858 by the architect Andrei Stackenschneider; the station formed part of the Kronstadt electromagnetic telegraph line. Open 10:30am–6pm; closed Mondays.

If you still have time and energy, walk to the town of Peterhof. To begin, the main street of Pravlenskaya runs along the east side of the Grand Palace and Upper Gardens. At number 4 is the **Museum of Playing Cards**, housed in the former 18th-century headquarters of the palace administration where over eight thousand objects are spread out over six rooms; one of the oldest exhibits is the Pack with Hawkers, dating to 1690. The cards come in all sizes and shapes (rectangular, oval, and zigzag). Visitors can also see packs used for bezique, bridge, whist and fortune-telling from countries around the world.

The **St Peter and Paul Cathedral**, built in 1751 by Elizabeth I, stands at the opposite end of the street with the Church Building Museum; closed Mondays. Here, Tsarevich Alexei, the last heir to the Russian throne, was baptized. Continue south and walk left around **Olgin Pond** to the **Tsaritsyn** and **Olgin Pavillions**, which sit on islands in the middle of the pond. Recently restored, they were built by Nicholas I for his wife and daughter, Olga Nikolayevna. Heading west down St Peterbursky Prospekt to number 60 brings you to the **Raketa Petrodvorets Watch Factory**, the area's oldest factory founded by Peter the Great in 1721. It has a great little shop that sells a variety of watches. (Closed Sat/Sun) www.raketa.su or www.raketa.com.

The **Belveder Peterhof**, a 3-star hotel with 22 rooms, is located in Lugovoi Park, a ten-minute taxi ride from Peterhof Palace. The **New Peterhof** is a 4-star hotel with 150 rooms also near the park and palace.

STRELNA

On the way to or from Peterhof from St Petersburg, a visitor may consider making a stop at the baroque **Konstantin Palace at Strelna**, located only 6 kilometers east of Peterhof. If you go by *elektrichka* train from the Baltiisky Station, get off at Strelna. Exit the station, make a right to the road and cross, then make another right down to the bus stop. Take bus 163 four stops to the Palace. After two stops you will pass an old residence of Peter the Great—the small yellow building on the other side of the street.

Strelna was first mentioned in Peter the Great's 1706-campaign journal when he ordered a wooden house built here as a stopping place. After the Swedes were defeated, work began on the estate. In 1716, under the supervision of Carlo Rastrelli, the marshy shore was first drained and then three canals were dug from the upper terrace to the sea. The architects Leblond and Michetti drew up plans for the park and Big Strelna Palace. But, Peter slowly lost interest in Strelna as he began directing his efforts to build Peterhof.

Over the years, the palace was never fully completed until, in 1797, Paul I presented the estate to his second son, Grand Duke Konstantin Pavlovich, when the palace became known as Konstantinovsky Dvorets. In turn, Alexander II then gifted it to his younger brother, Konstantin Nikolayevich. The palace and grounds were practically destroyed during the WWII German occupation, and then left to languish during the Soviet period. President Putin gave the order for the complex to be restored into a Presidential Palace for the 2003 St Petersburg tercentennial. Over $200 million was collected from charitable contributions, and a medley of architects, restorers and water engineers worked together (from old photographs and plans) to restore the palace and grounds. Twenty bridges were built, including three drawbridges connecting the park with Peter Island where the Pavilion of Negotiations stands on the original location of Leblond's Temple of Water. The Romanov coat-of-arms is on the palace's restored front façade, and a **Monument to Peter the Great** stands out in front. It's a lovely stroll about the grounds and along the Upper English Park, ponds and numerous canals. (See page 621.)

Today, the palace is known as the Palace of Congresses, and is used to host myriad government functions. When no state affairs are taking place, part of the palace's 50 or so rooms are open to the public. The central **Marble Hall** is decorated with yellow marble pilasters set amongst blue marble walls. Opposite is the **Blue Hall** with blue and mirrored ornamentations, and next door the pink **Oval Hall** is used for official meetings. The Billiard Room was always popular; Peter the Great introduced the game after he visited Holland. The wine cellar, dating back to 1755, contains over 13,000 bottles. On the third floor, a spiral staircase leads to an observation deck with breathtaking views of the grounds and Gulf of Finland.

In 2007, after the death of her husband, acclaimed cellist Mstislav Rostropovich, Galina Vishnevskaya put up for sale their unique art collection, which includes antique furniture, porcelain and works by artists such as Serov, Bryullov, Roerich and Repin. Russian billionaire, Alisher Usmanov, purchased it for $72 million and donated it to Russia. Today, this collection is part of a permanent display at the Palace that also includes other 18th- and 19th- century Russian paintings and decorative art works.

In 2008, the St Petersburg Konstantinovsky Charitable Fund (controlled by the office of the President) purchased the unique Lobanov-Rostovsky Russian Theater Art Collection, comprised of over 800 pieces of Russian stage and costume design devoted to the period between 1890 and 1930. Many of the works were made especially for Diaghilev's Ballets Russes and include costumes, drawings, paintings, posters and watercolors. Plans are to build a special venue near the Konstantinovsky Palace to exhibit the collection.

A visitor can buy a ticket just to enter the park and grounds. Excursions of the park are offered Thurs–Sun from 12:30pm–3pm. The Palace is open 10am–6pm; closed Wednesdays; group tours only. Tours in English are often available from noon to 6pm. www.konstaninpalace.ru. If continuing on to Peterhof, exit the Palace, make a right, and go down a few blocks to the bus stop, and take bus 352.

Peter the Great's Wooden Palace, nearby at 2 Bolnichnaya Gorka, was built in 1716 as a temporary residence. Today, it houses a small museum on the History of Strelna. Open 10.30am–6pm; closed Mondays. The **Trinity-Sergius Monastery**, also known as the Czar's Monastery, has a restored interior, originally modeled after St Catherine's Monastery in the Sinai. It also contains many aristocratic graves including that of Zinaida Yusupova, the mother of Count Yusupov who participated in the murder of Rasputin.

If you want to sleep like a czar, stay at the nearby **Baltic Star Hotel**; besides rooms, the facility also offers VIP cottages on the shore of the Gulf of Finland with a sauna and swimming pool. www.balticstar-hotel.com.

ORANIENBAUM (ОРАНИЕНБАУМ) OR LOMONOSOV (ЛОМОНОСОВ)

Oranienbaum, also known as Lomonosov, is situated only 10 kilometers (six miles) west of Peterhof on the Gulf of Finland, at 48 Yunovo Lenintsa. In 1707, while Peter the Great was building Monplaisir, he gave these lands to his close friend Prince Alexander Menschikov to develop. Menschikov was the first governor-general of St Petersburg and supervised the building of the nearby Kronstadt Fortress. (For his palace in the city see pages 59/64/520.) He wanted to turn the estate into his summer residence. Since the prince planted orange trees in the lower parks (first grown in hothouses), he named his residence Oranienbaum, German for Orange Tree. The first palace here was constructed in the 1710s, designed by Giovanni Fontana. Several years later Peter the Great came to visit Menschikov by ship, but because of the swampy shoreline, he was unable to land. Thus, in three days, Menshikov had a sea canal dug, over a mile long, from the palace to the sea, so that Peter could sail up to the palace.

Unfortunately Menschikov never fully enjoyed this estate—he ended up in Siberian exile three years after Peter I's death. The property was briefly made into a hospital before Peter III preferred living here to the Winter Palace. After Peter's death in 1762, his wife, Sophie Frederica Augusta von Anhalt-Zerbst-Dornburg (Catherine the Great) expanded the buildings and grounds around Rococo architecture and made it her private pleasure abode. Oranienbaum became the center of masked balls and parties that entertained Russian royalty and foreign

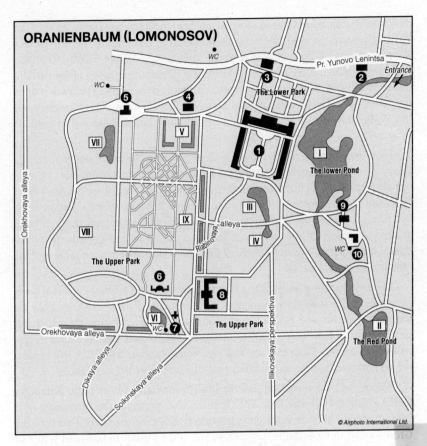

1   The Great Menshikov Palace

2   The Lower Houses

3   The Picture House

4   The Stone Hall

5   The Coasting Hill Pavilon

6   The Chinese Palace

7   The Chinese Kitchen Pavilon

8   The Countiers-in-Attendance Pavilon

9   The Honorary Gate

10 The Palace of Peter III

I   The Lower Pond

II   The Red Pond

III The Carp's Pond

IV   The Houseshoe-shaped Pond

V   The Pond near the Stone Hall

VI   The Pond near the Chinese Palace

VII The Pond near the Sliding Hill Pavilion

VIII The Figured Pondies

IX   The Crescent-shaped Pond

diplomats. It continued to be used by members of the Romanov family up until the 1917 Revolution. In 1948, the name was changed to Lomonosov after the famous Russian scientist who had a glassworks and mosaic factory nearby. (For the Lomonosov Museum see page 519.) The estate fortunately escaped major shelling during WWII and today restoration work continues on the palaces. The park is open daily 9am–8pm. The Menshikov Palace is open 10:30am–6pm; closed Tuesdays and last Wednesday of each month. (The Peter III and Chinese Palaces are closed on Mondays.)

There are a number of ways to get to Oranienbaum. The train from Petrodvorets (Novy Peterhof) is about four stops and a 20-minute ride to 'Lomonosov'. (A local bus also leaves for Oranienbaum next to the rail station, and there is a ferry from Kronstadt.) A commuter *elektrichka* train leaves Baltiisky (Baltic) Station in St Petersburg to Lomonosov and takes an hour. From Lomonosov station, walk southwest across the park, and keep going up the main road towards the green-domed Cathedral of Archangel Michael. From here, the park entrance is on your left (about a 10-minute walk).

The path into the park leads to a lake where visitors can sunbathe and rent boats in summer. The two-story baroque-style **Menshikov Palace**, built in 1725 by architects Fontana and Schädel, stands atop the hill overlooking the parks and formal gardens that were originally designed by Antonio Rinaldi. Three rooms house the exhibit, 'Oranienbaum and its Owners from 1720–1917.' The copper-roofed Japanese Pavilion also exhibits paintings and other works of art.

West of the palace, walking past the small **Stone Hall** leads up to the **Katalnaya Gorka** (Sliding Hill) **Pavilion**. This brilliant blue pyramid, the forerunner of a modern amusement ride, is the only structure of its kind in the world. Catherine the Great wanted to toboggan in summer, so she asked Rinaldi to construct a ride so that she and her guests could roller coaster along a long wooden tract, with hills and dips, from the pavilion's third floor balcony down through the lower gardens. The ground floor of the pavilion has a model of the original Sliding Hill, and the rococo-style Round Hall has a porcelain exhibit. The 1760s faux marble floors are the last example of its kind, since the process of how to produce this gypsum-based material has been lost.

A five-minute walk down the southern path leads to the Rococo-style **Chinese Palace** (Kitaisky-Dvorets), also built by Rinaldi from 1762–68. The palace gets its name from the sumptuous decorations of the rooms and halls. Hand-carved furniture, parquet floors, porcelain, portraits and paintings detail every room. Each painted ceiling was the work of masters from the Venetian Academy of the Arts. The designer Alexander Benois commented: 'The Chinese Palace is a pearl, the only one of its kind, a work of art ... with a purely musical effect of its own that has something in common with the sonatas of Haydn and Mozart.' The tour through the palace runs wing-to-wing from the rooms of Catherine the Great's then seven-year-old son, the future Paul I, across to Catherine's private suites. The central State Rooms include the Blue and Pink Drawing Rooms, Billiard Room, Hall of Muses and Damask Bedchamber. Nine seamstresses spent a year and a half embroidering ten panels with different colored silk and chenille for the Glass Bugle (glass beads) Study, with bases made from mother-of-pearl bugles. Mikhail Lomonosov created the mosaic furniture, decorated with opaque glass. The **Large Chinese Hall** pays homage to the fascination with the Orient and what was imagined at the time to be the style of the art of China. It is decorated with Chinese furniture and beautiful inlaid wooden chinoiserie-style walls. The exterior **Chinese Kitchens** stand adjacent to the old Cavalry Barracks. The complex is open 10:30am–6pm; closed Mondays and last Tuesday of the month (and from October to May). In between the Chinese and Peter III Palaces is the small **Deer Park** where deer are reared for eventual release onto the grounds.

Continue east through the Upper Park to the **Palace of Peter III**, another Rinaldi creation, built in 1752, and dubbed Peterstadt. Before Catherine's husband, Peter III, was assassinated in 1762, he had constructed here a model fort filled with thousands of toy soldiers. He also loved to drill and parade thousands of real soldiers about the grounds in strict Prussian disciplinary fashion around the **Honorary Gate**, which still stands today. His love of the military rubbed off on his son Paul, as well. Today, the second floor contains a Picture Hall and exquisitely lacquered panels and doors. Open 10:30am–6pm; closed Mondays. (It often closes during winter months.) The **Okhota** (Hunt) is the main restaurant in the area, situated on the road facing the main entrance at 64 Dvortsovy Prospekt; as its name suggests, game is the specialty on the menu.

The **Lomonosov Porcelain Factory** was founded in 1744 by Elizabeth I, Peter the Great's daughter, as Russia's first porcelain enterprise. The factory (named after the influential Russian writer and scientist Mikhail Lomonosov) was run by another scientist, Dmitry Vinogradov, who had invented a mass means of ceramic production. Eventually renamed the Imperial Porcelain Factory by Catherine the Great, the facility came to produce most of the imperial porcelain, including table settings and miniature items; and it went on to become one of the leading porcelain enterprises in all of Europe. Alexander I (1777–1825) ordered the famous Gurievsky dinner setting, celebrating Russia's 1812 victory over Napoleon; it included 4500 pieces which were gilded with several kilos of gold. The Imperial Porcelain Factory survived the Soviet period, and it still creates over 500 different items. The *cobalt net* blue and white pattern became the Factory's trademark. On the factory site is a Museum (closed Mondays), exhibiting objects produced from the mid 18th-century through today (other famous porcelain settings are also on display in the Hermitage Museum). In St Petersburg, the Imperial Porcelain Factory is located at 151 Obukhovskoy Oborony Prospekt, metro Lomonovskaya; open daily from 10am–8pm. www.ipm.ru or www.lomonosov-russia.com.

KRONSTADT (Кронштадт)

When Peter the Great founded St Petersburg in 1703, the Great Northern War (1700–1721) with the Swedes was in its early stages. To protect the gulf approach to his city, Peter began building the Kronstadt (German for 'Crown City') Fort in 1704. Located 29 km (18 miles) west of the city, it soon became one of the mightiest fortresses along the Baltic coast. Its construction, in the narrowest part of the Finnish Gulf, was overseen by Prince Menschikov and designer Domenico Trezzini. The brick canal, begun in 1719, was fitted with docks for building and repairing ships. By 1723, the fortress on Kotlin Island had grown into a town, designed by Peter I himself.

No work of engineering in Europe could rival the Kronstadt canal. At the time, dry docks could handle only one battleship. The water in the docks was filled and drained by pumps (often taking months), powered by horses or windmills. In contrast, the Kronstadt canal could remarkably contain up to twelve ships at a time, and the docks emptied (and refilled) in a matter of hours with the aid of a special system of discharge and storage ponds. In 1774 windmills were replaced by the largest steam engine in the world. By the start of the Crimean War in 1853, Kronstadt had become the mightiest naval citadel in all of Europe. By the early 20th century the fortresses of Kronstadt included 17 artificial islands and fortified batteries on the north and south shores of the Gulf of Finland.

Monuments on the island are linked to the history of the Russian fleet. On July 26, 1803 Ivan Kruzenshtern set off from Kronstadt to command Russia's first round-the-world expedition. He returned here on August 19, 1806, having sailed over 45,000 nautical miles. These Baltic sailors were always at the forefront of rebellion. During the 1917 revolution, Kronstadt ships, which patrolled the Neva River, played a vital role in the October takeover. Later, in 1921, during the difficult Civil War and famine, the workers of Petrograd were on the brink of revolt. On March 1, 1921, masses gathered in Kronstadt's **Anchor Square** to form their own revolutionary committee against the Bolsheviks. The rebellion lasted for 18 days, when Red Army troops, led by General Tukhachevsky, crossed the ice to capture Kronstadt. About 600 sailors were killed in the bloody assault, 900 were executed and thousands imprisoned. Tukhachevsky wrote in his memoirs: 'It was not a battle, it was an inferno.... The sailors fought like wild beasts, I cannot understand where they found the might for such rage.' During WWII, and siege of Leningrad, garrison, ships and submarines helped fend off violent enemy attacks. Over 6,000 residents were killed by bombings and starvation. Later, in 1990, during the attempted overthrow of Gorbachev, the Kronstadt naval base commander offered to safely house the St Petersburg mayor and the city cabinet. The city's centerpiece, the **St Nicholas's Seaman's Cathedral**, built between 1902–13 in neo-Byzantine style by Vasily Kosyakov (modeled on Constantinople's Hagia Sophia), honors all those sailors who perished at sea and during the Kronstadt rebellion. The 70-meter (230-foot) high cathedral with a 27-meter (88-foot) diameter dome stands on the highest point in Kronstadt. It is decorated with ornamental mosaic murals (many by painter Petrov-Vodkin) and the floors are made of marble set in brass. Today, the church also houses a museum, dedicated to the history of the fortress, which celebrated its 310th anniversary in 2014. Kronstadt town museums are open 11am–5pm; closed Mondays.

Only after 1997 were foreign visitors allowed into this closed military city of 45,000 residents, where some of the country's military and scientific vessels are still docked today. The former Menshikov Palace now hosts a club for island sailors, some of whom also attend the naval academy. At 5 Andreyevskaya is the **Museum of Underwater Diving**, which includes gear from the late 19th century, when Russia opened its first diving school on Kotlin Island.

The **Kronstadt Tide-Gauge** has its origins in a horizontal mark cut into the stone pier of a bridge over the Obvodny Canal that indicates the average water level of the Baltic between 1825 and 1840. Later a gauge for measuring sea level was installed alongside, a zero reading corresponding to the mark. A special float lying on the surface of water in a well (connected to the Gulf of Finland) is linked to a mareograph—a device that automatically records current sea levels of the Baltic. These readings provide the basis for measurements of height across Russia.

Offshore are several forts that were constructed between 1853 and 1856 during the Crimean War. The most interesting is the **Alexander Fort**, whose foundations were first laid in 1839; it was later used as an anti-plague laboratory. Today, it hosts evening dances during the summer White Nights, and yachts from the city also enjoy docking here in warmer months.

From April 25 through October, daily hydrofoils leave hourly from near the Tuchkov Bridge from 9am–6pm; the trip takes 30–40 minutes. Or try taking a local *elektrichka* train from Finland Station to Gorskaya, on the north shore of the Gulf of Finland, and then the ferry across to Kronstadt. An *elektrichka* also leaves from Baltic (Baltiisky) Train Station to Lomonosov, where ferries (or a bus over the dam) depart for the island. From Peterhof, there is a local bus or train to Lomonosov (Oranienbaum).

On the way, notice the 29-kilometer (18-mile) barrier built across a section of the Gulf of Finland (this was the area of the older Finnish border until 1939) to control the floods (over 300 in St Petersburg's history). Tidal waves sweep inland during severe storms. In 1824, the water level rose over four meters (13 feet), killing 569 people.

WEST OF THE CITY (NORTHERN GULF)
RAZLIV (Разлив)

The village of Razliv lies 35 kilometers (22 miles) northwest of St Petersburg on the Karelian Isthmus, near the former Finnish border. Lenin fled here in 1917 to hide from the Provisional Government.

Agents were searching everywhere for him and advertised a reward of 200,000 rubles in gold. Shaving off his trademark beard and wearing a wig, he ventured out at night from Finland Railway Station to the village, and stayed in a barn owned by the Yemelyanov family. The glass-covered barn and family house is now the **Razliv Sarai Museum**, at 3 Yemelyanova, housing some of the things Lenin used. On the outside wall, a plaque reads, 'Here in this barn for a period of several days from July 10, 1917, Vladimir Ilyich Lenin lived and worked while in hiding from the agents of the Provisional Government.'

After a few days of hiding here, Nikolai Yemelyanov rowed Lenin across Lake Razliv and built a hut out of hay for a more secretive shelter. Lenin lived and wrote articles in this *shalash*, or thatched hut, by the lake. The **Shalash Museum**, near the hut, exhibits some of Lenin's personal documents and belongings. Another inscription reads, 'Here in July and August 1917 in a hut made of branches the leader of the October Revolution went into hiding from the sleuths of the bourgeois government.' In August, Lenin left the hut and traveled ten kilometers to Dibuny Station, from where he left for Finland, only to return in October to lead the final stages of the Bolshevik revolution. A tourist boat takes visitors across the lake to the hut. Both museums are open 11am–6pm (in summer till 7pm); closed Wednesdays. www.razlivmuseum.spb.ru.

The easiest way to get here is by *elektrickha* train from Finland Station (about an hour) along the northern shore of the Gulf of Finland toward Sestroretsk; the stop is Razliv (Tarkhovka). Enroute, it is interesting to note the town of Lakta (before Olgino). Peter the Great built a country residence here called Blizniye Dubki (Nearby Oaks). In November 1724, as he was riding along the coast, Peter noticed a ship that was sinking in a storm, and he dove into the icy waters to help rescue the drowning people. As a result the czar became gravely ill and died on January 27, 1725. It was also in Lakta where the enormous boulder was found for the pedestal for the monument of The Bronze Horseman on St Petersburg's Senate Square (see page 534/546).

REPINO (Репино)

The road from Razliv along the Karelian Isthmus leads to Repino (at 411 Primorskoye Hwy), located about 45 kilometers (30 miles) northwest of St Petersburg. Repino is a small town in the Solnechnoye resort area once known as Kurnosovo. It bears the name of the celebrated painter Ilya Repin (1844–1930), who bought a cottage in the settlement in 1899 and made it his permanent residence until his death. (The Penates burned down during World War II, but was later totally reconstructed.)

Repin was one of the *Peredvizhniki* group of artists, dubbed The Wanderers, and considered the master of Russian realism who portrayed the rich texture of Russian life. One of his celebrated works is the *Reply of the Zaporozhian Cossacks to the Sultan* which he sold to Alexander III in 1891 for over 30,000 rubles, the most ever paid for a Russian painting.

Repin named his estate the Penates, after the Roman gods of home and well being. His friends and students gathered at the estate every Wednesday, and then Repin worked by himself the rest of the week. Painted here were: B*loody Sunday, Meeting of the State Council* and *Pushkin's Examination at the Lyceum*, as well as portraits of Gorky, Shalyapin and Tolstoy. (Many of Repin's works are on display in the Tretyakov Gallery in Moscow and at St Petersburg's Russian Museum where you can view one of his most famous works, *The Volga Boatmen*, see page 326.) Over 600 pieces that include artworks by Repin, his son Yuri, as well as by students and friends are on display. An old documentary film shows Repin at his house. Audio guides in English are available. Birch trees line the path up a small hill to his grave, above which stands a bust of the artist. Open 10:30am–5pm (in winter till 4pm); closed Mondays and Tuesdays. eng.nimrah.ru/musrepin.

Take an *elektrichka* train from Finland Station (or if already in Razliv, it is only about a 15 minute ride further west) in the direction of Zelenogorsk/Vyborg to Repino. From the station head towards the water, make a left on Repin Street and walk about 400 meters to the estate.

One train stop west of Repino brings you to the village of **Komarovo** (once a part of Finnish territory) where the famous poet Anna Akhmatova is buried near the dacha where she lived for many years. Her funeral was held in the city's St Nikoilai Marine Cathedral on March 10, 1966. In 1963, at the age of 74, Akhmatova wrote of Komarovo:

This land, although not my native land,
Will be remembered forever,
And the sea's lightly iced,
Unsalty water.

The sand on the bottom is whiter than chalk
The air is heady, like wine,
And the rosy body of the pines
Is naked in the sunset hour,

And the sunset itself on such waves of ether
That I just can't comprehend
Whether it is the end of the day, the end of the world,
Or the mystery of mysteries in me again.

NORTH OF THE CITY
VYBORG (Выборг)

When in St Petersburg, Vyborg is an easy day trip north of the city. Lying 122 kilometers (76 miles) northwest of St Petersburg and 240 kilometers (150 miles) south of Helsinki, Vyborg, one of the oldest cities in Europe (dating back to the 13th century), is a lovely town with Finnish influences of winding cobblestone streets, picturesque old buildings, and a medieval castle, built in 1293 when the Swedes captured the region of Karelia from Novgorod. Peter the Great annexed the area back in 1710, but, a century later, the city fell within autonomous Finland. After the 1917 Revolution, the area remained part of independent Finland, when it became known as Viipuri. Stalin's troops took back control in 1939, but, during WW II, Russia lost it again, this time to the Germans and Finns. After the war, when Stalin got the region back, he deported all the Finns north across the border. Shipbuilding and fishing remain important industries, and the bustling harbor is full of ships loading up timber.

Starting west of the castle, you'll come upon **Anna's Fortress** (Anninskaya Krepost), named after Empress Anna Ivanovna (1693–1740), and built as protection against the Swedes. Here, charming narrow streets meander through picturesque old neighborhoods. Returning east across Krepostnoi Bridge leads to the imposing medieval **Castle** (*Viipuri Linna* in Finnish), built upon a small rock island in Vyborg Bay. It is the city's oldest structure, and now contains a small museum (closed Mondays). After visiting the castle, continue back across the bridge to the land spit. The main thoroughfare of Krepostnaya leads to the **Belfry Watch Tower** of the Old Cathedral. A few blocks directly north, off Prospekt Lenina, stands the 16th century **Round Tower** (Kruglaya Bashnya). Across from the tower, standing in the central

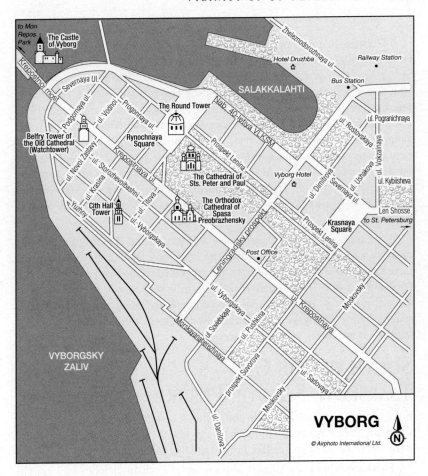

To Mon Repos Park — The Castle of Vyborg — Krepostnoi most — Severnaya Ul. — Podgornaya ul. — ul. Vodnoi — Progonnaya ul. — The Round Tower — Nab. 40-letiya VLKSM — SALAKKALAHTI — Hotel Druzhba — Zheleznodorozhnaya ul — Railway Station — Bus Station — ul. Pogranichnaya — Belfry Tower of the Old Cathedral (Watchtower) — ul. Novoi Zastavy — Rynochnaya Square — Krepostnaya ul. — ul. Storozhevoibashni — Prospekt Lenina — The Cathedral of Sts. Peter and Paul — Vyborg Hotel — ul. Rostovskaya — ul. Dimitrova — Severnaya ul. — ul. Ushakova — ul. Volkzalnaya — ul. Kybiisheva — ul. Krasina — ul. Titova — The Orthodox Cathedral of Spasa Preobrazhensky — Len Shosse — to St. Petersburg — Cith Hall Tower — ul. Vyborgskaya — Krasnaya Square — Prospekt Lenina — Yuzhny — Leningradsky prospekt — Post Office — ul. Vyborgskaya — ul. Sovietskaya — ul. Pushkina — ul. Krepostnaya — Moskovsky — VYBORGSKY ZALIV — Morskaya naberezhnaya — prospekt Suvorova — ul. Sadovaya — Moskovsky — ul. Danilova — VYBORG — © Airphoto International Ltd. — N

square, is the **Cathedral of Saints Peter and Paul** (Sobor Petra I Pavla), built in 1799. Back on Krepostnaya is the **Cathedral of the Transfiguration** (Spaso-Preobrazhensky Sobor), constructed in 1787. The **City Hall Tower** is a short walk southwest to Vyborgskaya Ulitsa. Many of the other buildings are architecturally interesting, as is the town library, designed by renowned Finnish architect, Alvar Aalto. All in all, Vyborg is home to a variety of architectural styles from medieval forts to pre-war functionalist masterpieces.

Spread throughout 440 acres of land, it is also well worth a visit to **Mon Repos Park** (French for 'My Rest'), which lies 2.6 kilometers (1.6 miles) northwest of the castle along the shoreline of the Zashchitnaya Inlet. From the train or bus station, take bus 1 or 6 that makes a stop 200 meters from the Park Gate entrance. Open daily 10am–9pm (Oct–April until 6pm). www.parkmonrepos.org.

The estate, first developed in the 1750's, was later bought in 1784 by Prince Friedrich Wilhelm of Württenberg, brother-in-law of Emperor Paul I; but the Prince had to leave a few years later because of a divorce scandal. The manor, now named Mon Repos, was then sold in 1788 to Ludwig Heinrich von Nicolai, the prince's acquaintance and librarian to Paul I; the estate remained in this family until 1942. The park, with over 50 plant species, consists of the main house and library and monuments of classical architecture, such as **Broglie's Obelisk**, the **Temple of Neptune** and **Ludwigstein Chapel**, also known as the 'Island of the Dead'. Among the designers of the landscaped rock park (with glacial formations up to 20 meters high) were architects de Thomon, Martinelli, Montferrand and Stackenschneider The Chamber Musical Festival, known as 'Evenings at Mon Repos' takes place in summer.

Five express trains a day depart from Finlandsky Station to Vyborg and take just under two hours. Cheaper *elektrichka* trains also leave about every hour and take three hours. In the station, departure times are posted on the board as Vyborgskoye. Buses enroute to Helsinki usually make stops in Vyborg as well. The bus station is situated just across the street from the old impressive façade of the Vyborg train station, both centrally located. Leningradsky Prospekt runs southwest from the stations towards town. www.infoservices.com.

SOUTH OF THE CITY
TSARSKOYE SELO OR PUSHKIN (Царское Село)

If you plan to visit Tsarskoye Selo and Pavlovsk in one or two days, note that the Catherine Palace is closed on Tuesday (and last Monday of month), and many museums in Pavlovsk on Tuesday, Friday (and first Monday of month).

Tsarskoye Selo (Tsar's Village), also known as Pushkin, is located 25 km (15 miles) south of St Petersburg. (The main entrance to the park is from Sadovaya Ulitsa.) The quickest way to Tsarskoye Selo is by *elektrichka* commuter train from Vitebsky Railway Station south to the stop of Detskoye Selo; the journey takes about half an hour (directly to Pavlovsk station is 40 minutes.) Buses and *marshrutka* 371 and 382 run from the station to Ekaterininsky (Catherine's) Park in about ten minutes (or it is a half-hour walk). Remember to check return train times before you leave the station! To journey via bus, from St Petersburg's Moskovskaya Metro (take the exit marked 'Buses for the airport') and *marshrutka* minibus numbers 342 or 545 make the journey to both Pushkin and Pavlovsk. Excursion kiosks located in front of Gostiny Dvor along Nevsky Prospekt also offer group tours to Tsarskoye Selo and Pushkin, including transportation.

Tickets for entry into **Catherine's Park** (open 7am–9pm) are sold near the entrance (you may need to show this ticket at the Catherine Palace ticket office, so hold on to it). A visitor can buy an **E-ticket online** in advance for a specific day, which grants entry to both the park and Catherine's Palace. A printed-out voucher needs to be exchanged for a Palace entry ticket at certain marked kiosks near the Palace lobby between noon and 4pm. If you do not have a voucher, start queuing early by the Palace for a ticket, as lines are long in summer. Entry hours are noon–2pm & 4pm–5pm, till 8pm on Mondays (often in summer, entries are noon–7pm); the palace is closed Tuesdays and last Monday of month. (From October to April, when the complex is less crowded, entry times are 10am–5pm, till 8pm on Mondays.) If you have a Petersburg City Card, from October 20 through April 30, entry to the park and Historical Interiors of the Palace are free (www.petersburgcard.com).

Check the website **eng.tzar.ru** for both E-ticket purchase and information on the Palace and other museums, some of which are closed other than Tuesdays, and also require a separate entrance fee. Visitors are brought into the palace as a group tour (guided tours in English are available, but find out the times); it is suggested to just enter with any first available tour, and slip away once inside to go at your own pace.

In 2010, Tsarskoye Selo celebrated its 300th anniversary. During the Northern War, Peter the Great won back the region between the Neva and the Gulf of Finland from the Swedes. In 1703, Peter I gifted some of these lands to his friend Alexander Menshikov; then, in 1710, the Czar gave some of Menshikov's land to his wife, the future Empress Catherine I. (Menshikov had introduced Peter to his future wife.) Catherine then commissioned Jacob Roosen to create the gardens, and the architect, Johann Friedrich Braunstein, to build a two-story stone palace. By 1728, the town was known as Tsarskoye Selo, the Tsar's Village. After Catherine I's daughter, Elizabeth I, inherited the estate, she commissioned Francesco Bartolomeo Rastrelli, in 1752, to enlarge and transform the palace into a grandiose summer residence. He added three-story wings, an entrance stairway, and ornamented façades with many columns and statues. Upon completion, the beautiful baroque masterpiece, with its opulent interior, stretched 300 meters (980 feet)—the longest palace in the world. The columns of the upper story were supported by 60 large figures of Atlas. When Empress Elizabeth and her court arrived to view the glistening gold and greenish-blue painted palace for the first time, the French Ambassador heralded, 'The only thing needed is a case in which to put this jewel!' In 2002 President Putin approved the allocation of 140 kilograms of gold for the restoration of the palace.

Catherine the Great made other additions to the palace. During her reign (1762–1796) many renowned architects, such as Charles Cameron, Antonio Rinaldi and Giacomo Quarenghi, worked in the neo-classical style on the palace. In the 1800s, other buildings and gardens were also assembled. For over a century, the monarchs of Russia ruled from this imperial residence for nearly six months a year. In 1887, a piped water system was installed along with a simple power station, making Tsarskoye Selo Europe's first town run entirely by electricity.

City residents used to flock here in summer for the beneficial effects of the climate. After the Revolution the name was changed to Detskoye Selo (Children's Village) because of the large number of orphanages in town; many of the buildings were turned into schools. Pushkin studied at the Lyceum from 1811 to 1817. In 1937, to commemorate the 100-year anniversary of the poet's death, the town was renamed Pushkin. Today the town is referred to either as Tsarskoye Selo or Pushkin, but the train station stop is still called Detskoye Selo.

The first Russian railway was constructed between Tsarskoye Selo and Pavlovsk in 1834. By 1837 the line had been extended all the way to St Petersburg. (A model of the inaugural train that took Nicholas I and his family to the summer palace in Tsarskoye Selo stands at the end of the platform in St Peterburg's Vitebsky Station; also take a look at the Royal Waiting Room.) One of the passengers who rode the first train to St Petersburg on 31 October 1837 wrote, 'The train made almost one *verst* (kilometer) a minute...60 *versts* an hour, a horrible thought! Meanwhile, as you sit calmly, you do not notice the speed, which terrifies the imagination, only the wind whistles, only the steed breathes fiery foam, leaving a white cloud of steam in its wake...' The line between St Petersburg and Moscow was built between 1843 and 1851. (See the Special Topic on the Trans-Siberian Railway.)

On September 8, 1941, less than three months after Germany invaded Russia, the German army took over Pushkin, setting up command centers in both the Catherine and Alexander Palaces, during which time they were horribly looted and damaged. (The town was finally liberated on January 24, 1944.) Compare the restored rooms to photographs on display of the German devastation.

Upon entering **Catherine's Palace** (Yekaterininsky Dvorets), the visitor climbs the magnificent **Marble Staircase**, built by Ipolit Monighetti in 1860. On the interior walking tour, you first pass through the gilded black iron gates to **Rastrelli's Cavaliers' (Knights) Dining Room** and **Great Hall**, filled with gilded mirrors and ceiling painting of the Triumph of Russia.

Then after passing through several exhibition halls, you arrive at one of the palace's most famous rooms, the **Amber Room**, once referred to as the 'Eighth Wonder of the World'. In 1701, the eccentric Prussian King, Friederich Hohenzollern I, ordered tons of amber extracted from the Baltic Sea coast so he could create an amber room for his palace in Charlottenberg. When the King died, his heir, the militaristic Friederich Wilhelm I, ordered the amber sections packed up and stored in the Berlin Stadtschloss. In 1717 when visiting Germany, Peter the Great saw them, and convinced the King to give him the panels. In exchange, the King requested 55 six-foot-tall "giants" for his Corps of Grenadiers. But after returning to Russia, Peter I never did anything with the panels. Later, his daughter, Elizabeth I, had her favorite architect, Rastrelli, install them in a room in the Winter Palace. He combined the panels with mirrors, jasper mosaics, and gilded woodcarvings. In 1755, Catherine the Great ordered them transferred and mounted in a room in Catherine's Palace in Tsarskoye Selo. The Amber Room (Yantarnaya Komnata) covered three walls and was arranged in three tiers. The Room remained intact for nearly two centuries until WW II, when the Nazis relocated them out of the country. Countless treasure hunters searched the world for decades, (the panels were said to have last been seen at Königsberg Castle), but no one ever discovered the room's whereabouts. Beginning in 1979, the Soviet government initiated the rebuilding of the famous site; and Russian craftsmen worked for more than 20 years to reconstruct the Amber Room (based on original surviving photographs). They used more than 500,000 amber pieces (finished as thin as a bar of chocolate) at a cost of over $15 million (some of which was donated by German companies). Rebuilding the Amber Room required six tons of amber, yet only 25% of the raw material is used; the other 75% becomes dust. In other words, from a kilogram of amber (2.2 pounds), only 150 grams (five ounces) is usable. Today, covered with more than a ton of forty-million-year-old amber, the room glows with more than 10 different yellowish to red and golden-honey hues. Additionally, copies of the original 1750's Florentine mosaics (made from quartz, onyx, jasmine and jade) adorn the walls. (One original mosaic, entitled *Smell and Touch*, does exist in the room; it was discovered in 1997 in Bremen, Germany, along with an amber chest.) A nearly exact replica of the original room was re-opened to the public on March 31, 2003 for St Petersburg's 300th-anniversary. (See page 615.)

The **Picture Gallery** stretches across the entire width of the building. Of the 130 French, Flemish and Italian canvasses that were here before the war, 114 were evacuated and can be seen today. The next exhibition halls contain *objets d'art* presented during the reign of Catherine the Great, **Alexander I's Study**, and the photo room which displays the great destruction of the grounds and palaces caused by the war and the challenging process of the immense restorations. Next comes Cameron's **Green Dining Room** with its mythological motifs, and later, the breathtaking **Chinese Blue Room**. The walls of this room are decorated with Chinese blue silk and oriental colored landscapes, and Empress Elizabeth is portrayed as Flora, Goddess of Flowers. Through the **Choir Anteroom** (used by the Empress during the church service), you enter the palace chapel.

The northeast section of the palace, in the chapel wing, contains the **Pushkin Museum**, made up of 27 halls displaying the beloved writer's personal belongings and manuscripts (rooms 10–13 relate to Pushkin's estate home in Mikhailovskoye, see vicinity section of Pskov).

In front of the palace's northeastern façade stands the **Statue of Alexander Pushkin**, commissioned in 1899 to mark the 100th-anniversary of his birth. The poet is wearing his Lyceum uniform and sitting on a garden seat. In his famous poem, *Evgeny Onegin*, Pushkin wrote:

> *...In the days, when in the Lyceum gardens*
> *I blossomed in untroubled ease...*
> *Close by the waters gleaming in the stillness,*
> *The Muse began to appear to me...*
> *And sang of childish merriments,*
> *And of the glory of our ancient times*
> *And of the heart's tremulous dreams.*

The four-story **Lyceum** is linked to the Palace by an archway. It was originally built by Catherine the Great as a school for her grandsons, but later expanded by Alexander I, who inaugurated the Lyceum on October 19, 1811 for children of the aristocracy. The Czar wanted to enact reforms for the country but was afraid his subjects would misunderstand them. So he decided to cultivate the younger generation by forming new learning institutions and reforming existing ones. The classrooms were on the second floor and the dormitory on the third (the ground floor housed the servants' and tutors' lodgings, and the first floor the mess and assembly halls). The Lyceum's first class consisted of 30 boys between the ages of 11 and 14, and one of these students was Alexander Pushkin.

The Lyceum is now a museum and the classrooms and laboratories are kept as they were during Pushkin's time. In the dormitory is a plaque that reads, 'Door no. 14 Alexander Pushkin,' and examples of a student's narrow bed, wooden desk, chest of drawers and inkstand. In the school's assembly hall, on 8 January 1815, Pushkin read aloud his school exam poem, *Recollection of Tsarskoye Selo*, in front of the great poet Gavrila Derzhavin. Today, October 19 is celebrated as Lyceum Day, the anniversary of its opening date in 1811.

Behind the Lyceum are the old royal stables, now the **Carriage Museum** with a collection of royal carriages (open 10am–6pm; closed Wednesdays and last Tuesday of month). The neighboring **Church of the Sign** (1734) is the oldest original building in town. Continuing north down Dvortsovaya (on the corner of Moskovskaya) brings you to **Pushkin's Dacha** where he lived with his wife from May to October 1831.

Catherine's Park consisted of three types: the French was filled with statues and pavilions, the English had more trees and shrubs, and the Italian contained more sculpted gardens. The grounds stretch over 567 hectares (1400 acres). Walking in an easterly direction into the French part of Catherine's Park leads to the **Upper**

Tsarskoye Selo

Cathedral of St Fyodorov
Dvortsovayo Ulitsa
Pushkin's Dacha
to train station
Moskovskaya Ulitsa
Ulitsa Kominterna
Malaya Ulitsa
Kitchen
Srednaya Ulitsa
Children's Pond
Alexander Palace
Bus to Pavlovsk
Sadovaya Ulitsa
Arsenal
Chinese Theater
Catherine Palace
Hermitage
Alexander   Park
Chinese Village
Granite Terrace
Grand Pond
Admiralty
13
Milkmaid Fountain
Great Caprice
Volkhonskoye Shosse
N
© Airphoto International Ltd
Orlov Gate

1 Lyceum
2 Carriage Museum
3 Church of the Sign
4 Upper Bath
5 Lower Bath
6 Grotto
7 Cameron Gallery
8 Agate Pavilion
9 Milkmaid Fountain
10 Marble Bridge
11 Pyramid
12 Turkish Baths
13 Chinese Creaking Pavilion

Bath (1777), modeled on Emperor Nero's Golden House of Rome, and used as baths for the Royal Family. The path, lined with mythological characters, then leads down to the **Lower Bath**, once used by the court and other visitors. Open 11am–6pm; closed Thursdays, (during winter months) and in rainy weather.

The route then leads to the ornamental 64-columed **Hermitage** (1744–1756), built to entertain guests. No servants were allowed on the second floor. The guests wrote requests on slates and then up to five tables could be lowered and raised with the appropriate food and drink, including such delicacies as elk lips and nightingale tongues! The adjacent fish canal provided seafood for the royal banquets. Open 11am–6pm (group tour only); closed Mondays, (during winter months), and in rainy weather. Tours with table raising demonstration are at noon, 12:30pm, 3pm & 3:30pm.

Heading south brings you out to the **Grand Pond** and **Grotto**, built by Rastrelli in 1753. Originally it was ornamented with over 200,000 seashells to give the illusion of a fairy-tale hideaway. During the reign of Catherine the Great the famous statue of Voltaire sitting in a chair was displayed here. Today it can be seen in the Hermitage Museum. The **Grotto Pavilion** is open 10am–6pm; closed Tuesdays and in rainy weather. Rastrelli built the 25-meter high **Orlov (Chesme) Column**, sculpted from multicolored marble, on an island in the middle of the pond as a monument to the victory of the Battle of Chesme on 25 June 1770. In summer you can take a ferry ride out to this little island. On the eastern bank stands the old **Admiralty Pavilion** that is now a restaurant. Open daily 11am–7pm. (Short **ferry rides** depart from the Granite west side of the Pond, and on the east side near the Admiralty.)

West of the Grotto is the **Cameron Gallery**, named after its builder, Charles Cameron. Greek and Roman bronze figures line the staircase and are placed in between the numerous Ionic columns. The gallery opens onto the **Hanging Gardens** and **Agate Pavilion** (with its semi-circular rotunda), named because of its interior is faced with this gemstone; it was once used as Catherine the Great's personal *banya*. From the **Granite Terrace** there is a magnificent view of the pond and English-style gardens.

Continuing south along the western bank of the pond brings you to the **Milkmaid Fountain**, sculpted in 1816 by Pavel Sokolov. At the southwest corner of the pond lies the bluish-white **Marble Bridge** (made from Siberian marble between 1770–76 and modeled on the Palladian Bridge in Wilton, England) which crosses a channel to the granite **Pyramid**, originally designed in 1781 as a summer house. On the opposite bank are the **Turkish Baths**, built in 1852 to resemble a Turkish mosque (and mark the Russian victory in the Russo-Turkish War of 1828–29). Open 11am–6pm; closed Wednesdays, (during winter months) and in rainy weather. North of the Marble Bridge, the **Concert Hall Pavilion**, built in the 1780's by Quarenghi and dedicated to the Goddess Ceres, hosts summer concerts, usually on Saturday afternoons (a ticket includes a ferry ride out to it). Open 11am–7pm; closed Mondays and Tuesdays.

At the northwestern end of Tsarskoye Selo stands the classical-style **Alexander Palace**, built by Catherine the Great (1792–96 by Quarenghi) for her grandson, the future Alexander I, and presented to him for his marriage. It was his younger brother, Nicholas I who first extensively used the palace, and then by Nicholas II who preferred it as his primary residence. The family would often take tea with Rasputin in the Maple Drawing Room with the polar bear rug. After the Czar abdicated in March, 1917, the family lived here under house arrest for six months. The Palace is currently undergoing an extensive multi-million-dollar restoration but several impressive rooms are open to visitors. Open 10am–6pm; closed Tuesdays and last Wednesday of month. **Alexander Park** (open 7am–11pm) makes up the western side of the grounds, and many of the structures within the park, such as the **Chinese Creaking Pavilion**, were designed in *chinoiserie* style. (See pages 620–621.)

In the semicircular wing of the Catherine Palace is the **Tsarskoselsky Present Café** (www.tsarpresent.com), and another smaller café operates in the central vestibule. The Bosquet Café is in the park by the entrance to the palace. The **Admiralty Restaurant** is in the old brick Admiralty Pavilion overlooking the Grand Pond. For more upscale fare try **Daniel** at 2/3 Srednaya where a Swedish chef offers culinary delights in an elegant setting. www.apriorico.com. **The 19th-Century Restaurant** is next door, broken up into four differently styled dining rooms that serve traditional Russian food. www.restaurantpushkin.ru.

If you would like to overnight in Tsarskoye Selo and continue on to Pavlovsk the following day, consider a stay at the mid-priced **Hotel Ekaterina**, at 5 Sadovaya, located at the southwestern end of Catherine's Palace in the old servant's block. Once crowds leave for the day, enjoy a tranquil stroll around the grounds. www.hotelekaterina.spb.ru.

In Pushkin's town center stands **St Catherine's Cathedral**, built in 1840 under the direction of architect Konstantin Ton. In 1939 it was demolished and then, later in 1960, a nine-ton statue of Lenin was erected on its spot. In 2004, the statue was toppled and two years later work began on a new church that opened on June 27, 2010 for the 300th anniversary of the town.

PAVLOVSK (Павловск)

Pavlovsk is located 29 kilometers (18 miles) south of St Petersburg, and only 4 kilometers southeast of Tsarskoye Selo. To get here, take an *elektrichka*, train from Vitebsky Railway Station to the Pavlovsk stop; they leave every half hour, and the trip takes about 40 minutes. (Or it is one stop further, a ten-minute ride, from the Detskoye Selo stop in Tsarksoye Selo.) It is about a fifteen-minute walk from the Pavlovsk station southeast through the park to the palace.

Regular *marshrutka* minibuses (numbers 342 or 545) also depart from St Petersburg's Moskovskaya Metro (follow exit marked 'Buses to airport') and stop first in Pushkin on their way to Pavlovsk. The bus stop in Pushkin (Tsarskoye Selo) to/from Pavlovsk is by the Orangerie near the corner of Oranzhereynaya and Srednaya Streets. Excursion kiosks located in front of Gostiny Dvor along Nevsky Prospekt also offer group tours to Tsarskoye Selo and Pushkin, including transportation.

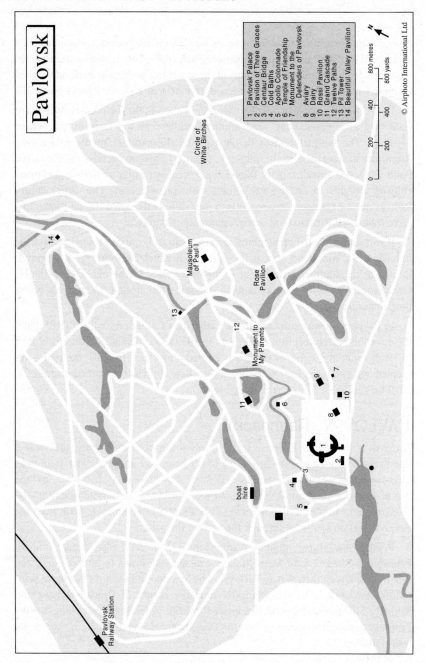

Pavlovsk

1   Pavlovsk Palace
2   Pavilion of Three Graces
3   Centaur Bridge
4   Cold Baths
5   Apollo Colonnade
6   Temple of Friendship
7   Monument to the
     Defenders of Pavlovsk
8   Aviary
9   Dairy
10 Rossi Pavilion
11 Grand Cascade
12 Twelve Paths
13 Pil Tower
14 Beautiful Valley Pavilion

© Airphoto International Ltd

800 metres

800 yards

0   200   400

0   200   400

Circle of
White Birches

Mausoleum
of Paul I

Rose
Pavilion

Monument to
My Parents

boat
hire

Pavlovsk
Railway Station

The Pavlovsk Park is open 10am–6pm (between 6am–10am and 6pm–midnight, entrance is free). The Pavlovsk Palace is open 10am–6pm; note that the first and third floor rooms of the palace are closed Tuesdays and Fridays, and the entire palace is closed the first Monday of each month. www.pavlovskmuseum.ru.

The flamboyant court life of Tsarskoye Selo scared away most of the wildlife, so the royal family went out to the nearby area of **Pavlovskoye** to hunt. Two wooden hunting lodges were known as Krik and Krak. In 1777, upon hearing of the birth of her first grandson, Alexander, Catherine the Great gifted her son Pavel (Paul) and his wife, Maria Fyodorovna (the former Sophie Dorothea Augusta de Württemberg), "one thousand acres of woodlands, ploughed fields and two villages with peasants," lying on the banks of the Slavyanka River. In 1779, Catherine invited her favorite architect, Charles Cameron, from Scotland to come and construct a palace for the couple. Cameron began his activities with the Temple of Friendship, (dedicated to Catherine the Great), the Apollo Colonnade at the park's entrance, the Obelisk, and Triple Lime Avenue; he also designed the areas of the Great Star and White Birch. Cameron greatly admired the 16th-century Italian architect, Andrea Palladio, whose creations interlaced modern ideas with the heritage of Ancient Rome.

In 1781, after gaining permission from Catherine the Great, the young couple, under the pseudonym of the Count and Countess Severny (du Nord), set off on a 14-month tour of Europe, where they bought up furniture, fabrics, sculptures and paintings for their new palace. They declared that Pavlovsk provided them with "more pleasure than all the beauty of Italy." Upon their arrival in Paris, King Louis XVI and Marie Antoinette gave them a ceremonial welcome, and Marie gifted them a unique toilet set decorated with her crest. Upon visiting the famed Sèvres pottery, the Grand Princess purchased porcelain goods for the then astronomical sum of 300,000 livres. When Pavel and Maria returned from Europe, life in Pavlovsk transformed into a realm of amusements and gala festivities. Maria Fyodorovna aspired to organize Pavlovsk after the fashion of Marie Antoinette in Trinon. The Dairy pavilion housed goats and Dutch cows, and sheep grazed on the riverbanks; she also helped design all the parks and gardens. Many of Maria's handicrafts and embroideries still adorn the walls of the palace today. A decade after the royal couple took up residence here, the palace was given a classical makeover by Vincenzo Brenna, who also worked on the park layouts and, built a popular Theater complex on the grounds. For over 40 years, the palace remained under the loving care of Maria Fyodorovna, who transformed the area into an important part of Russian cultural life; one poet called it "an Abode of Muses and Graces." During her 67 years, Maria bore and raised ten children, and continued to live here for another 27 years (until her death) after her husband's tragic death; Paul I was murdered in St Petersburg's Mikhailovsky Palace on March, 23, 1801.

When Pavel ascended the throne as Paul I in 1796, Pavlovsk became the official Imperial summer residence. During this same year, the village was also officially renamed Pavlovsk. Since the Czar was also the Grand Master of the Maltese Order, the estate hosted grand festivities each year for the knights. In all, Paul I was heir to the throne for forty years, and was Czar for exactly four years, four months and four days. Upon Maria's death, their youngest son, Grand Duke Mikhail Pavlovich inherited the estate. Pavlovsk remained in the Romanov family until the 1917 Revolution, when the estate was confiscated by the Bolsheviks.

Pavlovsk Park was created by Pietro Gonzaga (who lived here from 1803 to 1838) and covers over 600 hectares (1480 acres) making it (for its time) one of the largest landscaped parks in the world, with such designs as the **Valley of Ponds** and the **Circle of White Birches**. Near the palace's southern façade in the **Private Garden** is the **Pavilion of Three Graces**, designed by Cameron in 1801, with 16 white Ionic columns. Around to the west, across the river over the **Centaur Bridge**, are the **Cold Baths** and **Apollo Colonnade** (1783). On the north side, the **Great Stone Staircase** leads to the Slavyanka River and the **Temple of Friendship** (1782) with its white Doric colonnades. Further north along the riverbank are the **Twelve Paths**, lined with 12 bronze statues representing mythological figures. A westward path then leads to the **Monument to My Parents**, a pyramidal structure with a medallion containing the profiles of Maria Fyodorovna's parents. A simple inscription reads, 'To my parents.' A little further east across the river is the **Rose Pavilion** (closed Fridays) and then stroll to the **Mausoleum of Paul I** (1808); the murdered czar is actually buried in the Peter and Paul Fortress. East of the mausoleum, a very lovely part of the park is known as the **Big Star** where rows of white birch radiate from the center. (See pages 622–623.)

Many famous architects such as Brenna, Cameron, Quarenghi, Rossi and Voronikhin worked on the construction of **Pavlovsk Palace**, with its 64 white columns, green dome, and classical yellow façade. The palace contains an Egyptian vestibule, Paul's Library, French, Greek and Italian Halls, orchestral chambers, billiard and ballrooms, and the dressing rooms of Empress Maria Fyodorovna and Paul I. Paul had his suites along the north side that include the **Hall of War** (he was obsessed with the military, see Mikhailovsky Castle on page 542). In contrast, Maria created the **Hall of Peace**, decorated with flowers and musical instruments.

The State Bedchamber contains an elegant four-poster bed by Henri Jacob, and the famous 64-piece Sèvres toilet service, presented to Maria Fyodorovna during her visit to Paris in 1782 by Marie-Antoinette. Situated in the south block on the middle floor is Paul's **Throne Room**, the largest room of the palace, and the **Hall of the Maltese Knights of St John**—after the island of Malta was captured by the French in 1798, the knights chose Paul I as their Grand Master. In 1796, Paul I created the

Picture Gallery and some of the 200 works that were brought here from the Hermitage and purchased from other collections can still be viewed here today. Mignard's 'Christ and the Woman of Samaria' and Jouvenet's 'The Presentation of the Temple' come from the famous Crozat collection, purchased by Catherine the Great. After the death of her husband, the widowed Empress Maria built a ground floor study graced by her favorite works of mainly religious paintings.

On May 22, 1838, the first passenger railway line was opened in Pavlovsk, which included the construction of a Music Station, designed by Andrei Stackenschneider. The youngest son of Paul I, the Grand Duke Mikhail Pavlovich, gave his permission for the construction of a railway line that ran right into the Big Star region of the park. The Music Vauxhall attained great popularity, where grand concerts and dinner parties in the Large Room where conducted for over a century for St Petersburg society. It was here that Mikhail Glinka's *Waltz Fantasia* premiered; and Johann Strauss conducted and performed concerts for over a decade to great acclaim. Even Dostoevsky described the wonderful impression that the Music Station made on him in his novel *The Idiot*. The palace and grounds, and Music Station were virtually destroyed during WWII (over 70,000 trees were cut down for firewood), but were impressively restored by 1970. Luckily nearly 14,000 pieces of art and furniture were evacuated before the occupation, and later returned to their original places. The **Monument to the Defenders of Pavlovsk**, on the grounds east of the palace, is dedicated to all those who died clearing the park of mines after the war. Today, the palace, 17 pavilions, 12 bridges, parks and ponds of the estate mirror the highly poetic work of many artistic masters of the 18th and 19th centuries.

Café 'Near the Iron Gates' (U Chugunnikh Vorot), at 1 Krasnikh Zor (on the main road from the station to the palace), is open daily 9am–9pm. The **Bolshoi Kolonni Zal Restaurant**, at 20 Sadovaya, with the next door **Café Molochni Domik**, is open 10am–6pm. A short walk on the road back towards Pushkin (from the train station), at 16 Filtrovskoye Shosse (Highway), is **Podvore** (Town House), a lovely old traditional log cabin that serves hearty Russian food and delicious *shashlik* barbecued in the open air. Musical nights abound and often a wild Cossack ensemble is performing. www.podvorye.ru.

GATCHINA (Гатчина)

Gatchina is 45 kilometers (28 miles) southwest of St Petersburg. An easy way to get here is by *elektrichka* commuter train (about an hour's ride) south from Baltiisky Railway Station to the Gatchina stop. From here it is a leisurely ten-minute walk down the avenue behind the station building to the park grounds. From Moskovskaya Metro, *marshrutka* minibus or local bus 431,18 or 18A run directly to the park—just mention to the driver that you want to be let off in front of Gatchina

Palace (*Dvoryets*). Another easy way to Gatchina is to take a Russian excursion bus from the corner of Dumskaya (Gostiny Dvor) and Nevsky Prospekt. Check ticket kassa for times and prices. Buses also leave for Pushkin and Pavlovsk, often combining an excursion with Gatchina.

The Palace, at 1 Krasnoarmeisky Prospekt, is open 10am–5pm, closed Mondays and first Tuesday of each month. The Palace is located in the middle of town, and the extensive landscaped grounds are public, which means in summer there are lots of picnicking locals, especially on weekends. So join them by bringing along some food of your own! www.gatchinapalace.ru/en.

The village of Gatchina was first mentioned in 15th-century chronicles. In the early 18th-century Peter the Great presented his sister Natalya Alekseyevna with a farm in the area. In 1765, Catherine the Great acquired the land and gave the estate as a gift to her lover Count Grigory Orlov, the man who had helped her ascend to the throne. Between 1766 and 1781, Antonio Rinaldi designed a palace and park in early classicism style. (The Eagle Pavilion and the Chesme Column, both built to honor the Orlov brothers' military deeds, still stand in the park today.) After the Count's death in 1783, Catherine purchased the estate from Orlov's heirs and passed it on to her son and heir, Paul, who later redesigned the palace (1792–1798) to look like a medieval castle. During his reign Paul I was a terribly paranoid czar (and for good reason—he was later murdered in 1801); so he had the architect Vincenzo Brenna add sentry boxes, toll-gates, a military parade ground, and build a moat, fortress and drawbridges around the castle. After Paul's death the estate remained neglected until Alexander III made Gatchina his permanent residence. (Alexander was terrified of revolutionary elements and felt safe here after his own father, Alexander II, was assassinated in 1881.) The grounds were badly damaged during World War II; fortunately, a few old 1870s watercolors of some of the interiors survived, and artists have used these to help restore rooms close to their original designs.

Several dozen of the 500 rooms within the **Great Gatchina Palace** are now open to the public, with magnificent collections of antique furniture, porcelain and artwork. These include Paul I's Throne Room, the Marble Dining Room, Crimson Drawing Room, Chesme Gallery and the White Ball Room with a collection of sundials on the balcony. There is also an exhibit of old weaponry on the ground floor. A secret 130-meter (426-foot) long **underground passage** (created by Orlov) leads to a grotto on the edge of Silver Lake. After fleeing the Winter Palace on the night of the Bolshevik Revolution, Alexander Kerensky (leader of the Provisional government) escaped to Gatchina and used the tunnel to evade revolutionary mobs. Climb the **Signal Tower's** 191 granite steps to the top for a spectacular view of the park (open May 1–November1). (See page 623.)

Gatchina Park weaves around the estate's White, Black and Silver lakes and is filled with gardens, greenhouses, pavilions, gates, columns, wells and bridges. The grounds were mainly designed by a pair of Englishmen, Mr Sparrow and Mr Bush. Between the White and Silver Lakes is the largest section of the park, known as the **English Landscape Gardens**. At the end of **White Lake** there is a lovely little **Temple to Venus** on the Island of Love. Behind Long Island is **Silver Lake**, which never freezes over; the first Russian submarine was tested here in 1879. On the northeastern shore of White Lake is **Birch Cabin**, which looks just that from the outside, but inside is an unexpected suite of palatial rooms lined with mirrors, a gift to Paul I from his wife. Other areas include the **Lime Tree Garden, Upper and Lower Dutch Gardens** and **Botanical Gardens** with its Water and Woods Labyrinth paths. Toss a coin for good luck into the **Jordan Well!** The white **Priory Palace** stands in front of **Black Lake**, originally built for a French prior who never lived here. It was designed in 1799 by architect Nikolai Lvov (for the Knights of the Maltese Order), who introduced 'rammed-earth' structures to Russia, a cheaper, more fireproof method of construction. (It is the only example in the area to survive from the late 18th century.) One can see examples of the rammed-earth process on the first floor. In warmer months, rowboats are available for rent in the lakes.

In town, the baroque **Pavlovsky Cathedral**, at the end of the pedestrian street, has a striking restored interior. Nearby, on Ulitsa Chekhova, is the **Shcherbakov Literary Museum**, open 10am–6pm weekdays. Alexander Shcherbakov (1901–1945) was a founding member of the Soviet Writers' Union along with Maxim Gorky. A short walk west is the blue-domed **Pokrovsky** (Intercession) **Cathedral**.

The only eating options are in town. Near the Pokrovsky Cathedral, at 2 Dostoevsky is the **Slavyansky Dvor** and near the Pavlovsky Cathedral, at 3a Sobornaya, is the **Café Piramida** with a range of traditional Russian food, along with simpler cakes, coffee and tea.

For fans of the writer, **Vladimir Nabokov**, his family estate of **Rozhdestveno** can be visited in the village of Siversky, located 31 kilometers (19.5 miles) south of Gatchina. It was first bought by Nabokov's grandfather, Ivan Rukavishnikov, a gold manufacturer, and then inherited by his son in 1901. When the son died in 1916, the estate passed on to his nephew, Vladimir Nabokov; but, in 1919, the Nabokov family was forced to flee the country after the Revolution. Today the beautiful estate house, with its iconic floor of a huge wooden chessboard at the entrance, is open as the **Nabokov Museum**. (In St Petersburg, another Nabokov house museum is located at 47 Bolshaya Morskaya, metro Sadovaya.) These homes and the city of St Petersburg are lovingly described in his autobiography, *Speak Memory*. To get here from Gatchina, get on the train and ride it south to the stop of Siverskaya. From St Petersburg's Baltic Station, take an *eletricka* train that is heading south in the direction of Luzhskoye to Siverskaya. From here, take bus 500 or *marshrutka* minibus 121, and tell the driver to drop you at Rozhdestveno.

I particularly remember the cool and sonorous quality of the place,
the checkerboard flagstones of the hall, ten porcelain cats on a shelf,
a sarcophagus and an organ, the skylights and the upper galleries,
the colored dusk of mysterious rooms, and carnations and crucifixes everywhere.

Vladimir Nabokov on Rozhdestveno

VELIKY NOVGOROD (Великии Новгород)

Veliky Novgorod is about a three-hour drive (180 kilometers/108 miles) southeast of St Petersburg on the M20 Highway. (Do not confuse Veliky (Great) Novgorod with Nizhny (Lower) Novgorod.) Trains and commuter *elektrichka* leave from St Petersburg's Moskovsky Station (and Vitebsky Station) several times a day and take about three hours to Novgorod Na-Volkhove (the town lies along the Volkhov River). For regular train departure schedules (not *elektrichka*), see www.russiantrain. com; tickets can also be purchased online. From Moscow's Leningradsky Station, two overnight trains arrive in Veliky Novgorod early the next morning (8.5 hours). From St Petersburg's Avtovokzal 2 Bus Station (Metro Ligovsky Prospekt, 36 Obvodny Canal) buses run about every half hour or so to Veliky Novgorod's bus station (journey 3.5 hours), which is right next to the town's train station. (If you read Russian, times and schedules are posted on www.avokzal.ru.) Another way to Novgorod is by taking an inexpensive Russian excursion bus tour. Check the ticket *kassa* on the corner of Dumskaya (Gostiny Dvor) and Nevsky; prices and departure times are posted here. There are both one- and two-day excursions. One-day excursions last about 12 hours. (In summer, weekends are the most crowded times, and note that Novgorod's main museum is closed on Tuesdays.)

Novgorod is one of the oldest towns in Russia, founded almost 1,200 years ago. The first Varangian leader Rurik settled here by the shores of Ilmen Lake and named the town Novgorod, meaning 'New Town.' By 977, Novgorod had gained its independence from Kievan Rus. During the 11th and 12th centuries the town prospered when it served as a major center between the Baltic and Black Sea trading routes. Soon the city, with its 30,000 inhabitants, one of the most educated centers in eastern Europe, became known as Novgorod the Great—*Veliky Novogorod*. A century later, while other areas of the country were sacked by the invading Tatar hordes, this region escaped severe Mongol occupation. In 1240, Prince of Novgorod, Alexander Nevsky, also battled off the attacking Swedes.

The golden age of Novgorod lay between the 12th and 15th centuries when wealthy nobles and merchants built over 200 churches. Even though the city remained a center for trade and religion well into the 16th century, it eventually lost its independence to Moscovy when Ivan the Great's troops occupied the city in 1478. Later, when Novgorod questioned Moscow's rule, it is said that Ivan the Terrible built a wall around the town, preventing anyone from leaving. Then, after the population still refused his subjugation, it is said that he had thousands of people tortured and killed in front of him. By the early 18th-century, the city had lost its strategic significance and slowly fell into a state of relative obscurity.

The old town is divided by the Voklhov River—the right bank is known as the Trading Side where the merchants lived and markets were held. The left (west) bank, the Sofia Side, is the area of the kremlin and fortress; the prince once governed from within these walls. Novgorod is an excellent example of an old Russian town with its preserved medieval art and ancient architecture (over 50 ancient churches and monasteries remain), paintings (icons, frescoes and mosaics) and history (collections of birch-bark manuscripts).

The original earthen and log ramparts of the kremlin were laid in about 1000AD, and in 1484 Ivan the Great ordered the building of a brick wall with nine watch towers. Today the Novogorod Kremlin complex is a Unesco World Heritage Site. The most famous and oldest remaining structure within the *detinets*, or citadel, is the five-domed **Cathedral of St Sophia** (1045–50), constructed to glorify Novgorod's patron saint. The son of Yarloslavl the Wise modeled it after the great cathedral of the same name in Kiev, which his father had built. (The town's first wooden Church of St Sophia was built at this site in 989.) The structure's enclosed galleries, chapels and iconostasis were originally decorated with icons and frescoes by artists brought in from as far away as Constantinople. One of the most famous icons is **Our Lady of the Sign** which, according to legend, saved the city from an attack by a Suzdal Prince and his large army in 1170. (On view in the Novgorod State United Museum is a 15th-century icon depicting three scenes from this battle; it is considered one of the first icons ever painted of an historical event.) The western portal contains the magnificent bronze Sigtuna Doors, made in Magdeburg in the early 1050s. Today, the cathedral is still used as a place of worship. Open daily 8am–8pm; Sunday services at 10am & 6pm.

North of the cathedral is the Gothic-style **Palace of Facets** (Granitovaya Palata), built by Archbishop Yevfimy in 1433; today it is Russia's oldest civilian stone building. After seven years of restoration, it reopened in 2014 to host a permanent exhibition of religious artifacts and medieval Russian jewelry; open 10am–6pm; closed Mondays and first Wednesday of month. In the center of the kremlin stands the 16-meter (52-foot) high **Millennium of Russia Memorial**, erected in 1862 to commemorate the 1,000th anniversary of Rurik's arrival in Novgorod. At the top are Mother Russia and the Orthodox Church, and the monument also depicts figures of the country's most celebrated rulers, nobles, artists and military heroes.

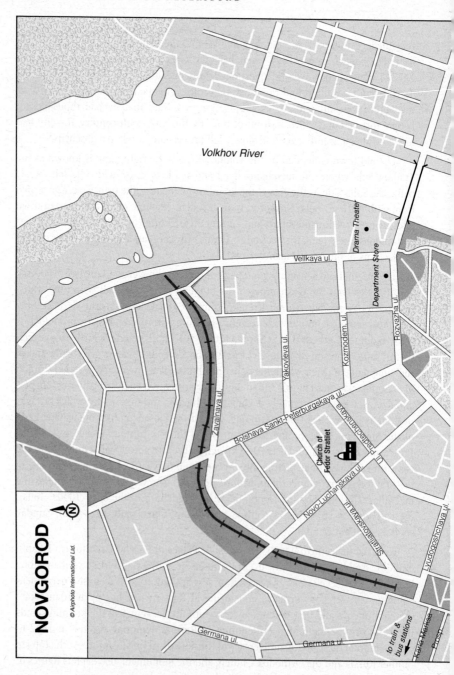

NOVGOROD

© Airphoto International Ltd.

N

Volkhov River

Drama Theater

Vellkaya ul.

Department Store

Rozvazha ul.

Yakovleva ul.

Kozmodem. ul.

Zavalnaya ul.

Bolshaya Sankt-Peterburgskaya ul.

Predtechenskaya

Church of
Fedor Stratilet

Novo-Luchanskaya ul.

Strallatovskaya ul.

Lyudogoshchaya ul.

Germana ul.

Germana ul.

Karla Marksa

to train &
bus stations

Prosp.

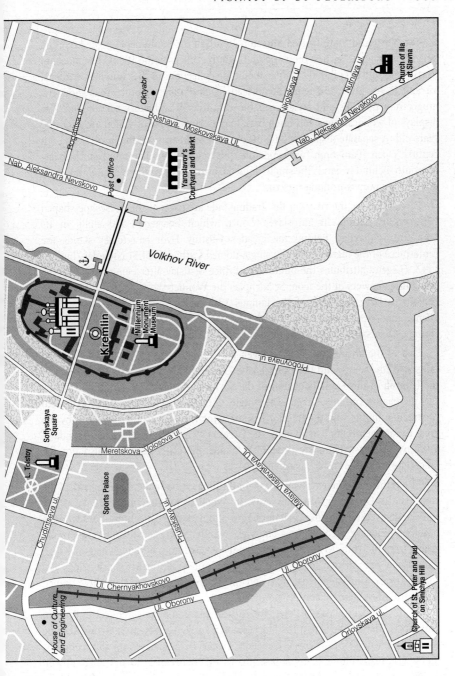

Church of Illa at Slavna

Nikolskaya ul

Nuthaya ul

Nab. Aleksandra Nevskovo

Oktyabr

Bolshaya. Moskovskaya UL

Bogutitsa ul

Nab. Aleksandra Nevskovo

Post Office

Yaroslavov's Courtyard and Markt

Volkhov River

Kremlin

Millennium Monument Museum

Probovnaya ul

Sofiyskaya Square

L. Tolstoy

Meretskova Volosova ul

Sports Palace

Malaya Vlasevskaya UL

Chudintseva ul

Prusskaya ul

Ul. Oborony

Ul. Chernyakhovskovo

Ul. Oborony

Orlovskaya ul

House of Culture and Engineering

Church of St. Peter and Paul on Sinichya Hill

The **Novgorod State United Museum** (south of the monument) is the kremlin's largest building; it was first built as administrative offices in the 1800s. The museum has 35 halls and over 8,000 exhibits, including collections of the churches' medieval art and icons. Over 250 icons are placed in chronological order that show the progression of skills and styles over the centuries. The history section includes displays of woodcarvings and birch bark manuscripts, some of which are over 800 years old. A separate display is on Novgorod's gold treasury, dating back to the 6th century. Open 10am–6pm (weekends till 7pm); closed Tuesdays and last Thursday of month. Behind it stands the single-domed **Church of St Andrew Stratelates**, built in 1360. www.novgorodmuseum.ru.

Directly across the river on the Trading Side are parts of the horseshoe-shaped 17th-century arcade in Yaroslavl's Court, which boasted 1,500 stalls in its 16th-century heyday. Behind the arcade's Gostiny Dvor gate-tower stands the centerpiece of the market side, the single-domed **Cathedral of St Nicholas**, built in 1113. (Legend attributes the building to Prince Mstislav after being healed by the miraculous powers of the icon, St Nicholas the Wonder-Worker.) The interior still contains a large fragment of the famous 12th-century fresco, *Job's Wife*. (Open 10am–6pm; closed Mondays, Tuesdays and last Friday of month.) Six other churches also stand in the area around the old trading complex.

East of the arcade, standing between the **Cathedral of Our Lady of the Sign** (closed Wednesdays) and the **Church of St Theodore Stratelates-on-the-Stream**, is the **Church of the Transfiguration of the Savior-on-Elijah-Street**, built in 1374 by the merchants on this street. The single dome and walls are decorated with ornamental motifs, and the interior has surviving frescoes, painted in 1378, by the great Byzantine master Theophanes the Greek. Open 11am–5pm; closed Mondays, Tuesdays and last Thursday of month. Numerous other churches also dot the landscape along the eastern bank of the river.

About three kilometers (two miles) south, situated along the western bank of the river, is the **Open Air Museum Park of Wooden Architecture**, known as the Vitoslavlitsky. (See page 624.) Here there is a remarkable collection of old wooden buildings and log architecture—churches, windmills, *izba* cottages, granaries—dating from the 16th- to 19th-centuries, and collected from outlying villages. (Open daily 10am–8pm, winter till 6pm.) Just a 15-minute walk further south brings you to the **Yuriev Monastery** ensemble and the magnificent asymmetric three-domed **Cathedral of St George**, commissioned in 1119 by Prince Vsevolod. One chronicle names the builder as 'Master Peter,' the earliest mention of any architect in Russian chronicles. Many believe that the oldest known surviving icon of St George (dating to 1030 and now in Moscow's Tretyakov Gallery) originates from this complex, along with many illuminated manuscripts written between 1120 and 1228, now in

Moscow's Historical Museum. For centuries, Novgorod had his own distinctive architecture and style of icon painting (see Special Topic on Icon).

In 1998, Novgorod town lawmakers voted to change the city's name back to Novgorod Veliky or Novgorod the Great, bestowed in the 12th-century to recognize the town's special status. Today the town has a population of over 220,000.

There are numerous restaurants and cafés scattered about town. These include, **Detinets Restaurant** in the Kremlin; three restaurants west of the Kremlin are **Nice People** (with daily specials and salads) at 1 Meretskova-Volosova, www.gonicepeople. ru; a few blocks north is **Ilmen** at 2 Gazon with a self-serve ground floor café and second floor restaurant; a few blocks west down Lyudogoshcha, at number 8, is **Café le Chocolat** with a wide selection from sushi to dessert. www.cafelechocolat.ru. On the right bank of the river is **Dom Berga**, at 24 Bolshaya Morskaya, with both a café and restaurant serving traditional Russian dishes.

For an overnight stay in Novgorod, there are plenty of hotels. The 4-star **Park Inn Veliky Novogord** is at 2 Studentcheskaya. Centrally located, just west of the Kremlin, are the mid-range **Volkhov Hotel** and **Akron Hotel**, located next to each other at 24 Predtechenskaya. www.hotel-volkhov.ru and www.hotel-akron.ru. Several blocks south, at 11 Prusskaya, is the **Hotel Cruise** that contains both a hotel and a cheaper hostel side with dorm rooms that share a bathroom in the hallway. For more listings, see www.booking.com and www.infoservices.com.

PSKOV (Псков)

Pskov is 190 kilometers (118 miles) southwest of Novgorod and 261 kilometers (162 miles) southwest of St Petersburg. It is suggested to try and combine Novgorod and Pskov in one trip with an overnight in Novgorod. Local buses run the Novgorod-Pskov route, twice daily, departing in the morning and mid-afternoon, taking about 4 hours. In Pskov train and bus stations are next to each other on Vokzalnaya Ulitsa. Buses run from the stations to the town center.

From St Petersburg, two long-distance trains depart daily from Vitebsky Station (early evening) bound for Lithuania (Vilnius) and Latvia (Riga), which make a stop in Pskov; the journey is about 5 hours. (www.russiantrain.com.) A longer *elektrichka* commuter train also runs from Baltic Station in the early morning for Pskov. From Moscow, an overnight train (taking over 12 hours) leaves Moscow from Leningradsky station and arrives in Pskov in the morning. Another option is to hop on a bus from Petersburg's Vitebsky Station; there are 15 daily buses bound for Pskov and take about 5 hours to get there. Pskov has an airport (located 6km southeast of town), and there are flights (less than 2 hours) several times a week from St Petersburg's Pulkovo Airport and Moscow's Domodedovo Airport.

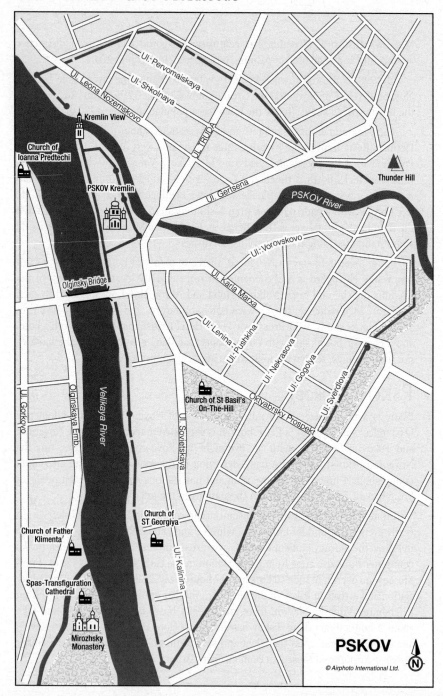

PSKOV

© Airphoto International Ltd.

Pskov is another of Russia's most ancient towns—it was first mentioned in a chronicle in 903 (2013 marked Pskov's 1110 Anniversary). Pskov began as a small outpost of Novgorod and later grew into a commercial center and developed its own school of icon painting. It is still filled with many beautiful churches and icons. In 1510, Vasily III, according to a chronicle 'took the city without a battle.' Later his son, Ivan the Terrible tried to annex Pskov, but the town resisted for many years before being subjugated. According to legend the bell on St Nicholas-on-Ushokha Church began tolling on its own as Ivan the Terrible rode by. Since the ringing startled his horse, Ivan ordered the bell's tongue cut out. Rimsky-Korsakov later wrote an opera based on the uprisings called *The Maid of Pskov*. On March 15, 1917, at a small railway station about 120 kilometers (75 miles) from Pskov, ironically named Dno (Bottom), Nicholas II relinquished the Russian throne, signing the official letter of abdication.

The oldest part of town stands where the Pskov and Velikaya (Great) rivers join. Here the 17th-century white **Trinity Cathedral**, the main church, towers above the other wooden buildings of the town's kremlin, known as The Krom, surrounded by a stone rampart. In the early 12th-century the stone Mirozhsky Monastery was constructed on the Velikaya River's southern left bank by the Mirozh River and, in 1150, its **Spas-Transfiguration Cathedral** was consecrated by the Archbishop of Novgorod and Pskov; the monks of the monastery painted all the interior frescoes (it is now a UNESCO heritage site). One Pskov monk also penned the famous 12th-century epic chronicle, *The Lay of Igor's Host*, based on the fighting campaigns of Prince Igor of Novgorod. (In 1795, Prince Musin-Pushkin discovered these chronicles in Yaroslavl's Savior Monastery (see page 341).

Walking north along the left bank (at the north end of Ul Gorkovo), lies the **Ivanovsky Monastery** and the white **Predtechensky Church**. Many of the town's churches were named according to their location, such as **St Basil's-on-the-Hill**, **Assumption Church-by-the-Ferry** and **St Nicholas-at-the-Stone Wall**.

There are plenty of centrally-located hotels and places to eat around town. The **Dvor Podznoeva Hotel**, at 1 Nekrasov (a five-minute walk from the Kremlin), has a popular restaurant by the same name, with a wine and cheese cellar, along with a bakery café. For a list of hotels, see www.booking.com.

PUSHKIN'S MIKHAILOVSKOYE

About 120 kilometers (75 miles) southeast of Pskov lies a cluster of estates known today as **Pushkin Hills**. The three estates were damaged during the war, but have been extensively restored to their former 19th-century appearance, along with the creation of a splendid nature reserve. The most famous is the family estate of the celebrated poet, Alexander Pushkin, known as Mikhailovskoye. (All three are closed on Mondays.)

From Pskov, you can catch a bus to Pushkinskiye Gory (Pushkin Hills) from the Pskov bus station. There are up to four daily buses; the journey takes about 2.5 hours. The Pushkinskiye Gory bus station is about 7km (4 miles) from the Pushkin estate of **Mikhailovskoye**. (Before leaving the bus station, find out the times of return buses to Pskov; the last may be in mid-afternoon; on weekends a few hours later.) If you don't want to jump on a local bus, take a taxi or it is a pleasant walk. To get there, make a left out of the bus station and walk about 1km along the road where you'll see the Svyatagorsk Monastery on the left. From there a road winds off to the right, which leads to Mikhailovskoe; keep following the signs from here. (To return, you can try and jump on an excursion bus that is driving back to the bus station or Pskov.)

The **Svyatogorsky Monastery** and its Assumption Church was founded by Ivan the Terrible in 1569. Pushkin's mother, Nadezhda, was buried here in April 1836, near the eastern wall of the church. Less than a year later, Pushkin was killed in a tragic duel. After the funeral in St Petersburg, the poet was laid to rest in a grave next to his mother. In 1840, a marble obelisk commissioned by Pushkin's widow, Natalya Nikolaevna, was placed over the grave with a simple inscription of the years of his birth and death.

The **Mikhailovskoye Estate** was established when Pushkin's great grandfather, Abraham Petrovich Hannibal (Peter the Great's Abyssinian general) received the lands from Empress Elizabeth in 1742. Pushkin stayed here after his graduation from Tsarskoye Selo's Lyceum in 1817, but did not return again for seven years, when he was exiled from the capital by Alexander I because of his so-called seditious writings. Pushkin's two-year stay at Mikhailovskoye, between 1824 and 1826, greatly enhanced his descriptions of country life in his novel-in-verse *Yevgeny Onegin*, and the exile certainly added to his tragedy, *Boris Godunov*. To break the tedium, Pushkin often visited the neighboring **Petrovskoye estate** of his great-uncle. The large white-column manor house is surrounded by a park that leads to Lake Petrovskoye.

Pushkin's favorite pastime was visiting the nearby **Trigorskoye estate**, owned by the extended Osipova family. Pushkin became quite enamored by Madame Praskovya Osipova's married niece, Anna Petrovna Kern, and was inspired to pen one of his most famous love lyrics:

I remember the miraculous moment
You appeared before me
Like a fleeting vision,
Like a spirit of pure beauty...

And my heart beats in ecstasy,
And once again is born in it,
Divinity, and inspiration,
And life, and tears, and love.

The new Czar Nicholas I allowed Pushkin to return to St Petersburg in September 1826, after deciding to take on the role of the poet's personal censor. The Pushkin Poetry Days Festival is held annually in Mikhailovskoe on the first Sunday of June, close to Alexander Pushkin's birthday (June 6).

The three estates are open 10am–5pm; closed on Mondays and last Tuesday of month (and usually second half of November). The information department is at 21 Novorzhevskaya; it is possible to overnight in two guesthouses on the museum-reserve. Other hotels and guesthouses are nearby, as the Hotel Druzhba (Friendship), at 8 Lenina, which is walking distance from the bus station. For more information on the three estates, lodging and restaurants, see www.pushkin.ellink.ru.

EAST OF THE CITY (LAKE LADOGA AREA)
PETROKREPOST OR SCHLÜSSELBURG (Петрокрепост)

Peter's Fortress, or Petrokrepost, situated on a small island near the southwestern shore of Lake Ladoga, was founded by Grand Prince Yuri in 1323 to protect trade waterways linking Novgorod with the Baltic. At that time, the small outpost was known as Oreshek (Nut). When Peter the Great captured the tiny fortress from the Swedes in 1702 (they took control of the lands in the 17th-century), he renamed it from the Swedish Nöteborg (Nut Fortress) to Schlüsselburg, the Key Fortress. The town of Schlüsselburg (35 kilometers or 22 miles east of St Petersburg) sprang up along the left bank of the Neva, where it flows out of the lake. After the Great Northern War ended in 1721, Peter converted the fortress into a prison. He had his sister Maria and first wife Evdokia Lopukhina imprisoned here, and many Russian revolutionaries suffered similar fates. On May 8, 1887, Lenin's brother Alexander Ulyanov, along with four others who attempted to assassinate Czar Alexander III, were hung in the prison yard. The German name of Schlüsselburg was changed to Petrokrepost in 1944 during World War II.

For day trips here, check out the ticket kassa at the corner of Dumskaya (Gostiny Dvor) and Nevsky Prospekt; inexpensive Russian excursion buses make tours to the fortress several times a week. Trains run from St Petersburg's Ladozhsky Rail Station to Petrokrepost, located on the bank of the Neva opposite the fortress. By car, take the M18 Highway east. (For Lake Ladoga/Valaam Boat tours, see page 672.)

Staraya Ladoga (Старая Ладога)

Once the capital of ancient Rus, Staraya (Old) Ladoga celebrated its 1260th anniversary in 2013, marking it as one of the oldest towns in Russia and Northern Europe. Lying 120 kilometers (72 miles) east of St Petersburg, the enchanting town, with only 3500 residents, is situated along the Volkhov River near Lake Ladoga. In the early 8th century, Varangians (Norsemen) established an outpost in the area where the Volkhov flows into the Ladozhka River (the earliest discovered timber structure dates back to 753). Since the town lay on important trade routes from the Baltic to the Volga and Black Seas, it quickly developed into a thriving center of culture, commerce and even decorative art; by the 9th century, the prominent 'City of Ladoga' had become the capital of the Slav-Varangian state. According to ancient chronicles, the Norseman Rurik and his army were summoned by Slavs in 862 to rule and settle the region. Ladoga thus became a capital city and the seat of the House of Rurik, the first ruling dynasty of Rus. Later Rurik's son, Prince Oleg, met his tragic end here. According to legend (and told in Alexander Pushkin's *Song of Oleg the Wise*) a fortune-teller told Oleg that his death would somehow be connected to his favorite horse; thus, Oleg abandoned it for another. Later, the Prince was mortally bitten by a snake that had slithered out of the dead horse's skull. Over the next eight centuries, control of Ladoga fluctuated between Swedish, Mongol and Russian rule. In 1702, Peter the Great set out from Ladoga with over 16,000 men to assault the Swedish fortress of Nöteburg (today's Petrokrepost)—a campaign that eventually drove out the Swedes and led to the founding of the new capital in 1703. It was then that Peter the Great decreed that administrative centers and all citizens of Ladoga (now prefixed with Staraya) be transferred to the newly founded town of Novaya (New) Ladoga, located 12 kilometers to the north, and nearer to the southern shores of Lake Ladoga. This cruel fate ultimately helped preserve the architectural wonders of this gem of a town where over 160 historical and cultural landmarks are still evident today.

This museum-reserve includes the ancient **Burial Mounds** or *sopki* ('barrows') that are still found along the banks of the Volkhov. One of the mounds is believed to contain the grave of Prince Oleg. The town's main attraction is the pentagonal **kremlin** and its numerous gate towers, now restored to their 17th-century configuration In the mid 12th-century, the town, now annexed to the mighty Novgorod Principality, erected as many as six stone churches, two of which, still stand today (the Assumption and St George). Ladoga was the first to introduce the cross-and-dome church style architecture with four pillars and three apses, later widely adopted by other Russian towns. Behind the kremlin walls lies the **Uspensky Monastery** with its main single-domed **Church of the Assumption**. In 1718, Peter I banished his first wife, Evdokia Fyodorovna Lopukhina to this monastery (she had supposedly plotted against him) where she remained for seven years before being transferred to Schlüsselberg, and finally to Moscow's Novodevichy Convent where she died in 1731. Overlooking the River Vokhov, outside the kremlin, is the small white **Church of St George the Victorious** (1165); frescoes still cover over 150 square meters of the interior. The medieval fresco of 'St George and the Dragon' is a masterpiece of Greco-Russian art. In 1445 the Monastery of St George was built around it. (In its heyday, the town contained six monasteries.) In 1695, on the grounds of St John Monastery, the five-domed masonry **Church of St John the Precursor** was built atop Malysheva Hill, where it still stands today. Another unique structure is the all wooden **Church of St Demetrius of Thessalonica**, consecrated in 1646. The **Church of Dmitry Solunsky** houses a small museum of peasant life. To the south stands the 17th-century **Monastery of St Nicholas the Miracle Worker**, the **Nikolsky Cathedral** and the tent-roofed **Church of St John Chrysostom**. On the right bank, the **Church of St Basil the Great** is all that is left of the monastery.

Numerous limestone cliff and cave formations are found along the banks of the Volkhov river. A short ride north brings the visitor to Novaya Ladoga, whose points of interest include the **Nikolo-Medvedsky Monastery**, two 15th-century churches and an old cemetery. The helmut-domed **Klimentovskaya Church** and belfry stands on Karl Marx Prospekt. Other pre-revolutionary buildings and old merchant homes also dot the town. One kilometer north of Novaya Lagoga, is the old **Village of Krenitsy**; on the other side of the river is the ancient **Old Believer's Village of Nemyatovo**. The picturesque **Village of Sviritsa**, 30 kilometers (18 miles) to the east, is situated on islands, surrounded by seven rivers. Resembling Venice, there are no streets here, and boats are used as the main means of transportation.

To get to Staraya Ladoga, trains (1–2 hours) or *elektrichka* suburban trains (2.5 hours) depart from St Petersburg's Ladozhsky station to Volkhovstroi-1 (Volkhov). Then take a taxi, or bus or *marshrutka* number 23 from the station's front square for the remaining 13-kilometer (8-mile) ride to the town (ask the driver to let you known when to get off; you'll see the Kremlin on the right). Group bus tours can also be purchased from travel kiosks on the corner of Nevsky (Gostiny Dvor) and Dumskaya; travel agencies also offer one and two-day excursions. To overnight, the Hotel Ladya is at 6 Sovetskaya.

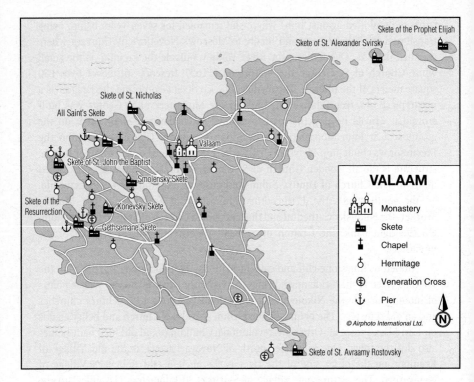

VALAAM ISLAND (Валаам)

The Valaam Archipelago (made up of over 50 islands) is situated 170 kms (105 miles) north of St Petersburg in northwestern Lake Ladoga, Europe's largest freshwater lake. Valaam Island is the largest with 600 residents. The word *valaam* is thought to derive from the Finnish *valamo*, meaning "high land." According to legend, two Greek missionaries, Sergius and Herman, first visited these northern Novgorod lands in the first half of the 10th-century during the conversion of the area to Orthodox Christianity. The island's main attraction, the 14th-century **Transfiguration** (Spaso-Preobrazhensky) **Monastery**, was first built as a fortress to protect the area from the Swedes. After Swedish armies destroyed the structure in 1611, Peter the Great had it rebuilt a century later, when the monastery doubled as a prison. In the 19th-century, Valaam attained its greatest prosperity under Abbot Damaskin, who was also an architect, agronomist, botanist, economist and writer. Damaskin established a regular shipping route to the island from the mainland, and a 32-kilometer (20-mile) railway was built to ship goods to and from the cloister. The monks also built a model farm and ponds where fish were reared for caviar. The highlight of Valaam was its orchards that contained over 60 varieties of apples, along with berries, melons and grapes. At one point, any traveler or pilgrim to the island was obliged to bring along a sack of black soil for the gardens. From 1811 to 1917, the archipelago was part of the Finnish Duchy of the Russian Empire. After the 1917 Revolution, it became part of Finland, and this lasted until the Russian-Finnish War of 1940. During WWII, the monastery was bombed several times, and its inhabitants evacuated. The island structures remained in total disrepair until 1989, when six monks arrived to restore cloistered life. Eight main *skity* (secluded monasteries with a small collective of monks who, though living the life of a hermit, work together for common needs), are scattered about Valaam island. The closest, near the ferry dock, is the **Voskresensky (Resurrection) Monastery**, with an upper church that holds liturgical recitals. Another skete within walking distance is the **Gethsemene Monastery** with a wooden church and monastic cells. A ferry takes the visitor to the **Transfiguration of the Savior Monastery** (located 6 kilometers/4 miles from the harbor), the heart of the island's religious life. On the cathedral's lower floor is the **Church of Saints Sergius and Herman**, completed in 1892, with an icon depicting the two saints kneeling before Christ. Today the complex consists of several hundred residents, who mostly get around by horse and boat. Even though tourist souvenirs and beer are sold outside, all visitors are required to respect the environment and honor the dress code. Men must leave their heads uncovered and wear long trousers (no shorts), and women wear long skirts and cover their heads (scarves and aprons are provided at the entrance).

Today, the clergy is helping to restore the gardens and three orchards with over two thousand apple trees, including some over 200 years old. One of the most beautiful roads starts from the main cloister and leads through an alley of 300-year-old Siberian Fir trees to the Abbot's cemetery. Father Damaskin is buried near the northern altar wall of the nearby church. The island's beauty has inspired many of Russia's artists and musicians—Tchaikovsky's First Symphony is thought to portray a musical landscape poem of the island.

The most common excursion to Lake Ladoga is by boat from St Petersburg, In addition to quicker day trips, cruises also leave at night (rooms are clean, yet spartan), arrive the next morning and then tour Valaam Island and the lake (about six hours), and return the following morning. (There is only one small hotel on Valaam, almost always full.) Although meals are provided onboard ship, it is highly recommended that you bring along your own food. If you add Kizhi, the trip becomes four nights/five days. Boats run from mid-May to mid-September, depending when the lake is navigable. St Petersburg's main river terminal is at 195 Obvodnovo Canal Embankment; metro Ploshchad Alexandra Nevskovo. Group tour tickets can also be bought from ticket kiosks on the corner of Nevsky (Gostiny

Dvor) and Dumskaya Street in town. A bus takes passengers to the ferry. (For a list of boat companies that tour Lake Ladoga, see Boat Excursions and River Cruises on pages 729–730). It is also possible to book a pilgrimage through the monastery: see www.valaam.ru.

KIZHI ISLAND (КИЖИ)

This island (one of almost 1,400) lies about 150 kilometers (90 miles) northwest of Lake Ladoga in Karelia's region of Lake Onega. (Lake Onega lies just south of the White Sea.) Its first settlers arrived in the sixth millennium BC, and ancient petroglyphs are still discernible on some of the rock formations. Between the tenth and 12th centuries inhabitants of Novgorod set out to colonize their own lands along the shores of the lake.

The **Church of the Resurrection of Lazarus**, on the islet of Mooch, is one of the oldest buildings in Russia. The main attraction, on the southwestern end of the six-kilometer long Kizhi Island is the 37-meter (121-foot) high wooden **Cathedral of the Transfiguration of the Savior**, built in 1714, to honor Peter the Great's victory over the Swedes. Pine logs form the octahedron structure, and over 30,000 curved silver aspen shingles were handmade to cover the 22 cupolas of the three-tiered roof. The Cathedral was used in summer and during major holidays. As it was customary to build paired churches, the adjoining octagonal nine-domed winter **Church of the Intercession** was added in 1764. It has an extended wooden vestibule that was used for town meetings and on display here are icons from both churches. (Other items are exhibited in the Museum of Fine Arts in the neighboring town of Petrozavodsk.) A climb to the top of the center tent-roofed **bell tower** provides a great panoramic view of the island. Bells of the **Chapel of Archangel Michael** are played in summer.

A **Museum of Wooden Architecture** hosts a collection of 19th-century exhibits from northern Russia. These include the simple log-hewn late 15th-century **Resurrection of Lazarus Church, Chapel of the Icon of the Savior** from the village of Vigovo; the **Church of the Three Prelates**, with its one large wooden tower, from the village of Kavgora; the rectangular **Sergeyev House**, built in 1908, with the living space on one side and the barn on the other; and the more elaborate two-story **Oshevnev House** (1876) from the Logmorychei village. It was customary to decorate the houses with colorfully carved window shutters and *kokoshnik* gables along the roof.

The national treasures of Kizhi Island have been established as a UNESCO site and are slowly being restored. (See Valaam for excursions, with more information on page 729.) For more information, www.kizhi.karelia.ru.

ANNA AKHMATOVA (1889–1966)

In 1889, the Gorenko family of Odessa added a new daughter, Anna. She was destined to become one of Russia's greatest 20th-century lyric poets.

When Anna was one year old, the family moved north to Tsarskoye Selo near St Petersburg, where she lived until she was 16. 'My first memories are those of Tsarskoye Selo,' she later wrote, 'the green grandeur of the parks, the groves where nanny took me, the hippodrome where small, mottled ponies jumped, and the old train station....'

She wrote her first poem at the age of 10. But poetry was a licentious pastime, according to her father, and he admonished her not to 'befoul his good and respected name.' So, Anna, while still in her teens, changed her surname to Akhmatova, honoring her maternal great-grandmother's Tartar heritage which, supposedly, was traced back to the last khan of the Golden Horde in Russia, Achmat Khan, a descendant of Genghis.

Her first book of poetry, *Evening*, appeared in 1912, and was an immediate success. 'Those pathetic verses of an empty-headed girl,' the astonished author wrote, 'have, no one knows why, been reprinted 13 times.' And yet every young person of the time could recite her *Gray-Eyed King*. Prokofiev later set the lyrics to music.

> Hail to thee, everlasting pain!
> The gray-eyed King died yesterday...
> I will wake up my daughter now.
> And look into her eyes of gray.
> And outside the window the poplars whisper.
> 'Your King is no more on this earth.'

Her second collection, *The Rosary*, was published in 1914. With the publication of Akhmatova's *White Flock* collection, Russian poetry hit the 'real' 20th-century. Her recurrent themes of romance and love and the wounded heroine of these poems speaks with intimacy and immediacy.

> There is a sacred boundary between those who are close,
> And it cannot be transcended by passion or love
> Though lips on lips fuse in dreadful silence
> And the heart shatters to pieces with love...
> Those who strive to reach it are mad, and those
> Who reach it are stricken with grief...
> Now you understand why my heart
> Does not beat faster beneath your hand.

In 1910, Anna married the talented poet Nikolai Gumilyov, who had begun to court her when she was 14. Together they traveled to Italy and then to France where Modigliani made a series of drawings using Anna as his model. Along with her talent, she had tremendous physical beauty. Anna was five-foot-eleven-inches tall, dark-haired, lithe and feline; someone once compared her light green eyes to those of a snow leopard. Positively stunning, she caught the eye of many an artist and sculptor. In addition, a whole volume could be filled with poetry and prose written just about her.

Recollections of the years with Gumilyov echoed many times throughout her poetry.

> He loved three things in the world,
> Singing at night, white peacocks
> and old maps of America.
> He hated when children cried,
> He hated tea with raspberry jam
> And women's hysterics.
> ...and I was his wife.

Gumilyov was the creator and leader of the Acmeists. After many years of romantic Symbolisism, their manifesto called for poetry of clarity and restraint. The cult lionized the city and Pushkin's Russia just as the imperial regime was about to collapse. Anna was 28 and at the center of Petersburg's artistic world of cabarets and intellectuals when the Romanov dynasty was ousted during the 1917 Revolution. She was 32 when, under Stalin, Gumilyov (by then her ex-husband) was arrested on a charge of plotting against the Soviet Government. He was executed soon afterwards. Her only son, Lev, was later twice arrested and sentenced to many years in a labor camp. (A noted scholar in later life, he died a natural death in 1992.)

Anna Akhmatova's name began to disappear from the literary scene and from 1925 until 1940 there was an unofficial ban on the publication of all her poetry. In 1935, her common law (third) husband Nikolai Punin, an art critic and historian of Western art, was arrested; he later died in a Siberian prison. The disappearance and death of friends, harassment by officials, no place to live, hours of waiting in lines for news of her arrested son, all took their voice in her prose-poem *Requiem*, dedicated to those times. Not daring to write anything down on paper, her friends memorized the verses. She wrote it between 1935 and 1940, but it wasn't allowed to be published in Russia until 1987.

In the terrible years of the Yezhov horrors, I spent 17 months standing in prison lines in Leningrad. One day somebody recognized me. There standing behind me was a woman with blue lips. She had, of course, never heard of me, but she suddenly came out of her stupor so common to us all and whispered in my ear (everybody there spoke only in whispers) 'Can you describe this'? and I said 'Yes, I can.' And then a fleeting smile passed over what had once been her face ...

Even though Akhmatova had opportunities to leave the country during Stalin's Terror, she refused to emigrate. To her, being Russian meant living in Russia, no matter what the government did to her or her loved ones. 'No! Not beneath foreign skies.... I was with my people then ... There my people, unfortunately, were...'

Pictures of Akhmatova show a beautiful woman with an aristocratic profile and a proudly raised head—a lioness with sad eyes. In the summer of 1936, a friend of hers wrote, 'She is extraordinary and quite beautiful. Those who have not seen her cannot consider their lives full.'

In November 1941, during the Siege of Leningrad, Akhmatova was evacuated to Tashkent. There she began writing her *Poem Without a Hero* set in the Fountain House (in the former Sheremeryev Palace off of the Fontanka Canal) in St Petersburg. The work consumed her for 22 years; she finished it in 1962. In 1946, after the war, Akhmatova returned to Petersburg, where her popularity was again immense. Because of her growing celebrity, and also possibly because of a meeting with Isaiah Berlin, she was expelled from the Writer's Union and denounced by Zhdanov, Stalin's cultural watchdog, who accused her of poisoning the minds of Soviets; he called her a 'half-nun, half-harlot'.

After this denunciation, Akhmatova was no longer published. She earned her money through translations and writing about accepted poets such as Pushkin. With no official residence, she lived off the help and kindness of friends. The West suspected that she was no longer writing poetry; many in Russia thought that she was no longer alive. But, somehow, she always knew that it was her fate to live through an epoch of interminable grief and upheaval.

In 1956, Akhmatova's son was released from the camps, and the last decade of her life became somewhat easier. She continued to live in the apartment on the Fontanka and was given the use of a tiny summer house in Komarovo, a writer's colony outside Petersburg. She was allowed to travel twice abroad. In 1964, Anna Akhmatova received the Etna Taormina Literary Prize in Catania, Italy; and in 1965, in England, she received an honorary doctorate from Oxford.

After her death on March 5, 1966, a memorial service was held at the Cathedral of St Nicholas the Seafarer, a 20-minute walk from her house on the Fontanka. It was said that the crowd attending her memorial looked like a human sea. The poet Joseph Brodsky, a close friend, wrote:

'At certain periods of history only poetry is capable of dealing with reality by condensing it into something graspable, something that otherwise couldn't be retained by the mind. In that sense, the whole nation took up the pen name of Akhmatova, which explains her popularity and which, more importantly, enabled her to speak for the nation as well as to tell it something it didn't know... her verses are to survive because they are charged with time....'

And timelessness. She captured the sense of the eternal in her last dated poem of February 1965, at the age of 75.

> So we lowered our eyes,
> Tossing the flowers on the bed,
> We didn't know until the end,
> What to call one another.
> We didn't dare until the end

To utter first names,
As if, nearing the goal, we slowed our steps
On the enchanted way.

A literary critic who visited the house on the Fontanka described her room: 'A bed, or rather a stretcher, covered with a thin, dark blanket stands by the wall: on another wall is a mirror in an ancient gilt frame. Next to it, on a shelf, is a porcelain object, not really valuable but antique. In the corner is a folding icon. By the wall next to the door stands a small rectangular table, with a simple inkstand and a blotter—the desk. There are also one or two old chairs and a worn armchair, but neither wardrobe nor bookshelves. Books are everywhere, on the desk, the chair and on the windowsill.' The Anna Akhmatova House Museum is in St Petersburgh at 34 Fontanka and displays these rooms, where she lived and wrote, along with photos, letters and her poetry (see pages 562 and 624).

Akhmatova never stopped writing about life's tumultuous truths.

These poems have such hidden meanings
It's like staring into an abyss.
And the abyss is enticing and beckoning,
But never will you discover the bottom of it,
And never will its hollow silence
Grow tired of speaking...

I know the gods transformed
Humans into objects without killing their minds.
So that my amazing sorrows will live forever...

...I am not allowed to forget
The taste of the tears of yesterday.

Today, four monuments in the city celebrate the great 20th century poet. One stands next to the Neva River between Shpalernaya and Robespierre Embankment. Erected in 2006 to mark the 40th anniversary of Akhmatova's death, this striking 3-meter high bronze statue is symbolically located opposite the former Kresty Prison, where her partner, the art critic Nikolai Punin, and son, Lev Gumilev, were incarcerated during the 1930s. Another stands in the courtyard of 17 Ordynka Street, where she once lived. Sculptor Vladimir Surovtsev modeled the elegant statue on her famous portrait painted in Paris by Modigliani. In the words of Osip Mandalstam, 'her poetry...will become one of the symbol's of Russia's greatness.' Two fascinating documentaries on the poet are *Fear and the Muse: The Story of Anna Akhmatova* (narrated by Claire Bloom and Christopher Reeve, 2000) and *The Anna Ahkmatova File* (1989), directed by Semyon Aranovich.

THE BRONZE HORSEMAN

Where lonely waters, struggling, sought
To reach the sea, he (Peter the Great) paused, in thought...
The haughty Swede here we'll curb and hold at bay
And here, to gall him, found a city.
As nature bids so must we do:
A window will we cut here through
On Europe, and a foothold gaining
Upon this coast, the ships we'll hail
Of every flag, and freely sail
These seas, no more ourselves restraining.
A century passed, and there it stood,
Of Northern lands the pride and beauty,
A young, resplendent, gracious city,
Sprung out the dark of mire and wood...
Now there rise great places and towers; a maze
Of sails and mastheads crown the harbor;
Ships of all ports moor here beside
These rich and people shores; the wide,
Majestic Neva slowly labors,
In granite clad, to push its way
'Neath graceful bridges; gardens cover
The once bare isles that dot the river,
Its glassy surface still and grey.
Old Moscow fades beside her rival.
A dowager, she is outshone,
Overshadowed by the new arrival
Who, robed in purple, mounts the throne...
...the weather raged wildly
The Neva swelled and roared,
Gurgling and welling up like a cauldron
Rushed on the city. Before her, all fled...

It was then on Peter's square...
Sat motionless, terribly pale,
Eugene. He was in terror, not for himself...
The widow and her daughter, his fiancée Parasha,

Alexander
Pushkin

Had been swept away...
Eugene shuddered...above him loomed...
A brazen head in the dusk,
Him by whose fateful will
The city by the sea was founded...
Awesome is he in the surrounding gloom!...
Where are you galloping, haughty steed,
And where will you plant your hooves?
Oh, mighty potentate of fate!
Was it not thus, aloft hard by the abyss,
That with curb of iron
You reared up Russia?...
Scowling, Eugene stood before the prideful statue...
'I'll show you!' And suddenly full tilt...
He runs down the empty square...
But, all night, wherever the wretched madman
Might turn his steps,
Behind him everywhere the Bronze Horseman
Was galloping with heavy clatter...

Alexander Pushkin (1799–1837)

Everything we have comes from Pushkin. His turning to the people so early in his career was so unheard of, so astonishing, such a new and so unexpected departure it can only have been a miracle or, failing that, the fruit of the singular grandeur of genius—one, I might add, we cannot fully appreciate even today.

Fyodor Dostoevsky, A Writer's Journal, 1876

The realm of poetry is as boundless as life itself; yet every object of poetry has been set, from time out of mind, into a specific hierarchy, and to confuse the high with the low or take the one for the other is a major stumbling block. In the great poets, in Pushkin, this harmonious precision in the ranking of objects has been brought to perfection.

Leo Tolstoy, 1874

ST PETERSBURG PRACTICAL INFORMATION

TELEPHONE NUMBERS

Country code for Russia (7)   St Petersburg city code (812)

EMERGENCY SERVICES

Fire   01
Police   02
Ambulance   03 (See also Medical)
Emergency from cell phone 112

The St Petersburg Tourist Information Bureaus have locations all about town and at the airport. The main office is at 14 Sadovaya, metro Gostiny Dvor (tel. 300-3333/310-2822). Other locations are at 12 Palace Square, Vosstaniya Square and St Issac's Square. Look for the blue box with the "i" in the middle. www.ispb.info, www.visit-petersburg.ru, www.stpetersburg.com and www.saint-petersburg.com.

St Petersburg City Smart Card, consider purchasing a 2-, 3- or 5-day electronic Smart Card which offers visits to 40 museums along with discounted transportation and other tours. www.petersburgcard.com.

Taxis

Taxi Million, tel. 600-0000, www.6-000-000.ru (in English, take credit cards). **Taxi Blues**, tel. 321-8888, www.taxiblues.ru. **Taxi-4**, tel. 633-3333, www.taxi-4.ru. **Petersburg Taxi**, tel. 324-7777 (or 068), www.taxi068.spb.ru. **Welcome Taxi**, tel. 643-4273, http://welcometaxi.ru and **New Yellow Taxi**, tel. 600-6666, http://peterburg.nyt.ru/en. About 15 minutes prior to pick-up, the dispatcher will phone to tell you the make, color and license number of the car, so they need to be able to call you back. Rates depend on distance, and airport runs are offered at a fixed price.

USEFUL ON-LINE SERVICES

St Petersburg's official website: www.saint-petersburg.com.

About St Petersburg for Tourists: www.travel.spb.ru.

Travel: www.ostwest.com, www.travelrussia.ru and www.waytorussia.net.

Traveller's Yellow Pages for St Petersburg: www.infoservices.com.

St Petersburg at your Fingertips: www.cityvision2000.comIn Your Pocket (towns around the city): www.inyourpocket.com.

St Petersburg Times: www.sptimes.ru.

Express Mail/Post

Post Offices are located at: 9 Pochtamskaya, 65 Nevsky Prospekt and 29 Liteiny Prospekt.

DHL International, 10 Nevsky Prospekt. Tel. 326-6400. www.dhl.ru.

Federal Express, 3 locations, 4a Finlandsky Pr. office 35/2. Tel. 495-8587. www.fedex.com.

TNT Express Worldwide, www.tnt.com.

United Parcel Service (UPS), 6 Voroshilova and 12 Shturmanskaya. Tel. 703-3939, www.ups.com.

Useful Publications in English

Many English-language newspapers and magazines can be found in hotel shops and magazine kiosks. *Pulse St Petersburg* is published monthly with city cultural news and events. *St Petersburg Times* is the leading English-language newspaper in the city (www.sptimes.ru). *Where in St Petersburg* is published six times a year with useful information on travel and culture (www.where.ru). The *Moscow Times* has information on both Moscow and St Petersburg, and the world (www.themoscowtimes.com). *Passport Magazine* is run by Expats www.passportmagazine.ru, as well as www.expat.ru. *Russian Life Magazine* is at www.russianlife.com.

Medical

Most top-end hotels have a resident doctor or nurse.

American Medical Clinic, 78 Moika Canal Emb. Tel. 740-2090. Metro Sadovaya. (Also provides **Dental Care**). www.amclinic.com.

EuroMed Clinic, 60 Suvorovsky Pr. Tel. 327-0301. Metro Chernyshevskaya. www.euromed.ru.

Medem International Clinic & Hospital, 6 Marata, Tel. 336-3333. Metro Mayakovskaya. www.medem.ru.

Pharmacies, the chain 36.6 Pharmacy has branches all around town. Look for signs Apteka / АПТЕКА.

Opticians, look for the Optika chain. Renome Optics Club is at 49/1 Suvorovsky Pr; open 11am–8pm.

CONSULATES

Armenia, 22 Dekabristov. Tel. 571-7236, www.armenianembassy.ru.

Australia (Honorary Consulate), 14 Petrovsky. Tel. 315-1100/325-7334. www.russia.embassy.gov.au.

Austria (Honorary Consulate), 43 Furshtatskaya. Metro Chernyshevskaya. Tel. 275-0502.

Belarus, 3a Bonch-Bruevicha, Metro Chernyshevskaya. Tel. 273-0078/4164.

Bulgaria, 27 Ryleeva. Metro Chernyshevskaya. Tel. 273-4018/7347.

China, 134 Griboyedov Canal Emb. Tel. 713-8009/714-7670. http://saint-petersburg.china-consulate.org.

Cuba, 37 Ryleeva, Metro Chernyshevskaya. Tel. 272-7506.

Czech Republic, 5–7 Tverskaya, Metro Chernyshevskaya. Tel. 271-0459/4612. www.mzv.cz/petersburg.

Denmark, 42 Moika Canal, Metro Nevsky Proskpekt. Tel. 703-3900/3529. http://rusland.um.dk.

Estonia, 14 Bolshaya Monetnaya, Metro Gorkovskaya. Tel. 703-3900/702-0920. www.peterburg.estemb.ru.

Finland, 4 Preobrazhenskay. Metro Chernyshevskaya. Tel. 331-7600. www.finland.org.ru or www.finland.org.

France, 15 Moika River Emb. Metro Admiralteyskaya. Tel. 332-2270. www.consulfrance-saint-petersbourg.org.

Germany, 39 Furshtatskaya. Metro Chernyshevskaya. Tel. 320-2400/2140. www.sankt-petersburg.diplo.de.

Hungary, 15 Marata. Tel. 312-6458/6753.

India, 35 Ryleeva St. Metro Chernyshevskaya. Tel. 640-7222. www.indianconsulate.ru.

Israel, 1/61 Bolshoi Kazachi (Grand Cossack) Lane. Tel. 272-7887/406-0500.

Italy, 10 Teatralnaya Pl. Tel. 318-0791/0792. Metro Nevsky Pr. www.conssanpietroburgo.esteri.it.

Japan, 29 Moika Canal Emb, Metro Nevsky Prospekt. Tel. 449-4770/4771. www.st-petersburg.ru.emb-japan.go.jp.

Kazakhstan, 15a Vilensky Lane. Tel. 335-2546. www.kazconsulate.spb.ru & www.kazembassy.ru

Latvia, 11 10-ya Liniya.Vasilyevsky Island. Metro Vasileostrovskaya. Tel. 336-3454/449-8290. www.mfa.gov.lv/en/stpetersburg.

Lithuania, 37 Ryleeva. Tel. 327-3167. consulate-stpetersburg.mfa.lt.

Netherlands, 11 Moika Canal. Metro Admiralteyskaya.
Tel. 334-0200, stpetersburg.niconsulate.org.

Norway, 13–15 Ligovsky Prospekt, 3rd floor. Tel. 612-4100. www.norvegia.ru.

Poland, 12/14 5-ya Sovetskaya. Metro Vosstaniya. Tel. 336-3140/3141.
www.sanktpetersburg.msz.gov.pl.

Spain, 9 Furshtatskaya, Metro Chernyshevskaya. Tel. 702-6266/6284.
www.espana.spb.ru.

Sweden, 1–3 Mal Konyushennaya, Metro Nevsky Prospekt. Tel. 329-1430/1440.
www.sweden.spb.ru.

Thailand (Honorary Consulate), 9/6 Bolshoi Pr. Metro Vasileostrovskaya.
Tel. 325-6271.

Ukraine, 1b Bonch-Bruevicha. Tel. 320-3200/3239 & 331-5969.

United Kingdom, 5 Proletarsky Diktatury, Metro Chernyshevskaya. Tel. 320-3200/3239,
www.british-consulate.net/St.Petersburg.html or www.ukinrussia.fco.gov.uk.

United States, 15 Furshtatskaya, Metro Chernyshevskaya. Tel. 331-2600 (operates
24 hours for emergencies) and 331-2888. http://stpetersburg.usconsulate.gov.

Airports

Pulkovo International Airport, located 17 kilometres (ten miles) south of the city.
(See Airport information page 71/506). Flight timetables see: www.pulkovoairport.ru.

Customs Regulations, any items over 100 years old, including art, icons,
instruments, coins, jewellery, etc. cannot be taken out of Russia. If you think it looks
old, it must be assessed at the Cultural Security Dept at 17 Malaya Morskaya (Mon–
Fri, 11am–5pm), metro Admiralteyskaya (or it could be confiscated). Bring
passport, sales receipt and item. The customs officer will issue a receipt for tax paid
and an exit certificate (certifying that the item is not an antique).

Airlines

Aeroflot, 1/43 Rubinshtein (off Fontanka). Tel. 438-5583, Metro Gostiny Dvor. (free
from RF 8-800-444-5555). Moscow (495) 223-5555, www.aeroflot.com.

Air France, 35 Bolshaya Morkskaya. Tel. 325-8252 (airport 324-3241).
Metro Gostiny Dvor. www.airfrance.com.

Austrian Airlines, 17 Startovaya, Tel. 346-8101, www.austrian.com.

British Airways, 1/3 Malaya Konyushennaya (14 Sotsialisticheskaya).
Tel. 380-0626/325-2565, Metro Nevsky Prospekt, www.britishairways.com.

Delta Airlines (code share Air France and KLM), www.delta.com.

Finnair, 44 Kazanskaya. Tel. 326-8170, Metro Gostiny Dvor. www.finnair.com.

KLM, 35 Bolshaya Morskaya. Tel. 311-6797, Metro Nevsky Prospekt. www.klm.com.

Lufthansa, 7 Voznesensky Prospekt. Tel. 314-4979/5917, Metro Sadovaya. www.lufthansa.com.

Rossiya Airlines, 61 Nevsky Prospekt, Metro Nevsky Prospekt. Tel. 633-3800. www.rossiya-airlines.com.

S7, 14/35 Spassky Lane. Tel. 457-0652, www.s7.ru.

SAS, 25 Nevsky Pr. Tel. 325-3225, Metro Nevsky Prospekt. www.scandinavian.net.

Swissair, 57 Nevsky Prospekt. Tel. 325-3250, www.swissair.com.

Transaero, 48 Liteyny Pr. Tel.602-0000/279-1974, Metro Chernyshevskaya. www.transaero.ru.

RAILWAYS

See Getting There page 71 & Getting Around pages 79–81, for more details on train travel and buying tickets. Ticket windows at each station sell same-day and advance (up to 45 days) tickets. Each station has both long distance and local *electrichki/* commuter trains. To check schedules, timetables and prices (and buy tickets online) see: www.russianrailways.com, www.express-2.ru, www.russianrail.com and www.russiantrains.com.

The **Central Railway Ticket Office** is at 24 Griboyedov Kanal Embankment. Tickets sold for any station or destination. Monday–Saturday 8am–8pm; Sunday 8am–4pm. Metro Gostiny Dvor.

Baltic Station (Baltiisky Vokzal), 120 Obvodnovo Kanala. Metro Baltiiskaya. Trains include those to Moscow, Peterhof, Gatchina, Oranienbaum and Baltic states.

Finland Station (Finlyansky Vokzal), 6 Lenin Sq. Trains include those to Helsinki, Finland, Vyborg, Lake Ladoga, Repino, Razliv and Olgino. Metro Ploshchad Lenina.

Ladozhsky Station, 73 Zanevsky Pr. Trains to Helsinki, Murmansk, Arkhangelsk, Ekaterinburg. Metro Ladozhsky. www.lvspb.ru.

Moscow Station (Moskovsky Vokzal), 85 Nevsky Pr. Trains include those to Moscow, Novgorod, Yaroslavl, Ivanovo, Kostroma and many other points north and south. Connection to Trans-Siberian express. Ticket windows on 2nd floor near train platforms. Commuter tickets sold on right side of station. Metro Ploshchad Vosstaniya, www.moskovsky-vokzal.ru.

Vitebsk Station (Vitebsky Vokzal), 52 Zagorodny Pr. Trains to southwest Russia, and direct trains to Budapest, Prague, Brussels and Berlin. Metro Pushkinskaya.

ACCOMMODATION

The old Soviet Hotel system is now a dinosaur of the past and today every type of accommodation is available—from five-star luxury and boutique & mini-hotels to bargain hostels and apartments. It is now much easier to select a hotel based on location, cost, service and style. (For more information see Being There/Hotels section, page 83.) Many hotels, particularly those located in the heart of the city, tend to get booked up, especially in summer months (when rooms are also much more expensive), so try and reserve as far in advance as possible. (Winter hotel rates can be up to 50% less.) Most establishments now have their own websites, where you can book directly online (often at a discounted rate), and take credit cards. Before booking, find out what amenities are included, such as breakfast, private bath, visa support, and airport/town center transportation. Ask if the VAT and city tax are already included in the price. How close is it to a Metro station? (You can easily pinpoint the hotel's location in the city by its nearest Metro stop.) Ask for a room with minimum street noise or the best view available. Cheaper hotels can be situated far from the city center; you may consider booking a slightly more expensive yet more centrally located hotel to save on travel time. Upon check-in you will be asked for your passport/visa for registration (always keep a copy of both). See each individual website for more information and pictures of the establishment. Other useful websites are: www.booking.com, www.hotels.com, www.st-petersburg-hotels-russia.com and www.allrussianhotels.com.

AIRPORT HOTELS:

Crowne Plaza is next to Pulkovo Airport with free shuttle service to the Metro Moskovsky. www.crowneplaza.com.

Park Inn Pulkovskaya, 1 Pobedy Square. Situated 5 kilometers from the airport, it provides shuttle service to/from airport and Metro Moskovskaya. www.parkinn.com.

DELUXE—Four and Five Star

Most luxury hotels provide visa invitation services and airport transportation. The complex contains restaurants, bars, fitness center, business and bank exchange centers, and all the other amenities usually associated with luxury hotels. The following (depending on season) can be from $250 to well over $1,000 a night.

Astoria Rocco Forte, 39 Bolshaya Morskaya, is located by St Isaac's Cathedral. Built in 1912 by architect Fyodor Lidval, it has been restored to its original five-star art-nouveau grandeur. Metro Admiralteyskaya. www.roccofortehotels.com.

Next door to the Astoria is the slightly cheaper four-star **Angleterre Hotel**. www.angleterrehotel.com.

Corinthia Hotel St Petesburg, 57 Nevsky Prospekt. Located in a former 19th-century mansion, it has over 350 rooms, an art-deco lobby and a roof-top health club (with pool and sauna) and shopping arcade. Metro Mayakovskaya, www.corinthiahotels.com.

Domina Prestige St Petersburg, 99 Moika Embankment. This 5-star hotel is located in the former Jomini Kleiber Mansion on the Moika Canal near St Issac's Cathedral. www.dominarussia.com.

Four Seasons Hotel Lion Palace, 1 Voznesensky Pr. Located in the former 19th-century palace of Prince Lobanov-Rostovsky near St Issac's Cathedral, this 5-star hotel is all about *luxury*. Metro Admiralteyskaya. www.fourseasons.com.

Grand Hotel Emerald, 18 Suvorovsky Pr. This deluxe hotel, with marble floors and chandeliers made from Swarovski crystal, has over 70 rooms and a fitness center. Metro Pl. Vosstaniya. www.grandhotelemerald.com.

Grand Hotel Europe Belmond, 1/7 Mikhailovskay (off Nevsky Pr.) One of the city's oldest and most iconic hotels, it is a cultural and culinary landmark by Arts Square (request one of the new Terrace rooms). Metro Nevsky Prospekt, www.grandhoteleurope.com or www.belmond.com.

Hermitage Hotel, 10 Pravda, official hotel of the Hermitage, it is decorated as rooms in the Winter Palace with the Catherine the Great Restaurant preparing menus once served at the Imperial Residence; a 10-minute ride to the museum. Metro Mayakovskaya. www.thehermitagehotel.ru.

Hotel Moika 22, named after its address, this 5-star Kempinski Hotel is located right off Palace Square with views of the Winter Palace and Moika River. The building dates back to 1853, and first designed by Dutch architect, Basil Von Witte. Metro Admiralteyskaya. www.kempinski.com.

Nash (Our) Hotel on Vasilyevsky Island, 50 11th Liniya, This four-star hotel is near Metro Vasileostrovskaya. www.nashotel.ru.

Novotel St Petersburg Centre Hotel, 3a Mayakovsky St. Opened in 2006, with 233 rooms, it was designed with business travelers in mind. Near Nevsky and Metro Mayakovskaya. www.accorhotels.com.

Park Inn by Radisson, 89 Nevsky Prospekt, with over 250 rooms near the Moskovsky Train Station. Metro Pl Vosstaniya. www.parkinn.com.

Radisson Royal Hotel, 49 Nevsky Pr. Five star hotel right in the heart of town. www.radissonblu.com.

Radisson Sonya Hotel, 5/19 Liteiny Pr, 4-star hotel near the Fontanka Canal and Summer Gardens. Metro Chernyshevskaya. www.radissonblu.com.

Renaissance Baltic Hotel, 4 Pochtamtskaya St, this 4-star hotel is located in a former 19th-century mansion, which served as the residence of Mikhail Yakovlev, a school friend of the poet, Alexander Pushkin. Great city views and of St Issac's Cathedral. Metro Admiralteyskaya. www.marriott.com.

Taleon Imperial Hotel, 15 Nevsky, four-star hotel located in a 18th-century palace that overlooks the Moika Canal; near St Isaac's Cathedral and the Hermitage. Metro Admiralteyskaya. www.booking.com.

W St Petersburg, 6 Voznesensky Pr, Opened in 2011 with 137 rooms next to St Issac's Cathedral, this luxury hotel set in a classic 19th-century building, with floor-to-ceiling windows, has the award-winning Alain Ducasse restaurant and miXup terrace with spectacular views, along with a swimming pool, gym, sauna and spa. Metro Admiralteyskaya. www.wstpetersburg.com.

MODERATE
These average between $130 and $250+ per night (single/double).

3Mosta, 3a Moika Embankment. This 24-room boutique hotel's name means 'Three Bridges' and is located near the Church of Spilled Blood off Nevsky. Well worth a stay! Metro Nevsky Prospekt. www.3mosta.com.

Alexander House, 27 Kryukov Canal Emb. A lovely 14-room boutique hotel, created by Alexander & Natalya (each room decorated for their favorite world cities), located close to the Nikolsky Cathedral and Mariinsky Theater. Nearest Metro Pl Sennaya. www.a-house.ru.

Amaranta Admiralteyskaya, 8 Alexander Blok, mini hotel, in 19th-century Silver-Age setting has 54 rooms on 5 floors near Mariinsky Theater in Kolumna District. www.amaranta.ru.

Art Hotel Trezzini on Vasilyevsky Island, 21 Bolshoi Prospekt. Named after the architect who originally designed the island's lay out, it is located a few blocks from the Art Academy and Neva River. Metro Vasileostrovskaya. www.trezzini-hotel.com.

Casa Leto, 34 Bolshaya Morskaya, the 5 rooms of this Italian-style boutique hotel are named after old St Petersburg architects: Trezzini, Rossi, Rastrelli, Quarenghi and Rinaldi; guests share a living/dining area. Metro Admiralteyskaya. www.caseleto.com.

Comfort Hotel, 25 Bolshaya Morskaya, this 18-room hotel is centrally located between Nevsky and St Issac's Cathedral. Metro Admiralteyskaya. www.comfort-hotel.ru. At the same location is also the **Herzen Hotel**, www.herzen-hotel.ru.

Courtyard Marriot on Vasilyevsky Island, 61 2-ya Liniya, more of a business-style hotel near Metro Vasileostrovskaya with views of the Malaya Neva and Tuchkov Bridge. The **Courtyard Marriot Pushkin Hotel** is in town at 166 Griboyedov Canal, Metro Pl. Sennaya. www.courtyardsaintpetersburg.ru.

Demidov Bridge, 50 Griboyedov Emb, 3-star mini-hotel with 16 rooms on the canal near Metro Sadovaya. www.demidov-hotel.com. **Comfitel** has three other locations: City Hotel at 249 Ligovsky Pr, Metro Vladmirskaya; Primavera Hotel at 90–92 Nevsky, Metro Mayakovskya; and Alexandria Hotel at 6 Spassky Lane, near Griboyedov canal and Metro Spasskaya. www.comfitelhotels.com.

Fifth Corner, 13 Zagordny Pr, this standard mini-hotel is located not far from Nevsky. Metro Vladimirskaya. www.5ugol.ru.

Helvetia Hotel & Suites, 11 Marata/Vosstaniya, located in an early 19th-century mansion, near Nevsky Prospekt. Metro Mayakovskya. www.helvetiahotel.ru.

Hotel Indigo, 17 Tchaikovsky, boutique hotel with 119 rooms on 7 floors near the Summer Gardens. www.ihg.com.

Hotel St Petersburg on Vyborg side, at 5/2 Pirgovskaya Emb opposite the Aurora Battleship. A large 3-star hotel with over 400 rooms. Ask for a river view. Metro Ploshchad Lenina. www.hotel-spb.ru.

Kristoff Hotel, 9 Zagorodny Pr, this 31-room hotel is located a few blocks from Nevsky and the Fontanka Canal. Metro Dostoevskaya. www.kristoff.ru.

Marshal Hotel, 41 Shpalernaya, three-star hotel set in a 19th-century building near the Smolny Cathedral and Tauride Palace; has the Mannerheim Museum with history of Czar's Chevalier guards. Metro Chernyshevskaya. www.marshal-hotel.spb.ru.

Moskva Hotel, 2 Alexander Nevsky Square, is just opposite the monastery at the end of Nevsky Prospekt. Metro Aleksandra Nevskovo, www.hotel-moscow.ru.

Nevsky Forum, 69 Nevsky Prospekt. Boutique hotel with 20 spacious rooms in different categories. Near the Moskovsky Train station. Metro Mayakovskya. www.forumhotel.ru.

Obuhoff Hotel, 1 Knipovich, a 3-star mini-hotel (40 rooms on 5 floors) located on bank of Neva River, just south of Alexander Nevsky Monastery and metro station. www.obuhoffhotel.ru.

Palantin Hotel, 6 Rizhsky Pr. 3-star mini hotel with 20 rooms on 5 floors; Metro Baliiskaya. www.palantinhotel.ru.

Petro Palace Hotel, 14 Malaya Morskaya near Nevsky Pr and the Hermitage. The building was originally designed for famous merchant Van Stahl in 1897. Popular with tourist groups. Metro Admiralteyskaya. www.petropalacehotel.com.

Park Inn by Radisson (Pribaltiiskaya) on Vasilyevsky Island, 14 Korablestroiteley at the far end of Vasilyevsky Island by the Gulf of Finland. Metro Primorskaya. It also has the Waterville Aqua Park & a wellness spa. www.parkinn.com.

Pushka Inn, 14 Moika Emb, this 34-room boutique hotel on the Moika Canal is next door to the Pushkin House Museum and near the Hermitage. Family-style apartments are also available. Metro Admiralteyskaya. www.pushkainn.ru.

Rachmaninov Art Hotel, 5 Kazanskya, 3rd floor. This mini-hotel on two floors has 26 rooms with antique furnishings and a contemporary art gallery. Metro Nevsky Prospekt. www.hotelrachmaninov.com.

Sokos Hotels on Vasilyevsky Island, Finnish-operated, one, at 11–13 8-ya Liniya, has over 200 rooms and is located near the main shopping area with views of the Neva. Metro Vasileostrovskaya. The second more expensive **Sokos Hotel Palace Bridge** on the Strelka at 2–4 Birzheovoi Lane is more of a family resort with pool, saunas, bowling alley. www.sokoshotels.com.

Stony Island have two hotels located at: 1 Lomonosov (Metro Gostiny Dvor) with 17 rooms near the heart of nightlife off Nevsky/Dumskaya, and 45 Kamennostrovsky Pr on the **Petrograd side** not far from the Peter and Paul Fortress (Metro Petrogradskaya). www.stonyisland.com.

Tradition Hotel on Petrograd side, 2 Dobrolyubova, is situated across the Neva river from the Hermitage, and near the Zoo and Peter & Paul Fortress. Metro Sportivnaya. www.traditionhotel.ru.

INEXPENSIVE

Average around $50–$125+ for single/double. Check to find out what amenities are included, such as television, fridge or air conditioning. Some offer cheaper room rates for shared bathroom, and there may be different classes of rooms, such as standard, upgraded or even semi-lux. Note location and nearest metro stop.

Amaranta Manifest, 5 Saperni Lane, 3-star mini hotel in a Russian avant-garde setting with 35 rooms on 3 floors. Off Liteiny Prospekt, near Metro Chernyshevskaya. www.manifest-hotel.ru.

Anichkov Pension, 64 Nevsky Prospekt, located on the 3rd floor this mini-hotel has just 6 rooms and apartments (entrance off Karavannya). Metro Gostiny Dvor. www.anichkov.com.

Arbat Nord Hotel, 4 Artilleriiskaya, this modern-style boutique hotel is near Metro Chernyshevskaya and the Neva River. www.arbat-nord.ru.

Arkadiya, 58 Moika Canal Emb, a quiet Boutique-style hotel on the Moika canal near the Admiralteyskaya metro. www.arkadiahotel.ru.

Austrian Yard Hotel & Apartments, 16 Furshtatskaya, a quiet, 4-room mini-hotel (with a courtyard sauna) located next to the Austrian Consulate, and several blocks from the Neva River and Tauride Gardens. The Apartment block is at number 45. Metro Chernyshevskaya. www.austrianyard.com.

Belvedere Nevsky, 29 Bol. Konyushennaya. Finnish-managed mini-hotel near Nevsky Prospekt. Metro Nevsky Prospekt. www.belveder-nevsky.spb.ru.

Brothers Karamazov, 11a Sotsialisticheskaya, this lovely boutique hotel is near the Dostoevsky Flat Museum where the writer penned *The Brothers Karamazov*. About a 20-minute walk to Nevsky, near metro Vladimirskaya. www.karamazovhotel.ru.

Dostoevsky House Hotel, 6/1 Kaznacheyskaya, Comfortable 10-room mini-hotel located in the house where Dostoevsky lived from 1861 to 1863. Rooms face either the Griboyedov canal, the street or Sennaya Square; these areas were all described in *Crime and Punishment*. Near Metro Pl Sennaya. www.ddspb.ru.

Fortecia Peter, 29 Millionnaya, this 8-room mini-hotel is just minutes away from the Hermitage located in a quiet courtyard. Metro Admiralteyskaya. www.fortecia.ru.

Greenwich Hotel, 14 Kovensky Lane, the theme of this quiet 8-room mini-hotel is English, complete with a red phone box in the lobby. Metro Pl Vosstaniya. www.greenwich-hotel.ru.

Guest House Nevsky 3, 3 Nevsky Prospekt, this mini-hotel has just four rooms facing a quiet courtyard just minutes from the Hermitage. Shared kitchen, laundry. Metro Admiralteyskaya. www.nevsky3.ru.

Hotel Griffon, 35 Griboyedov Kanal, named after the nearby Griffon Bridge, this 12-room comfy mini-hotel is in a great location behind the Kazan Cathedral. Metro Gostiny Dvor. www.grifonhotel.ru.

Hotel Vera, 25/16 Suvorovsky Pr, this stylish boutique hotel is in a 1903 building with stained-glass windows and slanted ceilings. Rooms facing the back courtyard are quieter. Has larger family suites with kitchenette. Near Nevsky and Vosstaniya Square and metro. www.hotelvera.ru.

Kronverk Hotel on Petrograd Side, 9 Blokhina, located a few blocks from the Neva River and Zoo/Peter & Paul Fortress, it occupies the top of a large business center. Metro Sportivnaya. www.kronverk.com.

Mini Hotel Dolce Vita, 38 Griboyedov Canal, this 8-room mini-hotel has a rather featureless interior but the central location makes up for it. Metro Nevsky Prospekt. www.hotel-dolce.ru.

Moika 5 is at 5 Moika Canal Embankment, with 24 rooms, behind the Church of Spilled Blood. Metro Nevsky Prospekt.

Nevsky Hotel Group, has three comfortable hotels located around Nevsky Prospekt, and two others by the Moika Canal and Neva River. **The Nevsky Hotel Astor**, at 25 Bolshaya Konyushennaya, has 26 rooms. **Nevsky Hotel Grand** is down the same street at 10, and the **SkyHotel** is across the street at number 17. Metro Nevsky Prospekt. www.hon.ru.

Okhtinskaya (Vyborg Side), a large 3-star hotel at 4 Bolsheokhtinsky Pr. on the Neva River across from the Smolny Cathedral. Nearest Metro Novocherskasskaya. www.okhtinskaya.com.

Okyabrskaya Hotel, was the Grand Hotel du Nord in czarist times; has a central location near Nevsky at 10 Ligovsky Pr. www.booking.com.

Pio on Griboyedov, 35 Griboyedov Emb. This cosy 6-room mini-hotel overlooks the canal. (The 6 rooms share 3 bathrooms.) Metro Nevsky Prospekt. The **Pio On Mokhovaya**, 39/10 Mokhovaya, has 11 rooms each with own bathroom. Metro Mayakovskaya. www.hotelpio.ru.

Polikoff Hotel, 64 Nevsky Prospekt, this modern mini-hotel is in a quiet location with the entrance at 11 Karavannaya. Metro Gostiny Dvor. www.polikoff.ru.

Rinaldi Art Hotels is a mini-hotel chain with many locations, including town center, the **Petrograd side** and **Vasilyevsky Island**. www.rinaldi.ru.

Rossi Hotel, 55 Fontanka Emb near Rossi St and Lomonosov Sq. The 46 rooms of this boutique hotel all have a different design, along with the restaurant and spa. Metro Gostiny Dvor. www.rossihotels.com.

Shelfort Hotel on Vasilyevsky Island, 26 3-ya Liniya, If you need to stay on the island, this quiet hotel, with old world charm, offers both rooms and suites. Metro Vasileostrovskaya. www.shelfort.ru.

Suvorov Hotel, 3–13 5th Sovetskaya, 3-star hotel mini-hotel located on the ground floor behind the Oktobrsky Concert Hall. Located a few blocks east of Nevsky near Metro Pl Vosstaniya. www.suvorovhotel.spb.ru.

BUDGET HOTELS
Less than $50 a night.

Aurora Hotel on Petrograde Side, 15 Malaya Posadskaya, this 4-room mini-hotel is tucked behind the Peter & Paul Fortress and offers rooms with both private and shared bathrooms, along with a communal kitchen. Metro Gorkovskaya. www.hotel-aurora.ru.

Golden Age Retro, 16 Grazhdanskaya (2nd floor), this mini-hotel is a great bargain located in a quiet courtyard near metro Sadovaya. www.retrohotel.ru.

Green Apple, 14 Korolenko, this mini-hotel hotel has 15 rooms on two floors inside the former 19th-century Prince Muruzi Mansion. Offers bargain rooms that sleep up to three people; shared kitchen. East of the Hermitage, near metro Chernyshevskaya. www.greenapplehotel.ru.

Hotel Nauka, 27 Millionnaya, this Academy of Sciences hotel has rock bottom prices (basic dorm-style rooms—with fridge and TV—and shared bathroom) and is located right next to the Hermitage. Metro Admiralteyskaya. www.hotel-nauka.ru. (Russian only).

HOSTELS

See.www.hostelworld.com, www.hostelbookers.com, www.hostels.com, www.famoushostels.com and www.hostelworld.com for a full listing of hostels and other budget hotels.

Lucky for the budget traveller there has been an explosion of new hostel choices throughout the city. Offering private and dorm rooms, they also provide—for free or a small added fee—visa support & registration, airport/train transfers, breakfast, shared kitchen & laundry, Wifi or free internet computers, and can help organize city tours; many also offer free local and international phone calls. Reservations can be made online through their own websites. These are just a few:

Friends Hostel, named after the popular American TV show, has five great locations in town. Offers doubles, triples (and up to 5 people) with 4–6 bed dorm rooms (that include all male or female) and shared bathroom and kitchen. Organizes tour events as historical walks, etc. The first, at 20 Griboyedov Canal, is right off Nevsky next to the Kazan Cathedral in a quiet courtyard. The second is at 3 Bankovsky Lane, near the Griboyedov Canal and Sadovaya, Metro Pl Sennaya. Friends on Nevsky is at 106 Nevsky on the 5th floor, located towards the end of Nevsky Prospekt near Metro Mayakovskaya. Nearby Friends on Vosstaniya is at number 11, right off Nevsky near Metro Pl. Vosstaniya. For information and booking of the hostels see: www.friendsplace.ru.

Artway Hostel Sleepbox has two locations at 3/54 Malaya Sadovaya near Ostrovsky Square off Nevsky with 4 to 12 bed dorms. The second, at 16 Nevsky, is by the Hermitage with 2–4 bed rooms and double lux with bathroom. www.hotelrachmaninov.com.

Cuba Hostel 5 Kazanskaya behind the Kazan Cathedral and Nevsky, offers 2 to 10 bed dorm rooms; shared bathrooms & kitchen. Metro Nevsky Prospekt. www.cubahostel.ru.

Graffiti L Hostel, 33-35 Ligovsky Prospekt, right off Nevsky and metro Pl Vosstaniya. Doubles, Family (3), Lux (with bathroom) and 4, 6, 10 bed dorm rooms; shared bathrooms & kitchen. www.graffitihostel.ru.

Hostel Life, 47 Nevsky Prospekt, Twins, Doubles, Lux and dorms for 4 to 8 people. Shared bathrooms & kitchen. Metro Mayakovskaya. www.hostel-life.ru.

Location Hostel has two locations: one at 8 Admiralteysky Prospekt by the Admiralty & Hermitage. The second is at 74 Ligovsky Pr in the cool new cultural space of Loft Project Etagi (a 10-minute walk to Nevsky; metro Ligovsky Pr). Dorm rooms from 6 to 14 beds and doubles. Shared bathroom & kitchen. (Ligovsky has 3 designer rooms with bathroom.)

Nord Hostel, 10 Bolshaya Morskaya (1st floor) right by arch of Palace Square & the Hermitage. With 10-bed dorm room and private doubles. Shared bathroom, kitchen & laundry. Metro Nevsky Prospekt. www.nordhostel.com.

Puppet Hostel, 12 Nekrasova, a 15-minute walk to Nevsky and Metro Mayakovskaya. Doubles and up to 5 bed dorm rooms. Free tickets to the Bolshoi Puppet Theater next door. www.hostel-puppet.ru.

Soul Kitchen Hostel, 62/2 Moika Canal Embankment, offers mixed and female or male dorm rooms, with double and family rooms, and larger suites; both private and shared bathrooms. Large kitchen and roof-top deck. A 10-minute walk from Kazan Cathedral and Admiralteyskaya metro. www.soulkitchenhostel.com.

BED & BREAKFASTS/HOMESTAYS
See www.bednbreakfast.sp.ru and www.airbnb.com for listings of bed & breakfasts, hostels and apartments. For Russian homestays, see www.hofa.ru.

Andrei & Sasha's Homestay, 49 Griboyedov Canal near metro Sadovaya. Three apartments rented out entirely or by room (2 to 4 bedrooms in each). Shared bathroom, kitchen & rooftop deck. Inquire at: asamatuga@mail.ru.

Nevsky Prospekt B&B, 11/8 Nevsky Prospekt, the five rooms offer a reasonable price for such a central location (with shared bathroom). Metro Gostiny Dvor, www.bnbrussia.com.

Nils Bed & Breakfast, 21 5-ya Sovetskaya off Nevsky near metro Pl Vosstaniya. German managed with 4 rooms for 1 to 4 guests; shared bathroom and kitchen. www.rentroom.org.

APARTMENTS SHORT/LONG TERM RENTALS
(If traveling with a small group an apartment rental may be cheaper, plus it offers more amenities such as a kitchen.) www.cityrealtyrussia.com and www.introbyirina.com and www.airbnb.com.

DINING
St Petersburg is now a culinary delight, filled with hundreds of eating establishments—from cosy cafés and gourmet restaurants to the most elegant settings in old palaces or plush new hotels. Aside from traditional Russian dishes, scores of other ethnic-style restaurants serving everything from Georgian and Italian to Japanese and Indian/Vegetarian have sprung up about town, many of which have nightly entertainment. (Some also offer discount business luncheons and happy hour.) Every type of cuisine imaginable is offered, as well as matching prices, which vary from the very cheap to amazingly expensive. The standard for tipping is 8–10%, but sometimes the service charge is included in the bill. Most cafés and restaurants are

open noon to midnight, and later on weekends; and many have their own websites, so you can check for more information on the menu, prices and location (even if you can't read Russia, pictures are posted!).

So many food stores and supermarkets have opened up that you just need to ask the staff of your hotel to direct you to the nearest one; a Westerner can now find practically everything that is available at home. Most hotels have Wifi (or an internet computer for use), and there are numerous Internet Cafés scattered about town.

Fast-food chains can be found everywhere as well, such as **City Grill Express**, **Fasta Pasta**, **Kroshka Kartoshka** (baked potato with toppings), **Teremok** (pancake blini), **Yolki-Palki** and **Shokoladnitsa**. Sushi is a craze, so Japanese-style chains—as **Dve Palochki** (Two Sticks), **Yakitoriya**, and **Planet Sushi** have multiple locations. **Coffee House**, **Idealnaya Chashka** (Ideal Cup) and **Chainaya Lozhka** (Tea Spoon) are some of the many coffee & tea hang outs.

The average price per person (without beverage/alcohol) is indicted by the symbols: $—up to $15; $$—up to 35; $$$—up to $50, and $$$$ over 50 and much higher. Be aware that a few cocktails can often double the bill.

CITY CENTER

22:13 Lyubimoe Mesto (Favorite Place) $$, 2 Konyushennaya Sq, two-story restaurant that overlooks Imperial Stables; four times a year the chef travels to new places that inspire an innovative menu, with mixology cocktail selection. Cosy place to work with your laptop or eat a hearty breakfast. Open 9am–2am. Metro Admiralteyskaya. www.22-13.com.

Barbaresco $$, 2 Konyushennaya Sq, housed in the former Imperial Stables on several floors, it is named after wine of the northern Italian Piedmont region. Classic Italian pastas & risottos, antipastos & bruschettas, meat & fish. Metro Admiralteyskaya. www.barbarescoitaliano.com.

Café Green Room $, 74 Ligovsky on the 3rd floor of the Loft Project ETAGI building. Tasty and inexpensive breakfasts, lunches, dinners; summer terrace. Metro Ligovsky Pr. www.loftprojectetagi.ru.

Cat Café $$, 22 Stremyannaya, Georgian restaurant including traditional meat dumplings and *khachapuri* bread. Metro Mayakovskaya.

Dom Beat $$, 12 Razyezzhaya, named after an old Soviet department store, this popular retro-style bar & restaurant has an international menu (breakfasts till 7pm). Music & dancing later in the evenings. Open noon to 6am. www.dombeat.ru. Across the street is the scrumptious **Bushe** Austrian bakery. Metro Ligovsky Prospekt.

Gosti (Guests) $, 13 Malaya Morskaya, Balkan specialities include greek salad, pumpkin soup, Serbian chorba-style fish, octopus & leg of rabbit; good breakfasts and home-made desserts. Live music on Tues/Thurs. Confectionary open from 8am, restaurant from noon. www.gdegosti.ru.

Ne Goru-ee $$, 3 Kirpichny Lane, The Georgian restaurant "Don't Grieve" has lots of tasty dishes from the Caucasus. Metro Admiralteyskaya. www.negoruy.ru.

Stolle $, 1/6 Konyushenny Lane. Freshly baked meat, fish & fruit pies. www.stolle.ru.

Yolki Palki $, 9 Malaya Konyushennaya, restaurant chain offering tasty Russian food (and salad bar) at affordable prices. Metro Admiralteyskaya.

KARAVANNAYA ULITSA

Kavkaz Bar $$, 18, generous portions of Caucasus-style dishes served both at the bar and in the restaurant. www.kavkazbar.ru.

Korovabar $$$, 8, named after the bar in the film 'A Clockwork Orange,' it specializes in steaks and other meat dishes. Metro Gostiny Dvor.

Khutor Vodogray $$, 2, interior is decorated in the style of a Ukrainian cottage even with its own tree; traditional hearty Ukrainian fare. Metro Gostiny Dvor. www.vodograi.ru.

Mama Roma $$, 3/35, everything Italian—pizza, pastas, grilled meats & fish. www.mamaroma.ru.

Tarkhun $$, 14, intimate and elegant with traditional Georgian food. www.restorantarkhun.ru.

KAZANSKAYA ULITSA

Mamalyga $$, 2, a wide variety of south Caucasian tastes from Armenian to Georgian & Swaneti—shashylks to khachapuris. www.mamaliga-mamaliga.com.

Office Pub, 5 Kazanskaya, off Nevsky. Draught beers, Sport-TV.

Sharlot Café $$, 2, sandwiches, salads, pasta, meats and seafood; breakfast until 4pm. www.sharlotcafe.ru.

Soup Vino $, 24 , great soups, salads, pastas! www.supvino.ru.

Terrassa $$, 3a, on top floor of shopping center with glass walls and amazing views of Kazan Cathedral. Serves a huge selection of delicious Russian & Georgian to Italian & Thai with resident DJ's; part of Ginza Project. www.terrassa.ru.

ULITSA MARATA

La Perla Fish House $$$, 54, Nautical inspired interior, one of the best fish restaurants in town; also serves meat dishes & other European fare with wine list. Metro Ligovsky Prospekt.

Les Amis de Jean-Jacques Rousseau $$, 10, classy French bistro with wines by the glass. Metro Mayakovskaya. www.jan-jak.com.

Orient Express $, 21, with delicious Russian dishes, the interior is filled with *eletrickhi*-type train benches. Metro Vladmirskaya. www.orient-express.spb.ru.

Ukrop (Dill) $, 23, Vegetarian, vegan & raw food; on the first floor you can order already prepared food; the second floor is a full service restaurant, www.cafe-ukrop.ru.

ULITSA RUBINSHTEYNA

Barslona $$, 26, Spanish bar and restaurant with tapas & Sangria. (Two other center locations.) Metro Vladimirkskaya, www.barslona.ru.

Fartuk (Apron) $, 17, family-run with tasty European dishes and even home-made Lemonade. Metro Mayakovskaya.

Mops $$$, 12, everything Thai…chef, food, décor and hospitality; a Spa is in the courtyard. Metro Mayakovskaya. www.mopscafe.ru.

O! Cuba $$, 36, interior made to look like a Cuban veranda complete with a 1950's Buick convertible. Latin-Cuban fare with a complimentary mini-mojito. Live music Fri & Sat nights. Metro Dostoevskaya. www.o-cuba.ru.

Tres Amigos, $, 25, Mexican fare from burritos to quesadillas. Metro Vladimirskaya.

Schastye $$, 15, the 'Happiness' Café & Bar serves excellent Italian meals with a superb selection of pastries. Metro Mayakovskaya. www.schaste.com.

NEVSKY PROSPEKT

All addresses are Nevsky Prospekt (and metro) unless otherwise indicated.

Biblioteka $, 20, located in the 3-story old Dutch Church. A café-delicatessen is on the ground floor, a restaurant and shops on the first, and a tapas-wine bar on the second; literary events also take place here.

Bistro Garçon $$, 95, Savory French-style bistro with a Parisian chef, wines and a great bakery. (Open 10am–midnight). Metro Pl Vosstaniya. www.garcon.ru.

Café King Pong $$, 16 Bolshaya Morskaya, Pan-Asian fare with a large menu that includes dim sum, soups, noodles and rice dishes. www.kingpong.ru.

Café Singer $, 28, in the Old Singer Building of Dom Knigi, it has both a café and bakery with a Russian menu and superb views over Nevsky Prospekt and the Kazan Cathedral. Open 9am–11pm.

Chopsticks $$, 8 Admiralteyskaya, specializes in Cantonese & Szechwan dishes with some Indian & Thai as well.

Dlinny Khvost (Long Tail) $$ 92 (open 24 hours), two-story Asian-decorated interior that offers Pan Asian for a reasonable price. www.dlinniyhvost.ru.

Dve Palochki (Two Sticks) $, 22, Japanese chain with over 20 locations. The American Editon, at 96, is decorated to look like an old-fashioned 1950's American diner, with baseball playing on TV screens.

Gogol $$, 8 Malaya Morskaya, Gogol's famous 'Overcoat' hangs in the atrium and the menu reads like a novel (Gogel wrote *The Overcoat & Dead Souls*), where each chapter is a course in itself. Traditional Russian food from 19th-century recipes. Metro Nevsky Prospekt. www.restaurant-gogol.ru.

Grey's Bistro $$, 5/3 Konnaya, large international menu; delicious breakfasts, Cakes, and wine, beer & cocktails. Metro Pl Vosstaniya. www.greys-bistro.ru.

Grot $, 38 (open 24 hours), cellar café-bar that serves Central Asian/Russian food as *manty* meat dumplings and *lagman* beef noodle soup.

Gusto $$$, 1 1a Degtyarnaya, classy Italian by gastrophile chef Fabrizio Fatucci; seasonal food themes such as 'Aromas of the Taiga.' Metro Ploshchad Vosstaniya. www.gusto.spb.ru.

Il Patio $, 182, popular pizza chain scattered all about town. Metro Pl Alexandra Nevskovo. www.ilpatio.ru.

Literatornoye Kafe $$, 18, Dates back to czarist times (in 1837, Pushkin left for his fatal duel from here); Russian cuisine, classical music and literary & poetry readings.

Madridsky Dvor $$, 14 8-ya Sovietskaya. This Madrid-style courtyard restaurant has different rooms for relaxing and Spanish dining. Metro Pl Vosstaniya. www.madrid-restoran.ru.

Marcelli's, $$, 21 & 43 Nevsky (open 24 hours), Italian restaurant chain with an extensive menu of starters, soups, salads, grilled dishes & pastas, and a wine list. Metro Nevsky Prospekt.

Palkin, 47 $$$$, this original eatery was opened in 1874 when it was frequented by Chekhov & Tchaikovsky; today it's still set in an elegant and formal atmosphere serving mainly Russian cuisine, with an extensive wine list. Large windows overlook Nevsky. www.palkin.ru.

Stray Dog Café $, 5 Arts (Iskusstva) Sq (in basement). Previous hangout of 20th-century artists and poets (such as Akhmatova, Mandalstam), and continues to act as a café-bar, gallery, cabaret & theater. Metro Nevsky Prospekt. www.vsobaka.ru.

Stroganoff Yard $$, 17, located in court of Stroganov Palace, live music in evenings. Metro Nevsky Prospekt.

Tandoor $$, 10 Admiralteysky Pr, has served up tantalizing Indian cuisine, from kebabs to curries, for over two decades in its two rooms. Metro Admiralteyskaya. www.tandoor-spb.ru.

Yakatoriya $$, 5/7 Ostrovsky Square, this chain of restaurants has good Japanese selections, including a sushi bar. www.yakitoriya.spb.ru.

SMOLNY & LITEINY (EAST OF NEVSKY)

Metro Chernyshevskaya unless otherwise noted.

Baltic Bread $, 25 Grechesky Lane, small chain of café-bakeries; stop by for any meal of the day or even a light snack. Metro Pl Vosstaniya. Another location is at 19 Vladimirsky. Metro Dostoevskaya. www.baltic-bread.ru.

Botanika $$, 7 Pestelya, large vegetarian menu (with soups, salads, pastas) and playroom for kids. Interiors designed by Alexei Haas. www.cafebotanika.ru.

Buddha Bar & Restaurant $$$, 78 Siponskaya Embankment. Trendy new hang out with an Asian ambiance and international menu from sushi and wok specialities to meat and fish. (Near the Bolshecktinsky Bridge, but not near a metro.) www.Buddha-Bar.ru.

Frida $$, 57 Chaikovskaya, named in honor of Mexican artist, Frieda Kahlo; copies of her paintings decorate the walls, offers Mexican, Italian and a full vegetarian menu (and cocktails & hookas).

Gin No Taki, $$ 17 Chernyshevskaya, Over 180 dishes that include everything Japanese: sushi, sashimi, tempura, yakitori, bento boxes, beer; photo menu, too. www.ginnotaki.ru.

Jakov $, 3 Chernyshevsky, perfect place to stop for coffee, tea and cake with choices from pastries to chocolates.

Gypsy Tapas Bar $$, 14 Liteiny (on corner of Furshtatskaya), Spanish/Middle Eastern décor, offering tapas and main meal selections; large cocktail menu & cover band on weekends. www.gypsybar.ru.

Jai Hind $$, 17/19 Ryleeva, Indian restaurant with curries and vegetarian. www.jaihind.okis.ru.

Igrateka $$, Located in the Tauride Gardens, this venue has a full menu and live music in the evenings; open till 6am Fri & Sat.

Il Grappolo $$$$, 5 Belinskaya (off Liteiny). Gourmet Italian and large wine list. Located above the **Probka Wine bar**; www.probka.org. Across the street, at no. 6, is **Putanesca**, serving Italian food and great cocktails and desserts. Metro Nevsky Prospekt.

Kompot Café $, 10 Zhukovsky, offers a wide selection from soups and sandwiches to breakfasts and heartier meals. Metro Pl Vosstaniya. www.kompotcafe.ru.

Lemonade $, 9 Belinskaya, a roof terrace bar where you pay for how long you spend here (and not what you eat) so you can help yourself to the lemonade, cream soda and sweets. Vegan food also available, and live music in the evenings. Metro Nevsky Prospekt. www.vk.com/lemonaderoof.

Novaya Istoria (New History) $$$, 8 Belinskaya, Specialty is fresh seafood, with fresh oysters and lobster brought in several times a week. Metro Nevsky Prospekt.

Makarov $$, 2 Manezhny Lane, Russian food with tasty breakfasts.

Mechta Molokhovets (Molokhovets' Dream) $$$, 10 Radishcheva, an iconic city restaurant that takes its recipes from the popular 19th-century cookbook *A Gift to Young Housewives* by Elena Molokhovets; it offers a wide range of tasty and traditional Russian cooking; wine list. Metro Pl Vosstaniya. www.molokhovets.com.

Sunduk $$, 42 Furshtatskaya, basement bohemian-style café, European-Russian menu with live (blues/jazz) music from 8:30pm–11pm. Metro Chernyshevskaya. www.cafesunduk.ru.

Vox $$$$, 16 Salyonoi/Pestelya, Upscale stylish Italian with home-made pastas, unique wine list and a lovely outdoor dining terrace in summer months. www.voxresto.ru.

Zavodnye Yaitsa (Mechanical Eggs) $$, 48 Furshtatskaya, eccentric café with everything bizarre covering the walls from airplane propellers to pipes and water meters. European menu with salad choices. Metro Chernyshevskaya. www.zavodim.spb.ru.

SENATE SQUARE (SENATSKAYA PLOSHCHAD) & ST ISAAC'S CATHEDRAL
Nearest metro is Admiralteyskaya unless otherwise noted.

Dekabrist $, 2 Yakulovicha, small selection of European, reasonably priced.

House of Architects Nikolai Restaurant, 52 Bol. Morskaya (five minutes walk from the Cathedral). European & Russian dishes.

Karavan $$$, 46 Voznensky Pr. Middle-eastern restaurant decorated with Turkish carpets and even a stuffed camel. Offers more than 30 varieties of kebabs. Metro Sadovaya.

Krokodil $$, 18 Galernaya, eclectic interior with a varied menu for both lunch and dinner. Another is at 46 Kazanskaya.

Mansard $$$, 3 Pochtamskaya, gourmet international menu with spectacular views of St Issac's. www.ginza-mansarda.ru.

MiX in St Petersburg $$$$, 6 Voznesensky Pr in W Hotel, The city's first celebrity-style restaurant by French chef Alain Ducasse. www.wstpetersburg.com.

Prospekt $$, 21 Malaya Morskaya, decorated with historial photos, serves up traditional Russian specialities, along with grilled fish. www.prospekt-restaurant.ru.

Russian Vodka Room No 1 $$$, 4 Konnogvardeysky, this restaurant (open noon–2:30am) is part of the Russian Vodka Museum and offers an opulent old-style Russian menu from suckling pig to venison and Gatchina trout plus a huge list of vodkas, including 100 gram shots. www.vodkaroom.ru.

Tandoori Nights $$, 4 Voznesensky Pr. Tasty Indian & vegetarian food, as clay-oven Tandoori and Peswari Naan bread with Indian beer, rum and 18 types of tea. Metro Admiralteyskaya. www.tandoorinightsspb.com.

Teplo $, 45 Bol Morskaya, the 'Warm' Restaurant in the House of Composers has intimate rooms with a menu that offers a variety of international choices, including Italian and vegetarian with freshly baked bread and pies. www.v-teple.ru.

Umao $, 11 Konnogvardeisky, the owners traveled widely and collected their favorite recipes, which include a little something from all around Asia. Metro Admiralteyskaya. www.umaocafe.ru.

MOIKA CANAL EMBANKMENT (NABEREZNAYA REKI MOIKI)
All addresses are Moika Canal Embankment (and Metro Admiralteyskaya) unless otherwise indicated.

Dom (Home) $$$, 72, in Ryleyev's House, an expensive wine bar compiled by Tatyana Sharapova, director of the Pro Sommelier School. The menu includes smoked duck salad, Dorado fillet with artichokes and pear cheesecake.

Entrecote $$$, 25 Bol Morskaya, French cooking with ribeye steaks as the speciality.

Entrée $$, 6 Nikolskaya Sq, Classic French restaurant with a side café that offers sandwiches and desserts. Metro Sennaya Pl.

Gastronom $$, 1/7, open 8am–midnight, varied cuisine from Russian & European to Japanese & Uzbek. Music Fri & Sat evenings. www.gastronom.su.

NEP $$, 37, Named after the 'New Economic Plan' started by Lenin in the early 1920's, this hip hangout, with a Russian-Thai menu, also offers nightly cabaret-style entertainment. www.neprestoran.ru.

PMI Bar $$, 7, Spread over three floors, it is known for its mixology and fusion cocktails and enoteca wine tasting. The owner, Yevgeny Finkelstein, creates menus for each new season.

Russkaya Ryumochnaya No 1 $$, 4 Konnogvardeisky (south of the Moika near New Holland), Exotic Russian dishes, caviar and a huge vodka list. www.vodkaroom.ru.

The Idiot $, 82, named after Dostoevsky's novel, this cosy 4-room basement environment aims to create a 19th-century St Petesburg, complete with fireplace, bookcases and chess boards. Provides lots of vegetarian selections and hearty breakfasts; a complimentary vodka shot is also served. (Open 11am–1am) Metro Sennaya Pl. www.idiot-spb.com.

Troiktsky Most $, 30, a great chain of vegetarian restaurants; another location is at 38 Zagorodny, Metro Pushkinskaya.

Valenki & Varezhka $$, 87, cosy vaulted-interior with Russian/European menu.

GRIBOYEDOV CANAL (NABEREZHNAYA GRIBOYEDOVA KANALA)

All addresses are Griboyedov Canal Embankment (and Nevsky Prospekt Metro) unless otherwise indicated.

Avlabar $$, 26/2 (open 11am–6am), Causasian food, often with singers and karaoke.

Bistro Garçon $, 25, Boulangerie-style with fresh sandwiches, baguettes and cakes. With other locations around town (as 95 Nevsky). www.garcon.ru.

Denis & Nikolaev $, 77, a fabulous confectionary that also offers Russian food, including hearty soups. Metro Sennaya Ploshchad.

Kilikia $$, 20, named after the Armenian region within Turkey, this ethnic restaurant, with six halls, serves tasty Armenian food, including shashlyk kebabs, tava stews, and bread made in stone ovens, with live music in the evenings. Metro Sennaya Ploshchad. www.kilikia.spb.ru.

Leica $, 29, Russian-Italian-style food with board games and Fri/Sat disco nights.

Mozarellabar $$, 64, for a relaxing lunch or dinner of salads and pizza or fish. Metro Sadovaya.

Park Giuseppe $$$, 2b, serving scrumptuous Italian in two rooms and a terrace overlooking the canal. www.park-restaurant.ru.

Pirogovoi Dvorik (Pie House) $, 22, hearty cheap pies with a choice of fillings.

Teplichnye Usloviya $, 25/3, rustic cottage atmosphere with traditional Russian fare (borsch & cutlets) along with Italian pastas and yummy desserts. www.teplichnie.ru.

FONTANKA RIVER EMBANKMENT (NABEREZHNAYA REKI FONTANKI)

All addresses are Fontanka River Embankment (and metro Nevsky Prospekt) unless otherwise indicated.

Aragvi $$, 9, Georgian cuisine with large portions; large windows overlook the canal.

Bulion $$, 55, home-cooked variety of soups, pastas and dumpings.

Grey's Bistro $$, 5/3 Konnaya, large choice from international menu. Metro Mayakovskaya.

Imbir $$, 15 Zagordony, tasty Russian cooking with full bar; popular with locals. Metro Dostoevskaya.

Kashmir $$, 7 Bol. Moskovskaya, Indian vegetarian. Metro Vladimirskaya.

Palermo $$, 50, Italian-style restaurant with a Mediterranean menu. Metro Dostoevskaya. www.palermo.spb.ru.

P.I.R.O.G.I $$, 40 Fontanka (open 24 hours), started in Moscow, this bohemian café-bar has both smoking and non-smoking rooms, and an international menu; DJ sets at night and French *chansons* by day. www.piterogi.ru.

Vkus Yest $$$, 81 Fontanka (near Bolshoi Drama Theater) featuring nouveau Russe cuisine in a cosy setting. Metro Mayakovskaya.

Shinok $$$, 13 Zagorodny Pr., Ukrainian dishes as *vareniki* dumplings served by waiters dressed in traditional costumes. Open 11am–5am. Metro Dostoevskaya.

SADOVAYA ULITSA
All addresses are Sadovaya Ulitsa (and Metro Sennaya Ploshchad) unless otherwise noted.

Baku $$$, 12/23, Azerbaijani cuisine that includes shashlyk kebabs and plov spiced lamb & rice dishes and tasty vegetable stews; two floors, one of which has evening entertainment that includes music and belly dancing. www.baku-spb.ru.

Conchita Bonita $$, 39 Gorokhovaya, Cuban owners with Tex-Mex and South American fare; often loud music.

Fasol $$, 17 Gorokhovaya, Stylish café offering both Russian and European choices.

Fish House $$, 4 Gritsova Lane, rich selection of fish and seafood dishes, steamed, baked or grilled, with large portions. Metro Sadovaya. www.fish-spb.ru.

Khinkalnaya na Neve $$, 13–15, Georgian cuisine with shashlyk and tasty vegetable dishes. www.hinkaly.ru.

Khochu Kharcho $$, 39–41 Sadovaya (open 24 hours), 'I Want Kharcho!' (a traditional lamb-vegetable stew), specializes in Megrelian western Georgian food which features spice and walnuts. www.hochuharcho.com.

Metropol $$$, 22, French cuisine and home-brewed Belgian beers.

Pelmeny Bar $, 3 Gorokhovaya, Metro Admiralteyskaya, this chain serves up traditional Siberian dumplings with mushrooms, fish, pork or beef, along with a soup or salad starter.

Sumeta $$, 5 Yefimova, Dagestani cuisine with Caucasian wines; the specialties are meat dumplings and Lula kebabs. Metro Sadovaya.

Testo $$, 5/29 Gritsova, home-made Italian cooking specializing in pasta. www.testogastronomica.ru.

Tsar $$$$, 12 Sadovaya, a place for noblemen to dine, with excellent Russian cuisine (try the Poharskaya cutlet a la Pushkin) and wine served in crystal goblets. Metro Gostiny Dvor. www.tsar-project.ru.

Zoom Café $$ 22 Gorokhovaya, intimate café with bookshelves and boardgames that serves everything from chicken teriyaki to potato pancakes. www.cafezoom.com.

THEATER SQUARE
Metro Sadovaya unless otherwise noted.

Curry House $$, 3–7 Glinka, Resident Indian chef with extensive menu offering lots of vegetarian choices. www.curryhousespb.com.

Dvorianskoye Gnezdo (Noble Nest) $$$$, 2 Dekabristov, located in the former teahouse of the Yusupov Palace. One of city's top formal restaurants, Russian & European cuisine with live classical music. Metro Sadovaya.

Hundertwassar Bar $, 4 Teatralnaya, named after the German artist, this cosy bohemian-style bar often hosts evening jam sessions by students from the nearby Rimsky-Korsakov Conservatory. Metro Sadovaya.

Lechaim $$ 2 Lermontovsky Pr by the Grand Choral Synagogue, serves traditional Jewish food, including kosher Russian and Georgian dishes. Metro Sennaya Pl. www.jewishpetersburg.ru.

Romeo's Bar & Kitchen $$$, 43 Rimsky-Korsakov, tasty Italian & Russian; includes special menus for "Before & After the Theater". www.romeosbarandkitchen.ru.

Sadko $$, 2 Glinka, next to the Nikolsky Gardens, a lovely dining option on the way to the Mariinsky Theater. Tasty Russian food; often the waiters break out into song. Metro Sennaya Pl. www.wadko-rst.ru.

Vincent $$ 16/11 Teatralnaya Sq, specializes in Mediterranean cuisine with great tartares and risottos; wine list.

Za Stsenoi (Backstage) $$$, 18/10 Teatralnaya, the Mariinsky's restaurant, overlooking the Kryukova Canal and decorated with theater props; Mariinsky dancers and opera singers have written on the walls. Good international choices.

VASILYEVSKY ISLAND
Metro Vasileostrovskaya unless otherwise indicated.

Black and White $, 25 6-ya Liniya. As the name implies, this coffee shop also offers breakfast, lunch and other snacks (open 11:30am–1am). Around the corner on Sredny Pr is the **Chainaya Lozhka** (Tea Spoon).

Brugge, 22 Makarov Emb, gastropub with over 70 types of Belgian beer. Food includes Flemish lamb stew and Liege-style waffles. Metro Vasileostrovskaya near Tuchkov Bridge.

Gintarus $$, 5 Sredny Pr, on the other side of the Strelka near the Malaya Neva, Lithuanian and Russian dishes.

Grand Petrov $$, 5 University Emb, if you enjoy German food, 'Peter's City' microbrewery offers everything from Sausage Salzburg and home-brewed Pilsners to Bavarian pretzels. www.gradpetrov.com.

Imperator $$, 5 University Emb near the Strelka. Russian & Caucasian choices with a pleasant outdoor summer terrace.

Helsinki Bar $$, 31 Kadetskaya Liniya near the Malaya Neva & Tuchkov Bridge. This Finnish retro bar is filled with vintage furniture, tasty Finnish-style cooking and very cool DJ's who keep on spinning the vinyl until 2am. www.helsinkibar.ru.

Kvartira 55 $$, 36 1-ya Liniya, 'Apartment 55, Open 9am–6am. Russian/European dishes with a wine list.

Lapsha $$, 9a Kadetskaya Liniya, Pan-Asian menu from noodles & curries to Pad Thai & Dim Sum.

Old Custom's House $$$$, 1Tamozhenny Lane, located inside an old 18th-century warehouse, this restaurant is known for its creative Russian dishes and excellent wine list; visit the Vodka & Caviar House next door. www.oldcustom.ru.

Mama Roma $$, 6 Sredny Prospekt, everything Italian from pizza to risotto. www.mamaroma.ru.

Restoran $$, 2 Tamozhenny Lane (University Emb), a wide selection of traditional Russian dishes. www.elbagroup.ru.

Russky Kitsch $$, 25 University Emb near the Art Academy Museum, this six-room restaurant is laden with Soviet realism artwork, including a ceiling painting of Brezhnev and Castro embracing; a glass-enclosed terrace looks out on the Neva River. Traditional Russian dishes from *blini* to *pirozhki* and vodka & caviar.

Stolle $, 50 1-ya Liniya near the Tuchkov Bridge, this café specializes in all types of pies from meat to fruit specialities.

Sakartvelo $$, 13 12-ya Liniya, 3 blocks west of Vasileostrovskaya metro. The island's special secret Georgian restaurant with live music in the evenings.

PETROGRAD SIDE (PETROGRADSKAYA STORONA)
Metro Petrogradskaya unless otherwise noted.

Chekhov $$, 4 Petropavlovskaya by the Tower House, the charming setting here is from a 19th-century dacha that presents traditional Russian dishes from Chekhov's time. www.restaurant-chekhov.ru.

Day & Night Barberry $$$, 10 Kamennoostrovsky Pr, all natural food menu, prepared organically and without any additives.

Il Lago dei Cigni (Krestovsky Island) $$$$, 21 Severnaya, the restaurant sits by 'Swan Lake' with beautiful views of the Finnish Gulf, and is run by Chef Remo Mazzucato. Gourmet Mediterranean food and live music. Metro Krestovsky Ostrov. www.illago.ru.

Langust $$$$, 84 Bol Prospekt, lots of live (tank) or fresh fish, lobster and shellfish (be aware prices are per 100 grams). www.restoranlangust.ru.

Les Amis De Jean-Jacques Rousseau $$, 2 Gatchinskaya off Bolshoi Prospekt; another of the town's French-style bistro wine-bars. Metro Chakalovskaya. www.jan-jak.com.

Le Menu $$, a1 Dobrolyubova, Stylish all Vegetarian café near Birzhvoi Bridge. Open 9am–11pm. Metro Sportivnaya.

Lujaika $$, 16 Aptekarsky, this "Lawn" restaurant is decked out like a whimsical wonderland with even resident rabbits hopping about. Asian fusion with open-air dining cabanas and a pond kids can fish in. Part of the Ginza Projects.

Mari Vanna $$$, 18 Lenina. Like being invited to dinner at a friend's home, you'll be served with delicious traditional Russian home-cooked dishes. (Reservations essential for the front door to open.) www.marivanna.ru.

Mesto (Place) $$, 59 Kronversky Prospekt behind the Zoo, this art-deco-style restaurant offers many imaginative international dishes and piano music in the evenings. Metro Gorkovskaya.

Orlandina Club $$, 3 Instrumentalnaya by Botanical Gardens. Owned by Caravan Records, this underground venue is a great place to hang out by the bar or listen to evening concerts. Open 4pm–11pm.

Na Zdorovye (To Your Health!) $$, 13 Bolshoi Pr, located right across from the Freud Dream Museum, this Soviet-style restaurant with its bust of Lenin, paintings of peasant life and 78-rpm records, prepares old Russian recipes into mouthwatering delights; try the kvas! Metro Sportivnaya.

Pryanosti I Radosti $$, 3 Posadskaya, a popular Ginza Projects restaurant serving everything from spicy Caucasian to European and traditional Russian. Metro Gorkhovskaya. www.ginzaproject.ru.

Salkhino $$, 25 Kronvserksy Pr, home-cooked Georgian dishes with paintings on the wall by local artists, which are often for sale. Metro Gorkhovskaya.

Staraya Derevnya (Old Village) **Vyborg Side**, $$, 72 Savushkina right across the river from Yelagin Island. Family-style home-cooked Russian food. Metro Chornaya Rechka. www.sderevnya.ru.

Tbilisi $$$, 10 Sytninskaya behind the Fortress, Georgian chefs whip up the best of Caucasian cooking from chicken *tabak* to meat dumplings; large selection of wines. Metro Gorkovskaya.

The Living Room $$, 20 Bolshaya Zelenina, American menu, anything meaty from burgers to beef cutlets, wine & beer. Metro Chkalovskaya.

Troitsky Most $, 9/2 Kamennoostrovsky, another branch of the town's Vegetarian restaurant chain, near the 'Trinity Bridge'. Metro Gorkovskaya.

Volga-Volga $$$, Petrogradsky Emb, Dock 1. The boat cruises the Neva while you enjoy the Asian fusion cuisine and views of Peter & Paul Fortress (from May to October). Metro Gorkovskaya. www.ginza-volga.ru.

Volna (Wave) $$, 5 Petrogradsky Emb next to Peter's Cabin. International menu includes Asian and Italian with daily specials; wine and cocktails. Summer terrace overlooking the Neva. Metro Gorkovskaya. www.volna.su.

Zhelaniya (Wishes), 23 Dobrolyubova, cosy room with just ten tables, offering exotic fusion that includes duck and reindeer. Metro Sportivnaya.

Yakitoria $$, 4 Petrogradskaya Emb next to Peter's Cabin, another of the city's Japanese chain restaurants with everything from sushi to tempura. Metro Petrogradskaya. www.yakitoriya.spb.ru.

BARS
There are hundreds of bars scattered about town; most are open noon to midnight. See also Nightclubs that follow.

Big Liver Place, 2 Shvedsky Lane, menu of over 100 creative mixology cocktails. Metro Nevsky Prospekt.

Buddha Bar & Restaurant (see listing under Smolny)

Café Stirka, 26 Kazanskaya, lounge sofas and, most peculiar, washing machines, so you can do your laundry while having a drink and light snack.

Dickens, 108 Nevsky, Beer (more than 10 beers on tap) & whiskeys, with good snack food and breakfasts. Restaurant on second floor. Metro Sennaya Pl. www.dickensrest.ru.

Fat Friar Bar, 2 Dumskaya (and other locations), bar chain and beer hall with tasty food; metro Gostiny Dvor, first floor is a bar & lounge, and second hosts the dance floor with a huge video wall.

Folks, 2 Lomonosov, popular with students and a younger crowd, the bars are spread over three floors, each with different types of music. Metro Nevsky Prospekt. www.folksbar.ru.

Harat's Irish Pub, 109 Nevsky, plenty of beer & whisky and hearty Irish-style breakfasts. TV's play popular sports.. Metro Pl Vosstaniya. www.harats.ru.

Liverpool, 16 Mayakovskaya, This Beatle-themed pub features Fab-Four alike cover bands, as the Sunflowers. Metro Mayakovskaya. www.liverpool.ru.

Nikakikh Orkhidey, 9 Kolomenskaya, just off Nevsky, this charming cellar piano bar's owner is Boris Bardash with the local band Ole Lukkoye; along with local singers, Boris often performs himself. Russian menu. Open 3pm–midnight. Metro Pl Vosstaniya.

Manhattan, 90 Fontanka, a basement art-club with live music; open 2pm–5am with concerts Wed–Sun at 8pm. Metro Pushkinskaya.

MiXup Bar, 6 Voznesensky, (1pm–midnight; Fri & Sat til 2am), On top floor of the classy W Hotel with great views and large selection of creative mixed cocktails. One floor above is the **MiXup Terrace** that has cabana seating that looks out over the city. Metro Admiralteyskaya. www.wstpetersburg.com.

Pickwick Pub, 6 Ryleeva, English pub with 20 types of beer on tap; football playing on the telly. Metro Chernyshevskaya.

Pivnaya 0.5, 44/2 Zagorodny Lane, The Pivnaya (pub) offers a good choice of beers along with playing classic Soviet films on Sundays. Metro Vladimirskaya.

Probka, 5 Belinskaya, charming Italian-style wine bar (wine by the glass) and menu of light snacks. Metro Gostiny Dvor. www.probka.org.

Terminal Bar, 13a Rubinshteyna, with an enormous bar, a good place to relax and have a drink with friends; piano and other live music. Metro Dostoevskaya.

The Other Side, 1 Bol Konyushennaya, popular expat bar and café with good chili and wrap sandwiches; live music (as jazz and blues) at 8pm, and 10pm on weekends. Metro Nevsky Prospekt. www.theotherside.ru.

Tinkoff, one the city's first microbreweries, with beers brewed on-site; enjoy both the food and live music. Metro Nevsky Prospekt. www.tinkof.ru (check website for new address.)

Trappist, 36 Radischeva, specializing in beers with European food and fresh mussels on the weekend. Metro Chernyshevskaya. www.cafetrappist.ru.

Zhopa, 6 Bakunina, Funky decorated bar, music, table football. Look for the Ж (Zh) on the front door. Don't ask to find it, as it is the Russian slang for 'arse!' Metro Ploschad Vosstaniya.

ZigZag, 59/92 Gorokhovaya, specializing in the art of mixology, with home-made liquers and creative cocktail menu. Metro Sennaya Ploshchad.

NIGHTCLUBS
Most nightclubs are open 6pm–1am weekdays and till 6am Fri & Sat; many have a cover charge (check individual websites). The popular areas, where numerous clubs are located, are along Dumskaya (by Nevsky & Gostiny Dvor), Rubinshteyna (along the Fontanka Canal), 50 & 53 Ligovsky Prospekt warehouse district, and by Nevsky Prospekt & Vosstaniya Square.

Bar Without a Name, 3 Bankovsky Lane, to enter walk into the courtyard behind Friends Hostel and make a right; in a basement with no markings is the bar with two rooms, one bar/lounge and the second a dance floor with DJ's. Metro Sennaya Pl.

BarakObamaBar, 2 Konyushennaya, in summer months lively outdoor dance floor, with interior two-floors of bars w/DJ's and a hookah lounge. Face control, so dress stylishly to get in. Metro Nevsky Prospekt. www.barbarakobama.ru.

Bermuda Bar Disco, 6 Bankovsky, bar that becomes a hopping disco after midnight. Metro Sennaya Pl.

Cosmonaut Club, 24 Bronnitskaya, a large former Soviet cinema converted into one of the city's most popular clubs, this venue has live music often with international bands. On the first level is a dance floor for 1300 people and two spacious bars. The VIP area is on the second floor with a lounge, bar & restaurant with views of the stage & dance floor. South of the Fontanka near metro Teknologichesky Institut. www.cosmonavt.su.

Dom Beat, 12 Razyezzhaya, named after an old Soviet department store, this popular retro-style bar & restaurant has an international menu (breakfasts til 7pm). Popular hang-out for music & dancing in the evenings. Open noon to 6am. Metro Admiralteyskaya. www.dombeat.ru.

DUMSKAYA—Dumskaya off Nevsky Prospekt (next to Gostiny Dvor) is one of the hippest places in town (especially on weekends) and just chocked full of hot spots for drinking and dancing; the music includes everything from Russian pop and techno to DJ's and live music. (Try to get in before 11pm to get stamped before the crowds.) Spots include **Belgrad**, **Dacha**, **Fidel**, **Ludovic**, **Punch**, and **Shine**.

Griboyedov, 2a Voronezhskaya (at intersection Kon. Zaslonova), considered one of the city's best clubs, it's situated in a bomb shelter, and founded by the ska band Dva Somalyota (Two Airplanes). Alternative bands and international DJs. Concerts start at 10pm, DJ parties after midnight. The Café Griboyedov Hill upstairs has a lounge and concerts as well on Saturdays (sketch, reggae) and Mondays (jazz); good food. Open noon–6am. Metro Ligovsky Pr., www.griboedovclub.ru.

Havanna, 21 Moskovsky Pr. smart Cuban-themed club with live bands and three dance floors playing Latin music. Metro Tek. Institute, www.havanaclub.ru.

Kitaisky Lyotchik Dzhao Da, 7 Pestelya, started in Moscow, the city now has a hopping 'Chinese Pilot Dzhao Da' all its own. A plane hovers over the bar, and in the back area, a stage hosts rock and indie bands in the evening. Metro Gostiny Dvor.

LIGOVSKY PROSPEKT: Metro Ploshchad Vosstaniya.

Dushe, 50 Ligovsky. Owned by local groups Spitfire and Leningrad, this art-punk club, with a New York Loft-style interior, has nightly DJ's, live music and occasional fashion shows. **Dyuni**, 50 Ligovsky Prospekt, situated in the back courtyard, this tendy hangout, with indoor bar, is especially popular in summer months, as the outside sand-covered pit area is filled with ping pong, table football and other games; open 24 hours. **Jesus Club**, 50 Ligovsky Prospekt, located in the warehouse complex, packs in clubbing crowds over the weekend. **Metro**, 174 Ligovsky Pr. Multiple bars and three dance floors, popular with a younger crowd. www.metroclub.ru.

PUSHKINSKAYA 10, 53 Ligovsky Pr, Contemporary music and art complex with cool music clubs including: **Experimental Sound Gallery (Gez-21)**, 3rd fl, like an artist's loft, wide range of music, along with film screenings, readings; open 5pm–midnight. www.gez21.ru; **Fish Fabrique**, ground fl, the bohemian faction of the city gathers here to listen to 8pm concerts Thursday through Sunday; open 3pm–6am; **Fabrique Novelle** also hosts concerts. www.fishfabrique.spb.ru.

Mod Club, 7 Griboyedov Canal Emb, three levels of bars and dance zones, that offers Russian, techno, RnB and Euro music; area also has an art space, summer terrace and *novus* billiard tables. Metro Nevsky Prospekt. www.modclub.info.

Par.spb (Petrograd Side), 5b Alexandrovsky Park. trendy spot that attracts some of the world's best DJs. (*Par* is the Russian word for steam—the site used to house a laundry.) Metro Gorkovskaya.

Petrovich, 56–58 Marata, first opened in Moscow, this fun and quirky club and restaurant is decorated with Soviet paraphernalia and has live music and dancing at night. (Soviet dance night on Saturdays) Metro Ligovsky Prospekt. www.petrovich-piter.ru.

Platforma, 40 Nekrasov. Hosts rock and jazz concerts, along with other literary events and film screenings. Open 24 hours. Metro Pl. Vosstaniya. www.platformaclub.ru.

RadioBaby, 7 Kazanskaya, a large bar space divided into different rooms with club DJ's after 10pm. (To enter, go through the arch at no. 5, and turn left through second arch.) Metro Nevsky Propsekt. www.radiobaby.com.

Revolution, 26 Sadovaya. A restaurant during the day, it becomes a multi-level dance club at night, decorated in revolutionary symbolism. www.revolutionclub.ru.

Tunnel Club, 7 Zverinskaya & Lubansky Lane (Vasilyevsky Island), half way between the Sportivnaya metro and Zoo, this bombshelter club with its military themes offers mainly techno and rock n' roll; open midnight–3am and till dawn on weekends.

XXXX, 34 3-ya Sovietskaya, a pub chain with food by day, and music & dancing all night. Metro Pl Vosstaniya. http://xxxxbar.ru.

Zoccolo, 2/3 3-ya Sovietskaya, is a café by day, and at night the underground space hosts concerts of different music genres at 8pm; on weekends the venue is open till dawn. Metro Pl Vosstaniya.

JAZZ AND BLUES

Many have a cover charge for the music. Check websites for programs.

Jazz Philharmonic Hall, 27 Zagorodny Pr. Created by jazz violinist and composer David Goloshchokin (and known as the Church of Jazz), resident and foreign bands play jazz and Dixieland in the Big Hall at 7pm (closed Mon/Tues) and other arrangements are played in the smaller Ellington Hall (Chamber Hall of Acoustic Jazz) at 8pm (Tues, Fri & Sat). Museum of St Petesburg Jazz is on the second floor. Metro Vladimirskaya. www.jazz-hall.ru.

JFC Jazz Club, 33 Shpalernaya. One of the most progressive jazz venues in town with other music styles as acid jazz and blues. Open 7pm–11pm. Metro Chernyshevskaya. www.jfc-club.spb.ru.

Jimi Hendriz Blues Club, 3 Liteiny Prospekt, intimate cellar venue with Russian & Georgian food. Russian Blues musicians. Open 2pm–midnight; concerts at 8:30pm. www.hendrix-club.ru.

Red Fox Jazz Café, 50 Mayakovsky, showcases all forms of jazz and everything from bebop to ragtime. Open jam sessions on Sunday nights. Large menu selection. Open 10am–2am and on Fri/Sat til 5am. Metro Chernyshevskaya. www.rfjc.ru.

Sunduk Art Café, 42 Furshtatskaya (near the US Embassy). Pleasant restaurant that features jazz, blues and rock performances from 8:30pm–11pm. (Opens at 10am). Metro Chernyshevskaya. www.cafesunduk.ru.

The Hat Bar, 9 Belinskaya, The Hat, an old-time American looking bar, boasts 30 types of whiskey, nine bourbons and cocktails. Daily live music and jazz always playing. Metro Nevsky Prospekt.

LGBT NIGHTCLUBS

Nonexistent during the Soviet era (homosexuality received up to three years imprisonment), LGBT culture has finally taken root, but with the new government laws banning so-called gay propaganda aimed at minors, discrimination still exists. In Russian, the slang for gay is *goloboy*, meaning 'blue,' and the word for lesbian is *lesbianka*, taken from the English. Check individual websites for music events and cover fees.

3L (Triel), 109 Moskovsky Prospekt. The city's most popular Lesbian club is located in the southern part of town next to metro Moskovskiye Vorota. Open Wed & Fri/Sat/Sun 10pm–6am. www.triel.spb.ru.

Malevich, right next door to 3L. By day it functions as a cosy café with early evening social events, and then it opens to all night party time with a mixed crowd. Same hours as the 3L. www.malevich-club.ru.

Cabaret, 43 Razyezzhaya, puts on popular drag shows at 2:30am; open Thur/Fri/Sat 11pm–6am. Metro Ligovsky Prospekt. www.cabarespb.ru.

Central Station, 1/28 Lomonosova, this area is the center of the city's gay scene with large bars and dance floors. (Lesbian Night is on Wednesdays.) The downstairs European bar-restaurant looks like a French boudoir, and a staircase leads up to seven more rooms of bars and dance floors. www.centralstation.ru.

Golubaya Ustritsa (Blue Oyster) 1 Lomonosov, The Blue Oyster (also called the Gay Trash Bar) is one of the main gay clubs in town. (By Central Station.) Metro Nevsky Prospekt. www.boyster.ru.

Greshniki (Sinners), 29 Griboyedov Canal, spread over four floors. Daily 6pm–6am. Metro Gostiny Dvor. www.greshniki.gay.ru.

The Club, 17 Scherbakov Lane, located in the basement, this gay-mixed club has several bars (including an outdoor summer courtyard bar), a large dance floor and stage where local groups and drag acts often perform. Dress fashionably. (Open 11pm–6am Thurs, Fri & Sat.) Metro Dostoevskaya.

SHOPPING
ANTIQUES, ARTS, CLOTHING, HANDICRAFTS, JEWELLERY, MUSIC...
Most open daily 10am–7pm.

Amber, 19 Malaya Morskaya, wide selection of amber.

Bee-Keeping, 51 Sadovaya, this lovely shop sells different flavors of *myod* honey along with natural creams and teas blended with pollen and beeswax. Metro Sennaya Ploshchad.

Hermitage e-Shop, offers high-quality replicas of masterpieces from the Hermitage Museum's collections. www.hermitagemuseum.org & www.hermitageshop.org.

Generator Nastroenia (Mood Generator), 7 Karavannaya. Collection of unique items as leather journals & Soviet propaganda-themed covers. Metro Admiralteyskaya.

Imperial Porcelain, 7 Vladmirsky, open 10am–8pm. Sells dishes and other objects made in the famous Lomonosov Porcelain Factory. Metro Vladimirskaya. Other branches are at 60 & 160 Nevsky Prospekt, and the factory outlet, at 151 Obukhovsky Oborony (metro Lomonoskaya), has discounted prices. www.ipm.ru.

Kisselenko Fashion Salon, 47 Kirochnaya. The store of popular fashion designer Lilia Kisselenko, specializing in woman's clothing & accessories. Metro Chernyshevskaya. www.kisselenko.ru.

Kommissiony Magazin, 17 Mayakovskaya. Basement shop full of interesting finds if you dig through the assortments of stuff. Metro Mayakovskaya.

Kosher Shop, 2 Lermontovsky Pr next to the Synagogue. This kosher food shop also sells a selection of Jewish-themed books, art and music. Metro Sennaya Ploshchad. www.jewishpetesburg.ru.

La Russe, 3 Stremyannaya, open 11am–8pm. A shop filled with a varied collection of 18th- to 20th-century antiques, and it helps with customs and international shipping. Metro Makayavskaya. www.larusse.ru.

Loft Project ETAGI (see Art Galleries).

Lyyk Design Market, 74 Griboyedov Canal Emb, latest in Russian fashion clothing designs. Metro Nevsky Prospekt.

Mariinsky Gift Shop, Mariinsky Theater, 1 Teatralnaya Sq, open 11am–6pm on days of performances. Theater-themed souvenirs along with books, posters, CDs and DVDs. Metro Sadovaya.

Miltary Shop, 26 Sadovaya, open 10am–7pm (entrance in courtyard). Buy anything military, from uniforms and striped sailor tops to boots and hats. Metro Gostiny Dvor.

Model Shop,7 Aleksandrovsky Park (in Artillery Museum), this shop sells all kinds of model cars, trains and planes. Metro Gorkhovskaya.

OFF, 8 Pechatnika Grigorevya, open noon–8pm. Vintage and second-hand clothing store. Metro Ligovsky Prospekt. www.offoffoff.ru.

Parfionova, 51 Nevsky Prospekt, open noon–8pm. The city's first fashion house was created by Tatyana Parfionova, and this boutique sells her clothing designs. Metro Mayakovskaya. www.parfionova.ru.

Phonoteka, 28 Marata, open 10am–10pm. This vintage music store sells records, CD's and DVD's. Metro Mayakovskaya. www.phonoteka.ru.

Soldier of Fortune, 37 Nekrasova, open 11am–9pm. Chocked full of everything from camouflage clothing and knives to military-type souvenirs. Metro Ploshchad Vosstanya.

Tanya Kotegova's Fashion House, 44 Bolshoi Prospect (Vasilyevsky Island), collection of exclusive ladieswear. Open noon–8pm; closed weekends. Metro Vasileostrovskaya. www.kotegova.com.

Tula Samovars, 11 Dzhambula, sells all types and sizes of samovars and other tea-related items. (The city of Tula is known for making samovars.) Metro Zvenigorodskaya. www.samovary.ru.

Yahont, 24 Bolshaya Morskaya, open 10am–8pm. Carl Fabergé once had his studio in the building, and Yakhont carries on the creative jewellery tradition here in the salon. Metro Nevsky Prospekt.

SOUVENIRS

Babushka, 33 Leytenanta Shmidta Emb (Vasilyevsky Island). The store is decorated in the style of an 18th-century nobleman's house, filled with traditional souvenirs; worldwide shipping. Metro Vasileostrovskaya.

Bazar, 54 Angliiskaya Emb & 4 Petrovskaya Emb (Petrograd side). Large selection of Russian folk art and souvenirs. Metro Admiralteyskaya and Gorkovskaya.

Heritage, 37 Moika Canal Emb. Paintings, jewellery, amber, crafts. Metro Admiralteyskaya.

Museum, 7/5 Mytninskaya Emb (Petrograd Side). Traditional souvenirs, paintings, jewelery, crystal and porcelain. Metro Sportivnaya.

Onegin, 11 Italyanskaya. Filled with paintings, icons, lacquer miniatures and other gifts; worldwide shipping. Metro Nevsky Prospekt. www.souvenirboutique.com.

Matryoshka, 83 Bolshoi Prospekt (Vasilyevsky Island), Everything from dolls and Easter eggs to lacquer boxes. Metro Vasileostrovskaya.

Nevsky Souvenir, 22–24 Nevsky, open 9am–10pm. Wide selection from icons and jewellery to lacquer boxes. www.nevskysouvenir.com.

Retro Shop, 22 Karavannaya. Great quirky shop filled with old Soviet paraphelnalia from records to posters & pins. Metro Admiralteyskaya.

Souvenir Market Vernissage, 1 Griboyedov Canal right behind the Church of the Spilled Blood. Over 150 outdoor shops that sell everything from *matryoshka* nesting dolls and art work to handicrafts, woodwork and other great souvenir items. Open 9am–9pm. Metro Nevsky Prospekt.

Udelnaya Flea Market, Vyborg Side, open Sat–Sun 8am–5pm. The city's largest flea market filled with everything imaginable from splendid old artefacts & antiques to furniture and kitschy junk. Take the metro north to Udelnaya, pass the large permanent market, and then you'll come to the large area of vendor stalls where you can browse for hours!

ART GALLERIES

ART re. FLEX, 5 Bakunina, open noon–7pm; closed Sun/Mon. This gallery exhibits contemporary paintings, graphics & sculptures by local artists. Metro Ploshchad Vosstaniya. www.artreflex.ru.

Borey Art Gallery, 58 Liteiny Prospekt, open noon–8pm; closed Sun/Mon. Contemporary art gallery, with works for sale. The shop also sells books on art and architecture. Metro Mayakovskaya. www.borey.ru.

Erarta, 2 29-ya Liniya (Vasilyevsky Island) Open 10am–10pm; closed Tuesdays. Set in a 20th-century columned building on the island's west side, the gallery focuses on works by local artists from the 1960's to present day. Includes paintings, graphic art, sculptures, installations. Nearest Metro Vasileostrovskaya.

KGallery, 24 Fontanka Emb. 19th- & 20th- century Russian artists and porcelain. Metro Nevsky Prospekt. www.kgallery.ru.

Loft Project ETAGI, 74 Ligovsky Prospekt, open noon–10pm (Sat/Sun from 10am). Multifunctual art space on five floors in the former Smolensky Bread Factory that has three galleries, two exhibitions halls, shops, a bookstore, hostel and the Café Green Room. Great place to wander and checkout the city's contemporary art scene. Metro Ligovsky Prospekt. www.loftprojectetagi.ru.

Liberty Arts Gallery, 17/25 Pestelya, open 11am–8pm; closed Mondays. Specializing in Soviet art from the 1930's to 1980. Metro Chernyshevskaya. www.sovietart.ru.

Manezh Central Exhibition Hall, 1 Issac Square, open 11am–7pm; closed Thursdays. Houses rotating art exhibitions of local artists. Metro Admiralteyskaya. www.manege.spb.ru.

Marina Gisich Gallery, 121 Fontanka, open 11am–7pm, Saturday noon–8pm; closed Sundays. One of the city's best small galleries, exhibiting both Russian and international artists. Metro Teknologichesky Institute. www.gisich.com.

MArt, 35 Marata, Gallery of modern art, including paintings, graphic art & sculpture for sale by well-known local artists. Metro Mayakovskaya. www.martgallery.ru.

Novy Museum, 29 6-ya Liniya (Vasilyevsky Island) displays paintings & sculptures by local artists. Metro Vasileostrovskaya. www.novymuseum.ru.

Perinnye Ryady Art Center, 4 Dumskaya/ground floor, open 11am–9pm. Art galleries with a collection of over 300 works by local artists. Metro Gostiny Dvor.

PUSHKINSKAYA 10 (Entrance at 53 Ligovsky Pr), open 4pm–8pm; closed Mon/ Tues. Founded in 1989, during the perestroika period, it continues to function as a 4,000 square meter arts cooperative with galleries and studios; and still functions as a central part of the city's progressive arts and music scene. Galleries include the **Museum of Non-Conformist Art** and the **New Academy of Fine Arts Museum** on the 4th floor, and the **Temple of Love, Peace & Music**, dedicated to John Lennon, is on the ground floor. Music clubs include **Fish Fabrique**, **Fabrique Novelle** and the **Experimental Sound Gallery (GEZ-21)** (see Nightclubs). Metro Ploshchad Vosstaniya. www.p-10.ru. (You can also book a tour thru the website.) Another art center down the street, at 39, is **100 Svoih** (100 of Our Own), open 4pm–9pm; closed Tuesday. www.100svoih.ru.

Rosphoto State Photography Center, 35 Bolshaya Morskaya, open 11am–7pm. Exhibitions of Russian & international contemporary photography & other mixed media works. www.rosphoto.org. Across the street, at 38, in the 18th-century building that belonged to Ivan Yelagin, is the **Exhibition Center of St Petersburg**

Artists' Union that displays over 9000 items from the 1960's to the 1980's including paintings, photography & sculpture. Here is also the **Blue Hall Gallery** with works for sale by Soviet painters from 1990 to 2008. www.ruspaintersallery.com. Open noon–7pm; closed Mondays. Metro Admiralteyskaya.

Rizzordi Art Foundation, 49 Kurlyandskaya, open 2pm–8pm; closed Mondays. A huge art space on the upper floors of a renovated 19th-century brewery. Rotating exhibitions of local artists are showcased here. Metro Baltiiskaya and a half-hour walk. www.rizzordi.org.

Sol-Art Gallery, 15 Solyanoi Lane, open 10am–6pm. Near the Decorative Arts Museum, with exhibitions of contemporary local art, both paintings and graphics, which is also for sale. Metro Chernyshevskaya. www.solartgallery.com.

BOOKSTORES
Angliya (English) Books, 38–40 Fontanka, open 10am–10pm. Collection of literature, history, art, travel books all in English. Metro Gostiny Dvor.

Bukvoed, 13 Nevsky Pr. Open 9am–10pm. Chain of bookstores with art books, calendars, maps and posters. Metro Admiralteyskaya. www.bookvoed.ru.

Dom Knigi (House of Books), 28 Nevsky in the old Singer Building; open 9am–midnight. The largest bookstore in the city; on first floor English-language books, calendars, postcards, etc. Metro Nevsky Propsekt. www.spbdk.ru.

England-Angliya Books, 40 Fontanka, fiction & artbooks in English.

Knizhnaya Lavka Pisateley (Writer's Bookcorner), 66 Nevsky, has a collection of Russian literature and travel guides in English, with other interesting art works. Metro Gostiny Dvor.

Staraya Kniga (Old Book), 3 Nevsky; open 10am–7pm. Antique bookseller of old Russian & Soviet books, along with art and maps and other unique items. Metro Admiralteyskaya.

DEPARTMENT STORES & SHOPPING CENTERS
Most are open daily10am–10pm. Metro Gostiny Dvor unless otherwise indicated.

Bolshoi Gostiny Dvor, 35 Nevsky Prospekt. Center of the 19th-century merchant arcades, today entirely rennovated and now contains many stores and souvenir shops.

DLT (Dom Leningradskoi Torgovi—House of Leningrad Trade), 21–23 Bol. Konyushennaya. Built in 1913, with its famous glass-ceiling atrium, the 7-story building has been completely restored. Metro Nevsky Prospekt.

Galeria, 30a Ligovsky Prospekt. Five floors filled with over 300 shops, food courts, a multi-screen cinema complex, supermarket and even a bowling alley. Metro Ploshchad Vosstaniya. www.galeria.spb.ru.

Grand Palace, 44 Nevsky Prospekt, open 11am–9pm. Grand shopping place filled with the latest designer clothing shops. www.grand-palace.ru.

Nevsky Center, 114 Nevsky Prospekt, open 10am–11pm. Seven stories filled with over 70 shops and the department store, Stockmann, which has a large supermarket in the basement. Metro Ploshchad Vosstaniya. www.nevskycentre.ru. Concept Store Nevsky is at 152.

Passazh (Passage), 48 Nevsky Prospek. Similar to Moscow's GUM Department Store, this arcade, that stretches between Nevsky and Italyanskaya, is filled with boutiques stores and souvenir shops. While here, look for **Prostranstvo Kultury** that offers items of local designers, including clothing, bags & jewellery. www.passage. spb.ru.

Vladimirksy Passage, 19 Vladimirsky Pr. Filled with over 100 stores, which include fashion boutiques and restaurants; the large supermarket Lend is in the basement. Metro Vladimirskaya. www.vpassage.ru.

FARMERS' MARKETS OR RINOK
Markets are usually open Mon–Sat 8am–8pm; Sun 8am–4pm.

Kuznechny Rinok, 3 Kuznechny Lane. Metro Vladimirskaya. Opened in 1927, this was the city's first indoor market. Still the best market with a wide selection of food, fruit and produce.

Maltsevsky Rinok, 52 Nekrasova. Wide selection of meats, fruits, vegetables, even spices and fresh honey. Metro Pl. Vosstaniya.

Sennoy (Hay) Market, 4 Moskovsky Prospekt. City market with meat & fish, fruit & vegetables. Metro Sennaya Ploshchad.

Sytny Rinok, 3/5 Sytninskaya Sq on Petrograd side, this market, one of the city's oldest, sells meat & produce as well as clothing & electronics. Metro Gorkovskaya.

MUSEUMS
Museum ticket kiosks usually close one hour before the closing of the museum. Aside from its usual closing days, a museum may be closed one extra day each month, known as sanitation day. Often a photo/video permit costs extra (and foreigners may be charged more than locals). For information on city museums and exhibitions, see www.saint-petersburg.com/museums and visit-petersburg.ru/en.

Consider purchasing a 2-, 3- or 5-day electronic Petersburg City Smart Card, which offers visits to 40 museums along with discounted transportation and other tours. www.petersburgcard.com/eng.

A combined savings ticket for four museums: the Marble & Stroganov Palaces, Mikhailovsky Castle and Russian Museum can be purchased, good for 3 consecutive days. www.rusmuseum.ru. A one-day ticket can be bought for the Hermitage which includes the five buildings on Palace Embankment; the two (consecutive) day Hermitage ticket also includes the Menschikov Palace, the General Staff Museum, Peter the Great's Winter Palace, Staraya Derevnya Restoration & Storage Center & Museum of Imperial Porcelain Factory. www.hermitagemuseum.org.

Academy of Arts Museum, 17 Universitetskaya Emb, Open 11am–6pm; closed Monday and Tuesday. (Ticket office on 2nd floor) Metro Vasileostrovskaya. Vasilyevsky Island. www.nimrah.ru.

Alexander Blok House, 57 Dekabristov. Daily 11am–6pm; Tuesday until 5pm; closed Wednesday. Metro Sadovaya. www.spbmuseum.ru.

Alexander Nevsky Monastery & Museum of Urban Sculpture, located at 179 Nevsky Prospekt in the Annunciation Church. Open 11am–5pm; closed Monday and Thursday. The Lazarevskoye and Tikhvinskoye Cemeteries are open daily 9:30am–6pm. Metro Ploshchad Aleksandra Nevskovo. www.gmgs.ru.

Anichkov Palace, 39 Nevsky Pr. Metro Gostiny Dvor Guided tour only.

Anna Akhmatova Museum, 34 Fontanka Emb. in the Fountain House of the former Sheremetyev Palace (entrance from 53 Liteiny Pr). Daily 10.30–6.30pm, Wednesday 1pm–9pm; closed Monday & last Wed of month. Metro Vladimirskaya. www. akhmatova.spb.ru.

Applied Arts Museum, 13–15 Solyanov Lane, Tuesday–Saturday 11am–5pm. Metro Chernyshevskaya.

Battleship Aurora, 4 Pedtrogradskaya. Metro Gorkovskaya, Currently under restoration in Kronstadt. www.aurora.org.ru.

Beloselsky-Belozersky Palace, 41 Nevsky Prospekt. Metro Gostiny Dvor. Guided tour by appointment only. www.beloselskiy-palace.ru.

Botanical Gardens, 2 Professora Popova. Open 10am–6pm. Greenhouse 11am–4pm (May–Sept); closed Friday. Metro Petrogradskaya.

Bread Museum, 73 Ligovsky Prospekt. Open 10am–4pm; closed Sat/Sun. Metro Ligovsky Prospekt. www.colobki.ru.

Brodsky House Museum, (the artist) 3 Pl. Iskusstvo (Arts) Square. Open noon–7pm; closed Monday and Tuesday. Metro Gostiny Dvor. www.nimrah.ru/musbrod.

Cathedral of Our Lady of Kazan, 2 Kazanskaya Sq. Open 9am–10pm; services at 10am–6pm. Metro Nevsky Prospekt. www.kazansky-spb.ru.

Cathedral of the Savior on Spilled Blood, 2 Griboyedov Canal Emb. Museum open 10:30am–6pm, evening admission 6pm–10:30pm from May 1–Sept 30; closed Wednesday, Metro Nevsky Prospekt. eng.cathedral.ru.

Central Navy Museum, 1 Truda Square (entrance by Kryukov Canal). Open 10am–6pm; closed Monday and Tuesday. Closest Metro Sadovaya. www.navalmuseum.ru.

Central Railway Museum, 50 Sadovaya, open 11am–5pm; closed Friday and Saturday. Metro Sennaya Pl. www.museum.ru/museum/railway. If you're a railway buff, ask here about the Museum of Railway Technology at 118 Obvodnov Canal, Metro Baltiiskaya, closed Monday; the Shushary Museum of Railway Technology in Paravozny Museum (from Vitebsky Station); the National Railway Bridge Museum at Krasnoye Selo; or the Lebyazhe Railway Museum Depot in the town of Lubyaze.

Communication Museum, 7 Pochtamtskaya. Tuesday–Saturday 9.30am–6pm. Metro Nevsky Pr.

Circus Arts Museum, 3 Fontanka Emb. By appointment only; excursions on Tues/Wed/Fri. www.circus.spb.ru. circusmuseum@mail.ru.

Derzhavin Museum, 118 Fontanka Emb. Open 10:30am–6pm, Thursday noon–8pm; closed Tuesday and last Friday of month. Metro Sadovaya. www.museumpushkin.ru.

Dostoevsky Literary Memorial Museum, 5/2 Kuznechny Lane. Open 11am–6pm, Wednesday 1pm–8pm; closed Monday & last Wed of month. Metro Vladimirskaya. www.md.spb.ru.

Erarta Museum, 2 29-ya Liniya. Open 10am–10pm; closed Tuesday. Metro Vasileostrovskaya (Vasilyevsky Island). www.erarta.com.

Fabergé Museum in the Shuvalov Palace, 21 Fontanka Canal. Metro Nevsky Prospekt. Entrance by pre-arranged tour. website: www.fsv.ru/en.

Freud Museum of Dreams, 18a Bolshoi Prospekt (Petrograd side). Open Tuesday and Sunday noon–5pm. Metro Sportivnaya.

General Staff Museum of the Hermitage, (in the Arch behind the Winter Palace at 6/8) open 10:30am–6pm, Sunday till 5pm; closed Monday.

Geological Museum, 74 Sredny Prospekt (Vasilevsky Island). Open 10am–4pm; closed Sat/Sun. Metro Vasileostrovskaya.

Grand Choral Synagogue, 2 Lermontovsky Prospekt. Metro Sadovaya. www.jewishpetersburg.ru.

Hermitage, 34 Dvortsovaya Nab. Open 10.30am–6pm; Wednesday 10:30am–9pm; closed Monday. Metro Admiralteyskaya. www.hermitagemuseum.org.

Hermitage Preservation and Storage Center, 37 Zausadebnaya. Guided group tours only, four times daily. Closed Monday/Tuesday. Metro Staraya Derevnya (Vyborg side). www.hermitagemuseum.org.

Gumilev Memorial Apartment Museum, 1/15 Kolomenskaya. Open 10:30am–5:30pm; closed Sunday and Monday. Metro Dostoevskaya.

Icebreaker *Krasin* Museum, moored 22L Lieutenant Schmidta Emb. Open 11am–5pm (guided tour on the hour); the engine room is shown on Sat/Sun at 1pm and

3pm. Closed Monday, Tuesday and last Wednesday of month. Metro Vasileostrovskaya, Vasilyevsky Island. www.krassin.ru/en.

Kirov Museum, 28 Kamennoostrovsky Pr. Open 11am–6pm, Tuesdays till 5:30pm; closed Wednesday. Metro Gorkovskaya. www.kirovmuseum.ru.

Kunstkammer/Museum of Anthropology and Ethnography, 3 Universitetskaya Emb and the **Lomonsov Museum**. Open 11am–6pm; closed Monday and last Tuesday of month. Metro Vasileostrovskaya. Vasilyevsky Island. www.kunstkamera.ru.

At 17 Universitetskaya is the **Museum of the Academy of Art** exhibiting works of Academy graduates. Wednesday–Sunday 11am–6pm.

Marble Palace, 5/1 Millionnaya. Open 10am–6pm; Monday until 5pm; closed Tuesday. Metro Nevsky Prospekt. www.rusmuseum.ru.

Mendeleyev Museum, 7/9 Mendeleyevskaya Liniya. Open 11am–4pm; closed Fri/Sat/Sun. (Entrance by pre-booked guided tour.) Metro Vasileostrovskaya.

Menschikov Palace, 15 Universitetskaya Emb. Open 10.30am–6pm, Sunday until 5pm; closed Monday. (Free admission first Thursday of month.) Metro Vasileostrovskaya on Vasilyevsky Island. www.hermitagemuseum.org.

Mikhailovsky Castle (now a branch of the Russian Museum), 2 Sadovaya. Open 10am–6pm; closed Tuesday. Metro Gostiny Dvor, www.rusmuseum.ru.

Museum of the Arctic and Antarctic, 24a Marata. Open 10am–6pm, Sunday till 5pm; closed Monday and last Friday of month. Metro Vladimirskaya, www.polarmuseum.ru.

Museum of the Artillery and Military, 7 Aleksandrovsky Park (Petrograd side). Open 11am–6pm; closed Mon/Tues & last Thursday of month. Metro Gorkovskaya.

Museum of the Avant-Garde (House of Matyushin), 10 Professora Popova. Open 11am–6pm, Tuesday until 5pm; closed Wednesday. Metro Petrogradskaya (Petrograd side). www.spbmuseum.ru.

Museum of the Defense and Siege of Leningrad, 9 Solyanoi Lane. Open 10am–5pm; Wednesday 12:30pm–9pm; closed Tuesday and last Thursday of month. Metro Chernyshevskaya. (Another museum is located in the Memorial to Heroes of the Defense of Leningrad on Victory Square. Metro Moskovskaya.) Metro Chernyshevskaya. www.blokadamus.ru.

Museum of Erotica, 47 Furshtatkskaya. Open 9am–6pm. Metro Chernyshevskaya.

Museum of Ethnography, 4/1 Inzhenernaya. Open 10am–6pm, Tuesday till 9pm; closed Monday and last Friday of month. Metro Gostiny Dvor. www.ethnomuseum.ru.

Museum of the History of Religion, 14 Pochtamtskaya. Open 10am–6pm, Tuesday 1pm–9pm; closed Wednesday. Metro Sadovaya. www.gmir.ru.

Museum of Musical Instruments, 34 Fontanka (in the former Sheremetyev Palace). Open 11am–7pm; closed Tuesday and last Wednesday of month. Metro Vladimirskaya. www.theatremuseum.ru.

Museum of History of Political Police, 2 Gorokhovaya. Open 10am–6pm; closed Sat/Sun. Metro Admiralteyskaya. www.polithistory.ru.

Museum of Political History, in the former Kshesinskaya Mansion at 2–4 Kuibysheva. Open 10am–6pm, Wed 10am–8pm; closed Thursday and last Monday of month. Metro Gorkovskaya. www.polithistory.ru.

Museum of Printing, 32 Moika Emb. Open 11am–6pm; Tuesday until 5pm; closed Wednesday. Metro Nevsky Pr. www.spbmuseum.ru.

Museum of Imperial Porcelain, 151 Obukhovskoi Oborony Pr. Open 10:30am–6pm, Sunday till 5pm; closed Monday. Metro Lomonsovskaya (in southeast part of town). www.hermitagemuseum.org.

Museum of Theatrical and Music Arts, 6 Ostrovskty Sq. Open 11am–6pm, Wednesday 1pm–9pm; closed Tuesday and last Friday of month. Metro Gostiny Dvor. www.theatremuseum.ru.

Nabokov House Museum, 47 Bol. Morskaya. Open 11am–6pm, Sat/Sun 12–5pm; closed Monday. Metro Sadovaya. www.nabokovmuseum.org.

Nekrasov Apartment Museum, 36 Liteiny Pr. Open 10:30am–6pm; closed Monday, Tuesday and last Friday of month. Metro Chernyshevskaya, www.museumpushkin.ru.

Novy Museum, 29 6-ya Liniya. Open noon–7pm; closed Mon/Tues/Wed. Metro Vasileostrovskaya, Vasilyevsky Island. www.novymuseum.ru.

Oreshek Fortress and Memorial Center of WWII, Schlüsselburg on Orekhovy Island. Open daily 10am–5pm from May 31 to October 31.

Peter and Paul Fortress, 3 Petropavlovskaya Krepost, Grounds open 6am–9pm. Museums open 10/11am–6/7pm. Closed Wednesday. Metro Gorkovskaya www. spbmuseum.ru.

Peter the Great's Cottage, 6 Petrovskaya Nab. Open 10am–6pm, Thursday 1pm–9pm; closed Tuesday. Metro Gorkovskaya.

Peter the Great's Summer Palace, Summer Gardens/Fontanka Canal. Open 10am–6pm; closed Tuesday and first Monday of month. Closest Metro Nevsky Prospekt/Chernyshevskaya.

Peter the Great's Winter Palace, 32 Palace (Dvortsovya) Embankment. Open 10:30am–6pm, Sunday till 5pm; closed Mondays. Metro Admiralteyskaya.

Police History Museum, 12 Poltavskaya St. By appointment only. Metro Pl. Vosstaniya.

Piskarevskoye Memorial Cemetery, 74 Nepokorennykh Pr. Open 10am–6pm (in summer, cemetery is open until 9pm). Metro Pl. Muzhestva and Bus 123/138. www. pmemorial.ru.

Planetarium, 4 Aleksandrovsky Park. Open 10.30am–8pm; closed Monday. Metro Gorkovskaya. www.planetary-spb.ru.

Popov Central Museum of Communications, 4 Pochtamtskaya. Open 10:30am–6pm; closed Sunday, Monday and last Thursday of month. Metro Nevsky Prospekt. www. rustelecom-museum.ru.

Pushkin Museum (Russian Literature Institute), 4 Makarov Emb. Open 11am–4pm; closed Saturday/Sunday. Metro Vasileostrovskaya (Vasilyevsky Island). www. pushkinskijdom.ru.

Pushkin House Museum, 12 Moika Emb. Open 10.30am–6pm, Monday noon–8pm; closed Tuesday and last Friday of month. Metro Nevsky Prospekt. www. museumpushkin.ru.

Rimsky-Korsakov Memorial House, 28 Zagorodny Pr. Open 11am–7pm, Wed 1pm–9pm; closed Mon/Tues and last Friday of month. Metro Vladimirskaya. www. theatremuseum.ru.

Rumyantsev Mansion & History of St Petersburg Museum, 44 Angliiskaya Emb. Open 11am–6pm, Tuesday until 5pm; closed Wednesday & last Tuesday of month. Metro Nevsky Prospket. www.spbmuseum.ru.

Russian Museum, 4 Inzhenernaya. Open 10am–6pm, Thursday 1pm–9pm; closed Tuesday. Metro Gostiny Dvor. www.rusmuseum.ru.

Russian Vodka Museum, 5 Konnogvardeysky Bul. Open daily noon–10pm. Metro Admiralteyskaya. www.vodkamuseum.su.

Shalyapin House Museum, 2-B Graftio. Open 11am–7pm, Wed 1pm–9pm. Closed Monday, Tuesday and last Friday of month. Metro Petrogradskaya. www. theatremuseum.ru.

Sheremetyev Palace, 34 Fontanka. Open 11am–6pm, Wed 1pm–9pm; closed Tuesday and last Wednesday of month. www.theatremuseum.ru.

Smolny Cathedral and Concert Hall with Bell Tower, open 10am–6pm; closed Wednesday. Nearest Metro Chernyshevskaya. eng.cathedral.ru.

St Isaac's Cathedral, Isaakievskaya Pl. Open 10:30am–6pm, evening admission 6pm–10:30pm May 1–Sept 30. The upper Colonnade walkway is open 10:30am–6pm (May 1–Oct 31 until 10:30pm), and during the White Nights (June 1–August 20) 6pm–4:30am; closed Wednesday. Metro Nevsky Pr.

Stieglitz Museum of Applied Arts, 15 Solyanoi Lane. Open 11am–5pm; closed Sunday, Monday and last Friday of month (and Academy Holidays in August). Metro Chernyshevskaya. www.stieglitzmuseum.ru.

Stroganov Palace, 17 Nevsky Pr. Open 10am–5pm; closed Tuesday. Metro Nevsky Prospekt.

Suvorov Museum, 43 Kirochnaya. Open 10am–6pm. Wednesday 1pm–9pm; closed Monday. Metro Chernyshevskaya. www.suvorovmuseum.ru.

Submarine *Narodovolets* (D2 Peoples' Will) is moored at 10 Shkipersky Protok. Open 11am–5pm; closed Monday and Tuesday. Metro Primorskaya (Vasilyevsky Island).

Theater and Musical Arts Museum, 6 Ostrovsky Sq. Open 11am–7pm; Wednesday 1–9pm; closed Tuesday and and last Friday of month. Metro Gostiny Dvor. www. theatremuseum.ru.

World of Water Museum, 56 Shpalernaya. Open 10am–6pm; closed Monday/Tuesday. Metro Chernyshevskaya.

Yelagin Palace, 1 Yelagin Island. Open 10am–6pm; closed Monday and last Tuesday of month. Metro Staraya Derevnya, Krestovsky Ostrov. www.elaginpark.org.

Yelizarov Museum, 32 Ul Lenina (3rd fl). Open 11am–4pm; closed Wednesday. Metro Chkalovskaya.

Yusupov Palace & Rasputin Museum, 94 Moika Canal Emb. Open daily 11am–5pm. Closest Metro Sadovaya. www.yusupov-palace.ru.

Zoological Museum, 1 Universitetskaya Nab. Open 11am–6pm; closed Tuesday. Metro Vasileostrovskaya. Vasilyevsky Island. www.zin.ru.

Zoo, 1 Aleksandrovsky Park, summer hours, 10am–8pm; winter hours, 10am–6pm. Metro Gorkovskaya. www.spbzoo.ru.

THEATERS AND CONCERT HALLS

Theater, concert and circus performances usually begin on weekdays at 7pm, 7.30pm or 8pm with matinée performances on weekends, with an earlier evening show. Be on time, as ushers are strict about curtain time! The date and time of the performance, along with your seat number are written on the ticket. It is usually required to leave your coat in the lobby cloakroom. Programs are sold, and opera glasses are also available for a small rental fee. During the intermission, drinks and snacks are often served in the lobby. Each theater has its own box office, open daily. Tickets can also often be reserved through a travel/service bureau in your hotel, or purchased from street/metro theater kiosks. Some major theaters offer ticket purchase on their website (but you need to print out the ticket for admission). Also try the Central Ticket Office at 42 Nevsky Prospekt (open 9am–8pm, closed Sunday, Metro Nevsky Pr). On the night of the performance you can also bargain for tickets from touts at the door. For information on performances, see www.balletandopera.com and www.ticketsofrussia.ru.

Aleksandrinsky (Pushkin) Theater, the oldest drama theater in Russia, at 2 Ostrovskaya Square. Metro Gostiny Dvor. www.alexandrinsky.ru.

Baltic House Theater, 4 Aleksandrovsky Park. Metro Gorkovskaya. www.baltichouse.spb.ru.

Beloselsky-Belozersky Palace Mirror Hall, 41 Nevsky Pr. Has symphonic musical concerts and theater performances. Metro Nevsky Prospekt.

Bolshoi Drama Theater, 65 Fontanka. Metro Sennaya Ploshchad. www.bdt.spb.ru.

Bolshoi Puppet Theater, 10 Nekrasov. Metro Chernyshevskaya. www.puppets.ru.

Circus, 3 Fontanka Embankment. Metro Gostiny Dvor. www.circus.spb.ru.

Comedian's Refuge (Priyut Komedianta), 27 Sadovaya. Metro Sennaya Ploshchad. www.pkteatr.ru.

Comedy Academic Theater, 56 Nevsky Pr. Metro Nevsky Propekt.

Demmeni Marionette Theater, 52 Nevsky. Metro Nevsky Prospekt. www.demmeni.org.

Feel Yourself Russian, 4 Truda Square in Nikolayevsky Palace. Metro Admiralteyskaya. www.folkshow.ru.

Glinka Kapella Concert Hall, 20 Moika River Emb. Metro Nevsky Prospekt. www.glinka-capella.ru.

Grand (Oktybrsky) Concert Hall, 6 Ligovsky Pr. Metro Pl. Vosstaniya. www.bkz.ru.

Hermitage Theater of Concerts and Ballets, 34 Dvortsovaya (Palace) Emb. In Hermitage complex. Metro Nevsky Prospekt. www.hermitageballet.com.

Ice Palace, 1 Pyatiletok. Metro Prospekt Bolshevikov (southeast). www.newarena.spb.ru.

Komissarzhevskaya Theater, 19 Italyanskaya. Metro Gostiny Dvor. www.teatrvfk.ru.

Lensovet Palace of Culture, 42 Kamennoostrovsky. Metro Narvskaya.

Maly Drama Theater, 18 Rubinshteina. (Directed by Lev Dodin) Metro Dostoevskaya. www.mdt-dodin.ru.

Mikhailvosky Theater, 1 Iskusstva (Art) Square. Metro Nevsky Pr. www.mikhailovsky.ru.

Mariinsky I Theater of Opera and Ballet, 1 Teatralnaya Pl. Metro Sennaya Pl. www.mariinsky.ru.

Mariinsky II, 34 Dekabristov, Metro Sennaya Pl. www.mariinsky.ru.

Mariinsky Concert Hall, 20 Pisareva, (entrance from 37 Dekabristov). www.mariinsky.ru. (Buy tickets online; Mariinsky ticket offices are open 11am–7pm, or other box offices are in Gostiny Dvor on Nevsky and at the Central Ticket Office at 34 Griboyedov Canal.)

Music Hall and Baltiisky Dom, 4 Aleksandrovsky Park. Metro Gorkovskaya.

Rimsky-Korsakov Conservatory, 3 Teatralnaya Pl. Metro Sadovaya. www.conservatory.ru.

Shostakovich Philharmonic Hall, 2 Mikhailovskaya Bolshoi Zal. Maly Hall is at 30 Nevsky. Metro Nevsky Prospekt. www.philharmonia.spb.ru.

Smolny Cathedral Concert Hall, 3/1 Rastrelli Pl. Metro Chernyshevskaya. www. cathedral.ru.

The Other Side, 1 Bolshaya Konyushennaya. Metro Nevsky Prospekt. www. theotherside.ru.

Yusupov Palace Theater, 94 Moika Canal Emb within the Yusupov Palace. Metro Sadovaya. www.yusupov-palace.ru.

RELIGIOUS DENOMINATIONS
RUSSIAN ORTHODOX
CATHEDRALS
Women should dress modestly and cover heads; men remove hats.

Cathedral of the Holy Trinity, 1 Monastery River Emb. in Alexander Nevsky Monastery. Open 8am–6pm; services at 6pm. Metro Pl. Aleksandra Nevskovo, www. lavra.spb.ru.

Cathedral of the Savior on the Blood, 2a Nab. Griboyedova Kanala; see listing under museums.

Cathedral of the Transfiguration, 1 Preobrazhenskaya Sq. Metro Chernyshevskaya.

Church of the Savior, 1 Konyushennaya Sq. Burial service for Alexander Pushkin was held here on 1st February 1837. Metro Nevsky Prospekt.

Kazan Cathedral, 2 Kazanskaya Sq. Metro Nevsky Prospekt.

Smolny Cathedral of the Resurrection of Christ, 3/1 Rastrelli Pl. Open 10am–7pm; closed Wednesday. Functions as a museum with no services. Metro Chernyshevskaya.

St Isaac's Cathdral, see listing under museums.

St Nicholas (Nikolsky) Cathedral, 1/3 Nikolskaya Sq, open 9am–7pm. Metro Sadovaya, south of the Mariinsky Theater.

St Peter and Paul Cathedral, in Peter and Paul Fortress, see listing under museums.

Trinity Cathedral, 7a Izmailovsky Prospekt, open 9am–7pm; services daily at 10am, and Fri–Sun at 5pm. Metro Teknologichesky Institute.

Vladimirsky Cathedral, 20 Vladimirsky Prospekt, open 8am–6pm; services daily at 6pm. Baroque-style 18th-century cathedral where Dostoevsky was a parishioner. Metro Vladmirskaya.

OTHER

Armenian Church of Holy Resurrection, 29 Smolenka Emb. Daily 10am–6pm. Metro Vasileostrovskaya on Vasilevsky Island.

Armenian Orthodox Church of St Catherine, 40/42 Nevsky Prospekt. Open daily 9am–9pm; metro Nevsky Prospekt.

Baptist Church of the Gospel, 52 Borovaya Metro Ligovsky Prospekt.

Buddhist Temple Monastery, 91 Primorsky Prospekt on Vyborg side. Open daily 9am–7pm. Metro Staraya Derevnya.

Cathedral of the Assumption of the Virgin, 11a 1-aya Krasnoarmeiskaya. Metro Teknologichesky Institut.

Church of St Catherine, (Lutheran) 1 Bolshoi Pr. Vasilyevsky Island. Metro Vasileostrovskaya.

Evangelical Lutheran Church of St Peter & Paul, 22/24 Nevsky Prospekt. Metro Nevsky Prospekt.

Mosque of the Congregation of Moslems, 7 Kronversky Pr. Metro Gorkovskaya on Petrograd side.

Roman Catholic, Our Lady of Lourdes, 7 Kovensky Lane. Metro Mayakovskaya.

Roman Catholic Church of St Catherine, 32/34 Nevsky Pr. Metro Nevsky Prospekt.

Grand Choral Synagogue, 2 Lermontovsky Pr, open 8am–8pm; Saturday service at 10am. On site is the Small Synagogue (open 11am–4pm, Fri/Sat 11am–1pm), a restaurant and Kosher shop. Metro Sadovaya. www.jewishpetersburg.ru.

MISCELLANEOUS

BANYA/SAUNAS

Most top-end hotels have fitness centers and saunas and/or swimming pools. Usually, for a fee, non-hotel residents can use the facility. See Special Topic on *Banya*)

Degtyarniye Bani, 1a Degtyarnaya, off 140 Nevsky, operates from 8:30am–9pm. On the upper floor of the building, this Banya complex is divided into women's and men's sections; both have a traditional *parilka* banya, Turkish steam room, cold plunge pool and lounging areas; each session is for two hours. (Private banyas can also be booked). Other types of services as body scrubs (with coffee, soap or birch leaves) and massage are extra. Check website for hours of operation/prices/services; call to reserve, as spots tend to fill up; tel. 717-7670/0116 or 969-5315. Metro Ploshchad Vosstaniya. www.d1a.ru (website in English).

Mytninskiye Bani, 17–19 Mtninskaya, by reservation, tel. 271-7119. Separate male/female sides (and private lux) with traditional banya, cold pool and lounge. Ploshchad Vosstaniya. www.mybanya.spb.ru.

Kazachiye Bani, 11 Bolshoi Kazachy Lane. Offers communal banya, but specializes more in private lux experience. Metro Pushkinskaya. www.kazbani.ru.

Krugliye Bani (Circle Baths), 29 Karbysheva (on Vyborg side); closed Wed/Thurs, tel. 297-6409. Offers both communal and private banyas with an upgraded lux communal option for women and men at different times. Metro Ploshchad Muzhestva.

MOPS SPA, 12 Rubinshteyna, open 11am–11pm. Run by the same management as the MOPS Restaurant, this lovely day spa offers traditional Thai & Indonesian massage, aromatherapy, facials, etc. Metro Dostoevskaya. www.mopsspa.ru.

BOAT PASSENGER DOCKS & TOURS

Boats are in service between May and October. During crowded summer months, try to purchase tickets in advance (which you can do directly at each pier's ticket kiosk).

Anichkov Pier is the most popular at the corner of Nevsky Prospekt and the Fontanka River. Small riverboats depart daily about every half hour from 11am to 10pm. The canal tours last about one hour.

Anglo Tourismo offers daily English boat (in summer) and walking (including night) tours of the city. www.anglotourismo.com. See also **Peter's Walking, Boat & Bicycle Tours** at www.peterswalk.com.

Griboyedov Canal Pier is on the corner of Nevsky and the canal. Boats operate between noon and 7pm and also tour the canals in summer.

Moika Pier is at the corner of Nevsky and the Moika River.

Hermitage Pier is across from the museum on Dvortsovaya (Palace) Embankment. From the upper deck, hydrofoils depart for Peterhof (from 9am to 3pm every 20 minutes), taking 20 minutes. From the lower deck, double-decker river boats depart for one-hour excursions along the Neva River. Another pier is situated across from Senate Square, near the Bronze Horseman Statue. Large riverboats leave for both one-hour trips along the Neva River, and across the Gulf to Peterhof.

Main River Terminal, at 195 Canal Obvodnovo, has river cruises (which depart every few days) to points north, such as Valaam and Kizhi (that last one to five days), and south to Moscow. Metro Proletarskaya.

Tuchkov Bridge Pier has daily hydrofoils to Kronstadt that depart every hour between 9am and 6pm.

BUS TRAVEL

City Tour, the red double-decker 'hop on, hop off' bus runs along the routes of the city's main sites. A day ticket is valid for as many trips as you like. www. citytourspb.ru.

St Peterburg's main bus terminal, Avtovokzal 2, is at 36 Obvodnov Kanal, Metro Obvodny Kanal. (There is no Avtovokzal 1) www.avokzal.ru.

For international Bus routes, see: Lux Express at www.luxexpress.eu and Ecolines at www.ecolines.ru. The Ardis Finnord line runs to Helsinki with a stop in Vyborg. Departs from the Moskva Hotel, entrance 3, metro Alexander Nevskovo. www. ardisfin.ru.

DUMSKAYA

From Dumskaya along Nevsky Prospekt and Gostiny Dvor Shopping Arcade there are numerous travel kiosks that offer group bus excursions both around the city and to outlying areas. Even though most tours are in Russian, the bus gets you there and into the palaces and grounds. Even though the cost is often more for foreigners, the options are usually cheaper than regular English-only tours.

CAR RENTALS

Many of the more expensive hotels have car rentals available. Car, minivan, and bus rentals (with and without driver) can be found. It is recommended not to drive within the city, unless planning on excursions out of town. Public transportation is quite adequate to use around town.

Autopole Rent, Tel. 607-7777. www.autopole.ru.

Avis, Pulkovo Airport and at the Moscow Hotel (Ent 3), Metro Pl Aleksandra Nevskovo. Tel. 324-6109/600-1213. www.avis-rentacar.ru.

Europecar, Pulkovo Airport. Tel. 385-5284. www.europcar.com.

Hertz, Pulkovo airport and at the Moskovsky Train Station in town. Tel. 454-7009. www.hertz.com.

Sixt, Pulkovo Airport, all main train stations in town and at the Angleterre Hotel, 39 Bolshaya Morkskaya (Metro Admiralteyskaya). Tel. 309-0355/244-0355. www. sixt.com.

FERRIES AND RIVER CRUISES

The **Marine Façade Terminal** is where most large cruise ships now dock. Vasilyevsky Island, metro Primorskaya. www.portspb.ru. The **Sea Passenger Terminal** is at 1 Morskoi Slavy Square, at the southern corner of Vasilyevsky Island. (Most ferries from Scandinavia dock here.) www.mvokzal.ru. Travel to Sweden is about 24 hours,

Estonia 14 hours, and Helsinki 10 hours. For timetables and prices, see www. stpeterline.com and www.saimaatravel.fi. Tickets can be bought at the Sea Terminal or at the **Ferry Center** at 19 Vosstaniya, near the Moskovsky Train station in town, Metro Pl Vosstaniya. Many boats from Moscow and within Russia arrive at the **River Port Terminal**, located at 195 Obukhovskoi Oborony Prospekt, Metro Proletarskaya.

Tickets can be purchased at each Passenger Terminal or through individual websites. Check the travel kiosks on the corner of Nevsky Prospekt and Dumskaya (along Gostiny Dvor); often they offer tours to such places as Valaam & Kizhi, Kronstadt, Peterhof and Schlüsselburg.

Infoflot, cruises include to White Sea's Solevetski Islands/Valaam and Golden Ring towns of Yaroslavl and Uglich—up to 12 days. www.infoflot.com.

Liberty, specializes in tours for the disabled, and has specially wheel-chair fitted vans. www.libertytour.ru.

Mosturflot, cruises between St Petersburg & Moscow. www.mosturflot.ru.

Orthodox Cruise Company, up to ten-day cruises between St Petersburg and Moscow, and Golden Ring towns. www.cruise.ru or through www.atorus.ru/en.

Sunny Sailing, 94 Ligovsky Pr/2nd fl. River cruises to Lake Ladoga, Valaam, Kizhi, and south to Moscow and Astrakhan. Yacht charters. www.sailing.spb.ru.

Vodohod, cruises up to two weeks to Golden Ring towns, Lake Ladoga/Kizhi and Nizhny Novgorod & Astrakhan. www.bestrussiancruises.com.

SPORTS
Bicycling SKAT PROKAT, 7 Goncharnaya, open 1pm–8pm. Bike rentals, along with Saturday and Sunday morning city bike tours. Rental by hour or by day. (Bring your passport or driver's license for deposit +$). Metro Ploshchad Vosstaniya. www. skatprokat.ru.

Rent Bike, 4a Yefimova (off Sadovaya), open 24/7; tel/sms 981-0155. Bike rentals (and delivery to your hotel, special conditions apply; deposit required). Metro Sennaya Ploshchad. www.rentbike.org.

Petersburg Bike Tours, run jointly with Skat Prokat, offers city bike tours, including a White Night Tour from mid-May until end of August. www.peterswalk.com.

Bowling City, 3 Yekimova (across from Rent Bike), open 24/7. A sports club that provides over 30 bowling lanes, pool tables, a sports bar and plenty of karaoke. Metro Sennaya Ploshchad. www.fitness.ru.

Bus City Tours, www.citytourspb.ru.

GYMS & POOLS: Plenty of **Planet Fitness Clubs** are scattered about town. Many have swimming pools, tennis courts and classes such as aerobics, spinning and yoga. (Largest location is on Petrograd side at 18 Petrogradskaya Emb.) See www.fitness.ru for locations. The **Sports Complex** on the Petrograd side at 9a Kronversky has weights and a 25-meter heated swimming pool under a glass roof. Metro Gorkovskaya. www.dfkpgups.ru. **Fitness Palace**, at 21a Konnogbardeisky, has a gym, cardio room & tennis court. Located near St Issac's Cathedral. www.fitpalace.ru.

Waterfille AquaPark, 14 Korablestroitelei in Park Inn Pribaltiiskaya Hotel, open 9am–11pm. The water park features scores of waterslide-type rides, jet streams and wave pools, along with a lap swimming pool, and shallower pools for kids. Metro Primorskaya. www.waterville.ru.

Skating & Cross Country Skiing—Yelagin Island; Metro Krestovsky Ostrov. In winter, the car-free island offers ice skating, sledding and cross-country skiing, skates and skis are available for rent. www.elaginpark.spb.ru.

WALKING CITY TOURS:

Anglo Tourismo offers daily English walking (including night) and boat tours (in summer) of the city. www.anglotourismo.com.

VB Excursions, walking tours of the city. www.vb-excursions.com.

Peter's Walking Tours offers over 10 walking (lasting 3 to 5 hours) and biking tours, and trips to environs, all led by experienced locals who are fluent in English. www.peterswalk.com and www.biketour.spb.ru.

USEFUL ADDRESSES

IN THE USA

Contact information for embassies and consulates of the Russian Federation around the world: www.russianembassy.net. Russian embassies & consulates in US: www.russianembassy.org.

Russian Embassy, 2650 Wisconsin Ave, NW, Washington DC 20007. Tel. (202) 298-5700.

Visa Consular Section, 2641 Tunlaw Rd, NW, Washington DC 20007. Tel. (202) 939-8907.

RUSSIAN CONSULATES GENERAL

New York, 9 East 91st St, New York, NY 10128. Tel. (212) 348-0926, www.ruscon.org.

San Franciso, 2790 Green St. San Francisco, CA 94123. Tel. (415) 202-9800/928-6878, www.consulrussia.org.

Seattle, 600 University St, Suite 2510, Seattle, WA 98101. Tel. (206) 728-1910.

Houston, 1333 West Loop South, Suite 1300, Houston, TX 77027. Tel. (713) 337-3300.

VISAS

Red Star Travel, 123 Queen Anne Ave N, Suite 102, Seattle, WA 98109. Tel. (800) 215-4378 or (206) 522-5995, www.travel2russia.com.

TDS Travel Document Systems, five offices in US, Washington DC (800) 875-5100, New York (877) 874-5104, Los Angeles (888) 424-8472, San Francisco (888) 874-5100, Houston (866) 797-2600, www.traveldocs.com.

Pinnacle TDS, 1625 K St, NW, Suite 750, Washington DC 20006. Tel. (888) 838-4867, www.pinnacletds.com.

CIBTvisas.com.

Go To Russia, Tel. (888) 263-0023, in Atlanta (404) 827-0099, www gotorussia.com.

Russian National Tourist Office, 224 West 30th St, Suite 701, NY NY 10001. Tel. (877) 221-7120, (646) 473-2233; Moscow, 8/10 Neglinnaya, Bldg 1 Ste 13/14. Tel. (495) 623-7978, www.russia-travel.com.

Visa House: in Moscow, Tel. (495) 721-1021, www.visahouse.com.

Visas Online: in Moscow, 29 Leninsky Prospekt. Tel. (495) 956,4422, toll-free US (800) 324-0492, (provides visa registrations) www.visatorussia.com.

AIRLINES

Aeroflot, tel. (866) 879-7647, www.aeroflot.com.

Air France, tel. (800) 237-2747, www.airfrance.com.

Alaska Airlines, tel. (800) 426-0333, www.alaskaair.com.

American, tel. (800) 433-7300, www.aa.com.

British Airways, tel. (800) 247-9297, www.britishairways.com.

Delta, tel. (800) 241-4141, www.delta.com.

Finnair, tel. (800) 950-5000, www.finnair.com.

KLM, tel. (800) 447-4747, www.klm.com.

Korean Air, tel. (800) 438-5000, www.koreanair.com.

Lufthansa, tel. (800) 645-3880, www.lufthansa.com.

United, tel (800) 241-6522, www.united.com.

SAS, tel. (800) 221-2350, www.scandinavian.net or www.flysas.com.

TRAVEL AGENCIES, TOUR AND SPECIALITY GROUPS

For Hostels & Homestays and Independent Russian Travel Agencies, see Practical Information Sections for both Moscow and St Petersburg.

Council on International Exchange (CIEE), www.ciee.org.

Exeter International, tel (800) 633-1008 www.exeterinternational.com.

MIR, 85 South Washington St Ste 210, Seattle, WA 98104. Tel. (800) 424-7289/ (206) 624-7289, www.mircorp.com.

Pioneer East-West Initiative, 203 Allstone St Cambridge, MA 02139. Custom designed Russian trips, specialty tours, and homestays. Tel. (800) 369-1322, www.pioneerrussia.com.

Rail Europe, Specializing in Russian, CIS & European train travel. Tel. (800) 622-8600, www.raileurope.com.

Red Star Travel, see listing under visas.

T.E.I. Tours and Travel, PO Box 23784, Pleasant Hill, CA 94523 (925) 825-6104, www.teiglobal.com.

Tour Designs, 713 Sixth Street SW, Washington DC 20024. Tel. (800) 432-8687, (202) 554-5820, www.tourdesignsinc.com.

ADVENTURE TRAVEL

Abercrombie & Kent, tel. (888) 785-5379, www.abercrombiekent.com.

Geographic Expeditions, tel. (888) 570-7108, www.geoex.com.

GW Travel Limited, (Golden Eagle Trans-Siberian Express) www.gwtravel.co.uk.

SteppesTravel, see listing under UK, www.steppestravel.co.uk.

Zegrahm Expeditions, tel. (888) 979-4787, www.zegrahm.com.

IN THE UK

Russian Embassy, 6-7 Kensington Place Gardens, London W8 4QP.
Tel. (0)207 229-6412/7281. www.rusemb.org.uk.
Russian Visa, 5 Kensington Place Gardens, London W8. tel (0)203 668-7474.
In Scotland, 58 Melville Street, Edinburgh, EH3 7HF.
Tel. (0)131 225-7098, www.rusemb.org.uk.

AIRLINES

Aeroflot, tel. (0)800 026-0033, www.aeroflot.com.
British Airways, tel. (0)844 493-0787, www.britishairways.com.
Finnair, tel. (0)870 241-4411. www.finnair.com.

TRAVEL AGENCIES

Andrew's Travel House (ATH), Skyline House, 1/F, 200 Union St, London, SE1 0LX, tel. (0)207 727 2838 (provides Russian visa support & invitations), www.athvisas. co.uk

CIBT Visas, www.cibtvisas.co.uk.

Findhorn Ecotravels, The Park, Findhorn, Moray, Scotland. IV36 3TD, tel. (0)1309 690995, www.findhornecotravels.org.

GW Travel Limited, (0)161 928-9410, (Golden Eagle Trans-Siberian Express) www. gwtravel.co.uk.

Real Russia, 5, The Ivories, Northampton St, Islington, London N1 2HY, (0)207 100 7370 (Moscow office: 9 Bolshaya Maryinskaya, #313, tel. (495) 616-8086; St Petersburg office, Alliance Travel, 7 2nd Sovetskaya, Rm 408, tel. (812) 579-9933, www.realrussia.co.uk.)

Regent Holidays, tel. (0)207 666-1244, www.regent-holidays.co.uk.

Russia Experience, 1d, The Court, Lanwades Business Park, Newmarket, CB8 7PN. Tel. (0)845 521 2910, www.trans-siberian.co.uk.

Russia National Tourist Office, London (0)207 985 1234, 202 Kensington Church St, W8 4DP; Edinburgh 16 Forth St, EH1 3LH.
Tel. (0)131 550 3709, www.visitrussia.org.uk.

STA Travel, tel. (0)333 321 0099, www.statravel.co.uk.

Steppes Travel, *Travel Beyond the Ordinary*, 51 Castle St, Cirencester, Gloucestershire GL7 1QD, tel. (0)843 636 8342; International 44 1285 601 495; Toll free US only 855-203-7885. Travel journeys all around Russia and the former republics. (See Steppes Traveller Magazine on the website) www.steppestravel.co.uk.

Voyages Jules Verne, 21 Dorset Square, London NW1 6QE, tel. (0845) 166-7003, (0)207 616 1000, www.vjv.com.

IN CANADA

Russian Embassy, 285 Charlotte Street, Ottawa, Ontario K1N 8LS.
Tel. (613) 235-4341, www.rusembassy.ca.

CONSULATES
Ottawa, 52 Range Road, Ottawa, Ontario K1N 8JS, tel. (613) 236-7220/0920.
Montréal, 3655 Avenue du Musée, Montréal, Quebéc H3G 2E1, tel. (514) 843-5901.
Toronto, 175 Bloor St East (South Tower), Suites 801/802, Toronto, Ontario M4W 3R8, tel. (416) 962-9911, www.toronto.mid.ru.

AIRLINES
Aeroflot, tel. (866) 221-7291, Toronto tel. (416) 776-3932, www.aeroflot.com.
Air Canada, tel. (888) 247-2262, www.aircanada.com.
Air France, tel. (800) 667-2747, www.airfrance.ca.
British Airways, tel. (800) 247-9297, www.britishairways.com.
Finnair, tel. (800) 950 5000, www.finnair.com.
KLM, tel. (866) 434 0321. www.klm.com.
Lufthansa, tel. (800) 563-5954. www.lufthansa.com.

TRAVEL AGENCIES
Canadian Gateway, 7851 Dufferin St, Suite 200, Thornhill, Ontario L4J 3M4.
Tel. (800) 668-8401/(905) 660-1100, www.canadiangateway.com.
Explore Worldwide Ltd, (888)-216-3401, www.exploreworldwide.com.
Rail Europe, tel. (800) 361-7245, www.raileurope.com.
Travel Cuts, tel. (800) 667-2887, www.travelcuts.com.

IN HONG KONG

Russian Consulate, Room 2106-2123, Sun Hung Kai Centre, 30 Harbour Road, Wanchai, tel. 2877-7188, www.russia.com.hk.

AIRLINES
Aeroflot, tel. 2769-8122, www.aeroflot.com.
British Airways, tel. 3071-5083 and 2216-1088, www.britishairways.com.

TRAVEL AGENCIES
Global Union Transportation Ltd, Room 505, Nan Fung Tower, 173 Des Voeux Rd, tel. 3713-2300, www.global.com.hk.

IN AUSTRALIA

Russian Embassy, 78 Canberra Avenue, Griffith ACT, Canberra 2603.
Tel. (06) 6295-9033, www.russianembassy-au.ru.
Sydney Consulate, 7–9 Fullerton Street, Woolahra, NSW 2025.
Tel. (02) 9326-1866/1702, www.sydneyrussianconsulate.com.

AIRLINES IN SYDNEY
Aeroflot, tel. (02) 9262-2233/1821, www.aeroflot.com.
British Airways, tel. 1300 767 177, www.britishairways.com.

TRAVEL AGENCIES
Gateway Travel, 48 The Boulevard, Strathfield, NSW 2135.
Tel. (02) 9745-3333, www.russian-gateway.com.au.
Russia Experience, tel. 1300-654-861, www.trans-siberian.co.uk.
STA Travel, tel. 134782, www.statravel.com.au.
VisaLink, www.visalink.com.au.

IN NEW ZEALAND

Russian Embassy, 57 Messines Road, Karori, Wellington.
Tel. (04) 476-6113, consular department (04) 476-6742, www.newzealand.mid.ru.

AIRLINES
Air New Zealand, tel. 0800 737 000 (0)9 357 3000, www.airnewzealand.co.nz.
British Airways, Auckland. tel. (09) 356-8690; outside Auckland (0800) 274-847.966 9777, www.britishairways.com.

TRAVEL AGENCIES
STA Travel, tel. 0800 474-400, www.statravel.co.nz.

(For listings of embassies, consulates, travel agencies and other useful addresses in Moscow and St Petersburg, see Practical Information sections.)

RUSSIAN ORTHODOX CHURCH HOLIDAYS AND FESTIVALS

There are 11 fixed Orthodox Church observances that fall on the same date each year. In 2010, then President Dmitri Medvedev declared a new holiday, Orthodox Christianity Day, to be celebrated on July 28, in honor of the Baptism of Rus and Russia's conversation to Christianity in 988 A.D.

Jan 6	*Sochelnik*	Christmas Eve
Jan 7	*Rozhdestvo Khristovo*	Nativity of Christ
Jan 19	*Bogoyavlenie Gospodne*	Epiphany
Feb 15	*Sretenie Gospodne*	Candlemas Day or Feast of the Purification and preparing for Lent
Apr 7	*Blagoveshchenie Bogoroditsy*	Annunciation of Our Lady
Aug 19	*Preobrazhenie Gospodne*	Transfiguration of Christ (Second Savior)
Aug 28	*Uspenie Bogoroditsy*	Assumption of the Holy Virgin
Sept 21	*Rozhdestvo Bogoroditsy*	Nativity of Our Lady
Sept 27	*Vozdvizhenie Zhivotvoryashchevo Kresta Gospodnya*	Exaltation of the Cross
Oct 14	*Pokrov Bogoroditsy*	Intercession of Our Lady
Dec 4	*Vvedenie vo Khram Bogoroditsy*	Feast of Presentation of the Blessed Virgin

The Orthodox Church celebrates numerous holidays and religious events; many of these Church holy days stem from old pagan rituals. The month of May, for example, is very significant in the Orthodox religion. The first Sunday after Easter is known as *Krasnaya Gorka* or Little Red Mountain. It originated as a pagan spring rite when newlyweds and their relatives celebrated fertility, both for the land and their future offspring. In May, some of Russia's most revered saints are also honored: Saint Georgy Pobedonosets (Victory-Bringer) is remembered on May 6 and Saint Nikolai Chudotvorets (the Miracle-Maker) on May 22. The Day of Slavic Language and Culture falls on May 24. This marks the birth of Saint Cyril (827–869) who helped create the first Slavic written language, based on Greek characters.

Fifty days after Easter the Church celebrates the holiday week of *Pyatidesyatnitsa* (50)—the feast of the descent of the Holy Spirit on the Apostles. The festival is also known as *Troitsa* (Trinity), an honoring of the Father, Son and

Holy Spirit. Centuries ago, this was merged with the old Slavonic pagan feast *Semik* (Seven Days) which heralded the beginning of summer. Villagers cut down a birch tree, decorated it with ribbons and flowers, and then held parties beneath it. Afterwards they threw the garlands into the river; how they floated predicted the village's future year.

Additionally, Slavs made sure to pay an annual visit to their ancestors' graves. They believed that the dead influenced the fate of the living. The cult of the dead is also linked with the legend of the mermaid. Spirits of young women or unbaptized children who died unnatural deaths were thought to be transformed into mermaids who, each spring, roamed the riverbanks to entice victims into the water. Anyone who had a relative die in this way paid extra attention to their gravesites. Mermaids were considered the female spirits of the water, and *Troitsa/ Semik* week is also nicknamed *Rusalnaya* (Mermaid).

In August the Orthodox Church celebrates three feast days connected with the life of Christ. Since both Russian farmers and Christians were concerned with their summer harvests and sowing seeds for the following year, they developed protective religious rites. Spas the First (Festival of the Savior's Cross or First Savior) falls on August 14; it is also known as 'Honey Day'. The holiday let people know it was time to gather honey from the beehives. A large festival was held on Moscow's Trubnaya Square where peasants sold crimson honey from large vats along with *barankas* (ring-shaped rolls). On this day peasants also brought their seeds to church and the priest sprinkled the fields with holy water. In old Rus, the cleansing of the water also took place; everyone down to livestock would be baptized in the rivers and blessed by the priests. This was thought to ward off evils and cure all ills.

August 19, Transfiguration Day of Christ (or Spas the Second/Second Savior), is also known as 'Apple Day'. On the morning of Apple Day, everyone would take their apples to local churches. They couldn't be eaten until blessed—people believed that worms would appear in their stomachs if they broke this rule. It was customary for thousands of vendors to pour into Moscow's Zamoskvorechye district across the river from the Kremlin to sell many varieties of this fruit.

Spas the Third or Third Savior-on-the-Veil falls on August 29; this is also known as 'Nut Day'. Nuts in the woods were gathered in sacks for the winter. Everywhere throughout Russia religious processions were also held leading with the Veronika Icon. According to legend, St Veronika gave Christ, while on the way to Calvary, her handkerchief with which to wipe his face. His image was miraculously left on it; in 944, the Veronika Icon (in Greek, *eikon* means image) was purchased by Byzantine Emperor Konstantine and moved to Constantinople.

RUSSIAN LANGUAGE

CYRILLIC ALPHABET

CYRILLIC	APPROXIMATE PRONUNCIATION
Аа	*a* as in 'father'
Бб	*b* as in 'book'
Вв	*v* as in 'vote'
Гг	*g* as in 'good'
Дд	*d* as in 'day'
Ее	*ye* as in 'yes'
Ёё	*yo* as in 'yonder'
Жж	*s* as in 'pleasure'
Зз	*z* as in 'zone'
Ии	*ee* as in 'meet'
Йй	*y* as in 'boy'
Кк	*k* as in 'kind'
Лл	*l* as in 'lamp'
Мм	*m* as in 'man'
Нн	*n* as in 'note'
Оо	*o* as in 'pot'
Пп	*p* as in 'pet'
Рр	*r* as in 'red' (slightly rolled)
Сс	*s* as in 'speak'
Тт	*t* as in 'too'
Уу	*oo* as in 'fool'
Фф	*f* as in 'fire'
Хх	*kh* as in 'Bach'
Цц	*tz* as in 'quartz'
Чч	*ch* as in 'chair'
Шш	*sh* as in 'short'
Щщ	*shch* as in 'fresh'
Ъъ	hard sign (silent)
Ыы	no equivalent, but close to *ee*
Ьь	soft sign (silent)
Ээ	*e* as in 'men'
Юю	*u* as in 'university'
Яя	*ya* as in 'yard'

BASIC RUSSIAN VOCABULARY

ENGLISH	RUSSIAN PHONETIC TRANSLITERATION
Hello	*zdravst'voitye*
Good morning	*do'broye oo'tro*
Good afternoon	*do'bree dyen*
Good evening	*do'bree vye'cher*
Good night	*spakoi'ne no'chee*
Goodbye	*da sveedahn'ya*
Yes	*da*
No	*nyet*
Please, You're welcome	*pozhal'sta*
Thank you	*spasee'bah*
Okay/good	*kharoshaw'*
Excuse me	*eezveenee'tye*
My name is ...	*menyah' zavoot' ...*
What is your name?	*kahk vahs zavoot'?*
Nice to meet you	*o'chin priyat'na svah'mee pahz nahko'mitsa*
How are you?	*kahk dyelah'?*
Do you speak ...?	*vii govoree'tye po ...?*
English	*ahnglee'ski*
German	*nemyet'ski*
French	*frantsooz'ski*
Russian	*roos'ski*
I speak English	*ya gavaryoo'po ahnglee'ski*
I don't speak Russian	*ya ne gavaryoo'po roos'ski*
I (don't) understand	*ya (ne) poneemah'yoo*
Speak slowly	*gavaree'tye myed'lenna*
Please repeat	*pazhal'sta paftaree'tye*
We (I) need a translator	*nam (menye) noo'zhen perevod'chik*
I'm a foreigner (male/female)	*ya eenastra'nets/eenastran'ka*
I'm from America/England	*ya eez Ahmer'eekee/ Ahn'glee ee*
I'm a tourist	*ya tooree'st*
Group	*groo'pa*
Tell me	*skazhee'tye menye'*
Show me	*pakazhee'tye menye'*
Help me	*pamaghee'tye menye'*

I (don't) want	*ya (ne) khahchoo'*
I want to rest/sleep	*ya khahchoo' ot dakhnoot'/spaht*
eat/drink	*yest/peet*
I can/can't	*ya magoo'/ne magoo'*
It (is) here/there	*e'to zdyes, tahm*
How old are you?	*skol'ka vahm lyet?*
Of course	*kahnyesh'na*
With pleasure	*soodavolst'veeyem*
Congratulations	*pazdrahvlah'yoo vahs*
where	*gedye'*
what	*shtoh*
who	*ktoh'*
when	*kagdah'*
how	*kahk*
why	*pachemoo'*
How much/many	*skol'ka*
How much does it cost?	*skol'ka stoi'eet?*
I	*ya*
he	*ohn*
she	*ahna'*
it	*ahno'*
you (informal)	*tii* (like German *du* and French *tu*)
we	*mii*
you (formal, plural)	*vii* (like German *sie* and French *vous*)
they	*ahnee'*
man	*moozhchee'na*
woman	*shchen'shcheena*
boy	*mahl'cheek*
girl	*dye'vooshka*
father	*otyets'*
mother	*maht*
brother	*braht*
sister	*sestrah'*
grandfather	*dye'dooshka*
grandmother	*ba'booshka*
husband	*moozh*
wife	*zhenah'*

AIRPORT

airplane	*samolyot'*
flight	*reys*
arrival	*prilyot'*
departure	*vylyet*
boarding	*pasad'ka*
baggage	*bagazh'*
my passport	*moy pas'port*
my visa	*maya' vee'za*
my ticket	*moy beelyet'*
suitcase(s)	*chemodahn' (ee)*
porter	*naseel'shchik*
I want to go to the airport	*ya khachoo' f aeroport'*

HOTEL

I want to go to the hotel	*ya khachoo' f gostee'neetsu*
Where is the hotel?	*gedye' gostee'neetsa?*
Where is Intourist?	*gedye' Intooreest'?*
floor lady	*dezhoor'naya*
maid	*gor'nichnaya*
key	*klyooch*
floor	*etazh'*
taxi	*tahksee'*
elevator	*leeft*
room	*kom'nata*
telephone	*telefon'*
lavatory	*tooalyet'*

TRANSPORT

map	*kar'ta*
street	*oo'leetsa*
crossing	*perekhot'*
Metro station	*stan'tseeya metro'*
bus stop	*astanof'ka afto'boosa*
tram stop	*astanof'ka tramva'ya*
taxi station	*stayahn'ka tahksee'*
train	*po'yezd*
station	*vokzahl'*
Must I transfer?	*na'do peresad'ku?*

Please tell me where/when	*skazheet'ye pazhal'sta gedye'/kagda'*
to get off	*na'da so' ytee*
I want to go to ...(by vehicle)	*ya khachoo' pahye'khat f ...*
Stop here	*astanavee'tyes zdyes*
Wait for me	*padazhdee'tye menyah'*
entrance	*vkhot*
exit	*vy'khot*
stop	*stoi'tye*
go (on foot)	*eedee'tye*
go (by vehicle)	*payezhai'tye*
Let's go (on foot)	*pashlee'*
Let's go (by vehicle)	*payekh'elee*
attention	*vneemahn'eeyah*
forbidden	*nelzya'*

THEATER

theater/ballet/opera	*teea'tr/balyet'/o'pira*
concert/cinema	*kantsert'/keeno'*
What is playing tonight?	*shto eedyot' sevod'nya vye'chiram?*
ticket office	*kas'sa*
Do you have tickets?	*oo vas yest bilye'tee?*
When does the show begin?	*kagda' nachinai'itsa predstavlyen'iye?*
museum/park/exhibition	*moozey'/Pahrk/Vees'tafka*

DAYS OF THE WEEK

Monday	*paneedyel'nik*
Tuesday	*ftor'nik*
Wednesday	*sreda'*
Thursday	*chetvyerk'*
Friday	*pyat'neetsa*
Saturday	*sooboh'ta*
Sunday	*vaskresyen'ye*
today	*sevod'nya*
yesterday	*fcherah'*
tomorrow	*zahf'tra*
morning	*oo'trom*
day	*dyen*
evening	*vye'cherom*
night	*noch*

week	*nedehl'ya*
month	*meh'syats*
What time is it?	*kator'ee chahs?*

CHARACTERISTICS

good/bad	*kharoshaw/plo'kha*
big/small	*ballshoy'/mal'enkee*
open/closed	*otkri'to/zakri'to*
cold/warm/hot	*kho'lodno/zhar'ko/gorya'chee*
left/right	*le'vo/prah'vo*
straight ahead	*preeyah'mo*
(not) beautiful	*(ne) krahsee'vo*
(not) interesting	*(ne) eenteres'no*
quick/slow	*bi'stra/med'lenna*
much (many)/few	*mano'ga/mah'lo*
early/late/now	*rah'no/poz'no/say chas'*
fun/boring	*ves'olo/skoosh'no*
(not) delicious	*(ne) fkoos'no*
possible/impossible	*mozh'no/nevozmozh'no*

NUMBERS

one	*adeen'*	nineteen	*devyatnaht'set*
two	*dvah*	twenty	*dvaht'set*
three	*tree*	thirty	*treet'set*
four	*chetir'ee*	forty	*so'rak*
five	*pyaht*	fifty	*peedesyaht'*
six	*shest*	sixty	*shestdesyat'*
seven	*syem*	seventy	*sem'desyet*
eight	*vo'syem*	eighty	*vo'semdesyet*
nine	*dye'vyet*	ninety	*dyevenos'ta*
ten	*dyes'yat*	one hundred	*sto*
eleven	*adeen'natset*	one thousand	*tee'syacha*
twelve	*dvenaht'set*		
thirteen	*treenaht'set*		
fourteen	*chetir'nahtset*		
fifteen	*pyatnaht'set*		
sixteen	*shestnaht'set*		
seventeen	*syemnaht'set*		
eighteen	*vosemnaht'set*		

MAP GLOSSARY AND ABBREVIATIONS

big	*Bolshoi (Bol.)*
boulevard	*Bulvar (Bul.)*
small	*Maly/Malaya (Mal.)*
bridge	*Mahst*
embankment	*Naberezhnaya (Nab.)*
new	*Novy*
lane	*Pereulok (Per.)*
square	*Ploshchad (Pl.)*
passage	*Proyezd*
avenue	*Prospekt (Pr.)*
highway	*Shosse*
old	*Stary*
street	*Ulitsa (Ul.)*
rampart	*Val*

MENU VOCABULARY

APPETIZERS

ZAKUS'KI

mushrooms in sour cream sauce	*gribi'so smetan'oi*
caviar	*ikra'*
salmon	*lososin'a*
black olives	*maslin'i*
sardines	*sardin'i*
herring	*seld*
salad	*salat'*
crab salad in mayonnaise	*salat kra'bi pod*
cucumber salad	*salat iz ogurtsov'*
tomato salad	*salat iz pomidor'*
salad made with potatoes, mayo, small chunks of meat, pickles	*stolich'ni salat*

SOUP

SUP

borsch	*borshch*
bouillon	*bulyon*
meat and potato soup	*pokhlyob'ka*
cabbage soup	*shchi*
fish or meat soup	*solyan'ka-riibni* or *myas'ni*

MEAT	*MYA'SO*
mutton	*bara'nina*
steak	*bifshteks'*
meatballs	*bitoch'ki*
filet	*file*
beef	*govya'dina*
goulash	*gulyash*
sausage	*kolbasa'*
meat patties	*kotle'ti*
lamb patties/kebab-style	*lyul'ya kebab*
shish kebab	*shashliik'*
schnitzel	*shnit'sel*
wieners	*sosis'ki*
pork	*svini'na*
veal	*telya'tina*
ham	*vetchi'na*
tongue	*yaziik'*

FOWL	*PTIITSA*
chicken	*kur'iitsa*
duck	*ut'ka*

FISH	*RII'BA*
crab	*kra'bi*
flounder	*kam'bala*
carp	*karp*
shrimp	*krevet'ki*
salmon	*lososi'na*
perch	*o'kun*
sturgeon	*osetri'na*
pike	*sudak'*
cod	*treska'*

OTHER DISHES	
blintzes	*blin'chiki*
pancakes with fillings	*blini'*
fried meat pastries	*chebur'eki*
hot cereal	*kash'a*
boiled meat dumplings	*pelmen'i*

baked dough with fillings	*piro'gi*
small hot pastries with fillings	*pirozhki'*
rice	*ris*
cheese pancakes	*siir'niki*
fruit or cheese dumplings	*varen'iki*
cold cheese tarts	*vatrush'ki*

BREAD (BLACK/WHITE) · *KHLEB (CHORNI/BELII)*

rolls	*bu'lochki*
jam	*dzhem*
preserves	*varen'ye*

DAIRY PRODUCTS · *MOLOCHNIYE BLYUDA*

thick buttermilk-like yoghurt	*kefir'*
butter	*mas'lo*
yoghurt	*prostok'vasha*
cream	*sliv'ki*
sour cream	*smetan'a*
cheese	*siir*
cottage cheese	*tvorog'*
egg	*yait'so*

VEGETABLES · *OVOSHCHI*

peas	*goroshek'*
mushrooms	*griibi'*
cabbage	*kapus'ta*
potatoes	*kartofel/kartosh'ka*
onions	*luk*
carrots	*morkov'*
cucumbers	*ogurtsi'*
tomatoes	*pomidor'i*
beets	*svyok'la*

FRUIT · *FRUKTI*

oranges	*apelsi'ni*
watermelon	*arbuz'*
melon	*dii'nya*
pears	*grush'i*
strawberries	*klubnika'*

lemon	*limon'*
raspberries	*malin'a*
peaches	*per'siki*
grapes	*vinograd'*
cherries	*vish'nia*
apples	*yab'loki*

CONDIMENTS	*PREPRAVA*
garlic	*chesnok'*
mustard	*garchee'tsa*
ketchup	*ketsup*
honey	*myod*
pepper	*per'ets*
sugar	*sak'har*
salt	*sol*

DESSERT	*SLADKOYE*
candy	*konfeti*
ice cream	*morozh'noye*
nuts	*orek'hi*
small cake/cookie	*pirozh'noye*
ice cream with fruit topping	*plombir'*
chocolate	*shokolad'*
pretzels	*sukhari'*
cake	*tort*

BEVERAGES	*NAPITKI*
tea	*chai*
coffee	*kofe*
near-beer	*kvas*
seltzered soda	*limonad*
beer	*pee'vo*
wine	*veeno'*
vodka	*vodka*
water	*voda'*
- mineral	*mineralnaya*
- seltzered	*gazir'ovannaya*
milk	*moloko'*
cognac	*konyak'*

juice	*sok*
orange	*apelsinovi*
tomato	*tomatni*
grape	*vinogradni*
apple	*yablochni*

TERMS

TERMEN

hot	*goryach'ee*
cold	*kho'lodno*
too	*slish'kom*
sweet	*slad'kee*
dry	*sukhoi'*
fresh	*svezh'ee*
not fresh	*he svezhee*
tasty	*vkus'no*
it's very good/delicious	*eto o'chen vkusno*
not tasty	*ne vkus'no*
with sugar	*s sak'harom*
without sugar	*biz sah'kara*
with milk	*s molokom'*
without milk	*biz moloka'*
rare (meat)	*s krov'yu*
medium	*sred'ne*
well-done	*prozhar'enye*

RESTAURANT

RESTORAN'

self-service	*samaapsloo'zhevaneye*
open	*otkri'to*
closed	*zakri'to*
(lunch) break	*(obyed) pereriv'*
dinner	*oo'zhin*
breakfast	*zaf'trak*
no space available	*mest nyet*
plate	*tarel'ka*
napkin	*salfet'ka*
cup	*chash'ka*
glass	*stakan'*
knife	*nozh*
fork	*vil'ka*

spoon	*lozh'ka*
table	*stol*
chair	*stul*
cigarettes	*ceegare'tee*
matches	*speech'kee*
waiter/waitress	*ofit'siant/ka*
I want	*Ya khachu'*
I want tea	*Ya khachu' chai*
menu	*menyoo*
bill	*schot*
bring me a bottle of	*preenesee'te bootil'koo*
wine/beer	*veena'/pee'va*
give me	*dai'te menye'*
pass me	*peredai'tye menye*
please	*pozhal'sta*
thank you	*spasee'bo*

The apostrophes in the phonetic transliteration indicate that the stress falls on the preceeding syllable (eg. in *spasee'bo* the stress is on *ee*).

A village near Yaroslavl as seen by the Illustrated London News, 1861.

RECOMMENDED READING

MAGAZINES & PUBLICATIONS

Glas: Contemporary Russian writing in English Translation, www.glas.msk.su.

Russian Life Magazine: www.russianlife.com.

Russian Life's Chteniya: Readings from Russia, www.russianlife.com/chteniya.

Passport Magazine: www.passportmagazine.ru.

Prakhin Literary Foundation: www.prakhin.org.

Pushkin House, Non-fiction Writing on Russia: London's Cultural Center for Russian arts with annual Russian Book Prize on non-fiction writing on Russia, www.pushkinhouse.org.

Zephyr Press: www.zephyrpress.org.

ON-LINE SITES ABOUT RUSSIA

Russian National Tourist Office: www.russia-travel.com.

Russia Travel: www.gotorussia.com.

Way To Russia: www.waytorussia.net.

Moscow: www.moscow.info.

The Moscow Times: www.themoscowtimes.com.

Expat in Moscow: www.expat.ru.

St Petersburg: www.saint-petersburg.com.

St Petersburg Times: www.sptimes.ru.

Russia Today: www.rt.com.

Russian National Group: www.russia-travel.com.

Russian National Tourist Guide: www.whererussia.com.

Gorbachev's Green Cross Intl: www.gcint.org.

Orthodox Church in America: www.oca.org.

RUSSIAN PRODUCTS IN THE USA

Hermitage Museum Gift Shop: www.hermitagemuseum.org (shop online).

Kremlin Gifts: www.kremlingifts.com.

Musica Russica: Russian choral music. www.musicarussica.com.

Russian Arts: www.russian-arts.com.

Russian Collection: www.russian-collection.net.

Russian Gift Shop: TheRussianShop.com.

Russian historical films & books: www.ihffilm.com.

Russia Online: offers books and magazines for Russian speakers. www.russia-on-line.com.

Sunbirds Russian Art: www.sunbirds.com.

Tolstoys: www.tolstoys.com.

GENERAL HISTORY AND CURRENT AFFAIRS

Applebaum, Anna, *Gulag, A History* (Doubleday, 2003)

Alliluyeva, Svetlana (Stalin's Daughter), *Twenty Letters to a Friend* (1967) & *Only One Year.*

Arutunyan Anna, *The Putin Mystique: Inside Russia's Power Cult* (Skyscraper, 2014)

Barker, Marie Adele & Grant, Bruce, *The Russia Reader: History, Culture, Politics* (Duke University Press, 2010)

Bobrick, Benson, *Fearful Majesty: The Life and Reign of Ivan the Terrible* (1987)

Conquest, Robert, *Reflections on a Ravaged Century* (2001); *The Great Terror: A Reassessment* (2007)

De Madariaga, Isabel, *Ivan the Terrible* (Yale University Press, 2005)

Duffy, J P & Ricci, V L, *Czars: Russia's Rulers for Over One Thousand Years* (1995)

Feinstein, Elaine, *Pushkin: A Biography* (Ecco Press, 1999)

Figes, Orlando, *Revolutionary Russia, 1891–1991: A History* (2014); *Natasha's Dance: A Cultural History of Russia* (Henry Holt, 2003); *A People's Tragedy: The Russian Revolution 1891–1924* (1998)

Furhmann, Joseph T, *Rasputin: The Untold Story* (2012)

George Arthur & George Elena, *St Petersburg: Russia's Window to the Future, The First Three Centuries* (2004).

Gessen Masha, *The Man Without a Face: The Unlikely Rise of Vladimir Putin* (Riverhead Books, 2013)

Gilyarovsky, Vladimir, *Moscow & Muscovites* (first published 1926) Amazon.

Gorbachev, Mikhail, *Memoirs*, (Doubleday, 1996)

Harford, James, *Korolev: How One Man Masterminded the Soviet Drive to Beat America to the Moon* (1997)

Keenan George, *Tent Life in Siberia* (first published 1870, University Press of the Pacific, 2001)

Knight Amy, *Who Killed Kirov? The Kremlin's Greatest Mystery* (Hill and Wang, 1999)

Knobloch Edgar, *Russia and Asia—Nomadic and Oriental Traditions in Russian History* (Odyssey Publications, 2007)

Lenin, Vladimir, *What is To Be Done?* (Written 1902, published by Penguin, 1988)

Levy, Adrian, *The Amber Room: The Fate of the World's Greatest Lost Treasure* (2009)

Lincoln, W. Bruce, *Sunlight at Midnight: St Petersburg and the Rise of Modern Russia* (2001); *The Conquest of a Continent* (Random House, 1994)

Massie, Robert, K, *Catherine the Great: Portrait of a Woman* (Random House 2012), *Peter the Great: His Life and World* (Ballantine Books, 1981); *Nicholas and Alexandra* (Atheneum Books, 1967); *The Romanovs: the Final Chapter* (Random House, 1995)

Massie, Suzanne, *Land of the Firebird: The Beauty of Old Russia* (Simon and Schuster, 1980); *Pavlovsk—The Life of a Russian Palace* (Little Brown, 1990)

McNeal, Shay, *The Secret Plot to Save the Tsar: New Truths Behind the Romanov Mystery* (William Morrow, 2003)

Milton Giles, *Russian Roulette: How British Spies Thwarted Lenin's Plot for Global Revolution* (Bloomsbury, 2014)

Montefiore, Simon Sebag, *The Romanovs: An Intimate Chronicle of the Russian Royal Family* (2014); *Catherine the Great and Potemkin: The Imperial Love Affair* (2010); *Young Stalin* (2007); *Stalin: The Court of the Red Tsar* (2005)

Nekrasov, Nikolai, *Petersburg: The Physiology of a City* (English publication, 2009)

Penningroth Phil, *Fugitive Moment*, (2012, Amazon)

Politkovskaya, Anna, *Putin's Russia*, (Metropolitan Books, 2006)

Radzhinsky, Edvard, The Rasputin File (2001); *Stalin: The First In-Depth Biography* (1997); *The Last Tsar: The Life and Death of Nicholas II* (Doubleday, 1993)

Rappaport, Helen, *The Romanov Sisters: The Lost Lives of the Daughters of Nicholas and Alexandra* (2014); *The Last Days of the Romanovs: Tragedy at Ekaterinburg* (2010)

Rasputina, Maria, *Rasputin: The Man Behind the Myth* (Prentice-Hall, 1977)

Reed, John, *Ten Days That Shook the World* (Written in 1919, published by International, 1967); *The Collected Works of John Reed* (The Modern Library, 1995)

Remnick, David, *Resurrection: The Struggle for a New Russia* (Random House, 1998); *Lenin's Tomb: The Last Days of the Soviet Empire* (Random House, 1994)

Richelson, Jeffrey, *A Century of Spies: Intelligence in the 20th Century* (1997)

Riehn, Richard, *1812: Napoleon's Russian Campaign* (McGraw Hill, 1990)

Roberts, Geoffrey, *Stalin's Wars: From World War to Cold War, 1939–1953* (2006)

Salisbury, Harrison, *The Nine Hundred Days: The Siege of Leningrad* (1970/2003) and *Black Night, White Snow: Russia's Revolutions 1905-1917* (1978)

Service, Robert, *Spies and Commissars: The Early Years of the Russian Revolution* (2012); *Trotsky: A* Biography (2009); *Stalin: A Biography* (2006); *Lenin: A Biography* (2002); *A History of Modern Russia: From Tsarism to the 21st Century* (Third Edition, 2009); *Comrades!: A History of World* Communism (2007); The *Russian Revolution 1900-1927* (Macmillan, 1986)

Smith, Douglas, *Former People: The Final Days of the Russian* Aristocracy (Farrar, Staus & Giroux, 2012), The *Pearl: A True Tale of Forbidden Love in Catherine the Great's Russia*, (2009)

Smith, Hedrick, *The New Russians* (Random House, 2012)

Ure, John, *The Cossacks: An Illustrated History* (Overlook Press, 2003)

Volkogonov, Dmitri, *Lenin: A New Biography* (2008); *Autopsy for an Empire: The Seven Leaders Who Built the Soviet Regime* (2008)' Trotsky: Eternal Revolutionary (2008)

Warnes, David, *Chronicle of the Russian Tsars: The Reign-by-Reign Record of the Rulers of Imperial Russia* (Thames and Hudson, 1999)

Yeltsin, Boris, *Against the Grain: An Autobiography* (Summit Books, 1990); *The Struggle for Russia* (1994)

PICTURE BOOKS, ART AND CULTURE

Afanasev, Alexander collected by: *Russian Fairy Tales* (Pantheon, 1976)

Before the Revolution: St Petersburg in Photographs 1890-1914 (Harry Abrahms, 1991)

Bird, Alan, *A History of Russian Painting* (Oxford, London, 1987)

Bowlt, John E, *Moscow & St Petersburg 1900-1920: Art, Life & Culture* (Harry Abrams); the author has numerous other books on Russian art and theater.

Brumfield, William Craft, *Landmarks of Russian Architecture: A Photographic* Survey (1997); *Lost Russia: Photographing the Ruins of Russian Architecture* (1995)

Bunin Ivan, *Ivan Bunin: Russian Requiem, 1885-1920*, Vol II *Ivan Bunin: From the Other Shore (1920-1933)*, Vol III *Ivan Bunin: The Twilight of Émigré Russia, 1934-1953*, by **Marullo, Thomas Gaiton**

Chandler, Robert, *Brief Lives: Alexander Pushkin* (2009)

Doran, Jamie & Bizony, Piers, *Starman: The Truth Behind the Legend of Yuri Gagarin* (Walker Publishing, 2011)

Ertl, Rett & Hibberd, Rick, *The Art of the Russian Matryoshka* (Vernissage Press, 2003)

Findeizen, Nikolai *History of Music in Russia From Antiquity to 1800*, Vol I, (Indiana Press 2008)

Galitzine, Katya, *St Petersburg: The Hidden Interiors* (Vendome Press, 1999); *Gifts to the Tsars, 1500–1700* (Harry R Abrams, 2001)

Garafola, Lynn & Van Norman Baer, Nancy, *The Ballet Russes and Its World*, (Yale University Press, 1999)

Goldstein, Darra, *A Taste of Russia: A Cookbook of Russian Hospitality* (2013)

Gray, Camilla, *The Russian Experiment in Art 1863–1922* (Thames & Hudson, 1984)

Hamilton, George Heard, *The Art and Architecture of Russia* (Pelican, 1992)

Himelstein, Linda, *The King of Vodka* (Collins, 2009)

Ho, Allan Benedict Ho & Feofanov, Dmitri, *Shostakovich Reconsidered* (1998)

Lewis, Ben, *Hammer & Tickle: A History of Communism Told Through Communist Jokes* (Amazon)

Maxym, Lucy, *Russian Lacquer, Legends and Fairy Tales Volumes I & II* (1992)

McPhee, John, *The Ransom of Russian Art* (Farrar, Straus & Giroux, 1994)

Moynahan, Brian, *Leningrad: Siege and Symphony* 2014); *A Russian Century: A Photographic History of Russia's 100 Years* (Random House, 1995); *Rasputin: The Saint Who Sinned* (1999)

Nice, David, *Prokofiev, A Biography: From Russia to the West 1891–1935* (Yale University Press, 2003)

Norman, Geraldine, *The Hermitage: The Biography of a Great Museum* (1998)

Plisetskaya, Maya, *Maya Plisetskaya*, autobiography (2001)

Pokhlebkin, William, *A History of Vodka* (Verso, 1993)

Prince Michael of Greece, *Royal Russia: The Private Albums of the Russian Imperial Family* (with Carol Townend, 2007); *Jewels of the Tsars: The Romanovs and Imperial Russia* (2006); *Nicholas and Alexandra: The Family Albums* (Tauris Parke, 1992)

Richmond, Yale, *From Nyet to Da: Understanding the New Russia* (2008)

Rudnitsky, Konstantin, *Russian and Soviet Theater 1905–32* (Harry Abrahms, 1988)

Robinson, Harlow, *Sergei Prokofiev: A Biography* (2002)

Scheijen Sjeng, *Diaghilev: A Life* (2010)

Shvidkovsky, Dmitri, *Russian Architecture and The West* (2007); *St Petersburg: Architecture of the Tsars* (1996)

Snowman, A Kenneth, *Carl Fabergé: Goldsmith to the Imperial Court of Russia* (1988)

Strizhenova, Tatiana, *Soviet Costume and Textiles 1917–45* (Flammarion, 1991)

Stuart, Otis, *Perpetual Motion: The Public and Private Lives of Rudolf Nureyev* (Simon & Schuster, 1995)

Sylvester, Richard, *Tchaikovsky's Complete Songs* (2003)

The New Grove Russian Masters: Glinka, Borodin, Balakirev, Mussorgsky, Tchaikovsky (1986)

Thomas, D M, *Alexander Solzhenitsyn: A Century in his Life* (1998)

Troitsky, Artemus, *Children of Glasnost* (1992); *Back in the USSR: The True Story of Rock in Russia* (Faber & Faber, 1987)

Vassiliev, Alexandre, *Beauty in Exile: The Artist's, Models and Nobility Who Fled the Russian Revolution and Influenced the World of Fashion* (Harry Abrams, 2000)

Volkov, Solomon, *Magical Chorus: A History of Russian Culture from Tolstoy to Solzhenitsyn* (2009); *Shostakovich and Stalin* (2004); *St Petersburg: A Cultural History* (1997); *Romanov Riches: Russian Writers and Artists Under the Tsars* (2010), and other books on Russian art and culture.

Von Solodkoff, Alexander, *Masterpieces from the House of Fabergé* (1989)

Walsh, Stephen, *Stravinsky: A Creative Spring* (Knopf, 1999)

Wilson, Elizabeth & Dee, Ivan R, *Mstislav Rostropovich: Cellist, Teacher and Legend* (2007)

York, Michael, *Are My Blinkers Showing?: Adventures in Filmmaking in the New Russia* (Da Capo Press [Member of Perseus Books Group], 2005)

NOVELS, POETRY AND TRAVEL WRITING

Andreyeva, Victoriya, *Treasury of Russian Love Poems* (1995)

Aitken, Gillon R, *Alexander Pushkin: The Complete Prose Tales* (1996)

Akhmatova, Anna, *The Complete Poems of Anna Akhmatova*, expanded edition. Translated by Judith Hemschemeyer and edited by Roberta Reeder (Zephyr Press, 1997)

Akhmatova, Anna, *My Half Century, Selected Prose* (Ardis, 1992)

Akunin, Boris, *The Winter Queen* (Erast Fandorin Mysteries, 2003); *Murder on the Leviathan!* (2005); *Pelagia and the White Bulldog* (2006); *The Death of Achilles* (2006); *The Diamond Chariot* (2012) and more…

Arndt, Walter (transl), *Pushkin Threefold (poems, lyrics, narratives)* (1993)

Babel, Nathalie (ed), *The Complete Works of Isaac Babel* (W.W. Norton, 2001)

Berlin, Isaiah, *The Soviet Mind* (Brookings, 2004)

Bitov, Andrei, *Pushkin House* (1998)

Blair, Elaine, *Literary St Petersburg: A Guide to the City and its Writers* (2007)

Brodsky, Joseph, *A Guide to a Renamed City* (essays from *Less Than One*, Farrar Straus Giroux, 1986)

Bulgakov, Mikhail, *The Master and Margarita; Heart of a Dog* (Penguin, 1993)

Bunin, Ivan—1933 winner Nobel Prize for Literature, *Collected Stories of Ivan Bunin* (2007); *About Chekhov: An Unfinished Symphony* (English publication, 2007)

Butov, Mikhail, *Svoboda*, winner of Booker Prize (2011)

Byron, Robert, *First Russia, Then Tibet* (Penguin, 1985)

Capote, Truman, *The Muses are Heard* (from A Capote Reader, Hamish Hamilton, 1987)

Chekhov, Mikhail, *Anton Chekhov: A Brother's Memoir*, (2009)

Chekhov: The Portable Chekhov (Viking, Penguin); Rayfield, Donald, *Anton Chekhov: A Life* (2013)

de Custine, Marquis, *Letters from Russia* (Penguin, translated from French), first published in the 19th-century (2014)

Dostoevsky, Fyodor, *Crime and Punishment; The Brothers Karamazov; Notes From Underground; The Idiot*

Eisler, Colin, *Paintings in the Hermitage* (1990)

Ginsburg, Evgenia, *Journey Into the Whirlwind* (2002)

Gogol, Nikolai, *Dead Souls; The Inspector General; Diary of a Madman; The Collected Tales of Nikolai Gogol*

Harrison, Marguerite, *Marooned in Moscow: The Story of an American Woman Imprisoned in Soviet Russia* (1921); *Unfinished Tales from a Russian Prison* (1923)

Ilf & Petrov, *The Twelve Chairs* (Northwestern University Press, 1997); *The Golden Calf* (2009)

Kates, J (ed.), *In the Grip of Strange Thoughts: Russian Poetry in a New Era* (Zephyr Press, 1999)

Lukyanenko, Sergei, *New Watch: Book Five* (in series, 2014)

Mandelstam, Osip, *Journey to Armenia); The Noise of Time: Selected Prose; The Selected Poems of Osip Mandalstam*

Mandelstam, Nadezhda, *Hope Against Hope: A Memoir and Hope Abandoned* (1999)

Marullo, Thomas Gaiton, *Cursed Days: Diary of a Revolution* (1998)

Mochulsky, K, *Dostoevsky: His Life and Work* (Princeton University Press)

Nabokov, Vladimir, *Speak, Memory* (Capricorn, first published in 1947); *Verses and Versions: Three Centuries of Russian Poetry* (Harcourt, 2008)

Pasternak, Boris, *Doctor Zhivago* (Vintage, 2011)

Pelevin, Victor, *Omon Ra (1998); Generation P (2000); Babylon (2001); Buddha's Little Finger (with Andrew Bromfield, 2001); A Werewolf Problem in Central Russia and Other Stories (2003)*

Reeder, Roberta, *Anna Akhmatova: Poet and Prophet* (1995)

Rotkirch Kristina, *Contemporary Russian Fiction: a Short List: Russian Authors* (2008)

Rybakov, Anatoly, *Dust and* Ashes (1996); Fear (Little, Brown & Co, 1992); *The Children of the Arbat* (Dell, 1988)

Rzhevsky, Nicholas, *An Anthology of Russian Literature from Earliest Writings to Modern Fiction* (1996)

Schmidt, Paul, *The Stray Do Cabaret: A Book of Russian Poems* (2006)

Shamalov, Varlam,*The Kolyma Tales* (1980)

Solzhenitsyn, Alexander, *One Day in the Life of Ivan Denisovich; The First Circle; The Gulag Archipelago; The Red Wheel* (1994)

Sorokin, Vladimir, *Telluria* (2013); *The Day of the Oprichnik* (Farrar, Straus & Giroux 2011)

Steinbeck, John & Capa, Robert, *A Russian Journal* (Paragon House, 1989); first published in 1948

Theroux, Paul, *Ghost Train to the Eastern* Star (2008); The *Great Railway Bazaar* (1975)

Thubron, Colin, *Where Nights are Longest* (Atlantic Monthly Press, 1983); *Among the Russians* (Penguin, 1985); *In Siberia* (Harper Perennial, 2000)

Tolstaya, Tatyana, *White Walls: Collected Stories* (2007); *On the Golden Porch* (1990); *Sleepwalker in a Fog: Stories* (1992); *You Love, You Love Not* (1997); *Sisters* (1998, with sister Natalya); *Pushkin's Children: Writing on Russia and Russians*, 2003.

Trifonov, Yuri, *The Old Man* (1999); *The Exchange & Other Stories* (1991); *Another Life and The House on the Embankment* (1999)

Tsvetaeva, Maria, *Milestones*, poems written in 1916 (2002)

Turgenev, Ivan, *Fathers and Sons; The Collected Works of Ivan Turgenev*

Tynyanov, Yury *Young Pushkin: A Novel* (Overlook, 2008, first published in serial form between 1935 and 1943)

Ustinov, Peter, *My Russia* (Little, Brown & Co, 1983)

Van Der Post, Laurens, *Journey in Russia* (Penguin, 1965)

Vitale Serena, *Pushkin's Button* (University of Chicago Press, 2000)

Voinovich, Vladimir, *Moscow, 2042* (1987); *A Displaced Person: The Later Life and Extraordinary Adventures of Private Ivan Chonkin* (2012)

Yevtushenko, Yevgeny, *Don't Die Before You're Dead* (Random House, 1995); *Selected Poems* (Penguin Classics, 2008); *The Collected Poems: 1952–1990* (1992)

Tolstoy reading list: The best English language translations of *Anna Karenina* and *War and Peace* are issued by Modern Library. W.W. Norton publishes *Tolstoy's Short Fiction*, *Confession*, and *Tolstoy*, a biography by A.N. Wilson. Northwestern University Press has issued *Tolstoy's Plays*, in three volumes. *Walk in the Light and 23 Tales* (collection of his short stories), 2000. For a fascinating glimpse of Tolstoy's marriage, try *Love and Hatred: The Stormy Marriage of Leo and Sonya Tolstoy*, by William Shirer. *The Last Station* (1990), by Jay Parini, reconstructs the last year of Tolstoy's life; it was made into a feature film, The Last Station (2009), with Christopher Plummer and Helen Mirren.

Trans-Siberian/Siberia: *Travels in Siberia*, Ian Frazier (2010); *In Siberia*, Colin Thubron (Harper Perennial, 2000); *Siberia, Siberia*, by Valentin Rasputin (Northwestern Univ Press, 1997); *Tent Life in Siberia*, George Kennan (first published 1870/Univ Press of the Pacific, 2001); *The Conquest of a Continent: Siberia and the Russians*, W. Bruce Lincoln (Random House, 1994); *East of the Sun: The Epic Conquest and Tragic History of* Siberia, Benson Bobrick (1992); The *History of Siberia: From Russian Conquest to Revolution*, Alan Wood (Routledge, 1991); and *Through Siberia by Accident*, Dervla Murphy (2006).

Genealogy of the Imperial Family

This table is only a partial listing of dynastic relatives.

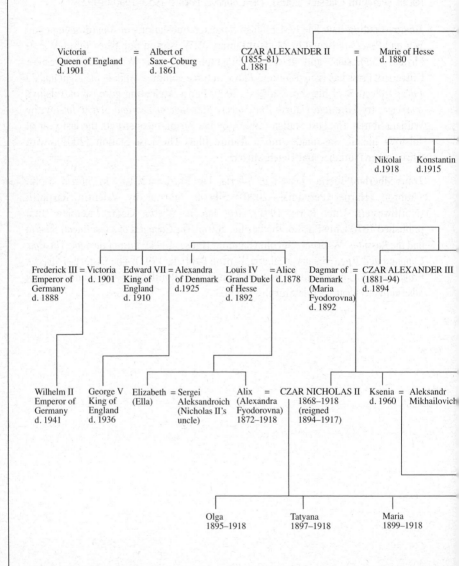

Victoria = Albert of   CZAR ALEXANDER II = Marie of Hesse
Queen of England   Saxe-Coburg   (1855–81)   d. 1880
d. 1901   d. 1861   d. 1881

Nikolai   Konstantin
d.1918   d.1915

Frederick III = Victoria Edward VII = Alexandra   Louis IV = Alice   Dagmar of = CZAR ALEXANDER III
Emperor of   d. 1901   King of   of Denmark Grand Duke d.1878 Denmark   (1881–94)
Germany   England   d.1925   of Hesse   (Maria   d. 1894
d. 1888   d. 1910   d. 1892   Fyodorovna)
                                                                     d. 1892

Wilhelm II   George V   Elizabeth = Sergei   Alix   =   CZAR NICHOLAS II   Ksenia = Aleksandr
Emperor of   King of   (Ella)   Aleksandroich (Alexandra 1868–1918   d. 1960 Mikhailovich
Germany   England   (Nicholas II's Fyodorovna) (reigned
d. 1941   d. 1936   uncle)   1872–1918   1894–1917)

Olga   Tatyana   Maria
1895–1918   1897–1918   1899–1918

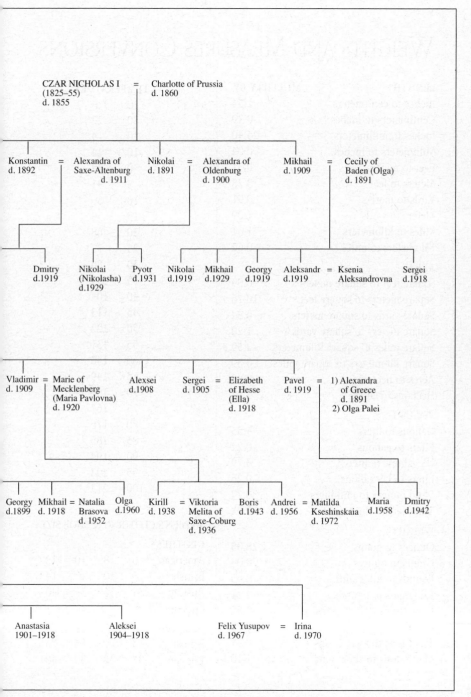

CZAR NICHOLAS I   =   Charlotte of Prussia
(1825–55)   d. 1860
d. 1855

Konstantin = Alexandra of   Nikolai = Alexandra of   Mikhail = Cecily of
d. 1892   Saxe-Altenburg   d. 1891   Oldenburg   d. 1909   Baden (Olga)
                    d. 1911   d. 1900   d. 1891

Dmitry   Nikolai   Pyotr   Nikolai   Mikhail   Georgy   Aleksandr = Ksenia   Sergei
d.1919   (Nikolasha)   d.1931   d.1919   d.1929   d.1919   d.1919   Aleksandrovna   d.1918
                 d.1929

Vladimir = Marie of   Alexsei   Sergei = Elizabeth   Pavel = 1) Alexandra
d. 1909   Mecklenberg   d.1908   d. 1905   of Hesse   d. 1919   of Greece
                  (Maria Pavlovna)   (Ella)   d. 1891
                  d. 1920   d. 1918   2) Olga Palei

Georgy   Mikhail = Natalia   Olga   Kirill = Viktoria   Boris   Andrei = Matilda   Maria   Dmitry
d.1899   d. 1918   Brasova   d.1960   d. 1938   Melita of   d.1943   d. 1956   Kseshinskaia d.1958   d.1942
                        d. 1952   Saxe-Coburg   d. 1972
                                                                 d. 1936

Anastasia   Aleksei   Felix Yusupov = Irina
1901–1918   1904–1918   d. 1967   d. 1970

WEIGHTS AND MEASURES CONVERSIONS

LENGTH	MULTIPLY BY
Inches to centimeters	2.54
Centimeters to inches	0.39
Inches to millimeters	25.40
Millimeters to inches	0.04
Feet to meters	0.31
Meters to feet	3.28
Yards to meters	0.91
Meters to yards	1.09
Miles to kilometers	1.61
Kilometers to miles	0.62

AREA	
Square feet to square meters	0.09
Square meters to square feet	10.76
Square yards to square meters	0.84
Square meters to square yards	1.20
Square miles to square kilometers	2.59
Square kilometers to square miles	0.39
Acres to hectares	0.40
Hectares to acres	2.47

VOLUME	
Gallons to liters	4.55
Liters to gallons	0.22
US gallons to liters	3.79
Liters to US gallons	0.26
Fluid ounces to milliliters	30.77
Milliliters to fluid ounces	0.03

WEIGHT	
Ounces to grams	28.35
Grams to ounces	0.04
Pounds to kilograms	0.45
Kilograms to pounds	2.21
Long tons to metric tons	1.02
Metric tons to long tons	0.98
Short tons to metric tons	0.91
Metric tons to short tons	1.10

TEMPERATURE

°C	°F
-30	-22
-20	-4
-10	14
0	32
5	41
10	50
15	59
20	68
25	77
30	86
35	95
40	104
45	113
50	122
55	131
60	140
65	149
70	158
75	167
80	176
85	185
90	194
95	203
100	212

WOMEN'S CLOTHING & SHOE SIZES

CLOTHES				
American	6	8	10	12
British	8	10	12	14
Russian	34	36	38	40

SHOES				
American	6	7	8	9
British	4.5	5.5	6.5	7.5
Russian	37	38	39	40

INDEX